REVIEW OF

Child Development Research

VOLUME FIVE

Advisory Board

REVIEW OF

Child Development
Research

VOLUME FIVE

Editor
E. MAVIS HETHERINGTON

Associate Editors
JOHN W. HAGEN
REUBEN KRON
ALETHA HUSTON STEIN

Prepared under the auspices of the
Society for Research in Child Development

THE UNIVERSITY OF CHICAGO PRESS

Chicago and London

Volume 1 (1964) and Volume 2 (1966) were published by
Russell Sage Foundation, New York
Volume 3 (1973) and Volume 4 (1975) were published by
The University of Chicago Press, Chicago

The University of Chicago Press, Chicago 60637
The University of Chicago Press, Ltd., London

International Standard Book Number: 0-226-35155-5
Library of Congress Catalog Card Number: 64-20472

Contents

Preface

This is the fifth volume in the series Review of Child Development Research. This series is intended to present a selected sample of reviews of research on important issues in child development, written in such a way that they will be interesting, informative, and comprehensible to professionals involved in work with children and families. Since these collections are oriented toward a broad interdisciplinary audience of people working with children in research or in applied areas, an attempt is made to minimize professional jargon and to present methodological details only when they are necessary for interpreting or drawing conclusions from the studies presented. The aim in these volumes is to provide the practitioner or researcher with a critical review and analysis of the research literature on selected topics, to present a summary of the current status of our knowledge and questions yet to be answered on these issues, and, when possible, to relate findings drawn from research to practical problems. In some cases, the reader may find that the isolation of the laboratory scientist is reflected in a relative dearth of research findings that can be directly related to relevant problems, and may feel confronted by more questions than answers. However, on most topics reviewed it is anticipated that the reader will be offered a solid research base and alternative points of view from which to examine and reconceptualize practical issues in child development and family relations.

The topics included in this volume are not intended to be a comprehensive survey of important contemporary issues in the study of the child; they are a selection of issues regarded as ripe for review and of sufficient general importance to interest a heterogeneous range of disciplines. A topic was judged ready for review if there was a substantial body of research accumulated in the area and if no other current review on the topic was available. In addition, topics were selected only when an outstanding scientist who was familiar with theory, methods, issues and findings in an area was available to write a chapter.

No attempt was made to focus on a single theme or theoretical orientation in this volume. The initial chapter by Robert Sears on the history of child development in the United States gives a unique, often personal perspective on the antecedents of contemporary developmental psychology by one of the visionary men who helped to shape its course.

The current concern with the role of ecological factors in children's behavior is reflected in the second chapter by Paul Gump. The author demonstrates the salience for the development of the child of the ecology in the community, home, and school.

The chapters by Aletha Huston Stein and Lynette Friedrich on the impact of television on children and by James Bryan on the development of prosocial behavior show the utility of a social learning framework in explaining important facets of child development. The former chapter also presents a thoughtful analysis of the advantages and disadvantages of experimental, naturalistic, and field studies in examining such an important domain.

When child psychology was trying to establish itself as an experimental science in the fifties and early sixties, developmentalists tended to think of themselves as specialists and worked within narrowly restricted areas. Although to many investigators the idea of being able to study "the whole child" seems embarrassingly grandiose, in the past decade it has been recognized that development doesn't proceed in narrowly encapsulated areas and that in order to understand most phenomena in development a broader approach to the study of the child must ensue. The review on the development of social cognition by Carolyn Shantz clearly reflects a new interest in the convergence of social and cognitive development.

In the chapter by Anne Pick, Daniel Frankel, and Valerie Hess, the status of our knowledge about attentional processes is examined. At one time concern with attention was largely confined to a series of restricted learning and perceptual problems in the laboratory. It is now recognized that an understanding of attentional processes will contribute to our understanding of an array of problems in information processing, social and personality development, learning in the classroom, and learning difficulties of children with reading disabilities or sensory handicaps. This is shown in the chapters by Joseph Torgesen on reading disabilities and by Kathryn Meadow on the development of deaf children.

Joseph Torgesen has provided a concise review of the research on reading disabilities. In doing this he has attempted to separate fact from fancy in the theoretical underpinnings of many intervention and training programs for children with such learning difficulties. It is to be hoped that such an objective analysis will help professionals working in this area to become more effective in coping with learning problems.

Kathryn Meadow has presented an analysis of the impact of deafness on the intellectual, social, and personality development of the child. This analysis is not presented solely in terms of the direct effects of the sensory limitations on the deaf child but in terms of the differences in life experiences of deaf children from those of nonhandicapped children.

Finally, in the chapter by Ross Parke and Candace Whitmer Collmer, a review of research and treatment programs related to child abuse, an issue of increasing social concern, is presented. The reviewers ask what can be derived from research findings that might minimize or alleviate this alarming problem.

The preparation and production of this book required the coordinated efforts and dedication of many people.

Guidance as to possible topics and authors were provided by the following members of the advisory board: John A. Clausen, Dorothy H. Eichorn, Willard W. Hartup, Frances D. Horowitz, and P. Herbert Leiderman.

Invaluable editorial assistance and counsel were provided by John W. Hagen, Reuben Kron, and Aletha Huston Stein, who served as associate editors on this volume. Only with their diligence, care, and sensitivity in coordinating the comments of reviewers and revisions by authors could the highly polished products represented by the chapters in this volume have been obtained.

In addition to the editorial efforts, each chapter was read by at least two and sometimes as many as four reviewers whose expertise and specialized knowledge of current research on individual topics were of great assistance to both authors and editors. The reviewers include: John H. Flavell, Hans G. Furth, Joan E. Grusec, Corinne Hutt, C. Henry Kempe, William Kessen, Lynn S. Liben, Robert M. Liebert, Eleanor E. Maccoby, John Money, Richard D. Odom, Ross D. Parke, Harriet L. Rheingold, Philip Schoggen, Robert L. Selman, Gerald M. Senf, Benjamin Shimberg, Alberta E. Seigel, Harold W. Stevenson, Murray A. Straus, and Marion R. Yarrow.

Finally, the knowledge and skill of the authors, their openness to editorial suggestions, and their willingness to labor through revisions served as the cornerstone of this book.

It is hoped that this volume will continue the tradition of previous volumes in this series by increasing communication and the exchange of ideas and information between scientists involved in basic research and individuals involved in the utilization and application of such knowledge in working with children and families.

E. MAVIS HETHERINGTON

1 Your Ancients Revisited: A History of Child Development

ROBERT R. SEARS

Stanford University
Boys Town Center

CONTENTS

I. Groundwork for a science
    A. The social history
        1. The empathic ethos
        2. The focus on children
        3. Science as a social instrument
    B. The professional history
        1. Education
        2. Medicine
        3. Social work
    C. The scientific resources
        1. Medicine and dentistry
        2. Statistics and measurement
II. Founding a science
    A. Child guidance clinics and mental hygiene
    B. Child development and child welfare research
        1. The Iowa program
        2. World War I
        3. The post–World War I boom
    C. The organizational steps
        1. The national scene
        2. L. K. Frank and the Institutes
        3. World War II

I am most grateful to a number of my colleagues who read an early draft of the historical section of this paper and gave me felicitous help in its revision. They are L. J. Borstelmann, Albert Hastorf, E. Mavis Hetherington, Pauline Sears, and Lois Meek Stolz. The final section on the state of the art is not history but opinion—only my own.

1

Child development as we know it today has all the characteristics of a science. It has many research practitioners, well-equipped laboratories, the normal media for scientific communication, and respected academic status. Its body of knowledge is growing with the aid of the same mixture of chance and wisdom that serves any of the other sciences. Like them, too, it is subject to the uneasy mixing of theory and empirical study, and to that unpredictable fadism in the popularity of problems which results from occasional stimulation of interest by a new research method or a new theoretical slant or some practical issue needing a quick solution.

Its history is rather different from that of the traditional scientific disciplines, however, even though theirs show most of these same qualities. The other life sciences have been largely self-contained and self-stimulating in their growth. In America, especially, they developed within the academic structure, depending for the improvement of their knowledge on the scientist's desire to know more about the special phenomena of his discipline, and to continue the orderly erection of the factual and theoretical edifice to which he is devoted. The histories of biology, psychology, biochemistry, and anthropology are largely intellectual histories, the records of developing theories, of accumulating facts, of more and more precise instrumentation, and of biographies of the scientists who performed these feats.

In contrast, child development was formed by external pressures broadly based on desires to better the health, the rearing, the education, and the legal and occupational treatment of children. These pressures came from many social sources. As the nineteenth century developed, their expression became more and more persuasive in the articulations of spokesmen for the deeply changing ethos of the times. By the end of the century there had developed a vaguely cohesive expertise within the professions of education and medicine, and the origins of social work as a helping profession were clearly visible. During the first 2 decades of the twentieth century these professions began relevant research to improve their abilities, but their main influence on the future science was their rapidly expanding services for children in the schools, hospitals, clinics, and social agencies.

This expansion continued after World War I, and it was in the next decade, the 1920s, that scientists from several non-professionally oriented ("pure science") disciplines began to join the researchers from the child-oriented professions to create what we now view as the scientific field of child development. But like the engineering sciences which evolved from physics and chemistry, child development is a product of social needs that had little to do with science qua science.

Now, a half century later, child development is a reflection of the tremulous partnership that always seems to exist when pure and applied science, and the services of scientists, are directed toward fulfilling social rather than purely intellectual needs. Today's novitiates in the "science" of child development must not complain when they feel the heat of social demands put upon them. The field grew out of *relevance.* Its content and its multidisciplinary structure are a product of the demands for social usefulness. Furthermore, there is some risk that it will fractionate into its component disciplines—and disappear as an entity in the world of science—if that relevance is not maintained.

The present paper is designed (1) to record the historical forces in the nineteenth and early-twentieth centuries that laid the groundwork for the new science of child development, (2) to provide a brief history of its founding and growth between the two World Wars, (3) to describe the many threads within psychology and other disciplines that have coalesced to form that part of child development called developmental psychology, and (4) to assess the accomplishments and take a candid look at the strengths and weaknesses of the latter field as it exists in today's society.

I. Groundwork for a Science

A. THE SOCIAL HISTORY

1. The Empathic Ethos

Man's inhumanity to man has decreased gradually through the centuries, but only by fits and starts. During the long Middle Ages there was little progress. The rack and the fire were used without compunction. The elite with power and position oppressed the weak who had neither. The slave, the peasant, the poor, the homeless, the insane were given short shrift, along with the Jew and all others who differed with the Establishment's religious and political orthodoxy. Among the weak who had few rights and little protection were women and children, the latter particularly being subjected to indignities now hard to believe (de Mause 1974).

By the end of the eighteenth century, however, the basic value systems of Europe had begun to change. An occasional philosopher had thought seriously about the nature of the child (see Kessen 1965), and the doctrine of original sin was being sharply questioned. In France, Britain, and the American colonies there was a stirring of rebellion against the church and its supportive monarchies. The violence of the French Revolution was a fierce exclamation of rebellion against the inequities of the past. No brief moment in time is good for specifying when social change begins. It does not start all that suddenly, nor with an official pronunciamento. But the last decade of the eighteenth century was a time when, in retrospect, one can see a clear increment in the empathic ethos in Western society.

Empathy means feeling oneself into the feelings of another, absorbing those feelings in some fashion that lets the self feel what the other is feeling. By and large, empathy appears to occur most strongly with others who are felt to be close to or like the self in some way. The apparent broadening of this category of empathizable others marked the beginning of an era of humanitarianism that, still by fits and starts, continues to the present day. The broadening was in the direction of the weak and the helpless, those who had few rights and little protection before, who had been the butt of hostility and little understanding.

A convenient first instance to use as a benchmark of this ethos was the French psychiatrist Pinel's pronouncement in 1792 that the mad were ill (Murphy 1949). The history of beliefs about the nature of madness is similar to the histories of man's efforts to understand many other mysteries. Madness, like the weather, was a perfect foil for the projection of hates and anxieties; the succession of theories seems to have run the gamut of possibilities, from machinations by the multifarious Greek gods through the influence of heavenly bodies to demoniacal possession (Goshen 1967). Inherent in all, however, was the implication of distance between the mad and those who considered themselves nonmad, a distance sufficient to make the treatment of the mad brutal and heartless through the ages. Pinel's edict put a new light on the matter. While the ill poor might not be of much empathic import to the upper classes, illness as such was a category of experience that applied to everyone at one time or another and was admittedly worth sympathy and the provision of kindly care. Pinel was not the first to define madness as illness (see Hippocrates and Paracelsus, e.g., in Goshen 1967), but it is interesting that his interpretation was the first one generally accepted in Western society and that this acceptance has now been unbroken for 2 centuries.

In the United States, a second benchmark was the establishment of secular groups for the institutional care of delinquent children (Hopkirk 1944). Since the fourth century, the church had adopted as one of its responsibilities the care of abandoned children. But the bad child, like the mad adult, was viewed as a moral problem by the church. In 1825 a private society established a House of Refuge for delinquent children in New York City, and in the following year a municipally owned House of Reformation was founded in Boston. These institutional names suggest the new spirit that invested the treatment of the delinquent; now he was viewed as in need of care and instruction rather than punishment for wickedness.

The institution of slavery was the ground for another benchmark in America. Early in the century abolition became a strong force in the northern states. The final militant stand that eventuated in the war between the states was preceded by 3 decades of agitation that contained in much of its verbal expression an overt recognition of the inhumanity of slavery. One need but reread Harriet Beecher Stowe's *Uncle Tom's Cabin* (1852) or Mark Twain's *Huckleberry Finn* (1883) to recognize the naked appeal to empathy as a weapon in the campaign for abolition. The cruel pain of slave husbands and wives separated from one another, of children sold away from their parents, was directly invoked as an emotional brief for change. Mark Twain, writing a half century after the fact, reflected the feelings and attitudes of those in the 1830s and 1840s who detested slavery and were outraged by its cruelties. Whatever political, economic, and moral forces may have loaned strength to the battle for abolition, the values to which many of the public appeals were made were humanitarian ones and the method of appeal was empathic.

2. The Focus on Children

Just why children's welfare should have been so especially served by those new values is not clear; that it *was* so served is very clear (Bossard & Boll 1960). In America there were supporting values and social and economic pressures that doubtless helped. For example, the realization grew during the first half century after the Revolution that a democracy could work only if its citizens were well educated. Horace Mann's campaign for the development of free public elementary education combined the democaratic and welfare values (Messerli 1972), and by the 1830s compulsory tax support for schools had been accepted in several states. Universality of the policy would not be achieved until the fading years of the century, but Boston had moved forward into free public secondary education in 1821, and Massachusetts made free high schools compulsory in 1827 (Anderson & Gruhn 1962).

Ever since the Revolution, too, there has been a strong emphasis on social mobility, particularly in urban environments. Education was early recognized as a channel for improved economic position, and by the 1930s would actually be used as one index of socioeconomic status. The duration of compulsory school attendance gradually lengthened, a phenomenon parallelled by growing pressures in the last half of the century for protective laws respecting child labor (Abbott 1938). Both longer schooling and less oppressive working conditions were supported by labor unions as well as social reformers. The unions had something to gain over the long term by increasing the education of their upward-mobile workers. More immediately, they wanted relief from the labor competition from children, a matter that became of increasing concern toward the end of the century as mechanized factories depended on fewer and fewer hands to turn out a given amount of goods.

Early in the century, at about the same time the refuges for delinquent children were being established, attention was turned to child rearing. The child, now become more precious as the "father" or "mother" of the democratic citizen, required a more effective rearing. The newly aroused empathic spirit dictated a change from punitiveness and brutality to kindness and compassion. This was by no means a new notion, for it had been expressed forcefully by John Locke in his 1690 *Some Thoughts Concerning Education.* Locke's views had already permeated British and American philosophy, and his position had but to be made popular for parents.

The clergy were among the leading protagonists in this movement, the first widely popular guide for mothers being *The Mother at Home* by the Reverend John S. C. Abbott, which was published in Boston in 1833 (Wishy 1968). Not surprisingly, the Calvinist tradition permeated such writing; children were little tyrants, and the aim of rearing was to break their willfulness (if not their wills), and to force them into a mold of high conscience, piety, respect for authority, and a deep sense of responsibility. The main burden of the new advice was a shift in disciplinary method from the use of physical punishment to that of withholding love. Quite rightly, the morally obsessed clergy perceived that this type of motivation was more effective for creating powerful guilt-ridden consciences (see Sunley 1955).

There were signs of lightening of these strictures, however, and in the same year that Abbott published his book, Bronson Alcott, the father of Louisa May Alcott, began an experiment in child rearing with his own daughters which was at least slightly more oriented to the giving of love than to its withholding (Strickland 1973).

The major emphasis in child-care advice remained moral until the last part of the century, however; the building of self-control and proper character as defined by the Protestant ethic were the essential goals. Then, with the sudden blooming of scientific medicine in the 1870s and 1880s, a new element was introduced. The child's physical welfare now became an important focus. Sleep, exercise, nutrition were beginning to be better understood, and Holt's *The Care and Feeding of Children* (1894) was a landmark in the public adoption of more scientific procedures for insuring children's health and well-being. From this it was not a far cry to the development of pediatric clinics, state-supported institutions for neglected children, special school programs for retarded children, stringent child-labor laws, and the formation of social welfare programs to insure the minimum economic and working conditions for mothers which would permit them adequate opportunity to perform child care. In the half century from the early 1870s to the end of World War I, the conception of the child as a responsibility of society-at-large became solidly established (see Abbot 1938). Subtly, too, in this half century, the child's role had changed. No longer was he but a redeemable and educable pre-adult; he was now becoming a future citizen and perhaps a redeemer (Wishy 1968).

3. Science as a Social Instrument

There were other significant value changes during this period also, ones not immediately related to children but eventually important to child development. From early in the nineteenth century, the infusion of science and engineering into various aspects of life in the Western world had improved the average standard of living dramatically by increasing the amount of material goods available for distribution. Watt and his condensing steam engine marked a major beginning of this process. The railroad and steamboat followed quickly to transform transportation. By the 1870s and 1880s the telegraph, telephone, and linotype machine had contributed totally new dimensions to communication. Cut-and-try genetics began to improve the quality of corn and hogs, and by the end of the century the application of biology and chemistry to agriculture had added another example of the way in which science could solve problems to the manifest benefit of mankind.

That not all the by-products of these applications of science to transportation, communication, commerce, and agriculture were advantageous to all parts of mankind is another story. The history of the Industrial Revolution needs no resume here. What was significant for the present record is that science itself became respected and admired. It was almost like a new genie, to be called upon for the solution of old and difficult problems. Mark Twain, who so often reflected (sometimes bitterly) the changing values of the last half of the century, displayed the popular feeling most clearly in *A Connecticut Yankee in King Arthur's Court* (1888). This fantasy of a practical scientist-engineer of the 1880s transplanted into a prescientific society expressed the adulation of the layman for the accomplishments of the new methods and disciplines. Many had the sense that man had finally found a method of mastering his environment. This spirit, coupled with recognition of the great European advances in scientific medicine, created a new kind of belief—that science could solve everything. The late-nineteenth century was the time when "wise men" gave way to empiricists, when belief and opinion were replaced by scientifically determined facts, and when *Science* began to be spelled with a capital *S*.

B. THE PROFESSIONAL HISTORY

During that half century three professions became intimately involved in work with and for children. The command of scientific methods and findings grew most rapidly in medicine, but education was faced with such severe pressures for improvement that the climate was right for the rapid development of new technical skills in that field also. The problems of social advising and help were rapidly creating a new profession of social work, and it, too, began to develop principles and a special expertise.

1. Education

Public education required many teachers. The proportion of children 5–17 years old who were enrolled in elementary schools rose from 57% in 1870 to 73.5% in 1910; the proportion of children graduating from high school increased more than fourfold during that same period (Bossard & Boll 1960). In 1867, the Congress authorized the establishement of the Department of Education, which would become the U.S. Office of Education in 1929. Normal schools and institutes for training teachers were widely established; major universities created departments or schools of education; and states implemented the educational process by state offices. These were all symptoms of the growth of a profession, one to which the community gradually learned to turn for expert help in the care and education of its children.

By the end of the century the construction was complete, and during the next 2 decades educational research grew into a recognizable part of the applied social sciences. The research did not grow in a vacuum, however; it was a direct response to the crucial questions facing schools—*how* to teach *what* to *whom.* In the beginning, how to teach was dealt with by opinion, as was child rearing, but the learning process, and motivation to bring it into action, soon became subjects of study. E. L. Thorndike, newly Doctored by Cattell, after 2 years' work on chicks in William James's Cambridge basement, was brought to Columbia's new Teachers College in 1899 to develop the study of educational psychology. How to teach was attacked indirectly through a study of how the child learns; Thorndike's first major approach to this was his joint study with Woodworth on transfer of training. Characteristic of the age was his emphasis on the learner rather than the teacher (Thorndike 1903).

The second question, that of curriculum, was more tangled in social values than the other two. It remained as a matter of debate, the lines being drawn between the elitism of liberal education and the practicability (for many children) of vocational training.

The third question—who was capable of learning—gradually resolved itself into the field of the psychology of individual differences. The origin of the problem appears to have been the compulsory school-attendance laws. These laws, beginning in Massachusetts in 1821, were originally coupled with the problems of child labor, but the school aspect gradually was strengthened. New York passed a truly compulsory law in 1874, but within a few years it was discovered that many children—probably those who would not have attended school at all in earlier years—were simply incapable of profiting from the regular elementary school program. Paris discovered the same thing after its compulsory education act was passed in 1882, and in 1904 the school board employed Binet and Simon to devise a method for selecting those children who either required a special kind of schooling or should be excused altogether (Peterson 1926). The intelligence test which was the result of these efforts became the opening segment of one major area of psychological science and can be considered further as one of the mainstreams in the history of child psychology.

The lack of intellectual ability was not the only reason for school retardation and failure. The great influx of Southern and Eastern European families in the 1890s deluged the schools with children who not only suffered language handicaps but many of the emotional problems of cultural displacement. The ensuing school difficulties soon led to the development of clinics for the study of disturbed children and the application of remediation procedures for their treatment (Levine & Levine 1970).

2. Medicine

The role of medicine in this sequence of events was significant for both substantive contribution and the infusion of scientific method into a new area of human affairs. Until mid-century, in America, medicine's competence and its public respect were modest. In 1873, the novelist Charles Dudley Warner could safely inject this humorous query into his part of *The Gilded Age:* "Whether medicine is a science, or only an empirical method of getting a living out of the ignorance of the human race, . . ." (see Clemens & Warner [n.d.], p. 234).

By the end of the century such humor was archaic even in the United States. From early in the century in Europe, at Vienna, Berlin, Leipzig, Paris, London, anatomy and the new science of experimental physiology had been exploding, partly in parallel with physics and chemistry and partly with their help. Most of this life-science development was in a medical context, but the application to medical practice was only moderate until Pasteur's discoveries in the 1870s created the new science of bacteriology, providing a rational basis for chemical therapeutics in the treatment of disease and public health techniques for its prevention. By the end of the century, scientific medicine was pretty well master of the macrophysiology of the human body and was deep into its chemistry and the more molecular aspects of its neural functioning. The consequent benefits to the practice of medicine were of immediate import to the ill, and contributed significantly to the belief in the power of science mentioned earlier.

3. Social Work

Parallel with these developments in the United States were several social and political reform movements. The chief ones of importance in the present context were those directed to the liberation of women and the welfare of children. By now the earlier era of the empathic ethos had grown into an activist phase, and what had once been a subject for humane feelings now became a battlefield of rights. For women, the demand for equal political rights and conditions of employment were as much a part of the atmosphere of the 1870s as they are a hundred years later. In sharp contrast between then and now, however, was the linkage of *child welfare* to women's rights—the right to have time and opportunity for child care was part and parcel of women's rights in general.

From mid-century there had been a growing dissatisfaction with the minimal child care of the public almshouses, and throughout the next 75 years there was constant improvement in both public and private institutional care for abandoned or neglected children (Hopkirk 1944). As the emphasis on individual maternal care increased, however, the function of protective and helping agencies changed. They became more involved in aid and advice to mothers in their own homes and in the selection of foster homes. This kind of technical help constituted one of the earliest forms of social work and ultimately came to include the work of the visiting nurse and visiting teacher as well.

A final benchmark from which to gauge how far the child welfare movement had come since the Revolution was the establishement of the U.S. Children's Bureau in 1912 (Abbott 1938). It was now public policy at least to monitor the working conditions of children, although there was no change in the principle that children belong to their parents. While the Bureau was charged with collecting and maintaining statistics on child labor, its most important contribution was in providing an official center for the dissemination of information on the effective care and rearing of children. The first edition of the booklet *Infant Care* was published in 1914, and through its successive editions for 60 years it has provided a constant input of advice to parents, in recent decades decreasingly based on "expert" opinion and increasingly on the findings of child research (see Wolfenstein 1953).

C. THE SCIENTIFIC RESOURCES

The history of any science has its limits somewhat determined by the subject matter with which a succeeding generation of scientists concerns itself. Hence, history must constantly be rewritten; as new problems arise, or new theories are invoked, new progenitors can become important.[1] For present purposes, the reference point chosen is the content of scientific child development as it first displayed itself during the 2 decades between World Wars I and II. If we were to use the subject matter of the 1970s as the criterion, of course, not only would contributions of those 2 earlier decades become a part of the history itself but certain nineteenth-century aspects of medical research, particularly those of endocrinology, biochemistry, and human genetics, would have to be included in the matrix of the earlier scientific history.

The social and professional history that laid the groundwork for a science of child development belonged to the early and middle parts of the nineteenth century. The newly developing scientific resources that contributed to the style and content of the science in the between-the-wars period, however, were mainly from the 1890s and the first 2 decades

1. Old ones can lose some of their precursor importance, too. Phrenology had a historical relevance to mid-nineteenth century brain-behavior study (Boring 1950), but its faulty assumptions brought it to a dead end. It is no longer a significant part of the "working history" of science. It is a part of the history of unworkable ideas, however, and he who ignores the history of mistakes suffers the risk of reinventing a square wheel.

of the twentieth century. Those which were mainly psychological—for example, normative study, psychoanalysis, intelligence testing, and behavior theory—need no comment here. They are integral parts of certain psychological mainstreams which will be discussed later. Two others, however, do deserve mention, for they were clear nonpsychological contributors to child development. These were the new scientific medicine and mathematical statistics.

1. Medicine and Dentistry

Since child development was directed mainly to the study of normal development rather than to pathology, nutrition was a focus of major interest. Nutrition was an area in which normal development could be enhanced. Physiological chemistry was an essential discipline for this study, and its methods were as fundamental as were those of the whole area of digestive physiology (see Ackerknecht 1955). The interest of child developmentalists rather rapidly turned to the behavioral aspects of ingestion as well. The orientation of Holt's *The Care and Feeding of Children* (1894) remained the most strongly identifying characteristic of the study of nutrition as it was incorporated into child development. The emphasis was on normal growth and nutritionally proper feeding.

Physical growth itself became a central focus of developmental study after World War I. From the mid-nineteenth century there had been interest in the sheer external size of children of different ages, sexes, and nationalities, including prenatal size (Thompson in Carmichael 1946).[2] Normative morphological data were gradually accumulated, but the development of internal structures was not extensively recorded. Prenatal growth represented a peculiarly difficult field (and still does). The methods of experimental embryology were applicable to other animals but not to man. The study of fetal growth was a tedious process, for it depended on the availability of fetuses of different ages. Developmental anatomical study could only be "cross-sectional," not longitudinal.

So far as skeletal structure was concerned, however, Roentgen's discovery of X-ray photography in 1895 represented a major instrumental breakthrough for growth study. By the end of the war, X-rays were in widespread use for diagnosis and provided an enormous resource for the longitudinal study of skeletal growth.

For reasons to be mentioned later, heavy emphasis was placed on tooth development, both from a descriptive standpoint and a nutritional one, and the period between the wars saw a substantial follow-up on the early dental research from the 1890 to 1920 period.

2. To save space in the list of references, chapters in the five great *Handbooks* are referred to in this fashion rather than by separate listing at the end of the paper.

Medicine's historical contribution went far beyond X-rays and the various aspects of nutrition, of course. The child guidance movement and the successful creation of a theory of personality development would not have happened in the form they did without the substantive contributions of clinical medicine. Brain damage, hormonal imbalances, auditory and visual dysfunction, nutritional deficiency, and a host of other conditions were incorporated into an understanding of children's disorders. These understandings, in turn, became a part of the matrix from which a theory of personality development would be constructed. Hence, much of the historical contribution of medicine to the field of child development must be traced through the clinical channel rather than through the research developments more appropriately labeled Child Development in the period prior to World War II.

2. Statistics and Measurement

The experimental methods of physiology, the case studies of medicine and psychiatry, and the single-subject methods of psychophysics and introspective psychology had never required the use of precise probability theory for evaluating the significance of data. In most instances the phenomena being studied were sufficiently exact in their manifestations, and differences between conditions were sufficiently great, that single cases could be used with no difficulty. When Galton began to interest himself in human genetic characteristics, however, he discovered that the variability in traits and behavior was sufficiently great that some type of probability statement had to be provided to indicate degrees of correlation or the significance of differences between groups. Probability theory was already at hand and, during the last 2 decades of the nineteenth century and the first 2 of the twentieth a usable statistical science was constructed. Without it, test construction and normative study would have been impossible, and the complexities of multiple causation of behavior characteristics could not have been untangled. Child development was by no means unique in its dependence on statistics, for the methods developed prior to World War I were immediately applicable to all of the social and behavioral sciences. Wherever within-group variation existed in the data of any science—agriculture, pharmacology, and virtually all of the life sciences—probability theory and its statistical corollaries were needed.

II. Founding a Science

The confluence of these social and scientific resources led to the parallel growth of two somewhat separate approaches to the science of child development. One was clinical, stemming directly from the medical and psychological developments of the last part of the nineteenth century. The other was a more formally structured discipline, oriented to experimentation and measurement, and modeled after the research methods of the standard biological and psychological disciplines. The former was organized around case studies from the clinic and created the field and theory of personality development that was a major substantive contribution during the subsequent decades. The latter was organized around laboratories and carefully controlled field studies and was a more immediate antecedent of what is today labeled Child Development.[3]

The clinical developments were a little ahead of the laboratory science, but about the turn of the century both became recognizable efforts to cumulate knowledge, improve methods, and construct theories suitable to their own problems. In this present section the sequences of development for both will be described, not only before the war but in those magic years of the 1920s and 1930s when both came alive and formally organized.

A. CHILD GUIDANCE CLINICS AND MENTAL HYGIENE

These various developments among the child-oriented professions provided resources with which to attack some of the problems children suffered. Deviant behavior exhibited in schools and in the form of delinquency gave major impetus to child guidance clinics as channels for reparative procedures.

In 1896, Lightner Witmer opened the first psychological clinic at the University of Pennsylvania, with emphasis on school problems (Witmer 1911). In 1909, William Healy started a psychiatric clinic in connection with the Juvenile Court in Chicago (Healy 1915). These pioneering efforts immediately determined one of the salient characteristics of the later scientific field of child development—its multidisciplinary character. Children might be referred to Witmer's clinic for their difficulties in the school setting, or to Healy's because of conflicts with the law. Neither the settings nor the symptoms were of singular import, for neither could reveal, in advance of individual case study, just where the best point of intervention for remediation would be. Always it was a whole child who was in trouble and needed help, regardless of where the trouble started or how sometimes limited was the help needed. As scientific medicine, clinical psychology, social work, and educational diagnosis

---

3. For a more detailed and personalized history of this period, particularly of the 2 decades between the wars, see Senn (1975). His chronicle is organized around the lives and influences of the leading figures of that time, the data coming from a fascinating set of 80 oral-history tapes collected during the 1960s and 1970s.

and remediation developed through the 3 decades after 1890, their practitioners increasingly found that the diversity of causes and the ensuing treatments went beyond the coping capacity of any single profession. Hence it was hardly surprising that schools began hiring psychiatrists, clinics added staff psychologists, legal aid societies consulted with many types of specialists, and pediatricians were brought into the family welfare agencies. And from the turn of the century, social workers were in demand for every agency that dealt with children.

The child guidance type of clinic was largely an outgrowth of Healy's Chicago experience (Stevenson & Smith 1934). Commonly it was staffed by a psychiatrist, a psychologist, and a social worker, each of whom examined a referred child with his or her own diagnostic techniques. The social worker interviewed the child's parents and teacher as well, and if the case involved some apparent medical problem the psychiatrist would consult the child's physician. When the necessary body of information had been secured, the case would be discussed in a staff meeting, an understanding of its essential character would be formulated, and agreement on remediation procedures would be reached. This last step involved the allocation of responsibility for treatment either to one of the staff members or to some accepting outside professional such as a remedial reading teacher, a probation officer, the family physician, a religious counselor, or a social worker from some other agency who would work with the child's parents.

The importance of the child guidance clinic movement as a part of the professional history of child development stemmed from the understandings achieved with respect to the personality and social development of children. Although the youngsters referred to clinics were "problem children," it quickly became evident not only to the clinic staffs but to many parents, teachers, and others with whom they consulted and worked in the treatment process that the same principles of development observed in clinic cases were applicable to nonclinic children as well. Healy and many other psychiatrists engaged in this work had been strongly influenced by Freud's psychoanalytic theory, and hence the concepts of psychosexual development, unconscious motivation, and defense mechanisms entered centrally into the developing theory. The influence of social work in clinic programs led to a rich understanding of the role of social elements—especially those of intrafamilial tensions—in the emotional development of children. By 1920 a fairly sophisticated understanding of both school problems and delinquency had become widespread among professionals dealing with children, and the juvenile court had proved its value as an arm of the sociolegal handling of delinquent children and their families.

By this time, too, Alfred Adler's individual psychology had become widely familiar in both Vienna and the United States. His emphasis on the conflicts induced by family relationships and by social structures, as determinants of childhood neurosis, was congenial to the theory of personality development being created from guidance-clinic experience (Adler 1924, [1930] 1963; for an excellent review, see Murphy 1949). Indeed, by 1930 the motivational aspects of the theory had more in common with Adler's conceptions than with Freud's.

The child guidance movement was greatly strengthened in 1921, when the Commonwealth Fund began the support of a set of demonstration clinics. The first, and perhaps the best known, was the Bureau of Children's Guidance, established by the New School of Social Work in New York City as a practicum-training facility for student social workers (Lee & Kenworthy 1929). Its stated purpose was the prevention of juvenile delinquency. In its 5 years of operation about 90% of its case load was children between 5 and 19 years of age, nearly half being referred by schools. The 10–14-year age group accounted for half the cases. This was a sample not unlike those of later clinics. From 1922 to 1927, when the "demonstration" ended, new clinics were started in Saint Louis, Norfolk, Dallas, Los Angeles, Cleveland, and several other cities. Some were successful, and the communities picked up support. Others were failures; neither the Commonwealth Fund nor the community leaders had had much experience with community activities requiring entrepreneurial expertness to keep them going. But regardless of the fate of individual clinics, the clinic idea thrived.

Healy had gone to Boston in 1917 to head the new Judge Baker Clinic, and from there, in collaboration with Augusta Bronner and others, published *Reconstructing Behavior in Youth* (1929). This report gave careful attention to foster home placement as a remedial procedure and involved extensive follow-up studies to connect treatment outcomes with clinic diagnoses and recommendations. During this same period, in Los Angeles, Miriam Van Waters, the referee for the Juvenile Court, was developing a strong integrative program between the court and the public schools in collaboration with the clinical psychologist Elizabeth Woods (Van Waters 1925). In the meantime, Douglas Thom had established his Habit Clinics in Boston, and by the end of the 1920s there were several guidance clinics operating effectively in every large metropolitan center. Thom's Habit Clinics, in contrast with those oriented toward school problems or the prevention of delinquency, were devoted to the problems of infancy and pre-school-aged children (Thom 1924).

There were a number of major publications between 1915 and the end of the 1920s that reported case findings in considerable detail. The first, and most immediately influential, was William Healy's massive *The Individual Delinquent* (1915). There followed quickly a succession of detailed reports of clinic cases, both in books and in the journal *Mental Hygiene,* which began publication in 1917. At Smith College, a school of social work opened in 1921 and provided a new journal that published not only case reports but many small research projects contributing to the new theoretical area. The stream of reports grew broader and deeper through the 1920s (e.g., Thomas & Thomas 1928), and gradually a coherent theory of personality development began to emerge, a theory that was heavily psychological in emphasis but that rested on the assumption of interdependence of physical, psychological, and social variables as determinants of behavioral outcomes.

During this postwar decade, too, the developing theory was applied to the problem of rearing normal children. Such books as Groves's *Personality and Social Adjustment* (1923), Blanton and Blanton's *Child Guidance* (1927), Thom's *Everyday Problems of the Everyday Child* (1927), and Blanchard's *The Child and Society* (1928) brought the social, psychological, and psychiatric principles into focus for an understanding of the child's development in the family and in peer-group settings. It was these textbooks, together with the clinical case materials, that provided the formulation of personality development theory with which the field of child development was endowed when it became a self-conscious field of science about 1930.

In 1924 the child guidance clinicians coalesced into a professional group of their own, the American Orthopsychiatric Association, and in 1930 began publication of the *Journal,* which provided a medium for data communications and symposium discussions concerning both professional and theoretical problems of child guidance and personality development. Not surprisingly, the orientation of this professional group, and the editorial direction of its *Journal,* were toward problems of behavior deviance. But since the conviction in most quarters was that the same principles applied to both normal and abnormal personality development, there remained close professional affiliation between the orthopsychiatric group and those non-clinically oriented students of child development who were shortly to form the Society for Research in Child Development (1934) and in the following year to start publishing its three associated journals *(Child Development, Child Development Abstracts,* and the *SRCD Monographs).*

Today, in child development circles, there is frequent, even compulsive, reference to the value of interdisciplinary research, although the reasons are rarely mentioned. To the researcher, half drowned in the minutia of his own little problem puddle, this emphasis on the whole child as the unifier for a science may seem a hollow appeal to some forgotten piety. Regrettably enough, it often is. But to those who struggled with the infinite variety of human problems presented in the child guidance clinics of the 4 decades before World War II, the piety is alive and genuine, for the need was—and is—ineradicable.

B. CHILD DEVELOPMENT AND CHILD WELFARE RESEARCH

1. The Iowa Program

The movement began in Iowa in 1906. It was sparked by a very thoughtful woman, Mrs. Cora Bussey Hillis. She had had several children and lost some. As she saw the situation, her losses had been due to a lack of knowledge about children's health and development. She viewed the research of the agricultural college at Ames with respect, and came to the conclusion that if research could improve corn and hogs it could also improve children. She visualized a child research organization comparable to the Ames agricultural station but connected with the university at Iowa City to be in close interaction with the schools of medicine and education. It would have the same three functions, too: research, teaching, and dissemination. The research would be directed to all problems of children's development and welfare, with the goal of building a body of solid factual knowledge that would benefit children and enable both parents and child specialists to work more effectively. The teaching was to be directed mainly toward developing a larger cadre of researchers but also to training professional personnel who would work directly with parents and children. Dissemination of the research findings was an essential element in the program, for Mrs. Hillis was anxious to see the flow of new knowledge reach the public as soon as possible.

With the aid of Carl Emil Seashore, a psychologist serving as dean of the Graduate School at the State University of Iowa, a proposal for the Iowa Child Welfare Research Station was prepared (Seashore 1942). The notion of such an organization was novel. The agricultural public believed in science for hogs, but children were another matter, and it was shaken in a different area of values. Could the human soul be subjected to Science? There was considerable wrangling on the matter, particularly in a rather conservative legislature, but slowly people began to believe it could. Labor unions, service clubs, women's clubs, and a host of other organizations got behind the campaign, and in 1917 the Iowa legislature approved the plan and appropriated $50,000 to open the Station.

2. World War I

The history of child development might have been different, and per-

haps reflected a slower course of growth, had World War I not intervened. The university at once appointed Bird T. Baldwin, an educational
psychologist, as the first director of the new station. But Baldwin was
needed in Washington, along with a score of other psychologists who
collaborated to construct the army selection tests. To Mrs. Hillis's disappointment, the university postponed opening the laboratories until Baldwin could return. The delay was brief, however, and in 1919 he did
return and the Iowa Child Welfare Research Station was underway.

But some shockingly murky water washed under the bridge during
those 2 war years. America had come a long way in the 60 years since the
Civil War. No longer could affluent young men buy the services of substitutes for military duty, nor could great masses of the indigent, the
faraway, or the lackadasical be simply ignored in the search for man-
power. In World War I there was a universal draft. Almost all young
American males were tested by the new mental tests and given physical
examinations. And in two respects they were, in the mass, found sadly
wanting. Neither their teeth nor their literacy were adequate for military
service. An army travels on its stomach, and teeth must be sufficient to
fill the stomach. Soldiers must be able to read and understand orders,
and the cost of transporting an army across the Atlantic did not admit of
carrying deadheads who could not fulfill the role of a fighter.

3. The Post–World War I Boom

Public pressure was brought on various branches of government to
increase the support for education and for dental research. President
Wilson labeled 1919 as the Children's Year; scientists responded vigorously and in considerable numbers to the call for child welfare research.
But most important, what the federal government could not do until
after World War II was done by private philanthropy. Just as the Commonwealth Fund had supported the demonstration clinics, so the Rockefeller interests dedicated about $12 million in memory of Laura Spelman
Rockefeller to *research, teaching,* and *dissemination* in the field of child
development. Had the Iowa station had to go it alone, its influence
would no doubt have been great, but it would have attracted others to its
mission more slowly. The Rockefeller millions multiplied many times the
efforts which would construct the new science.

C. THE ORGANIZATIONAL STEPS

1. The National Scene

The first official step was the establishing of a subcommittee on child
development in the Division of Anthropology and Psychology of the
National Research Council in the winter of 1922–1923. The chairman of

the division was Robert S. Woodworth, a Columbia experimental psychologist. In the following year, 1924, a full committee was formed, and Woodworth took the chairmanship. To many he was the Mr. Psychologist of his day, and his enthusiasm and support were symptomatic of the widespread child development interest of nonclinical scientists in the early twenties. The committee, with support from the Laura Spelman Rockefeller Memorial, called several research conferences, distributed funds for postdoctoral research fellowships, and in 1927 started publication of *Child Development Abstracts and Bibliography.* The clientele of child development had grown rapidly. In that year a listing of such scientists by the committee contained 425 names. In 1933, its last research conference in Chicago was the setting for a decision among the developmentalists to create an independent Society for Research in Child Development. On November 3–4 the following year the committee was the organizational host at the National Academy of Sciences building in Washington for the first meeting of the new society (Poffenberger 1933). At this meeting there were more than 200 active participants in fields ranging widely through orthodontics, nutrition, early childhood and parent education, psychology, pediatrics, psychiatry, sociology, and many other professional and scientific disciplines *(Committee on Child Development* 1934).

2. L. K. Frank and the Institutes

In the meantime, with the Memorial's support, the universities had not been laggard. Teachers College created its Child Development Institute in 1924, the University of Minnesota established its Institute of Child Welfare in 1925 with a structure similar to Iowa's Station. At Yale, where Gesell's Psycho-Clinic had been founded in 1911, the clinic's special research facilities were greatly expanded in the same year; the University of California at Berkeley gave an earnest of its intent to have an institute when in 1926 it brought Herbert Stolz, then director of parent education for the state department in Sacramento, to Berkeley as director of the new institute. Relatively small grants had facilitated these developments, but in 1927 and 1928 the groundwork for expansion had been laid, and the memorial made very substantial long-term grants to Iowa, Minnesota, Yale, Teachers College, and the University of California, Berkeley. The latter was thus enabled to start its Institute of Child Welfare in 1927 and two of its three longitudinal growth studies the year after.

The moving spirit behind this program was a young economist, Lawrence K. Frank. He, like Mrs. Hillis 2 decades before, was strongly convinced that parent education was an essential process for the future well-being of children, and the grants to universities contained a plentiful element of support for such activity. At Teachers College after 1930, indeed, parent education became the primary area of effort under the direction of Lois Hayden Meek (later Stolz), although the intent of the grant was to infuse all aspects of education with child development. Strong programs were developed at Iowa and Minnesota, too, but at both, and at Yale and Berkeley, there was especially vigorous development of pure child development research and graduate training for research careers. Some of the institutes received funds with which to purchase preferred stock in the new *Parents Magazine* enterprise and hence had a part in a visible and popular parent education activity.

The nature of the grants to the universities provided high autonomy for the programs. The research centers became small empires, each with a powerful and dominant director. Partly this was the style of the times, for many university departments as well as research organizations were similarly structured. The style led to enormous productivity and often brilliantly coordinated programs. Its major weakness was that it did not develop equally dynamic leadership at the second echelon within the centers themselves.

The 1930s were a golden era for developmental research, particularly in child psychology. In addition to the five Rockefeller-supported centers, several others achieved a sufficiently critical mass of research personnel to warrant the label "center," each with its own style and substantive emphasis (Stoddard 1939).

The Iowa Child Welfare Research Station was the bellwether. In its first decade, Bird Baldwin established a strong tradition for the study of physical growth, and after his death in 1928 George Stoddard's program on mental growth stamped the station as an environmentalist stronghold during the 1930s. At the *University of Minnesota Institute of Child Welfare* John Anderson developed a research program with emphasis on the development of school-aged children, on personality development, and on objective behavior measurement methods. *Yale's Clinic of Child Development* was the creature of Arnold Gesell, whose meticulous studies of motor development in infancy finally permitted the publication of an *Atlas of Infant Behavior* based on 3,200 photographs, providing a kind of anatomy of infant action. The clinic's observational research extended into the preschool years and led to an important stage theory of early development widely publicized in popular books for parents (see Stolz 1958). *Teachers College's Child Development Institute* began as a general child research organization, with major emphasis on personality development under the direction of Helen Thompson Woolley. When she retired in 1930, Lois Meek became director and served until the Institute closed in 1936 and its functions were absorbed into other departments.

The *University of California's Institute of Child Welfare* at Berkeley was established in 1927 by Herbert R. Stolz and Harold E. Jones with funds from the Memorial. Its program was concentrated on longitudinal study. The Guidance Study under the direction of Jean Macfarlane was started in early 1928, the major focus being on personality development. Later that year, Nancy Bayley began the Berkeley Growth Study, the chief concern of which was intellectual development. In 1932, Stolz and Mary Cover Jones began the adolescent growth study, with primary attention to physical, physiological, and social development. All three studies were eventually extended to full life-cycle scope (Jones et al. 1971).

The *Fels Research Institute* was established in congenial proximity to Antioch College at Yellow Springs, Ohio, in 1929. Its program called for the study of man from conception forward, and its first and long-time director, Lester Sontag, promptly began a life-cycle longitudinal study oriented toward physiological and personality development. A famous interim report is *Birth to Maturity* (Kagan & Moss 1962).

Child research groups developed in many other places as well. Those at Merrill-Palmer School, Mooseheart Laboratory, St. George's School for Child Study at the University of Toronto, Johns Hopkins, Catholic University of America, Cornell, Bank Street School, the Universities of Michigan, Ohio, and Washington, the University of Colorado Medical School, and in the schools of Public Health and Education at Harvard had all produced substantial research by the end of the 1930s.

3. World War II

By the beginning of the United States' participation in World War II (1941), the Society for Research in Child Development had been a going concern for 7 years. Its three journals had been published under its imprint for 6 years, and at least three of the institutes had their own vigorous monograph series. The National Research Council Committee seemed to be in a position to release its now mature child to find its own way in the world. The study of child development had extended into most of the life sciences, and the professions which dealt with children had been widely influenced by the developmental point of view.

But disaster struck. World War I had helped bring child development alive. World War II nearly killed it. The reason was unexpected but simple. Most child development researchers belonged also to some discipline or profession and were masters of its skills, knowledge, and technology. They were needed in the war effort. Dentists, psychiatrists, and clinically trained psychologists were drawn into the armed services. Pediatricians were converted to psychiatrists and internal medicine. Psychologists, physiologists, anthropologists were drawn into war-relevant research or administrative work. The developmentalists left in the universities were needed to substitute for them as teachers.

The publication situation was serious. In 1935 the society had taken over *Child Development* from the Williams and Wilkins Company, which had started it in 1930. As early as 1939 there were beginning to be financial problems, and the war exacerbated matters. By 1945, the supply of manuscripts for the journals was negligible, the membership was scattered and exhausted by the war, there had been no meetings between 1940 and 1946, and the society was almost bankrupt. Two decades earlier the National Research Council Committee had built the field, and now once again it took a supportive role. In 1948, with a $3,000 grant from the Cattell Foundation, it paid the society's bills. Once more it helped with the organizational work, getting both the journal subscription lists and the membership list into viable condition (McLean 1954). Federal funding on a massive scale replaced the private philanthropy of the 1920s and 1930s. And a new generation of young scientists quickly renewed the enthusiasm which had been so high before the war. The rest must be classed as *current* history and will be considered later.

D. THE SUBSTANTIVE ACHIEVEMENT

The amount of factual information and research methodology accrued in the 2 decades between the wars was enormous. No brief review could do justice to the scope of the field. Both child psychology and physical growth came fully of age. The latter developed mainly normatively, with primary emphasis on external morphology and skeletal growth (Thompson in Carmichael 1946). In the late thirties and early forties, a good half of the articles in *Child Development* were in this field. Developmental psychology probed extensively into the various mental functions—memory, perception, intelligence, sensory capacities, emotions—and into the broad spectrum of problems loosely called personality and motivation. Normative data were obtained in most of these areas for all ages from the neonatal hours to young adulthood. The 1,000 pages of the first edition of Carmichael's *Manual of Child Psychology* (1946) give a fair and solid review of the field's substance at the time of World War II.

Similar progress was made in the many other specialized areas that composed child development. No one scholar could have pretended to competence in the field as a whole. The creation of the cross-disciplinary doctoral Committee on Human Development at the University of Chicago in 1941, under the chairmanship of Robert Havighurst, was a valiant attempt to coordinate knowledge, but its faculty soon discovered that the doctoral candidates were necessarily specializing in the knowledge and techniques of specific disciplines, mainly psychology. No sooner had

anabolic integration brought the new discipline to its zenith than cata-
bolic fractionation began. Final destruction is not in sight for two good
reasons, however. At the level of *practice*—in the home, the school, the
courts, the clinics, in education, dentistry, work, the law—there are still
whole children to be dealt with and practitioners who must integrate
what the researchers have fractionated. And second, every year reveals
new and provocative problems to imaginative workers at the edges of
their research disciplines where their own problems become embroiled
with those of neighboring disciplines.

III. MAINSTREAM DEVELOPMENTS IN CHILD PSYCHOLOGY

A. INTRODUCTION

For reasons of its social history, child psychology developed within
both the child development movement and academic psychology. Hall,
Thorndike, Watson, and Terman, for example, contributed many of the
early findings that helped form child development, but all considered
themselves psychologists. Hall was the first president of the American
Psychological Association; Thorndike, Watson, and Terman followed in
their turns. In the twenties and thirties, the years of the great institutes,
much of the support for child psychology was linked to child development, but later, in the decades after World War II, federal research
funding made possible a more vigorous expansion of the field into regular psychology departments. Not a few younger scholars were attracted
from other areas of psychological research, and in consequence the history of child psychology, as defined by its contents in the seventies,
contains a substantial infusion of events and theories that derived less
from multidisciplinary developmental science than from the main body
of psychology itself.

This present section is a history of certain mainstreams that have contributed to child psychology as we know it in the seventies. Some of them
may have become dim in memory; others are a living part of current
theory and research. Obviously they do not constitute a complete record
of all the intellectual events that have influenced the content of contemporary developmental psychology, but they may help to expose the con-
tinuities in our science. The main emphasis is on history, and references
to the post–World War II sequellae will be sufficient only to make the
connections, and in some cases to record important research or theoretical developments that even in these 3 decades have themselves become
history.

The history of a science is a various and halting thing. Some methods
and findings that are properly part of its content seem to have had little
impact on future work, as happened with the baby diaries of the late-

nineteenth century. Others become a permanent part of the developing science. This may happen quickly, as with Roger Brown's work on developmental psycholinguistics, or more slowly as in the case of Jean Piaget's work on cognition. This latter had no significant precursors, but it hardly can be called a *historical* mainstream, for it has become central to the developmental psychology of the seventies, Piaget began publication in the late twenties and perhaps qualifies as one of our Ancients on that ground—but his influence is that of a contemporary not historical figure. Again, sometimes old events that were once irrelevant become central to the history of the new structure when the content and methods of the science itself change. For instance, the animal behavior studies of the pre–World War I period were little connected with child psychology at the time, but by the forties had become salient in theory-building around the developmental problems of learning, motivation, and reactions to frustration (e.g., Miller & Dollard 1941; Sears 1948). As of the seventies they are an essential part of the history of ethology and other comparative studies of development (e.g., Hess in Mussen 1970).

To trace these complexities the historian must be both reconstructive and developmental, reporting the events which have proved in retrospect to be relevant to the state of affairs at some criterion date, but not neglecting to record also those events which were immediately causal in the growth of the social and intellectual enterprise being examined. This present section is written from the developmental point of view, as were the previous ones. The relevance of the reported mainstreams is clearly dependent on a reconstructive view, however, and, in shifting from the history of the broader field of child development to the narrower one of child psychology, the criterion date moves from World War II to the substance of the field as represented by Mussen's *Carmichael's Manual* (1970).

1. The Great Handbooks

At any given moment a science has three main aspects, its empirically determined substantive content, its research methods, and its theories. All these are recorded for child psychology in the five major handbooks published during the last 40 years. The first, edited by Carl Murchison, appeared in 1931, when the first full decade of the burgeoning developmental field had made its mark. The book contained 22 chapters by as many authors, six of whom were European: Kurt Lewin, Susan Isaacs, Jean Piaget, Charlotte Bühler, C. W. Kimmins, and Anna Freud. The other handbooks, appearing in 1933, 1946, 1954, and 1970, changed the number of chapters, somewhat, but the chief changes were in content and organization.

In table 1 are listed the chapter topics by abbreviated labels. The order of listing does not correspond to any one of the handbooks' tables of contents but has been arranged to place connected topics adjacent to one another. In the subsequent columns are given the chapter numbers and authors' names for the relevant chapters in each of the successive volumes. Where no name is shown for a later handbook, the topic can be understood to have been dropped, sometimes because active research had ceased and sometimes because the substance was incorporated into other topical areas as the organization of knowledge changed. When new topics were added, no names appear for the previous volumes. In the two years between the first and second editions of the Murchison *Handbook* (1931, 1933), for example, six topics were dropped and seven new ones were added. Of the dropped topics, two were reinstated in 1946 and remain through 1970. Several more topics were dropped after the second volume, and some of them were later reinstated. In general, separate chapter coverage at successive stages in handbook publication seems to have been associated with the vitality of the research topic. Some estimate of the growth of research in the different areas can be gotten from the fanning out to the right of the space devoted to each. The biological area boomed early; cognitive and personality study have come to the fore more recently. There is one notable exception to this general principle—psychoanalysis. It had its own chapter in the first volume, but in later ones was widely incorporated into other topics dealing with personality development, socialization, and psychopathology.

The apparent disappearance of method and theory in the latest handbook is misleading, of course. By 1960, research methods had become of sufficient importance that the still active National Research Council Committee on Child Development commissioned an entire handbook devoted to them (Mussen 1960). As to theory, by 1967 it was possible for Baldwin to write a sophisticated textbook on *Theories of Child Development* (Baldwin 1967), and 2 years later a full handbook was devoted to theories of socialization alone (Goslin 1969). The topics of these last three books are not included in the table 1 list, which is primarily topical, but the existence of the volumes indicates a significant directional development of child psychology and child development in the last dozen years.

Listing the substantive content of a science does not tell how it came to be there. History is properly a developmental study, and it must say something of the influences that produced the changes in content and organization. Knowledge feeds on knowledge, but there is also a *Zeitgeist;* and there are also people, people whose ambitions, enthusiasms,

TABLE 1

AUTHOR AND CHAPTER NUMBER FOR EACH CHAPTER TOPIC IN THE FIVE HANDBOOKS OF CHILD PSYCHOLOGY

Chapter Topics	Murchison 1931	Murchison 1933	Carmichael 1946	Carmichael 1954	Mussen 1970
Research methods	1. J. Anderson	1. J. Anderson	1. J. Anderson	1. J. Anderson	
Genetic influences on behavior					2. G. McClearn
Prenatal growth of behavior		2. L. Carmichael	2. L. Carmichael	2. L. Carmichael	6. L. Carmichael
Ethology					1. E. Hess
Animal infancy			3. R. Cruikshank	3. R. Cruikshank	
The neonate and infancy		3. K. Pratt	4. K. Pratt	4. K. Pratt	5. W. Kessen, M. Haith, & P. Salapatek
Twins and maturation	6. A. Gesell	4. A. Gesell	6. A. Gesell; 7. M. McGraw	6. A. Gesell	
Early experience					7. W. Thompson & J. Grusec
Organic drive systems	2. H. Woolley	18. W. Blatz			
Physical growth	8. B. Wellman		5. H. Thompson	5. H. Thompson	3. J. Tanner
Physiological development					4. D. Eichorn
Motor development	8. B. Wellman	5. M. Shirley			
Sensory and perceptual development					11. H. Pick, Jr., & A. Pick
Eidetic imagery	21. H. Klüver	17. H. Klüver			
Mental growth measurement		7. F. Goodenough	9. F. Goodenough	8. F. Goodenough	16. N. Bayley
Education, environment, and mental growth	5. S. Isaacs		11. H. E. Jones	10. H. E. Jones	16. N. Bayley
Learning	10. J. Peterson	10. J. Peterson	8. N. Munn	7. N. Munn	12. H. Stevenson
Language	9. D. McCarthy	8. D. McCarthy	10. D. McCarthy	9. D. McCarthy	15. D. McNeill
Cognitive processes	11. J. Piaget	12. J. Piaget			8. S. White; 9. J. Piaget; 10. J. Langer; 13. D. Berlyne; 14. J. Flavell; 18. J. Kagan & N. Kogan

Cognition and education....	13. V. Jones		14. V. Jones	13. V. Jones	19. W. Rohwer, Jr.
Moral behavior and character		13. V. Jones		19. H. Anderson & G. Anderson	23. M. Hoffman
Social behavior; peer interaction....	12. C. Bühler	9. C. Bühler			24. W. Hartup
Adolescence....		23. L. Hollingsworth	12. W. Dennis	11. J. Horrocks	
Emotions....	3. M. C. Jones	6. M. C. Jones	15. A. Jersild	14. A. Jersild	
Attachment and dependency.					21. E. Maccoby & J. Masters
Aggression....					22. S. Feshback
Sex differences; sex typing...		15. B. Wellman	19. L. Terman	17. L. Terman & L. L. Tyler	20. W. Mischel
Ordinal position.	7. H. E. Jones	13. H. E. Jones			
Drawings....	14. F. Goodenough				
Plays, games, recreation....	15. H. Marshall				
Dreams....	16. C. W. Kimmins				
Psychoanalysis....	17. A. Freud				
Adjustment problems; psychopathology....		22. P. Blanchard		18. C. Banda	28. E. Anthony & W. Goldfarb
Speech pathology....		16. L. Travis			
Gifted children....	18. L. Terman	19. L. Terman & B. Burks	18. C. Miles	16. C. Miles	
Feeblemindedness....	19. R. Pintner	20. R. Pintner	17. E. Doll		27. H. Robinson & N. Robinson
Special abilities....	20. L. Hollingsworth	21. L. Hollingsworth			17. M. Wallach
Creativity....					
Social class and ethnic influences....					25. R. Hess
Primitive children; cross-cultural....	22. M. Mead	24. M. Mead	13. M. Mead	12. M. Mead	26. R. Levine
Field theory....	4. K. Lewin	14. K. Lewin	16. K. Lewin	15. K. Lewin & S. Escalona	

successes, failures, and idiosyncratic interests are only embalmed in the successive handbook chapters. It is to this sequential process we turn now, with a look backward into seven great mainstreams that constitute the headwaters of Child Psychology 1970.

B. THE NORMATIVE TRADITION AND TESTING

1. The Normative Problem

G. Stanley Hall went from his psychology professorship at Johns Hopkins to become the first president of Clark University in 1889. Clark was to be a small school, mainly graduate, with a focus on psychology and the hard sciences. Hall's interests were vigorously educational, however, and he soon developed the child study movement, a somewhat zealous orientation toward incorporating child development into educational training. It became a highly polemicized educational fad, but it had one significant side effect.

Hall, like his contemporaries, knew little about children's behavior, motives, capacities, and interests. He had already done some work with children at Johns Hopkins, and now he set about studying them more extensively. He began holding summer workshops for teachers and school administrators who were interested in child study. He and his students constructed elaborate questionnaires on a host of topics and distributed them to the teachers, who then submitted them to thousands of children, sending the data to Hall for processing. The studies examined children's play, interests, fears, anger, dreams, imaginary playmates, reading habits and preferences—almost everything that children could tell about themselves. Some of the ensuing reports, published in Hall's journal, *Pedagogical Seminary* (later to become *Journal of Genetic Psychology* under Murchison's editorship), were descriptively interesting, but as normative data results from the questionnaire method were of little value; by 1900 the method had come into disrepute. The samples were unknown, the conditions of data collection were unstandardized, there was sometimes a strong aura of moral conformity in the children's reports that suggested teacher influence.

The more precise methods of sampling had not yet been much developed, but Galton and Pearson, in England, had already developed the rudiments of statistical methods required for massive normative study. In 1903, Thorndike published his first little volume on *Educational Psychology,* which laid out the procedures for testing and for data analysis of test results. It was supplemented in the following year by his book on measurement (1904), which provided a methodological sophistication for research that destroyed Hall's all too casual methods and the value of his findings. But while the factual outcomes of his studies were of questionable value, the conception of normative study did take hold of educators' and psychologists' imaginations and provided a directing interest for later developmental research (see Ross 1972).

2. Tests and Measurements

Hall was an intense and articulate leader not only for child study but for the very able graduate students and faculty with whom he surrounded himself at Clark, especially in the early 1900s. Among the students were Arnold Gesell and Lewis M. Terman. Testing had become a focus of strong interest, and Binet's new intelligence test looked especially provocative to Terman. Although Hall was far from enthusiastic, Terman undertook, for his doctoral dissertation, a massive testing program applied to two small groups of children characterized, respectively, as bright and dull by their teachers (Peterson 1926).

The passing of the questionnaire left a vacuum, however. The testing movement was just starting, so far as higher-level functions were concerned, and for all its usefulness and relatively sound methodology it was not at first directed toward the noncognitive aspects of children's behavior. There was no reason why it should have been, for the crying needs of education were for techniques by which individual differences in ability could be measured and the effectiveness of different methods of teaching could be evaluated by reference to the accomplishment of pupils. Intelligence tests for the former purpose and standardized achievement tests for the latter were in the offing. Both would be put to use for the broader study of individual differences in intellect and for the better description and understanding of such deviant groups as the gifted, the feebleminded, and those with special abilities and disabilities. Once the parameters of intelligence had been somewhat determined, differences between demographically defined groups—by sex, age, ordinal position, race, socioeconomic status, national origin, parental occupation, amount of schooling—would be examined. And inevitably, intelligence tests entered into the long history of the nature-nurture controversy.

The first American use of Binet's test was H. H. Goddard's 1910 translation of Binet's 1908 revision. Goddard, at the Vineland (New Jersey) Training School, wanted a more exact measure of the individual abilities of the children assigned to the school. A number of other tests, or translations of Binet's, were published in the next few years, but the most successful was L. M. Terman's revision called the Stanford-Binet (1916). Terman added many new tests and standardized the whole on a sample of 1,000 children. He adopted Stern's convention of referring to mental age/chronological age ($\times$ 100) as IQ, and shortly thereafter published evidence indicating that the IQ remained fairly constant over the childhood years. The first Stanford-Binet remained serviceable as the primary reference point for the measurement of intelligence for 20 years, and then was revised and restandardized by Terman and Maud A. Merrill in 1937 (McNemar 1942). The latter made still another revision in 1960. In the meantime, David Wechsler had constructed an entirely new test in 1949, a test which had the advantage of providing a better form for adults. Since then his test and the Stanford-Binet have held more or less similar status, with the former perhaps more commonly used for clinical purposes.

Two kinds of normative data were gathered with intelligence tests. One was population descriptive and the other correlational. By 1920, the approximately normal distribution of intellectual ability in the general population had been established. The consistency of repeated measures had been demonstrated and an accurate estimate of the error of measurement was available. There was strong presumption of the relative constancy of the IQ. The range of scores in the general population, with the proportion of children falling in each class interval, had been determined.

The correlational findings were beginning to be of some theoretical and practical interest. The original validation of Terman's revision was based on teachers' ratings of children's ability, and now the proof of the pudding was that IQ was usefully predictive of school achievement. On the other hand, while both teachers' ratings and school grades revealed sex differences in achievement—with girls learning to read earlier and boys being better at science—there were no sex differences in IQ. A few studies had shown small positive correlations between IQ and some measures of physical fitness, height and weight, anatomical maturity, nutritional status, health history, and motor development, but these relationships were by no means as strong as those between IQ and both socioeconomic status and educational opportunity, a finding that made clear the limitations on the use of intelligence tests for the study of race differences. Indeed, until after World War II the normative study of race differences had provided little information beyond the fact of higher IQs among more white than black samples of children. The confabulating variables of education, selection, and cultural appropriateness of tests were so obvious that by 1946 the whole issue of race differences had been transferred to the nature-nurture area.

The 1910s were a period of beginning vigor in research on the qualities of deviant children. The feeble minded were the first focus of study because they were a social problem. They were examined with respect to language development, educational modifiability, and various intellectual attributes and personality functioning (see Pintner in Murchison 1931). The frequent association of mental deficiency with physical anomaly was noted, and the fact of a *continuous range* of abilities among children who had been indiscriminately labeled "feebleminded" in the previous century was made crystal clear.

3. Return to the Normative

The heyday of normative study was the decade of the twenties, however. For example, Terman turned his attention to a problem which had fascinated him since his graduate school days—charting the characteristics of the gifted child. In 1921 he selected about 1,500 California children with IQs of 140 or over, and began what, in the mid-seventies, has proved to be the longest-lasting longitudinal study in history. Its intent was normative in the correlational sense. By the end of the decade Terman had shown beyond doubt that good things go together, that "genius" was associated with better health, greater mental stability, and greater educational accomplishment than existed in the rest of the population.

The vacuum in objective study of personality development, left by the discard of the questionnaire, had to be filled. As the guidance clinics began to reveal the importance of motivational and personality variables for school achievement, as well as for the development of morality, some educators turned their attention to character development (e.g., Hartshorne & May 1928). By the mid-twenties the test construction expertise that had been developed with intelligence and achievement tests could be turned to the measurement of personality variables, providing an objectification of assessment much needed by the rapidly growing profession of clinical psychology. Once again, as with the questionnaire, disenchantment was in store, however, for the paper-and-pencil tests relied on a questionable trait assumption, and response sets were soon recognized as strong influences on test results. Individualized projective tests began to develop in the 1930s (doll play, Thematic Apperception Test, the Rorschach).

At the more molecular end of the molar-molecular dimension of normative research were the meticulous studies of newborns by Gesell, Thompson, Halvorson, and their colleagues in the Yale Clinic of Child Development. The development of prehension and other patterned motor activity was precisely charted, and an important start was made on teasing out the relative contributions of maturation and learning by the use of the co-twin control method (see Gesell in Murchison 1931, 1933; and both Gesell and McGraw in Carmichael 1946).

The two demographic variables that attracted most interest initially were sex (gender) and ordinal position. As with giftedness, the folklore about both was substantial, and the iconoclasm inherent in the new methods of measurement—indeed, in psychological science as a whole—

made the search for differences (and nondifferences!) a challenging opportunity to exploit objective methods. Ordinal position did not prove immediately rewarding, for as Jones (in Murchison 1931, 1933) showed, the confabulation of this variable with age, family size, and other correlated demographic factors made investigation difficult and conclusions (especially about intelligence) uncertain. The problem went on the back burner for 2 decades until it was resurrected in the fifties as a part of the problem of role learning and personality development.

Sex differences were more rewarding to researchers. Folklore associated a number of personality characteristics with gender, and in the several decades of Darwinian influence the implication of biological causation had undoubtedly been strengthened. The testers now turned their skills to new variables, particularly those involving motivation, interests, recreational likes and dislikes, emotions, and neurotic qualities. Jersild's studies of age and sex differences in emotions and dreams, in the thirties (see Jersild's chaps. in Carmichael 1946, 1954), were important sources of normative data. By 1950, this normative approach had been replaced by the growing interest in sex typing. But old problems recur with new interests and methods. Suddenly, in the seventies, the growing movement of women's liberation, together with the rapid development of methods for psychophysiological study of neonates and of techniques for behavioral observation of complex motivational and social behavior in older children, has led to a recrudescence of pure normative study of sex differences (e.g., Maccoby & Jacklin 1974).

Normative findings are not easy to summarize. The facts learned about motor and mental development, language and vocabulary development, physical growth, and personality characteristics (interests, motives) in the 1920s formed the basis for more sophisticated research on developmental processes in the thirties. The acquisition of skills, both motor and intellectual, the mechanics of speech development, the influence of praise, blame, and other factors in the learning process, were all problems that could be attacked once the descriptive knowledge of children's behavior, and the correlations among behaviors, were at hand. Unhappily, not all the cross-sectionally determined age differences proved sound. In the thirties longitudinal methods replaced them, and in the sixties the longitudinal methods themselves have had to be revised. This problem will be discussed in a later section.

4. Since World War II

So far as the basic psychological functions are concerned, the day is long past for sheer frequency counts of some dependent variable in children of demographically different groups. As with sex differences, however, normative measurement is still needed when hitherto unexplored variables become interesting. In the first decade after the war, child-rearing practices and their presumed consequents in children's personalities were important topics, and a substantial amount of conventional normative data was collected. In the sixties, age-relevant cognitive processes attracted interest; normative study charted the exact qualities of the stage changes which Piaget had noted. In that same decade, too, the normative study of language development was reactivated by the evident advantage to be gained from shifting to a linguistic description of the behavioral output.

For other processes, however, the sophistication of normative study has increased rapidly in the last 3 decades. Indeed, it may come as a shock to students of perception, learning, and more recent work in linguistics and cognition to hear that their elaborate experimental studies belong in that category at all. Obviously this work has other historical antecedents as well, and sometimes other purposes, but fundamentally much of the research on these topics, as summarized in Mussen (1970), is essentially descriptive of *how children behave.* What is new are two additional questions being asked—*Under what conditions?* and *What is the sequence of development?*

The last 2 decades of research on infancy is a notable case in point. The visual cliff phenomenon was first meticulously described and then variations in conditions of evocation were examined. Studies of startle reactions or of visual attention have been directed to discovering the exact nature of stimuli which elicit them. Sequential studies of infants at trimonthly intervals have charted for individual children the developmental sequence of changes in looking, speaking, manipulating objects, reacting to separation or reunion, and many other behaviors. With respect to mother-infant relationships, parallel studies with nonhuman primates and with other mammals have revealed striking similarities to human infants in the potential for anxiety reactions and depressions as responses to separation. So far as infancy is concerned, answers to the three basically normative questions have been tumbling out at a high rate, and there is no end in sight.

C. PSYCHOANALYSIS

1. Background

The latter part of the nineteenth century saw a development of dynamic conceptions of mental processes in connection with psychiatric problems. In Paris, since 1892, Janet had been working with a concept of dissociation as a device for explaining the development of hysterical symptoms (Janet 1907). By 1895, Breuer and Freud had extended the study of hysteria in the genetic direction. Their book, *Studies On Hysteria* ([1893–1895] 1957), described a number of cases of symptom development in terms of the childhood experiences which induced a dissociative process. The therapeutic method of psychoanalysis proved effective for eliciting memories of childhood experiences, particularly those connected with emotional conflicts. By 1905 Freud had learned enough from the free associations of his adult patients to be able to construct a theory of childhood sexuality, a theory which was by no means novel (Kern 1973) but which was formulated in such a way as to give a more precise conception of the stagewise development of sexual feelings and object choices from birth to adulthood. As with his theory of dreams, Freud had built on the observations of his predecessors, but he provided a novel formulation that brought the child's emotional development into a systematic theoretical framework. Although Freud's own clinical observations were based entirely on adults, his sexual theory was strictly developmental.

2. Introduction into Child Development

The early infusion of motivational and emotional variables into child development grew from Freud's psychoanalytic studies and from the need of the guidance-clinic workers for an understanding of personality development. The ubiquitous G. Stanley Hall was a key figure in the introduction. In 1909 he celebrated Clark University's twentieth anniversary by bringing Freud and Jung before a distinguished audience of American psychologists, and Freud's lectures (1910) at once became both controversial and influential. (Forty years later, Clark would celebrate its sixtieth anniversary by bringing Anna Freud to Worcester for an honorary degree. Her speech on that occasion [Freud 1951] demonstrated clearly that psychoanalysis had lost neither influence nor its controversial quality.)

By the end of World War I sides had been chosen. Watson and Lashley, for psychology, were critical of psychoanalysis, while Healy and many other child psychiatrists were cautiously accepting. It was the old conflict between the methods of the laboratory and the clinic, and the 1920s saw the gradual division of child and clinical psychologists into two groups, the clinical practitioners (American Orthopsychiatric Association) and the more research-oriented developmental researchers (Society for Research in Child Development). Lest this imply more divisiveness than in truth existed, let it be noted that David Levy held the elected presidency of both organizations at one time or another, and child psychologists with an interest in personality commonly were members of both.

This joint interest was especially strong among researchers on personality and psychodynamics. Through the thirties there was a vigorous effort to combine psychoanalytic theory with other theoretical approaches and to test the validity of psychoanalytic concepts by other research methods (see Sears 1943). At Harvard, H. A. Murray's Psychological Clinic was the focus of this effort; at Illinois, Sears was starting his "objective" studies of projection and repression; toward the end of the decade, a parallel effort was going on in Yale's Institute of Human Relations, with an experimental rather than clinical approach (for an excellent history of this movement, see Shakow & Rapaport 1964).

3. Child Analysis

In the meantime, the direct psychoanalytic study of children had had a long and profitable history. After World War I, two streams of development must be noted, one centering in London and the other in Vienna. They were as much in conflict as many other subschools of psychology have been from time to time and for the same reasons: different observed data were interpreted in terms of different basic assumptions. Melanie Klein, a student of Ferenczi's, headed the London group. By 1921 she had begun the analysis of children as young as 2 years of age, using their manipulation of play materials as a substitute for adult free associations. From a theoretical standpoint, she viewed the object relation of the child to mother as primary, and the development of the superego as a derivative of the fear of loss of love inherent in this relationship rather than as a product of the resolution of the Oedipus complex.

In Vienna, Anna Freud had begun her treatment of children, but with a difference. Her own earlier interest had been in education, and while maintaining an orthodox view of psychosexual development she had introduced a new dimension to psychoanalytic practice—nonverbal behavior. She was doubtful of the desirability of therapeutic intervention before the onset of the latency period and hence worked mainly with school-aged and adolescent patients. While Melanie Klein had had to use doll play and other such techniques because of linguistic deficiency in very early childhood, Anna Freud supplemented her approach through language by play activities because these added alternative sources of data. Play procedures became standard for investigating hidden feelings and the defenses against them. Except for Sigmund Freud's observations on parapraxes, nonverbal behavior had previously played

but a slight role in analytic writings. Now, just as with psychologists who
wanted to study the mental operations of the lower animals, nonverbal
behavior was introduced as a substantive content for psychoanalysis.
Erik Erikson, working with Anna Freud in a quasi-educational setting,
developed an interpretative approach to children's play with standardized play materials and later, both at Yale and Berkeley in the thirties
and forties, used them for character diagnostic purposes. In New York
David Levy began using play materials and dolls for diagnostic, therapeutic, and research purposes. By the mid-thirties, play therapy was a
standard part of the child psychoanalytic armamentarium. From this
background there was but a short step to the nonanalytic study of fantasy and ego defenses by means of projective doll play, a problem field and
method that was actively pursued during the forties and fifties, and represented one of the continuing inputs of psychoanalysis to the more
experimental side of child psychology.

4. The Effects of World War II

Developmental theory within psychoanalysis proper continued to
grow vigorously. World War II created a number of real-life exigencies
that permitted observation, and required treatment, of children's psychic
disasters. Anna Freud, who had moved to England with her father in the
face of the Nazi holocaust of the mid-thirties, was heavily engaged in the
care and study of both foreign refugees and English children displaced
from their homes and families by London bombings. Her classical study
(Freud & Dann 1951) of six orphaned refugee children, whose basic
cathexes and identifications were with one another during the first 5
years of life, raised important questions about the primacy of orality in
infantile emotional development. The Burlingham and Freud (1944)
study *Infants without Families* had already focused attention on the importance of peer relations. These studies, together with the persuasive
observations·(not the theories) of Klein, Fairbairn, and others of the
object-relations school of English psychoanalysis, were the precursors of
work on what has now become the concept of *attachment* under the
skillful theorizing of John Bowlby (1969, 1973).

The direct observations of children in nurseries, schools, emergency
caretaking, and clinical settings before and during the war years was of
great importance in the construction of purely psychoanalytic developmental theory. The play analyses of Erikson during the thirties and
forties, together with his observations of Indian behavior in the Pacific
Northwest, led to an extensive expansion of the kinds of motives and
feelings covered by the theory. By 1950 he had incorporated the sequence of observable changes into a life-cycle conception of personality

development (Erikson 1950), a conception which placed social interactive feelings, such as trust, into the same stage-theory developmental context as the original libidinal stages of Sigmund Freud.

5. Adolescence

Adolescence had attracted little analytic interest until Anna Freud's *The Ego and the Mechanisms of Defence* (1937) utilized it as a demonstration ground for the defensive processes. In New York, however, Peter Blos, who had worked with her and with Erikson in Vienna in the twenties, had become active in the treatment of disturbed adolescents. In 1941 he published *The Adolescent Personality*, which, though psychoanalytic in theoretical orientation, made wide use of behavioral observations by teachers, parents, and social workers as well as of the more conventional data from therapeutic intervention. This book made a first and most significant step toward incorporating adolescent personality into the theoretical framework that had been growing through the work of guidance-clinic workers since Healy's early formulations in 1915. By 1961, Blos had perfected a highly sophisticated five-stage theory of the child's emotional development from prepubescence to late adolescence.

6. Since World War II

Following World War II, clinical psychology was reincorporated into the academic departments of psychology. The need for clinicians in the Veterans' Administration was very great, and U.S. Public Health Service support insured that clinical work with children would be well represented in both training and research programs in both clinical and academic settings. Hence, in the late forties and through the fifties, psychoanalysis regained its influence, and for about 2 decades there was a recrudescence of the earlier mating between psychoanalysis and behavior theory that had begun with the work of G. V. Hamilton and English Bagby in the teens and twenties. This latter development can be discussed more fully in the next two sections, for it involved the absorption of anthropology and behavioral psychology into the developmental field as much as it did the influence of psychoanalysis. That the sixties saw a falling off of psychoanalytic influence was in part a result of the shift of interest from personality or motivational aspects of development to the cognitive. But in part the self-imposed isolation of the analytic group was responsible.

7. The Isolation of Psychoanalysis

The historical relationship between psychoanalysis and other systematic approaches to developmental psychology has been largely unidirectional. Sigmund Freud's lifelong insistence on confining his theoretical formulations to data obtained by a single method of investigation created a theory that excluded all of the other knowledge about children's development obtained during those 5 decades. The findings about intellectual processes, perception, learning, language development—indeed, the great bulk of the factual information contained in the first four handbooks listed in table 1—was ignored during the half century when Freud was the dominant figure in the psychoanalytic movement (1890–1940). Only haltingly, in the 3 decades since, have child analysts moved beyond the scriptures (as has occurred with Anna Freud, Erikson, and Bowlby) to develop a broader perspective within analytic theory itself.

This state of affairs has no doubt helped to create the division between laboratory and clinical students of child psychology. It need not have occurred and probably would not have if the chief architects of orthodox theory had not been themselves so dominated by Sigmund Freud. In England in the twenties, for example, Susan Isaacs was strongly influenced by the psychoanalytic group, but her imaginative development of progressive educational methods incorporated all she could discover about children's development (Isaacs in Murchison 1931). In the United States, both then and through the thirties and forties, Healy, Levy, and many other guidance-clinic child therapists were able effectively to conceptualize human development with a more eclectic use of the empirical findings of clinical and laboratory research, not only from psychology but from other social sciences as well. An excellent interim report on the status of both theory and practice within the clinic milieu is given by Pollack (1956), a psychoanalytically oriented sociologist whose detailed case reports illustrate the effective conjunction of analysis and other approaches to the disturbed child.

These efforts, together with the research orientations discussed in the next two sections, have not borne the fruit of scientific unification for which one might have hoped in earlier years. Instead, during the last 3 decades, other developmentalists have found alternative antecedents for many behavioral qualities of children and have constructed different kinds of theories to incorporate them. Nonetheless, many of the problems attacked by the analytic method, and the motivational variables conceptualized by analytic theory, have played a central role in forming the personality development field during the same period. Object relations, attachment, dependency, aggression, sibling rivalry, gender-role development, child-rearing influences, and achievement motivation all owe their existence as research areas in developmental psychology to their initial discovery as essential variables for psychoanalytic theory. As of the 1970s, however, psychoanalysis as a theory, a method, and a body of findings can best be viewed as a historical mainstream for child psychology.

D. ANTHROPOLOGY

1. Background

The early history of anthropology is of no great significance here. For centuries, historians, explorers, and missionaries had been fascinated by peoples whose customs varied from their own. From the sixteenth century, the accounts of travelers became more and more systematic, and by the end of the nineteenth century a substantial literature had been developed by ethnographers whose primary purpose was scientific. Their methods were well standardized, reasonably objective, and directed toward securing a body of data on a broad list of tacitly agreed-upon topics—mainly customs and societal structure, and only incidentally the more intimate behaviors of parents and children. As with the other mainstreams considered here, anthropology began its contribution hesitantly at about the turn of the century, and then with great vigor turned directly to the problems of child development in the twenties (for an excellent brief history, see Mead in Murchison 1931).

2. The 1920s

Psychoanalytic theory was the first stimulus to this research, and Bronislaw Malinowski was the first contributor. His field work in the Trobriand Islands was performed during the preceding decade and came to its most relevant publication in *Sex and Repression in Savage Society* (1927). Freud had conceived of the Oedipus conflict as an inevitable universal in the boy's development in a nuclear family. Skeptical as only an anthropologist can be, Malinowski went to a matrilineal society to study a crucial control case. In the islanders' culture, the two adult male roles of mother's lover and son's dominant father were separated, the latter role being allocated to the mother's brother. Malinowski's observations of father-son relationships showed fairly conclusively that the Oedipus conflict as known in Western patrilineal society simply did not exist among the Trobriand islanders.

The logic of Malinowski's work was followed by Mead in her classical studies of adolescent girls in Samoa (1928) and New Guinea (1930). The pair of studies, together with Mead's careful examination of deviant cases within each society, indicated a strong probability that the turmoil and emotional distress associated with pubescence in American society were a function of the latter's characteristic homogeneous and relatively isolated nuclear household, together with a lack of a strong peer culture.

3. The 1930s

Mead's exposition of the cross-cultural control method (in Murchison 1931) was influential with other anthropologists (e.g., Linton, Benedict, DuBois, Kluckhohn) as well as with psychologists and a few psychoanalysts. She proposed the testing of developmental hypotheses by the comparison of children from cultures that differed in theoretically relevant ways. Such comparisons were to be used as naturalistic experiments, ones in which the variations between groups could be considered as variations in independent variables. During the thirties there was a great expansion of fieldwork directed specifically to the study of children. World War II put an end to fieldwork, and hence much of this material was published in the early to middle forties. Of major influence at the time were the studies by Dennis of Hopi children (1940), by DuBois of the Alorese (1944), and by Erikson of the Sioux (1950). At Columbia, Kardiner (1939) and Linton were examining ethnographic data in the light of psychoanalytic theory in an attempt to understand the interactive effects of child-rearing experiences and social structure. Whiting's *Becoming a Kwoma* (1941) belonged to this period but would have its greatest influence a decade later.

In the meantime, however, following her Bali fieldwork with Gregory Bateson, Margaret Mead changed her views of the most appropriate use of cross-cultural data. Bateson's sensitive photographs of mothers and children helped to reveal the pervasiveness of behavioral, postural, and gestural differences among cultures, variations as great as those of the more formally described linguistic, lineal authority, and economic dimensions. By the end of the period between the wars (in Carmichael 1946), Mead had rejected her original comparative method and had adopted the position that every culture was unique. This was another reflection of the seemingly insoluble conflict between what Gordon Allport (1937) called the idiographic and nomothetic approaches to science; in his case the distinction was applied to personality study, in Mead's to the relation between child development and culture. One can, without undue distortion, speak of the Mead I period (in Murchison 1931, 1933) and the Mead II period (in Carmichael 1946, 1954).

4. After World War II

Mead was correct in pointing to the difficulty of using the cross-cultural method with single cultures. Each culture varied from every other in many different ways, not just in some one single theoretically relevant characteristic. Culture trait variants were not independent of one another, either, and it seemed impossible to untangle causal relations.

Mead's idiographic reaction to this complex state of affairs was only one alternative, however. To an anthropologist and a psychologist who were sophisticated in measurement, there was another. John Whiting and Irvin Child (1953), following the customary psychological method of comparing groups of children, proposed the comparison of groups of *cultures* which differed in less one respect. Hopefully, as with groups of children, there would be a random assortment of covarying qualities, and the single theoretically relevant variable common to the group could be matched with outcome variables. They carried this logic to effective conclusion in their quantitative study of more than 70 cultures whose methods varied significantly with respect to several child-training practices. They found that the projective belief systems about the origins of disease were correlated with severe child-training practices, the type of belief being determined by the aspect of child training most severely expressed (e.g., weaning, toilet training, etc.).

The data for this study were obtained from the Cross-cultural Area Files at Yale, where a vast library of earlier ethnographies had been catalogued, page by page, in terms of content. The files were only moderately satisfactory, however, because the field studies had been done before Whiting and Child selected their independent and dependent variables. Often there were no data on the relevant matters. In the fifties, therefore, an elaborate study of six cultures was initiated by Whiting, Child, and William Lambert, with field teams trained in a common method of data collection. The methodological advances made by child psychology during the thirties and forties now came into play. Direct behavior observation replaced verbal reports of informants; careful sampling of subjects replaced generalized summaries about the culture as a whole; variability of behaviors was given attention as well as central tendencies.

So far as findings were concerned, six cultures were far better than one, but neither the large number of cases from old ethnographies nor the more precise data on a small number of new ones has provided a perfect solution to the problem of how best to use cross-cultural variation as nature's experiment. As LeVine (in Mussen 1970) has described, the problem continues.

E. BEHAVIORISM AND THE LEARNING PROCESS

1. Background

At the turn of the century, while Freud was drawing together his observations about psychosexual development in Vienna, a new behavioral psychology was being created in the United States. Although its British biological precursors had been oriented mainly toward a study of instinctual or tropistic behavior, the main American focus was on the learning process, with chicks, cats, and rats serving as the initial reagents. Psychoanalysis, constructed by a neuroanatomist turned psychiatrist, was essentially descriptive in its developmental aspect, a stage theory of the unfolding of psychic propensities. It was in a European philosophical tradition that would nurture two other significant stage theories a few decades later, those of Heinz Werner and Jean Piaget.

The behavioral psychology of Thorndike and John B. Watson came from an altogether different philosophical tradition, one whose roots lay deep in the soil of British Empiricism, and for which John Locke's *tabula rasa* was a pervasively influential ideological element. Inherent in American folk philosophy was a belief in the controllability of human events, and one corollary of this, as it had been for Locke (1690), was a belief in the experiential determination of character and conduct. Man was what his environment made him. When Thorndike defined the law of effect, and Watson denoted the conditioned reflex as the basic unit of learning, they were selecting a process for study that was of central importance in the American conception of man's nature and were proposing operational principles that were strictly in accord with American philosophic tradition. It was inevitable, therefore, that behavior and the learning process would ultimately be incorporated as a part of American developmental psychology.

2. The First Theory: John B. Watson

Shortly after the turn of the century, Watson got his Ph.D. at Chicago with a dissertation on rat behavior. In 1908 he accepted a professorship at Johns Hopkins, and it was there that he formulated the basic tenets of behaviorism. Orthodox experimental psychology had taken consciousness as its subject matter, conceiving of the science's goal as a description of the "normal, adult, human mind." When Titchener was the titular head of the Establishment, and when he was confronted with the growing and widespread interest in study of abnormal, animal, and child psychology, he denied the possibility of such study (simply by definition), and said: "The wish is father to the thought, and the thought is but the wish become dogmatic."

The day of Titchener's orthodoxy was done, however, and in 1913 Watson published his manifesto for behavior as the basic subject matter of psychology. In the following year he published *Behavior: An Introduction to Comparative Psychology* (1914), and in 1918 his introductory textbook, *Psychology from the Standpoint of a Behaviorist* (1918). Not everyone may have realized it, but the revolution was complete. Shortly thereafter he and Rosalie Rayner (1920) performed their famous experiment on Albert, a 9-month-old boy, first conditioning him, with a loud sound, to be frightened at the sight of a rat and then testing him successfully for stimulus generalization to objects such as a rabbit and a dog. A small but noisily viable behavioristic child psychology was in being. Watson's theoretical model was very simple indeed, consisting essentially of the concatenation of Pavlovian conditioned reflexes. He applied it to child rearing in his *Psychological Care of Infant and Child* (1928), which he wrote as a successor to Holt's book.

3. The Second Theory: G. V. Hamilton

Even before Watson's programmatic adoption of behavior as the subject of psychology, a young American psychiatrist, G. V. Hamiltion, was laying the groundwork for a much more sophisticated theory of learning, one which would account not only for simple trial-and-error learning but for higher-level reasoning as well (1911). Trained as a psychobiologist (with Yerkes) and as a psychiatrist, Hamilton was as much interested in motivation as in the dynamics of action and the principles of learning. His work with primates promptly led him into an examination of the effects of frustration on both cognition and emotion (1916). He performed a number of difficult problem-solving experiments, with several species of animals, that permitted him to analyze their reactions to baffling disadvantage. He isolated several types of reaction to frustration, systematizing them under the general category of *persistent nonadjustive affective* behavior. Having formulated a theory of learning and frustration from his animal data, he then spent a year in a small midwestern city, treating patients referred to him by other physicians in the community. The 200 cases were reported, some in considerable detail, in the first half of *Objective Psychopathology* (1925). The cases were interpreted in terms of the quite sophisticated behavioral theory presented in the second half of the book. The interpretations—and the theory—eschewed any dependence on the mentalistic concepts of psychoanalysis, though it is evident that Hamilton was fully familiar with analytic observations and principles. These case studies provided a body of data more detailed than any Freud had published since the 1893–1895 volume with Breuer and were very persuasive in the suggestion of an alternative method of interpretation.

Hamilton's study of marriage (1929) applied this theoretical position to an understanding of personality and its developmental sequences. By now he was more systematically attentive to the developmental variables of psychoanalytic theory, particularly those having to do with sexual development. The study in depth of the psychical development of 100 married persons of each sex provided the first "objective" (nonpsychoanalytic) study of these forms of behavior. It was the beginning contribution to what was to become, over the next 4 decades, a continuous effort on the part of nonanalytic developmentalists to combine learning theory and psychoanalysis for an understanding of motivational development through the life cycle.

Hamilton's work fit well with that of the vigorous young behaviorists at North Carolina who were carving out other areas of psychology for behavior theory—Dashiell in learning and problem solving (1928), F. H. Allport in social psychology (1924), and English Bagby in the psychology of personality (1928). Their books, combined with Watson's studies of emotions and Hamilton's psychopathology, created a strong systematic behavioral psychology applicable to developmental problems.

4. The Third Theory: Clark L. Hull and the Yale Group

In 1929, Clark Hull moved from Wisconsin to Yale. With him he took an active program of research on hypnosis and a newly vitalized dedication to the learning process. Briefly the two interests were at war for his time and attention, but learning soon won. At his first seminar meeting (on hypnosis) Hull banged the table with his fist and said, with a mixture of pride and defiance, "I'm a behaviorist!" Within the month his first paper on learning was published (Hull 1929). From a theoretical standpoint it was simply the latest in a long line—from Thorndike, Watson, Hamilton, Dashiell, and many others—but from the standpoint of child psychology it was the beginning of the Hullian period in behavior theory.

Hull's importance lay not so much in the details of his theory as in his seriousness about the mission of the Yale Institute of Human Relations, which was to construct a unified science of human behavior. The first 5 years of the Institute's existence had proved a disaster so far as the mission was concerned. Several prestigious professors had been appointed but with no attention to their communality of interest or their relevance to the task to be undertaken. A radical reorganization in 1935 found Mark May, as the new director, enthusiastically supporting Hull as the de facto intellectual leader. The latter immediately began his cross-disciplinary seminars, the initial topic of which was to see whether psychoanalytic and behavior theory could be combined. The first fruit was *Frustration and Aggression* (Dollard et al. 1939), one chapter of which traced the socialization of aggression through childhood. This theoretical account was the forerunner of the full-scale social learning theory soon afterward presented by Miller and Dollard under the title *Social Learning and Imitation* (1941), an account based in part on experiments on imitation in young children.

Inherent in Hull's theory, and in the various later derivations from it that were applied to child psychology, were the notions of drive and drive reduction. The latter was a clear successor to Thorndike's law of effect, stated many years earlier. The former, drive, was a continuing concept in the long history of biologically oriented psychology. Freud's evident use of a drive concept (libido) made it easy to combine Hull's behavior theory with the elements in the psychoanalytic observations about motivational development in childhood. It was this body of principles that Miller and Dollard called social learning theory, a now ubiquitous term that has been applied to a variety of theory structures in the ensuing 3 decades.

5. Personality Development and Child Rearing

When World War II intervened, the Institute's young supporting staff scattered, some leaving permanently, others returning to Yale years later but with new interests. The preparatory period was over, and in the immediate postwar years the direct effects of the Hullian era were manifested in child psychology. There were three main extensions of the Institute program, partly at Yale but more actively at the Iowa Child Welfare Research Station, where Sears had replaced Stoddard as director in 1942, and to which he brought John Whiting in 1947. One extension was the self-conscious construction of an empirically based theory of personality development that was formed out of a combination of psychoanalysis and behavior theory (Dollard & Miller 1950; Sears 1943, 1948). The second was the big push on studies of child rearing and its effects on children's personalities (e.g., Sears, Maccoby, & Levin 1957; Sears, Rau, & Alpert 1965; Sears, Whiting, Nowlis, & Sears 1953). The third was the quantum jump in the methodological sophistication of the cross-cultural study of child development and child rearing, as described in the previous section on anthropology.

The first study of child rearing, made at Iowa between 1947 and 1949, was a correlational one in which the mothers' child-rearing practices and attitudes were correlated with their 4–5-year-old children's behavior in preschool (Sears et al. 1953). The child behavior dependent variables were several types of dependency and aggression. The mother behavior independent variables were such practices as style of nursing, weaning, and toilet training in infancy, and nurturance, punitiveness, and types of discipline currently being used or expressed. The maternal measures were coded from 3-hour interviews; the child behaviors were measured by time-sample observations and teacher ratings in the preschool. Measures of the strength of fantasy expression of aggression were obtained from projective doll play. Several significant relationships were found between punitiveness and aggression and between nonnurturance and dependency behavior.

While many of the findings were replicated in similar studies during the next decade, certain ones very definitely were not. The ones that were replicated related mainly to *current* parental attitudes and practices as inferred antecedents of children's current behavior. The ones that were not replicated related mainly to matters such as weaning and toilet training. For these latter practices, *retrospective* interview reports were eventually shown to be highly inaccurate.

Although a number of major studies followed the methodological patterns of the first Iowa study and depended on the same general theory of personality development, evidence began to accrue that the gross trait-like measures of both parental and child behavior were not the most suitable for analyzing the effects of rearing on child behavior. Much of the difficulty stemmed from the drive concept when it was applied in the form of secondary or acquired drive.

In the sixties one major change in the theory was the elimination of drive. As learning principles began to be applied in detail to motivational development, especially in the context of child rearing as a training process, the inexactness and lack of an independent operational definition of drive made the notion more and more useless. Skinner (1938) had found it possible to conceptualize the learning process without drive or drive reduction, limiting the active agency to reinforcement. When researchers realized that much motivation could be defined by reference to incentives and reinforcing situations only, child psychology moved toward a more simplified theory of personality development (e.g., Bandura & Walters 1963; Gewirtz 1972) that derived most of its areas of substantive interest but little of its theoretical structure from psychoanalysis. Thirty years after the beginning of this sequence of events, the theory has finally been returned to clinical use in the form of behavior modification techniques. So far as contemporary personality development theory and research are concerned, a substantial part derives quite directly from this behavioristic mainstream.

F. NATURE-NURTURE

1. Background

The relative contributions of nature and nurture to human ability and conduct have been a matter of controversy for centuries. Even Locke, with all his emphasis on the importance of child rearing and education, acknowledged that there were great individual differences in children's potentials and temperaments. Darwinian biology hotted the arguments in the mid-nineteenth century, and by the end of the century not a few British biologists were arguing that instinct was a logically simpler explanation of much animal behavior than was reasoning or learning. Freud and McDougall built their theories around instincts, and in the United States between 1910 and 1930 much animal research was directed toward an untangling of what behavior was learned and what was un-learned (bird songs, nesting, infant caretaking, flying, fighting, copulation, cats killing rats, etc.). By 1924 there was a revolt against the too-ready acceptance of instinct (Bernard 1924), and the behavioristic emphasis on learning took over as the explanatory wastebasket for all behaviors of unknown origin.

For child psychology the major reflection of the nature-nurture controversy was with respect to intelligence. There were two general methods of approach to the problem. One involved the direct study of family similarities, an attempt to estimate the influence of inheritance either by tracing intellectual defect or superiority through family lines, or by comparing degrees of similarity in ability between family members having different degrees of communality of inheritance (identical twins, fraternal twins, etc.). In effect, genetic variation was the independent variable. The other method sought to measure the influence of variations in the environment, and the latter served as the independent variable.

2. The Genetic Method

The genetic method got a modest start with the studies of Galton on first- and later-born children, and of Dugdale on the family history of the Jukes. A more direct and better controlled approach came in 1913, however, with the publication of Goddard's study of 10 generations of the Kallikak family. During the Revolutionary War a young buck of good family inadvertently sired a baby by a probably feebleminded barmaid. Later he married within his own class and sired again. Both strains were viable, and Goddard was able to secure sufficient records of successive generations of each strain to demonstrate the overwhelming preponderance of intellectual defect in the barmaid line. Defect could only be inferred in these historical persons, of course; the bases for estimate were social, occupational, and educational failure. The method was by no means conclusive, for there was as much succession of social disadvantage as biological in the Kallikak strain.

Studies of parent-child, sibling, and twin correlations began in the twenties, increased in the thirties, coming to include comparisons of identical twins reared apart, and have been proliferating ever since. The data show with no ambiguity a strong genetic influence on intelligence as measured by IQ.

3. The Environmental Method

In the meantime, although earlier generations of scholars were still strongly influenced by nativistic beliefs, in both Britain and the United States younger educational and social psychologists began to examine systematically the effects of various environmental factors on IQ. Parental education, the family's socioeconomic status, and rural and urban conditions of living were the initial variables studied. Later in the twenties and through the thirties the effects of institutional environments (principally orphanages) and foster homes were compared with home of origin as conditions providing variation in the amount of social and intellectual stimulation. Much of this work led to the conclusion that environmental stimulation was responsible for some variation in IQ. It also demonstrated clearly that intelligence tests were by no means categorically different from achievement tests and that the initial construction of the Stanford-Binet had made it most suitable for the testing of white middle-class children. Studies of Kentucky mountain children, canal boat children, migrants, and rural children in Scotland and several parts of the United States suggested that isolation from the mainstream of the culture led to a gradual deterioration of IQ. How much this was a function of environmental influence, how much of selective out-migration, and how much of decreasing applicability of the tests with age was not at first clear.

Three kinds of experimental studies, undertaken mainly at Iowa in the thirties under the direction of Stoddard, Wellman, Updegraff, Skeels, and Skodak, helped to clarify the matter. One was the study of the effect of preschool attendance on IQ, and the others were the effects of selective foster home placement and modification of orphanage practices in respect to the social and intellectual stimulation of children. The results of all three types of study suggested that environment had a significant influence on IQ, but all three kinds of research were difficult to perform and were amenable to substantial methodological criticism.

4. Conflicts in Values

Terman's prepossession with nature as a source of variance was affronted, and he and McNemar unleashed their criticisms with full vigor. Stoddard replied in kind, feeling rightly that there was too much evidence to be ignored and that not all of the consistently directed difference could be accounted for by one ad hoc explanation after another. For a few years, there was great brouhaha. Then—more for personal reasons than because anything had really been decided—the excitement subsided.[4] Jones, a nativist at heart, in his evaluation of the data (in Carmichael 1946) concluded that, while there was some possible evi-

---

4. Stoddard left the research field permanently for university administration in 1942, and Terman retired a couple of years later. Woodworth's calm analysis of the twin and foster child literature (1941) focused attention on problems remaining to be solved rather than the data already in.

dence for a modest influence of environmental conditions of rearing and experience on the IQ, a great deal more research would be required to define either the amount or kind. It is still not clear that his cautions were fully deserved. If there had been overstatements on both sides, one could blame them on the heat of controversy—a state of affairs no less distressing in the seventies than in the thirties, as has been demonstrated in the recent attacks on Jensen and Herrnstein.

Inevitably, the history of the nature-nurture problem was bound up with the continuing attempt to understand the nature of measured intelligence. Because of the close link of the latter to social survival and achievement, and its correlation with high status and financial rewards within American society, research has occurred in a value-laden atmosphere that has quite evidently taken toll of objectivity. The Iowa-Stanford imbroglio was no more than a sample of comparable controversies over race differences, social class differences, and social policies with respect to extrafamilial child care and early childhood education that have extended over the last 4 centuries. The whole range of contemporary social issues relating to racial conflict and to the treatment of the poor and the disadvantaged is embedded both philosophically and scientifically in the question of nature and nurture as determinants of human potential and conduct. It would be too much to expect that the reports and evaluations of research findings, as chronicled in the sequence of handbook chapters, could be entirely dispassionate or without unconsciously hidden agenda. Such an accomplishment would not seem to accord with either the nature or nurture of man.

G. KURT LEWIN AND FIELD THEORY

1. The Man and His Theory

Although educational and developmental psychology had been interested in performance as well as learning, and psychoanalysis had laid great stress on psychodynamics and defense mechanisms, there was little in the way of a systematic approach to principles of action until the mid-twenties, when in Berlin Kurt Lewin began his studies of action and emotion in children. At the 1929 International Congress of Psychology in New Haven, he presented a brief review of his findings and of a theory of environmental influence on behavior. His first major presentation to an American audience, however, was his paper on "Environmental Forces in Child Behavior and Development," published in Murchison's *Handbook* (1931).

After service in the German army during World War I, Lewin worked as a student with Koffka and Kohler, two of the main architects of Gestalt theory. He began his research on nonsense-syllable learning but quickly turned to more dynamic problems such as motivation, incentives, conflict, frustration, and anger. Modeling his theory after field theory in then contemporary physics, Lewin defined an elaborate set of field force and behavior parameters which provided a structure within which environmental influences (*stimuli* were anathema to Gestalters) could be related to changes in the child's actions. He used such concepts as need, valence, vector, force, satiation, and barrier. These were all propert es of the *organism in a field* and belonged to neither organism nor field alone. Conflict, for example, could be understood as simultaneously presented objects having positive (or negative) valence. This established a tension, which could be resolved by action following the vector toward (or away from) the objects. The theory was essentially one describing the resolution of forces in a field composed inseparably of the organism and its perceived environment. It was an intensely visual theory and required diagrams rather than algebraic equations for its expression. Lewin thought spatially and his theory reflected his thoughts.

Lewin came to the United States to teach summer school at Stanford in 1932, and was on his way home to Berlin when he was warned of the Nazi takeover. He knew he had little future as a Jew in Germany, so he quickly got his family and some furniture out of the country and returned to the United States, where over the next 15 years he was successively at Cornell, the University of Iowa, and the Massachusetts Institute of Technology. Although his first paper, cited above, ended with an earnest and more than perfunctory statement of the applicability of his field theory to development as well as action, Lewin in fact never developed that part of the theory. The brief comments there suggested that changes resulting from the resolution of field forces would be changes in the perceptual qualities of the environment. It was a view consistent with the action theory, the changes resulting from experience being as allocable to the environment as to the child, really indivisibly.

2. Influence

This theory had a mixed influence. It was marvelously descriptive for scholars with good spatial imagery. It seemed a perfect solution to the problem of systematizing action and incorporating motives, perceptions, and environmental influences into a single structure. But while it attracted a few afficionados, its influence was limited. On the other hand, Lewin's enormous fertility for conceptualizing new facets of behavior led to a broadening of developmental psychology into social behavior and motivational problems that have formed permanent testimony to his influence. One need but mention a few of the concepts he brought to the laboratory to see how his empirics have outlasted his theory.

Barriers.—Just as "baffling disadvantage" had provided a starting point for Hamilton's research, so barrier situations fascinated Lewin. His earliest observations of infants and toddlers led him to formulate some basic reaction forms, for example, *aus dem Felde gehen* and *Umweg.* Observations of conflict behavior were interpreted in terms of positive and negative valences, and types of reaction were related not only to the nature of valence but to other aspects of the field, for instance, the degree of restriction on direction or vigor of movement. The qualitative distinction between internalized and externalized conflicts, later invoked by S-R psychologists, was unnecessary for Lewin, since to him all forces involved both internally and externally defined forces. The publication in 1935 of *A Dynamic Theory of Personality* presented the detailed observations, with field theoretical interpretation, of the basic behaviors related to reward, punishment, barrier situations, and conflict. It was from this work, along with Hamilton's, that much of the later study of conflict and of nonaggressive reactions to frustration flowed. Barrier situations in the study of toddler personality in the seventies are one direct outgrowth.

Task interruption.—Another type of frustration study was that of task interruption, which led to research on the so-called Zeigarnick effect and on substitution. Both phenomena were behavioral representations of psychodynamic processes earlier incorporated in psychoanalysis, but Lewin's dependent variables were just as behavioral as Watson's, not the contents of consciousness or the unconscious. For an excellent summary and evaluation of the 4 decades of research, see Van Bergen (1968).

Level of aspiration.—This was another concept that came from Lewin's Berlin laboratory in the late twenties. The difference between a child's past performance and his expectations as to how well he might do on another try was found to be related to previous experiences of success and failure (Sears 1940). The extensive research literature of the thirties and forties brought together by Lewin et al. (1944) led in two directions for child psychology. One was the study of achievement motivation as represented in the work of McClelland (1953) and his successors, and the other was the set of problems combined under the labels of self-concept and self-esteem. Both continue to be areas of research vitality in the seventies, even though work on the experimental paradigm of level of aspiration as it was performed in the thirties and forties has virtually ceased.

Group psychology.—During his years at Iowa, from the mid-thirties to mid-forties, Lewin broadened his interest from the personality of the child to the social psychology of groups. The famous study of regression (Barker, Dembo, & Lewin 1941) overlapped with the equally famous study of authoritarian and democratic group atmospheres (Lewin, Lippitt, & White 1939; Lippitt 1940), which was the precursor of all the future research on small group dynamics. In psychology this work burgeoned during the forties after Lewin left Iowa for MIT, where he established the Research Center for Group Dynamics. He died suddenly of coronary occlusion, in 1947, and the subsequent development of small group research is more a part of the history of social psychology, sociology, and group therapy than of child psychology.

Students.—Lewin's formal theory did not long survive him. His influence remains powerful, rather, through the successive generations of students who trained with him. The names of Dembo and Rickers-Ovsiankina from his brief but fruitful Berlin period are still well known in American developmental psychology, and in other fields the names of Bavelas, Cartwright, Lippitt, Festinger, J. R. P. French, Kounin, Escalona, and Jerome Frank give a representation of his legacy to psychological science. Of these, Lippitt, Kounin, and Escalona remain developmentalists.

Perhaps the most extensive and productive sequel of Lewin's earlier work with children is that of Barker, whose *Ecological Psychology* (1968) has provided a sophisticated conceptualization of the operation of environmental forces in naturalistic settings. Barker was a postdoctoral student with Lewin in the thirties, and indeed published the first American study of conflict following Lewin's theory. He established a field station, with H. F. Wright, in a small Kansas town in the mid-forties. The ensuing 3 decades have seen the construction of a solid propositional theory that defines environmental variables and relates them to both immediate action and longer-term community changes. The work can be seen as clearly influenced by Lewin's field theory but is in the tradition of propositional theory rather than the spatial symbolism of Lewin.

H. LONGITUDTIAL STUDIES

1. The need

Although the stage theories of Freud, Piaget, Werner, and later Erikson and Blos seemed to emphasize uniformities in behavioral development, none of these theorists was blind to the existence of wide individual differences in both rate and style of development. Learning theorists were even more oriented toward such idiosyncratic qualities. Early normative studies of age differences were cross-sectional, however, and although they revealed wide individual differences in performance or abilities at any given age, the age comparisons revealed only the group uniformities in change. For purposes of studying individual differences in development, longitudinal studies were needed. The same children had to be observed at successive ages.

2. The Beginning

Except for the baby diaries, which were brief longitudinal single-case studies, there were no truly longitudinal researches before World War I. Terman's 1921 selection of his Gifted Group was the beginning of the first. His interests were mainly related to the social, educational, personality, and achievement characteristics of his sample, and he resolved to follow the group as long as was feasible. The latest follow-up, nearly 15 years after Terman's death, was under way in 1973. The findings of the approximately 50 years of study are well known and embedded as facts in the substance of developmental psychology (see Terman & Oden 1959). One serious defect in the design should be mentioned, however, for it has limited the usefulness of the study. Terman did not provide comparison groups; three kinds would have been helpful—one, a random population sample from the same community sources as the Gifted Group; two, a comparable group of gifted subjects who could have been used for treatment variation over the years; three, and most important, a couple of cohorts from later periods in time, followed for a decade or so (see Section 5 below).

3. The Berkeley Studies

In 1928, two studies were begun at Berkeley. One was the Guidance Study under the direction of Jean Macfarlane. It was originally designed to discover whether a heavy infusion of parental guidance during a child's first 6 years would reduce the number and severity of behavior pathologies during that period. A random sample of 248 Berkeley infants aged 21 months was divided into experimental and control groups. The wealth of information obtained in the early years, and the not-too-serious loss of subjects over time, induced the institute to continue the study through later years of the life cycle. At the end of the third decade, 68% of the sample were still available.

Surprisingly, the original question has never received a clear answer. But many others have. Virtually all that we know about early- and late-maturing children has come from those files, as have many other of the facts of individual patterns of child development from infancy through adolescence, particularly in the social and personality realms.

In the same year, Nancy Bayley commenced the Berkeley Growth Study with a nonrandom group of 74 newborns, mainly white and middle class. This group contributed heavily to the sequential study of mental abilities. It, too, became a life-cycle study, and the latest follow-up measures are focused on the subjects at age 36.

The Oakland Growth Study of adolescents was begun in 1932 by Mary Cover Jones and Herbert Stolz. The initial 212 subjects were 11 years old and were followed intensively during the succeeding 6 years. Additional measures have been taken at the subjects' ages 33 and 43. The emphasis of the Oakland Growth Study was on physical and physiological measures and on social development. The massive data on individual growth curves constituted the earliest and best source in this field (Stolz & Stolz 1951).

All three of these studies were begun and continued under the Institute of Child Welfare (now Development), and hence a substantial amount of basic measurement method was common to the three. Only to the initiate is the full scope of these enterprises knowable. The research populations have provided literally dozens of significant sets of cross-sectional data in addition to those that are fully longitudinal. Unhappily, as has been the case with other sequential works, there was no tidy way to publish. The investigators have released one set of findings after another in a steady stream of disparate articles and monographs over the 35 years since the work began. In 1971, 61 of the most substantive papers were collected in a single volume (Jones et al. 1971) with additional summarizing chapters on methods and perspectives.

4. The Fels Study

Another study that needs special mention was that begun at the Fels Institute in 1929 under the direction of Lester Sontag. Initially directed to a study of personality development, with special emphasis on the relation of such variables to child-rearing experiences, this research was the setting for the construction of the earliest rating scales for measuring parental behavior through home observations. The correlational data between early-childhood behavior and samples measured at later ages have provided some of the soundest long-term sequential findings on personality development. The well-known greater consistency of dependency in girls and of aggression in boys (Kagan & Moss 1962) is a case in point.

5. The Outcomes and a New Method

The longitudinal studies, by their long-term nature, are less lost in history than are some of the other events described in preceding sections. Many of their findings have been essentially normative in nature. In one respect they have made obsolete much of the normative data of the early part of the century. The Stolz individual growth curves from the Oakland Growth Study, and the individual mental ability measures from both the Terman and the Bayley researches, have qualified markedly the findings based on cross-sectional age samples. The crucial comparison of such data with longitudinal measures came in a study by Schaie and Strother

(1968), who combined the two methods by measuring several mental abilities in a number of age groups between ages 20 and 70 and then repeating the measures 7 years later. The earlier cross-sectional evidence had shown marked decrement in certain abilities, especially in the 50–70-year age range. The repeated measures, that is, the longitudinal procedure, showed that this decrement was greatly overestimated for any specific individual.

The same findings were disquieting methodologically, however. It was apparent that there were significant generational differences in mental ability. The younger cohorts got higher scores on the mental tests. A lot of normative mental-test data from earlier years have now been reexamined, and there is little question that within American samples of both children and young adults there is a monotonic curve of increasing mental ability. Recent studies have shown, also, that adolescent cohorts as few as 2 years apart may show significant differences in certain personality variables (Nesselroade & Baltes 1974).

For normative purposes and for tracing the path of individual growth and development, the longitudinal studies replaced the earlier cross-sectional age-group comparisons. Now the method of the single longitudinal group, measured sequentially through time, will have to be replaced by the multiple-overlapping-groups longitudinal study. It turns out—to no one's great surprise when the matter is put this way—that not only do individuals change with time but so does a society itself. Age cohorts are representative of a time in history, and society's history must be treated just as developmentally as the histories of the individuals who compose it. The multidimensional character of child development is thus once again reinforced, and the science of child psychology must return once more to the larger science of child development. The sudden incorporation of psychohistory into the whole means future historians of the science will have still a different outline to follow. As was said before, there is nothing static about history.

IV. THE STATE OF THE ART

Developmental science has come a long way in the century that covers its growth to maturity. The 3 decades since World War II have provided a very visible gain. When the war ended, *Child Development* was 3 years behind in its publication schedule, and university faculties had been decimated of developmentalists. The science itself was still essentially normative and atheoretical, although psychoanalysis, behavior theory, and Lewin's field theory were beginning to point the way to a more sophisticated era.

The situation soon changed radically. The normative missions of the previous quarter century had been largely fulfilled, and theoretical advances in several areas—for example, learning, perception, linguistics, cognition—introduced a new cohesiveness to the study of the developmental process itself. The sharply increased availability of research and training funds through the National Institute of Mental Health quickly augmented the research force. The meteoric rise in research output soon began, and by 1956 the previously starving journals had to be increased both in size and number.

Because this is a history of the ancients, little has been—or will be—said about current research and theory. There have been three trends since World War II, however, that deserve comment and evaluation. One is the reflection of an ideological conflict that began centuries ago in Western philosophy and has continued to plague modern biobehavioral science. The other two reflect ideological conflicts, too, but these conflicts are of more modern origin and belong to science, not philosophy.

A. NATIVISM-EMPIRICISM: AN IDEOLOGICAL IMPASSE

The empathic ethos has been revitalized in the last 2 decades. In the quest for civil rights, equal employment and educational opportunities, the rights of privacy and the self-determination of conduct, the *haves* have begun giving support to the *have nots*. Feelings are strong and actions often militant. In child development, these rearoused values have been expressed through a resurgence of research on early childhood education as a means toward bettering the individual's capacities, and on sociological analyses of the social systems, as reflected in the law, personnel practices, and school organization, as a possible channel for enhancing people's life chances. Both endeavors are consonant with an underlying empiricist philosophy—a belief that the child's behavior is capable of great modification both through his individual learning and through changes in the social stimuli and manipulanda of his life.

But in philosophical matters there is never action without reaction. Simultaneously there has been a rearousal of nativistic beliefs—that is, the conception of the child as an autonomous being with immanent capacities who unfolds and grows at his own pace and in his own way. This underlying ideology is reflected in the widely reactivated research on genetic contributions to intelligence and in the enthusiastic delving into stages of cognitive development.

There are strong historical roots for both nativism and empiricism. The two have been polarized extremes, existing side by side, within belief systems about the nature of man. Most of the early representations of the conflict are irrelevant to modern child development, but its reflection in the nature-nurture controversy is not. John Locke and his successors in

British Associationism laid the groundwork for what can be seen in the last 2 centuries in America as a strong prepossession with the empiricist view. This was the burden of the earlier background statement about both the normative tradition and the behavioristic movement. It must not be forgotten that Locke was a revolutionary, however. He was challenging, in a monarchical and elitist society, a deeply pervasive belief in the betterness of some than of others. When Darwin came along in the mid-nineteenth century, a new strength was given to nativism. By World War I Darwinism was as powerful an unconscious determinant in the biobehavioral belief system as was Locke's empiricism.

In child development, the two positions are exhibited in a number of ways. Nature versus nurture is one, the conception of qualities of the person as being determined either by inheritance or by environmental influence. The child as active agent versus the child as passive object is another. The former view sees the child as unfolding, self-controlling, initiative of behavior, dominative toward the world around him, while the latter sees him as responsive to stimuli, modified by his experience, passively changing to the dominative world outside. Still another representation is commonly (though neither necessarily nor always) seen in stage versus continuity theories of development. Freud's psychosexual stages, Werner's and Gesell's unfoldings, and Piaget's cognitive stages are nativistic, while social learning theories are clearly a reflection of empiricism. (Terman's continuity description of intelligence is an exception, for he was as nativist as they come.)

The tension between these two positions lies like a San Andreas earthquake fault beneath child development. When the tension becomes great enough, there are shakings in the laboratory. Shifts in research interests sometimes seem faddish, but some of them are partly the product of natural corrections in the nativist-empiricist conflict. The predominance of interest in child rearing and social learning in the forties to sixties was premonitory of a shift to cognitive stage explorations and the study of genetic determination of sex and race differences in the sixties and seventies. By the eighties, it is safe to predict that there will be a reversal.

To anyone familiar with children and with the data of child development research, neither nativism nor empiricism alone seems an accurate lead to assessing the determinants of child behavior. And that, of course, is the beauty of science. It forces reality into these deeper and imprecise belief systems. But scientific knowledge grows slowly, and when there is an absence of hard fact, traditional belief-systems become the guides to thought. The lacunae in knowledge are always filled with belief. Too bad that *science* cannot be divorced somehow from the *scientists,* for it is they who have these confabulating systems that sometimes interfere with the objectivity sought through the precision of research. On the intellectual level such value-laden philosophies have some of the quality of primary process thinking and can create as much confusion for the orderly development of science as the actual primary process does for the orderly development of a child's emotional life.

Inevitably there is a swing back and forth between these half-hidden polarizations. In nature, they form a false dichotomy, stemming from prescientific philosophy, and are inapplicable to contemporary thought. They created controversy in the twenties and thirties, as was reported in the nature-nurture section, and they are still doing it in the seventies. They need comment here because they are a too often unrecognized element in determining not only the path of child development research but the actual interpretation of research findings.

B. TWO TYPES OF RESEARCH

One notable change during the last 2 decades has been in the style and purpose of child development research. A conflict of ideologies is involved here, too, but it is refreshingly free of philosophy. Rather, it is related to what kind of principles researchers want to elucidate. There are two kinds: those that are intended to be universal, and those that are intended to apply to specific developmental situations. For the first kind of principle, *process* research is required; for the second, *substantive*.

Process research is related to theories of a general nature that apply to all behavior at all times. For example, research on learning, perception, work and fatigue, and cognitive processes is related to the general theory of human development. The principles discovered in such research apply to all children everywhere. Or at least this is the intent.

There is a second type of theory about development that includes propositions concerning the substantive character of nonuniversal forms of behavior developed under nonuniversal situations. This is the kind of theory that puts together specific developmental stages with specific types of experience and attempts to find generalizations that apply wherever these particular circumstances occur in conjunction. Examples of this would be Freud's conception of the Oedipus conflict and its resolution in nuclear family structures; Malinowski's work was a case in point. Other examples are the development of sex typing in certain cultural circumstances, relating the development to such variables as father and mother presence or absence; the influence of specific forms of child-rearing behavior (e.g., physical punishment) on the development of specific action systems (e.g., aggression). Studies of the adoption of certain developmental tasks, such as walking, toilet training, the child's coping with his own regressions in early adolescence, the various crisis reactions connected with marriage, childbirth, occupational role changes, etc., are other examples.

Clinical, naturalistic, and experimental research methods have all been widely used for developing knowledge of this second type. Experimental methods have commonly been used much more effectively, however, for the study of process. In the last 2 decades, there has been a strong tide running toward process research rather than toward the substantive kind. This was not true of Piaget's own studies of cognitive development, to be sure, but it has characterized much of the research which has developed from it. The frequent efforts to extend Piaget's analyses cross-culturally represent a further orientation toward the problem of universal propositions, that is, process theory and research.

It seems likely that as such process theories as those of social learning, cognition, and perception develop more fully, there will be a return to an interest in the specific substantive problems of development. For example, the famous problem posed by Freud in his little paper on the consequences of children's discovering the anatomical differences between the sexes is essentially a problem in cognitive development. Although many investigators were impressed with the importance of the problem that Freud was fumbling with, the absence of an understanding of stage differences in cognitive capacity prevented any serious undertakings to solve the problem. No direct effort has yet been made to link cognitive stages with the specific kinds of sexual experiences that boys and girls undergo during their early years, but doubtless this problem will be attacked in due course.

The swing back and forth between process and substantive research is almost inevitable. The latter depends on the principles derived from the former. When substantive investigation finds itself without an adequate base in universal propositions, its findings become clouded. For example, when social learning theory was applied to understanding the development of secondary oral drive, it worked well, and results of certain experiments confirmed predictions derived from it. But when the same theory was used for the study of more complex socially motivated behavior, it proved incomplete. Necessarily, there has had to be time-out on such research until the newer form of social learning theory could be constructed.

During the last 3 decades, developments in measurement theory have played much the same role as process research, and as of the seventies aptitude-treatment-interaction devices, cross-lagged correlation methods, and regression analysis have permitted a sharp increase in the effectiveness of genetic research and evaluations of intervention techniques.

Where do we stand now on process versus substantive research? Perspective on the up-close is always hard to get, and of course there is no single answer for all parts of child development. Social learning theory has become sufficiently mature that it should be applied substantively without further ado. There is no profit in sight for further *i* dotting and *t* crossing on modeling, imitation, discrimination, or S-R connective principles. What is needed now is a program of application to substantive developmental problems. The same may be said of Piaget's cognitive stages. The broader field of cognition is a different matter, however, and considerably more process research will be warranted before investigators divert their full attention to substantive issues. The acquisition, maintenance, and modification of motivation (e.g., achievement, dependency) has now had 3 decades of substantive study and seems to have reached a dead end. Perhaps a return to the processes themselves will provide new life. The study of language acquisition seems to have reached that stage, too, and is in serious need of some general principles to supplement the present body of descriptive and normative data.

The solution of substantive problems in child development is difficult if not impossible without the prior construction of propositions about the processes involved. By the same token, however, the sheer delineation of process has little value until the propositions are used substantively.

C. A METHODOLOGICAL CONFLICT

1. Experimentalism

Another trend closely associated with heavy emphasis on process research has been that away from naturalistic methods and toward experimental ones. The arguments favoring the latter need no repetition. Research in naturalistic settings, even with "nature's experiments," is commonly indecisive because it so often must rest on purely correlational research design. For problems embedded in process theory, the experimental method is almost essential. Since several fields were entering the process stage in the late fifties, and since much of the research was fruitful, the experimental method was associated with valued outcomes.

In retrospect we can see that it was the process quality of the research that was important, but the method was too closely associated to be viewed independently. A mild cultism soon developed, a conviction that the use of experiments was the *sine qua non* of good research. This attitude accompanied, and was one of the causes of, the relative slowdown in the study of substantive theoretical problems. There are many varieties of these latter that cannot be studied experimentally; they must be approached either by observational methods in naturalistic settings or by the use of social experiments in which societal interventions differ in different places and thus permit an experimental design treatment. (Those latter opportunities are of limited frequency, of course.) There is no good blinking at this fact and there is no point in adherence to the principle of experimentalism when such a strategy is doomed to leave great areas of developmental psychology unexamined. Experimental methods applied in the laboratory can only discover what antecedents *can* influence action or development. They never can determine what *does*. In the laboratory, modeling has been proven unequivocally to be a determinant of aggressive behavior in young children. In field studies, so have physical punishment, nonnurturance, covert invitation, and direct permissiveness. But until meticulous research in naturalistic settings is undertaken, the complex interactions of these and many other variables cannot be understood with respect to the behavior of real people in the real world.

2. Reinforcement by Government Policy

Both experimentalism and process research were further stimulated by an adventitious aftermath of the war. All wars have increased birth rates, and World War II was no exception. Demographers predicted heightened school enrollments, *McCall's Magazine* featured togetherness, college girls talked endlessly and blissfully of having six or eight children as rapidly as possible, the National Research Council estimated needs for college teachers in halcyon terms, and the federal government poured out millions for research and training grants to universities. These latter were eager to support their faculties, accepted the largess, and by 1960 were utterly flooded with graduate students.

This increase placed severe burdens on faculty with respect to supervising the work of graduate students. The high frequency of joint papers between faculty and graduate students suggests that the faculty were trying desperately to put together their more extensive and integrated research programs by concatenation of a lot of small (and quickly accomplishable) researches by graduate students. Experiments in laboratories can usually be done more quickly than either experimental or naturalistic studies in field settings. Hence the former were favored, and process problems got the nod.

The financial research-support policies of the federal government were effective in providing a base for this development. Grants of 2–4-year terms made it possible to provide graduate student support. So-called project funding was valuable in supporting many kinds of research that could be done on brief term bases. This was what most university based researchers wished. Short-term support and frequent review was not conducive to innovation in either methods or scientific problems, however, and the lack of a well-publicized policy of long-term grants (either pro-grammatic or for longitudinal researches) probably contributed to what now seems to have been an excessive emphasis on the process aspects of developmental psychology.

Other branches of child development seem not to have suffered this excess. Anthropology, medicine, and education, for example, have con-tinued with a good balance of the two kinds of research. To be sure, educational child developmentalists have continued to be subordinated to the measurement experts in schools of education, just as child psy-chologists have often been departmentally dominated by "experimental" psychologists. But there has been a difference, because the measurement specialists have helped to improve research.

In sum, the last decade has seen a scientifically unnecessary devotion to process research, which can be considered only instrumental to solv-ing the substantive problems of child development. External forces in universities and the federal government's support policies have rein-forced this imbalance. The period has left us with an abundance of data, but whether the quantity will be matched by its usefulness will be known only when it is applied to the guiding of substantive research in the next decade.

D. THE CLIMATE FOR RESEARCH

With all its productivity, child development finds itself in the seventies with the worst climate for research in its history. Federal funds for sup-port of training and basic research have been sharply reduced. The Con-gress has begun to play the accountability game, with mission-oriented research appropriations and a bluntly stated expectation of useful out-comes. Zealots for the protection of children's rights, or the rights of minorities, have combined their social mission with an antiscience cru-sade to make any kind of research with human subjects difficult. Com-munities, through their schools, have shown a not infrequent impatience with academic researchers and are reluctant to give them access to chil-dren for research participation.

The reasons lie in the unhappy transactional relationship between so-ciety at large and the research community. He who pays the piper calls the tune, and it is evident the piper has been playing the wrong tunes. He may not, in fact, be able to play all the tunes demanded, but it is also inescapably true that too often and for too long he has been giving more attention to his fellow pipers than to the paying customers.

1. What Society Asked For

Nothing new or mysterious has been asked for in the last decade. The social forces operative on child development today are the same ones chronicled, in the first pages of this history, as having created the field. All that has changed is the intensity of the demand and perhaps the articulateness of the demanders. The empathic ethos, the focus on children, and the faith in science still describe the values and expectations inherent in society's demand. But the intensity has been greater in the last decade than it was in the 5 before. Whole new classes of unprivileged people have become empathizable others. Once upon a time the homosexual was mad; then for nearly 2 centuries he was ill; now he is merely different and is reluctantly allowed to assert his right to be different. Once American blacks were slaves; then they were disfranchised freedmen; now their right to equality is acknowledged, and the battle to end discrimination is being won. For other minorities and for women the same Sierra-like progress has been made. The only surprise in all this is that anyone should be surprised or taken unaware when another upswing in the pressure for human rights occurs, for progress in these matters is always monotonic when viewed over a long enough period of time.

The focus on children has not been lost in this process. At the turn of the century the greatest needs were in the fields of health, education, and social conflict. Science and the child-oriented professions responded directly to these needs and by World War II had made great strides in satisfying them. But now two other areas of need have been identified, and both are commonly couched in terms of *rights*. One is the right of all children to the opportunity for optimal development not only in the physical realm but in the intellectual, emotional, and social ones as well. The other is the right to be treated with the same dignity and equality of respect for feelings that adults receive. Children must be treated as changing individuals, not as a homogeneous herd; they must be accorded increasing autonomy with age.

These values have been widely articulated in White House Conferences and in polemical literature for a decade or more. As is usual with society's changing values, the spokesmen for them are ahead of the populace. In the present case, however, there has been a revolt from "children" themselves, a revolt quite like that of the other unprivileged groups who have joined the class of empathizable others. Age-group pressures from the young have supported their adult spokesmen. The voting age has been reduced, college students sit on faculty committees, high schools have developed student councils, and peer participation in counseling and social control have become commonplace.

It is these pressures toward individuation and respect for children that provide some of the rationale for restrictions on scientists who wish children to participate in research. Unfortunately, much of the leadership for the restrictive movement is in the hands of lawyers, for whose profession an adversary position best describes its view of the fundamental social relationships between people. Hence, that between the researcher and the child is seen as one of exploitation, because the individual child who is being studied gains nothing and the researcher gains his research.

Lawyers are not the only ones who view research on children as exploitation. Among the unprivileged there is fear that the results of some kinds of social and psychological research may be used to justify continuing discrimination. The ill-advised use of white-appropriate intelligence tests for black inner-city children and for Mexican-American children has given them good reason not to trust the academic Establishment. And regrettable as it may be, child development researchers are not easily discriminated from the rest of the dominant part of society, much of which has been exploitative or worse.

Yet, while some parts of society are resentful toward the researchers, other parts are demanding greatly of them. The shift from health needs to the wider developmental areas is simply one more example of the popular expectation that science can solve society's problems. Medicine and the physical engineering sciences have fulfilled the expectations that disease could be controlled and that great benefits in communication, transportation, indeed in the provision of all material goods, could he achieved by research and development. It is not surprising that child developmentalists themselves were caught up in this belief. Certainly they encouraged it. For 2 decades after World War II, there was repeated testimony before Congress that the funds sought for the National Institute of Mental Health would eventually buy just what society wanted.

So, the same forces that created child development in the nineteenth century pressed hard once again for the expanded and intensified needs of the latter half of the twentieth. To understand the ambivalence in the relation between society and the researchers we must consider what the latter have provided in return for the support they solicited and got.

2. The Social Contribution

It has been a commonplace in popular scientific writing to point to dramatic breakthroughs in research and theory. Willard Gibbs and Einstein, Pasteur and Roentgen are justly celebrated. The discoveries of insulin and the antibiotics have provided dramatic controls for fatal disease. These are but the high peaks of accomplishment, of course, and the many smaller and less spectacular achievements on which they are based are commonly ignored.

Neither child psychology nor the other branches of developmental study has produced any awesome breakthroughs that have had sudden beneficial problem-solving effects with high social visibility. This is never likely to happen either, for the problems on which society wants help are ones that represent massive difficulties in the relationships between people (e.g., within-family conflicts), or between individuals and the social system (e.g., child neglect in poverty homes). Regardless of how much is known about the causes of a given social trouble, implementation of cure by change either in individuals (e.g., parents) or in institutions (e.g., schools) is a very slow process. There are no antisociotics that can have the quick and dramatically visible effects on delinquency, depressive states, or mental retardation that antibiotics had on scarlet fever or pneumonia.

One can point to a few early child development researches that have had significant longer-term effects for children's welfare, but they were long ago. The development of achievement and intelligence tests led to great advances in educational methods and clinical procedures. The work on foster homes for delinquents and for institutionalized retarded children led gradually to a widespread rejection of orphanages and reform schools. But such illustrations of breakthrough findings are hard to find.

More often, it seems, there has been an accumulative effect of long series of studies that have had a general influence on attitudes toward children rather than any categorical effect on immediate practices. These influences are easier seen when the events that produced them occurred a good many years ago. For example, in the early 1930s, Kurt Lewin's notions concerning level of aspiration became coupled with the results of American research on the effects of success and failure and of praise and reproof for performance. The cumulative effect of researches between 1925 and 1940 was to make a major change in the attitude of educators toward motivating children. The use of punishment and derogation have by no means disappeared from general educational practice in elementary schools, but there is little question that the dissemination of research findings indicating deleterious effects from punitive treatment, and from the creation of feelings of failure and loss of self-esteem, have led to a modification of educational practice. In comparison with values of 3 decades ago, contemporary educational policy leans strongly in the direction of ego-supportive practices and the avoidance of punitive efforts at motivation. In consequence, there has been a widespread increase in children's liking for schoolwork and in their achievement. The increase in contemporary research on the dimensions of self-concept and locus of control in children is a direct outcome of the results of this earlier set of studies and may be expected to result in further changes in educational practices.

Likewise in a general way, Terman's and Leta Hollingsworth's gifted-child research changed a cultural value system and set of stereotypes; it led to an entirely new image of the gifted child. While this new image probably had little direct representation in practice, over a 40-year period it did change the social attitudes toward children who were school-bright in the early years of their lives and led to a respect for them rather than an enviously derogating attitude.

More recent research discoveries, such as those relating to the effects of mother-child separations, have not yet produced extensive social changes. On the other hand, we have some 25 years of clinical observation of mother-child separation situations which permit us to state categorically that the period between 6 months and 2 years is a dangerous time for allowing the child to be long separated from his primary object of attachment. The knowledge of this period of danger is already well communicated to pediatricians, social workers, child psychologists, psychiatrists, and others who are in a position to advise with parents, and the recognition of the situation is gradually becoming introduced into the general culture via women's magazines and other sources of parental education. On the other hand, the consequences of our new knowledge, and its effect on the reduction of clinically disturbed children and adults, is too recent to provide statistics or evidence. As with the effect of the early studies on success and failure on performance and self-concept, it is likely that the effects of this research on attachment and dependency will be much more manifest 30 years from its inception than it is today. Indeed, there is a cumulative effect of the last quarter-century's research on the relations of adults to children—not only mothers to babies, and vice versa, but fathers to sons, fathers to daughters, and teachers to pupils (and again vice versa)—that is already being noted informally as the implications of the findings are gradually introduced into the culture. Over the long term they will have a significant effect in changing the experiences of children and their outcomes.

What cannot escape notice is that all these examples are of substantive research—none is process. Yet for the last 2 decades child development research has been heavily process oriented. Even when process research is of highest quality and most productive for establishing the next base from which substantive research can be undertaken, it gives no immediate service to the changing of practices with children in the real world. Its relevance is to science, not to society. Regrettably, one must add that by no means all of such research in the last few years has been of the highest quality. In the frantic scramble for respectability in the academic psychological Establishment, too many child psychologists and their graduate students have dashed madly after the wild hares of experimentalism and elegant statistical methodology while ignoring the spoor of the worthy substantive fox.

This period of emphasis on process (and the massive amount of trivia that has come with it) would be merely an interlude in the longer usefulness of the science were it not that, with federal research financing since World War II, child development has become a more visible and official part of society than it ever was before. No longer are the auditors to the researchers' explanations of their progress patient and knowledgeable foundation executives. Now they are congressmen, equally wise but less patient. They were promised solutions to the problems of mental health and retarded emotional, intellectual, and social development. Navel-contemplating theories, elegant designs, and ANOVA do not sound like the tune the customer called for.

The result of this delay in substantive research has been impatience on the part of the consumer. Congress has been blunt in judging the wide-open-field-with-peer-evaluation method to be unsatisfactory as a way of selecting researchers for support. It has added some boundary conditions in the form of mission-oriented appropriations. Funds are provided for work on specific diseases, or on mental retardation, or on violence, or on delinquency. This is a clear message to return to substantive research.

3. What Will Be the Outcome?

Process research has been essential during these last 2 decades. And while substantive research has lagged, there has been a necessary accretion of normative data in research areas that had been badly underdeveloped in earlier years. The increasing pressure for truly social problem-solving research comes at a time when child development is probably ready to turn back to relevancy as a guide to action. One thing can be guaranteed—that when it *does* turn to a heavy investment of that kind, a now impatient society will quit interfering with human research and the financial support will again flow at appropriate levels. Neither the needs nor the forces that created child development have changed, nor will they.

REFERENCES

Abbott, G. *The child and the state.* Chicago: University of Chicago Press, 1938.
Ackerknecht, E. H. *A short history of medicine.* New York: Ronald, 1955.
Adler, A. *The practice and theory of individual psychology.* New York: Harcourt, Brace, 1924.

Adler, A. *The problem child.* Published in German, 1930. New York: Capricorn, 1963.

Allport, F. H. *Social psychology.* Boston: Houghton Mifflin, 1924.

Allport, G. W. *Personality: a psychological interpretation.* New York: Henry Holt, 1937.

Anderson, V. E., & Gruhn, W. T. *Principles and practices of secondary education.* (2d ed.) New York: Ronald, 1962.

Bagby, E. *The psychology of personality.* New York: Henry Holt, 1928.

Baldwin, A. L. *Theories of child development.* New York: Wiley, 1967.

Bandura, A., & Walters, R. *Social learning and personality development.* New York: Holt, 1963.

Barker, R. G. *Ecological psychology.* Stanford, Calif.: Stanford University Press, 1968.

Barker, R.; Dembo, T.; & Lewin, K. Frustration and regression. (Studies in topological and vector psychology: II) *University of Iowa Studies in Child Welfare,* 1941, *18* (1).

Bernard, L. L. *Instinct: a study in social psychology.* New York: Henry Holt, 1924.

Blanchard, P. *The child and society.* New York: Longmans, Green, 1928.

Blanton, S., & Blanton, M. G. *Child guidance.* New York: Century, 1927.

Blos, P. *The adolescent personality.* New York: Appleton-Century, 1941.

Blos, P. *On adolescence.* New York; Free Press, 1961.

Boring, E. G. *A history of experimental psychology.* (2d ed.) New York: Appleton-Century-Crofts, 1950.

Bossard, J. H. S., & Boll, E. S. *The sociology of child development.* (3d ed.) New York: Harper, 1960.

Bowlby, J. *Attachment and loss, I: Attachment.* New York: Basic, 1969.

Bowlby, J. *Attachment and loss, II: Separation.* New York: Basic, 1973.

Breuer, J., & Freud, S. *Studies on hysteria.* 1893–1895. New York: Basic, 1957.

Burlingham, D., & Freud, A. *Infants without families.* London: Allen & Unwin, 1944.

Carmichael, L. (Ed.) *Manual of child psychology.* New York: Wiley, 1946.

Carmichael, L. (Ed.) *Manual of child psychology.* (2d ed.) New York: Wiley, 1954.

Clemens, S. L. (Mark Twain), & Warner, C. D. *The gilded age.* (1873). (Author's National ed.) New York: Harper, n.d.

Committee on Child Development, National Research Council. Proceedings of the 1st biennial meeting, Society for Research in Child Development. Mimeographed. National Research Council, Washington, D.C., November 3–4, 1934.

Dashiell, J. F. *Fundamentals of objective psychology.* Boston: Houghton Mifflin, 1928.

de Mause, L. Childhood and the psychogenic theory of history. In L. de Mause (Ed.), *The history of childhood.* New York: Psychohistory Press, 1974.

Dennis, W. *The Hopi child.* New York: Appleton-Century, 1940.

Dollard, J.; Doob, L. W.; Miller, N. E.; Mowrer, O. H.; & Sears, R. R. *Frustration and aggression.* New Haven, Conn.: Yale University Press, 1939.

Dollard, J., & Miller, N. E. *Personality and psychotherapy.* New York: McGraw-Hill, 1950.

DuBois, C. *The people of Alor.* Minneapolis: University of Minnesota Press, 1944.

Erikson, E. H. *Childhood and society.* New York: Norton, 1950.

Freud, A. *The ego and the mechanisms of defence.* London: Hogarth, 1937.

Freud, A. The contribution of psychoanalysis to genetic psychology. *American Journal of Orthopsychiatry,* 1951, *21,* 476–497.

Freud, A., & Dann, S. An experiment in group upbringing. *Psychoanalytic Study of the Child,* 1951, *6,* 127–168.

Freud, S. *Three contributions to the theory of sex.* (1905) New York: Nervous and Mental Disease Publishing Co., 1925. (2d ed.)

Freud, S. On psychoanalysis. *American Journal of Psychology,* 1910, *21,* 181–218.

Gewirtz, J. L. Attachment, dependence, and a distinction in terms of stimulus control. In J.

L. Gewirtz (Ed.), *Attachment and dependency.* Washington, D.C.: Winston, 1972.

Goddard, H. H. *The Kallikak family.* New York: Macmillan, 1913.

Goshen, C. E. *Documentary history of psychiatry.* New York: Philosophical Library, 1967.

Goslin, D. A. *Handbook of socialization theory and research.* Chicago: Rand McNally, 1969.

Groves, E. R. *Personality and social adjustment.* New York: Longmans, Green, 1923.

Hamilton, G. V. A study of trial and error reactions in mammals. *Journal of Animal Behavior,* 1911, *1.*

Hamilton, G. V. A study of perseverance reactions in primates and rodents. *Behavior Monographs,* 1916, *3* (2).

Hamilton, G. V. *Objective psychopathology.* Saint Louis: Mosby, 1925.

Hamilton, G. V. *A research in marriage.* New York: Boni, 1929.

Hartshorne, H., & May, M. A. *Studies in deceit.* New York: Macmillan, 1928.

Healy, W. *The individual delinquent.* Boston: Little, Brown, 1915.

Healy, W.; Bronner, A.; Baylor, E. M. H.; & Murphy, J. P. *Reconstructing behavior in youth.* New York: Knopf, 1929.

Holt, L. E. *The care and feeding of children.* New York: D. Appleton, 1894.

Hopkirk, H. W. *Institutions serving children.* New York: Russell Sage Foundation, 1944.

Hull, C. L. A functional interpretation of the conditioned reflex. *Psychological Review,* 1929, *36,* 498–511.

Janet, P. *The major symptoms of hysteria.* New York: Macmillan, 1907.

Jones, M. C.; Bayley, N.; Macfarlane, J. W.; & Honzik, M. P. *The course of human development.* Waltham, Mass.: Xerox Publishing Co., 1971.

Kagan, J., & Moss, H. A. *From birth to maturity.* New York: Wiley, 1962.

Kardiner, A. *The individual and his society.* New York: Columbia University Press, 1939.

Kern, S. Freud and the discovery of child sexuality. *History of Childhood Quarterly,* 1973, *1,* 117–141.

Kessen, W. *The child.* New York: Wiley, 1965.

Lee, P. R., & Kenworthy, M. E. *Mental hygiene and social work.* New York: Commonwealth Fund, 1929.

Levine, M., & Levine, A. *A social history of helping services.* New York: Appleton-Century-Crofts, 1970.

Lewin, K. *A dynamic theory of personality.* New York: McGraw-Hill, 1935.

Lewin, K.; Dembo, T.; Festinger, L.; & Sears, P. S. Level of aspiration. In J. Mc V. Hunt (Ed.), *Handbook of personality and the behavior disorders.* New York: Ronald, 1944.

Lewin, K.; Lippitt, R.; & White, R. K. Patterns of aggressive behavior in experimally created "social climates." *Journal of Social Psychology,* 1939, *10,* 271–299.

Lippitt, R. An experimental study of the effect of democratic and authoritarian group atmospheres. (Studies in topological and vector psychology: I) *University of Iowa Studies in Child Welfare,* 1940, *16* (3), 45–195.

Locke, J. Some thoughts concerning education. (1690) In *The Works of John Locke.* Vol. *8.* London: C. Baldwin, 1824.

McClelland, D. C.; Atkinson, J. W.; Clark, R. A.; & Lowell, E. L. *The achievement motive.* New York: Appleton-Century-Crofts, 1953.

Maccoby, E. E., & Jacklin, C. N. *The psychology of sex differences.* Stanford, Calif.: Stanford University Press, 1974.

McLean, D. Child development: a generation of research. *Child Development,* 1954, *25,* 1–8.

McNemar, Q. *The revision of the Stanford-Binet scale.* Boston: Houghton Mifflin, 1942.

Malinowski, B. *Sex and repression in savage society.* New York: Harcourt, Brace, 1927.

Mead, M. *Coming of age in Samoa.* New York: Morrow, 1928.

Mead, M. *Growing up in New Guinea.* New York: Morrow, 1930.

Messerli, J. *Horace Mann*. New York: Knopf, 1972.

Miller, N. E., & Dollard, J. *Social learning and imitation*. New Haven, Conn.: Yale University Press, 1941.

Murchison, C. (Ed.) *A handbook of child psychology*. Worcester, Mass.: Clark University Press, 1931.

Murchison, C. (Ed.) *A handbook of child psychology*. (2d ed. rev.) Worcester, Mass.: Clark University Press, 1933.

Murphy, G. *Historical introduction to modern psychology*. (Rev. ed.) New York: Harcourt, Brace, 1949.

Mussen, P. H. *Handbook of research methods in child development*. New York: Wiley, 1960.

Mussen, P. H. (Ed.) *Carmichael's manual of child development*. New York: Wiley, 1970. 2 vols.

Nesselroade, J. R., & Baltes, P. B. Adolescent personality development and historical change: 1970–1972. *Monographs of the Society for Research in Child Development*, 1974, *39* (Serial No. 154).

Peterson, J. *Early conceptions and tests of intelligence*. Yonkers, N.Y.: World Book Co., 1926.

Poffenberger, A. T. In *A history of the National Research Council, 1919–1933*. Reprint and Circular Series, N.R.C., 1933. Pp. 39–43.

Pollack, O. *Integrating sociological and psychoanalytic concepts*. New York: Russell Sage Foundation, 1956.

Ross, D. *G. Stanley Hall: the psychologist as prophet*. Chicago: University of Chicago Press, 1972.

Schaie, K. W., & Strother, C. R. A cross-sectional study of age changes in cognitive behavior. *Psychological Bulletin*, 1968, *70*, 671–680.

Sears, P. S. Levels of aspiration in academically successful and unsuccessful children. *Journal of Abnormal and Social Psychology*, 1940, *35*, 498–536.

Sears, R. R. *Survey of objective studies of psychoanalytic concepts*. Bulletin No. 51. New York: Social Science Research Council, 1943.

Sears, R. R. Personality development in contemporary culture. *Proceedings of the American Philosophical Society*, 1948, *92*, 363–370.

Sears, R. R.; Maccoby, E. E.; & Levin, H. *Patterns of child rearing*. Evanston, Ill.: Row, Peterson, 1957.

Sears, R. R.; Rau, L.; & Alpert, R. *Identification and child rearing*. Stanford, Calif.: Stanford University Press, 1965.

Sears, R. R.; Whiting, J. W. M.; Nowlis, V.; & Sears, P. S. Some child-rearing antecedents of aggression and dependency in young children. *Genetic Psychology Monographs*, 1953, *47*, 135–234.

Seashore, C. E. *Pioneering in psychology*. Iowa City: University of Iowa Press, 1942.

Senn, M. J. E. Insights on the child development movement in the United States. *Monographs of the Society for Research in Child Development*, 1975, *40* (Serial No. 161).

Shakow, D., & Rapaport, D. *The influence of Freud on American psychology*. New York: International Universities Press, 1964.

Skinner, B. F. *The behavior of organisms*. New York: Appleton-Century, 1938.

Stevenson, G. S., & Smith, G. *Child guidance clinics: a quarter century of development*. New York: Commonwealth Fund, 1934.

Stoddard, G. D. The second decade. *University of Iowa Studies in the Aims and Progress of Research*, 1939 (58).

Stolz, H. R., & Stolz, L. M. *Somatic development of adolescent boys*. New York: Macmillan, 1951.

Stolz, L. M. Youth: the Gesell Institute and its latest study. *Contemporary Psychology*, 1958, *3*, 10–15.

Strickland, C. A transcendentalist father: the child-rearing practices of Bronson Alcott. *History of Childhood Quarterly*, 1973, *1*, 4–51.

Sunley, R. Early nineteenth century American literature on child rearing. In M. Mead & M. Wolfenstein (Eds.), *Childhood in contemporary cultures*. Chicago: University of Chicago Press, 1955.

Terman, L. M. *The measurement of intelligence*. Boston: Houghton, Mifflin, 1916.

Terman, L. M., & Oden, M. *The gifted group at mid-life*. (Genetic studies of genius, Vol. *V*) Stanford, Calif.: Stanford University Press, 1959.

Thom, D. A. *Habit clinics for the child of pre-school age*. Washington: U.S. Children's Bureau, 1924.

Thom, D. A. *Everyday problems of the everyday child*. New York: D. Appleton, 1927.

Thomas, W. I., & Thomas, D. S. *The child in America*. New York: Knopf, 1928.

Thorndike, E. L. *Educational psychology*. New York: Science Press, 1903.

Thorndike, E. L. *Theory of mental and social measurements*. New York: Teachers College, Columbia University, 1904.

U.S. Children's Bureau. *Infant care*. Washington, D.C.: Government Printing Office, 1914 (and subsequent eds.).

Van Bergen, A. *Task interruption*. Amsterdam: North-Holland, 1968.

VanWaters, M. *Youth in conflict*. New York: Republic, 1925.

Watson, J. B. *Behavior: an introduction to comparative psychology*. New York: Henry Holt, 1914.

Watson, J. B. *Psychology from the standpoint of a behaviorist*. Philadelphia: Lippincott, 1918.

Watson, J. B. *Psychological care of infant and child*. New York: Norton, 1928.

Watson, J. B., & Rayner, R. Conditioned emotional reactions. *Journal of Experimental Psychology*, 1920, *3*, 1–14.

Wechsler, D. *Wechsler Intelligence Scale for Children*. New York: Psychological Corp., 1949.

Whiting, J. W. M. *Becoming a Kwoma*. New Haven, Conn.: Yale University Press, 1941.

Whiting, J. W. M., & Child, I. *Personality and child training*. New Haven, Conn.: Yale University Press, 1953.

Wishy, B. *The child and the republic*. Philadelphia: University of Pennsylvania Press, 1968.

Witmer, L. *The special class for backward children*. Philadelphia: Psychological Clinic Press, 1911.

Wolfenstein, M. Trends in infant care. *American Journal of Orthopsychiatry*, 1953, *33*, 120–130.

Woodworth, R. S. *Heredity and environment: a critical survey of recently published material on twins and foster children*. (Bulletin 47) New York: Social Science Research Council, 1941.

2 Ecological Psychology and Children

PAUL V. GUMP
University of Kansas

CONTENTS

Dr. E. V. James made substantial contributions to this review; his assistance is very much appreciated. Part of the bibliographic work was supported by a grant from the National Institute of Child Health and Human Development.

I. INTRODUCTION

Research dealing with environment and behavior comes from a variety of scholarly disciplines: anthropology, ethology, geography, political science, psychology, and sociology. Many applied areas have also contributed: architecture, engineering, environmental design, natural resource management, and regional and urban design. A bibliographic contribution by Craik (1973), with 280 references and 13 content areas, demonstrates the heterogeneity of studies under the behavior-and-environment label. Bibliographic periodicals are now available—for example, Esser and Archea's *Man-Environment Systems* (1969), and *Exchange Bibliographies* (1971), contributed by the Council of Planning Librarians. Moos (1973) has suggested six major types of environmental conceptions in an effort to bring order to the mélange of environment-and-behavior studies. There exists, then, a plethora of quite diverse research reports, reports whose "environment" label suggests their potential candidacy for this discussion; therefore, some initial description of what I have accepted (and rejected) is appropriate.

Material involving the physical environment might have been selected for review, that is, material in which behavior is related to physical factors of the natural or the man-constructed milieu. These kinds of environmental investigations have been included in publications by Kates and Wohlwill (1966), Proshansky, Ittelson, and Rivlin (1970), Moos and Insel (1973), and Ittelson et al. (1974). In all physical environment studies, the separation between environment and behavior is easily maintained; however, the degree to which the physical world includes all important variables of a child's external world is quite limited. Such physical milieus as living rooms, streets, playgrounds, and classrooms have programs or action structures; although these are behavioral, they are still external, environmental facts of the child's life. At different times the same milieu may support contrasting environments. To participate in a Little League contest is to be in a very different environment than to help the groundskeeper on the day before the big game—although the baseball diamond is the physical milieu in both cases. The major distinction in these examples is one of program, or of "standing pattern of behavior" (Barker & Wright 1955). Other words implying this program side of environments are "action structure," "agenda," "regime," or "standard procedure." The child environments reported here are those that deal with *physical milieu and/or program.*

One set of studies not reported here are those in which the environment is defined as it is experienced by the subject. Thus, environmental descriptions analogous to Murray's "psychological press" (1938) or studies on the perception of the environment are not included. The exclusions imply no judgment regarding the importance of such approaches; they reflect only the belief that the ecological environment, what Barker (1968) has labeled "the pre-perceptual environment," provides a useful arena for understanding child behavior; this nonpsychological yet still behavioral context provides variables which significantly condition a child's living.

Another kind of "environment" is at the interface of a sequence of subject-related environmental inputs and subject responses. This temporal juncture of subject acts and environmental stimuli represents the moment-by-moment coupling of subject and environment; this is an individual-behavior-and-environment *seam.* For behavior theory, the environment at the seam is the important environment, the one in a mutually contingent relationship with subject behavior. Gewirtz (1968), referring to inputs to child subjects, has well described such an environment and the rationale for its use. Two aspects of the seam environment are distinctive: first, the environment at the seam is not an independent ecological unit but is continuously subject dependent; second, since the seam environment remains coupled with subject behavior, it represents a "line" across space and through time, not an ecological "enclosure."

In his discussion Gewirtz does refer briefly to "ecological factors," thereby pointing to the environment which is the primary target of this review. For example, in a child care situation, "ecological factors" would include the number of caretakers, the number and age mix of children, amount and kinds of play material, and the general child activities supported by the situation. However, Gewirtz is interested in such factors only as they might yield contrasting environment-behavior seams for study; in spite of using terms like "setting" or "environment," he gives these ecological factors scant attention in their own right (see also Gewirtz & Gewirtz 1969). The ecological factors, and the *subject-independent ecological units* in which they are found, are central to our research review. The research limited to the seam environment is an important literature but will not be reviewed here. Eventually, we may expect that researchers will coordinate the ecological environment and the seam en-

vironment in order to understand environment-and-behavior relationships.

A third area of studies concerns the expanding field of human ethology. Those ethological investigations which center on the evolutionary
significance of child behaviors and invest little effort in environmental
measurement are beyond the boundaries of this review. However, an
increasing amount of ethological material is relevant to ecological psychology, and I was able to include several illustrations. Regrettably, the
coverage is incomplete; interested readers are directed to reviews by
Jones (1972) and McGrew (1972) and to a recent paper by Charlesworth
and Spiker (1974).

A final explanation is appropriate regarding the attention given to
matters of conceptualization and method. Ideally, the major thrust of a
research review would relate to findings: to what we now know in the
field. In the present case, sturdy, replicated findings are not bountiful. At
this time, the field is necessarily struggling with conceptual issues, with
how to think about the problem, and researchers are inventing and de-
bating methods of data collection. The presentation here reflects these
preoccupations with concepts and methods.

Contributions have been organized on the basis of kind and scope of
child's environment; this arrangement puts together materials of the
same general subject matter but also implies some repetition of basic
concepts and variables at various points throughout the presentation.

The description begins with an account of the ecological concepts and
methods developed by the group identified as ecological psychologists;
subsequent sections deal, in order, with the general community, with
housing, with day care centers and nursery schools, and with public
school environments. A final section reflects on the current status of
research and knowledge regarding children's environments.

II. Contributions from Ecological Psychology

In the late 1940s, Roger Barker and Herbert Wright began investigation of child life in a small midwestern town. Barker (1965) has described
salient developments in that effort. This naturalistic research not only
occurred in "real life" settings, but it avoided investigator input to either
the subject's environment or his behavior. This type of research attempted to avoid the circularity of an investigator picking up from his target
phenomena effects of what he, by measurement or control methods, put
into those phenomena. The label for such research is *transducer* research;
others later discussed it under the heading of "unobtrusive measures"
(Webb et al. 1966). The contrasting method, one usually avoided by

ecological psychologists, is *operator* research, in which the subject's environment and/or his response activity is quite deliberately put under investigator control.

A. THE ISSUE OF UNITS

One problem quickly surfacing in transducer research is that of appropriate units of analysis. Without specific experimental and testing probes to subjects, without constraints on subject behavior, what shall be the pieces of action and context which are the research base? The ecological psychologists developed units for both.

The *behavior episode* was identified as a unit of action. The episode was described in narrative records of the free-running behavior stream of children in natural contexts. These specimen records are illustrated by Barker and Wright's *One Boy's Day* (1951). The methodology of analysis of specimen records has been explicated by Wright (1967); it is based primarily on the start and the end of a unidirectional segment of a subject's behavior. Because these units have time span, they display a greater variety of properties than responses to discrete stimuli; for example, they manifest duration, conditions of initiative and termination, and qualities of the actor such as emotionality and sociality. The qualities of episodes are sensitive to ecological differences; such differences can often be identified hy analyzing the behavior episodes of the same children in different settings. For example, Gump, Schoggen, and Redl (1957, 1963) described the nature of camp settings by analysis of the episodes of boy campers.

Environmental force units (EFUs) are stretches of time in the record during which a child's associates attempt to get the child to behave in a particular fashion. Although EFUs may be initiated by either the subject or his associates, EFU description and bounding are determined directly by what environmental agents want from the child, not what the child seeks. The EFU was developed by Schoggen (1963) and is a subject-centered part of the environment. The EFU units do not directly describe the objective context within which the child behaves; rather, these units refer only to that part of the social context which actually engages the child.

A naturally occurring part of the unit developed from ecological psychology which attempts to bound the objective environment is the *behavior setting*. This unit is independent of a subject's perceptions. One may speak of a behavior setting being a subject's environment in the sense that the subject inhabits it at a given time. Beyond this, the setting unit is described in ecological, not subject behavior, terms.

The behavior setting stands as a unique unit in environmental psychology, a field in which units are rare although variables abound. Since behavior settings are so central to the research to be reported, a brief explanation is appropriate.

As explained by Barker (1968), a behavior setting consists of elements from two realms; it has a *milieu* (spatial enclosure, ground, facilities) and a standing pattern of behavior or *program* (a regime, a set of procedures, a way of doing). There is a pattern to both the milieu and the program; these patterns are similar in shape—they are "synomorphic." The passing, food-selecting line of children in a school cafeteria has a behavioral shape that is synomorphic to the tray, the sliding track, and the food offerings. The milieu-with-behavior segments are technically "synomorphs," and these exist in various degrees of inclusiveness: the cafeteria line is a part of the cafeteria, which is only a section of the entire school. There are technical means by which a synomorph of particular size can be bounded. Examples of the synomorphs of size employed in ecological research are cafeteria, Mrs. Baker's second-grade academic class, principal's office, drugstore, and grocery. Synomorphs of this span, this degree of inclusiveness, have been called behavior settings.

Several characteristics of behavior settings are important. They are objective, noninferred realities; they are solidly located in time-space loci; they are bounded contexts existing apart from any single person's (or investigator's) perception. Behavior settings are environments where people live, they are not abstractions. A second setting aspect relates to the two positions of a person within the setting; he is a component of the setting—a customer or a functionary; he is also an individual who will use the setting for his own purpose.

The third quality is implied by the second: the individual, once in a setting, is markedly influenced by its milieu and program; his behavioral opportunities and constraints come from the setting; that which he can experience is markedly influenced by the setting he inhabits.

The research contributions from ecological psychology are, then, closely tied to problems of units: units which divide the subject's behavior stream into subject episodes or spans of environmental forces, and units which delineate natural sections of the subject's objective environment.

The work of ecological psychologists on total communities is presented first; this material can be conveniently divided between investigations for which behavior settings and derivative measures are the central research target and those studies which focus on specific subject children and their behavior with regard to settings.

B. CHILDREN AND THE GENERAL COMMUNITY: BEHAVIOR SETTING CENTERED

Communities can be described in terms of the behavior settings which are their primary ecological parts. Such descriptions, at the setting level, are complete pictures of the environment under study. An early investigation, *Midwest and Its Children* (Barker & Wright 1955), described a town of 700 people (120 of whom were children) as it functioned over a year's time. If one town can be described, two can be compared. Barker and Schoggen (1973) measured the environments and the environmental usage of Midwest, Kansas, and Yoredale, England. Both towns were described with identical methods, at two points in time, a decade apart. An important aspect of the study was the introduction of a measurement of environmental size. We are accustomed to indicating the size of a community by reporting the number of its inhabitants. Logically, this would be similar to measuring the size of a pasture by counting the number of cows in it. The size of an environment can be based on the extent of its behavioral opportunities; for Barker and Schoggen, size is the amount of behavior-setting functioning which is "at hand" for inhabitant behavior. With the size measurement, data may be reported keeping environmental size distinct from environmental use. Material describing the relation of the American and English communities to their children and adolescents illustrates this point.

One question that may be asked about the status of any population class concerns its range of free movement. For example, in what proportion of a community's environment are children free to choose entry or nonentry? Put negatively, in what percentage of the community's environment are they not coerced to come into or stay out of settings? Results showed that the American children (Midwest) were presented with more noncoercive environments than were the English (Yoredale) children. Further, the percentage of child hours spent in "free settings" was also greater for the Midwest children.

A second set of data regarding the place of young people in these American and English communities refers to setting power. In settings, persons may be assigned relatively low power (guests, audience persons), moderate power (members, customers), or high power (functionaries, leaders). Young people in Midwest found more of their environment using them as relatively high-power functionaries than did the English youth. Barker and Schoggen show that if the nonadults of Midwest were to cease their functionary activity, and if the level of community activity were maintained, a very heavy additional load of activity would fall on the town's adults; the additional effort for the Yoredale adults would be very much less. Thus, in the ecological sense, children and adolescents were more needed in the American than in the English community.

Other data show that substantial portions of the environments in both towns made children *beneficiaries* of other age groups; however, Midwest children were much more likely to act as *benefactors* to other age groups when compared to Yoredale children.

The Barker and Schoggen work draws together these and other results to contrast the child rearing practices and philosophies. To oversimplify, the English system tends to reserve significant participation in community life for adulthood; then, after a long period of care and education, the young will be competent for adult tasks. Midwest, on the other hand, uses young people in some of the significant action whether or not they are assumed fully ready. While the above can be expressed as a contrast in values, it is important to consider the accompanying ecological conditions. Midwest manages a large environment with a small population; to maintain its settings, the town must accept—even instigate—significant contributions from children and adolescents. One can speculate that the ongoing environment generates the value system; at the least, it supports the system.

More traditional cross-cultural comparisons of child rearing attend to beliefs expressed by adults, sometimes to specific actions by caretakers toward children. The Barker and Schoggen approach is radically different; it asks how ecological units of the overall habitat deal with children and how children function as participants in these units; finally, it suggests the "ecological need" that underlies some of the contrasts.

C. CHILDREN IN THE COMMUNITY: SUBJECT CENTERED

The preceding studies targeted behavior settings and measures derived from the setting unit. Questions about children were usually pursued by analyses of how the class "children" was dealt with by the settings of a community. Ecological studies in which individual children served as subjects have been carried out by Wright and his colleagues (Wright 1969, 1974a, 1974b). The major research curiosity has been the relation between community size and child life; accordingly, the investigations have centered mainly on four small midwestern towns (populations: 500–1,400) and one large town (33,000).

The Wright researches present a wide range of methods for investigation of human habitats; they also offer a wide range of dependent variables expressive of child life within various habitats. Wright has sought to infer the processes which underlie relationships between various ecological and behavioral (or cognitive) variables; and, to a degree, he is able to show that such relations go beyond mere correlations, to "limited necessity."

The *activity range* of the child is prominent among the targets of these studies. It consists of the specific community parts in which the child actually behaves. These ecological units, behavior settings, have been identified, and the child's life has been described in terms of settings entered. The investigators concentrate on the range of the child abroad, that is, away from his home and school.

The range or "trail" methodology can involve self-report through a day diary as well as through an interviewer. A major work by Roemer (1968) with adolescents in a black community just outside an eastern metropolis involved use of diary reports to identify settings typically inhabited by youth and to describe patterns of peer association and group activity.

The hope in these ecological efforts is that one can learn how associations between an ecological condition and an aspect of a child's behavior or development can occur. The associations by themselves are often not difficult to establish. For example, Hathaway et al. (1959) were able to show that variations in adolescent MMPI scores were associated with residence in farms, small farms, or cities. But the mediating conditions, the linkages for such association, are left unclear.

Fuller reporting by Wright of his work, its methodology, and its theory context is forthcoming.

III. Children and Housing

Housing provides the immediate environment of a child's early life; as the child becomes more mobile, the proximal environment outside the house also is used. The behavior opportunities available to a child are determined to a large extent by how much space is available within and around the home and how that space is structured and furnished. A useful review of housing research and presentation of normative data on families' use of space within the home has been offered by Altman, Nelson, and Lett (1972). Discussions of housing areas in relation to children's play and many photographed examples of problems and solutions are available in Allen (1968), Bengtsson (1970), and Friedberg (1970). Pollowy (1973) has analyzed 36 user studies dealing with the play needs of boys and girls and with the circumstances of play. The analysis proceeds from consideration of spaces inside the dwelling (livingroom, kitchen) through areas immediately outside (access areas, courtyards) to more distal portions of residential settings (playgrounds, shelters). A stimulating aspect of Pollowy's work is specification of the design implications for each space as implied by available research findings. Research prohlems and findings in the area of sociological studies in housing have been discussed by Glazer (1967), Michelson (1970), Raven (1967), Schorr (1963), and Wurster (1951).

A. SLUM CLEARANCE

Research interest in the area of housing environment and human behavior had its impetus from the urban ecology studies of the Chicago
School (Faris & Dunham 1939; Park & Burgess 1925; Wirth 1938). Using "natural areas" as units of analysis and census records as data, it was
possible to locate regions which exhibited characteristic social behavior
patterns. Specifically, slums could be identified mostly on the basis of
location and physical characteristics of their housing; such slums showed
symptoms of social pathology such as high incidence of crime and mental illness. The location of slums was explained by economic behavior in
speculative buying near central business districts, and the social pathology was explained by a population of highly mobile single men and wom-
en. The density of such a population under poor housing conditions with
accompanying anonymity was hypothesized to have provided the conditions for the social pathology.

Following the general concern about slum environment, slum clearance and urban renewal programs got under way in several cities in the
1930s. As people moved from slum areas to public housing, questions
about the social and health effects of housing became amenable to research. Chapin (1938, 1941, 1951) documented the benefits of public
housing for former slum dwellers. It was found that social participation
of such families increased; for example, when they moved to public
housing, their membership in organizations such as clubs and church
groups increased. Further, qualitative attributes of living rooms improved; use crowding (measured by multiple uses of the same space)
decreased (Chapin 1941).

Wilner et al. (1962) reviewed 40 selected studies concerning the effects
of improved housing on health and social life. Several studies in Europe
and in the United States showed clear negative correlations between
conditions of housing and incidence of tuberculosis; crowding was often
the housing condition investigated. Studies on aspects of health such as
general morbidity and hospital admissions showed similar results.
Among social phenomena, mental hospital admissions and delinquency
rates were found to be related to such characteristics of housing environment as overcrowding and percentage of buildings needing major repair.

In a study in Great Britain, Petzing and Wedge (1970) found that
7-year-olds from crowded homes were 9 months behind in reading age
compared to children from noncrowded homes even when other variables relevant to reading were controlled. Hole (1959) reported that when
families moved from crowded dwellings to public housing and privacy
became available, they experienced a decrease of interpersonal tension.

In Baltimore, Wilner et al. (1962) conducted a longitudinal study from 1955 to 1958; 300 families who moved into new public housing projects and 300 matched families (those living in slums but applicants for public housing) were studied for 3 years by periodic data collection. The investigators documented the improvement in housing by comparative measures of persons per room, of kitchen and bath facilities, and of physical condition of various dwelling factors and areas. A morbidity survey was conducted by interviewers 11 times during the study to record health conditions of the members of the families; adjustment and mental health data were similarly collected five times, and the quality of housing was rated twice.

The test group was compared to the control group with regard to episodes of illness, severity of illnesses, hospitalizations, and mortality. Comparisons were made within each age group. On each index and within most age groups, the data generally supported the hypothesis that the test families maintained better health than the control families.

For the young (below 20 years of age) episodes of illnesses increased during the period immediately after moving to public housing; later, the number of illnesses decreased to a level below that of the control group. This phenomenon was accounted for by an initial increase in communicable diseases among the children newly assembled in the housing project; they apparently needed time to develop immunity.

Social adjustment within the families and with neighbors was studied through interviewing. A number of measurements showed directional trends confirming the expectations of better adjustment in new housing, but only a few reached statistical significance. The test families reported an increase in satisfaction with housing and space and with interaction with neighbors; however, interpersonal relations within these families did not show significant improvement.

Although the Wilner research indicates that scores on intelligence and achievement tests showed no difference between the children who moved to public housing and the control group, records showed that the new-housing children were more regular in school attendance and experienced more promotions than those who stayed in slum dwellings.

From the above results, slum clearance and urban renewal could be looked upon as having a positive effect on people who have to move from slums to public housing. However, Fried (1963, 1967) and Gans (1959, 1962) have shown that there are other important problems. Disturbing a slum community and dispersing people into public housing projects can eliminate existing community life and result in no satisfactory substitutes for many of the families. Most families affected by slum clearance and urban renewal resented the forced relocation process. An answer to this dilemma was suggested in urban rehabilitation or a physical improvement of dwellings in slums instead of clearing the area for reconstruction. Colean (1960) has reported case studies of such neighborhood rehabilitation of housing in several cities; these case studies indicate some improvement in health and social life of the inhabitants, though no systematic quantitative data are presented.

Improved housing in the above studies meant facilities such as hot and cold water supply, internal plumbing, screens for windows, pest control, and more space and rooms per inhabitant. The hypotheses regarding social benefits have found some, though equivocal, support. It has been found that people appreciate facilities such as more space per person, and such facilities have reduced tension arising from use crowding or multiuse of space. On the other hand, massive forced relocation of families from slums to the "benefits" of better housing has also been found to disturb the ongoing social life to the extent that the net result might be termed negative. In general, less confidence exists now than in the 1930s and 1940s that slum clearance alone will yield more benefit than harm. In the early 1970s a number of housing projects across the United States were being viewed as expensive failures (Newman 1972).

B. DESIGN OF HOUSING

Improvement in physical health can be shown to relate to general improvements in housing facilities; variations in social behavior, however, seem more influenced by details of housing design. Issues in design include: high-rise versus low-rise construction, houses placed around a courtyard versus row housing, provision of large playgrounds versus distribution of small playgrounds, and provision of large projects with structures of similar form versus establishment of a variety of housing in a project.

Studying the housing conditions of nonnatives living in special Alaskan communities, Smith (1972) found that children became less active after staying there some time. Some women were depressed, and about two out of three were found taking psychotropic medicines. The housing facilities for these people were poor and small; there was not enough space or facilities for vigorous play and other activity inside. Outside the home, it was too cold and dark for half the year for any outdoor activities. The severe cold interacting with the given facilities (including housing) resulted in social isolation and low stimulation. The latter conditions, it is reasoned, produced apathy and depression in women and severely affected the physical and emotional condition of children.

The separation of inhabitants from the facilities which might enliven their existence is a serious complaint also reported by Srivastava and

Good (1969). These authors note that adult inhabitants of a midwestern urban housing project see activities of the many children as a threat, although they are aware that lack of recreational facilities for children contributes to the problem.

1. Site Plan

Reporting on studies of several housing projects for low-income families in the San Francisco area, Cooper (1972) has called for more attention to and research on exterior environment and site planning as opposed to emphasis on interior design. Public housing projects have generally succeeded in providing safe and sanitary interior spaces; however, Rainwater (1966, 1970), studying the Pruitt-Igoe projects in Saint Louis, and Cooper (1970, 1972), investigating projects in San Francisco, have found that when housing projects were beset with problems and were labeled failures, the inhabitants' complaints focused on the public spaces and communal facilities rather than on facilities inside apartments. These residents were often so afraid of the neighborhood that they had a "house as haven" attitude (Rainwater 1966).

In studies of the external environment, several issues have been pursued: the placing of houses or apartments in relation to each other within a project; location of housing at high-speed heavy-traffic streets or light-traffic streets; structuring of space between the apartment door and the public street; the kind of building structure, namely, high-rise apartments or low-rise and single-story buildings; design; and use of space for children's play areas. Investigations in which such issues were pursued are summarized below.

Festinger and his associates (Festinger 1951; Festinger, Schachter, & Back 1950) studied a housing project containing one section of apartment buildings and another section of single-family houses. There were 10 apartments in each apartment building, five on each floor, all opening to a long porch in front. The single-family homes were of attached and unattached types but were organized so that about 10 houses faced a courtyard. It was hypothesized that both physical distance and functional distance, produced by positional relationships, would affect the pattern and number of passive contacts, which in turn influenced the pattern of friendships developed. The research data supported the hypothesis. Sociometric choices of residents showed that close friendships of residents were mostly with families who lived nearby. In the courtyard arrangement, families living in houses facing each other or next-door neighbors were most likely to form such friendships. In the apartment buildings, those living in apartments near staircases and postal letter delivery points had more friends than others. Families living in houses around a courtyard were found to form a cohesive group. Some houses were located at the end points of the U-shaped courtyards but facing a main street instead of the courtyard; families living here were found to be socially isolated from the rest.

Two households facing each other across a street could be as well acquainted as next-door neighbors but only if the street had very light traffic. Appleyard and Lintell (1972) compared three kinds of streets: heavy traffic, moderate traffic, and light traffic. All three streets were located in the same general neighborhood, and data were collected by interviewing the residents. The proportions of apartment dwellers and homes without children were found to increase as the traffic level on the street increased. On the light-traffic street, children often used sidewalks for play or for walking to a neighborhood store; such activities on the heavy-traffic street were practically nonexistent.

Jacobs (1961) has written extensively to show that, in successful and lively neighborhoods, sidewalks are used to assimilate children in a variety of activities and play, to provide safety for residents and pedestrians, and as a setting for social contacts. For sidewalks to serve these functions, traffic on the streets concerned should not be too heavy or too fast. In other words, these streets should be more like neighborhood streets and less like highways. Appleyard and Lintell's study has shown how high level of noise and high risk of accidents created by heavy traffic prevent sidewalks from functioning as settings for social contacts and children's play.

Other consequences of traffic noise were demonstrated by Cohen, Glass, and Singer (1973); they studied auditory discrimination and reading ability of children living in 32-story towers over a Manhattan expressway. Apartment noise was negatively related to height of residence. For children who had lived under these conditions 4 or more years, height of residence was positively related to auditory discrimination, and the latter was positively related to reading ability. Thus, through the mediation of noise and its effect on auditory discrimination, children living on lower floors read significantly more poorly than children living on the higher ones.

2. High-Rise versus Low-Rise Buildings

High-rise constructions, by definition, imply some positional relationships, like one dwelling over the other; they restrict the possibility of some others, such as a courtyard. Wallace (1952) has provided a discussion of the influence of housing on social structure with particular reference to high-rise and low-rise public housing projects. On the basis of his own observation and conversations with tenants in one project in Philadelphia with low-rise row houses and in one project in New York with high-rise apartments, Wallace proposed 44 specific hypotheses about housing and social life. Verification of these hypotheses was not within the scope of that study, but Wallace recommended that the total population of a project be kept under 1,500 persons, that density be kept at a minimum, and that each dwelling unit include some privately controlled outdoor space in the form of a porch or yard.

Fanning (1967) studied the medical records of families in the British armed services while they were housed in Germany. Respiratory complaints, especially of children, were more frequent from apartment dwellers than from families in houses; "psychoneurotic complaints" were more frequent for apartment women. Further, the latter complaint increased on the higher floors of the apartments. Physical isolation in small space was used to account for the respiratory problems; social isolation, for the emotional complaints. It was assumed that developing social contact was important for all of the families, since they were uprooted from previous associations; it was further assumed that apartment dwelling, particularly on the higher floors, made spending time outside in yards and walks less likely; this in turn made less probable the development of social contacts. The Fanning study unfortunately did not actually measure social contact, so this is an assumed mediating variable in a correlational study.

The negative effects of high-rise buildings on families have been reported in several other studies. After reviewing investigations from several countries, Stewart (1970) concluded that the great majority of families with children were not satisfied with living in an apartment, either high rise or low. Cooper (1972) has provided data to show that high-rise buildings for low-income housing contributed to an institutional environment, negative social status, unsafe and unhealthy environment, lack of community life, and high crime rates.

Cooper has pointed out that the cultural value associated with single-family housing and against multifamily high-rise buildings operates as an intervening variable to yield several effects. The norm of aspirations of families in the United States is for a single-family dwelling. The stigma attached to high-rise buildings leads to the perception of an institutional environment and negative social status. These perceptions, coupled with other problems in site plan and management policies, are supposed to lead to such sociopathological symptoms as crime, delinquency, and a lack of community life.

The idea that sociological and ecological phenomena interact to produce the problems of high-rise housing for low-income families can be supported by other investigations. Reporting about housing in Helsinki,

Sweetser and Sweetser (1968) have pointed out that most of the new housing construction there was multifamily projects and that most of the single-family housing in Helsinki was substandard. It seems that middle-income families chose to buy apartments in multifamily projects. While social class or cultural attitudes toward single or multifamily dwellings may be important, it should also be noted that there are associated ecological factors. For example, the multifamily projects were planned with amenities like shopping, transportation, and schools, while the single-family houses were located far away in the outskirts of the city. In this country also, high-rise apartments have been more successful when accompanied by a large janitorial and security staff (Newman 1972) and when the populations consist almost exclusively of young, single, middle-income professionals (Werkerle & Hall 1972).

The specific characteristics of high-rise housing which are related to problem behaviors need to be isolated and investigated. Height away from the ground by itself can result in reduced visits to any place outside the building. Littlewood and Sale (1972) found that smaller percentages of children from high-rise apartments played in the yards than from low-rise apartments.

The kind of access is another important factor; the access to high-rise apartments may be from a balcony, a corridor, or some variation of these. Balconies can facilitate informal contacts between residents. Long "double-loaded corridors" usually function strictly as trafficways; to talk to a neighbor one has to go to a closed door and gain formal admittance. Thus Stewart (1970) found that only 9% of the dwellers in balcony-access apartments professed loneliness as against 57% in corridor-access apartments.

Newman (1972, 1973) compared two apartment complexes in New York occupied by low-income families of very similar characteristics and located in the same neighborhood; one was a high-rise apartment complex, the other low-rise. About three times as much crime was reported in the high-rise complex as in the low-rise complex. Newman used the concept of defensible space to account for this phenomenon. The high-rise buildings were not designed to make the space between the apartment door and the public street defensible; this space was blind to direct surveillance from either the public street or from apartments, thus making it a no-man's-land. But the apartments in the low-rise project had small patches of land with only short distances from the street and building entrance; these small pieces of land were shared by a small number of families. Because of the surveillance from the apartments and from the street, these spaces had the characteristics of defensible space.

A habitat's safety is obviously related to the kind of life a young child can lead. Young children in the low-rise project played on landings and up and down stairwells, their activity monitored by mothers listening through partially opened apartment doors. Usually children in the high rise were not permitted to use these extra play spaces; doors were locked, with young children inside. Safety and location of child play can be mutually supportive qualities: a safe area is used by children; once so used, the area is watched over by their caretakers, thereby increasing the safety of the space for all.

Older children's depredations can increase the danger of a project. In New York projects, youngsters found ways to ruin both elevator cages and shafts. With elevators out of action, residents on the higher floors felt especially exposed to danger. Children themselves suffered maiming and death in their elavator recreations. The New York City Housing Authority reported 21 children killed in elevator accidents between 1969 and 1971 (Newman 1972). Threat to the peace and security of the project can also come from young people who are not residents but who utilize the facilities. Newman reports that a project in one city borders on three different schools and residents complain of much teenage harrassment. Projects near popular hamburger joints or playgrounds often show higher crime rates. The threat of the collective youth culture to children was expressed by parents in the Pruitt-Igoe project (Rainwater 1970).

While Newman notes instances in which high-rise construction was successfully managed by middle-class families and their children, he declares that use of high-rise construction by welfare families is proving disastrous. Housing officials find that such projects, in even 5 years, may be physically destroyed—a destruction heavily assisted by the children and youth who lived there. We are accustomed to study environments in terms of the two-way ecological relation between environments and species. Children shape environments as well as inhabit them.

C. USE OF LANDSCAPE

Open spaces around homes and apartments are provided with the intention and expectation that the spaces would have utility. Some utilities, such as providing circulating fresh air, are not dependent on human behavior. Nevertheless, human use of these spaces for activities can become very important. We have already noted that, under certain conditions, undesirable human behavior (crime) can prevail in the nonprivate, nonpublic landscape. We now turn to more positive uses of the landscape. Such uses include vigorous games, social contacts, domestic activities, and children's play. We need to understand the conditions under which such positive uses flourish so that such conditions can be created and conditions supporting crimes and other pathological uses can be minimized.

Researches systematically describing and documenting uses of open spaces around homes and apartments are rarely reported. It seems that when a designer provides space for positive uses, such uses by the occupants are assumed to take place. The studies of Cooper (1972), Newman (1972), and Rainwater (1970) have clearly shaken that faith.

The functions and structure of neighborhood parks and open space in housing projects may be considered generally similar. But since our attention is on housing environments, we will deal with neighborhood parks only briefly. Gold (1972) has provided a useful review and discussion on the use and nonuse of neighborhood parks; Bangs and Mahler (1970) and Dee and Liebman (1970) have also studied use of such parks in urban areas. Holme and Massie (1970) studied facilities for play provided in housing projects and outside. Evidence so far developed suggests that parks and playgrounds do not accommodate a substantial portion of an area's play requirements. The single most important determinant of park use is physical proximity; playground facilities tend to be used mostly by children living quite near; even these youngsters visit briefly—one investigator (Wade 1968) reports 15 minutes as an average stay.

Some residual effects of arrangements of the open landscape on behavior, such as friendship patterns, have already been reported. We turn to the kinds of behavior that occur on the landscape and to the characteristics of their location.

Saile, Borooah, and Williams (1972) have reported one of the most comprehensive studies of this kind. In addition to interviewing both architects and residents, observers recorded data on actual behavior occurring on the grounds of two housing projects in Rockford, Illinois. The behavioral data were used to compare design intentions to actual use. The houses were placed around partially enclosed service courts with a back door from the kitchen to the service court. Results showed that the back door was used much more as an entranceway than was the main door on the living room side. Also, the kitchen itself became an area for social interactions, a finding more pronounced for black residents than for white. Children used the courts for their play more often than an area specifically designed for play. A central sidewalk, designed to connect pedestrian traffic to the main road, was found to be used mostly by cyclists, while pedestrians often took a shortcut through the playground. Investigations to understand why such inconsistencies occur between design intentions and actual use can be very useful for the design profession.

Coates and Sanoff (1972) used a similar observational method to develop a behavioral map of a residential project. Attention was focused on children, and observations were conducted during after-school hours, once a day on four weekdays and two Saturdays. A community open space provided with facilities for several kinds of games was found to be well used. Ambiguous places, places without built-in cues for specialized use, such as backyards and streets, were used less often; but behavioral diversity (the ratio of number of different kinds of uses to total number of uses) was high in such ambiguous spaces. In general, fewer teenagers than younger children used the facilities in the housing project. Small groups of two to three persons were more common than single individual or larger group activities.

From England, where a larger proportion of the population lives in public housing, several studies on children's play in housing projects have been reported (Hole & Miller 1966; Holme & Massie 1970; Littlewood & Sale 1972; Stewart 1970; White 1953).

Stewart (1970) interviewed almost 300 apartment dwellers in six English localities. No observational data or control groups were established. The study offers parental opinion regarding apartment life for children: 92% of adults with children under 5 years said that they would prefer houses to apartments. Parents (usually mothers) reported that children in apartments were too "restricted," were not "content." Unfortunately, a systematic analysis of specific reasons for the unsuitability of apartment life for children was not developed. There was agreement that playgrounds and play groups did not solve the problem for the younger children.

Loneliness, especially of mothers, was a widespread complaint. Lack of sufficient social interaction for mothers can affect children through two quite different routes. The "psychological carryover" from mother to child is an obvious possibility. Also, if loneliness means that the activity range of the mother is restricted—if, for example, she does little visiting with other mothers, if she does not frequently get to a variety of settings—this can affect the young child directly. Since a young child's activity range is quite dependent on that of the mother, a "lonely" mother can present the child with an understimulating, socially restricted environment.

Data which go beyond opinion of parents to actual behavior of children have been offered by Littlewood and Sale (1972). Data were collected by observations similar to the behavior mappings previously reported; 16 housing estates from five different cities with locations in central city areas and on the outskirts were observed. About 50,000 observations were recorded.

During these summer observations, when outdoor play was expected to be at its peak, about 20% of the children were observed outdoors at any time. The 5–10-year-olds were the most frequent users; about 30% of such children were observed in the outdoor space of the projects. The secondary-school-age children were seen least often; being old enough to wander away, they were free to use public parks and other facilities far from the projects.

The proportion of children seen playing was positively correlated with the proportion of children living on ground-floor apartments and negatively correlated with density of persons per acre. When multistory buildings had wide access decks, children were often found playing outside their apartments on these access decks. With such access decks the difference between high-rise and low-rise buildings in the proportion of children was minimal.

Most outside play, more than 75% of all observations, took place near dwellings. The preference for nearness was true irrespective of what kind of place was available nearby; thus, where roads and pavements were near dwellings, even such places were often used by children for play. Child use of gardens, planted areas, and wild areas was also highly related to nearness to dwelling entrances.

Use of play areas was related to the kind of equipment they provided. Thus playgrounds with swings, slides, and wading pools were found well used, while unconventional architectural equipment, like a concrete maze, pyramid, or play platforms, often very expensive, was seldom found in use.

In addition to presentation of their findings, Littlewood and Sale (1972) also provide helpful discussions, explaining the phenomena and specifying their implications for housing planners and administrators.

Newson and Newson (1968) have presented a detailed report of child behavior and child-rearing practices expressed by English mothers of various social class and housing statuses. These authors make clear that housing, use of housing, and social class are tightly interrelated. For example, the extent to which the kitchen is the center of family activity is greatest in the lower classes. The child's use of various spaces—and mother's behavior related to that use—are well described in the research account. In some analyses, the Newsons controlled class variables and presumably tested the relation of housing alone to family and child life; for example, punishment of lower-class children was significantly more frequent in the unimproved and more densely populated housing.

The Newsons remark on one other matter that also appears in studies conducted in the United States: the separation between the familial behaviors expressive of sharing, fairness, and mutual help existing inside the dwelling and the more "might makes right" activity in the areas just outside. As the Newsons express it, lower-class young learn that in the yards and streets beyond their homes, "the weakest go to the wall" (p. 135).

D. SUBURBS AND NEW TOWNS

Although millions of children are now growing up in suburbs, accounts of how life goes for children as a consequence of suburban conditions are not easily found. However, there is one proposal for construction of housing in the suburbs that brings together propositions about central developmental problems, life for children, and design specifications. Alexander (1972) begins with the assumption that flight to the suburbs represents a withdrawal from stress. However, suburban life, with its very low density of children, its individual yards and lack of communal space, makes it very difficult for children to find one another. The suburb, says Alexander, "virtually destroys the children's play group." (Researchers should test this undocumented yet very important assertion.) With the loss of the play group, the development of a pathological "autonomy-withdrawal syndrome" begins. As a consequence of his psychological and ecological diagnosis, Alexander offers a 12-point design solution. The major qualities most relevant to children would involve a relatively high density of families (28) in a cluster about common land. The land itself, shielded from street traffic, would be accessible and visible from every dwelling. Although the common land would be continuous for the 28 families, it would be provided with a variety of small play spaces with grass, earth, water, and mud available. The ingenious fashion by which Alexander would provide for density yet create an open, even rural-appearing environment need not detain us here. The central point is that he has made a highly explicit statement about the ecological condition of children and the presumed effects of that condition. The research required to test Alexander's propositions is fairly obvious. What is the psychological condition of children with and without frequent play group experiences? What community and housing arrangements support the development of children's play groups?

Much literature is available describing new towns such as Reston, Virginia, or Columbia, Maryland. Lansing, Marans, and Zehner (1970) have discussed such towns in terms of density, availability of recreational settings, and so forth. The U.S. Department of Housing and Development (1970) has published an annotated bibliography of over 600 entries dealing with almost 200 communities. However, systematic studies of child behavior and adjustment in the towns are not provided.

E. HOUSING AND CHILDREN—CONCLUDING THOUGHTS

The research on housing in relation to children's lives and children's development tends to be diverse rather than cumulative. The variety of orientations and methodologies makes it difficult to integrate findings. However, there are repeated concerns in the research that can be employed to provide a way of looking at the material.

Research has indicated that improvement of interior dwelling arrangements and facilities will not solve the problem of secure and active living
in the community. Inhabitants, especially children, are very much affected by conditions exterior to the dwelling area.

One important dimension appearing explicitly in the community work
of ecological psychologists and more implicity in housing research is the
availability of behavioral opportunities. A fundamental question that
one may ask of a small town or of a housing project is: to what extent are
the places, things, persons, and events which support interesting activity
and sociality available here? The first level of unavailability is the literal
absence of possible supports; for example, outdoor play space may simply be lacking, or those commercial settings often frequented by school-
age children (drug stores, eateries, variety stores, etc.) do not exist. Children themselves may be only sparsely present, a condition which surely
reduces play opportunities and which may become an increasing problem for communitites with low birth rates. Certain facilities may be physically present but functionally unavailable. Children have traditionally
used sidewalks, streets, and alleys as their urban playgrounds; when traffic becomes too rapid or heavy, these play spaces are lost. On a more
complicated level, children become unavailable to one another if danger
prevents an informal outdoor space from being used as a get-together
place. Some research findings have documented this limitation on
children's lives; there are a few hopeful findings on how the relatively
safe domain of the apartment may be extended to hallways, landings,
and outside ground space. Balcony access, as opposed to double-loaded
corridors, appears to facilitate children's outside play; space that, for one
reason or another, is easily monitored increases the likelihood of play
beyond the child's dwelling; spaces that can be seen as extensions of a
home area are quite useful to young children; spaces farther abroad (e.g.,
playgrounds) are often not.

A more fundamental problem presented by recent research is the conflict between the requirements for hospitable housing and the depredations of children and adolescents. Research on providing children with
play opportunities and on how areas might be protected from children
does exist. The more fundamental question as to how behavior of the
young might contribute to housing hospitality is yet to be answered.

IV. ENVIRONMENTS FOR PRESCHOOLERS

A. DAY CARE

An analysis of research findings related to day care has been presented
by Grotberg (1971). Chapman and Lazar (1971) have reviewed present

conditions and future needs in the area. Clearly, description of day care arrangements should be preceded by consideration of their context. Political and ideological antagonists are using day care as a battleground (Ellis & Petchevsky 1972); there are economic facts of life forcing the day care problem to our attention. Of women with children under 6 years, one in three works (U.S. Bureau of the Census 1971, 1972). Since the proportion of women in the work force has been increasing rapidly, the need for some kind of care for preschool children will probably continue.

Although there have been strong pressures for the establishment of day care centers, two economic facts of life are pertinent. At present, day care at centers is *not* an arrangement made by a large proportion of working mothers; it has been estimated at 8% (Low & Spindler 1968). The second hard fact about center day care is that the real expense (for "good care") far exceeds what most working mothers actually pay now or can be expected to pay in the near future. Center day care which would serve poor and near-poor working mothers translates, under today's circumstances, into heavily subsidized day care (Angrist & Lave 1973).

The major alternatives to child care at a center include care in the child's home by father (10%) and by other relatives (18%) and care in other homes by relatives (18%) and nonrelatives (20%). (Percentages are from Low & Spindler [1968]). Use of private family care thus far exceeds center care. Although most citable research on children refers to centers, such research touches only a fraction of the environments provided for the children of working mothers.

Clearly, factors operate which will sustain family care arrangements in the future. Family care is less expensive than unsubsidized center care. Accessibility is a second obvious advantage for family care. Ruderman (1968) reports that 70% of family care users are within 5 minutes of the sitter, but only a third of the center's users are so close. Other advantages of the family system have been listed by Emlen (1972). Many of the advantages are not research supported, but some appear self-evident. For example, it is common knowledge that most care givers have had experience in care of their own children. Emlen's list deals with several classes of factors: the suitability of the family arrangement from the point of view of the mothers, of the caretakers, of the child, and of the larger society. There are 32 advantages proposed, which I will not recite here; I recommend the Emlen references for vigorous detailing of support for the family day care arrangement.

There are studies presenting a less optimistic picture of family day care; Willner's publication (1969) is an example. It is perhaps suggestive that the more favorable reports come from Spokane, Portland, and Pasadena, and the pessimistic ones from New York City.

The research effort by Emlen, Donoghue, and LaFarge (1971) has been directed to questions about the locations of sitters and the concerns and reactions of sitters' mothers to the arrangements. What actually happens to children and with what effects was not investigated. However, one Emlen measure did approach the question of input to children: the number of children cared for per home, or population size. Some discussions of the size issue and the child's welfare have included "horror stories" to create revulsion against child care models of which the author disapproves. One cited case involved 47 children in a home licensed for six; in this environment, the younger ones were tied to cribs and chairs (Keyserling 1971). More useful information is offered by Emlen, who makes two points about size: for his Portland, Oregon, sample, the average number of children in a day care home was 3.30; only 5% of his sample were in homes involving more than six children. Further, since frequencies dropped off very rapidly after three children, it was inferred that large numbers of children in a home represented a different environment, a deviant enterprise. Emlen suggests that the heavily populated arrangement probably does provide inadequate care of young children.

1. Center Care Compared to Alternatives

Very few comparative data are available regarding what happens to children and children's behavior in various preschool environments. A study proposed by the Center for Applied Behavior Analysis (1972) deserves attention even though it was not carried out. The investigative plan established five types of care as contrasting environments: sponsored home care, proprietary home care, AFDC (own mother) care, sponsored center care, and proprietary center care. Dependent variables referred to language and intellectual development and "personality." The research plan was developed from consultation with a sophisticated group of researchers and practitioners; the inventory of variables and measurement possibilities and the excellent child care bibliography should be useful to those planning research in this area.

While the above plan put most emphasis on possible lasting effects of preschool environments, on "residual variables," the ongoing input and reaction of children were studied by Prescott (1973). Four different environments were investigated: closed centers (most activity decisions made by teachers), open centers (much activity choice by children), family (proprietary) care, and nursery-and-home care. Details on care definitions are available in Prescott (1972). Variables dependent on environmental types included: time in transition between activities; whether activity was initiated and terminated by external pressure, external instigation, or spontaneous direction; and amount and type of adult input.

Briefly, it was found that, relative to all other environments, the closed center used up much child time in official transitions (24%) and presented the most adult pressure and least spontaneous activity change. Even the open centers (although in clear contrast to the closed ones) showed more transition time and more adult pressure in the initiation and termination of segments than did the nursery-home combination. Children in closed centers were found relatively often in closed activities, that is, those which intrinsically restrict the possibilities of action: copying, coloring in color books, or working puzzles. In the homes, such activities were infrequent; on this variable open centers again placed between the closed ones and the homes. Prescott (1973) also found that exploration was most frequent in the nursery-home environment, least in the closed center.

The Prescott sample of environments and of children was necessarily limited; each was selected as representative of "good quality" for its type, and all were located in southern California. Yet there are variables and measurements here suggesting that life for a child in a center, particularly one of closed structure, is substantially different from life in a home or home-and-nursery environment.

2. Manipulations of Center Care

The Living Environments Group, directed by Todd Risley, has investigated variations in day care milieu and program as related to staff and child behavior. The most prominent dependent variable has been appropriate engagement of the child with the presented section of the day care environment; a "PLA-CHECK" method of evaluating such engagement has been offered by Doke and Risley (1971). Engagement is taken as a measure of the suitability of the surround for the child. Day care is not viewed as preparation for life in yet another environment but as the environment for life now.

One set of studies concerns how children are put into contact with activities and materials. A program may present simultaneous options or a required sequence. Greater material and personnel resources can be invested in the fixed sequence; however, children may lose interest in activities they cannot choose. Research by Doke and Risley (1972) indicated that child interest was not less in the fixed sequence—if two conditions were met: materials in the ongoing activity were sufficient, and children who were finished with an activity could proceed to the next.

Other arrangements for child movement were manipulated. LeLaurin and Risley (1972) compared the condition by which a teacher supervises one group as it proceeds from one activity to another (man-to-man defense) with an arrangement by which teachers supervise one activity area and groups come to them (zone defense). The zone defense yielded much less loss of child time (time not in appropriate contact with activities) than did the man-to-man defense.

During a play period, children may have access to all available toys, or they may be required to check them out one at a time (Montes & Risley, in press). An interesting result was that limited access resulted in an increase in sociodramatic play. Children apparently learned to assign responsibilities to one another for checking out items. One child would get pots and pans, another "fruits," etc. Then the items were used in group play. On a larger scale, use of activity areas may be routed through a "switching task," as when children are required to accomplish some little academic activity in order to change activity places. The magnitude of the task can control the rate of activity change; the "switching task" condition also permits introduction of learning exercises which might be avoided under a free-access condition (Jacobsen, Bushell, & Risley 1969).

Child attendance at activities in a choice situation was studied by Hursh et al. (1973). Although activities themselves showed different degrees of attractiveness, the teacher's relation to the activity was more influential. For example, teacher attention to the activity supported child interest more than mere teacher presence.

Another program consideration is sequencing. Does it make a difference what activity follows what? According to data from Krantz (1974), vigorous activities lengthened transition times and increased disruptive behaviors in subsequent activities.

Simple variations in milieu (as opposed to program proceedings) can also have useful effects. For example, Twardosz, Cataldo, and Risley (1974b) demonstrated that an interior partition in the day care center markedly increased the effort necessary to monitor children or to supervise staff. The superiority of open architecture for visual access is clear enough; however, it has been widely assumed that this "unprotected milieu" can distract the child. The investigators systematically compared sleep and activity behaviors under wall-less and under partitioned arrangements. Openness yielded no loss of sleep or activity engagement.

The physical milieu has enclosures but also things; the latter can be selected to influence children's behavior. For example, crib toys can provide pre-sleep supports to play and yet not delay or shorten sleep periods (Twardosz, Cataldo, & Risley 1974a). Toys can be introduced which yield social or isolate play (Quilitch & Risley 1973). The kinds of food will influence the amount eaten and extent to which spoons are used (Twardosz, Cataldo, & Risley 1975).

As the above samples illustrate, the Living Environments Group manipulates clear environmental variables and measures the impact upon immediate child behavior. (Sometimes staff behavior is targeted.) The studies are straightforward and of obvious practical interest.

3. Attachment Behavior and Day Care

Ainsworth (1973), in a previous volume of this series, reviewed material dealing with the correlates of day care to the child's attachment behavior. Measurement taken by Caldwell et al. (1970) did not show reliable differences between day care and home care children on mother attachment or on related variables. A marginally significant trend appeared for day care children to be more dependent upon other people in the environment. Blehar (1974) compared two groups of middle-class children who had entered day care at age 2 and at age 3 with well-matched control groups. Children's reactions to mother separation and reunion and to proximity to a stranger were carefully measured in a standardized situation. Compared to controls, both groups of day care children showed relatively less favorable reactions to their mothers and more avoidance of the stranger. Results appeared more emphatic for the 3-year-olds, who, relative to the home care children, cried more upon separation, searched more for the absent mother, and touched her more, yet resisted her more; the older day care group also engaged in markedly less exploratory behavior. The investigator describes the younger day care children as showing more avoidant behavior, possibly indicating a detachment process; the older ones were said to manifest a more anxious, ambivalent attachment.

If Blehar's results are confirmed by others—especially if these negative behaviors are shown in daily life situations—sober concern about developmental effects of early day care will be justified. Obviously effort must be directed toward determining whether variations in the day care arrangements and environments can affect attachment development. Continuity and accessibility of the substitute caretaker are dimensions of probable importance. Further, there are other developmental variables (feelings and skills in peer relations, for example) which may relate to dimensions of day care environments.

Although not covered here, reports of day care arrangements and child effects from cultures other than that of the United States deserve attention. Particularly pertinent would be accounts of day care systems which are well accepted in their respective countries (see Grotberg 1971).

B. INVESTIGATIONS OF NURSERY SCHOOL ENVIRONMENTS

As in other areas, the nursery school studies which have an ecological emphasis must take account of two sides of the problem: recording and analysis of free-running child behavior *and* measurement of the environmental context. A methodological contribution by Caldwell (1969) illustrates current tendencies in this area. The description of child behavior is managed by specimen records which are translated into a computer language (called APPROACH). This behavioral side of the nursery school action is analyzed according to 13 major categories and 85 subdivisions. To transform complicated and rich behavioral data into manageable computer bits is a major accomplishment. But, as Caldwell points out, this is not enough: for ecological analysis, a useful coding system must also report the context "as faithfully as it reports emitted behavior" (p. 89). Yet the APPROACH system offers only four quite simple and obvious categories of the setting. The peripheral place of setting variation is also indicated by the display of data used to illustrate the system, setting variables being given little attention. The APPROACH code is presented as a contribution to behavioral ecology; it does reveal psychologists' expertise in describing individual behavior—but also reflects their reluctance to differentiate the environment and make it a central research target.

1. Studies on Nursery School Subsettings

In *Understanding Children's Play,* Hartley, Frank, and Goldenson (1952) have illustrated how each nursery school activity (e.g., blocks, art, music and movement, and so forth) provides unique opportunities for the expression of children's interests or needs. Blocks invite, for example, cooperation on group projects; they can also be involved in conflict, in the activities of the "brigands of the block corner" (p. 143). Although not quantitative, this book remains a rich source of hypotheses for researchers interested in the subsettings, the ecological parts of nursery school functioning.

Shure (1963) investigated five nursery school subsettings: art, books, dolls, games, and blocks. Subsettings were truly areas with facilities (milieu), not simple child behaviors or activities. Although the number of children was small (seven boys and seven girls), some of Shure's results were congruent with the Hartley work and with later findings. The block area was most frequently inhabited by boys, art by girls. Active social interchange reached its highest percentage in the doll area, was moderately high in the block area, and was relatively low in art. Although destructive behavior was low in all subsettings, it was twice as high in blocks as in any other.

In the process of studying interchild positive reinforcement in the nursery school, Charlesworth and Hartup (1967) discovered that generalized reinforcers were more frequently exchanged at "dramatic activities" (blocks, puppets, and so forth) and less frequently at "table activities" (art, puzzles, stories, and so forth). The authors point out that the dramatic activities were conducive to peer exchange, while the projects or stories (table activities) were not.

More thorough tests of the relation of subsettings to child behavior comes from a group of studies at the Education Research Project, directed by Jacob Kounin. The basic data sources have been videotape recordings of 598 lessons and 37 half-day sessions; in the latter a different child was targeted during each session. The research foci have been studied to determine "what goes on"—as opposed to testing of already derived propositions.

For example, children's involvement in their preschool settings can be measured by checking setting attendance; Rosenthal (1973), studying each of 37 children for a full taped session, noted that a setting's usage could be expressed as an attraction (how many children appeared) or in terms of holding power (how long children remained with the setting). The two measures are relatively independent. Rosenthal found, as did Shure, that art and blocks were the most popular subsettings (as measured by attractiveness); however, the holding power of art was significantly greater than that of blocks. Settings also differed in their yield of play groups of mixed sex or age; thus, children at the climber were of one sex or the other, those in the kitchen area, of both.

An interesting dimension of Rosenthal's effort referred to *freedom*. The question was the extent to which child behavior for the total session was free. The operational definition of freedom was: If, whatever the child is doing, external sources (teacher, peers) have not pressed him into it, he is "free." This freedom measure is similar to the activity initiation and termination quantifications used by Prescott. The TV tapes presented very special advantages over actual behavior because of the rerun possibility; Rosenthal could identify an activity and then reverse the tape to study that portion which showed the circumstances of the activity's beginning. Fifty-five percent of these beginnings were "free." Future research may provide comparative data on the degree of such "freedom" in various kinds of day care and nursery school environments.

Using the same TV tapes, Houseman (1972) examined interpersonal conflicts in the nursery school. With records available for minute and repeated inspection, some surprising findings emerged. For example, interpersonal conflicts, in a nursery school that appeared peaceful enough, were quite frequent (one every 5 minutes per child). However, the great majority were of short duration and of no measurable consequence. Two-thirds of all conflicts related to ongoing activity, involving possession or use of materials, actions, and space; by contrast, person-centered conflicts accounted for less than a quarter of the disagreements. Although variables of race, sex, or age showed few relationships to interpersonal conflict, there were clear situational determinants. As in previous studies, the block area was associated with relatively high conflict, art with low. Further, events preserved on tape indicated why this relation was obtained. Houseman noted more frequent and varied sources of conflict in the block play program than in art. Material conflicts occurred when one child needed another child's block for his own construction; space became a problem when areas were taken over for "boardwalks"; egos were bruised when "insiders" built walls and turned "outsiders" away; role competitions arose when the blocks became stores or houses.

In contrast, an activity area such as art had fewer sources of conflict; children could come into conflict only over materials or harm to a child's picture. Houseman also noted, among her ecological explanations of conflict, the importance of boundary; art tended to present "clarity of demarcation" for each participant, block play did not. The Houseman investigation did *not* establish that naturally occurring variations in population density were related to interpersonal conflicts; as the analysis of block play versus art play indicated, there are a number of ecological sources of interpersonal conflict beyond a restricted amount of space per person.

Involvement and sociality have dominated the measurements of children's immediate response to their environments. Sherman (1975) identified another aspect of child action which he labeled group glee—a combination of laughter, yelling, and physical gyration which erupted in about 40% of the 598 nursery lessons. After a search of the TV tapes had located glee incidents, re-searches were instituted to learn the conditions associated with these happy raucous events. Sherman learned that rate of glee was 10 times higher in lessons involving intense props and movement (drums and dance) than in lessons asking for individual construction; he discovered that large and mixed-sex groups were more gleeful than their opposites. Sherman's repeated examination of the tapes also identified specific events, prior to the gleeful bursts which served as a triggering function. For example, a call for volunteers resulted in children chorusing their willingness to do the job; then, apparently stimulated by their own vocal output, they began to chant and move in a gleeful fashion. That glee stimulates more glee was indicated by Sherman's analysis of whether the gleeful incident began as a simultaneous reaction to a precipitating event or developed as one child followed another in gleeful reaction. Sherman found that at least 70% of incidents were of the latter, the "contagious," type.

The lessons were analyzed from a more comprehensive perspective by Kounin and Gump (1974). The major dependent variable was the on-task behavior of pupils. However, the program, the format, of the various lessons was analyzed in terms of its signal system. The research identified and categorized the kind of signal sources offered in various lesson formats and the continuity of these signals. As illustration, when the teacher reads a story, the signal source is continuously emitting and the children attach themselves to this continuity; group discussions, by contrast, present lulls, signal lacunae, during which children often lose connection to the lesson stimuli, and their on-task rate drops as a consequence. Kounin and Gump were able to show significant variations in on-task rates meaningfully associated with various signal systems. The identification of the "action control dimensions" of programs and their sensible connection to participant behavior is manifestly necessary if we are to have a theory of eco-behavioral phenomena.

It might be important to observe that in all four of the investigations at the Kounin project, child demographic variables (e.g., age, sex, race) were infrequently associated with the selected dependent variables; at the same time aspects of the ecology repeatedly showed strong relationships to these same variables.

2. Studies on General Nursery School Variables

Some investigators have dealt with a major variable of the nursery environment without particular regard for subsettings. Berk (1971) compared the environmental force units (Schoggen 1963) impinging upon children in a permissive university nursery school with those engaging children in a Montessori school. A notable feature of Berk's presentation is her conceptualization of linkage between the environment and child response. The general program requirements of a nursery school constrain the teacher-to-child inputs, which in turn shape the child's response. For example, relative to the university nursery, the Montessori program yielded more teacher expectations in conflict with children's desires and more complying behavior on the part of the children.

A series of studies observed aggressive interaction as a function of crowding or density (Hutt & Vaizey 1966; Jersild & Markey 1935; Krantz 1974; Swift 1964). Although the tendency is for crowding to be associated with increases in aggressive interaction, analysis reveals that

the relationship is neither simple nor consistent. Ethologists have probably done most to clarify the issue at the preschool level.

McGrew (1972) has reviewed recent literature on population density
and presented experiments of his own. As McGrew explains, density can
refer to a high number of persons (social density) or to a number of
persons in a restricted area (spatial density). (A similar distinction has
been drawn by Stokols [1972].) The two densities or "crowdings" do not
necessarily yield the same behavioral outcomes. McGrew found that
changes in space changed the frequency of running behavior—whether
his large or his small group were subjects; on the other hand, running
behavior was not affected when space was held constant and group size
was changed. More important changes were associated with changes in
social density than in spatial density; however, some of these changes
were surprising, not following the simple predictions from the group-size
literature. Partial evidence indicated that increase of group size increased
hitting behavior. Other negative consequences of "crowding" did not
appear; negative expletives actually decreased under increased group
size—for both full-space and restricted-space conditions. McGrew suggests that children kept their social interaction rate moderate in the face
of increased social density, thus avoiding some of the conflicts which
might otherwise be generated.

Following the work by McGrew, Smith and Connolly (reported in
Smith 1972) noted that density should refer to population in relation to
resources, not space. Reasoning that, for children at free play in a nursery school, the most important resource was play equipment, the investigators varied this dimension. Amount of equipment had greater impact
on social behavior than did amount of space. For example, decreased
equipment was associated with more sharing of toys and apparatus,
larger groups, fewer "loners," and more aggressive and stress behaviors.
Some of Smith's results would have been predicted by early, seminatural-
istic research by Johnson (1935). When playground equipment was reduced, children showed more social interaction and more conflict. The
Smith report also considers differences in children's behavior when they
are provided with different kinds of play equipment—that is, with apparatus only (e.g., chairs, tables, Wendy house, climbing frame, pram), with
toys only (e.g., chairs, tables, puzzles, tea set, blocks, telephone) and with
a control condition of both apparatus and toys. Most intriguing results
appeared when apparatus only was compared to the control situation;
with only the apparatus available, children increased verbal and physical
contacts with one another, cooperative group play, and unusual uses of
equipment. The unusual-behavior differences were very substantial in
both samples of subjects and were of special interest to Smith. As he

describes them, they are more like *behavior episodes* (Barker & Wright 1955) than the behavioral categories which ethologists have employed. Two episodes were: "Sitting in a line of chairs, as a pretend train," and "Walking prams along tables put end to end." These behaviors seemed to Smith to be creative; they evolved as children's responses to the limitations as well as the possibilities in the apparatus condition.

Material now reported from a variety of sources (Johnson 1935; Mc-Grew 1972; Montes & Risley, in press; Smith 1974) points to a general conception regarding play facilities and children's reaction. A presumed "deprivation" in equipment does not necessarily lead to "deprived behavior." Under some conditions, children will compensate, even invent. One condition which may be favorable is novelty; children facing a new situation take new action. Another condition which can result in "deprivation" is the intrinsic quality of the resources which remain. When only apparatus remained in the Smith study, highly social and creative behavior resulted; however, when only toys were present and the apparatus was gone, similar positive behavior was not developed.

3. A Note Regarding Nursery School Efforts to Increase Intellectual Competence

Among the many intervention efforts, the work of Weikart (1972) has special interest because of its attention to program management; he concluded that the type of program in operation might not be as significant as the intensity with which it was carried out. Forces mobilized by adequate planning sessions and corrective and supportive supervision can increase or sustain intensity. Weikart speculates that program type and supervision interact, that the more open-ended programs require more supervision.

The variety of programs which have operated under Head Start have been evaluated. Horowitz and Paden, in volume 3 of this series (1973), have contributed a full review of such programs and other environmental interventions; their work will not be repeated here.

4. Concluding Remarks on Environments for the Preschooler

Research focusing on preschool environments has been increasing rapidly. However, only the smallest portion of this effort informs us about the most common of all out-of-family environments for preschool children, the caretaker's home. Valuable as it may be, sophisticated research carried out in centers and schools cannot tell us how children fare in these homes or what variables operate to yield beneficial care. Clearly research in this area, though difficult, is urgently needed.

By now, investigations within centers or schools relating to subsettings have demonstrated that these ecological parts strongly affect the sociality, the activity involvement, even the mirth, of their child inhabitants. In some cases similar subsettings in various institutions seem to push in similar directions; this may be true of block corners, for example. The more fundamental issue is not the label of the subsetting but the ecological dimensions or variables operative; work in this direction is primitive but is beginning as investigators try to identify the properties of the ecological situation responsible for the child reactions. Experimental demonstrations of certain variables (e.g., density) have been obtained by ethologists; many simple and applied variables have been tested by the Risley group.

The relation of these environments to developmental dependent variables such as intellectual competence or social adjustment has been a basic problem for many years. Findings from the area of attachment behavior and day care are more recent examples. However, these findings, though they may refer to variables of most concern to students of child development, cannot stand alone. To understand the relation between variables under the rubric "early day care" and disturbed attachment behavior, the dimensions of that care need to be identified and measured, and the immediate reaction of children to variations in these dimensions is required as well. With information from these two areas, the variations in attachment behavior can be understood.

V. Public School Environments

The task of schools to prepare children for the future is so obvious that it can cloud another function of these institutions: Schools are where people live. The here-and-now quality of life for millions of children (and their teachers) is shaped by the conditions of the school environment. Each child between 6 and 16 spends about 1,200 hours a year in a setting cluster of society's choosing. The quality of these clusters and of children's experiences within them—apart from their capacity to train for the future—is surely an important issue. For a nonquantitative yet systematically drawn picture of pupil life in the traditional elementary classroom, the reader might examine the chapter, "The Daily Grind," by Jackson (1968).

Since every dimension involved in teaching methods and in educational regimes can be considered a dimension of environment, the amount of research material which could be considered for discussion is unmanageable. Although I will not discuss it, one major effort to change the educational environments of disadvantaged children should be mentioned. Project Follow Through represents a national investment in the establishment of a score of different programs, measurements of program operation, and evaluation of program effects. At this writing, data from Follow Through are not ready for publication. However, descriptions of the various programs are available in Maccoby and Zellner (1970); Bissell (1973) also has published a succinct statement of the Follow Through history and philosophy as well as a few program descriptions and sample evaluation data. In addition, external evaluation agencies have developed interim reports (for example, Stallings 1973).

For this review, I limit discussion to three main areas: the possibility of a description of schools based on units of an operating environment, the relation of open architecture to students' behavior, and the relation of some variables of high school environments to student action and experience.

A. ENVIRONMENTAL UNITS IN SCHOOLS

The direct observation of schools reveals separate sections or units operating with moderate autonomy: Mr. Jones's algebra class carried out its questioning, calculating, and explaining parallel to but mostly unaffected by the histrionics of Mrs. Mark's drama class next door. Ecological units of this size are called behavior settings and are discussed in the introduction to this chapter. Smaller, and less autonomous, environmental units or segments can exist within the class session. The testing periods within Mr. Jones's class are different environments from the periods spent going over homework assignments. These smaller units, which can be labeled segments, can operate in a one-at-a-time sequence or simultaneously (see Gump 1967). In an elementary classroom, for example, some children sit in front in a reading circle while others remain at their desks carrying out "seatwork." What a child can do, what he can experience, is shaped by the quality of his inhabited segments, and the quality of segments can be described along a number of dimensions. The reading circle involves direct and persisting teacher intervention, much interdependence of pupils with considerable verbal exchange, and outside pacing of pupils' behavior. On the other hand, seatwork usually lacks immediate teacher intervention and exhibits independence or privacy among pupils, and pacing comes from the pupil rather than from repeated outside stimulations. These differences are ecological differences, not those of psychology or of individual motivations; these differences arise from an action structure, which shapes the possibilities for inhabitant behavior.

The degree to which pupils are involved in ongoing official activity relates to segment qualities. Pupil focus on official action was significantly higher in an externally paced small group (reading circle) than in self-paced larger groups (seatwork). Teacher behavior also is related to the segment structure of the classroom. One crucial time in teaching is the transition from one classroom segment to another, from art work period to arithmetic session. Teacher moves dealing with deviating behavior increase at transitions and subside during the middle portions of a segment (Gump 1969).

Results reported by Kounin (1970) are consistent with the preceding findings. The involvement of elementary school pupils in ongoing activity was greater in the teacher-led recitation groups than in the teacher-absent seatwork groups. Further, teacher skill on a number of transition management dimensions was significantly related to pupil involvement in schoolwork.

Some, but by no means all, segments are equivalents of "lessons." Other investigators have confirmed the general proposition that variations in lessons' activity structure and subject matter are systematically associated with variations in teacher and pupil behavior. For example, Kowatrakul (1959) found that the open-discussion format yielded relatively high off-task pupil behavior; data from Hughes and Associates (1959) show that teachers express higher rates of negative affectivity in activity periods (e.g., arts and crafts) than in academic lessons. Adams and Biddle (1970) uncovered a chain of effects: social studies lessons were associated with teachers dealing with the class as a whole, while mathematics frequently involved the teacher working with individuals or being "disengaged" as students solved problems at their desk. The latter arrangement in math meant more pupils engaging in off-task behavior and, in turn, more teacher correction.

B. OPEN VERSUS TRADITIONAL EDUCATIONAL ENVIRONMENTS

The physical world of children is being markedly changed by construction of open schools. In some cases, these milieu changes have been accompanied by even more radical changes in environmental program. The open school, as a program, not a physical design, relies on high individualization of schooling. Unless otherwise stated, the word "open" used here will refer to physical design. The open school displays unpartitioned interior space and stands in contrast to traditional "egg crate construction"; in the latter, a series of equal-sized classrooms are arranged along corridors. Open design also implies centrally located resource centers which insure that the school's total learning materials will be continually accessible. In fact, *accessibility* is a key concept in open architecture; not only are facilities (sites, objects) to be readily available, but teachers and teachers, teachers and pupils, and pupils and pupils are to be allowed freer, easier contact. An attractive set of photographs, drawings, and verbal descriptions of open schools has been provided by the Educational Facilities Laboratories (1965). This same group, generously endowed by the Ford Foundation, has presented numerous publications showing the varieties of open plans and describing how they were developed. (Case Studies of Educational Facilities and Profiles of Significant Schools are two of the series in the EFL output.)

The earlier open schools were large rooms or "pods" serving as a base for three to six class-sized groups. More recent developments have gone in reverse but complementary directions; that is, larger unpartitioned spaces have been established, spaces capable of housing all of a school's students and staff; the same design often provides for small closed spaces as well, the latter often employing removable or "flexible" partitions.

If accessibility is one key concept in open design, *flexibility* is doubtlessly the other. The avoidance of permanent partitioning enables space to be structured in a variety of forms suited to whatever educational program is planned. Such flexibility also operates in relation to traffic spaces. Conventional classrooms require corridors; yet corridor floor space is fully used only during a fraction of the day. In an open school, similar space is used for school work or for traffic as needed. One estimate is that only 66% of the "egg crate" space is fully usable space compared to 80% for open schools (Educational Facilities Laboratories and Experimental Schools 1972).

The increase of open school construction has been phenomenal. In 1960 open schools were rare indeed; in 1974, even in the traditional Midwest, a school architect could report that *all* construction of elementary schools (of which he was aware) was open construction (Kenneth O. von Achen, Chartered Architects, Eudora, Kans., personal communication, 1973).

A thorough review of how the domination of open construction came about could be the basis of an excellent doctoral dissertation. Suggestions of causes include the facts that, relative to traditional schools, open ones provide increased accessibility and flexibility; are better looking (the open schools with the extended line of sight in their interiors are pleasant indeed); seem more in tune with the humanistic, child-centered philosophy going with open education programs; and cost less. The last item may have been crucial; some estimate that a 20%–25% savings can be obtained from open construction. Examples of saving include the fact that interior walls cost money to build and to paint; they require doors which may cost $300 each, and the cutting and fitting of carpet or ceiling material is more expensive where there are many walls. Relative economy of open construction appears most definitely in the construction of the building shell. When the furnishing process begins, cost mounts rapidly. Open schools require rugs, traditional ones can survive without them. If the open architecture is to facilitate an open *program,* with individualization of instruction, more learning materials will be required than in traditional programs. The initial costs, those which exist at the time a bond issue must be passed, are lower for the open school; however, there is debate about the long-term savings of open construction.

Absent from our reasons for the takeover of open school construction is the proposition that evaluation research established its educational superiority. The omission is quite necessary; very little research has been accomplished. The studies available in the area have been assembled in an annotated bibliography by the Metropolitan Toronto School Board (1972).

What has been found out regarding effects of open schools? To look for achievement test differences, or other residual differences, is probably premature; unless it can be shown that spatial arrangements influence school operations (curriculum, staff relations, instructional strategies, etc.), it can hardly be expected that such arrangements would reliably affect the distal variable of academic competence. In view of what we now understand, the useful studies in the area of open design are those which point to "what really happens" and to inhabitants' ongoing reaction to these happenings. A sample of these types of studies follows.

A comprehensive contribution in this area comes from Brunetti (1971, 1972), who has studied work of others and contributed data of his own. A first concern of both laymen and teachers is that of noise; it has been assumed that without walls, noise from simultaneous activities would create serious distraction. Of course, the amount of possible noise in the usual open school is reduced by acoustical treatments (rugs, ceiling tiles, etc.); still, when children are active and expressive, these provisions are often insufficient. Further, any acoustical arrangements which absorb sound also absorb the major means of classroom communication. Thus the noise problem, intrinsically, cannot be entirely solved by physical treatments. The problem with noise is not how much is produced but whether it actually annoys or distracts. Brunetti's findings on these issues are as follows: (1) Noise bothers teachers much more than pupils—if we accept the self-reports of each. (2) Noise distracts depending on the subject's activity; a high noise level in a laboratory activity is not nearly so distracting as similar noise in a study session. (3) Noise distracts depending on its content, its message value. Students report much higher distraction from overheard social conversations than from subject-matter talk (see also Burns 1972). (4) Noise distracts more when conditions are crowded (see also Burns 1972). Reflections on these findings indicate that noise cannot be equated with annoyance or distraction; noise abatement is necessary or not, depending on who the inhabitants are, their current activity, and the noise content.

Although the effects of noise are often minimal, the *prevention* of noise can have persisting and important program effects. An interview study of 12 teachers in an open school showed that most were quite concerned that their groups not cause noise, and they took one or another of the following precautions: they admonished children not to express enthusiasm too vigorously; they avoided use of learning aides such as record players; they were "careful" about outside speakers; and they strictly limited vigorous physical and vocal activity to recess or to an assigned time and place (Gump & Iliff 1971). The noise prevention problem is interesting, since it underlines the fact that some effects of environmental variables are found in what does not happen.

The preceding studies are "defensive"; they tell us the extent to which obvious worries about open conditions are justified. On the other side of the issue is whether some of the presumed benefits of open design actually occur. Conditions which open designs were thought to encourage included less structured or fixed grouping of children and their learning materials, more pupil activity and more pupil self-direction, and closer and more individualized teacher-pupil relationships. It was also supposed that teachers, taken out of their traditional classroom enclosures, would interact more with one another.

Brunetti reported that grouping in open schools tended to be less en masse. His data indicated that perceived self-direction of activity was greater in open as opposed to traditional schools. That self-perception data can be tricky to interpret was indicated when teachers in open schools—engaged in cooperative teaching—reported relatively *more* self-control (i.e., autonomy in operations). Since many teams involved four teachers, the objective autonomy of the team teacher was necessarily lower than that of a teacher who ran her classroom without significant dependence on colleagues; yet open-classroom teachers were generally more satisfied, felt support from their colleagues—and *said* they experienced more autonomy.

A recent paper by Traub et al. (1972) notes that the contribution of research evidence to program innovation in education has been slight; this failure of research arises partly from the incapacity of educational researchers "to describe and quantify programmatic environments" (p. 69). Traub and his colleagues have made significant steps toward correcting this deficiency, at least as it relates to research on open schools.

Their review of the literature resulted in identification of a number of aspects of school functioning which could be examined and quantified in terms of each aspect's support for the principles of open education. An instrument labeled Dimensions of Schooling (DISC) was developed using 26 items by which responding teachers could quantitatively describe practices in their schools. Description of clusters of items from a factor analysis study by Musella (1973) will illustrate the qualities of school operations which were measured by the DISC questionnaire. The first factor was *individualization of instruction* and reflected the extent to which students had choice in the methods, materials, and pacing of their own learning; *student independence,* a second factor, indicated the amount of free or independent study time available to students and the degree to which students evaluated their own work. Other clusters were: *environmental flexibility, nongradedness, flexibility of student evaluation,* and *flexibility of curricular materials.*

Fisher (1974) showed that DISC questionnaire measurement could predict actual operations and pupil perceptions as these appeared in elementary school lessons in language arts. For example, Fisher discovered that teachers in programs measured open by DISC spent less time giving directions and leading recitations and more time in individual and small-group consultation. Pupils in open programs spent less time watching or listening to other students or to teachers and more time at construction activity or with audiovisual equipment. Students in the DISC-measured open program perceived their schooling as offering more diversity and less formality. Fisher also found that open architecture correlated with certain variables apart from the DISC scores. In open-space environments, pupils were more likely to be "unengaged" or spending more time in transit; teachers in open spaces were more likely to spend time in maintainance activity.

Using completely different methods, Gump (1974) obtained some similar findings. Compared to pupils in traditional schools, primary pupils in open architecture experienced more different teachers and learning facilities during a school day. However, the pupils in open space also spent more time in "nonsubstance" phases of school operations (the between times, the preparatory periods). Nonsubstance times result from system delays, not from pupil disinterest. This problem of delay seemed to accompany the large amount of moving about in the open schools observed. When pupils are reported "unengaged," it is important to know whether they or the systems they inhabit are directly responsible.

The measurement of outcomes of school regimes on pupil variables was also facilitated by the DISC instrument. Preliminary data on school achievement tests are interesting. Weiss (1973) reported Toronto studies involving schools where 85% or more of the children came from homes where English was the first language (Type I) and from schools where less than 70% of the families used English as the first language (Type II). Open-program schools and closed-program schools were associated with similar achievement test scores for the Type I schools; however, achievement scores were *lower* in open programs when Type II schools were tested. Weiss reports other data for the Type I schools which indicate that both open programs and open architecture were associated with better attitudes toward school, teacher, and self than were closed programs and traditional architecture (Weiss cautions that the newness of the open-architecture schools might be affecting the scores). Certain presumed advantages of the open program did not show in test results: measures of curiosity, of creativity, and of group problem solving revealed few differences between open and closed programs.

The outcome findings of the Traub group are tentative and are reported here in the spirit of illustrating the kinds of research achievements which become possible once a dependable and inexpensive method of measuring programs becomes available.

Research on open-space schools has established that physical openness, by itself, does not lead to those desirable outcomes presumed for open education. But this result should not be taken as proof that open space has no important consequences. Evidence accumulates that open design, of itself, tends toward pupil mobility, teacher-teacher contact, teacher concern about creating distraction, and other conditions. These conditions will be managed in different ways by different schools and may not lead to any common outcomes on such dependent variables as academic achievement or change in personal and social adjustment. However, in schools as in other setting clusters, physical milieu and behavioral program cannot remain separate, they must "come to terms."

C. HIGH SCHOOL LIFE

Two large investigations by Kelly bear on the problem of the high school environment and behavior of its inhabitants. In one study (Kelly 1969), the coping behavior of students was related to the schools' rates of population exchange. Compared to a school with a relatively constant student group, students in the school with high turnover showed more behavioral variations, more multiple group membership, and more "exploratory activity." A second series of Kelly-led investigations followed two cohorts of boys from the eighth grade through high school (Kelly et al., in press). Through questionnaires, boys were measured for the degree to which they preferred to deal with the environment through exploratory effort. Although this measure turned out to be less predictive than hoped, findings on other aspects of male youth in suburban high schools appear quite useful. The array is too rich and heterogeneous for more than examples here. Research areas include a study of help-giving actions and attitudes of students who find a modicum of support in the school's offerings ("the citizens") and those who do not ("the tribe"). Relations among administrators, teachers, and pupils, and certain ecological factors that correlate to these associations, were also examined.

The relation of school size to student behavior and experience has been carefully investigated by Roger Barker and his colleagues. The effects of school size on students' actions in their schools' extracurricular settings and on the attitudes and feelings they associate with these settings are substantial. Further, these differences are predictable from an eco-behavioral theory; the highlights of this theory follow.

As institutions or communities become larger, number of inhabitants increases at a faster rate than number of settings; as a result, small institutions have less man power available per setting; their settings are undermanned compared to the settings of larger institutions. When settings are undermanned, the forces to maintain settings' operations fall more heavily on their few inhabitants. Youth in a small high school experience more invitations and more pressure to assume setting work than do youth in a large school. As a result, youth in small schools should be found working harder and assuming more responsible and difficult setting positions in extracurricular affairs. Finally, since persons who take more active, more central positions in an activity have different experiences than those who are audiences or members, small-school students should report different attitudes and feelings regarding their settings than large-school students (Barker & Gump 1964). (See also Barker [1968] for a more formal and detailed statement of this theory.)

Research verified the theory at its crucial points. Student population, from smallest to largest schools in a midwestern region, rose by a factor of 65; number of settings in the schools, only by a factor of eight. The median number of students present in the small-school settings was about one-third of those present in the large school. Relative to large-school students, those in the small schools reported twice as many pressures to take part in settings programs; they occupied 2.5 times as many leader and functionary positions. Small-school students reported more satisfactions related to development of competence, engaging in important actions, being valued by others, and being a part of significant group efforts. In contrast, large-school students emphasized vicarious enjoyment and gaining "points" for participation.

Various aspects of the undermanning theory as it predicts high school life have been confirmed by Baird (1969) and Wicker (1968). An initial study and its replication by Willems (1967) compared the sense of obligation reported by academically adequate and academically marginal students in large and small schools. The marginal students in the large school rarely reported a sense of obligation to support their school's extracurricular settings; however, the marginal students in the small schools reported just as many obligations as did their academically adequate classmates. The fact that the undermanned school must invite and press all students in order to maintain its extracurricular operations means that the academically marginal students are very likely to become a part of the enterprise; they respond by feeling obligations to it. In the large school, the academically marginal are also marginal in their participation and in their feelings of being responsible for their school's settings. The ratio of number of persons to some measure of behavioral opportunity clearly influences the actions and experiences of a setting's inhabitants. This proposition has a history too long for review here. In 1934, Dawe demonstrated that group size in kindergarten discussions was inversely related to child participation. The work of ethologists described previously uses space and play resources as measures of behavioral opportunity. Research of ecological psychologists emphasizes that behavioral opportunities (also obligations) can be related to positions in the program action of settings. These positions are objective, external behavioral opportunities just as surely as are spaces or playthings. Further, the issue of who will occupy these positions is very sensitive to changes in amount of man power (or child power).

The implications of the undermanning idea extend to arenas other than schools. In some respects, the elderly, youth, and children are all marginal people. What happens to them in particular environments depends on how much those environments need their contributions. Those interested in the welfare of children and youth might pay close attention to environments which contain many young people—but do not need them.

VI. RESEARCH ON CHILDREN'S ENVIRONMENTS

If there could appear, at this point, a summary of findings for the area just reviewed, it would be a satisfaction to writer and reader alike. But such a summary could only become a repetitive listing of rather heterogeneous material. Except for density research, the field has not been organized by dominant questions; without shared, organizing questions, it has been inevitable that there should be a diversity of concepts, of variables, and of methods. It is not surprising that the findings have not been cumulative.

One noticeable aspect of the review is the number and recency of its references. Research on children's environments has become legitimate, and that research is rapidly expanding. The word "environment" has been used in a general or heuristic sense for a long time. Studies have been carried out on the subjective ("life space") environment, and on the objective, yet "functional," environment located at the seam of subjects' acts and external input. More recently, however, investigators have begun measuring elements and parts of the operating environment, of the milieu-with-program niches in the world. Several factors may have contributed to the change. There is general interest in matters ecological; second, there is the widening recognition that environmental variables are coercive, that housing projects, day care programs, or classroom arrangements truly influence children. A final development may have been the realization that environments as units, or settings, can be conceptualized and measured. This development may be seen from several sources. From the early 1950s, Barker and his associates have been continuing contributors. Later investigators have also helped, for example, the work by the Traub group in describing school programs (Traub et al. (1972); Wolfensberger and Glenn (1973) have recently proposed a well-conceptualized system to measure the "normalization" potential in treatment environments of children and dependent adults. Research is like other activity; participants do what they can. Now that it seems that eco-behavioral research can be done, one may presume that more of it will be done.

Of the many dimensions along which the child-and-environment research could be divided, an important one seems to be that of span. A number of researches presented here have dealt with restricted portions of an environment. These portions were usually contexts such as the art or the block area of the nursery school; however, the restriction could refer to a single environmental dimension: the noise entering an apartment and its relation to reading ability. A collection of such studies has reported that various dimensions of the environmental part can be sensibly related to the degree to which a child is involved in the legitimate activity, the social behavior shown by children, the social behavior by adults to children, the emotional reaction of children, and so on. The narrow-span investigations have the advantage of simplicity and feasibility; findings are often concrete and practical.

There are, however, certain ecological interests which can only be pursued by wide-span research. For one thing, we are often curious not simply about how children react to a playground but about how they live; what, for example, is the range of their activity, their social contact? For such questions, some way must be found to deal with whole institutions and neighborhoods. Material of this span has been offered by

Wright (1969). Other efforts (Barker & Schoggen 1973) deal with whole communities.

The problem with wide-span studies is that width is often gained at the expense of concreteness. The environment is given a label (slum housing) or described by dimension (lower-class residential area), and then specific inhabitant variables are measured and related to the label or dimension. The wide-span environment can become more specific if analysis can begin with its ecological segments or parts. Thus a neighborhood, a day care center, a school is seen as a cluster of settings; the qualities of these settings and the relations between them can be used to describe the larger unit; the use of the larger unit by inhabitants can be related to these concrete entities, not simply to the general environment. Once investigators gain facility and confidence in their measurement of environmental parts, more comprehensive and illuminating studies of children's environments will result. If this stage is followed by agreement on the major questions to be asked, findings will become more cumulative.

REFERENCES

Adams, R., & Biddle, B. *Realities of teaching: exploration with video tape.* New York: Holt, Rinehart & Winston, 1970.

Ainsworth, M. D. The development of infant-mother attachment. In B. M. Caldwell and H. Ricciuti (Eds.), *Review of child development research.* Vol. 3. Chicago: University of Chicago Press, 1973.

Alexander, C. The city as a mechanism for sustaining human contact. In R. Gutman (Ed.), *People and buildings.* New York: Basic, 1972.

Allen, M. G. (Lady Allen of Hurtwood). *Planning for play.* Norwich, G.B.: Jarrold & Sons, 1968.

Altman, I.; Nelson, P. A.; & Lett, F. E. The ecology of home environments. Final Report, January 1972, Project No. 0-0502, U.S. Department of Health, Education, and Welfare, Office of Education, Bureau of Research.

Angrist, S., & Lave, J. Issues surrounding day care. *Family Coordinator,* 1973, *22,* 457–464.

Appleyard, D., & Lintell, M. The environmental quality of city streets: the residents viewpoint. *Journal of American Institute of Planners,* 1972, *38,* 84–101.

Baird, L. L. Big school, small school: a critical examination of the hypothesis. *Journal of Educational Psychology,* 1969, *60,* 253–260.

Bangs, H. P., & Mahler, S. Users of local parks. *Journal of American Institute of Planners,* 1970, *38,* 330–334.

Barker, R. G. Explorations in ecological psychology. *American Psychologist,* 1965, *20,* 1–14.

Barker, R. G. *Ecological psychology: concepts and methods for studying the environment of human behavior.* Stanford, Calif.: Stanford University Press, 1968.

Barker, R. G., & Gump, P. V. *Big school, small school.* Stanford, Calif.: Stanford University Press, 1964.

Barker, R. G., & Schoggen, P. *Qualities of community life: methods of measuring environment and behavior applied to an American and an English town.* San Francisco: Jossey-Bass. 1973.

Barker, R. G., & Wright, H. F. *One boy's day*. New York: Harper & Row, 1951.

Barker, R. G., & Wright, H. F. *Midwest and its children.*New York: Harper & Row, 1955. (Reprinted by Hamden, Conn.: Archon Books, 1971.)

Bengtsson, A. *Environmental planning for children's play*. London: Crosby Lockwood, 1970.

Berk, L. E. Effects of variations in the nursery school setting on environmental constraints and children's modes of adaption. *Child Development*, 1971, *42*, 839–869.

Bissell, J. S. Planned variation in Head Start and Follow Through. In J. C. Stanley (Ed.), *Compensatory education for children, ages 2–8*. Baltimore: John Hopkins University Press, 1973.

Blehar, M. C. Anxious attachment and defensive reactions associated with day care. *Child Development*, 1974, *45*, 683–692.

Brunetti, F. A. Open space: a status report. Mimeographed. School Environment Study, School Planning Laboratory, School of Education, Stanford University, Stanford, Calif., 1971.

Brunetti, F. A. Noise, distraction, and privacy in conventional and open school environments. In W. Mitchell (Ed.), *Environmental design: research and practice. Proceedings of EDRA conference*. Washington, D.C.: American Institute of Architects, 1972.

Burns, J. A. Development and implementation of an environmental evaluation and redesign process for a high school science department. In W. Mitchell (Ed.), *Environmental design: research and practice. Proceedings of EDRA conference*. Washington, D.C.: American Institute of Architects, 1972.

Caldwell, B. M. A new approach to behavioral ecology. In J. P. Hill (Ed.), *Minnesota symposia on child psychology*. Vol. 2. Minneapolis: University of Minnesota Press, 1969.

Caldwell, B. M.; Wright, D. M.; Honig, A.S.; & Tannenbaum, J. Infant day care and attachment. *American Journal of Orthopsychology*, 1970, *40*, 397–412.

Center for Applied Behavior Analysis. An experiment to facilitate national day care policy decisions. AA 313 Bristol Terrace, Lawrence, Kansas 66044, 1972.

Chapin, F.S. The effects of slum clearance and rehousing on family and community relationships in Minneapolis. *American Journal of Sociology*, 1938, *43*, 744–763.

Chapin, F. S. Social effects of good housing. In C. E. A. Winslow (Ed.), *Housing for health*. Lancaster, Pa.: Science Press, 1941.

Chapin F. S. Some housing factors related to mental hygiene. *Journal of Social Issues*, 1951, *7*, 164–171.

Chapman, J., & Lazar, J. A review of the present status and future needs in day care research: a working paper. Prepared for the Interagency Panel on Early Childhood Research and Development, Washington, D.C., November 1971.

Charlesworth, R., & Hartup, W. W. Positive social reinforcement in the nursery school peer group. *Child Development*, 1967, *38*, 993–1002.

Charlesworth, W., & Spiker, D. An ethological approach to observation in learning settings. In R. Weinberg and F. Woods (Eds.), *Systematic observation in school settings*. Minneapolis: University of Minnesota Printing Press, 1974.

Coates, G., & Sanoff, H. Behavioral mapping: the ecology of child behavior in a planned residential setting. In W. J. Mitchell (Ed.), *Environmental design: research and practice. Proceedings of EDRA-3/AR-8 Conference*. Washington, D.C.: American Institute of Architects, 1972.

Cohen, S.; Glass, D. C.; & Singer, J. E. Apartment noise, auditory discrimination and reading ability. *Journal of Experimental Social Psychology*, 1973, *9*, 407–422.

Colean, M. *Human side of urban renewal*. Baltimore: Fight Blight, Inc.; New York: Ives Washburn, 1960.

Cooper, C. Resident attitudes towards the environment of St. Francis Square, San Francisco: a summary of the initial findings. Development Research, University of California, 1970.

Cooper, C. Resident dissatisfaction in multi-family housing. In W. M. Smith (Ed.), *Behavior, design, and policy aspects of human habitats.* Green Bay: University of Wisconsin—Green Bay, 1972.

Council of Planning Librarians. Exchange bibliographies. Box 229, Monticello, Illinois 61856, 1971.

Craik, K. Environmental psychology. In P. Mussen and M. Rosenzweig (Eds.), *Annual review of psychology.* Vol. *24.* Palo Alto, Calif.: Annual Reviews, 1973.

Dawe, H. C. The influence of size of kindergarten group upon performance. *Child Development,* 1934, *5,* 295–303.

Dee, N., & Liebman, J. C. A statistical study of attendance at urban playgrounds. *Journal of Leisure Research,* 1970, *2,* 145–159.

Doke, L., & Risley, T. The PLA-CHECK evaluation of group care. Paper presented at the annual meeting of the Kansas Psychological Association, Overland Park, Kansas, April 1971. (Available from Department of Human Development, University of Kansas)

Doke, L., & Risley, T. The organization of day-care environments: required vs. optional activities. *Journal of Applied Behavior Analysis,* 1972, *5,* 405–420.

Educational Facilities Laboratories. *Schools without walls: profiles of significant schools.* New York: Educational Facilities Laboratories, 1965.

Educational Facilities Laboratories and Experimental Schools. *Places and things for experimental schools.* New York: Educational Facilities Laboratories, 1972.

Ellis, K., & Petchevsky, R. Children of the corporate dream: an analysis of day care as a political issue under capitalism. *Socialist Revolution,* 1972, *2,* 9–29.

Emlen, A. C. Family day care research—a summary and critical review. Family Day Care West, a Working Conference, Pasadena, Calif., Community Family Day Care Project of Pacific Oaks College, 1972.

Emlen, A.; Donoghue, B. A.; & LaFarge, R. *Child care by kith.* Portland, Ore.: Field Study of the Neighborhood Family Day Care System, 1971.

Esser, A., & Archea, J. (Eds.) *Man-environment systems.* Orangeburg, N.Y.: Association for the Study of Man-Environment Relations, 1969.

Fanning, D. M. Families in flats. *British Medical Journal,* 1967, *4,* 382–386.

Faris, R. E. L., & Dunham, H. W. *Mental disorders in urban areas: an ecological study of schizophrenia and other psychoses.* Chicago: University of Chicago Press, 1939.

Festinger, L. Architecture and group membership. *Journal of Social Issues,* 1951, *7,* 152–163.

Festinger, L.; Schachter, S.; & Back, K. *Social pressures in informal groups.* New York: Harper, 1950.

Fisher, C. W. Educational environments in elementary schools differing in architecture and program openness. Annual conference of the American Educational Research Association, April 1974. (Available from author: Far West Laboratory, 1855 Folsom Street, San Francisco, California 94103)

Fried, M. Grieving for a lost home. In L. J. Duhl (Ed.), *The urban condition.* New York: Basic, 1963.

Fried, M. Functions of the working class community in modern urban society: implications for forced relocation. *Journal of American Institute of Planners,* 1967, *33,* 90–103.

Friedberg, M. P. *Play and interplay.* New York: Macmillan, 1970.

Gans, H. J. The human implications of slum clearance and relocation. *Journal of American Institute of Planners,* 1959, *25,* 15–25.

Gans, H. J. *The urban villagers.* New York: Free Press, 1962.

Gewirtz, H. B., & Gewirtz, J. L. Caretaking settings, background events and behavior differences in four Israeli child-rearing environments: some preliminary trends. In B. M. Foss (Ed.), *Determinants of infant behavior.* Vol. *4.* London: Methuen, 1969.

Gewirtz, J. L. On designing the functional environment of the child to facilitate behavioral development. In L. L. Dittmann (Ed.), *Early child care: the new perspectives.* New York: Atherton, 1968.

Glazer, N. Housing problems and housing policies. *Public Interest,* 1967 (7), 21–51. (Also reprinted in J. K. Hadden, L. H. Masotti, & C. J. Larson [Eds.], *Metropolis in crisis.* Ithaca, Ill.: Peacock, 1967)

Gold, S. Nonuse of neighborhood parks. *Journal of American Institute of Planners,* 1972, *38,* 369–378.

Grotberg, E. H. (Ed.) *Day care: resources for decisions.* Washington, D.C.: Office of Economic Opportunity, June 1971.

Gump, P. The classroom behavior setting, its nature and relation to student behavior. Final report; mimeographed, 1967, U.S. Office of Education Cooperative Research Branch, Project No. 5-0334. (Available from author: Department of Psychology, University of Kansas)

Gump, P. Intra-setting analysis: the third grade classroom as a special but instructive case. In E. Willems and H. Raush (Eds.), *Naturalistic viewpoints in psychological research.* New York: Holt, Rinehart & Winston, 1969.

Gump, P. Operating environments in open and traditional schools. *School Review,* 1974, *84,* 575–593.

Gump, P., & Iliff, D. Interviews of teachers at open-area school. Unpublished manuscript, Department of Psychology, University of Kansas, 1971.

Gump, P. V.; Schoggen, P.; & Redl, F. The camp milieu and its immediate effects. *Journal of Social Issues,* 1957, *13,* 40–46.

Gump, P. V.; Schoggen, P.; & Redl, F. The behavior of the same child in different milieus. In R. G. Barker (Ed.), *The stream of behavior.* New York: Appleton-Century-Crofts, 1963.

Hartley, R. F.; Frank, L.; & Goldenson, R. M. *Understanding children's play.* New York: Columhia University Press, 1952.

Hathaway, S.; Flio, D.; Laurence, S.; & Young, A. Rural-urban adolescent personality. *Rural Sociology,* 1959, *23,* 331–356.

Hole, V. Social effects of planned rehousing. *Town and Planning Review,* 1959, *30,* 161–173.

Hole, V., & Miller, A. Children's play on housing estates: a summary of two BRS studies. *Architects Journal,* 1966, *143,* 1529–1536.

Holme, A., & Massie, P. *Children's play: a study of need and opportunities.* London: Michael Joseph, 1970.

Horowitz, F. D., & Paden, L. Y. The effectiveness of environmental intervention programs. In B. M. Caldwell and H. N. Ricciuti (Eds.), *Review of child development research.* Vol. *3.* Chicago: University of Chicago Press, 1973.

Houseman, J. An ecological study of interpersonal conflict among preschool children. Unpublished doctoral dissertation, Wayne State University, 1972.

Hughes, M. M., & Associates. Assessment of the quality of teaching in elementary schools. Unpublished report, Cooperative Research Project No. 353, Office of Education, U.S. Department of Health, Education, and Welfare, 1954.

Hursh, H. B.; Cooper, A. Y.; Reuter, K. E.: & LeBlanc, J. M. The part teachers play in attracting children to activities. Paper presented at the meeting of the American Psychological Association, Montreal, August 1973.

Hutt, C., & Vaizey, M. Differential effects of group density on social behavior. *Nature,* 1966, *209,* 1371–1372.

Ittelson, W. H.; Proshansky, H. G.; Rivlin, L.; & Winkel, G. H. *Introduction to environmental psychology.* New York: Holt, Rinehart & Winston, 1974.

Jackson, P. *Life in classrooms.* New York: Holt, Rinehart & Winston, 1968.

Jacobs, J. *Death and life of great American cities.* New York: Vintage, 1961.

Jacobson, J. M.; Bushell, D., Jr.; & Risley, T. R. Switching requirements in a headstart classroom. *Journal of Applied Behavior Analysis,* 1969, *2,* 43–47.

Jersild, A. T., & Markey, F. V. Conflicts between pre-school children. *Monographs of the Society for Research in Child Development* 1935, No. 21.

Johnson, M. W. The effect on behavior of variations in amount of play equipment. *Child Development,* 1935, *6,* 56–68.

Jones, N. B. *Ethological studies of child behavior.* Cambridge: Cambridge University Press, 1972.

Kates, R., & Wohlwill, J. (Eds.) Man's response to the physical environment. *Journal of Social Issues,* 1966, *22,* 1–140.

Kelly, J. Naturalistic observations in contrasting social environments. In E. Willems and J. Raush (Eds.), *Naturalistic viewpoints in psychological research.* New York: Holt, Rinehart & Winston, 1969.

Kelly, J. G., et al. *The high school environment: an introduction to a longitudinal study of person environment fit.* New York: Behavioral Publications, in press.

Keyserling, M. D. Day care challenge: the unmet needs of mothers and children. *Child Welfare,* 1971, *50,* 434–441.

Kounin, J. S. *Discipline and group management in the classroom.* New York: Holt, Rinehart & Winston, 1970.

Kounin, J., & Gump, P. Signal systems of lesson settings and the task related behavior of preschool children. *Journal of Educational Psychology,* 1974, *66,* 554–562.

Kowatrakul, S. Some behaviors of elementary school children related to classroom activities and subject areas. *Journal of Educational Psychology,* 1959, 121–128.

Krantz, P. Ecological arrangements in the classroom. Unpublished doctoral dissertation, University of Kansas, 1974.

Lansing, J.; Marans, R.; & Zehner, B. *Planned residential environments.* Ann Arbor: Survey Research Center, Institute for Social Research, University of Michigan, 1970.

LeLaurin, K., & Risley, T. The organization of day-care environments: "zone" versus "man-to-man" staff assignments. *Journal of Applied Behavior Analysis,* 1972, *5,* 225–232.

Littlewood, J., & Sale, R. *Children at play: a look at where they play and what they do on housing estates.* London: Department of Environment, 2 Marsham St. SW1. 1972.

Low, S., & Spindler, P. G. *Child care arrangements of working mothers in the United States.* (Children's Bureau Publication No. 46.) Washington, D.C.: Government Printing Office, 1968.

Maccoby, E. E., & Zellner, M. *Experiments in primary education: aspects of project Follow Through.* New York: Harcourt Brace, 1970.

McGrew, W. C. *An ethological study of children's behavior.* New York: Academic Press, 1972.

Metropolitan Toronto School Board. Study of educational facilities. (Annotated bibliography of research on open plan schools) Toronto, 1972.

Michelson, W. *Man and his urban environment: a sociological approach.* Reading, Mass.: Addison-Wesley, 1970.

Montes, F., & Risley, T. R. The organization of day care environments: access to play materials and play behavior. *Child Care Quarterly,* in press.

Moos, R. H. Conceptualization of human environments. *American Psychologist,* 1973, *28,* 652–665.

Moos, R. H., & Insel, P. M. *Issues in social ecology: human milieus.* Palo Alto, Calif.: National Press Books, 1973.

Murray, H. *Explorations in personality.* New York: Oxford University Press, 1938.

Musella, D. Closure on openness in education: dimensions of schooling, II. Annual conference of the American Educational Research Association, New Orleans, February 1973.

Newman, O. *Defensible space.* New York: Macmillan, 1972.

Newman, O. *Architectural design for crime prevention.* National Institute of Law Enforcement and Criminal Justice, March 1973, Stock No. 2700-00161, Superintendent of Documents, Government Printing Office, Washington, D.C. 20402.

Newson, J., & Newson, E. *Four-years old in an urban community.* Chicago: Aldine, 1968.

Park, R. E., & Burgess, E. W. *The city.* Chicago: University of Chicago Press, 1925.

Petzing, J., & Wedge, P. Homes for our children. *New Society,* 1970, *16,* 448–459.

Pollowy, Anne-Marie. Children in the residential setting: a discussion paper toward design guidelines. University of Montreal, Center of Research and Urban Innovation, Montreal, 1973.

Prescott, E. Group and family day care: a comparative assessment. Paper prepared for Family Day Care Work, a working conference, Pacific Oaks College, Pasadena, Calif., February 1972.

Prescott, E. A comparison of three types of day care and nursery school–home care. Paper presented at the meeting of Society for Research in Child Development, Philadelphia, Pennsylvania, 1973. (Author: Pacific Oaks College, 417 West California, Pasadena, Calif.)

Proshansky, J.; Ittelson, W.; & Rivlin, L. *Environmental psychology: man and his physical setting.* New York: Holt, Rinehart & Winston, 1970.

Quilitch, H. R., & Risley, T. R. The effects of play materials on social play. *Journal of Applied Behavior Analysis,* 1973, *6,* 573–578.

Rainwater, L. Fear and the house as haven in the lower class. *Journal of American Institute of Planners,* 1966, *32,* 23–31.

Rainwater, L. *Behind ghetto walls: black families in a federal slum.* Chicago: Aldine, 1970.

Raven, J. Sociological evidence on housing, I and II. *Architectural Review,* 1967, *142,* 68, 236.

Roemer, D. V. Adolescent peer group formation in two Negro neighborhoods. Unpublished doctoral dissertation, Harvard University, 1968.

Rosenthal, B. An ecological study of free play in a nursery school. Unpublished doctoral dissertation, Wayne State University, 1973.

Ruderman, F. *Child care and working mothers: a study of arrangements made for day time care of children.* New York: Child Welfare League of America, 1968.

Saile, D. G.; Borooah, R.; & Williams, M. G. Families in public housing: a study of three localities in Rockford, Illinois. In W. J. Mitchell (Ed.), *Environmental design: research and practice. Proceedings of EDRA-3/AR-8 Conference.* Washington, D.C.: American Institute of Architects, 1972.

Schoggen, P. Environmental forces in the everyday lives of children. In R. G. Barker (Ed.), *The stream of behavior.* New York: Appleton-Century-Crofts, 1963.

Schorr, A. L. Slum and social insecurity. Research Report No. 1, Social Security Administration, Division of Research and Statistics, Department of Health, Education, and Welfare, Washington, D.C., 1963.

Sherman, L. An ecological study of glee in small groups of preschool children. *Child Development,* 1975, *46,* 53–61.

Shure, M. B. Psychological ecology of a nursery school. *Child Development,* 1963, *34,* 979–992.

Smith, P. Aspects of the playgroup environment. In D. Cantor and T. Lee (Eds.), *Proceedings of the conference: psychology and the built environment.* London: Architectural Press, 1974. (Author: Department of Psychology, University of Sheffield, England)

Smith, W. M. Behavioral influences of arctic community environments. In W. M. Smith (Ed.), *Behavior, design, and policy aspects of human habitats.* Green Bay: Office of Community Outreach, University of Wisconsin—Green Bay, 1972.

Srivastava, R. K., & Good, L. R. *St. Margaret's Park public housing project: an environmental and behavioral profile.* Environmental Research Foundation, Topeka, Kans.: Milieu, 1969.

Stallings, J. A. *Follow Through program classroom observation evaluation, 1971–1972.* Menlo Park, Calif.: Stanford Research Institute, 1973.

Stewart, W. F. R. *Children in flats: a family study.* London: National Society for the Prevention of Cruelty to Children, 1970.

Stokols, D. On the distinction between density and crowding: some implications for future research. *Psychological Review,* 1972, *79,* 275–277.

Sweetser, F. L., & Sweetser, D. A. Social class and single family housing. In S. F. Fava (Ed.), *Urbanism in world perspective.* New York: Crowell, 1968.

Swift, J. W. Effects of early group experience: the nursery school and day nursery. In M. Hoffman and L. Hoffman (Eds.), *Review of child development research.* Vol. *1.* New York: Russell Sage Foundation, 1964.

Traub, R. E.; Weiss, J.; Fisher, C. W.: & Musella, D. Closure on openness: describing and quantifying open education. *Interchange,* 1972, *3,* 69–84.

Twardosz, S.; Cataldo, M. F.; & Risley, T. R. Infants' use of crib toys. *Young Children,* 1974, *29,* 271–276. (a)

Twardosz, S.; Cataldo, M. F.; & Risley, T. R. An open environment design for infant and toddler day care. *Journal of Applied Behavior Analysis,* 1974, *7,* 529–545. (b)

Twardosz, S.; Cataldo, M. F.: & Risley, T. R. Menus for toddler day care: food preferences and spoon use. *Young Children,* 1975, *30,* 129–144.

U.S. Bureau of the Census. *Statistical abstract of the United States.* Washington, D.C.: Government Printing Office, 1971, 1972.

U.S. Department of Housing and Urban Development. *New communities.* Washington, D.C.: Government Printing Office, 1970.

Wade, G. R. A study of free-play patterns of elementary school-age children in playground equipment areas. Unpublished master's thesis, Pennsylvania State University, 1968.

Wallace, A. F. C. *Housing and social structure.* Philadelphia: Philadelphia Housing Authority, 1952.

Webb, E. J.; Campbell, D. T.; Schwartz, R. D.: & Sechrest, L. *Unobtrusive measures: nonreactive research in the social sciences.* Chicago: Rand-McNally, 1966.

Weikart, D. P. Relationship of curriculum, teaching, and learning in preschool education. In J. C. Stanley (Ed.), *Preschool programs for the disadvantaged.* Baltimore, John Hopkins University Press, 1972.

Weiss, J. Openness and student outcomes: some results. (A part of the symposium with D. Musella, Closure on openness in education) Symposium presented at the meeting of the American Educational Research Association, New Orleans, February 1973.

Werkerle, G., & Hall, E. High rise living: can the same design serve young and old? *Ekistics,* 1972, *33,* 186–191.

White, L. E. Outdoor play of children living in flats. In L. Kuper (Ed.), *Living in towns.* London: Cresset, 1953.

Wicker, A. W. Undermanning, performances, and students' subjective experiences in behavior settings of large and small high schools. *Journal of Personality and Social Psychology,* 1968, *10,* 255–261.

Willems, E. P. Sense of obligation to high school activities as related to school size and marginality of student. *Child Development,* 1967, *38,* 1247–1260.

Willner, M. Unsupervised family day care in New York City. *Child Welfare,* 1969, *48,* 342–347.

Wilner, D. M.; Walkley, R. P.; Pinkerton, T. C.; & Tayback, M. *The housing environment and family life.* Baltimore: Johns Hopkins University Press, 1962.

Wirth, L. Urbanism as a way of life. *American Journal of Sociology,* 1938, *44,* 1–24.

Wolfensberger, W., & Glenn, L. *PASS: Program analysis of service systems. Handbook. Field manual.* York University Campus, Downsview, Toronto: National Institute on Mental Retardation, 1973.

Wright, H. F. *Recording and analyzing child behavior.* New York: Harper & Row, 1967.

Wright, H. F. Children's behavior in communities differing in size, I, II, III, and Supplement. Report of Project Grant MH 01098 (NIMH), Department of Psychology, University of Kansas, 1969.

Wright, H. F. Community size and the child's activity range. Unpublished manuscript, Department of Psychology, University of Kansas, 1974. (a)

Wright, H. F. *Urban space as seen by children of school age.* Milton Keynes, G.B.: Open University, 1974. (b)

Wurster, C. B. Social questions in housing and community planning. *Journal of Social Issues,* 1951, *7,* 1–33. (Also reprinted in W. L. C. Wheaten, G. Milgram, & M. E. Meyerson [Eds.], *Urban housing.* New York: Free Press, 1966)

3 Children's Cooperation and Helping Behaviors

JAMES H. BRYAN

Northwestern University

CONTENTS

Parts of this study were supported by the National Institute of Child Health and Human Development under research grant HD03234 to James H. Bryan. Thanks are due to Robert Prentky, Jean E. Slater, and Edward Marston for their assistance in the preparation of this manuscript. I am also grateful to the anonymous reviewers and to Aletha Stein, who suffered through initial drafts of the chapter and so ably and helpfully commented upon them.

I. Introduction

During the past decade, research on the development and correlates of helping and cooperative behavior has been abundant. Indeed, within the past 4 years of psychological literature, two review articles of research on helping behavior have been published in the *Psychological Bulletin* (Bryan & London 1970; Krebs 1970), while one entire journal issue (Wispé 1972) and one book (Macaulay & Berkowitz 1970), have been devoted exclusively to the theoretical and empirical presentations relevant to this topic. As Wispé writes, "Behaviors with 'positive' social consequences are now being studied in both the laboratory and in the field, and an interest in such things as altruism, charity, and sympathy is no longer enough to assure one's automatic expulsion from the behavior research community" (1972, p. 1).

Several factors have appeared to pique psychologists' interest in these behaviors. The factors cited have included the growth of humanistic psychology, student activism, the peace movement, and the apparently increasing brutality of many of our citizens toward themselves and others (Bryan 1972; Wispé 1972). Practical concerns to produce a "better society" have provided some motivation and reward to researchers interested in such behaviors. As a variety of writers have indicated, the helping of another, the sacrifice of some comfort to produce a better distribution of resources between the haves and have nots, is a value that is probably held by virtually everyone within this culture. Arguments and debates among citizens might arise from differences as to how much to sacrifice to whom, under what circumstances, and for how long, but agreement on the Good Samaritan principle seems widely accepted within our society. Adherence to the principle is widespread in terms of verbal endorsement, at least within the United States. Many people, and the institutions serving them, are quite dependent upon the generosity and activities of a concerned citizenry. But is it possible to increment the degree to which adults and children alike not only verbalize the Good Samaritan principle but also act in accordance with it? Can the educational institutions, the parents, and the mass media better teach behavioral allegiances to the value of concern for others and thereby reduce social and economic inequalities, the distress of victims, and brutality of the citizenry toward themselves and others? Many investigators feel that the answers must be in the affirmative and have begun their efforts to determine what might be done to affect such changes.

In addition to the practical concerns generating investigation in helping and cooperative activites, research has been stimulated by theoretical and more narrow technical interests. Of particular importance is the now current emphasis of many psychologists upon the power of material and social rewards in affecting human behavior, an emphasis which Campbell (1965) has described as "skin-surface hedonism." Psychologists expend considerable effort in delineating the power of reinforcement to affect behavior. The effects of what, when, and how rewards are given to a bird, rat, or child have received rather widespread attention by psychologists. However, relatively little attention has been paid to the fact that adults and children alike do sacrifice things that they value in order to benefit others. People do try to aid others even when there appears little obvious payoff for the risk or sacrifice involved (Bryan & London 1970; Krebs 1970; Rosenhan 1970, 1972). What are those circumstances which lead one to give up valued resources or run the risk of injury or inconvenience when neither material reward nor social acclaim seems imminent or likely? What is motivating the helping adult or child?

Most of the initial studies on helping behavior were addressed to the behavior of adults, not children, and it is difficult to estimate the degree to which such studies directly influenced the somewhat later investigation of children. In some studies of children's helping behavior, the hypothesis tested was explicitly linked to other investigators' ideas concerning this behavior exhibited by adults. For example, Bryan and Walbek (1970a, 1970b) conducted investigations to test whether children felt that they had a social responsibility to aid needy or dependent others, an explanation which had been advanced by Berkowitz and Daniels (1964) to account for helping behavior by college students. Staub (1970) was influenced by the work of Darley and Latane (1970), who had found that adults were less likely to show prompt helping of another adult in trouble when in the presence of a group than when alone. Staub conducted a series of investigations addressed to the question of whether the group would retard children's helping behavior in emergencies as it apparently inhibits such behaviors by adults. More typically, however, studies of the helping behavior of children have been most influenced by the theories and procedures of Bandura (1969). The emphasis in many studies of helping and sharing behavior is upon the role of observing others give, the impact of observing whether the aider got something for his troubles, the effects of observing more than one giving or selfish person, and the impact of hypocritical people upon the child's own behavior and attitudes. Essentially, most of the work on children's aiding behavior is concerned with the impact of what they observe other people do and what happens to these other people when they do it.

Whatever the sources of influence generating studies of such behavior, it is clear that considerable material and some knowledge is now available. This chapter presents evidence relevant to the determinants and correlates of helping and cooperative behaviors by children.

Before doing so, however, several limitations and biases of this chapter should be outlined. It would be well beyond the space limits of this chapter and the personal limits of the author to review all such studies conducted during the past several decades. Exclusions of worthwhile studies and topics had to be made and were based upon several considerations. First, most of the studies selected for review are of relatively recent origin, over 50% having been or to be published in the 1970s. Second, most of the studies included were experiments rather than correlational or survey investigations. As such there is a heavy emphasis upon laboratory-based behavioral measures of the dependent variables.

II. COOPERATION

A. CONCEPTS AND CHARACTERISTICS

Cooperation is thought to be reflected when individuals coordinate their actions in order to obtain what they want (Nelson & Madsen 1968). Interest in the development of cooperation among children stems more from practical than theoretical concerns insofar as theorizing is almost absent in this area of research. Two major sources of concern seem to be the stimulants to investigations on cooperation. On the one hand, cooperative responses are frequently used as a form of behavior to be changed through a variety of influence attempts. For example, cooperative responses are frequently used as the behavior to be changed in studies involving operant conditioning. There have been attempts to demonstrate that reinforcement affects cooperation between two or more children.

On the other hand, the second major concern seems to be determining the cultural and developmental influences which may affect such behavior by children. Comparisons are thus made of the cooperative behavior between children raised in different nations or different ethnic or social class groups. Will the personally deprived child be more competitive than his more affluent peers; are children raised in the United States more competitive or less cooperative than those raised in Mexico or on a kibbutz in Israel?

The usual laboratory procedure for investigating cooperation among children is to expose them to a task wherein their coordination of responses will get them something they both want. There are certain characteristics of this area of research which should be noted. First, studies of cooperation focus upon successful, not unsuccessful, cooperation. That is, cooperation measures typically index the degree to which children integrate their individual responses correctly, not the degree to which one child attempts to be cooperative but is thwarted by his partner. Second, cooperation is usually not costly to the child. The child can gain but not lose something by cooperating. Essentially there is no self-sacrifice involved. Third, laboratory investigations of cooperation which have focused upon subject differences have emphasized the operation of cultural and social influences, but not personality characteristics which may affect cooperative behavior. Age, sex, and culture are varied; personality traits which might be associated with cooperation are not. The evidence concerning personality differences and parental influences upon the development of cooperation comes primarily through the observation of children's behavior in vivo, mostly of nursery school age children during play within the school setting (e.g., Friedrich & Stein 1973; Hartup & Keller 1960). Insofar as these latter studies are generally concerned with children's consideration for others, they will be discussed under the topic of altruism.

B. REINFORCEMENT

Many of the investigations of cooperative behavior have focused upon the influence of reinforcement. Apparently, interest in the power of rewards to affect such behavior was stimulated particularly by the laboratory study of Azrin and Lindsley (1956). These investigators found that pairs of children between the ages of 7 and 12 cooperated more readily if each was rewarded for so doing. With the withdrawal of reward, their cooperation with each other decreased. The results of this study have had a rather profound influence on the development of this field of research. Various forms and procedures of reinforcement of such behavior have now come under scrutiny. Vogler, Masters, and Morrill (1970, 1971) have outlined, in some detail , methods by which cooperation between children can be influenced by the administration of rewards to the individual children involved.

While many investigators have employed pairs of children in studying cooperation, Mithaug (1969) and Mithaug and Burgess (1968) studied the impact of various reinforcement procedures on triads of children. These investigators again found that reinforcement which was based upon both individual and group performances increased the cooperation of 5–10-year-olds.

Rewards administered to children on the basis of their individual performances have been compared with rewards that are contingent upon the group's activity. Essentially, when an individual wants something and can obtain it only when the group reaches a particular standard of performance, is it likely that cooperation between those involved will be increased? The answer seems to be quite clearly in the affirmative. Investigators have *consistently* found that group-administered rewards are more effective in increasing cooperativeness than individually administered rewards, even when such behavior may produce fewer reinforcements to the child (Madsen 1967; Madsen & Shapira 1970; Nelson & Madsen 1968; Richmond & Weiner 1973; Shapira & Madsen 1969). Indeed, Nelson and Madsen found that group-administered rewards tend to produce a strategy of "taking turns" in reaching the goal among pairs of children, while individually administered rewards tended to produce a dominance-submissive relationship between children. Bronfenbrenner (1970) has reported that school systems within the USSR often employ group-administered rewards rather than rewards on the basis of individual behavior and that such a system seems to greatly increase cooperation among and responsibility toward one another by school-age children. In a most ingenious study, Fraser et al. (1973) found that among college students academic performance will be increased if grades are assigned not on individual merit but on group performance. Apparently this increase in achievement was related to an increase of cooperation among the students with regard to the sharing of materials and ideas.

The evidence gathered from laboratories and naturalistic settings suggests then that cooperation is facilitated by group-administered rewards rather than rewards to individuals on the basis of their own achievements. Students in classrooms, if cooperation is desired, should be rewarded with stars, tokens, or praise, not on the basis of their individual performance but on the basis of the entire group's actions. While such a system may offend our sense of justice being meted out on an individual basis, it is likely to produce friendlier, more cooperative, and less antagonistic relationships among children. All individuals working with groups of children should give serious consideration to the idea of rewarding, not individual enterprise, but collective productivity.

Unfortunately, there have been few studies concerned with the mediators of reinforcement effects or the relative efficacy of reinforcement relative to other types of training, such as modeling influences. Hopefully, the future will bring fewer demonstrations of the power of reinforcement and greater concern with the social and cognitive processes which compete or interact with reinforcement in affecting cooperation. For example, Shapira and Madsen (1969) found that the impact of individual versus group-administered rewards differed for children sampled in a kibbutz and those sampled in an urban setting. While children from both of these samples responded similarly to group-administered rewards by increasing their cooperative responses over the trials, they reacted quite differently to the individually administered rewards. Children sampled from the kibbutz continued to display cooperative responses under individual reinforcement, but the urban children were significantly less cooperative. The authors felt that two features of the kibbutz socialization practices were relevant to the findings. Compared with urban-raised Israelis, children on the kibbutz are trained from an early age to cooperate and work as a group and to minimize the importance of competition among themselves. The milieu and the socialization practices in the kibbutz may develop values focused on welfare of the group rather than self-interest.

Kagan and Madsen (1971) provide some experimental evidence that such group-oriented rather than self-oriented sets can lead to increased cooperation. These investigators, though not specifically studying the effect of reinforcement, provided some information which might account for the differential effects of individual and group-administered rewards. They found that instructional sets which induced a subject to perceive himself as an individual or as a member of a group differentially affected cooperative actions. Young children 4–5 years of age were unaffected by the varying instructions, but 7–9-year-olds were more likely to display cooperative behavior under the group than individually oriented instructions. The production of an "I" set greatly increased children's competition, even at the expense of obtaining rewards. One might suspect then that the administration of rewards based upon individual rather than coordinated group responses may produce such "I" sets and thus increase competition and inhibit cooperat on.

In summary, contingently administered reinforcements have been demonstrated to affect cooperative behavior of children. Reinforcement procedures which suggest to the child that he is being rewarded on the basis of his individual performance will elicit competitive, and occasionally nonadaptive, behavior rather than cooperative responses which are more likely to be reinforced.

C. SUBJECT VARIABLES

A variety of characteristics of cooperative and noncooperative children have been studied. These include social class, culture, race, and age. As previously noted, virtually no attention has been paid to the personality characteristics which might be associated with such behavior.

1. Developmental Trends

The results of several investigations suggest that cooperation is developmentally linked, decreasing as the child ages. Noteworthy however are two features of most investigations in this area. First, the child is confronted with but two possible responses, either cooperating or competing with others. What may be reflected in those findings which suggests a developmental decline in cooperation is simply an increase in the aging child's competitiveness. It is likely in the naturalistic setting that the child can cooperate without sacrificing competition and can compete without decreasing cooperation. Second, the children used in the studies of developmental changes in cooperation reflect a narrow age range, typically preschool to grade 6. Little is known about the cooperative behavior of adolescents.

The existing evidence does suggest, however, that when competition and cooperation are posed as alternative responses to the child the older child will be more likely than the younger one to compete. For example, in groups of same sex, and presumably same aged Mexican children, 4–5-year-old children were more cooperative in a "tug-of-war" game than 7–8-year-olds or 10–11-year-olds (Madsen 1971). Kagan and Madsen (1971) found that 4–5-year-olds were more cooperative in another type of game, a circle matrix task, than were 7–9-year-olds. In the circle matrix task pairs of children take turns moving a marker to adjacent circles in an array of seven rows and seven columns. Either child can win a prize if the marker is moved to his side of the array, but both children must move the marker in the same direction in order to reach a given side. The adaptive or cooperative strategy is to take turns moving it to one child's goal then to the other child's goal. If the children do not cooperate, the marker may remain in the middle of the array so that neither gets the prize.

The results of these two studies stimulated Madsen and Conner (1973) to investigate the relationship of intelligence to cooperation using a tug-of-war game. Six and 7-year-old retarded children were more cooperative than 11- and 12-year-old retardates. Both groups of retarded children cooperated more than normal children of the same chronological ages. Of interest was the author's observation that ". . . several retarded subjects expressed concern about what was the right thing to do or about the goodness of taking turns, while the non-retarded subjects more often expressed concern about winning or pulling the string before the other child" (pp. 177–178).

It should be kept in mind, however, that the above mentioned studies were conducted within a laboratory setting in which the child is presented with but two possible responses, to cooperate or to compete. Results based upon observations of children's behaviors within a naturalistic setting may yield different results. For example, Parton (1933) observed 2–5-year-olds, and Friedrich and Stein (1973) observed 4–5 ½-year-olds. Both found that cooperation was positively correlated with age for both boys and girls. Whether discrepancies in these findings are due to differences in the ages of the children tested, the setting in which they were tested, or the means by which they were tested, remains to be determined. However, it would seem reasonable to assume that preschool age children are initially socialized with a view to developing their cooperation with others. As the child develops, the socialization emphasis may well change toward greater stress on achievement of individual skills. For older children, when there is opportunity to compete or cooperate, they compete. When there is opportunity for cooperative activity which is not costly to them and which lies within their motor skills, it would seem reasonable to predict they would be more, not less, cooperative as they age. It does seem that most adults cooperate when costs to themselves are not involved.

2. Cross-cultural Studies

Are American children less likely to be cooperative than children from other cultures? Kagan and Madsen (1971) compared performances of Anglo-American, Mexican-American, and Mexican children on the circle matrix task. Mexican children were significantly more cooperative than Mexican-American children, who were in turn significantly more cooperative than Anglo-American children. Madsen and Shapira (1970) used performance on the Madsen Cooperation Board to compare the cooperative responses of Anglo-American, Afro-American, and Mexican-American children 7–9 years of age. In this task, children are instructed to manipulate a pen with strings so that it passes through a circle outlined closest to them. Children can cooperate by taking turns and not "pulling" against one another. The number of circles crossed serves as the measure of cooperation. All groups were equally cooperative under the conditions of group reward. However, when individual-reward procedures were initiated, Mexican-American boys were less likely to initiate maladaptive competitive behaviors than were the remaining groups. In a second experiment, Madsen and Shapira created conditions where competitive performance would be adaptive, that is, would lead to greater rewards, and compared the performance of the same subjects who participated in experiment 1. No differences in competitive behavior were found attributable to ethnic groups. In a third experiment, subjects from these three ethnic groups and from a Mexican village were tested without having had prior experiences with group-administered rewards. Only the Mexican village children cooperated fully, while the three ethnic groups from the United States showed considerable nonadaptive competition. The Mexican-American children evidenced "less vigorous" competition than did the remaining two United States groups. Using a "tug-of-war" task, Madsen (1971) again found Mexican children considerably more cooperative than Anglo-American children.

3. Sex Differences

By and large, most studies in which the cooperation of boys and girls are compared report no differences. For example, Lindskold et al. (1970) found no sex differences in cooperation in the performance of fourth- and fifth-grade children on a Prisoner's Dilemma Game. This game "is a two-choice, two-person game; each player must independently choose to cooperate or to compete on each play of the game and is unable to explicitly communicate his intentions to the other. If both players cooperate, both gain; if both players compete, both lose; but, if one competes while the other cooperates, the competitor gains more than he does in the event of joint cooperation, and the cooperator loses more than he does in the event of joint competition" (Lindskold et al. 1970, p. 277). Madsen (1971) found no sex differences among 4–11-year-olds on a tug-of-war task, nor did Sampson and Kardush (1965) or Richmond and Weiner (1973) find sex differences in their studies on cooperation. When sex differences are reported, boys generally evidence more cooperation than do girls (Friedrich & Stein 1973; Madsen 1967; Wasik, Senn, & Epanchin 1969).

It is not likely that a broad generalization can be made as to which of the sexes is the more cooperative. The complexity of cooperation is evidenced by the results reported by Tedeschi, Hiester, and Gahagan (1969). On the basis of studies with adults, these investigators expected that male children would be more cooperative than females, at least when such activity is measured by the Prisoner's Dilemma Game. Contrary to expectations, they found that which sex was the more cooperative depended upon the magnitude of the payoffs. When rewards were relatively great or small, females demonstrated more cooperation and more trust in their partner's behavior than did males. Results were generally reversed when the rewards and losses associated with the game were intermediate in magnitude. If cooperation is affected differently in boys and girls as a result of the payoffs within the environment, little confidence can be placed in any general statement concerning sex differences in cooperative behavior.

4. Social Class and Race

Several reasonable assumptions have led a number of investigators to study the impact of social class and race upon cooperative behavior. McKee and Leader (1955) suggested that persons deprived of resources or status are more likely to pursue them vigorously than persons not so deprived. On the other hand, Richmond and Weiner (1973) argue that the likelihood of deprived children obtaining a resource will be increased by training in cooperative rather than competitive behavior, and that such children should show the most cooperation.

Studies comparing the cooperative behavior of lower- and middle-class children have yielded inconsistent results. Studies by Brotsky and Thomas (1967) and Nelson and Madsen (1968) failed to find differences in cooperation between white middle- and lower-class 4-year-olds. Madsen (1967) did find that Mexican urban middle-class second-grade children were more cooperative than urban poor children when under group-reward conditions, but tended to be more competitive than the urban poor under conditions of individual rewards. McKee and Leader (1955) reported that upper-middle-class 3- and 4-year-olds showed less competition with another child of the same sex and socioeconomic studies than did children from lower socioeconomic backgrounds. McKee and Leader did not assess cooperative behavior.

With the current emphasis upon and interest in school integration and in the development and effects of ethnic or racial pride, it is somewhat surprising that, with the exception of the studies by Madsen and his colleagues discussed under cross-cultural studies, few studies have been published regarding cooperative interactions within and across ethnic and racial groups. Wasik et al. (1969), in their study of lower-class black and white kindergarten children, found that black children were less cooperative than white in a task requiring the matching of responses with a stylus. Harford and Cutter (1966) tested 6–12-year-olds, white and black, in a Prisoner's Dilemma Game and found that black boys were the least, and black girls were the most, cooperative. They found, as did Wasik et al., that the race of partners did not affect the children's cooperation with one another. On the other hand, the studies conducted by Sampson and Kardush (1965) and Richmond and Weiner (1973) found black children were generally more cooperative than whites under conditions of group-administered rewards, whereas white children interacting with other white children were the most competitive under conditions of individually administered rewards. Finally, Nelson and Madsen (1968) failed to find any race effects in their study of 4-year-olds.

5. Summary

Very few empirical generalizations concerning the subject variables associated with children's cooperation can be offered. The results pertaining to cooperation and its relationship to children's sex, race , and social class have not yielded strong and consistent information. There are developmental correlates of cooperation, but apparently the direction of the correlation depends upon the context and/or method used to observe the child. There does appear evidence that the child, particularly the older child, who is socialized within the United States might be particularly likely to show competitive rather than cooperative actions when only those two response strategies are available to him. Finally, there is a paucity of data concerning the personality characteristics associated with children's cooperation.

D. REACTIONS TO COOPERATION

There are few studies concerning the impact of cooperation upon the participants outside of their responses during the task. Little is known concerning how children view cooperative others, or what effects cooperation has upon subsequent social behavior. There is some evidence to suggest that cooperative behavior elicited within the laboratory setting will generalize along both stimulus and response dimensions. Altman (1971) trained cooperative behavior between pairs of 3–6-year-olds. While not all pairs reached the criterion specified for the learning of cooperation, those who did subsequently demonstrated more friendly and less hostile approaches to other children during spontaneous play. Blau and Rafferty (1970) found that friendship between partners was increased by experiencing reinforcement during a cooperation task.

Gottheil (1955) also found that eighth-grade children were likely to perceive members of their group in a more favorable light after having participated in a cooperative enterprise than were those children who had been involved in competition with their classmates or those who had neither competed nor cooperated. These findings parallel those reported by Sherif et al. (1961) in their study of competition and cooperation by 22 11-year-old boys during their stay at a summer camp. These investigators arranged competitive encounters between two groups of children. The members of each group lived together and for the initial part of the study were isolated from members of the other group until competitive interactions were introduced. At that point, intense rivalry and dislike developed between members of the two groups. Verbal barbs and physical assaults between the members of the rival camps were not unusual. When the boys of each camp were forced by necessity to cooperate with each other in order for them all to receive something they wished, interpersonal relationships and perceptions became considerably more benevolent. Cooperation increases attraction toward cooperating others, whether assessed in the laboratory or in vivo.

E. CONCLUSIONS AND SPECULATIONS

While there are relatively few conclusions which can be offered with much confidence concerning the development and determinants of cooperative behavior, as studied within the laboratory, two findings seem robust. First, children within the United States are likely to be trained, at a relatively young age, into a competitive response style. Second, the basis upon which rewards are given to children will have important effects upon their cooperation with one another.

While the socialization of children into a competitive response style may well enhance achievement, mastery of skills, and general success within a competitive society, it may have at least two negative consequences. First, competition may become an end in and of itself. That is to say, children may be socialized in such a way as to prefer interpersonal superiority to that of obtaining useful or pleasure-giving commodities. Second, competitive styles may attenuate cooperative activities. It is true, of course, that in many naturalistic settings, unlike laboratory ones, children are not faced with but two alternative responses: to cooperate or compete. Indeed, in many situations, such as in organized sports, children both cooperate with their teammates and compete against their opponents and do both with intensity (Sherif et al. 1961). But when cooperation and competition are mutually exclusive, for example when grades are assigned on the basis of rankings of the students in a classroom, it is likely that the American child, as he develops, becomes more competitive and less cooperative. Moreover, evidence will be presented subsequently to indicate that competitive atmospheres and competitive children are likely to show an indifference to the plights of unfortunate others. An emphasis upon competition may well attenuate a child's compassion for others.

The findings reported by Madsen and his colleagues that individually based reward systems are likely to increase competitiveness are particularly important. Much of the informal control by parents and the formal control in token economies are based upon just that form of resource distribution (Kazdin & Bootzin 1972). Yet, we know very little about the impact of such individually based reward systems upon the development of a child's attitudes toward his peers or the powerful. Additionally, no information is available concerning the effects of such reinforcement practices upon children's attitudes and judgments concerning the appropriateness of various bases for giving rewards. The notion that individuals should and do get what they individually deserve is no doubt a pervasive one within this culture. People do believe that individuals get what they personally merit (e.g., Lerner & Matthews 1967; Lerner & Simmons 1966). Moreover, even preschool age children distribute rewards to others based upon the other's productivity (Leventhal, Popp, & Sawyer 1973). But no information appears available as to the interaction of such beliefs and the usage of various forms of resource distribution during the socialization period. Finally, other forms of reward allocation are possible, yet their relative merits and demerits in the production of prosocial behaviors and the attitudes which underlie them have not been explored.

III. HELPING BEHAVIOR AND ALTRUISM

A. DEFINITIONS AND METHODS OF STUDY

Many investigations of helping behavior have been concerned with those circumstances in which sacrifices are made to benefit another without apparent gain and have been described as studies of altruism. Perhaps because of the long-standing importance of this term in philosophy, there continues to be some debate concerning the definition of altruism (e.g., Katz 1972). The central issue has been the assumption of unselfishness. Since Comte, the term has been used to refer to a helpful act which was unmotivated, an act which had no positive consequences to the helping agent. This emphasis put an impossible burden upon the social scientist, demanding of him that he demonstrate the null hypothesis. That is, to study altruism as historically defined, the investigator must demonstrate that a motive, the fulfillment of which would bring personal gratification, did not propel the altruist into action. This definition is still used to challenge the relevance of current investigations to "real altruism" (Ekstein 1972; Katz 1972). This definitional burden has inhibited the development of systematic studies of children's helping behavior.

Recently, altruism has been redefined in such a way as to generate much information of practical and theoretical use concerning children's helpful behaviors. Definitions do vary, of course, but probably not, as yet, to very significant degrees. Leeds (1963) defined altruism as a voluntary act intended to produce a beneficial outcome for another for which there would not be personal gain for the actor. Campbell (1972) suggested that altruism is self-sacrifice for the good of a social group, while Macaulay and Berkowitz (1970) defined altruism as "behavior carried out to benefit another without anticipation of rewards from external sources" (p. 73). Bryan and London suggested that such behaviors are those ". . . intended to benefit another but which appear to have a high cost to the actor with little possibility of material or social reward" (1970, p. 200).

Altruistic behavior is generally studied by providing the child with a situation where he might give up something he wants so as to benefit a needy other or where he must exert some effort to help a needy other. In order to minimize social coercion and the child's anticipation of rewards for his altruistic act, his sacrifice is made privately and usually is directed toward a stranger rather than a friend. This is not to say that such an act is not controlled, that the child is unmotivated, or that the child does not anticipate some rewards for his sacrificing act. Rather the emphasis is upon the reasonableness of the action in terms of immediate external reinforcements. It is assumed that most children would not anticipate an immediate external reward for the act, and the situation is so structured that it is reasonable to assume that most children who helped in fact intended to help the recipient of their generosity.

Typically, two types of altruistic or helping behavior have been studied: rescue and donation. In the rescue situation, the child is faced with an emergency wherein another child or adult, out of the subject's view, is apparently hurt. Measures of the child's rescue behavior include the speed in which he attempts to help the hurt other and the means by which this attempt is made (Staub 1970, 1971a, 1971b; Weissbrod 1974). Does the child seek the experimenter, attempt to aid by going directly into the room where the hurt other is, or does he not make any intervention efforts? If he does something, how quickly does he do it? In studies involving donations, the child is given the option of donating prizes he has won in a game and then is left unobserved to place them in a box for a needy other. The amount of the resources given constitutes the measure of the child's altruistic behavior. In both types of situations, the child typically does not see or interact with the recipient of his generosity.

Before discussing the results of the vast number of investigations available, several characteristics of work in this area should be noted. First, most investigations of helping behavior have been conducted within the context of the laboratory, not in "real world" settings. Most investigators seek to isolate a few processes that might influence such behavior within the laboratory setting. Other important processes which might interact with those being investigated are wittingly isolated or controlled within laboratory settings. It is generally hoped that, like the natural sciences, the findings generated from the laboratories of the psychologist will be applicable to the real world. As of now, however, confidence in the relevance of laboratory findings to other settings remains a matter of faith. There is little evidence concerning the limitations or real-world usefulness of laboratory-based findings in the area of helping behaviors.

An important issue for those working in the area of altruism is the degree to which the behavior they are measuring is related to other helping behaviors. For example, can one predict whether a child will sympathize, console, rescue, cooperate, or otherwise try to help another on the basis of his willingness to contribute money to needy others? When donation is used as a measure of helping, is it in fact related to other forms of helping? Studies conducted in the laboratory have generally not found high correlations among various forms of helping such as donating and rescuing (deLuca 1968; Mussen et al. 1970; Staub 1969; Staub & Sherk 1970; Weissbrod 1974). However, Elliot and Vasta (1970) did report a sizable correlation between donating candy and money to a stranger, and Midlarsky and Bryan (1972) found that children's donations in the laboratory predicted their giving within a classroom setting. Observational studies conducted in naturalistic settings and employing more global indexes of helpfulness have produced results which suggest that helping behaviors are intercorrelated. Friedrich and Stein (1973) found that nurturant and cooperative behavior were highly correlated in their sample of preschool boys and moderately correlated for girls. Likewise, Baumrind (1971) observed that nurturance and sympathy to other children, selfish behavior, helping others, bullying, thoughtlessness, understanding the viewpoints of peers, and insulting behaviors were all related in such a way as to suggest an underlying disposition to be socially responsible. Dlugokinski and Firestone (1973) found correlations among self-report measures, sociometric ratings, and a behavioral measure involving donations that indicated some individual consistency in children's consideration for others.

Finally, it should be noted that the overwhelming number of laboratory studies conducted on this topic are addressed toward helping an unfortunate other who is a stranger to the child. This point takes on some importance insofar as children judge the fairness of giving or taking something from another on the basis of the other's deservedness and the gains possible to the child who is giving or taking (Brickman & Bryan, in press; Lane & Koon 1972; Leventhal et al. 1973). Many of the laboratory findings regarding helping may not be applicable to situations involving friends.

The remainder of this chapter will discuss the research relevant to children's helping behavior. The initial section will be devoted to a discussion of the effect of observing others who help, the influence of the context in which this is observed, and the model's characteristics that influence the child toward generous behavior. In the second section, the role of the child's affective states as influences on helping will be discussed. The third section will review those studies involving the impact of comparison and competitive processes as they relate to helping. Finally, individual differences, such as age, sex, and personality traits, which might be associated with children's aiding, will be reviewed.

B. OBSERVING HELPING OTHERS

The literature shows that altruistic and helpful models affect children. If the child witnesses another person giving, the likelihood that the child will help is increased regardless of whether the other person is a peer or adult or is observed live or on videotape (Bryan 1972). Imitation has been demonstrated with regard to rescue acts (Staub 1971a) and to the donation of money (Schwartz & Bryan 1971a, 1971b); redeemable gift certificates (Bryan & Walbek 1970a, 1970b; Rosenhan & White 1967; White 1972); candies, marbles (Harris 1971); and tokens (Grusec & Driscoll 1973; Liebert & Poulos 1971; Midlarsky & Bryan 1972; Rushton, in press). These effects have been found with first to sixth graders (Elliot & Vasta 1970) as well as adults (Bryan & Test 1967).

Of considerable importance are the recent findings that the effects of altruistic models may be relatively enduring. Rushton found that children exposed to an altruistic model were more likely to donate during a posttest 2 months following exposure to the model than children exposed to a selfish model. Both Midlarsky and Bryan (1972) and White (1972) found similar results in that children exposed to a helping model within a laboratory setting were more likely to contribute to a charity at least five days later in another setting than children exposed to a selfish model.

1. The Social Responsibility Norm

One explanation of the modeling effect is that most people learn a standard or a "norm of social responsibility" which dictates that individuals should help others who are dependent upon them (Berkowitz & Daniels 1964; Krebs 1970). The helping behavior of the child, or the adult, is a function of having learned this norm and being reminded of it. There is some evidence to suggest that children do learn and accept this norm, at least by the time they are in the third or fourth grade. If asked, most children indicate that it is good to help the needy (Bryan & Walbek 1970a). Additionally, when children are asked to rate a model on such dimensions as niceness and goodness, they view a giving model more favorably than a selfish one (Bryan, Redfield, & Mader 1971; Bryan & Walbek 1970a, 1970b; Schwartz & Bryan 1971a). Finally, children will urge others to give in spite of hearing a model encourage them not to give (Bryan & Walbek 1970a). However, the question is whether the *actions* of a model are influential *because* such actions remind the child of this norm. This does not appear to be the case. Studies have been conducted where some children are verbally reminded of the norm and compared with other children who were not reminded. The results have not indicated that making the norm salient increases children's helping. Statements such as "It is good to give" or "Giving will make other children happy" or "If you give, it will make them very happy" have not been found effective (Bryan & Walbek 1970a; Liebert & Poulos 1971; Rushton, in press; Walbek 1969). If imitative donation is considered to reflect the influence of the salience of the norm of social responsibility, it would be necessary to assume that the motor behaviors of the model would be better norm reminders than restatements of the norm, an unlikely assumption.

2. Demand Characteristics

A second explanation of imitative altruism is that such behavior reflects the operation of "demand characteristics" of the experimental situation. This term as applied to imitative altruism reduces to the idea that children will do what they think is expected of them and that they interpret the model's actions as the expected behavior in that context. Interestingly, few have as yet asked the children what they thought was expected of them. Instead, a variety of manipulations and measures which would presumably reflect the operation of such expectancies have been designed.

It is presumed that the model's actions are influential because they define to the child the appropriate behaviors within the setting. Expectancies can also be induced by verbal statements concerning what the model has done, or will do. Thus, instead of employing such comments as "it is good to give," as in tests involving the Social Responsibility Norm, statements are made by the model describing his past behavior or probable future behavior (Grusec 1972; Grusec & Skubiski 1970). Grusec and Skubiski tested the effects of such verbal statements on third- and fifth-grade boys and girls. One group of children heard the model indicate that "they expect us to share," that "one had better do it," and that the model would in fact share. Such remarks affected the child's giving only when that child was a girl and only when there had been a warm interaction between the model and the child prior to starting the experimental task. In a follow-up study, Grusec (1972) used essentially the same procedures and instructions with 7- and 11-year-olds except that model warmth was not varied. The model's verbal statements describing his intent to donate were effective in eliciting children's donations as was his demonstration of charity for all children except 7-year-old boys. Grusec suggested that by age 11 most children have internalized the norm of social responsibility and are likely to respond to verbal cues suggesting donation. It should be noted that the negative results pertaining to this norm reviewed in the last section were based upon children considerably younger than 11 years of age. It is possible then that Grusec's explanation to account for the performance of her 11-year-old subjects is correct. She further suggested that 7-year-old girls are likely to be more concerned with social approval and conforming to adult expectations than are 7-year-old boys, and thus are more likely to be influenced by the model's verbalized expectancies.

Finally, Grusec and Driscoll (1973) compared the impact upon the child's willingness to donate of a model's verbalizations concerning his past donation behavior, his verbalizations regarding the experimenter's expectations concerning the desirability of donations, and his actual donation behavior. The results indicated that verbalizations, be they of past donation behavior or experimenter expectancies, did not affect the donation behavior of 7–10-year-old boys and girls. As usual, the generous actions of the model affected the donation behavior of the child. Grusec and Driscoll suggested that the critical difference among these three studies consisted of the behavior of the experimenter. In the first two studies, the experimenter indicated that it was acceptable albeit optional for the model and child to donate some of their winnings. In the Grusec and Driscoll experiment, the experimenter made no reference to this possibility. Presumably, this omission reduced the conflict experienced by the child to take or to give, thus they did not give.

The effects of the model's behavior might be attributable to several sources. Grusec and Driscoll suggested that the child's observation of the generous model evokes a comparison process between the child and model. The assumption is that the child compares himself with the model, and if the model actually donates the child's self-esteem will be reduced if he does not do likewise (cf. Bryan & Test 1967). A second possibility is that, in the absence of experimenter approval, the child requires more than verbal statements about donations from the model in order to believe that donations are in fact acceptable. It is one thing to be told that novel actions are acceptable to the experimenter by a model and quite another to observe a model actually perform the act with no untoward consequences.

Staub (1970, 1971b) has provided evidence suggesting that children are very sensitive to the rules of the situation and, in the absence of explicit permission for helping behavior, make the assumption that no action rather than helpful action is the rule to be followed. Merely informing the child that he would be allowed to enter a second room to sharpen a pencil increased the likelihood that the child would attempt to rescue a distressed other located in the second room (1970). In the absence of permission, seventh-grade girls acted similarly to same-age girls who had received explicit prohibitions about entering the room. Those who had received permission to enter this room showed more rescue behavior than the remaining two groups (Staub 1971b).

Evidence exists and common sense dictates that children are sensitive to the actions and demands of the experimenter and the model. They do follow instructions, are concerned with not violating the experimenter's rules, and generally leave or stay and conduct themselves appropriately when told to do so. The point is, however, whether the concept of "demand characteristics" is heuristic in the study of imitative altruism. One assumption implicit in the concept is that the behavior being reliably produced is doomed to brief, situationally specific, existence. While this is likely to characterize most behavior produced within the laboratory setting, it is presumed to be even more relevant to the actions produced by "demand characteristics." However, there are now several studies available which suggest that the altruistic model will affect altruism at a time rather removed from the treatment manipulations and will affect such behavior in settings other than the particular laboratory site (Midlarsky & Bryan 1972; Rushton, in press; White 1972). The evidence suggests that the impact of the altruistic model is not of extremely limited duration nor is it as situationally specific as implied in the concept of "demand characteristics."

Whatever the adequacy of the demand and social responsibility hypothesis in accounting for imitative altruism, important information has been obtained from such studies on the development of altruism and helping behavior. It is hardly profound, but it is nonetheless true, that adult and peer expectancies concerning children's behaviors are likely to have a very strong influence upon their conduct. The critical question is how should such expectancies be communicated to the child. Reminding the child of his social responsibility appears particularly ineffective in controlling helping behavior. On the other hand, verbal descriptions of aiding behavior and actual demonstrations of such behavior appear to have strong influence over the child, perhaps because they communicate so completely the methods and consequences associated with giving and the expectancies of authorities. Perhaps, as Grusec and Driscoll suggest, children do enter a social comparison process with the model, and when the model commits a helping act, the child, to maintain his self-esteem, must do likewise. We do not know.

Why the modeling effect has durability is still open to question. Perhaps children who give in the laboratory are consequently rewarded by parents, peers, or teachers for their behavior and thus maintain such behavior when given the opportunity. Perhaps nongivers are castigated. As yet, no attention has been paid to the long-term social consequences of charitable behavior by the child.

3. Personal Characteristics of the Exemplar

Not surprisingly, there has been considerable effort devoted to determining the personal characteristics of the model that facilitate children's helping. Warmth, affective expression, power, social status, popularity, and moral consistency have all been investigated.

Warmth of model.—Warmth is a central concept in theories of identification (Bandura 1969; Mowrer 1950), and it has demonstrated importance in imitative behavior in general (e.g., Hetherington & Frankie 1967). Therefore, it has been expected that helpfulness by a warm or nurturant model would be imitated more than such behavior by one who was indifferent or cold toward the child. The experimental procedures manipulating warmth typically include a brief (10 minutes or so) interaction between model and child in which the model is either warm or indifferent. The model then demonstrates helpful or unhelpful behavior, and the child's subsequent willingness to donate or rescue is assessed. The results are relatively consistent with regard to donation behavior. Model warmth either has little effect or generally retards donation. Two investigations failed to find that model warmth increased imitative altruism by third- through fifth-grade children (Grusec & Skubiski 1970; Rosenhan & White 1967). In two subsequent investigations, model warmth generally diminished the amount donated by 7–11-year-old children (Grusec 1971; Weissbrod 1974).

By contrast, model warmth facilitates rescue behavior. Staub (1971a) suggested that in an emergency situation it is to the child's benefit to reduce another's distress so as to reduce his own empathically produced anxiety. A "warm" model may reduce the child's fear of the experimenter's disapproval for initiating the rescue activity, which usually requires acts which have not been previously explicated as legitimate. As children who receive no permission for such behavior act similarly to those who have received specific prohibitions concerning such acts (Staub 1971b), it seems that rescue activity not previously legitimized by an authority requires courage on the part of the child. The less threatening the authority, the easier it is to have courage. Staub (1971a) tested this idea by exposing some kindergarten children to a warm and friendly experimenter-model who helped and others to a neutral and indifferent one. As expected, children who witnessed a warm model were more likely to initiate helping acts than those who had interacted with a cold or indifferent model.

Yarrow, Scott, and Waxler (1973) conducted a study of rescue activity by nursery school children in a naturalistic setting. Care was taken to document the fact that the teacher was either warm or cold toward the target children. Additionally, while specific attempts were made to train the child to be helpful, the measure of rescue activity was unrelated to the training tasks. That is, treatment effects were assessed on behaviors reflecting considerable generalization. Finally, unlike the usual 5–10-minute laboratory interactions for purposes of manipulating the model's warmth, the Yarrow et al. investigation employed models who were either warm or cold toward children for a period of 6 weeks. As expected, children were more likely to rescue after having had a warm rather than a cold relationship with an authority who had modeled helping acts.

The influence of warmth upon both rescue and donation behaviors of first-grade boys was investigated by Weissbrod (1974). Following a "warm" or "cold" interaction with a female model, children viewed a videotape of the model playing a bowling game and donating some of her winnings to a charitable organization. Some boys were subsequently given the opportunity to play the same game, win money, and make anonymous donations. Following this they heard cries of distress from a tape-recorded voice of a young boy, and rescue behavior was assessed. Other groups of children were exposed to a warm or cold model, then were directly exposed to the emergency situation without an opportunity to play the game or to donate. When both donation and rescue opportunities were available, warmth decreased donations, but did not affect rescue behavior. When the donation measure was omitted, model warmth increased rescue behavior.

The impact of an authority's or a model's warmth or permissiveness may well differentially affect rescue and donation behaviors, increasing the former while inhibiting the latter. In both instances, however, the dynamics involved may be the communication of a message to the child that he may do what he wishes: in the case of the donation, to not donate; in the case of rescue activity, to reduce his empathically produced distress by relieving the distress of another.

These findings are consistent with recent results pertaining to the effects of nurturance upon other behaviors involving self-denial. For example, Bandura, Grusec, and Menlove (1967) found that children adopted a less stringent standard for rewarding themselves when the model demonstrated warmth than when she displayed indifference or coldness. Likewise, Parke (1967) found that girls' resistance to temptation was lessened after exposure to an adult who demonstrated continuous warmth as opposed to one who demonstrated a withdrawal of warmth. While the impact of nurturance or warmth is clearly a complicated matter, it is likely that one consequence of a stranger's warmth is to facilitate a child's self-indulgence and hence may be more important as a communication about the consequences of transgressions than a facilitator of important forms of imitation involving self-sacrifice. Noteworthy however is the fact that studies of model warmth do involve the child's interaction with a strange adult in a strange setting. This liberating effect of warmth likely would be attenuated as the child became familiar with the adult's standards and enforcements and came to value the adult's approval more. Attention should also be drawn to the fact that in laboratory studies of model warmth care is taken to ensure that the warm model does not demonstrate helping behavior along with his warmth. In the naturalistic setting, it is likely that warm, friendly adults are likely to be helpful ones as well and thus both provide frequent examples of helping acts and help the children directly.

Affective reactions of the model.—Aronfreed (1968) has stressed the importance of conditioned emotional responses in the development and maintenance of altruistic behavior. He suggested that if the observing child experiences a change in affect which is increasingly positive, and if this change is associated in time with the donation act, the affect will become attached to the act. Bryan (1971b) and Midlarsky and Bryan (1972) investigated the impact of a model's affective response to his own donation behavior upon children. These investigators tested the idea that children will empathize with the model and, if the model demonstrates happiness when donating to needy others, the child's observations of the model will be associated with his empathically produced positive affect. The child then might be more likely to donate because he expects an increase in his positive affect or because this affect has become conditioned to such motor responses. Midlarsky and Bryan (1972) predicted that a model who demonstrated positive affect immediately following a donation or a selfish act would be more likely to be imitated than when such affect displays were not associated with giving or keeping. The results were as predicted. Children who were exposed to a selfish model who expressed happiness about keeping his gains donated the least, while children who viewed a model happy about his giving gave the most. In between these two groups in their generosity were the children who viewed either a selfish or a generous model whose happiness was not associated with his own giving or keeping. In another study (Bryan 1971a), children donated more and imitated the particular motor movements of the model more when the model had demonstrated affective responses immediately after donation than after a few seconds' delay. It appears that self-generated affective responses are powerful determinants of a model's influence on a child's imitation of aversive or self-sacrificing behavior. People who are trying it and liking it are probably most effective in serving as exemplars of aiding to children.

Power of the model.—The power of the model is influential in affecting imitation by observing children (Bandura 1969; Mussen & Distler 1959), and it is not surprising that this model attribute has been investigated in relation to imitative helpfulness. Experimentally, power is assigned to the model by his control over rewards and punishments, either implicitly or explicitly. Grusec (1971) found that 7–11-year-old children were more likely to imitate an adult male who would be selecting a child from the school for a special prize than one who did not have power to distribute any prize. Hartup and Coates (1967) found that the effectiveness of the child model depended upon the degree to which the child rewarded other children within the classroom and the degree to which the observing child received rewards from his classmates. Children who have had a history of reinforcements from their classmates were more likely to imitate a model who typically dispensed such reinforcements to their classmates. In contrast, children who infrequently received such reinforcements from their peers were more likely to imitate models who gave few such rewards to their peers.

Other methods designed to attribute power to the model have not been successful in affecting imitation. Bryan and Walbek (1970b; Marshall 1972) had one group of children view the experimenter who served as the model and another group of children view a model who was not the experimenter. They assumed that the experimenter, being in charge of the laboratories, games, and rewards, would be perceived by the child as being more powerful than a nonexperimenter model. Neither investigation found that the experimenter model was more effective than the comparison model. Moreover, Walbek (1969) failed to find that a model described as the child's possible future teacher was more effective in eliciting imitative helping than the same model not so described. One hypothesis advanced by Shirley (1973) to account for these discrepancies is that in the several studies in which the effect of power was found the powerful model actually functioned as an agent of reinforcement. Perhaps power, to affect altruism, must be directly tied to the control and dispensations of reinforcements.

Hypocrisy of the model.—It is likely that parents, educators, or friends are not entirely consistent in matching their verbalized morality with their motor acts. Indeed, it would seem likely that preaching morality is generally less costly than its practice and much easier to exhibit (Brown 1973; Bryan 1973). When behavior contradicts the moral position which has been espoused, hypocrisy has been demonstrated.

Studies concerned with the effects of inconsistency in preachings and practices have generally failed to find effects. In these studies, some children are presented with a model who both preaches charity (e.g., It is good to give; One should give) and practices it by donating to a charity. Other children are presented with a model who exhorts selfishness (e.g., It is not so good to give; One should not give) and practices it by keeping the funds. Yet other groups of children see inconsistent models who practice selfishness but preach charity or who preach selfishness but practice charity. Still others observe a model who does not preach anything but does or does not contribute his winnings. Little evidence has been forthcoming that hypocrisy concerning altruism reduces the child's own helpfulness or affects his judgments of the niceness or goodness of the model. The model's actions do affect the child's donations; the model's verbal statements do affect what the child preaches; and both words and deeds affect the child's perception of the model. Inconsistency between words and deeds, however, has not been found to affect the child's perceptions or imitation of the model (Bryan & Walbek 1970a, 1970b; Bryan et al. 1971; Midlarsky & Bryan 1972; Schwartz & Bryan 1971a; Walbek 1969).

Three experiments have been concerned with the effects of hypocrisy or inconsistency concerning charity upon the model's subsequent ability to influence the child's donations to charity through social approval. Bryan et al. (1971) failed to find that hypocrisy affected the power of the model's social approval when testing second and third graders on a self-sacrificing task which was dissimilar to the task presented to the model. However, Midlarsky, Bryan, and Brickman (1973), in two separate experiments, did find that when a model exhorted charity but failed to be charitable, his social approval following the child's donation acts served not to increase, but to *inhibit* donation acts. Social approval from someone who is inconsistent in his preachings and practices, or inconsistent in his behavior from the "demands" he places upon the child, becomes aversive to the child. Just which of the two forms of inconsistency produces the aversive quality to the reinforcement could not be separated within the designs of these two experiments. The results suggest, however, that the "moral" quality of the reinforcer may put constraints upon the reinforcer's power to influence the child.

4. Multiple Models

Although children obviously view a variety of models, little work has been devoted to understanding the impact of multiple models on any behavior, much less altruism (Bandura & Menlove 1968; Hildebrandt, Feldman, & Ditrichs 1973; McMains & Liebert 1968). Liebert and Fernandez (1970) studied the effects upon 4-year-old children of two models who contributed identical amounts to a charity. One model was as effective as two in eliciting donations, but there was more precise matching of amounts given when the boys were exposed to two rather than a single model. As yet no experiment has been conducted where several models were inconsistent with one another in their charitable activities.

5. Helping and Interpersonal Perceptions

While the effects of altruistic acts upon interpersonal relationships have not been experimentally manipulated. considerable data indicate that children evaluate helpful peers favorably. In most studies, children are asked to judge the niceness or goodness of a model who does or does not donate and does or does not preach the norm of social responsibility. The charitable model is consistently evaluated more favorably than the selfish one. In addition, models who preach generosity (regardless of their actions) are viewed more favorably than those who preach selfishness despite the fact that such preaching has little effect on subjects' donations (Bryan et al. 1971; Rushton, in press). These verbal reports are correlated with a behavioral measure of attraction—the child's choice of a balloon with either the model's or experimenter's name printed upon it (Schwartz & Bryan 1971a, 1971b). Considerably more information is needed about the impact of altruistic acts upon the interpersonal, and intrapersonal, life of the altruistic child.

6. Modeling and Context Effects

One hypothesis concerning altruistic giving is that the child anticipates receiving subsequent reinforcements for his generosity. On this basis one could reasonably assume that if a child observes the model being rewarded for his generous act, the probability of imitative helping would be increased. Harris (1970) failed to find that fourth- and fifth-grade children were more likely to imitate a generous adult model who had received praise for donating her earned tokens than one who had not received praise. Elliott and Vasta (1970) found that 5-, 6-, and 7-year-olds were more likely to imitate a peer model only when the vicarious reinforcements contained explanations of the relationship between giving and being rewarded. Presbie and Coiteux (1971) found that first-grade children were more likely to imitate the actions of the model, selfish or generous, either when the model praised himself following the action or when the experimenter praised the model. There are a number of differences between these studies which make comparisons difficult. For example, in the Harris and Elliott and Vasta experiments, donations were anonymous; in the Presbie and Coiteux study, the experimenter was present.

One point does need stressing. In most reports of experiments on vicarious reinforcement effects, little descriptive information is given regarding the model's response to the reinforcement. If vicarious reinforcement produces affect, is an experimental effect attributable to the model receiving a prized object or precious praise; or, is the effect attributable to the model's affective response to the reinforcement? The descriptions given of the interaction of model and reinforcer are typically not detailed enough to make a judgment. What is known is that the model's affective response does make a difference in the imitation of altruistic behavior (Bryan 1971b; Midlarsky & Bryan 1972) and may be more important than the reward being given (Lerner & Weiss 1972). Much greater care should be taken in controlling and/or specifying the affective responses of models to reinforcements in studies of vicarious reinforcement processes.

In naturalistic settings, it is extremely likely that models get involved with their charges in ways other than simply displaying the relevant behavior. White (1972) compared the effects of an experimenter coercing donations from the child with the effects of various forms of modeling demonstrations upon fourth- and fifth-grade children. Some of the children were told by the experimenter that on each occasion of winning two gift certificates they would be expected to give one to charity. This procedure was called "guided rehearsal." Another group of children observed the experimenter contribute some of her winnings and were provided an opportunity to donate some of their resources in the presence of this experimenter-model. This procedure was labeled "observation-plus-unguided-rehearsal." In the "observation condition," children observed the experimenter-model donate but were not provided an opportunity to donate in the presence of the model. Finally, another group of children received no "guided instruction" and no observation of a model. Half of the children from each of these groups were allowed to contribute anonymously to a charity immediately following the imposition of the treatments and then approximately 5 days later. The remaining half of the children were allowed to donate only after a lapse of 5 days following the treatments. Guided rehearsal produced the most giving, and observation and control conditions produced the least giving in the immediate test situation. During the second testing session, however, children in the observation-plus-unguided-rehearsal treatment donated as much as those in the guided rehearsal treatment. Both of these groups donated more than those who had simply seen the model and those who did not view a model. As White indicates, it is not clear how a "demand characteristic" explanation of the observation-plus-unguided-rehearsal condition could account for the results obtained in this study. Likewise, notions that donations are primarily motivated by attempts to obtain social approval seem inadequate to account for the results. Children in the unguided rehearsal condition had already donated in the presence of the experimenter-model and were not reinforced for it. It seems unlikely that giving in the private context, either during the immediate or later tests, reflects motivations to please or obtain approval from an absent experimenter-model who had previously given no reinforcement for such behavior.

Many of the studies of imitative altruism have employed videotaped models rather than live ones and have suggested the power of television to affect the prosocial activities of the young child (Shirley 1973). While television effects upon children are covered in another chapter of this volume, several points relating to these effects on the development of altruism will be made here. First, there are few studies directly testing the impact of currently presented television programs upon such behavior. Additionally, little is known regarding the content of television as it relates to prosocial activity. Is prosocial activity presented, and in what context, and is it rewarded or punished? For example, casual observation would suggest that many of the aggressive activities depicted during the weekend cartoon deluge are in the service of rescuing others in distress. Certainly content analysis of prosocial activities in cartoons, particularly aggressive prosocial behavior, is needed.

There is some theoretical reason to suppose that television violence may not only produce imitative aggression but may well also reduce some forms of helping activity. Children's fears can be reduced by the careful production of experimental films and tapes (Bandura & Menlove 1968; Weissbrod & Bryan 1973). If empathic or sympathetic responses, like fear, can be unlearned, then presentation of violence and continuing exposures to victims' distresses might serve to extinguish sympathetic or empathic responses (Lazarus et al. 1962). That is, the viewer may well become trained to be indifferent to the suffering of unfortunate others.

7. Summary of Imitative Helping

It is quite clear that the actions of peers and adults, whether live or televised, influence the observing child. The list of responses shown to be affected by a model's behavior is almost endless and includes behaviors which reflect self-denial by the child. Thus, standards of self-reinforcement, delay of gratification, and acts of courage have been shown to be so influenced. Not surprisingly, altruistic behavior can be added to the list.

While altruistic models generally do increase children's altruistic behavior, some do more than others. Power, reinforcement, affect, and consistency have all been linked to the facilitation of children's helping. As might be expected, the powerful model, a model who has some control over resources, is likely to influence altruism more than one lacking such control. The teacher and the parent may be particularly effective models, not only on the basis of their frequent exposure to the child but because of their relatively great power over him. Many socializing agents are probably reluctant to employ sanctions and power or to recognize the utility of these techniques. Yet there is reason to believe that demanding that children conform to standards produces stable dispositions toward aiding others, at least sharing wealth with them. The role of sanctions, demands, and control over the child's behavior is becoming increasingly recognized as being important in the development of a considerate other (Baumrind 1971; Staub, in press).

By contrast, a model's friendliness, or warmth, may differentially affect different forms of helping. Some forms of aiding, such as interventions in an emergency context, appear to be facilitated by a warm or friendly model. It is likely that in those situations in which helping requires novel actions, the proprieties of which may well be ambiguous to the child, the presence of a warm or friendly model will increase helping behaviors by the child. The warm teacher or parent might well facilitate novel, unusual, or courageous forms of helping when the child is highly motivated, by virtue of his own empathically produced distress, to help. On the other hand, in situations such as requests for donations, in which helping activity is not highly motivated, where the child is conflicted about giving or keeping, the warm model may be less effective in eliciting such charity than a cold and potentially punishing one.

Vicarious reinforcement has not beeen unequivocally demonstrated as a potent influence on children's imitative generosity. Even if such effects are powerful, the question should be asked as to whether they are frequent sources of influence. To me, it would appear unlikely that the parent frequently receives M&M candies, bubble gum, or social approval for his prosocial behaviors. Another plausible mechanism affecting the child's behavior is the self-generated affect of the model. Existing evidence leads to the inference that a model's own affective response to his behavior is likely to influence the behavior of the child. The model who is trying it and liking it appears to be a most influential model in affecting self-sacrifice. By the same token, the model who is trying it and disliking it may well do more to retard the development of prosocial activity than if he had refrained from committing the altruistic action at all.

It is likely and probably inevitable that most socialization agents demonstrate inconsistency between their preachings and their practices. One outcropping of such adult hypocrisy may well be the development of children who themselves preach charity but practice selfishness (Bryan 1973). Moreover, there is suggestive evidence that inconsistency by the model attenuates his subsequent ability to affect, through social approval, the child's altruism. Parents and teachers who give verbal approval for altruistic behavior should be wary of its use if they themselves have shown marked inconsistency in their words and deeds concerning prosocial activity.

Recently, increasing concern has been evidenced regarding the kinds of verbal inputs which might affect the child's willingness to help others. Preachings such as "it is good to give" are either ineffective or have very weak effects. Other forms of verbal statement are more successful, however, in eliciting such behaviors. If heavy emphasis is placed upon the consequences of helping the recipients, donations increase (Midlarsky & Bryan 1972). Likewise, verbal descriptions of past or future charitable actions increase the child's generosity, at least that of children above the age of 10.

Finally, a question must be raised as to the robustness of the modeling effect. The results of studies completed by Midlarsky and Bryan (1972), Rushton (in press), and White (1972) suggest that exposure to an altruistic model produces enduring effects. But studies involving other forms of behavior would lead one to expect that such modeling effects should be short-lived. For instance, when children are presented with a model who imposes different standards upon himself than on the child, the child will adopt whichever standards maximize his gains (Hildebrandt et al. 1973; Mischel & Liebert 1966; Rosenhan, Frederick, & Burrowes 1968). Children are more likely to cheat for purposes of obtaining a reward if the model, either through words or deeds, implies that the standards of self-reward that were set by the experimenter can or should be violated (Stein & Bryan 1972). Likewise, if children are exposed to multiple models who vary in their standards for self-reward, the child will tend to adopt the standards of the most lenient model (Bandura et al. 1967; McMains & Liebert 1968). As yet, multiple modeling studies which involve exposing the child to both a generous and a selfish model have not been completed, but it is likely that a selfish model would greatly attenuate the altruism of the observing child. Given the high probability of exposure to selfish or nonaiding models in many environments, modeling effects are likely to be short-lived. Perhaps the durability of imitative altruism that has been reported reflects the fact that children may be infrequently exposed to opportunities for donations and thus infrequently observe selfish others.

While the last decade of research has provided an abundant amount of information on imitative altruism, major questions remain to be tested. There has been little research completed which has attempted to investigate the relationship between the model's actions and the child's view of himself, the recipient, beneficiaries, or of charity itself. We know virtually nothing concerning the cognitive processes which facilitate a child's imitation of the model.

C. AFFECT AND HELPING

Within the United States, there are norms and values dictating a variety of actions, many of which are contradictory to each other (Darley & Latane 1970). Thus one should be helpful, but one should mind his own business. One should help the needy, but one should also get what he deserves. If norms dictate contradictory behaviors, it may be that moods and affective states are particularly important in directing behavior, especially the behavior of a child who has had relatively little opportunity to arrange these norms in a system of moral priorities. Additionally, it has been shown that affect is important in determining adult helping (Isen 1970; Isen & Levin 1972).

1. Methods of Inducing Moods

Several methods often used in studies of helping behavior may alter the child's moods while in the experiment. As indicated previously, the model's warmth toward the child might reasonably be thought of as increasing the positive affect experienced by the child (e.g., Rosenhan & White 1967). Moods might be manipulated through recall procedures by asking the child to "think about" an event which produced either considerable sadness or happiness for him (Moore, Underwood, & Rosenhan

1973). Another method, often used with adults (Berkowitz & Conner 1966; Kazdin & Bryan 1971), and occasionally with children (Staub 1968), is to provide the subject with either a success or failure experience which presumably creates a positive or negative mood. Finally, there may be an attempt to condition positive affect to external cures provided by the experimenter (Aronfreed & Paskal 1965; Midlarsky & Bryan 1967).

2. *Effects of Moods*

The influence of moods upon children's helping seems critically dependent upon how and when they are induced and the particular measure of helping employed. As previously indicated, the model's warmth, which would presumably induce a positive mood in the child, either does not increase charitable behaviors or decreases them. On the other hand, children's rescue behaviors are sometimes increased under these circumstances.

Moore et al. (1973) found that when some 7- and 8-year-old children were asked to recall events which had made them happy, they were more likely to donate money to other children than were the same-age children who were not given such instructions. The authors suggest that "people who are experiencing positive affect tend to be kind to themselves and to others in a variety of ways. They tend to reward themselves and others, to attend to their own assets more than their liabilities. . ." (p. 102). It is not clear why these two methods of generating positive affect in children, the warm model and the recall method, lead to such different effects on donations. There are two possibilities. As previously discussed, it is possible that the child views the warm model as someone who is not likely to punish selfish behavior. Second, there is an emphasis within these studies upon having fun, upon being self-indulgent. Children have fun with the model, fun with playing the game, fun at winning the prizes. In the recall method used by Moore et al. the task was presented as a serious one (testing hearing equipment) and interpersonal contact was minimized; games were absent. Positive affect then might play an important role in facilitating generosity in those conditions where the benevolence of the authority is not clearly established and/or in a situation with a focus other than self-indulgence.

Negative affective states have generally not been found to depress donations, at least when such states are produced by having subjects experience failure on some experimental task (Berkowitz & Conner 1966; Isen 1970). Moore et al. did find, however, that children who were asked to recall a sad event in their lives donated less than children who did not receive such instructions. Isen, Rosenhan, and Horn (1973) have suggested that whatever effects failure has upon negative affect which might depress donations are offset by children's desire to repair their images. These investigators demonstrated that third- and fourth-grade children who experienced failure in a task donated more than nonfailure subjects, but only under the condition where their contributions were going toward a charity explicitly linked to the experimenter. Thus the first lead that image reparation may serve as a motive for children's altruistic behavior has been produced and will no doubt receive further investigation.

One negative affective state that has been linked to altruistic behavior by adults is guilt (Carlsmith & Gross 1969; Freedman, Wallington, & Bless 1967; Wallace & Sadalla 1966). In studies of children, the effects of guilt that presumably results from minor transgressions have been examined. Silverman (1967) failed to find that sixth-grade children who cheated on a task were more likely to volunteer to help in a subsequent experiment than children who were not induced to cheat. In a very carefully controlled study, Test (1969) failed to find that children who had broken a peer's toy were more likely to donate winnings to that peer than children who had either not broken the toy or who had witnessed the experimenter inadvertently break it. Subjects appeared more interested in avoiding discovery than in redemption. There are no data then to suggest that aiding activity by children is increased by their guilt about interpersonal or academic transgressions.

3. Empathy and Conditioning

Several theorists have called attention to the importance of empathy in children's helping behavior (Aderman & Berkowitz 1970; Aronfreed 1968; Berger 1962; Hoffman 1973). Aronfreed proposed that altruistic helping is based upon the conditioning of empathically produced positive affect to the helping act. Essentially, if the child experiences some pleasure associated with helping, his disposition to help will be increased. He might experience this pleasure by empathizing with the responses of the recipient to his or another's help. Or, he might empathize with the pleasure shown by a helping model. The child's ability to empathize with another and the latter's expressiveness in demonstrating his own happiness while helping or being helped are stressed as important processes in establishing a child's motive to aid others.

Several experiments have been concerned with conditioning a child's positive affect to another individual's state of joy. It was expected that through conditioning procedures children can be taught to experience similar affective responses to those whom they are observing. In effect, they can be conditioned to be empathic. Once this empathy is established, acts which produce joy in others, such as helping acts, will produce a similar state in the child and thus will serve as either the motive or reinforcement for those acts. Aronfreed and Paskal (1965) and Midlarsky and Bryan (1967) tested these ideas using primary school age girls. In both studies, when an experimenter paired her expressions of joy with hugging the girl, inducing positive affect in the girl, the girl was more likely to sacrifice a prize. Girls given this conditioning continued to sacrifice their prize even when the experimenter no longer hugged them or expressed joy. When statements of joy were not initially paired with hugs, children were no more likely to be helpful than those who were never hugged or heard no joy statements. Finally, Bryan and Midlarsky found that the children's willingness to give up their prizes generalized; when they were allowed to make an anonymous donation to poor children, they gave more than children who were not given the conditioning session.

Aronfreed and Pascal (1966) extended this conditioning model to rescue activity. In this experiment, children were given three phases of training and testing. In the first, the child and experimenter heard an aversive noise through earphones, with the experimenter demonstrating distress as a result. In the second phase, only the child heard the noise and the experimenter acted to terminate it, but by so doing lost an opportunity to gain a reward. In the third phase, the child was tested to determine if she would imitate the experimenter's self-sacrifice in order to end the aversive noise presented to another child. Children who were given this sequence of training were more likely to forego the possibility of winning a prize than children who served in various control conditions eliminating either phase of the training.

There is supporting evidence then that conditioning children's empathic responses facilitates helpfulness. Essentially, if the child's own affect is aroused at the same time as another person's affect, the child's emotional responses will become conditioned to the other's expressions of happiness or distress. If the child learns, through modeling or tutorials, a response which will help the other and, at the same time, create a pleasant affective state within himself, he will be more likely to aid unfortunate others than children without such training. The elements deemed important are the similarity between the affective states of the child and the victim, the timing of the affective state of the child with the victim's expressions of his affect (the closer the better), and the effectiveness of the aiding response in producing a more pleasant or less aversive affective state in the helper.

4. Summary

There is increasing evidence concerning the importance of children's affective states in affecting their helping behavior. If the child's positive affect is conditioned to the observation or performance of the helping act, or if it is simply present, he will be more likely to be helpful toward others. It is possible, though not yet directly tested, that the facilitating effects of positive affective states might be offset if such states are induced in the child by his pursuit of fun. Self-indulgence may attenuate the increments in helpfulness associated with such positive affect. If the child's affect is negative, he will be less likely to be helpful unless he can either remove the source of his distress or repair his lowered status in the eyes of his beholder.

D. DESERVEDNESS, COMPETITION, AND HELPING

Social comparison processes, the norm of deservedness, and competitive atmospheres have recently been examined as influences upon the helping behavior of children. The studies are few but do suggest future directions of research.

Masters (1971) proposed that social comparison processes affect sharing, particularly toward an absent other. He tested the hypothesis that if a child receives an inequitable low reward compared with rewards given a competitor or nonparticipating children, he will be less likely to donate his funds to an absent friend or to his classmates than when he receives the rewards he deserves or more rewards than competitors or classmates. Testing 4- and 5-year-olds, Masters found that children donated most to an absent partner when they received their fair share of the rewards. Donations to an absent classmate were greatly reduced if the child had been led to believe that classmates had already received a greater number of rewards than had the subject. These results indicate that even the very young child is sensitive to equitable or inequitable distribution of resources.

In most experiments on children's altruism, the subjects' rewards are presumably merited by virtue of their actions. That is, they get what they deserve. What about giving under conditions where children get what they do not deserve? Long and Lerner (1974) suggested that children who believe in a just world, a world wherein you get what you deserve, would be more reluctant to donate a deserved than an undeserved reward. They argued that one measure of a child's belief in a just world is the child's willingness to delay gratification, presumably because such delay implies a trust that rewards will be forthcoming. In their study, some fourth-grade children were given money that they had earned. Other children were "overpaid"; they were told that the received money should have gone to older, more qualified children who, unfortunately, were unavailable. Children who had high delay-of-gratification scores were the most generous contributors when they were overpaid. That is, these children, as expected, gave away undeserved rewards.

One basis upon which children obtain rewards is competition with others in a task or game. What are the effects of competition upon children's donations? In a correlational study, Rutherford and Mussen (1968) found that highly competitive nursery school boys, categorized on their behavior in a "racing game," shared less with their friends than their less competitive peers. This finding suggests that children involved in competition are less likely to demonstrate altruism than children who obtain their resources by other means. However, the effects of competition are likely to depend on the outcome of the competition. One might reasonably expect that "winners," either because of feelings of competence (Kazdin & Bryan 1971) or because of the positive affect generated through success (Moore et al. 1973), would be more likely to donate to less fortunate children than children who either lost to or tied a competitor, Finally, the effects of competition might be more pronounced for older than younger children. Barnett and Bryan (in press) tested second and fifth graders in one of four conditions. In three conditions, the child played against an absent partner, winning, tying, or losing in the competition. A fourth group played the game without competing against another. Results were as predicted. The second graders' contributions of money to a charity were unaffected either by competition or the results of competition. Fifth graders who tied or lost in competition donated less than those who did not compete. Only those children who won in competition donated as much as, but not more than, children not involved in competition. The results suggest that any competition, whatever its outcome, is unlikely to enhance altruistic behavior.

1. Summary

Apparently children do consider the equality or equity of reward distributions when affecting a donation, and this may be particularly true for children who have the ability to delay gratification. It is possible that children who have obtained their rewards through competitive interactions do not donate simply because they feel they deserve their gains. No doubt this summary is making much ado about three studies, but it is reasonable to expect that many more studies concerned with the role of equity and equality in affecting helpfulness will be forthcoming.

E. SUBJECT VARIABLES

A variety of studies has provided information concerning the possible personal and social characteristics associated with altruistic activity by children. Subject variables have been included for study within experiments as a secondary interest and thrown into the analysis primarily because of design demands rather than theoretical interest. Only within the very recent past have attempts been made to explore systematically those subject differences which, on some theoretical basis, should be associated with aiding activity.

1. Age

There is considerable evidence that altruism is positively correlated with age, at least during the latter half of the first decade of life. With some exceptions (Dlugokinski & Firestone 1973; Harris 1970; Hartshorne, May, & Maller 1929; Liebert, Fernandez, & Gill 1969), most investigators do find that older children are more likely to donate and to rescue than younger ones (Barnett & Bryan, in press; Handlon & Gross 1959; Harris 1971; Midlarsky & Bryan 1967; Rushton, in press; Ugurel-Semin, 1952; Walbek 1969; Wright 1942).

An intuitively compelling explanation of this correlation is that the older children have had more opportunity to learn a norm of social responsibility or a norm dictating equality of resource distribution than younger children. The existing data, however, indicate that neither the norm of social responsibility nor the norm of equality of resource distribution can account for the age and generosity correlation. Solomon et al. (1972) found that the great majority of lower-class Mexican-American children verbally indicated the value of equality in resource distribution by the time they were in the second grade. The verbal expression of this norm was not correlated with age; second graders verbalized it as frequently as did eighth graders. Yet, behavioral measures of this value were correlated with age. Older children demonstrated greater equality in resource distribution, as measured by sharing during a dart-throwing game, than younger children. No correlation was found between verbalizations concerning equality in sharing and actual sharing behavior. Likewise, Bryan and Walbek (1970a) found that children, by the age of 8 or 9, have learned the norm of social responsibility, at least enough to verbalize their agreement to it when when questioned. Nevertheless, the correlation between verbal endorsements of the norm and behavior relevant to it was minimal. It is certainly possible that there is a different developmental course for learning the verbal statements of a value and the behavioral consequences of that value. If such is the case, however, it is incumbent upon those who explain the altruistic act as reflecting the learning of particular norms to specify with greater clarity just what criterion is being employed to infer the presence of a learned norm.

Another explanation of the relationship between age and generosity has been that of "behavior freeze." According to this hypothesis younger

children are more timid within the experimental situation and too frightened to initiate a charitable action. Some support for this proposition
comes from the findings that boys were more likely to eat and share a
candy reward than girls and that the need for social approval correlated
negatively with the amount eaten and shared (Staub & Sherk 1970).
Rosenhan subsequently (1969a) challenged this hypothesis on the basis
that nothing in the developmental literature suggests such "freezing" by
the younger child. Moreover, data gathered from studies on altruism
contradict this hypothesis. For example, Barnett and Bryan (in press)
videotaped second and fifth graders' responses within the experiment
and found younger children were more, not less, affectively expressive
during the experiment. Moreover, Weissbrod (1974) found that children
were more likely to donate their winnings to a charity after having previously experienced a "cold" rather than "warm" relationship with the
experimenter. Presumably, the cold experimenter ought to have induced
more timidity in the child than a warm one. The weight of the evidence
suggests that behavior freeze does not account for the correlation between age and generosity.

   A third explanation of the correlation between age and generosity, at
least within the experimental setting, is that the value of the prizes to be
donated may change with age. It is possible that older children donate
more than younger ones simply because the object to be donated is of
less value to them. As yet, no adequate scaling of incentives by developmental level of the child has been accomplished, so this hypothesis
remains to be adequately tested. Nevertheless, Midlarsky and Bryan
(1967) found the expected age effects on donations of M&M candies
even when both age groups verbally indicated the same degree of liking
for those candies. Age effects have also occurred when the objects to be
donated were tokens which might be exchanged for valuable, but unspecified prizes (Barnett & Bryan, in press; Harris 1971). Presumably,
children of varying age groups would anticipate receiving some reward
of approximately equal incentive value to them.

   A fourth explanation advanced to explain the relationship of generosity to age pertains to changes in children's moral and cognitive processes.
It is frequently hypothesized that the lower egocentrism of older children
enables them to assume another's view of the world and his effective
states; thus they are more motivated to aid a distressed or needy other
(Rosenhan, 1969a, 1969b). Rubin and Schneider (1973) provided data on
this question for 7-year-old boys and girls. Egocentrism in communicating a message to another was measured. Children were provided an opportunity to donate some of their earned candies and to help another
child on a clerical task. Following these tests, each child was given a test

of maturity of moral judgment. The higher the level of moral judgment and the lower the level of egocentrism, the greater the donations and help. (See Shantz's chapter in this volume for further discussion.)

The highly replicable finding that generosity increases with age has been obtained in the laboratory. In more complex naturalistic settings, such positive associations are not necessarily found. For example, Severy and Davis (1971) demonstrated that within a naturalistic setting both age and relatively advanced cognitive development may retard, not facilitate, helping. These investigators observed two age groups, 3–5- and 8–10-year-olds who were either mentally retarded or possessed normal intelligence, during free play activities in school. When controlling for opportunity to help, they failed to find that either age or intellectual level was associated with total helping. The authors distinguished two types of help: psychological (the child attempts to relieve a peer's psychological distress) and task (the child attempts to aid a peer in completing a task). Retarded children engaged in more psychological help than nonretarded ones. Older retardates and younger normal children engaged in more task help than the young retardates and older normals.

Severy and Davis's interpretation of their findings was that older normals have greater capacities to recognize and offer competent help to another, but "they have also been socialized into other norms which serve to inhibit helping among same-age peers. Primary among these norms are the achievement and independence norms which fuel much of the competitiveness of 8–10-year-old children. In the more sheltered milieu of the retarded children, no such stress on achievement and independence has developed, so acquired inhibitions (reasons not to help) do not mask the greater competence of the older retardates" (pp. 1029–1030). In the light of previously reported correlational (Rutherford & Mussen 1968) and experimental studies (Barnett & Bryan, in press) which suggest a negative relationship between competition and generosity, this explanation is quite reasonable. Thus the positive correlation between self-sacrifice and age found in laboratory settings might be limited to those situations in which competitive cues are relatively absent. While changes occur toward more mature moral judgments, less egocentrism, and greater empathy and role-taking skills as children age, it also appears that children learn norms or develop motives which mitigate against helping behavior as they mature.

2. Sex

By and large, differences between boys and girls are not found (Grusec 1971; Grusec & Driscoll 1973; Harris 1970, 1971; Madsen 1967; Masters 1971, Wasik et al. 1969) or are found to interact with particular treatments (Grusec & Skubiski 1970; Rosenhan & White 1967). When sex differences are found, girls are usually more generous than boys (Midlarsky & Bryan 1972; Moore et al. 1973; Rosenhan 1969b: White 1972). Apparently, girls are not only more likely to be generous in the immediate situation, but their donation behavior shows more stability over time than does that of boys (White 1972). Finally, while Grusec and her co-workers (Grusec 1972; Grusec & Skubiski 1970) failed to find that boys were less generous than girls after observing a model's charity, young girls (7 years of age) were more influenced by verbal descriptions of such actions by the model than were boys of the same age.

The greater generosity of girls than boys might be explained on the basis of their experiencing a greater number of interactions with nurturant, and probably helpful, adults than boys. For example, Yarrow et al. (1973) found that boys who frequently sought help from either a nurturant or nonnurturant adult were more likely to elicit negative or rejecting interactions than were girls who sought aid. It is possible that, in early childhood, boys who seek aid from others receive the help and then are punished for requesting it. This contradiction may be less frequent in the early experiences of girls, generalizing from the data presented by Yarrow et al. Additionally, helping and nurturance may be more sex appropriate for girls, while competition may be more acceptable for boys.

3. Social Class

The economic status of the child, or the child's family, appears to bear little relation to helping by children (Bryan 1971a; DePalma & Olejnik 1973; Madsen 1967; Rosenhan, 1969b). However, Berkowitz and Friedman (1967) did find differences between middle- and lower-class adolescents' helping behavior. Most interesting was their division of the middle-class sample into two groups: those whose parents were in occupations involving service and those from families involved in entrepreneurial occupations. Adolescents from the entrepreneurial group were more oriented toward reciprocity considerations in their helping than those of either the other middle-class or the lower-class families. They would help someone who had previously helped them but were less likely than other adolescents to offer help simply on the basis of the recipient's need. Perhaps similar distinctions among middle-class children of younger ages should be made in further investigations of social class correlates of helping.

4. Personality Correlates

There have been two approaches to the study of personality and helping. One approach has focused upon the general question of individual consistency in helping. If the child is helpful in one fashion, is he likely to be helpful in other ways as well? The second approach is concerned with isolating particular personality characteristics which might be associated with various forms of aiding. Are children who donate more likely to have high need for social approval, be more trusting, more socially responsible, or more obedient than those who do not donate?

Three studies conducted in vivo suggest that different types of helpfulness and consideration for others are positively related. Friedrich and Stein (1973) found that nurturant and cooperative behaviors were correlated in their observations of preschool boys. Dlugokinski and Firestone (1973) combined self-report measures, peer ratings, and a behavioral measure involving donations in their attempt to determine whether there is some individual consistency in children's consideration for others. Using fifth- to eighth-grade children, these investigators assessed understanding of the meaning of kindness as measured by a self-report scale, peer ratings of their kindness, and the amount children donated to UNICEF. By and large, for both boys and girls, positive but small relationships were obtained among these measures.

Baumrind (1971) rated preschool children on sympathy and nurturance to others, helping, selfishness, thoughtlessness, and insulting behavior. All of these behaviors were related in such a way as to suggest an underlying disposition of consideration to others. It appears then that children who are helpful are helpful in a number of ways, although the relationships among different forms of helpfulness are far from perfect.

A second major set of questions pertains to what other personality correlates of helping exist. By and large, the personality attributes studied have been selected on investigators' intuition rather than on the basis of some well-formulated hypothesis or theory. The search for such correlates is particularly compelling because individual differences in aiding behavior are often large. The personality characteristics studied include trust, social responsibility, social desirability, need for social approval, obedience, conformity, and delay of gratification.

Midlarsky and Bryan (1972), using Harris's (1957) scale of Social Responsibility, found small correlations between donations and social responsibility in both an immediate testing situation involving the donation of money and posttesting session involving the donation of candies. Scores on both a Social Desirability scale (Crandall, Crandall, & Katkovsky 1965) and a Trust scale (Hochreich 1966), did not correlate significantly with children's donations on both donation measures, although Trust scores did predict donations in the immediate testing situation.

Long and Lerner (1974), as previously discussed, found that children

with high scores on a delay-of-gratification test donated more undeserved rewards than children who had lower scores on delay of gratification. In addition, delay of gratification interacted with the nature of the
donation situation. When the donation was public, children with low
delay-of-gratification scores gave slightly more than did high scorers.
When donations were to be anonymous, high scorers gave substantially
more than did the low scorers. Thus the relation of delay of gratification
(belief in a just world in Long and Lerner's term) to donations depended
upon whether the obtained rewards were deserved and whether someone
else would know of the donation.

The need for social approval is an often suggested motive for altruistic
acts, especially donations. In a recent unpublished study, Bryan and
Prentky (1973) found that less than half of the children who donated
money to the March of Dimes mentioned that fact when leaving tape-
recorded messages for a person of their choice. Only three of 72 children
tested in a second experiment mentioned to the experimenter that they
had donated (Weissbrod 1974). Staub and Sherk (1970) found that children with high need for social approval assessed by a questionnaire
shared *less* than those with lower concern about approval. However, they
were also less likely to take their own rewards. It appeared that children
with high need for approval were hesitant to claim their rewards and
therefore less likely to donate them to others. Bryan and Walbek, in an
unwritten study (1968), found subjects with high need for social approval
scores donated slightly more than those with low scores. In this experiment, children were explicitly told how many prizes they should award
themselves. A reasonable hypothesis is that children who are concerned
with social approval are most likely to be helpful in situations where
standards of conduct are clearly known but least likely to be helpful in
those situations where there exists any ambiguity concerning the acceptability of such behavior.

The search for individual differences has extended into observations
and ratings of children's behavior in naturalistic settings. Rosenhan
(1969b) obtained teachers' ratings of subjects' obedience and helpfulness
within the classroom and observed children's public and private donations. Rosenhan assumed that the public donations represented conformity behavior motivated by the child's concern for rewards and punishments, while private donations reflected the child's concern for the
welfare of others. Ratings of helpfulness did not predict public donations, but obedience ratings did, particularly for 6–7-year-old children.
For the young child, public donations may simply reflect obedience to
an adult. Obedience was not related to private donations of 6- and 7-
year-olds. High donations characterized the more obedient 8-year-olds,

but low donations were typical of the obedient 10-year-olds. Ratings of helpfulness were positively correlated with private donations for the older, but not for the younger, children.

Emotional expressiveness, willingness to seek aid, and aggressiveness are associated with helping. Nursery school age children who were more likely to aid a puppet in distress also expressed emotional distress most readily during their everyday activities (Lenrow 1965). Hartup and Keller (1960) observed the behavior of 3–5-year-olds in a preschool setting. While they, like others (Hoffman 1970), found that helping behavior is infrequent in such young children, they did determine that nurturance, defined primarily as giving positive attention to peers, was positively related to the child's own seeking of help. There are any number of explanations that might account for these correlations. Perhaps children who express their distress and/or who seek help are more easily affectively aroused and respond more to threats both to themselves and to others. Perhaps children who express their distress and/or directly seek aid are more likely to be helped and therefore observe more aiding models. Perhaps the rendering of aid requires a quality of outgoingness, or a lack of interpersonal timidity (Hartup & Keller 1960), which is also often required of the child in expressing his distress or the seeking of help. Certainly, the possibility that some courage in interpersonal relationships might facilitate some forms of helping is suggested by the findings of Friedrich and Stein (1973) that cooperative behavior by girls and cooperative and nurturant behavior by boys was positively related to interpersonal aggression. Whatever the explanation of the correlation, it would appear that children who have the freedom to express the need for help are likely to render help to others.

5. Summary

There is abundant evidence indicating that the older the child, the more helpful he is likely to be. There is some evidence to suggest that girls are likely to be more helpful than boys. As yet, neither of these correlations has been adequately explained. There does appear reason to believe that there is a certain consistency in children's helpfulness, at least when assessed in the naturalistic settings. Children who help in one manner are also likely to help in other manners as well. As yet, however, it is not known whether these correlations reflect true relationships or the biases or halo effects of the raters employed to observe the children. Some personality characteristics associated with helping appear to be emotional expressiveness, willingness to seek aid, social responsibility, and aggressiveness, but clearly more research is needed to verify and explain these associations. Finally, the relationship between social class or wealth of the child and donation activity, the existence of which is so intuitively compelling, has not been established. If there is such a relationship, then the settings in which it is demonstrated are, as yet, to be determined.

F. SOCIALIZATION PRACTICES

Throughout this chapter, a number of laboratory investigations have been reviewed which provide clues as to effective socialization procedures in developing a helpful, considerate, and cooperative child. Modeling of helping, both verbally and motorically, expressions of affect, group-based rewards, and consistency between moral preachings and practices, to name a few, are probably important antecedents of children's helping and cooperation. A few studies have attempted to establish directly those parental discipline practices which facilitate the development of helping children. These will now be reviewed along with some recent theoretical speculations concerning those practices most conducive to training children's helpfulness.

1. Parental Discipline

Several investigations have been addressed to the parents' use of authority. Baumrind (1971) observed parents and their nursery school offspring. Of the various patterns of parental authority, Baumrind found that parents who could "specify aims and methods of discipline, promoted their own code of behavior, could not be coerced by the child and set standards of excellence for the child" were the most likely to produce cooperative and friendly children.

Hoffman and Saltzstein (1967) related methods of parental discipline to sociometric ratings by middle-class seventh-grade children of peers who demonstrated consideration for others. Both parents were classified as to whether they employed power assertion, love withdrawal, or induction techniques when disciplining their children. Power assertion is "associated with the relatively frequent use of discipline techniques involving physical punishment and material deprivation." Induction techniques consist of discipline in which the negative consequences of transgressions upon the lives of others are stressed. Love withdrawal, like induction, may suggest parental anger, hurt, or disapproval, but explication of the negative consequences of the child's action upon others is not offered. Induction techniques, used either by the mother or the father, enhanced girls' consideration of their peers. Boys' consideration of others was associated with the use of power assertion by either parent.

While suggestions have been made that prosocial behavior is attenuated by the fact that parents pay more attention to developing inhibitions than prosocial behavior (Staub 1971b), only one study has been completed which compared parental value orientations and young children's aiding behavior. Olejnik and McKinney (1973) categorized parents of 4-year-old children into those who administered rewards and punishments on the basis of a prescriptive value system, in which the emphasis is placed upon teaching the child what he ought to do, and those whose value system is proscriptive—the emphasis is upon what not to do. Whether the parent used rewards or punishments in disciplining the child, parents with prescriptive values had more generous (as measured by willingness to donate candy to poor children) offspring than parents with proscriptive values. Primary reliance on reward or punishment was not correlated with generosity. Greater emphasis by parents and teachers alike on training children in the do's as well as the don'ts of life might increase concern for others.

2. Speculations

Recently, both Baumrind (1971) and Staub (in press) have speculated as to those parental practices which might facilitate the development of prosocial behavior by children. Among the factors suggested by both as being critical are the modeling of such behavior by the parent, firm enforcement policies wherein both positive and negative reinforcements are employed, parental acceptance or at least nonrejection of the child, and finally, the employment of just and fair standards accompanied by the use of reasoning to justify directives given the child. Additionally, Staub speculates that the assignment to the child of meaningful responsibilities for which he is accountable may facilitate the development of prosocial behavior. Finally, Staub presents an interesting hypothesis that indirect training of prosocial behavior may be more effective than direct tutorials. That is, such an indirect training technique as having one child teach another to be helpful may be more effective than the more direct techniques of reinforcement, exhortation, or example.

IV. DEVELOPING COOPERATION AND HELPING:
CONCLUSIONS AND SPECULATIONS

The research of the past decade has demonstrated the variety of ways by which helping and cooperative behavior can be produced within the laboratory setting. Reinforcement, situational determinants, attitudes, personality, and temperamental factors have all been implicated. Evidence exists that children are not simply taught to place money in a can but are rather sensitive to the fact that the money is to be directed towards some needy other (Fouts 1972; Midlarsky & Bryan 1972). Children do appear to be concerned with others, this concern being stimulated by a variety of determinants.

Of the variables studied, the impact of models has been the most extensively investigated. Little doubt remains that the helping model, particularly the model who is trying it and liking it, can be an important stimulant to the child's self-sacrificing behavior, even under circumstances where the model is a videotaped one and one who will not know of the child's behavior. Moreover, it is the model who acts, not the one that simply gives lip service to generosity, that affects the child's apparent concern for others. Imitation of an altruistic model may show surprising durability and even transfer to dissimilar circumstances. A benevolent child may well reflect a benevolent environment, a fact which appears to be relatively ignored in our violence-prone culture. But why does the model affect such actions? Most imitative behavior is thought to be emitted for purposes of obtaining reinforcement. That is, imitation is a result of previous reinforcement for imitative action (Gewirtz 1969) or anticipation of such reinforcement (Bandura 1969). What is the power of reinforcement, and just what types affect the child's willingness to sacrifice an incentive? Both direct and vicariously administered material and social rewards appear to affect children's self-sacrificing actions (Fischer 1963; Midlarsky et al. 1973). The faith in the power of such reinforcement to account for self-sacrificing, however, is considerably greater than the evidence that either anticipation or a history of reinforcement does in fact produce imitative altruism. Needless to say, it is difficult to demonstrate the absence of motive. Certainly children do donate more in front of an audience than in the absence of one, and this does suggest that children are affected by the reward matrix of the donation situation. But what of the private donation context, the setting used in most experiments of aiding behavior? One might argue that such donations are prompted by the child's anticipation of subsequent rewards, from teachers, peers, or parents. Unfortunately, there is not much systematically gathered data on this matter and what there is does not lend much support to this interpretation.

Although it does not appear that rewards account for most altruistic actions within the naturalistic setting, it is clear that reinforcement can increase both cooperative and altruistic behavior (Azrin & Lindsley 1956; Midlarsky et al. 1973; Mithaug & Burgess 1968). What is important is to determine those conditions where reinforcement does not facilitate or indeed depress generosity and to delineate with more precision the processes involved. At least two studies have suggested that positive reinforcement is not only ineffective but aversive when given to the child by an adult who has preached charity but practiced greed. The impact of reinforcement is affected by the characteristics, moral and otherwise, of the reinforcer (Stevenson 1965).

Vicarious reinforcement is perhaps the most frequently investigated form of reward in studies of altruistic activity. Those conditions that increase helping behavior by a witness who has observed another receive rewards for aiding remain to be determined. By and large, the attempts to demonstrate the power of vicarious reinforcement have been unsuccessful or have shown that the effects depend on other variables. Of the forms of vicarious reinforcement studied, those which are likely to evoke empathic responses on the part of the observer seem most powerful. Affect arousal, not grunts of approval or the administration of rewards, is likely to form the basis of sustained altruism (Hoffman 1973; Rosenhan 1972).

Simple reminders of norms concerning helping activity are not sufficient, although they may be necessary, to affect such actions. Children appear to learn, by middle childhood years, that one should help another. But reminding them of this norm does not produce helping. Attitudes relevant to the distribution of rewards do appear to affect altruism. Donation behavior by children as young as 3 and 4 years of age is considerably affected by the distribution of rewards to peers (Masters 1971). Children judged relatively more mature in their moral judgments and in their ability to take another's view are likely to demonstrate self-sacrificing responses. But there is evidence, from studies within the laboratory and naturalistic settings, that children may well learn attitudes, as they age, that mitigate against self-sacrificing activities. Thus, some children will not sacrifice a reward that they deserve; others well trained in competition or exposed to a competitive situation, will be disinclined to help a needy other or to cooperate. Finally, there is some evidence which leads to the inference that within some naturalistic settings mental and chronological age may be negatively related to aiding peers.

A variety of values and procedures are likely to affect adversely a child's willingness to aid others. The spirit of private enterprise in which, under conditions of competition with others, one accumulates property which he somehow deserves seems to inhibit concern for others. Atmospheres which stress competition and socialization practices which encourage it are likely to mitigate against helpful or cooperative behavior. Property accumulated by skill rather than by chance is likely to be retained, not donated. Rewards, administered to an individual for his performance rather than administered to groups for group performances, are more likely to create competition than cooperation (Madsen & Shapira 1970; Richmond & Weiner 1973). While competition, achievement values, and the emphasis upon the accumulation of property might all have desirable products for the society, one is forced to conclude that such factors will attenuate helping and cooperation at the individual level.

What kinds of socialization experiences might be critical in generating the socially concerned child? It is likely that the adult who models altruism, who maintains a warm but also demanding relationship with the child, will generate dispositions to helping. The nurturant parent is likely to model helping, while parental demandingness is likely to train the child to adopt a socially responsible stance within family and social settings. It is likely that parents produce a helpful and cooperative child when they, through the use of induction techniques of discipline, provide an outward and empathic orientation toward others and emphasize the child's personal responsibility in settings where helping may be required. Those parents who emphasize achievement at the expense of others, an orientation toward the acquisition of limited resources, and conformity to the proprieties of the situation, are not likely to be breeders of helping children. As Staub (1971b) has suggested, it is likely that parents give more attention to training suppression of antisocial activity than in developing dispositions to prosocial ones. But many prosocial activities require courage, and it is likely that courage is boosted with rationales. Thus, as in most emergencies, a strange situation in which relatively novel actions must be performed and performed toward unfamiliar others probably requires performance in the face of anxiety. The lack of timidity and conformity may be critical in determining many types of aiding actions. Considerably greater attention should be paid, both within the home and within the classroom, to explicating the principles and circumstances which dictate helping and the techniques and channels by which such action can be initiated. The presence of values which run contrary to such training makes such efforts controversial, particularly large-scale efforts. Neither the personnel of the media nor the local PTAs are likely to reach great unanimity in attempting to decide which value and behavior should be taught, in which order, by what method. Nonetheless, it would probably be worthwhile to investigate more systematically the routes by which children can be developed into citizens genuinely concerned with the plights of others.

It should not be assumed that the development of helpful citizens will be without cost. As indicated elsewhere, "A helpful person may well be intrusive (e.g., invade our privacy), moralistic (e.g., prevent us from 'doing our thing'), or simply conforming to the status quo of proprieties (Bronfrenbrenner 1970). That is, a helpful person with all his 'good' intentions may well violate a variety of personal freedoms that we cherish. Whatever the nature of the costs, it is naive to assume that there will be none. Perhaps the price will be worth paying. At least it should be known" (Bryan 1972, pp. 101–102).

REFERENCES

Aderman, D., & Berkowitz, L. Observational set, empathy, and helping. *Journal of Personality and Social Psychology*, 1970, *14*, 141–148

Altman, K. Effects of cooperative response acquisition on social behavior during free play. *Journal of Experimental Child Psychology*, 1971, *12*, 387–395.

Aronfreed, J. *Conduct and conscience: the socialization of internalized control over behavior.* New York: Academic Press, 1968.

Aronfreed, J., & Paskal, V. Altruism, empathy and the conditioning of positive affect. Unpublished manuscript, University of Pennsylvania, 1965.

Aronfreed, J., & Paskal, V. The development of sympathetic behavior in children: an experimental test of a two-phase hypothesis. Unpublished manuscript, University of Pennsylvania, 1966.

Azrin, N. H., & Lindsley, O. R. The reinforcement of cooperation between children. *Journal of Abnormal and Social Psychology*, 1956, *52*, 100–102.

Bandura, A. *Principles of behavior modification.* New York: Holt, Rinehart & Winston, 1969.

Bandura, A.; Grusec, J. E.; & Menlove, F. L. Some social determinants of self-monitoring reinforcement systems. *Journal of Personality and Social Psychology*, 1967, *5*, 449–455.

Bandura, A., & Menlove, F. L. Factors determining vicarious extinction of avoidance behavior through symbolic modeling. *Journal of Personality and Social Psychology*, 1968, *8*, 99–108.

Barnett, M. H., & Bryan, J. H. The effects of competition with outcome feedback on children's helping behavior. *Developmental Psychology*, in press.

Baumrind, D. Current patterns of parental authority. *Developmental Psychology Monograph*, 1971, *4*, (1, Pt. 2), 1–103.

Berger, S. M. Conditioning through vicarious instigation. *Psychological Review*, 1962, *69*, 450–466.

Berkowitz, L., & Conner, W. H. Success, failure and social responsibility. *Journal of Personality and Social Psychology*, 1966, *4*, 664–669.

Berkowitz, L., & Daniels, L. Affecting the salience of the social responsibility norm: effects of past help on the response to dependency relationships. *Journal of Abnormal and Social Psychology*, 1964, *68*, 275–281.

Berkowitz, L., & Friedman, P. Some social class differences in helping behavior. *Journal of Personality and Social Psychology*, 1967, *5*, 217–225.

Blau, B., & Rafferty, J. Changes in friendship status as a function of reinforcement. *Child Development*, 1970, *41*, 113–121.

Brickman, P., & Bryan, J. H. Moral judgments of theft, charity, and disinterested transfers that increase or decrease equity. *Journal of Personality and Social Psychology*, in press.

Bronfenbrenner, U. *Two worlds of childhood: U.S. and U.S.S.R.* New York: Russell Sage Foundation, 1970.

Brotsky, S. J., & Thomas, K. Cooperative behavior in preschool children. *Psychonomic Science*, 1967, *9*, 337–338.

Brown, R. Schizophrenia, language and reality. *American Psychologist*, 1973, *28*, 395–403.

Bryan, J. H. Exhortations without modeling: a failure to produce an effect. Unpublished manuscript, Northwestern University, 1971. (a)

Bryan, J. H. Model affect and children's imitative behavior. *Child Development*, 1971, *42*, 2061–2065. (b)

Bryan, J. H. Why children help: a review. *Journal of Social Issues*, 1972, *28*, 87–104.

Bryan, J. H. "You will be well advised to watch what we do instead of what we say." Paper delivered to the symposium on contemporary issues in moral development, Loyola University, Chicago, 1973.

Bryan, J. H., & London, P. Altruistic behavior by children. *Psychological Bulletin,* 1970, *73,* 200–211.

Bryan, J. H., & Prentky, R. Public responses to children's altruism. Unpublished manuscript, Northwestern University, 1973.

Bryan, J. H.; Redfield, J.; & Mader, S. Words and deeds about altruism and the subsequent reinforcement power of the model. *Child Development,* 1971, *42,* 1501–1508.

Bryan, J. H., &Test, M. Models and helping: naturalistic studies in aiding behavior. *Journal of Personality and Social Psychology,* 1967, *6,* 400–407.

Bryan, J. H., &Walbek, N. H. Unpublished study, Northwestern University, 1968.

Bryan, J. H., &Walbek, N. H. Preaching and practicing generosity: children's actions and reactions. *Child Development,* 1970, *41,* 329–353. (a)

Bryan, J. H., & Walbek, N. H. The impact of words and deeds concerning altruism upon children. *Child Development,* 1970, *41,* 747–757. (b)

Campbell, D. T. Ethnocentric and other altruistic motives. In D. Levine (Ed.), *Nebraska symposium on motivation: 1965.* Lincoln: University of Nebraska Press, 1965.

Campbell, D. T. On the genetics of altruism and the counterhedonic components in human culture. *Journal of Social Issues,* 1972, *28,* 21–38.

Carlsmith, J. M., & Gross, A. E. Some effects of guilt on compliance. *Journal of Personality and Social Psychology,* 1969, *11,* 232–239.

Crandall, B. D.; Crandall, V. J.; & Katkovsky, W. A children's social desirability questionnaire. *Journal of Consulting Psychology,* 1965, *29,* 27–36.

Darley, J. M., & Latane, B. Norms and normative behavior: field studies of social interdependence. In J. Macaulay & L. Berkowitz (Eds.), *Altruism and helping behavior.* New York: Academic Press, 1970.

deLuca, J. F. Altruism as a personality trait in children. Unpublished master's thesis, Humboldt State College, 1968.

DePalma, D. J., & Olejnik, A. B. Effects of social class, moral orientations, and severity of punishment on boys' generosity. Unpublished manuscript, Loyola University, Chicago, 1973.

Dlugokinski, E., & Firestone, I. J. Congruence among four methods of measuring other-centeredness. *Child Development,* 1973, *44,* 304–308.

Ekstein, R. Psychoanalysis and education for the facilitation of positive human qualities. *Journal of Social Issues,* 1972, *28,* 71–86.

Elliot, R., & Vasta, R. The modeling of sharing: effects associated with vicarious reinforcement, symbolization, age, and generalization. *Journal of Experimental Child Psychology,* 1970, *10,* 8–15.

Fischer, W. F. Sharing in preschool children as a function of amount and type of reinforcement. *Genetic Psychology Monographs,* 1963, *68,* 215–245.

Fouts, G. T. Charity in children: the influence of "charity" stimuli and an audience. *Journal of Experimental Child Psychology,* 1972, *13,* 303–309.

Fraser, S. C.; Kelem, R. T.; Diener, E.; & Beaman, A. L. Two, three or four heads are better than one: modification of college performance by peer monitoring. Unpublished manuscript, University of Southern California, 1973.

Freedman, J. L.; Wallington, A.; & Bless, E. Compliance without pressure: the effect of guilt. *Journal of Personality and Social Psychology,* 1967, *7,* 117–124.

Friedrich, L. K., & Stein, A. H. Aggressive and prosocial television programs and the natural behavior of preschool children. *Monographs of the Society for Research in Child Development,* 1973, *38,* (4, Serial No. 151), 1–64.

Gewirtz, J. L. Mechanisms of social learning: some roles of stimulation and behavior in early human development. In D. H. Goslin (Ed.), *Handbook of socialization theory and research.* Chicago: Rand-McNally, 1969.

Gottheil, E. Changes in social perceptions contingent upon competing or cooperating. *Sociometry,* 1955, *18,* 132–137.

Grusec, J. E. Power and the internalization of self denial. *Child Development,* 1971, *42,* 93–105.

Grusec, J. E. Demand characteristics of the modeling experiment: altruism as a function of age, and aggression. *Journal of Personality and Social Psychology,* 1972, *22,* 139–148.

Grusec, J. E., & Driscoll, S. A. Saying and doing: effects on observer performance. Unpublished manuscript, University of Toronto, 1973.

Grusec, J. E., & Skubiski, L. Model nurturance, demand characteristics of the modeling experiment and altruism. *Journal of Personality and Social Psychology,* 1970, *14,* 352–359.

Handlon, B. J., & Gross, P. The development of sharing behavior. *Journal of Abnormal and Social Psychology,* 1959, *59,* 425–428.

Harford, T., & Cutter, H. S. G. Cooperation among Negro and white boys and girls. *Psychological Reports,* 1966, *18,* 818.

Harris, E. B. A scale for measuring attitudes of social responsibility in children. *Journal of Abnormal and Social Psychology,* 1957, *55,* 322–326.

Harris, M. B. Reciprocity and generosity: some determinants of sharing behavior. *Child Development,* 1970, *41,* 313–328.

Harris, M. B. Models, norms and sharing. *Psychological Reports,* 1971, *29,* 147–153.

Hartshorne, H.; May, M. A.; & Maller, J. B. *Studies in service and self-control.* New York: Macmillan, 1929.

Hartup, W. W., & Coates, B. Imitation of a peer as a function of reinforcement from the peer group and the rewardingness of the model. *Child Development,* 1967, *38,* 1003–1016.

Hartup, W. W., & Keller, E. D. Nurturance in preschool children and its relation to dependency. *Child Development,* 1960, *31,* 681–689.

Hetherington, E. M., & Frankie, G. Effects of parental dominance, warmth, and conflict, on imitation in children. *Journal of Personality and Social Psychology,* 1967, *6,* 119–125.

Hildebrandt, D. E.; Feldman, S. E.; & Ditrichs, R. A. Rules, models and self-reinforcement in children. *Journal of Personality and Social Psychology,* 1973, *25,* 1–5.

Hochreich, D. J. A children's scale for measuring interpersonal trust. Unpublished master's thesis, University of Connecticut, 1966.

Hoffman, M. L. Moral development. In P. H. Mussen (Ed.), *Carmichael's manual of child psychology* Vol. 2. New York: Wiley, 1970.

Hoffman, M. L. A theoretical perspective: the development of altruistic motives. Paper delivered at the symposium on contemporary issues in moral development, Loyola University, Chicago, 1973.

Hoffman, M. L. & Saltzstein, H. D. Parent discipline and the child's moral development. *Journal of Personality and Social Psychology,* 1967, *5,* 45–57.

Isen, A. M. Success, failure, attention, and reaction to others: the warm glow of success. *Journal of Personality and Social Psychology,* 1970, *15,* 294–300.

Isen, A. M., & Levin, P. F. The effect of feeling good on helping: cookies and kindness. *Journal of Personality and Social Psychology,* 1972, *21,* 384–388.

Isen, A. M.; Rosenhan, D. L.; & Horn, N. Effects of success and failure on children's generosity. *Journal of Personality and Social Psychology,* 1973, *27,* 239–247.

Kagan, S., & Madsen, M. C. Cooperation and competition of Mexican, Mexican-American, and Anglo-American children of two ages under four instructional sets. *Developmental Psychology*, 1971, *5*, 32–39.

Katz, J. Altruism and sympathy: their history in philosophy and some implications for psychology. *Journal of Social Issues*, 1972, *28*, 59–69.

Kazdin, A. E., & Bootzin, R. R. The token economy: an evaluative review. *Journal of Applied Behavior Analysis*, 1972, *5*, 343–372.

Kazdin, A. E., & Bryan, J. H. Competence and volunteering. *Journal of Experimental Social Psychology*, 1971, *7*, 87–97.

Krebs, D. Altruism—an examination of the concept and a review of the literature. *Psychological Bulletin*, 1970, *73*, 258–302.

Lane, I. M., & Coon, R. C. Reward allocation in preschool children. *Child Development*, 1972, *43*, 1382–1389.

Lazarus, R. S.; Speisman, J. C.; Mardkoff, A. M.; & Davison, L. A. A laboratory study of psychological stress produced by a motion picture film. *Psychological Monographs*, 1962 (Whole No. 553).

Leeds, R. Altruism and the norm of giving. *Merrill-Palmer Quarterly*, 1963, *9*, 229–240.

Lenrow, P. B. Studies in sympathy. In S. S. Tomkins & C. E. Izard (Eds.), *Affect, cognition, and personality: empirical studies*. New York: Springer, 1965.

Lerner, L., & Weiss, R. L. Role of value of reward and model affective response in vicarious reinforcement. *Journal of Personality and Social Psychology*, 1972, *21*, 93–100.

Lerner, M. J., & Matthews, G. Reactions to suffering of others under conditions of indirect responsibility. *Journal of Personality and Social Psychology*, 1967, *5*, 319–325.

Lerner, M. J., & Simmons, C. H. Observer's reaction to the "innocent victim": compassion or rejection? *Journal of Personality and Social Psychology*, 1966, *4*, 203–210.

Leventhal, G. S.; Popp, A. L.; & Sawyer, L. Equity or equality in children's allocation of reward to other persons? *Child Development*, 1973, *44*, 753–763.

Liebert, R. M., & Fernandez, L. E. Effects of single and multiple modeling cues on establishing norms for sharing. Paper presented at the meeting of the American Psychological Association, Miami Beach, 1970.

Liebert, R. M.; Fernandez, L. E.; & Gill, L. Effects of a "friendless" model on imitation and prosocial behavior. *Psychonomic Science*, 1969, *16*, 81–82.

Liebert, R. M., & Poulos, R. W. Eliciting the "norm of giving": effects on modeling and the presence of a witness on children's sharing behavior. Paper presented at the meeting of the American Psychological Association, Washington, D.C., 1971.

Lindskold, S.; Cullen, P.; Gahagan, J.; & Tedeschi, J. T. Developmental aspects of reaction to positive inducements. *Developmental Psychology*, 1970, *3*, 277–284.

Long, G. T., & Lerner, M. J. Deserving, the "personal contract," and altruistic behavior by children. *Journal of Personality and Social Psychology*, 1974, *29*, 551–556.

Macaulay, J., & Berkowitz, L. (Eds.), *Altruism and helping behavior*. New York: Academic Press, 1970.

McKee, J. P., & Leader, F. B. The relationship of socio-economic status and aggression to the competitive behavior of preschool children. *Child Development*, 1955, *26*, 135–142.

McMains, M. J., & Liebert, R. M. Influence of discrepancies between successively modeled self-reward criteria on the adoption of self-imposed standard. *Journal of Personality and Social Psychology*, 1968, *8*, 166–171.

Madsen, M. C. Cooperative and competitive motivation of children in three Mexican sub-cultures. *Psychological Reports*, 1967, *20*, 1307–1320.

Madsen, M. C. Developmental and cross-cultural differences in the cooperative and competitive behavior of young children. *Journal of Cross-cultural Psychology*, 1971, *2*, 365–371.

Madsen, M. C., & Conner, C. Cooperative and competitive behavior of retarded and nonretarded children at two ages. *Child Development,* 1973, *44,* 175–178.

Madsen, M. S., & Shapira, A. Cooperative and competitive behavior of urban Afro-American, Anglo-American, Mexican-American, and Mexican village children. *Developmental Psychology,* 1970, *3,* 16–20.

Marshall, H. M. The effect of vicarious punishment on sharing behavior in children. *Dissertation Abstracts International,* 1972, *32,* (11-a), 6539.

Masters, J. C. Effects of social comparison upon children's self-reinforcement and altruism toward competitors and friends. *Developmental Psychology,* 1971, *5,* 64–72.

Midlarsky, E., & Bryan, J. H. Training charity in children. *Journal of Personality and Social Psychology,* 1967, *5,* 408–415.

Midlarsky, E., & Bryan, J. H. Affect expressions and children's imitative altruism. *Journal of Experimental Research in Personality,* 1972, *6,* 195–203.

Midlarsky, E.; Bryan, J. H.; & Brickman, P. Aversive approval: interactive effects of modeling and reinforcement on altruistic behavior. *Child Development,* 1973, *44,* 321–328.

Mischel, W., & Liebert, R. M. Effects of discrepancies between observed and imposed reward criteria on their acquisition and transmission. *Journal of Personality and Social Psychology,* 1966, *3,* 45–53.

Mithaug, E. D. The development of cooperation in alternative task situations. *Journal of Experimental Child Psychology,* 1969, *8,* 443–460.

Mithaug, E. D., & Burgess, R. L. The effects of different reinforcement contingencies in the development of social cooperation. *Journal of Experimental Child Psychology,* 1968, *6,* 402–426.

Moore, B. S.; Underwood, B.; & Rosenhan, D. L. Affect and altruism. *Developmental Psychology,* 1973, *8,* 99–104.

Mowrer, O. H. *Learning theory and personality dynamics.* New York: Ronald, 1950.

Mussen, P., & Distler, L. Masculinity, identification, and father-son relationships. *Journal of Abnormal Social Psychology,* 1959, *59,* 350–356.

Mussen, P.; Rutherford, E.; Harris, S.; & Keasey, C. B. Honesty and altruism among preadolescents. *Developmental Psychology,* 1970, *3,* 169–194.

Nelson, L. & Madsen, M. C. Cooperation and competition in four-year-olds as a function of reward contingency and subculture. *Developmental Psychology,* 1968, *1,* 340–344.

Olejnik, A. B., & McKinney, J. P. Parental value orientation and generosity in children. *Developmental Psychology,* 1973, *8,* 311.

Parke, R. D. Nurturance, nurturance withdrawal, and resistance to deviation. *Child Development,* 1967, *35,* 1101–1110.

Parton, M. B. Social play among preschool children. *Journal of Abnormal and Social Psychology,* 1933, *28,* 136–147.

Presbie, R. J., & Coiteux, P. F. Learning to be generous or stingy: imitation of sharing behavior as a function of model generosity and vicarious reinforcement. *Child Development,* 1971, *42,* 1033–1038.

Richmond, B. O., & Weiner, G. P. Cooperation and competition among young children as a function of ethnic grouping, grade, sex, and reward condition. *Journal of Educational Psychology,* 1973, *64,* 329–334.

Rosenhan, D. L. Determinants of altruism: observations for a theory of altruistic development. Paper presented at the annual meeting of the American Psychological Association, Washington, D.C., 1969. (a)

Rosenhan, D. L. Studies in altruistic behavior: developmental and naturalistic variables associated with charitability. Paper presented at the meeting of the Society for Research in Child Development, Santa Monica, Calif., 1969. (b)

Rosenhan, D. L. Conceptual structures for prosocial behavior. Paper presented at the annual meeting of the American Psychological Association, Miami Beach, 1970.

Rosenhan, D. L. Learning theory and prosocial behavior. *Journal of Social Issues,* 1972, *28,* 151–163.

Rosenhan, D. L; Frederick, F.; & Burrowes, A. Preaching and practicing: effects of channel discrepancy on norm internalization. *Child Development,* 1968, *39,* 291–301.

Rosenhan, D. L., & White, G. M. Observation and rehearsal as determinants of prosocial behavior. *Journal of Personality and Social Psychology,* 1967, *5,* 424–431.

Rubin, K. H., & Schneider, F. W. The relationship between moral judgement, egocentrism, and altruistic behavior. *Child Development,* 1973, *44,* 661–665.

Rushton, J. P. Generosity in children: immediate and long term effects of modeling, preaching, and moral judgments. *Journal of Personality and Social Psychology,* in press.

Rutherford, E., & Mussen, P. Generosity in nursery school boys. *Child Development,* 1968, *39,* 755–765.

Sampson, E. E., & Kardush, M. Age, sex, class and race differences in response to a two-person non-zero-sum game. *Journal of Conflict Resolution,* 1965, *9,* 212–220.

Schwartz, T., & Bryan, J. H. Imitation and judgments of children with language deficits. *Exceptional Children,* 1971, *38,* 157–158. (a)

Schwartz, T., & Bryan, J. H. Imitative altruism by deaf children. *Journal of Speech and Hearing Research,* 1971, *14,* 453–461. (b)

Severy, L. J., & Davis, K. E. Helping behavior among normal and retarded children. *Child Development,* 1971, *42,* 1017–1031.

Shapira, A., & Madsen, M. C. Cooperative and competitive behavior of kibbutz and urban children in Israel. *Child Development,* 1969, *40,* 609–617.

Sherif, M.; Harvey, O. J.; White, B. J.; Hood, W. R.: & Sherif, C. W. *Intergroup conflict and cooperation: the robbers cave experiment.* Norman: Institute of Group Relations, University of Oklahoma, 1961.

Shirley, K. W. Television and children: a modeling analysis. Unpublished manuscript, University of Kansas, 1973.

Silverman, I. W. Incidence of guilt reactions in children. *Journal of Personality and Social Psychology,* 1967, *7,* 338–340.

Solomon, D.; Ali, F. A.; Kfir, D.; Houlihan, K. A.; & Yaeger, J. The development of democratic values and behavior among Mexican-American children. *Child Development,* 1972, *43,* 625–638.

Staub, E. The effects of success and failure on children's sharing behavior. Paper presented at the meeting of the Eastern Psychological Association, 1968.

Staub, E. Determinants of children's attempts to help another child in distress. Paper presented at the meeting of the American Psychological Association, Washington, D.C., September 1969.

Staub, E. A child in distress: the influence of age and number of witnesses on children's attempts to help. *Journal of Personality and Social Psychology,* 1970, *14,* 130–140.

Staub, E. A child in distress: the influence of nurturance and modeling on children's attempts to help. *Developmental Psychology,* 1971, *5,* 124–132. (a)

Staub, E. Helping a person in distress: the influence of implicit and explicit "rules" of conduct on children and adults. *Journal of Personality and Social Psychology,* 1971, *17,* 137–144. (b)

Staub, E. *The development of prosocial behavior in children.* New York: Warner Modular Publications, in press.

Staub, E., & Sherk, L. Need for approval, children's sharing behavior, and reciprocity in sharing. *Child Development,* 1970, *41,* 243–252.

Stein, G. M., & Bryan, J. H. The effect of a television model upon rule adoption behavior of children. *Child Development*, 1972, *43*, 268–273.

Stevenson, H. W. Social reinforcement of children's behavior. In L. P. Lipsett & C. C. Spiker (Eds.), *Advances in child development*. Vol. 2. New York: Academic Press, 1965.

Tedeschi, J. T.; Hiester, D.; & Gahagan, J. P. Matrix values and the behavior of children in the prisoner's dilemma game. *Child Development*, 1969, *40*, 517–527.

Test, M. A. Children's responses to harm-doing: a behavioral study. Unpublished dissertation, Northwestern University, 1969.

Ugurel-Semin, R. Moral behavior and moral judgement of children. *Journal of Abnormal and Social Psychology*, 1952, *47*, 463–474.

Vogler, R. E.; Masters, W. M.; & Morrill, G. S. Shaping cooperative behavior in young children. *Journal of Psychology*, 1970, *74*, 181–186.

Vogler, R. E.; Masters, W. M.; & Morrill, G. S. Extinction of cooperative behavior as a function of acquisition by shaping or instruction. *Journal of Genetic Psychology*, 1971, *119*, 233–240.

Walbek, N. H. Charitable cognitions and actions: a study of the concurrent elicitations of children's altruistic thoughts and deeds. Unpublished master's thesis, Northwestern University, 1969.

Wallace, J., & Sadalla, E. Behavioral consequence of transgression, I: The effects of social recognition. *Journal of Experimental Research in Personality*, 1966, *1*, 187–194.

Wasik, B. H.; Senn, S. K.; & Epanchin, A. Cooperation and sharing behavior among culturally deprived preschool children. *Psychonomic Science*, 1969, *17*, 371–372.

Weissbrod, C. S. The effect of non-contingent adult warmth on reflective and impulsive children's donation and rescue behavior. Paper presented at the annual meeting of the Midwest Psychological Association, Chicago, 1974.

Weissbrod, C. S., & Bryan, J. H. Filmed treatment as an effective fear reduction technique. *Journal of Abnormal Child Psychology*, 1973, *1*, 196–201.

White, G. M. Immediate and deferred effects of model observation and guided and unguided rehearsal on donating and stealing. *Journal of Personality and Social Psychology*, 1972, *21*, 139–148.

Wispé, L. G. Positive forms of social behavior: an overview. *Journal of Social Issues*, 1972, *28*, 1–19.

Wright, B. A. Altruism in children and the perceived conduct of others. *Journal of Abnormal and Social Psychology*, 1942, *37*, 218–233.

Yarrow, M. R.; Scott, P. M.; & Waxler, C. Z. Learning concern for others. *Developmental Psychology*, 1973, *8*, 240–261.

4 Impact of Television on Children and Youth

ALETHA HUSTON STEIN
AND LYNETTE KOHN FRIEDRICH
Pennsylvania State University

CONTENTS

I. INTRODUCTION

Social scientists are the camp followers of technological advances. Thus, the rapid spread of television through the United States during the 1950s was accompanied by considerable research on and interest in the impact of the new medium. Several classic studies were conducted during that period (e.g., Bailyn 1959; Himmelweit, Oppenheim, & Vince 1958; Schramm, Lyle, & Parker 1961). These investigations can be broadly distinguished from more recent television research by their focus on the effects of television per se rather than the effects of specific content. It seemed to many that such a vivid and compelling form of home entertainment should produce marked alterations in people's lives. They examined a wide range of behavior, asking questions such as, What activities were replaced by television viewing? Did viewing result in reduced peer interaction? Did it interfere with schoolwork? Was it used as an escape from unpleasant life circumstances? The research of this period is reviewed by Maccoby (1964).

Almost as soon as television had become an accepted part of everyday American life, however, the attention of social scientists turned to the impact of specific types of television content, particularly violence. Widespread public concern about violence led to periodic rounds of congressional hearings dealing with the relation between television violence and the increasing violence in society. The result of hearings in 1969 was an appropriation of one million dollars to provide new research on television and the social behavior of children and adolescents. A series of 23 empirical projects and numerous other papers and literature reviews resulted from this appropriation and are published in five volumes (Comstock & Rubinstein 1972a, 1972b; Comstock, Rubinstein, & Murray 1972; Murray, Comstock, & Rubinstein 1972; Rubinstein, Comstock, & Murray 1972). These documents formed the basis for recommendations to the Surgeon General concerning the effects of television violence (Surgeon General's Scientific Advisory Committee on Television and Social Behavior 1972). Summaries of this research are available (Liebert, Neale, & Davidson 1973; Murray 1973) as well as an annotated bibliography (Murray, Nayman, & Atkin 1971).

Most of the new research deals with the narrow issue of the relation of television violence to aggressive behavior. Hence, the bulk of our discussion is concerned with that issue and with the conditions that enhance or reduce the likelihood that behavioral aggression will result from television violence. Other areas covered in this chapter are the relation of television to children's understanding of social roles and stereotypes, cognitive development, and prosocial behavior. Although the effects of advertising are of considerable interest, that topic is not covered because there is so little adequate research (see Liebert et al [1973] and Ward [1972] for available studies). Similarly, there is virtually no literature investigating noncontent features such as pace, photographic techniques, animation, and the like, perhaps because they are not easily conceptualized in most of the theoretical approaches used.

Our orientation is developmental, so we have examined literature on children ranging from 3 to 18, with particular attention to age differences. Studies of college students and adults are not given comprehensive coverage, because it is not clear that one can generalize their results to younger age levels. Further, this survey is restricted primarily to studies conducted in the United States. While there is a considerable amount of media research in other countries, cross-cultural comparisons are difficult because American television differs dramatically from available programming in many nations (Liebert et al. 1973). Obviously, many other factors vary across cultures as well.

One principal theoretical basis for the research reviewed is social learning theory, particularly the refined conceptualization of observational learning developed by Bandura (1969a, 1969b). One of the most important propositions of this theory is the distinction between acquisition and performance of behavior. Behavior observed on television may be learned without any immediate acting out by the child. This learned behavior is stored, however, and may be acted on later if appropriate circumstances arise. A considerable amount of observational learning can occur without any obvious reinforcement either to the model observed or to the person observing. In fact, the situation where reinforcement is absent is the very one in which learning without immediate performance is most likely to occur (Bandura 1969b).

II. TELEVISION VIEWING PATTERNS

Television occupies a great deal of time in children's lives. Exact estimates of the number of hours per week are difficult to make because of the unreliability of different methods of assessment (Bechtel, Achelpohl, & Akers 1972) and seasonal and situational variation in viewing. Furthermore, there is such wide variation among individuals that an average figure is meaningless. In a sample of 100 preschool children, mothers reported that their children watched from 5 to 88 hours of television per week (Stein & Friedrich 1972). Lyle and Hoffman (1972a) found that, on a given day, about one-fourth of their sixth graders reported no viewing; at the other extreme, about a fourth reported over 5 hours of viewing. There are consistent findings, however, concerning mean group differences in the amount of viewing based on age, sex, social class, ethnic group, and intelligence.

A. AGE, SEX, SOCIAL CLASS, ETHNIC GROUP, AND INTELLIGENCE

The amount of television viewed increases gradually from age 3 to approximately the beginning of adolescence. Total number of hours viewed then declines among high-school-age adolescents (Lyle 1972). Although viewing of violent programs also declines, the proportion of violent programs watched increases in adolescence and preference for violent programs increases (Lyle & Hoffman 1972a).

Boys and girls watch approximately equal amounts of television during childhood, but girls watch slightly more than boys in adolescence (Lyle 1972). In early childhood, boys like cartoons better than girls, but there are few other differences in the types of programs liked or watched (Stein & Friedrich 1972). Male adolescents also like violent programs better than females do, but other preferences are similar. Thus, although female adolescents view a little more television than males do, they view less violence.

Children from lower-social-status homes watch more television and watch more violence than those from higher-status homes. Blacks also watch more television and more violence than whites, even when social status is controlled (Lyle 1972). Programs preferred by black children were different from those preferred by white children in two surveys. Both groups liked situation comedies, but blacks reported higher liking for family group shows and less liking for variety shows than whites (Fletcher 1969; Surlin & Dominick 1970). Violent shows were not among the most preferred programs for either group of children and adolescents interviewed.

Early research suggested that very intelligent children were heavy television viewers in the elementary years but not in adolescence (Schramm et al. 1961). Most recent studies have found that the amount of television watched bears little relation to intelligence or school achievement. Where relations do appear, heavy television viewing is associated with low intelligence or poor achievement (Friedrich & Stein 1973; Lyle & Hoffman 1972a; Stein & Friedrich 1972).

B. FAMILY INFLUENCES ON VIEWING PATTERNS

With the social concern about negative effects of television, particularly television violence, it might be expected that many parents would limit their children's viewing time or restrict the types of programs they are allowed to see. However, parents put very few restrictions on their children's viewing, even in the preschool years (Friedrich & Stein 1973; Lyle & Hoffman 1972b; Stein & Friedrich 1972). When parents do attempt to control children's viewing, such controls seem to have some effect in the early years (Friedrich & Stein 1973; Stein & Friedrich 1972) but may have a different meaning by the time children are preadolescents or adolescents. Parental attempts to control television viewing are associated with heavy viewing by older children (Chaffee & McLeod 1972; Lyle & Hoffman 1972a). At this age it may be that parental control arises primarily as a response to high television use.

Parents probably do influence their children's television viewing by serving as models. Children's viewing violent and nonviolent programs is related to their parents' viewing similar programs (Chaffee & McLeod 1972; Friedrich & Stein 1973; Greenberg, Ericson, & Vlahos 1972; Lyle & Hoffman 1972a; McLeod, Atkin, & Chaffee 1972a; Stein & Friedrich 1972). Adolescents' viewing patterns, however, are less like their parents' than those of younger children. Parent-child similarities in viewing could be due to mere convenience or opportunity rather than modeling. That is, people living in the same house may watch the same programs simply because someone has turned them on. This explanation seems incomplete for two reasons: the similarities in viewing are just as great in houses with more than one television set as in those with a single set (Chaffee & McLeod 1972), and there is decreasing parent-child similarity in adolescence when children might be more likely to be watching television during the same hours as their parents.

Children may also influence their parents' viewing. Chaffee and McLeod (1971) argue that this is a more plausible interpretation of similarities between adolescent and parental viewing. Parents did report seeking recommendations concerning television programs from their adolescent children. However, one would expect greater similarity with increasing age if this were the case. It is likely that all family members influence one another's viewing, particularly as children grow into adolescence and acquire a familiarity with the youth culture that forms the basis of so much adult television programming.

III. TELEVISION VIOLENCE

A. CONTENT OF TELEVISION PROGRAMS

The social concern and research focus on crime and violence in television become more understandable from content analyses showing the extent of violence on commercial television. The most elaborate content analyses have been performed by Gerbner and his associates (Gerbner 1972; Gerbner & Gross 1973). These analyses are based on a 1-week sample of dramatic fiction programs on the three major networks during prime time and Saturday morning hours for the years 1967–1972. Violence was defined as "the overt expression of physical force against others or the self, or the compelling of action against one's will on pain of being hurt or killed" (Gerbner 1972, p. 31). Verbal abuse, idle threats, or comic gestures were not included.

Some of the bare figures may best indicate the extent of violence in the world of television fiction. About 80% of the plays contained at least one incident of violence; the frequency of about five per play or eight per hour did not decline over the 6 years sampled. Programs directed at young children were particularly violent. Cartoons had the highest frequency of violence, although the average of 30 incidents per hour in 1969 was reduced to 17 by 1972. In another sample of Saturday morning programs, 30% of the programs were considered "saturated" with violence; in 58%, violence was incidental or minor (Barcus 1971).

The perception of violence is not the exclusive domain of content analysts. Both television critics and adults in the general public agreed closely on which programs contained extensive physical violence (Greenberg & Gordon 1972a). Adolescents and children also rated films and programs that researchers selected as violent or nonviolent. The subjects clearly perceived the differences in content in the same way professionals did (Greenberg & Gordon 1972b; Katzman 1972; Parke et al. 1974).

It is sometimes argued that showing violence with its negative consequences may inhibit people from acting violently, but television violence is rewarded at least as often as it is punished. The "good guys" are as violent as the "bad guys," and they often break the law, as well, in the service of supposedly good ends (Lange, Baker, & Ball 1969). In an analysis of the means-ends relations in television, Larsen, Gray, and Fortis (1968) concluded that socially disapproved means—that is, use of violence or illegal means of escape—were successful in attaining goals more frequently than legal or socially approved means. This was particularly true in children's programs.

Not only are the social consequences of violence frequently positive, but the actual negative, painful aspects of physical violence are virtually eliminated from television fiction. The network codes forbid showing blood, gore, and the like. In Gerbner's analysis (1972), painful consequences were so infrequent that coders could not rate them reliably.

Clearly, television fiction presents an inordinate amount of murder, mayhem, fistfights, gunfights, and most other kinds of physical violence. A child who watches even a moderate amount of television sees a great deal of violence. Violence is presented as a laudable and successful means of dealing with conflicts. Perhaps most important, no alternatives are shown that are equally successful in coping with difficulties.

Virtually all of the research on television content and behavior limits the definition of violence to physical injury or damage. The verbal abuse, aggressive humor, and control over other people by threat or imperative that are so prevalent on television are not included in most investigations. The repartee in the Archie Bunker family, for instance, is filled with hostility; yet the program would probably receive a fairly low rating using any of the methods described because physical attack is infrequent. This limitation on research makes the variables investigated more uniform, but probably precludes some important content.

B. DEFINITIONS AND MEASURES OF AGGRESSION

Just as a limited area of television content has been examined, a rather small domain of children's behavior has been the focus of most research on the effects of television violence. The viewer behavior studied in most cases is physical aggression. Less frequently, verbal aggression, aggressive attitudes, and perceptions of violence are examined. The measures include observation of solitary play behavior, interaction of small groups of children, free-play behavior, laboratory tasks, self-reports of behavior, reports of aggressive attitudes, and ratings by others, such as peers or adults.

One reason for the focus on physical aggression is probably that it is more easily observed and agreed on by others as well as by the individual being rated. Among adolescents studied by McLeod, Atkin, and Chaffee (1972b), the similarity between self-reports and peer ratings was greater for assaultive behavior than for verbal aggression; there was no agreement at all on ratings of irritability. Similarly, Leifer and Roberts (1972) found that teacher ratings of aggression correlated with children's choices of physical aggression on a questionnaire but not with choices of verbal aggression. Agreement between self and others' ratings appears best on the most dramatic and readily observable aspects of behavior; others may find it more difficult to assess verbal aggression and irritability because these are more subjective. On the other hand, subjects' own perceptions of verbal aggression and irritability may be inflated or depressed by the value and importance they attribute to aggression.

C. EXPERIMENTAL STUDIES OF EFFECTS OF VIOLENCE ON AGGRESSION

According to Bandura's (1969a) theory of observational learning, exposure to aggressive models instigates aggression through two related processes: learning new aggressive acts and disinhibition of behaviors already in the individual's response repertoire. Increased aggression is likely unless environmental conditions or fear of punishment inhibit behavioral expression.

The traditional opposing theory is based on the notion of catharsis. Some researchers have argued that viewing violence provides the person with a vicarious outlet for aggressive impulses; thus, it should reduce behavioral aggresssion. This position predicts, therefore, reductions in aggression as a result of watching television violence or engaging in aggressive fantasy (e.g., Feshbach & Singer 1971).

Reductions in aggression may also occur if aggression anxiety is aroused (Goranson 1970). Because many people are socialized to view aggression as unacceptable, they feel anxious and guilty when their aggressive impulses are aroused. Viewing violence may, therefore, lead to increased aggression if this anxiety is relatively low, or it may lead to no change or reduced aggression if anxiety is high.

1. Experimental Studies Using Laboratory-constructed Films

Laboratory studies in which children have been shown either a live model or a film constructed by the researcher unanimously support the prediction that aggressive models lead to increased aggressive behavior (Bandura, Ross, & Ross 1963a, 1963b; Christy, Gelfand, & Hartmann 1971; Davids 1972; Grusec 1972; Hanratty et al. 1969; Hanratty, O'Neal, & Sulzer 1972; Kuhn, Madsen, & Becker 1967; Leifer & Roberts 1972; Nelson, Gelfand, & Hartmann 1969; Rosekrans & Hartup 1967; Savitsky et al. 1971; Walters & Willows 1968). The results occur across a wide age range for both males and females and for emotionally disturbed and delinquent populations as well as for normal children. The format of most of these studies is similar. A modeling sequence containing several acts of physical and verbal aggression is shown to the child. An adult or peer hits bobo dolls, pounds toys with hammers, throws things, and the like. It apparently makes little difference whether the model is live or filmed (Bandura et al. 1963a). The child is then placed alone in a room with the toys or objects used by the model. Both specific imitation of the model's aggressive acts and nonimitative aggression have been observed quite consistently in children following exposure to aggressive models. Although most of the studies measure only aggression to objects, some work in Liebert's laboratory has employed an adult dressed as a clown as a target of aggression. The model shoots toy darts and performs other acts of aggression directed toward the "clown." This variation indicates that children will imitate interpersonal aggression in this relatively permissive and nonthreatening context.

Laboratory studies of this kind have the important advantage of a clearly defined and refined independent variable. One can be fairly sure that it is the aggressive behavior of the model that is affecting the child's behavior. Generalization from these studies to the effects of television in natural contexts is, of course, questionable. Aggression in television programs may be less clear or less salient than it is in a laboratory-made sequence. Children's attention may be less focused in a natural setting. Factors in the plot may alleviate the impact of the violence itself. The fact that a permissive adult has exposed the child to the model in the laboratory may be an important disinhibitor that is not present in "real life." Most behavioral observations are conducted immediately after exposure in situations very similar to the ones in which the models were observed. Therefore, these studies do not indicate how durable the behavioral changes are nor how much disinhibition would generalize to other situations. They also provide no information about generalization to other types of aggressive behavior, particularly behavior that is more serious and potentially harmful than the play activities measured in most studies.

Nevertheless, these laboratory studies provide very important information about the basic psychological processes involved in observing violence. They indicate that aggressive modeling stripped of any other elaborations leads to imitation and disinhibition, not to a cathartic "draining off" of aggressive impulses. This is true even when children are frustrated or presumably angry, a condition that is sometimes considered necessary for catharsis to occur. Under the most carefully controlled conditions, viewing aggression leads to increases, not decreases, in aggressive behavior. Therefore, when reduced aggression does occur in studies using more complex content, it is sensible to look for explanations other than catharsis.

2. Experimental Studies Using Real Television Content

In order to answer many of the questions raised above, numerous studies have been conducted using commercially produced television programs or films. In some of these studies, a brief segment of a program has been shown and aggression measured immediately afterward. For the most part, the measures of aggression tap interpersonal physical and verbal aggression rather than play behavior toward objects, so they are closer to the types of aggressive behavior of social concern. The behavior measured is also very different from that observed in the television programs; it is not simple replication of models' actions. In addition to the short-term studies, there are several "field experiments" in which children or adolescents, exposed to violent or nonviolent television diets over a period of time, have demonstrated changes in their behavior in natural settings. Both types of studies are summarized in table 1.

Early childhood.—Cartoons have the highest quantity of violence of any type of program. While some people have suggested that the animation and humor of cartoons reduce their effects because they are obviously unrealistic, young children have relatively little ability to make distinctions between fiction and reality. As cartoons are a predominant feature of young children's viewing, most studies with young children have employed them.

Several studies have demonstrated that one exposure to a violent cartoon leads to increased aggression (Ellis & Sekyra 1972; Lovaas 1961; Mussen & Rutherford 1961; Ross 1972). Siegel (1956) found a similar trend, though it was not statistically significant. In a conflict situation where only one toy was available to two children, Hapkiewitz and Roden (1971) found no effects on physical aggression of violent cartoons, but boys who saw the violent cartoons were less likely to share than the control groups. In no case has reduced aggression been found after watching violent cartoons. Nonaggressive cartoons have often been used as control films, so the increased aggression can be attributed to the violent content rather than to other qualities of cartoons.

Repeated exposure to violent cartoons also seems to increase aggression, although the findings are slightly less clear-cut. In a carefully controlled experiment (Steuer, Applefield, & Smith 1971), two groups were matched for home viewing and baseline measures of aggression. Eleven sessions followed in which children saw either aggressive cartoons or cartoons with physical aggression edited out before a free-play period. The group seeing the aggressive cartoons became significantly more aggressive during free-play periods than those seeing the nonaggressive cartoons. The difference increased steadily with time. In another field experiment (Friedrich & Stein 1973; Stein & Friedrich 1972), interpersonal aggression in nursery school classrooms was observed for children who were shown violent cartoons, neutral films, or prosocial television programs. For the half of the group which was initially above average in aggression, violent television was associated with higher interpersonal aggression than the neutral or prosocial films. This difference continued during the 2-week postviewing period. When the children in this experiment were observed in a mildly frustrating situation immediately after one program, there was a tendency for children who had seen the violent cartoons to be more aggressive, but the differences from other conditions were not consistent across sexes. Boys were also less cooperative after violent television, suggesting that they were relying on aggressive behavior more exclusively than the other groups (Stein, Friedrich, et al. 1973).

Summary.—Overall, it appears that violent cartoons instigate young children to aggressive behavior on a short-term basis. Repeated exposure

TABLE 1

SUMMARY OF EXPERIMENTAL STUDIES OF TELEVISION VIOLENCE

Short-Term Studies; Cartoon Stimuli; Early Childhood

Author(s) and Date	Subjects	Independent Variables	Dependent Variables	Results
Lovaas (1961).............	Preschool M & F	Aggressive cartoon vs. nonaggressive film	Play with a toy where 1 doll hit another in preference to a nonaggressive toy—adult absent	Aggressive cartoon > non-aggressive film
Siegel (1956).............	Preschool M & F	Aggressive cartoon vs. neutral cartoon	Play sessions—2 children: *a)* aggression to peer and anxiety—adult absent *b)* Anxiety during films	*a)* Nonsignificant trend for higher aggression and anxiety following aggressive cartoon *b)* Aggressive film > neutral
Ross (1972).............	Kindergarten M & F	Aggressive cartoon vs. nonaggressive cartoon vs. no viewing	Play sessions—2 or 4 children: *a)* "Normative" aggression—appropriate to the play materials *b)* "Transgressive aggression"—inappropriate object aggression or peer aggression *c)* Interpersonal aggression to peer—adult absent	*a)* Aggressive cartoon > no cartoon; nonaggressive cartoon between—females only *b)* No differences *c)* Aggressive cartoons > other 2 conditions—both sexes
Mussen & Rutherford (1961)...	6–7-year-old M & F	1) Aggressive cartoon vs. nonaggressive cartoon vs. no viewing 2) Half of children in each group were frustrated	Fantasy: stated desire to break balloons	1) Aggressive cartoon group > other 2 conditions 2) No effects of frustration
Hapkiewitz & Roden (1971)...	2d-grade M & F	Aggressive cartoon vs. nonaggressive cartoon vs. no viewing	Conflict situation: 2 children attempting to see another film through one peephole—adult present: *a)* Physical aggression *b)* Sharing	*a)* No differences *b)* Aggressive cartoon group shared less than other 2 groups —males only
Ellis & Sekyra (1972).........	1st-grade M & F	Aggressive cartoon vs. nonaggressive cartoon vs. no film	Classroom behavior during free activity: physical aggression	Aggressive cartoon > non-aggressive cartoon = no film

Field Studies; Cartoon or Noncartoon Stimuli; Early Childhood

Study	Subjects	Treatment	Measures	Results
Steuer, Applefield, & Smith (1971)	Preschool M & F	11 days of aggressive or nonaggressive cartoons	Play sessions: 5 children, physical aggression to peers, adult present but inattentive; Baseline (10 days); experimental (11 days)	Aggressive cartoon > nonaggressive cartoon
Stein, Friedrich, et al. (1973)	Preschool M & F	4–12 days of aggressive cartoons, neutral films, or prosocial programs[a]	Play session: 2 children in mildly frustrating task: a) Interpersonal aggression b) Cooperation with peer—adult absent	a) Aggressive cartoon and neutral film more aggressive than prosocial TV—males only; aggressive and prosocial TV > neutral—females only b) Aggressive cartoon less cooperative than neutral and prosocial TV—males only
Stein & Friedrich (1972), Friedrich & Stein (1973)[a]	Preschool M & F	12 days of violent cartoons, neutral films, or prosocial programs[b]	Observation in classroom; free play: a) Interpersonal aggression b) Self-control c) Positive interpersonal behavior; Baseline (7 days); experimental (12 days); postviewing (6 days)	a) Violent cartoons > neutral films only for Ss who were above median on baseline aggression b) Violent cartoon < neutral film c) No difference
Sawin (1974)	Preschool deprived M & F	12 days of noncartoon violent programs vs. neutral programs (not cartoon)	Play sessions: 5 children, aggression to peers, adult sometimes present; Baseline (9 days); experimental (12 days); follow-up (6 days)	Few differences; in first 6 days of viewing, neutral TV increased in aggression more than violent TV; neutral < aggressive TV during baseline

Short-Term Studies; Noncartoon Stimuli; Middle Childhood and Adolescence

Study	Subjects	Treatment	Measures	Results
Liebert & Baron (1972)	5–6-year-old and 8–9-year-old M & F	Brief excerpt of violent TV program vs. neutral program	a) Delivery of noxious stimulus to an anonymous peer through a "hurt" button, adult absent b) Solitary play session—aggression toward objects scored	a) Violent TV group pressed "hurt" button longer than neutral group b) Violent TV group higher than neutral—younger males only
Thomas (1972)	5½–8½-year-old M	1) Excerpt from violent film vs. neutral film vs. no film 2) Field dependence or independence of child	Delivery of noxious stimulus (loud noise) to a known visible adult, second adult present	Aggressive film lower than other 2 groups—field dependent 6½- and 7½-year-olds only

TABLE 1 (Continued)

Author(s) and Date	Subjects	Independent Variables	Dependent Variables	Results
Feshback (1972): Study I	4th–6th-grade M & F	Excerpts of "real" and "fictional" violent films vs. neutral films vs. no film	Same as Thomas (1972)	No difference between violent films and no film
Study II	4th–6th-grade M & F	Excerpt of "real" and "fictional" violent film vs. control groups in Study I	Same as Thomas (1972)	"Real" violent film more aggressive than no film; "fictional" violent film less aggressive than no film
Biblow (1973)	5th-grade M & F	1) Aggressive filmstrip vs. nonaggressive humorous filmstrip vs. control group asked to solve math problems 2) Pretest ratings of fantasy predisposition 3) Pretest observations of aggression and mood ratings in a frustrating situation with peers	Play session—adults present a) Verbal and physical aggression to peers—change from pretest; frustrating session b) Mood ratings—fear, sadness, shame, fatigue, elation, contrition—change from pretest frustrating session	a) For Ss with high predisposition to fantasy, aggression lower after both aggressive and nonaggressive films than for control; for Ss with low fantasy predisposition, aggression nonsignificantly higher after aggressive film than other conditions b) For high-fantasy Ss only, aggressive film led to increased fear, shame, sadness, fatigue; nonaggressive film led to increased elation and decreased fear, sadness, shame, fatigue; no change for controls
Leifer & Roberts (1972): Study I	Kindergarten & 3d-, 6th-, 9th-, & 12th-grade M & F	1 of 6 unedited TV programs varying in adult-rated amount of violence	Response hierarchy questionnaire assessing likelihood of using physical aggression in conflict situations	Choice of physical aggression positively related to the amount of violence in the program viewed
Study II	Preschool & 5th- & 12th-grade M & F (very small Ns)	4 edited violent programs vs. 1 neutral travelogue	Response hierarchy questionnaire	No difference
Collins (1973)	3d-, 6th-, & 10th-grade M & F	Edited violent film vs. neutral travelogue	Response hierarchy questionnaire	No difference
Walters & Thomas (1963)	Adolescent 15-year-old M	Excerpt from violent movie vs. neutral film	Delivery of noxious stimulus: shock to anonymous peer	Violent movie > neutral

Study	Subjects	Independent Variable	Dependent Variable	Results
Leifer & Roberts (1972)	13-year-old M	Same as Walters & Thomas 1963		Nonsignificant tendency for violent movie > neutral
Hartmann (1969)	Adolescent delinquent M	1) 2 films of fights vs. nonviolent film 2) Anger arousal or nonarousal	Same as Walters & Thomas (1963) Delivery of noxious stimulus: shock to provoking peer	1) Violent films > nonviolent film

Field Studies; Noncartoon Stimuli; Adolescence

Study	Subjects	Independent Variable	Dependent Variable	Results
Feshbach & Singer (1971)	8–18-year-old M from middle-class residential schools and lower-class boys' homes	6 weeks violent program diet vs. nonviolent program diet	a) Daily ratings of aggressive behavior by counselors b) Fantasy aggression c) Peer ratings d) Questionnaire measures of aggressive values and preferences Experimental (6 weeks); follow-up (1 week)	a) Nonviolent diet > violent diet; difference increased over time —boys' homes only b) Violent diet > nonviolent diet c) No difference d) Slight tendency for nonviolent diet > violent diet
Wells (1973)	7th–9th-grade M from middle- and lower-class residential schools	6 weeks violent program diet vs. nonviolent diet	Ratings of aggressive behavior by counselors and observations of aggressive behavior by trained researchers a) Physical aggression b) Verbal aggression Baseline (3 weeks); experimental (6 weeks)	a) Violent TV slightly > nonviolent TV b) Nonviolent TV slightly > violent TV
Parke et al. (1974)	14–18-year-old M in penal institutions —American and Belgian samples	5 days of violent movies vs. nonviolent movies; smaller group saw 1 violent or nonviolent movie	Observations of aggressive behavior by trained researchers Baseline (1–3 weeks); experimental (1 or 5 days); follow-up (1–3 weeks)	Violent movies > nonviolent movies—American sample and high-initial-aggression subjects in Belgian sample
Sebastian et al. (1974)	American sample in Parke et al. (1974)	1) Same as Parke et al. (1974) 2) Severe distraction and criticism vs. mild distraction by peer	Verbal aggression and criticism to peer in laboratory situation	1) Violent films > nonviolent films 2) Severe distraction > mild distraction; no interaction of films and distraction

[a] A detailed report of this study appears in Stein and Friedrich (1972). A briefer version is presented in Friedrich and Stein (1973).
[b] Findings for prosocial programs are presented in a later section.

either increases or maintains whatever effects are initially created. Data from small-group play sessions or dyads are most consistent. Observations of naturalistic play in the classroom indicate that long-term changes are most clear-cut for children who are already above average in aggression.

The impact of cartoon violence is important because cartoons are a pervasive part of the television diets of young children across almost all social groupings. Increases in aggression as a result of such viewing appear to occur for both sexes across a wide range of social conditions. Nevertheless, young children also watch a considerable amount of noncartoon violence on television. One field experiment with preschool children (Sawin 1974) was modeled in many respects on the procedures used by Friedrich and Stein (1973), except that noncartoon violent programs were used. For a population of deprived, primarily black children, Sawin (1974) found few differences in aggression in group play during repeated exposure to the "real life" version of "Batman" compared with exposure to a situation comedy. The absence of differences may have been due to a lower interest in the situation comedy, resulting in restlessness in the control group, or to the fact that the "real life" version of "Batman" is much less violent than most cartoons. Finally, deprived black children may react differently than the predominantly middle-class, white samples used in other studies.

Middle childhood.—Developmental changes in middle childhood might lead children to be less affected by television violence than preschool children. Older children have more behavioral and cognitive controls and more ability to distinguish fiction from reality, and are more sensitized to adult values and prohibitions about aggression. Indeed, the literature for this age group presents more contradictory results than do the studies of preschool children, but developmental changes are difficult to infer because of distinct differences in methods. All of the studies of middle childhood are short-term, laboratory-based experiments, and most use measures of aggression that are contrived and considerably removed from natural behavior.

The most frequently used measure involves administration of a noxious stimulus, such as a loud noise or shock to an unseen person in another room. While there is some evidence that behavior on such tasks is related to naturally occurring aggression for both children and adolescents (Hartmann 1969; Williams et al. 1967), these measures are probably subject to a variety of social influences that are specific to the laboratory situation.

It appears that the contradictions in the literature can be best explained as a function of aggression anxiety. To the extent that children have internalized social prohibitions of aggressive behavior, exposure to television violence would be expected to arouse anxiety about aggression as well as instigation to aggressive behavior. (Evidence is presented later that violent television does produce anxiety.) In situations where there are cues suggesting inhibition of aggression, such anxiety might be increased and aggressive behavior inhibited. Where the situation is permissive, aggressive behavior might be more likely. In the experimental studies reviewed, it appears that aggressive behavior increases following violence in situations that are relatively permissive but remains stable or decreases when the situations have many anxiety-arousing cues. Personality differences among children might also lead some children to respond to violence with high anxiety (and hence to inhibit aggressive behavior), while others may react with little anxiety. Again, available evidence suggests that subgroups of children who show increases in aggression appear to be less predisposed to anxiety reactions than those who do not show increases.

The measurement situations in which increased aggression followed television violence appear to have been permissive in at least some of the following ways (see table 1 for specific studies): the person toward whom the aggression was directed was a peer rather than an adult; no adult was present or (in studies with multiple sessions) an unresponsive adult was in the room; observations were collected in a familiar classroom setting where teachers supervised relatively large groups of students; or questionnaires tapping hypothetical responses were administered.

By contrast, in those studies in which aggression either did not increase or declined following viewing, the measurement situations appear anxiety provoking. In some instances, a familiar adult was the target of the aggression (Feshbach 1972; Thomas 1972). Children are certainly socialized to be much more inhibited about being aggressive to adults than to peers. In addition, the children were in an unfamiliar situation outside their classrooms, and an adult experimenter was present. In fact, examination of table 1 indicates that adult presence or absence in situations where children were removed from the classroom is a very good predictor of whether television violence has an effect. Only in studies with multiple sessions did children show increased aggression in the presence of an adult. Some early research (Siegel & Kohn 1959) suggested that preschool children became more aggressive with an adult present than they were without an adult in the room over several sessions, presumably because they interpreted the absence of censure from the adult as permission to behave aggressively. Sawin (1974) varied adult presence or absence and found a similar increase in aggression with an adult present for 3-year-olds, but 4-year-olds showed lower aggression in the presence of an adult than they did with an adult absent. He did not find differences in the effects of the television conditions between adult-present and adult-absent groups, but the numbers of children were very small and adult intervention was frequently necessary in both groups to prevent injury or damage. In any case, it appears that children enter a new situation with the expectation that an adult will disapprove of aggression. In a short-term study with only one session, this expectation probably inhibits aggressive behavior. Where multiple sessions occur and the adult does not react with disapproval, inhibitions on aggression are probably reduced and the effects of television violence appear.

Individual differences in anxiety reactions also predict reactions to television violence. Children who are prone to anxiety are less likely to behave aggressively after seeing violence than those who respond with little anxiety. In one study (Biblow 1973), children were initially observed in an anger-provoking situation. One group was rated high on signs of fear, sadness, contrition, and fatigue, but was fairly nonaggressive. These children, who appeared to be prone to anxiety, became still less aggressive and appeared still more anxious and distressed after seeing a violent film. They were also less aggressive after seeing a funny, nonaggressive film, but they appeared happier and less fearful. Thus, lowered aggression was associated with increased anxiety following the aggressive film; the humor in the nonaggressive film may have defused the instigation to aggression and provided, as well, a pleasant, positive experience.

The children who were relatively aggressive in the initial frustrating task were rated low on signs of anxiety. These children manifested slight, but nonsignificant, increases in aggression following the aggressive film, with no change in apparent anxiety.

Observations of children's emotional reactions while viewing the violent film in the Liebert and Baron (1972) study also suggest that boys who respond to violence with anxiety are less likely to show increased aggression than are those with relatively low anxiety about aggression. Facial expressions while viewing the films were videotaped and analyzed. Boys who appeared sad while viewing were relatively low in aggression; boys who had pleasant and happy expressions were most aggressive. These relationships did not occur, however, for girls (Ekman et al. 1972). It appears, then, that children who are most prone to aggression anxiety are least likely to be aggressive, particularly after exposure to violence. Those with less predisposition to anxiety are likely to behave aggressively if situational constraints are not too great.

Finally, whether or not children manifest increased aggression following exposure to violence probably depends on the age and sex appropriateness of the behavior measured. In the Liebert and Baron (1972) study, children were observed in solitary play with an assortment of toys. Only the younger boys had higher aggression after the violent program, probably because the toys, such as guns and bobo dolls, were less appropriate for older children and for girls.

The discussion thus far suggests that one means of combating the effects of violent television might be arousal of aggression anxiety. However, negative emotional reactions to violence apparently decrease with repeated exposure. In one study (Cline, Croft, & Courrier 1973), children who were frequent television viewers manifested lower physiological arousal while watching a violent film than did infrequent viewers. This finding is consistent with a number of experimental studies demonstrating that people's physiological reactions to unpleasant events gradually decline with repeated exposure (Bandura 1969a; Goranson 1970). Such findings lend credence to many critics' concern that the continued bloodletting and killing on television will harden children to violence in the real world.

Although anxiety reactions to violence apparently become habituated over time, the aggression-arousing effects of violent television do not decline with repeated exposure. If anything, they accumulate. The end result of this process is probably increased aggressive behavior and decreased susceptibility to inhibition of aggression as children watch more and more violence. In discussions of habituation to television violence, it is critical to distinguish between emotional reactivity and behavioral instigation. As emotional reactions decline, behavior instigation and positive attitudes toward aggression are likely to increase.

Summary.—In middle childhood, television violence can instigate aggressive behavior directed at people as well as objects. However, behavioral expression is more likely to be modulated by situational and personality variables for this age group than for preschool children. The laboratory studies of aggressive models indicate that imitation often depends on additional variables such as frustration. In the television studies, the degree to which aggressive behavior increases or is inhibited appears to depend on the anxiety-arousing properties of the testing situation. Aggressive behavior following violent television is most likely when the target is a peer or when the child is responding to a hypothetical situation. It is least likely when the target is a familiar adult. It is more likely when no adult is present than when an adult observes the behavior.

Children who show signs of anxiety and distress when they are exposed to violence or to frustration are less likely to behave aggressively than those who evidence little distress or even positive emotions. These findings are diametrically opposed to the predictions that would be made from catharsis theory. According to that interpretation, positive affect and enjoyment of violence should lead to reduced aggression. Instead, it appears that proneness to aggression anxiety serves to inhibit the behavioral instigation produced by television violence; when such anxiety is minimal, increased aggression is likely. Finally, anxiety reactions are likely to decrease with repeated exposure to violence, whereas aggressive reactions do not decline. This pattern probably results in more aggressive behavior and less anxiety for children who are frequent viewers of violence than for infrequent viewers.

Adolescence.—With greater cognitive sophistication and more internalization of societal prohibitions of aggression, one might expect adolescents to show even less global reaction to television violence than younger children and greater inhibition when the situational and personality variables identified in the previous section are operating. This developmental hypothesis cannot be evaluated on the basis of available experimental studies, because most of the studies of adolescents have used atypical populations and almost all are restricted to males. In addition, the situations used for measurement are similar to those that facilitated the expression of aggression in elementary-age children; none of the measures appears to involve anxiety-arousing conditions.

The short-term studies are consistent in showing increased aggression following exposure to aggressive films. Male adolescents who saw a violent movie segment gave a greater shock to a peer whom they had met briefly than did those who saw a neutral film (Hartmann 1969; Walters & Thomas 1963). In the study reported earlier, Leifer and Roberts (1972) found that, with adolescents of both sexes, physical aggression as a response to hypothetical conflict situations increased with the degree of violence of the television programs they had seen.

Three field experiments investigating more long-term effects have produced conflicting results, however. In each of these experiments, viewing violent or nonviolent films was experimentally manipulated in a natural setting over a period of time, and natural behavior was observed.

In the first experiment of this kind (Feshbach & Singer 1971), boys from 8 to 18 living in residential settings were randomly assigned violent or nonviolent television "diets" for a period of 6 weeks. Counselors and adult supervisors rated the amount of aggression demonstrated by the boys they worked with daily. In three upper-middle-class schools, there were no differences between viewing groups. In four lower-class institutions, aggression of the group with the nonviolent diet increased slightly over the 6 weeks while that of the group with the violent diet decreased.

The end result was that the group watching violent television was significantly less aggressive than the nonviolent viewing group.

A number of methodological reservations make these results difficult to interpret (see Feshbach & Singer [1972] and Liebert, Sobol, & Davidson [1972] for a detailed debate of the interpretation of this study). The two groups differed in aggression from the beginning of the viewing period, and there was no way of knowing whether this difference existed before viewing. Little information was obtained on the amoung of previous television viewing or program preferences, nor was the amount of viewing during the experiment carefully monitored. Complaints from boys receiving the nonviolent diet made it clear, however, that their assigned programs were less attractive than the violent programs. Their increased aggression may have resulted from the resentment generated by deprivation of their television favorites and from boredom created by the unavailability of their usual television fare. When adolescent boys have nothing to do, they are likely to engage in fights, roughhouse play, and complaints.

Fortunately, it is possible to clarify many of the issues raised by the Feshbach and Singer findings because Wells (1973) replicated their study with added controls. A baseline period was included and experimental and control groups were matched on the basis of initial aggression. Television preferences were assessed. Both outside observers and the residential staff rated the boys' behavior, whereas in the Feshbach and Singer study, only the residential staff did so. The age range was limited to boys in the seventh to ninth grades (the predominant age group in the first study). Ten residential schools were studied in different geographic areas. Half were upper middle and middle class; the other half were lower middle and working class.

There were virtually no significant differences in aggressive behavior between the boys in the two television diets. Where differences occurred, boys exposed to the violent diet were slightly higher in physical aggression. Boys receiving the nonviolent diet were slightly more verbally aggressive, but the author suggested that their verbal aggression consisted primarily of complaints about their television fare. Questionnaires indicated that boys liked the violent diet better and that it approximated their usual viewing more closely than did the nonviolent diet. Wells suggested that it might be more appropriate to call the group with the violent diet the control condition and the nonviolent diet group the experimental condition. In fact, both studies appear to investigate deprivation of usual television viewing patterns more than they do the impact of television violence. One reason this deprivation may have had more effects on the lower-class boys in Feshbach and Singer's sample could be that they had more time available to watch television. They lived in "boys' homes" and attended public schools, whereas the middle-class boys in both studies and the lower-class boys studied by Wells attended residential schools. The residential schools structured most of the boys' time, leaving little room for television viewing of any kind. In the boys' homes, there was, apparently, less structure.

Male residents of penal institutions in the United States and Belgium were subjects in a third set of field experiments (Parke et al. 1974). The boys ranged in age from 14 to 18. In each of the three studies, aggressive behavior was rated before, during, and after exposure to five full-length commercial movies shown during a 1-week period. Some groups saw violent films; the others saw nonviolent films. All television viewing was eliminated during the "movie week," and required study hours were canceled. Whole cottages of boys constituted experimental groups, and there were relatively few groups, so the film condition differences are to some extent contaminated with differences in atmosphere, staff, and the like, between cottages as well as differences in baseline levels of aggression. The observers were well-trained members of the research staff. Observations were more objective and less global than those used in previous studies, but the observers were aware of what films the boys were seeing. Nonaggressive films were eventually found that were as appealing as violent ones.

In the Belgian sample, subjects who watched violent movies were more aggressive than nonviolent film viewers only in cottages where the baseline level of aggression was high. Subjects who were initially low in aggression did not differ on the basis of film exposure. In the American sample, aggression in boys who saw the aggressive films increased, while that of boys who saw the nonaggressive films decreased. The viewers of violent films also showed greater verbal aggression toward peers in an experimental task administered at the end of the movie week (Sebastian et al. 1974).

Perhaps the most important contribution of this set of studies is the control of deprivation both by eliminating the usual television viewing for both groups and by selecting films with equal appeal. Thus, where film violence was varied independent of deprivation, naturally occurring aggressive behavior increased as a function of the violence viewed.

Summary.—The results indicate that filmed violence leads to increased aggression for adolescents in laboratory research and in experimental field studies when deprivation of preferred viewing is controlled. These results are derived primarily from males and from atypical populations ranging from boys in preparatory schools to institutionalized delinquent boys.

3. Summary

Across age groups, the predominant finding is that television violence instigates aggressive behavior. In laboratory studies where there are few additional variables to cloud the picture, children and adolescents consistently show increased aggression after viewing aggressive models. When real television programs are used, the same pattern occurs except where situational factors appear likely to inhibit aggressive behavior or where control groups have experienced frustration. Repeated exposure leads to increased aggression under most circumstances, but anxiety reactions to violence appear to decline with increased viewing.

D. EFFECTS OF TELEVISION VIOLENCE ON BEHAVIOR OTHER THAN AGGRESSION

The narrow focus of most studies of the effects of television violence on aggressive behavior may result in loss of information about the impact of television violence on other aspects of children's behavior. Prosocial behavior, self-control, ability to delay gratification, fear, anxiety, and dreams represent areas of children's functioning that might be influenced.

1. Prosocial Behavior

Viewing violence sometimes leads to decreased cooperation, helping, sharing, and the like, but mainly in situations involving frustration or conflict. In two studies discussed earlier in which boys who had seen violent cartoons showed reduced cooperation or sharing, the situations involved frustration or conflict (Hapkiewitz & Roden 1971; Stein, Friedrich, et al. 1973). In a third study, however, groups of children who had seen a war film manifested reduced constructiveness of play and reduced social interaction (Noble 1970). As the film was a war documentary rather than a cartoon, these changes may have reflected anxiety arousal rather than reduced disposition to prosocial behavior. In a task that did not involve interpersonal conflict, Liebert and Baron (1972) found no differences in the amount of helping exhibited by children who had seen violent and nonviolent television. Similarly, Friedrich and Stein (1973) found no differences in prosocial interpersonal behavior (free play) between groups which saw violent television and those which saw neutral films.

Self-control and willingness to tolerate delay were negatively affected by violent television in the Friedrich and Stein (1973) study. For children who saw violent television, their tolerance of delays in receiving things they needed or wanted dropped rather dramatically. Their willingness to accept responsibility for behavior in accord with rules of the nursery school without adult supervision also declined.

2. Fear, anxiety, and dreams

Some types of violence frighten young children, but fear reactions vary greatly, depending on the context of the violence. Violent programs led to greater physiological arousal than did nonviolent programs for preschool children in one study (Osborn & Endsley 1971). The children also stated that the violent scenes were more "scary." The program showing human violence led to more arousal than did cartoon violence, but this is probably due to the content rather than the format. The human film depicted a grandmother being strangled in front of a child; the cartoon portrayed "Spiderman" trapped in a cave. Siegel (1956) also found that preschool children manifested more observable signs of anxiety during an aggressive cartoon than during a nonaggressive cartoon. About half of the first graders interviewed by Lyle and Hoffman (1972a) said that they were sometimes frightened by television. The programs they feared were the "chiller-monster" types, not other forms of violence. The authors point out that these same programs were often favorites of young children, so in some instances fear may have an attractive, tantalizing quality.

About one-third of Lyle and Hoffman's (1972a) first-grade sample said they sometimes dreamed about television, but experimental studies of the dreams of older elementary school children show little effect of television violence (Foulkes, Belvedere, & Brubaker 1972). In two studies of elementary school boys, there were no indications that boys who saw violent Westerns had dreams that were more hostile or frightening than those of boys who saw nonviolent programs, nor were there differences between subjects who were very heavy home viewers of violence and those who were very infrequent home viewers. These studies leave a host of questions to be answered. If frightening dreams are stimulated by television programs, this effect would be more likely for younger children and in response to the monster-chiller programs that children consider most frightening. Thus, the negative results of Foulkes et al. (1972) do not exclude the possibility of television influences on dreams. Studies are needed in which both initial emotional reactions and subsequent dreams are assessed.

3. Summary

In addition to the effects of television violence on aggressive behavior reviewed earlier, violence also apparently leads to reduced self-control and tolerance for frustration as well as fear and anxiety for many children. In some situations, positive interpersonal interactions are reduced as well.

E. SOME COMMENTS ON METHODS

Before we proceed to the correlational studies, some remarks on various methods of study are in order. The laboratory experiment is often viewed as the preferred method by psychologists. It has the virtue of control over independent variables that permits causal inference, but generalizations to natural settings are limited because of the time constraints and artificial nature of most experiments. Correlational studies permit assessment of naturally occurring relationships, but they lack precise controls, and causal inferences are at best controversial. The field experiment appears at first glance to be the ultimate method because it combines the advantages of experimental control with observation of behavior in natural settings over a period of time. Although field experiments have produced some valuable results, there are serious problems that do not occur in other types of studies. When you intervene arbitrarily in people's lives by governing what they watch on television over a period of time, there are many side effects that are difficult to assess. Violent and nonviolent programs often have differential appeal; the resulting frustration and dissatisfaction become greatly magnified when viewing extends over a period of time. If naturally occurring groups such as cottages or classrooms are used, individuals cannot be randomly assigned to conditions. Baseline levels of behavior in the groups often differ, and it is very difficult to interpret results when this occurs. It is impossible to separate television effects on individuals from group processes that may spread the effects. Television viewing cannot occur under completely natural circumstances; subjects must be either taken to a special area for viewing or instructed about what to watch. Either process focuses attention on television. The unique advantage of the correlational method is the absence of interference in the process being studied. Correlational studies provide information about the naturally occurring relation between viewing violent television and aggressive behavior without the distortions introduced by experimental interventions in subjects' lives.

Our intention here is not to discount the value of the field experiment but to point out some of the problems unique to this method and perhaps to caution future investigators. The soundest conclusions can still be drawn from a combination of methods, so that the advantages and disadvantages of each at least partially compensate for one another.

F. CORRELATIONAL STUDIES

The correlational studies attempting to relate television violence viewing to aggression are summarized in table 2. Two indices of viewing were

TABLE 2

CORRELATIONAL STUDIES RELATING VIOLENT TELEVISION VIEWING TO BEHAVIOR

Author(s) and Date	Subjects	Measure of Viewing	Measure of Behavior	Relation[b]		
				Male	Female	Both
Stein & Friedrich (1972), Friedrich & Stein (1973)[c]	Preschool M & F	Frequency and preferences: parent report	Observations in nursery school	0	0	
Eron (1963)	3d-grade M & F	Preferences: parent report	Peer ratings	+	0	
Lefkowitz et al. (1972), Eron et al. (1972)[e]	13th-grade M & F	Preference: 1) 3d-grade parent report 2) 13th-grade self-report	a) Peer ratings in 13th grade	1a) +	1a) 0	
			b) Self-reported antisocial behavior	1b) +	1b) 0	
			c) MMPI: scales indicating aggressive tendencies and lack of behavior controls (scales 4 and 9)	1c) + 2a) 0 2b) 0 2c) 0	1c) 0 2a) 0 2b) 0 2c) 0	
McIntyre & Teevan (1972)	7th–12th-grade M & F	1) Preference: 4 favorite programs	Self-reported: a) Aggressive deviance	1a) 0		+[d]
			b) Serious delinquent behavior	1b)		+++
			c) Petty delinquent behavior	1c)		
			d) Approval of violence	1d)		
Lovibond (1967)	6th–7th-grade M	Preference	Attitudes: approval of force and violence	+		
Robinson & Bachman (1972)	13th-grade M	Preference	Self-reported: a) Aggression b) Serious delinquent acts	a) ++ b) +		

| | | | | | Relation[b] | |
Author(s) and Date	Subjects	Measure of Viewing[a]	Measure of Behavior		Male	Female	Both
Chaffee & McLeod (1971)......6th–10th-grade M & F		Preference	Self-reported aggression		0	0	0
McLeod et al. (1972a).........7th- & 10th-grade M & F		Frequency	Self-reported aggression		+	+	+
McLeod et al. (1972b).........6th- & 9th-grade M & F		1) Frequency 2) Past frequency	a) Self-reported aggression	1a)	+	+	+
				1b)	+	+	+
			b) Ratings of aggression by others	2a)	+	+	+
				2b)	0	0	+
			c) Positive attitudes about aggression	1c)	0	0	+
				2c)	+	0	+
Dominick & Greenberg (1972)..4th–6th-grade M & F		Frequency	a) Approval of aggression	a)	+[e]	0	
			b) Willingness to use violence	b)	+[e]	+	
			c) Suggested violent solutions	c)	+	+	
			d) Perceived effectiveness of violence	d)	+	+	

[a] Preference ratings are generally based on the amount of violence in the individual's three or four favorite programs. Frequency is based on the subjects' reports of viewing selected violent and nonviolent programs.
[b] Plus sign indicates a significant positive correlation; zero indicates a nonsignificant correlation.
[c] The first reference is a detailed report. The second reference is a briefer, more widely available report.
[d] Correlations not reported separately by sex.
[e] Middle class only.

used: preference for violent programs and frequency of viewing violence. In the few instances where both indices were used, they are only modestly related to one another (Chaffee & McLeod 1971; Stein & Friedrich 1972), perhaps because different ways of measuring each produce somewhat different results (Bechtel et al. 1972). Although Chaffee (1972) argued that frequency of viewing violence was more consistently related to aggression than was preference, our summary of the evidence suggests that preference for violence is also associated with aggression, particularly for males. The correlational studies provide information on attitudes and beliefs about aggression as well as about aggressive and deviant behavior.

1. Aggressive Attitudes

Children and adolescents who are heavy viewers of violence are more likely to approve of it and consider it an effective means of conflict resolution than are light viewers. In a study of middle- and lower-class boys and girls (Dominick & Greenberg 1972), correlations between viewing violence and several measures of attitudes about aggression were found, but the most consistent findings appeared for middle-class boys and the least consistent findings for lower-class boys. The relative absence of findings for lower-class boys may have been due to ceiling effects on the measures of aggressive attitudes or to a lack of refinement in the measure of viewing frequency. Because lower-class boys view more violence in general, the extremes of violence viewing may not have been discriminated from more moderate viewing levels. The measure which was most extensively related to television violence for all groups was the perceived effectiveness of violence. As the authors note, "Television violence works, for both the good guys and the bad guys; it gets things done" (Dominick & Greenberg 1972, p. 331).

Using a more refined measure of viewing frequency, McLeod et al. (1972b) found that exposure to violent television was related to positive attitudes about aggression for a sample of males and females of varying social class. The children's estimates of their past viewing of television violence were also associated with positive attitudes about aggression. Finally, adolescents whose favorite programs were quite violent approved of aggression more than did adolescents with nonviolent favorites (McIntyre & Teevan 1972).

These positive attitudes to aggression are likely to lead to aggressive behavior and to openness to learning and imitating violence when it is observed. Among adolescents, aggressive attitudes were positively related to both self-reports and peer ratings of aggressive behavior (McLeod et al. 1972b). Hicks (1968a, 1968b, 1971) demonstrated that elementary school girls' attitudes about aggression were good predictors of how much they would learn and perform aggression demonstrated by a model.

2. Realism and Learning

Despite the fact that older children and adults know that television drama is fiction, they frequently report learning modes of behavior to be used in their own lives; they also report that they consider television to be a realistic portrayal of life. Heavy viewers of television violence learn violent solutions, and they perceive violence as more realistic than do light viewers. McLeod et al. (1972a, 1972b) found that the more violent were the programs their subjects watched, the more aggression they reported learning from television. One-third of the adolescents studied by McIntyre and Teevan (1972) believed their favorite television shows were true to life regardless of whether these programs were fictional or real. In three other studies of adolescents, heavy viewers of violence considered violence more realistic than did light viewers (Lefkowitz et al. 1972; McLeod et al. 1972a, 1972b).

Adults who watch a lot of television are also more likely to believe the picture of the world presented than are light viewers. When a large sample of adults were asked factual questions about matters that are frequently distorted in television programs, heavy television viewers differed from light viewers in overestimating the percentage of crimes that are violent, the probability that they would be personally involved in violence, and the percentage of the population employed as law enforcement officials (Gross 1974).

Even for relatively mature people, therefore, the messages of television that violence is pervasive and that violence is an effective and positive means of goal attainment do have an impact. People who watch a lot of violent television are more likely to approve of aggression, to see it as an effective mode of conflict resolution, and to believe that it represents the real world.

3. Aggressive Behavior

There is a modest, but consistent, positive relation between viewing violence and aggressive behavior as reported either by the subject or by others who know him. The correlations in most studies range from .10 to .32. Given the many factors affecting aggressive behavior, it would be surprising if very high correlations occurred. The fact that violent television viewing is a significant predictor despite all the variations contributed by other factors suggests that the relation is a powerful one.

The frequency of viewing violence was positively related to self-reported aggression in samples in both Maryland and Wisconsin studied by McLeod et al. (1972a, 1972b). The relation held for both sexes from sixth to tenth grade. Ratings of aggression were also made by peers, teachers, and parents for the Wisconsin sample (McLeod et al. 1972b). All of these ratings, except those made by parents, were positively related to watching television violence. The intercorrelations of the different ratings of aggression were moderate. Peer ratings were more similar to self-ratings than were assessments by teachers. Parent ratings were negatively related to self-ratings.

It is likely that peers have a better opportunity to observe the aggressive behavior of adolescents than do parents and teachers, so these findings probably reflect real differences in behavior in different settings. In the Wisconsin sample (McLeod et al. 1972b), subjects' reports of past violence viewing were also related to self-reported aggression and to others' reports of aggression at about the same level of magnitude as current violence viewing. Preference for violence was not related to aggression in the Maryland sample (Chaffee & McLeod 1971).

Among the junior and senior high school students studied by McIntyre and Teevan (1972), however, the amount of violence in their favorite programs was related to self-reports of aggressive behavior and to reports of serious deviant behavior, such as encounters with the police. A similar pattern appeared in a survey of 19-year-old males (Robinson & Bachman 1972). Self-reports of aggressive behavior and of serious delinquent acts were associated with preferences for violent television programs. It is particularly interesting that 44% of their sample could not name three favorite programs. Those subjects with little television involvement had patterns of aggression that were similar to males whose favorites were low in violent content.

In one study of preschool children (Friedrich & Stein 1973; Stein & Friedrich 1972), the present authors obtained from mothers measures of both preference for violent programs and frequency of viewing. There was no relation between home viewing and observed aggression in the nursery school. As aggressive behavior was affected by small amounts of viewing in the nursery school, it is likely that the lack of relation to home viewing was due to the situation specificity of young children's behavior. In addition, there is some question, given the popularity of cartoons for this age group, of how discriminating the mothers' reports of violent preferences and frequency of viewing were.

While both preference for and frequency of viewing violent television are associated with aggressive behavior, the thorny issue is, of course, the causal direction to be inferred, if any. It could be argued that these studies demonstrate the effects of television violence on behavior or that they show that aggressive children are likely to select violent programs, or both. Perhaps the most ambitious effort to derive causal inferences was a 10-year longitudinal study (Eron et al. 1972; Lefkowitz et al. 1972) in which television preferences and peer-rated aggressive behavior were assessed at the third, eighth, and thirteenth grades. As the eighth-grade sample was relatively small, the principal points of focus were the third and thirteenth grades. In the third grade, there was a positive correlation ($r = .21$) of preference for violent television and aggressive behavior for boys. The boys' third-grade preferences for violent television were even more strongly related to their aggressive behavior 10 years later ($r = .31$). Aggression in both the third and thirteenth grades was unrelated to thirteenth-grade television preferences. Television preferences were not related to aggression for girls. For boys, the authors inferred that violent television preferences lead to aggressive behavior rather than the reverse. They suggested that violence has a cumulative effect that shows up more over time than it does when aggression is measured at the same point in time as the viewing. Their findings that third-grade violence viewing also predicted eighth-grade aggression ($r = .16$), but eighth-grade viewing did not, is consistent with this argument.

The causal inferences drawn from this study have aroused considerable controversy. The interested reader may find the methodological pros and cons discussed in Becker (1972), Howitt (1972), Kaplan (1972), Kay (1972), Kenny (1972), and Neale (1972). For our purposes, it is not necessary to rest our case on this study alone. The mere correlation over a 10-year period is impressive, particularly in view of the fact that third-grade television preferences were better predictors of late adolescent aggression than were several child-rearing variables, social status, educational variables, and other personality characteristics measured in the third grade.

The search for a one-way causal link in the correlational studies is undoubtedly an oversimplification. It is much more likely that the two variables affect each other in a two-way fashion. Nevertheless, many defenders of current television content attempt to dismiss the correlational findings by making the opposite one-way causal argument: that high aggression leads children and adolescents to watch television violence. They reason that causation cannot be inferred from correlations, and it is unlikely that television has one-way effects on passive viewers; therefore, aggressive children must choose violent media experiences (Klapper 1968). However, this argument is as oversimplified as the other. If violent television content and viewer characteristics both contribute to the correlation, then each contributes to the outcome in a "causal" fashion. Together, they produce a result that probably would not occur without both components. If television content were changed, the outcome might be different even though viewer characteristics are also important. We will present evidence later to show that this appears to be exactly the case. The more aggressive a child is, the more likely that child is to seek out violent television *and* the more likely that child is to show increased aggression as a result of seeing that violent television. Aggression predisposes not only choice of the medium but imitation of it as well.

The correlation between violence viewing and aggression does not appear to be a result of some third variable that is associated with both. That is, it is possible that viewing violence and aggression might be associated because both are more typical of lower-social-class children than middle-class children, or that both are more typical of children whose parents are aggressive than those with nonaggressive parents rather than because they are directly related to each other. Various studies of elementary and adolescent children have examined social class, IQ, school achievement, age, parental aggression, parental warmth, restrictiveness, punitiveness, aspirations for the child, parental viewing of violence, control of television viewing, and styles of family communication as possible "third variables" (Chaffee & McLeod 1972; Lefkowitz et al. 1972; McIntyre & Teevan 1972). None of them accounts for the relation of television violence to aggressive behavior. The third-variable hypothesis can never be fully disproved because there are always unexamined third variables, but the evidence cited strongly indicates that the correlation of viewing and aggression is not due to a third variable.

G. SUMMARY

The correlational and experimental studies indicate that viewing violence often instigates aggressive behavior. Such viewing is also associated with positive attitudes toward violence and with the belief that events on television reflect reality. These effects occur across a wide age range for both sexes and for children from varying social class backgrounds. The fact that the same findings result from differing methods and measures strengthens the conclusion drawn; although methodological weaknesses can be identified in any study, the strengths and weaknesses across studies fall in different areas. There is virtually no evidence that violence reduces aggressive behavior tendencies through catharsis. Under the most carefully controlled laboratory conditions, aggressive models lead consistently to increased aggressive behavior. In studies involving more complex sets of variables, manifestations of behavioral aggression following violence viewing appear to be influenced by situational and personality differences that may inhibit or permit such behavior.

Developmental changes are difficult to infer because the methods used at various age levels are so different. Preschool children have been studied in experimental settings, small-group play sessions, and natural environments in both short- and long-term experiments. Cartoon violence is associated with increased aggression in most of these studies, and there is little evidence of inhibition among young children. For elementary school children, the findings are mixed. While it is possible that increased behavior controls and cognitive sophistication enable children in this age range to inhibit aggression better than younger children, this conclusion cannot be drawn with any certainty, because all of the studies are short-term investigations with laboratory measures. Situational variables, such as expectations of adult disapproval, are particularly likely to operate in laboratory settings. Positive associations of aggression with viewing violence appear in the correlational studies and in those laboratory experiments where the situation is relatively permissive, but do not appear where the situation appears to be anxiety arousing. Individual differences in anxiety reactions to violence also appear to affect aggressive responses at this age.

The adolescent findings indicate fairly clearly that the effects of television violence do not decrease linearly with age. Most of the experimental and correlational studies show positive associations. Aggression is associated with natural viewing of violence in correlational studies, and it increases in experimental studies in which violent and control films are equal in appeal. Results occur for normal males and females, but they are more pronounced for males who are delinquent or highly aggressive.

Although viewing violence has immediate effects on aggressive behavior of adolescents as well as younger children, there is some evidence that both aggressive attitudes and aggressive behavior patterns are built up over time as a function of long-term exposure to high levels of violence. Some short-term longitudinal studies are needed in which cohort effects are controlled, intervals between measurement are short, and similar measures are used at different age levels. Such studies could clarify developmental patterns.

Finally, the narrow focus of most of the research leaves open questions about what characteristics of the violent stimulus are important as well as what other kinds of behavior may be affected. More refined coding of violent content such as that done by Leifer and Roberts (1972) is needed. In addition, some investigators have suggested that other types of content, such as competition (Feshbach 1973), may induce aggression. Similarly, a much wider range of characteristics, including self-control, positive forms of social interaction, and fear, may be affected by violence.

IV. FACTORS AFFECTING THE RELATION OF VIOLENCE TO BEHAVIOR

Although violent television can instigate aggressive behavior over a wide span of time and settings, many factors increase or decrease the likelihood that such behavior will be learned or acted out. Several of these factors are examined in the following section. The first set are individual differences—sex, habitual level of aggression, degree of motivational arousal, and age. Characteristics of the program itself, such as motives and consequences portrayed for violent action, the use of animation, and the depiction of violence as fictional or real, are then examined. Finally, family influences are discussed.

A. INDIVIDUAL DIFFERENCES IN RESPONSES TO VIOLENT TELEVISION

1. Sex Differences

Although females of almost every age watch less violent television and are less aggressive than their male counterparts, most of the evidence suggests that they are equally susceptible to aggressive models and to violent television. Experimental and correlational studies using real television or movie content have found relationships when both sexes were studied (see tables 1 and 2). The comparability of findings is surprising, partially because the focus on physical aggression in assessments of both television content and subjects' behavior is less appropriate for females than for males. Such assessments may underestimate relations for females, because verbal aggression and other more sex-appropriate forms are generally not measured.

The fact that many researchers have studied only males—and no studies of aggression are limited to females—reflects the assumption that males are more likely to be affected by aggressive models. Although females are also affected by exposure to violence, social concern is properly directed at males because females start from a much lower base level and are, therefore, less likely to be aroused to extremes of violent or delinquent behavior. In addition, relatively high aggression for females may be more adaptive than it is for males. On a continuum of interpersonal aggression that includes both males and females, the more aggressive females and the less aggressive males are near the middle of the curve. Moderate assertiveness probably characterizes these individuals. Those at the low end (mainly female) are extremely timid, and those at the high end (mainly male) engage in frequent uncontrolled, impulsive physical attacks. This hypothesis is similar to Maccoby's (1966) suggestion that extremes of passivity and activity are maladaptive for females and males, respectively.

Although both males and females become more aggressive on the limited measures used, there may be even greater effects for females on measures of aggressive behavior that are more sex appropriate. It is only when such dimensions as anxiety, irritability, tolerance of delay, and other more subtle forms of behavior are measured that the range of impact of violent television can be assessed. In addition, females who develop positive attitudes toward aggression as a result of television viewing may approve and encourage aggressive behavior in their children when they become mothers. Thus, the more subtle forms of hostility and attitude change in females which may be fed by violent television may also multiply through later generations.

2. Habitual Levels of Aggression

The report of the Surgeon General's Scientific Advisory Committee (1972) concluded that television violence was most likely to affect children who were already relatively high in aggressive behavior. In several studies furnishing information about habitual levels of aggression, television violence had a greater effect on the more aggressive children and adolescents (Friedrich & Stein 1973; Parke et al. 1974; Robinson & Bachman 1972; Stein & Friedrich 1972; Steuer et al. 1971; Wells 1973).

Although violent television appears to have its greatest impact on individuals who are already aggressive, the effects are not limited to this group. Many studies have found relations for the entire sample. Furthermore, the "highly aggressive" children who are most susceptible are not a highly deviant minority. They are frequently a rather large segment of the samples studied. They are above average in aggression but definitely within the "normal" range.

Defenders of television violence sometimes attempt to dismiss the possibility that television violence is harmful to society as a whole because of the greater reaction shown by aggressive children (Baker & Ball 1969; Efron 1972). Contrary to logic, they suggest that such children would be aggressive in any case, or that society should not regulate a condition that affects only a portion of the population with poor behavior controls. Of course, society does regulate many things that are harmful only to a minority, such as tobacco, alcohol, and speeding on the highway. The physical harm that may be done by an already violent minority inspired to new and greater acts of violence by television is of considerable social concern.

3. Motivational States of the Observer

A person who is angry or frustrated may be particularly attentive to film violence and especially prone to imitate it. In research with college males, it has repeatedly been demonstrated that an aggressive film is most likely to lead to aggressive behavior for subjects who have been angered. The person to whom the aggression is directed is the person who made the subject angry. In most of those studies, subjects who are not angered do not show increased aggression when they see a violent film (Berkowitz 1970; Goranson 1970).

Whether frustration leads children to imitate aggression more easily is open to question. Of four experimental studies varying both frustration and exposure to aggressive models (Hanratty et al. 1972; Kuhn et al. 1967; Mussen & Rutherford 1961; Savitsky et al. 1971), only Hanratty et al. (1972) found any effects of frustration. In some instances, however, the frustrations were very mild; in others, frustration consisted of reprimands from an adult that would probably lead children to inhibit aggressive reactions.

There is some evidence that participation in competition increases children's imitation. Christy et al. (1971) found that boys who experienced competition imitated either an aggressive or an active nonaggressive model more than did boys who did not experience competition. A similar trend appeared in an earlier study (Nelson et al. 1969). While the authors considered competition frustrating, this interpretation is questionable because the effects were similar regardless of whether the child succeeded or failed. It appears more reasonable that competition is generally arousing, especially for males.

In the studies where either frustration or competition led to high levels of imitation, the arousal *followed* exposure to the models. Thus, learning occurred under neutral conditions; arousal affected performance of already learned behavior. These findings confirm Bandura's (1969b) prediction that modeled behavior patterns are learned and stored even when they are not immediately used; when reinforcement conditions are favorable or emotional arousal occurs, the learned behavior serves as a guide to action.

4. Age Changes in Preference for Violence

In the previous section we concluded that behavioral reactions to television violence occur from preschool through adolescence. There is some evidence for cumulative, long-range effects of violence as children grow up (e.g., Lefkowitz et al. 1972). In addition, enjoyment or preference for violent content increases with age. Television producers often claim that violence is necessary to attract audiences; it may be that this taste for violence is cultivated as a child matures in the wasteland. Among the preschool children interviewed by Lyle and Hoffman (1972b), cartoons were the only category of programs in which preferences increased from age 3 to 5. Preferences for "Sesame Street," by contrast, declined. Comparisons of first, sixth, and tenth graders again indicated an increase in preference for "adult" violent programs with age. Tenth graders especially liked the "hip, youth-oriented" types of violent programs, but they also more often liked cop shows, Westerns, and movies than did younger children (Lyle & Hoffman 1972a). These changes in preference may be partly due to other elements in the content of the programs. Violence is more often contained in programs with appealing identification figures and "mature" plot lines designed for adolescents and adults than in programming that appeals to elementary school age children.

The findings from a study by Katzman (1972) suggest that violence itself is less appealing and more disturbing to younger children. Violent and nonviolent versions of the same television program were produced by editing 3 minutes of content. Fourth-grade boys liked the low-violence version better than the high-violence version; sixth and ninth graders liked both equally well. Fourth graders perceived both versions as more violent than did the older boys. Moreover, the younger boys learned more from the low-violence version; sixth graders learned equally well from both; and ninth graders learned more from the violent version. This pattern is consistent with the notion that older boys react to violence with less anxiety than do younger children.

Although firm conclusions cannot be drawn, it appears likely that some of the age changes in preference for violence result from habituation over the course of repeated exposure to violent programming. As children become accustomed to small amounts of violence, they may seek more dramatic instances in their entertainment for renewed excitement. The current trend of extreme brutality and sadism in movies may be an extreme outcome of this type of habituation on the part of the adult population. More research is definitely needed to separate the impact of cumulative exposure from other developmental and social changes.

B. CHARACTERISTICS OF THE PROGRAM

1. Consequences and Motives Portrayed

Television industry spokesmen often justify the portrayal of criminal and violent acts by pointing out that the villain is ultimately punished (Baker & Ball 1969). As we have seen, violence and illegal activities on television are rewarded with success as often as they are punished. Even those instances that are punished probably arouse aggression in young viewers.

Laboratory studies of consequences to the model.—Imitative behavior is more likely if the model is rewarded and less likely if the model is punished (Bandura 1965; Bandura et al. 1963b). When an aggressive model receives no consequences, children imitate as much as those who have seen an aggressive model rewarded (Bandura 1965). Other studies have replicated this difference for white children, but it is less consistent for black children (Rosekrans & Hartup 1967; Thelen 1971; Thelen & Soltz 1969).

Reward or punishment to a model may affect imitative behavior because it tells the child what consequences to expect in the same situation. This information is especially important in a laboratory setting where the child's play situation is similar to the film and an adult is in charge. One study found that it was only the children who expected to be placed in a situation similar to that of the model who were affected by observed consequences (Thelen et al. 1972).

Punishment to a model does not inhibit learning of the observed behavior. Children who saw an aggressive model punished remembered just as much of his behavior as those who had seen reward or no consequences (Bandura 1965). When children observed an adult stating preferences for different objects, they recalled the preferences of a punished adult at least as well as those of an adult who received no consequences. In one case, punishment to the model actually increased recall (Liebert & Fernandez 1970a; Liebert, Sobol, & Copeman 1972).

On the basis of this laboratory work, several questions can be raised about the salience of reward and punishment to television characters. If consequences to models serve as indicators of what would happen to children in similar situations, then generalization will be very limited. Program settings are often distant in time and locale from children's environments. The instigating effects of violence generalize broadly across situations and behaviors. If consequences draw attention to behavior, they may, in some instances, increase learning of violent or deviant acts. Finally, the link between behavior and punishment in many television programs may be confounded by stupidity or cowardice on the part of the villain. The message learned may be that stupid and weak people get caught, not that violent and criminal acts are punished.

Consequences and motives in real television programs. —Investigators have sought to answer some of these questions by examining children's understanding and behavioral reactions to varying motives and consequences for violence as they are portrayed in real television programs (Leifer & Roberts 1972). Motives as well as consequences were included because numerous studies of college men indicate that aggressive reactions are more likely when filmed violent acts are justified (in the service of good) than when they are not justified (Berkowitz 1970; Goranson 1970).

In a cross-sectional study of children from kindergarten through twelfth grade, six television programs were selected in which the motives and consequences varied from predominantly positive to predominantly negative. Understanding both motives and consequences increased with age in a linear fashion. The youngest children understood very little of either. In a second study, programs were edited to produce versions in which the motives and consequences were consistent and clear, but young children still failed to understand many of the motives and consequences.

Later work by Collins, Berndt, and Hess (1973) suggests that one reason for this lack of understanding is the inability to understand means-end relations. Another reason may be difficulty in distinguishing relevant from incidental content. Elementary-school-age children are inclined to notice and remember more incidental information from a film or a television program than are adolescents (Collins 1970; Hale, Miller, & Stevenson 1968). Adolescents usually remember content that is central to the plot, although no age differences were found in one study (Katzman 1972). Finally, the separation in time between a violent action and the motives and consequences associated with it may make it difficult for young children to make the connections. In one study (Collins 1973), third-grade children were more aggressive when they saw a program in which negative motives and consequences were separated from a violent action by commercials than when they saw the entire plot uninterrupted. Sixth- and ninth-grade children were not affected by the temporal separation, but for younger children it appears that this separation obscured the message that violence was unjust and was punished. When the criminal is caught or killed in the last 2 minutes of a program, many children may not connect this consequence with his violent actions in the early part of the story.

The second purpose of Leifer and Roberts's (1972) research was to determine whether motives and consequences affect children's dispositions to behave aggressively. Using the response hierarchy questionnaire, they found that positive or negative consequences for aggression in television programs had no effect on children's choice of aggression as a conflict solution at any age from 5 to 17. (The reader may recall that these choices did vary with the amount of violence in the programs.)

There were also no differences in aggressive choices associated with motivations for aggression as portrayed in complete television programs. When programs were edited so that each contained only good or bad motives, elementary school children showed slightly increased aggression after seeing good motives depicted and somewhat decreased aggression after viewing bad motives. In another study the winner of a filmed boxing match was described as justified or unjustified. High school students responded more aggressively when the violence was described as justified. Fourth and seventh graders did not react differentially, but there were differences in the expected direction when their perceptions of the justification for violence were examined. Thus, their behavior may have been affected by the justification they perceived, but they did not perceive what was intended by adults.

Not only do negative consequences in television often fail to inhibit aggression, but in some instances showing the pain involved in violence may increase it. In a study of adolescent male delinquents, Hartmann (1969) showed two versions of a fight—one focused on the victor's aggressive actions, the other on the loser's painful reactions. When the subjects were angered, they were subsequently more aggressive after seeing the "pain cues" version than the successful aggression version. Nonangered subjects were more aggressive after the successful aggression film. In short, for a population that is already highly aggressive, it appears that showing pain may arouse aggressive behavior under certain circumstances. Some studies of adults have found reduced aggression when blood and pain are shown (Goranson 1970), but, as our earlier discussion indicated, it is possible that repeated exposure might desensitize people to such unpleasant consequences.

Summary.—Unpleasant consequences or bad motives for violence performed by a television character do little to reduce the impact of his aggressive behavior. Before adolescence, children do not understand very well the intended motives and consequences for behavior. Even when they have some understanding, there is little change in their aggressive response tendencies. Adolescents understand program content better. They are somewhat more likely to be influenced by the motives portrayed for violence, but consequences have little effect.

2. Format of the Program: Cartoons versus Real People

It is sometimes suggested that cartoons have less effect on children's behavior than films of real people because the cartoons are more obviously fictional. Neither theory nor empirical data support this argument. The only study in which the same content has been presented in both formats found that imitation was slightly greater when the model was portrayed as a cartoon-like animal on a television set than when she was dressed as an adult (Bandura et al. 1963a). In television programs, the rates of violence in cartoons are two to three times the rates in noncartoons, so cartoons differ from noncartoons in frequency of violence as well as use of animation and related techniques. In the studies reviewed earlier, increased aggression occurred more consistently following cartoons than it did after programs with real people. At this stage, there is no reason to think that cartoons have less effect than films of people. They may have greater effects on preschool children, but the two formats need to be compared with controls for content before conclusions can be drawn.

3. Fictional versus Real Violence

In two studies discussed earlier (Feshbach 1972), filmed violence that was real was compared with fiction. In the first, real and fictional films of war scenes and campus riots were shown. None of the films led to differences from the no-film group. In a second study, children were shown one campus riot film with instructions indicating that it was real or fictional. Subjects who were told the riot was real were more aggressive than the no-film group; those who thought it was fictional were less aggressive than the no-film group. We proposed earlier that the lower aggression of the fictional violence condition may have resulted from anxiety-arousing conditions in the measurement situation. Why, then, should the real violence increase aggression even in this threatening situation?

Meyer's (1972) study of adult subjects provides one possible answer. Meyer compared the responses of male college students to real and fictional war scenes. Within each type, the violence was presented as justified or unjustified. After being angered, the subjects were more aggressive following justified violence, regardless of whether it was real or fictional. Those who were told it was unjustified did not differ from control groups. In the campus riot film used by Feshbach, most of the violence was committed by the police. It is possible that children perceived the violence as more justified when they were told it was a real event than when they were told it was made in Hollywood. In any case, the absence of differences between real and fictional films for adults suggests that some other variable accounts for the differences shown by children. Further study of the effects of reality versus fiction is badly needed.

C. FAMILY INFLUENCES

It is commonly assumed that parents have a stronger impact on children than does television. We often believe that, if parents provide clear values and use effective socialization techniques to discourage aggression, their children will not be much affected by television violence. On the other hand, the notion of a "socialization void" has been proposed (Surgeon General's Scientific Advisory Committee 1972). Where parents provide little guidance, children may acquire much of their social learning from television.

Strong parental disapproval of violence probably counteracts some of the effects of violent television, but the relative weight of parental socialization may not be as great as has been supposed, particularly for young children. In three experimental studies, children watched an aggressive film with an adult who either approved, disapproved, or made no comments about the model's behavior. For children from 5 to 8, aggressive imitation in a subsequent play session was affected by the adult reactions only if the adult was still present (Hicks 1968a). If the adult was absent, previous disapproval did not reduce imitative aggression (Grusec 1973; Hicks 1968a). Ten-year-old children did manifest reduced aggression even when the adult was absent (Grusec 1973), perhaps because they internalized the disapproval.

In a study discussed earlier, Dominick and Greenberg (1972) asked fourth- to sixth-grade children to rate their parents' values concerning aggression, as well as to indicate their own attitudes toward aggression. The only group for which parental disapproval of violence modulated the effects of frequent viewing was middle-class boys. For that group, aggressive attitudes were not related to the amount of violence watched when parents clearly disapproved of violence; when parents' attitudes were unclear, boys who viewed a lot of violence did respond more aggressively. For lower-class boys and for girls of all social classes, the relations of aggressive attitudes to television violence were not reduced by parents' disapproval of violence. McLeod et al. (1972a, 1972b) also found that the correlation of violence viewing and aggression was lower for adolescents whose parents emphasized nonaggression than for those whose parents did not.

It appears from these studies that parents can counteract the effects of televised violence to some extent if they convey strong disapproval of aggression. For young children, however, this disapproval may not carry over into situations where there is no adult supervision. Even for older elementary school children and adolescents the evidence is mixed, possibly because parents are often not present to react as the child watches television. The instigation to aggressive behavior provided by frequent exposure to violent television may be difficult for parents to counteract.

D. SUMMARY

Children of both sexes across a wide range of ages and social class backgrounds respond to television violence with aggression. The effects are not limited to males, to the very young, or to the poor, as some people have expected. Children who are habitually aggressive are most likely to be instigated to even higher levels of such behavior; those who are prone to aggression anxiety are least likely to react with behavioral aggression. If a child is frustrated or aroused by a competitive experience, he is somewhat more likely to act out witnessed aggression.

The literature provides some guides about what parents and television producers can and cannot do to alleviate the effects of television violence. The most effective action parents can take is to limit viewing in the early years. If they also convey a definite value system disapproving of aggression, violence may have slightly less impact. If disapproval is combined with child-rearing practices that lead the child to be relatively nonaggressive, the child will probably be less responsive to violence. But parents' ability to counteract the teaching of television appears limited.

The most effective modification of programming that producers can make is to reduce the amount of violence presented. Showing negative motives and consequences for violence does little to reduce its impact, particularly for young children who do not understand the connections of motives and consequences with the behaviors portrayed. The unreality supposedly conveyed by the cartoon format does not reduce the impact of violence; it may merely lead children to think some destructive actions are funny and harmless. Similarly, fictional presentations may have slightly less effect than programs showing real violence, but both instigate aggression.

V. Prosocial Television

Potentially, television could teach children many forms of prosocial behavior that would provide them with alternatives to the violent and deviant problem solutions so often shown. Until very recently, few researchers devoted attention to research on prosocial television content. We believe that the development of knowledge in this area is one of the most effective means of counteracting the pervasive violence that currently exists. If networks are given viable alternatives, they may be more willing to reduce violence. A better balance in television programming between prosocial and violent content might afford viewers a greater variety of behavioral models and reduce heavy reliance on violent problem solutions.

A. LABORATORY RESEARCH

Theory and laboratory research on modeling prosocial behavior has developed extensively in the last 10 years. In laboratory situations where models are presented either live or on film performing some type of prosocial behavior, children generally imitate that behavior. Imitation of adult or peer models has been demonstrated for affectionate behavior, helping another child, altruism and sharing, setting high standards for self-reward, giving up rewards after poor performance, delay of gratification, mature levels of moral judgment, and overcoming fears (see chap. 3 by Bryan in this volume and Hoffman [1970] for reviews of this literature).

Any attempt to generalize these findings to naturalistic effects of television raises the same questions that arose when laboratory studies of aggression were discussed. In most studies, the child is tested in a situation exactly like the one in which the model was observed. The extent to which imitation generalizes to other instances of prosocial behavior is open to question. In some studies involving children's verbal responses, generalization has been demonstrated. Children who observed a model making mature or immature moral judgments, for instance, imitated either type of moral judgment when presented with new items (Bandura & McDonald 1963; Cowan et al. 1969). Similarly, high or low delay of gratification responses generalized to new items and, in one study of late adolescents (Stumphauzer 1972), to related forms of behavior.

Although behavior is usually measured immediately after the model is observed, some studies have used follow-up tests as well, ranging from 1 to 4 weeks after the modeling experience. In most instances, the initial differences produced by modeling were still present on delayed follow-up (Bandura & Mischel 1965; Staub 1972; Stumphauzer 1972; White 1972), so there is some basis for thinking that behavioral changes endure over time.

B. STUDIES USING PROSOCIAL TELEVISION PROGRAMS

The program chosen by most researchers for the study of prosocial effects of television is "Mr. Rogers' Neighborhood." This program is perhaps the most widely viewed and skillfully designed program with a primary focus on social and emotional development. One of the most striking differences between real television programs and laboratory modeling films is the complexity of content. We identified the following list of themes in a subset of scripts: cooperation, sympathy, sharing, affection, friendship, understanding the feelings of others, verbalizing one's own feelings, delay of gratification, persistence and competence at tasks, learning to accept rules, control of aggression, adaptive coping with frustration, fear reduction, self-esteem, and valuing the unique qualities of each individual (Friedrich & Stein 1973; Stein & Friedrich 1972). The studies of "Mr. Rogers' Neighborhood" are summarized in table 3.

1. Learning from Content

Preschool children learn some surprisingly complex ideas from prosocial television programs, and they generalize their learning to new situations. Kindergarten children who saw four episodes of "Mr. Rogers" learned and generalized several themes—helping a friend, trying to understand another's feelings, knowing that wishes do not make things happen, and valuing a person for inner qualities rather than appearance (Friedrich & Stein 1975). Collins (1974) found that kindergarten children who saw four "Mr. Rogers" programs revealed more positive attitudes toward individual differences and were more willing to make unique choices on a generalized test than were the control group.

2. Social Interaction

Cooperation, helping, sharing, understanding others' feelings, and other positive forms of interaction increase when children see prosocial programs, although the results are qualified in various ways. Children who saw a brief episode stressing sharing demonstrated increased generosity to a friend immediately after viewing (Shirley 1974). Exposure to a series of programs was associated with helping another child, but only when the content was rehearsed after each program (Friedrich & Stein 1975). In a third study, children who saw "Mr. Rogers" made more empathic remarks about an absent child, but they shared candy more than a control group only when they believed they had spilled the other child's candy (Cosgrove & McIntyre 1974).

Given the complexity, slow pace, and subtle interweaving of themes, it is perhaps not surprising that longer exposure seems to be necessary to obtain more durable behavioral effects. In two experimental studies, preschool children saw 12 or 13 programs as a part of their curriculum (Friedrich & Stein 1973; Shirley 1974; Stein & Friedrich 1972; Stein, Friedrich, et al. 1973). In each, behavior was observed in free play as well as in experimentally designed tasks. The positive interpersonal behavior of lower-social-class children increased following exposure to "Mr. Rogers" in the Stein and Friedrich (1972) study, but middle-class children did not change. When these children were observed in pairs in a mildly frustrating situation, boys who had seen "Mr. Rogers" were slightly more cooperative than were the other television groups, but there were no differences for girls. In a middle-class sample, Shirley (1974) demonstrated increased sharing among children who saw the prosocial programs, but there were no changes in cooperation and helping. Sharing continued to increase during the follow-up period.

Aggression toward others may decline as a result of viewing the "Mr. Rogers" program, at least when the viewing experience itself is not disrupted. The interpersonal aggression of children who saw "Mr. Rogers" in Shirley's (1974) study declined steadily; the decline continued during the follow-up period. In a frustrating situation, boys studied by Stein, Friedrich, et al. (1973) were less aggressive after "Mr. Rogers" than they were after neutral programs, but girls who had seen "Mr. Rogers" tended to be more aggressive. Aggression in free play remained unchanged for both sexes (Friedrich & Stein 1973; Stein & Friedrich 1972). Finally, Singer and Singer (1974) found that children who watched the program in large groups without adult supervision became more aggressive, prob-

TABLE 3

SUMMARY OF EXPERIMENTAL STUDIES OF THE EFFECTS OF "MR. ROGERS' NEIGHBORHOOD"

Author(s) and Date	Subjects	Independent Variables	Dependent Variables	Results
			Brief Exposures (1–5 Programs)	
Shirley (1974)	3–4-year-old middle-class M & F	2 7-min segments of "Mr. Rogers" concerning sharing vs. no TV	Sharing 2 tasks with opportunity to share with other child who was present; before and immediately after TV	Prosocial TV > no TV
Cosgrove & McIntyre (1974)	3–6-year-old middle-class M & F	5 full-length "Mr. Rogers" programs stressing restitution, sharing, & empathy vs. no TV	Sharing: a) In hypothetical situations b) Task with opportunity for restitution of spilled candy to absent friend c) Empathic verbalization	a) No differences b) Prosocial TV > no TV c) Prosocial TV > no TV
Friedrich & Stein (1975)	5–6-year-old middle-class M & F	1) 4 edited "Mr. Rogers" programs (15–25 min) stressing helping, sharing, & understanding others vs. neutral TV 2) Rehearsal treatments for "Mr. Rogers" viewers: verbal labeling & role playing	a) Learning and generalization of program content—two measures b) Helping task with opportunity to repair a picture for an absent child c) Helping; fantasy measure	1a) Prosocial TV > neutral 2a) Prosocial TV with verbal labeling rehearsal > role playing or no rehearsal 1b & 2b) Prosocial TV with role playing rehearsal > other groups 1c & 2c) Prosocial TV with role playing rehearsal > other groups
Stein, Friedrich, & Tahsler (1973), Tahsler (1973)	4–5-year-old middle-class M & F	1) 4 full-length "Mr. Rogers" programs stressing persistence and effort vs. neutral films 2) Cues from "Mr. Rogers" contained in tasks or not	a) Persistence—task with intermittent success and failure b) Persistence—task with success followed by continual failure c) Motor inhibition tests d) Reflection-impulsivity	1a) Prosocial TV > neutral—females only 1b) Prosocial TV < neutral—females only 1c) Prosocial TV > neutral—females only 1d) Prosocial TV tended to be more reflective than neutral—females only 2a & 2b) Few differences.

Study	Sample	Design	Measures	Results
Collins (1974)	5–6-year-old middle-class M & F	4 edited "Mr. Rogers" programs stressing value of individual differences vs. neutral TV	a) Generalized content test; b) Puppet interview to measure learning of concepts; c) Play sessions: 2 children, pre- and postviewing; rules stated for conformity of toy choice in first session; no rules stated in second session; scored for frequency of choice of different toys	a) Prosocial TV > neutral; b) Tendency for prosocial TV > neutral; borderline significance; c) Prosocial TV > neutral—females only

Longer Exposures (11–13 Programs)

Study	Sample	Design	Measures	Results
Stein & Friedrich (1972), Friedrich & Stein (1973)[a]	4–5-year-old middle- and lower-SES M & F	12 "Mr. Rogers" programs vs. neutral films vs. aggressive programs	Free-play observation: a) Prosocial interpersonal behavior—cooperation, nurturance, verbalizing feelings; b) Self-regulation—task persistence, rule obedience; c) Interpersonal aggression. Baseline (7 days); experimental (12 days); postviewing (6 days)	a) Prosocial TV > other groups—lower SES only; b) Prosocial TV > other groups; c) No difference from neutral
Stein, Friedrich, et al. (1973)	Same as Stein & Friedrich (1972)	Same as Stein & Friedrich (1972)	Mildly frustrating task with another child: a) Cooperation; b) Interpersonal aggression	a) Prosocial TV slightly higher than neutral but not significant—males only; b) Prosocial TV < neutral—males only; prosocial TV > neutral—females only
Shirley (1974)	3–4-year-old middle-SES M & F	13 "Mr. Rogers" programs vs. neutral TV vs. no TV	Free-play observation: a) Cooperation; b) Sharing; c) Helping; d) Interpersonal aggression. Baseline (8 days); experimental (13 days); follow-up (7 days)	a) No differences; b) Prosocial TV > control groups; c) No difference; d) Prosocial TV < control group
Singer & Singer (1974)	3–4-year-old lower-SES M & F	11 "Mr. Rogers" programs with or without adult present vs. live instruction vs. no treatment	Free-play observation and ratings: a) Imaginative play; b) Concentration; c) Aggression. Baseline (2 weeks); follow-up (2 weeks)	a) Live instruction > prosocial TV > control; b) No difference; c) Prosocial TV—adult absent > other groups

[a]The first reference is a detailed report. The second reference is a briefer, more widely available report.

ably because there was a great deal of noise and distraction in these groups. Aggression did not change for children who watched with an adult.

The social interaction of preschool children is strongly influenced by specific settings. One would not predict exact conformity of results in naturalistic behavior, given different children, program content, and situations. The results are promising, as they indicate that various forms of positive social interaction can be instigated by prosocial television programming, even with relatively short exposure. In most studies, generalization to settings quite different from those in the program has been demonstrated.

In some cases, aggressive behavior has also been reduced following viewing of "Mr. Rogers." However, many prosocial behaviors are positively associated with aggression in naturalistic interactions (Murphy 1937; Wright 1960), and reduction of aggression is not necessary for the emergence of increased interpersonal skills, nor would it be expected in all situations.

3. Self-Regulation

Persistence and effort to learn to do things well, learning to wait, and understanding the reasons for rules are frequently emphasized in the "Mr. Rogers" programs. One of the biggest changes in free-play behavior for children who watched "Mr. Rogers" in the Friedrich and Stein (1973) study was increased task persistence. Those children also became somewhat more likely to follow classroom rules without adult supervision. Singer and Singer (1974) did not, however, find changes in concentration on tasks when children were observed in a follow-up period. Similarly, in a short-term experiment (Stein, Friedrich, & Tahsler 1973), preschool girls who saw "Mr. Rogers" were higher on some indices of persistence and self-regulation but not on others. There were no effects for boys.

4. Imaginative Play

There are frequent efforts to stimulate creativity and imagination in the "Mr. Rogers" program as well as attempts to help the child differentiate between fantasy and reality. The imaginative play of children studied by Singer and Singer (1974) did increase after watching a series of programs, particularly when an adult was present during viewing to focus attention on relevant aspects of the programs.

5. Other Prosocial Messages

In recent seasons, "Sesame Street" has shifted from an almost exclusive emphasis on cognitive and intellectual skills to inclusion of social and emotional concerns of children. Segments stressing cooperation, safety, fear reduction, and understanding another person's point of view are now being aired. Although most of the research evaluating these parts of the program is still in progress, Paulson, McDonald, and Whittemore (1973) have reported findings. During one season of "Sesame Street," six vignettes showing cooperation were broadcast nine times each. Children who had the program available in their day care centers could identify and label cooperation in situations similar to those in the show, but generalization was not tested. These children were also more cooperative than nonviewers but only in test situations like those shown on the program.

As the cooperation segments occupied a very small portion of the total "Sesame Street" programming and the children were not required to watch the program even when it was being shown in their classroom, these results are fairly impressive. The children had clearly learned the content of the program and implemented it in their behavior when situational cues were similar to the program.

Prosocial programming for older children is rare. There are some indications that alternatives to the usual formulas for children's programs are being explored. For example, "Fat Albert and the Cosby Kids" was the focus of a study attempting to determine the messages received and understood by elementary-school-age viewers (CBS Broadcast Group 1974). The themes in the five programs studied included: the arrival of a new baby, divorce of parents, safety and paying attention to signs, the cultural uniqueness of American Indians, and being proud of a father's job even when it is menial. Children who watched a program at home or in the laboratory reported many of the messages correctly in an interview. There was little relation between enjoyment and understanding the content of the program, though most children liked the program. There was no difference between naturalistic and captive-viewing conditions. Although no attempt was made to determine behavioral effects, this study at least demonstrates the potential of good programming for attracting audiences of older children and conveying a variety of messages to them.

6. Summary

This new wave of studies confirms the assumption that children can learn a host of prosocial skills and messages from carefully designed programming and that this learning affects positive social behavior, self-regulation, and imagination. More evaluative research is needed to determine the efficacy of efforts in current programming to promote fear reduction, improved self-image, and taking another's perspective. Even more important is the need to explore the possibilities of prosocial programming for older children, adolescents, and adults.

C. FACTORS THAT ENHANCE EFFECTS OF PROSOCIAL TELEVISION

If the potentially beneficial effects of prosocial television programming are to be realized, it is crucial for researchers to determine what factors within the program or within the child's environment enhance the impact of these programs. One set of suggestions can be derived from observational learning theory and related research.

1. Reward and Punishment to the Model

Although observing reward to a model generally increases the likelihood of imitation, it appears that such reward is more effective if it is an intrinsic outcome of the model's behavior rather than praise or some other reinforcement that is incidental to the behavior. Even in laboratory studies, observing an adult praise a child model for some prosocial act does not necessarily result in increased imitation (Elliot & Vasta 1970; Harris 1970). If the model looks pleased or rewards himself, imitation is somewhat more likely (see chap. 3 by Bryan in this volume). Illustrating the positive instrumental outcome of the behavior being taught might be quite effective. For example, in one of the "Sesame Street" vignettes on cooperation, two children help each other button clothes which they could not manage alone.

Reciprocity in peer interactions is another form of naturally occurring reward suggested in a study by O'Connor (1972). A film to encourage social interaction was made in which children approached other children and were greeted with smiles, offers of toys, and other gestures of friendship. Socially withdrawn children who saw the film dramatically increased their frequency of initiating social contacts in the nursery school. The message is that others will behave toward you as you behave toward them. This type of reciprocity does occur in free play among young children (Charlesworth & Hartup 1967) as well as in laboratory studies of sharing (Harris 1970, 1971). Thus, positive reactions by others are a realistic consequence to encourage prosocial behavior.

Demonstrating punishment for antisocial behavior appears to be less effective than modeling and rewarding prosocial behavior. When children see models punished for yielding to temptation, their levels of yielding are about the same as children who have seen no model at all (Hoffman 1970). Punishment appears to be more effective if the model looks distressed or unhappy or shows disapproval of his own behavior (Porro 1968; Slaby & Parke 1971).

As in the case of aggression, depicting rewards and punishments for televised prosocial behavior may be effective only if the child viewer is likely to experience similar consequences. Instrumental outcomes that are intrinsic to the behavior and reciprocal reactions by peers and adults appear to be more relevant consequences to portray than is adult approval. Signs of internalized pleasure or disapproval by the actor performing the behavior also affect imitation.

2. Portraying a Contrast

A time-honored dramatic and pedagogical technique involves presenting the "wrong" actions that get the protagonist into trouble and then resolving the dilemma with a prosocial action. This technique makes exciting drama, but it may reduce or distort the prosocial message, especially for young children who have difficulty understanding the connections between sequences or between behavior and consequences. In experimental modeling studies, children who have seen two models exhibiting conflicting behavior are less imitative than those who see only the more prosocial model (Allen & Liebert 1969; Bandura, Grusec, & Menlove 1967; see also Bryan, chap. 3 in this volume). Some investigators and advisers to "Sesame Street" have also expressed concern about possible confused messages or boomerang effects (Leifer 1973). For instance, portrayal of a common fear may suggest the fear to a child who has not experienced it. This is particularly likely if much of the sequence is devoted to dramatizing a fear with resolution coming only at the end. In one such sequence, a puppet shivers and quakes in his bed worrying about the dark. Resolution occurs briefly at the end when an approaching monster turns out to be Mommy. On the basis of available modeling literature (Bandura 1969a), characters should be shown overcoming fears or approaching objects fearlessly, not experiencing the fear.

3. Nurturance

When children have direct contact with an adult, warmth or nurturance by that adult can increase imitation of many types of behavior (Bandura 1969a). At first glance, it appears difficult for an adult to be warm and nurturant to a child who exists only at the end of an electronic circuit. However, a character like Mr. Rogers does convey a strong sense of warmth, support, friendship, and respect for a child. In his program, Mr. Rogers stresses the individual nature of each viewer; he refers to the audience as "my friend," he looks directly into the camera and talks about the worth of each individual child, and so on. This warmth may be as important as specific content in promoting prosocial behavior among children.

4. Verbal Persuasion

In a number of experimental studies, "preaching" by the model has been explored as well as his "practice." In general, verbal statements that sharing is good or should be done are not very effective influences on children's altruistic behavior (Bryan, chap. 3 in this volume). However, Staub (1972) recently demonstrated that verbal persuasion was very effective in increasing delay of gratification for seventh graders. The difference in findings may be due to the fact that the subjects were older than the elementary school children who participated in the altruism studies, or it may indicate that Staub found a more powerful form of verbal persuasion. Some other literature suggests that explaining why the prosocial behavior is good leads to increased imitation (Elliot & Vasta 1970). Such an explanation may be particularly important in television presentations where the content is more complex than laboratory films.

5. Verbal Labeling, Rehearsal, and Role Playing

For young children, simple verbal labeling of observed behavior appears to be important for learning. Coates and Hartup (1969) demonstrated that 4-year-old children learned and remembered a model's behavior better when an adult labeled it than when they simply watched the model. This difference was attributed to a "production deficiency" for verbal labels that characterizes preschool children (Flavell, Beach, & Chinsky 1966). They do not spontaneously label their experiences, although they can use labels if someone provides them. Seven-year-old children learned equally well regardless of adult intervention, presumably because they generated their own labels.

Rehearsal and role playing also increase children's altruistic and helping behavior. Elementary school children who rehearsed donating to charity after observing it were more likely to donate anonymously than those who did not rehearse, particularly on a follow-up test after several days (Rosenhan & White 1967; White 1972). Staub (1971) found that role playing of helping behavior (without a model) led to increased helping for girls and increased sharing for boys.

Both verbal labeling and role playing of prosocial television content were explored in a recent study by the present authors (Friedrich & Stein 1975). A series of four "Mr. Rogers" programs were shown to groups of kindergarten children. In the verbal labeling group, important elements from the television series were identified in books of short stories following each program. The role-playing treatment entailed rehearsal with hand puppets of some of the events in the programs. In both of these treatments, generalization of the themes from the plot in the program to situations involving children was included.

Verbal labeling was most effective in increasing children's learning and understanding of program content and generalization to new situations. Performance or behavioral effects were measured only for helping behavior. Both direct imitation of the helping actions in the program and being helpful to another child in a situation different from that shown were assessed. Children who received role-playing training were the only ones who were more helpful than the neutral control group. That is, short-term exposure to the program alone did not increase helping behavior, but exposure plus role playing did. It appears, then, that both labeling and role playing of program themes are a potent means of facilitating their adoption in everyday behavior.

6. Similarity of Television Characters to Child

Although children are more likely to imitate models who are similar to themselves than people unlike themselves (Rosekrans 1967), many other attributes may be more important than similarity. Even in experimental studies, children do not necessarily imitate people who are similar in sex, age, or race (Bandura 1969a; Kunce & Thelen 1972; Stouwie, Hetherington, & Parke 1970; Thelen & Fryrear 1971). They may be more likely to imitate people who are warm, powerful, or who have high status than to imitate peers, for instance. For purposes of television programming, the obvious solution is to use a variety of models—children, adults, puppets, cartoon characters—in a variety of settings and formats. This procedure would capitalize on different sources of appeal, and it would facilitate generalization by the child to a wide range of behavior settings.

D. SUMMARY AND IMPLICATIONS FOR EDUCATIONAL PROGRAMMING

Preschool children can learn a wide array of prosocial behavior from well-designed television programs such as "Mr. Rogers' Neighborhood." Children who have been exposed to programs even for relatively short periods of time have demonstrated increased cooperation, sharing, understanding of others' feelings, and verbalizing of their own feelings. In some instances, these changes were accompanied by reduced aggression. Self-regulation—task persistence and accepting rules—and imaginative play have also improved in some studies. Prosocial programs for older children are more recent in origin, but there is some evidence that such programs are attractive and successful in conveying their intended messages.

A number of principles for the construction of effective television portrayals of prosocial behavior can be extrapolated from the experimental imitation literature. Prosocial behavior should be followed by positive consequences that are intrinsic to the behavior and that would be likely to occur for the child viewer who imitated. Care should be taken not to negate a sequence of cooperative or helpful behavior with a slapstick ending. Emphasis should be placed on the efficacy of prosocial behavior: it succeeds.

Although depicting the "wrong" behavior before demonstrating the positive alternative is a standard dramatic technique, it may weaken the prosocial message, particularly for young children who do not connect sequences well. If contrasting behavior is shown at all, the consequences should be negative and should follow immediately. A variety of models—both similar and dissimilar to child viewers—embodying warmth, power, and status should be employed in order to maximize appeal and generalization. For young children, warm, supportive adults may be very potent models.

Clear narration and verbal labeling of action appear to enhance learning and imitation for young children. For older children, explanation and persuasive reasoning about the behavior may add to the impact of the model, but the model's example is crucial. Models in any format should act out the behavior as well as label it.

Rehearsal of content may be stimulated by the toys available to children. Batman capes and Sesame Street puppets probably instigate fantasy play that elaborates on their respective program contents. The current toy market is dominated by sex-stereotyped toys that provide little opportunity for boys to rehearse nurturant or empathic behavior and little opportunity for girls to rehearse active forms of cooperation. Toys representing characters and artifacts from prosocial programs as well as more general toys reflecting a variety of socially beneficial occupations and activities might stimulate children to rehearse and elaborate televised prosocial behavior in their play.

Finally, we have avoided the fundamental question, Who decides what is prosocial? Attempting to sway children in any direction involves a value judgment that may not meet agreement by everyone in a pluralistic society. While this question deserves extensive consideration by all people concerned with children, we would like to suggest two elements that may help establish a common ground. In "Mr. Rogers' Neighborhood," the unique worth of each individual is stressed, and an effort is made to convey a sense of worth to the members of the audience. Enhancement of self-esteem may be one goal that can be agreed on by people with widely differing values. Second, there is no way of eliminating values and influences on children's behavior from television. Therefore, information should be provided by television producers to the public identifying the values incorporated by programs. Hopefully, enough diversity will be reflected in programming to provide alternative choices for the public.

VI. COGNITIVE FUNCTIONING

The potential of television for positive contributions to children's learning and cognitive functioning has also been utilized in recent educational programs. Early studies of commercial television indicated that relatively little learning occurred (e.g., Schramm et al. 1961), but recent literature shows that modeling and other televised techniques can teach a wide variety of cognitive skills. In the laboratory, observational learning of language rules, concepts, problem-solving strategies, and conservation has been demonstrated (see Zimmerman & Rosenthal [1974] for a review of these studies). This learning is not restricted to mere reproduction of a model's responses; children generalize the principles they observe to new instances. The most widely known effort to create beneficial television programs for children has been carried out by the Children's Television Workshop, the producers of "Sesame Street" and "The Electric Company."

A. "SESAME STREET"

"Sesame Street" is designed to teach cognitive skills such as symbolic representation (e.g., letters and numbers), problem solving and reasoning (e.g., relational terms and classification), and understanding the physical and social environment. Fast action and slapstick humor are used to attract interest and attention, particularly among the disadvantaged preschoolers who are the principal target audience. A general background and discussion of the program by a psychologist closely involved in its creation appears in Lesser (1974).

Extensive evaluations of "Sesame Street" were carried out during the first 2 years of broadcasting by Educational Testing Service (Ball & Bogatz 1970, 1972; Bogatz & Ball 1971). The populations studied were predominantly disadvantaged children in different geographic areas, but smaller numbers of advantaged and Spanish-speaking children were included. In both studies, the investigators attempted to manipulate viewing experimentally by encouraging the parents of some children to have their children watch it. Comparison groups were given no special information about the program. In the first year, this manipulation did not succeed because, to everyone's surprise, most of the children watched at least occasionally. In the second year, however, sites were chosen where the program was available only on cable or UHF television. Reception capacity was supplied to the encouraged group but not to the control group.

Tests administered before and after the viewing season were specifically designed to measure skills taught on the program, although generalization to related tasks was included. Children who watched the program frequently gained more on these skills than did those who watched infrequently or never. This finding occurred when the experimentally encouraged group was compared with the control group in the second year as well as when naturally occurring variations in viewing were assessed. Generalization of viewing effects to a wider range of verbal skills was demonstrated in the second year by a significant difference between the encouraged and control groups on the Peabody Picture Vocabulary Test.

Although the gains associated with viewing occurred for all groups of children tested, younger children (3-year-olds) gained more than older children (5-year-olds). Disadvantaged children who watched frequently gained as much as advantaged frequent viewers. However, the advantaged children who watched infrequently also learned some of the skills being taught, probably because they had other learning sources. Disadvantaged infrequent viewers gained little. Thus, "Sesame Street" does not close the gap between advantaged and disadvantaged children, particularly because advantaged children watch it more often. It can, however, help to prevent that gap from increasing.

Encouragement of parents to expose their children to the program also increased its impact even when the amount of viewing was equated, probably because encouraged parents watched it with their children more often than did control parents. Teaching parents about what to teach their children may be an important subsidiary function of educational programming, especially for preschool children.

There is no doubt that "Sesame Street" has been remarkably successful in attracting its target audience and in teaching some important cognitive skills. These accomplishments are dramatic and important not only because of the effects of the show per se, but because the old shibboleth that children would not watch an educational program was proved false. Networks and commercial interests began to be convinced for the first time that there might be an alternative to their tried-and-true formulas for drawing audiences of children. Recent efforts to improve children's television programming are in large measure due to the ground broken by "Sesame Street."

With success, however, comes criticism. Some educators have expressed concern that the style of the show will lead children to be bored in school (where learning is presumably less exciting). However, children who were frequent viewers of "Sesame Street" during its first year of broadcasting were ranked higher in performance by their teachers after they entered school than those who were infrequent viewers (Bogatz & Ball 1971). Viewers also had more positive attitudes toward school.

Other critics have suggested that the fast pace of the show may lead to difficulty in attending to tasks that require sustained effort. In fact, an analysis of the structural properties of "Sesame Street" indicates that it represents a rapid or impulsive conceptual tempo compared with "Mr. Rogers' Neighborhood," which has a slower, more reflective style (Wright 1974). The experimental literature on modeling suggests, however, that children do not become more impulsive in solving problems as a result of observing impulsive models but that reflective models do lead to increased reflectivity (Debus 1970; Denney 1972; Ridberg, Parke, & Hetherington 1971; Yando & Kagan 1968). Thus, although "Sesame Street" probably does not promote cautious, painstaking effort on tasks, it probably does not reduce ability to sustain such effort either.

There is apparently a ceiling on how much children can learn from "Sesame Street." Frequent viewing for 2 years led to little gain during the second year. Those gains that did occur were primarily in new content areas (Bogatz & Ball 1971). This ceiling may be inherent in the medium because lack of control over previous viewing makes it impossible to build learning sequences. Each segment must be independent rather than build on previous content.

The program is not a substitute for live, formal instruction. Sprigle (no date) conducted two small-scale studies in which kindergarten classes of Head Start children who saw "Sesame Street" and used related curriculum materials were compared with classes receiving intensive instruction. In one study, the two groups did not differ on reading-readiness tests at the beginning of first grade or on achievement at the end of the first grade. In the second, the control group performed better on reading readiness, although the adequacy of the initial matching is open to question. The program was not designed as a substitute for formal education, particularly at the kindergarten level, but these findings should caution those teachers who have embraced it as an easy curriculum.

Finally, in adopting the techniques of commercial programs, "Sesame Street" has incorporated a considerable amount of physical aggression (e.g., in slapstick endings of sequences) and verbal aggression (e.g., calling people "Dumb-dumb"). Although blacks and Spanish-speaking groups are presented in a variety of roles, females are underrepresented and usually behave in passive or sex-stereotyped ways. These incidental aggressive and stereotyped content features probably contribute to the same patterns of belief and behavior that were discussed in the previous section of this paper.

B. "THE ELECTRIC COMPANY"

Techniques of commercial programming are also used in "The Electric Company," which is designed to teach elementary reading skills. The effects of this program were studied in 400 first- through fourth-grade classrooms in four communities (Ball & Bogatz 1973). Pairs of class-rooms in predominantly poor areas were matched for achievement level and randomly assigned to viewing or nonviewing conditions. In two cities, experimental group children saw the program in the classroom; in the other two, home viewing was encouraged. Control groups and the experimental home-viewing group received the usual classroom reading instruction.

Only the children who watched the program in school showed improvement in reading associated with viewing. They gained significantly more than the nonviewers on the Electric Battery, a test designed to measure the reading skills taught on the program, but there were few differences between the two groups on the Metropolitan Reading Tests. Although gains occurred across age, sex, and ethnic group, those in the bottom 10 % of the initial reading distribution did not benefit. The television techniques used were apparently not sufficient for the extremely poor reader.

There were no differences in performance associated with home viewing, despite the fact that many children watched the program. Viewing in school probably promoted closer attention to the program, and teachers undoubtedly provided added rehearsal and curriculum materials. It appears that the program was useful in the school context but that home viewing did not improve on the learning that children gained from ordinary school reading instruction.

C. OTHER EDUCATIONAL PROGRAMS

On a much smaller scale than the Children's Television Workshop productions, "Carrascolindas," a series for Mexican-American children, was produced and shown to first and second graders (Williams & Natalicio 1972). Cognitive skills and positive attitudes to a multinational cultural environment were emphasized in both English and Spanish. Children who saw the programs had better language fluency in both languages and gained more on a test of program content administered in English than a control group of nonviewers.

Radio supplements for commercial children's programs are also being explored in a "dual audio TV" project (Borton, Belasco, & Echewa 1974). A narrator inserts word definitions, concepts, and explanations of social relations in silent parts of a cartoon or situation comedy. In three studies of inner-city children, those who used this dual audio TV system at home showed improved vocabulary. It is difficult to ensure that children will use the radio during home television viewing, but the technique has promise for making educational use of some of the time children spend viewing cartoons and commercial programs.

D. SUMMARY

Observing others is an effective way of learning a variety of complex cognitive skills. Recent efforts to produce educational programs for young children, such as "Sesame Street" and "The Electric Company," have been successful in attracting audiences and teaching them while they are entertained. The learning gained may be very important in development, particularly for disadvantaged children who are relatively deprived of opportunities for education in the preschool years. Nevertheless, it appears that there are limits inherent in the medium that make it less efficient than direct instruction.

"Carrascolindas" and "dual audio TV" represent two of a number of small-scale efforts to use public television for educational purposes. With the development of cable television and its possibilities for local programming, small-scale programs specially suited for different localities, age groups, and cultural groups may become increasingly possible to broadcast. Professionals interested in the possibilities of television for cognitive development have examples and a potential medium available.

VII. SOCIAL KNOWLEDGE AND STEREOTYPES

Television is a source of information about the world, its social relationships, and its social structure. But it is not a mirror of society; it is a prism that selects and focuses attention on the values of the dominant culture. Gerbner (1972) has pointed out that the countless dramas cannot be taken at face value; they are symbolic of the values and power relationships that may be manifested in more subtle forms in real life. He suggests that the most important aspect of violence is its symbolic representation of power: "The distribution of roles related to violence, with their different risks and fates, performs the symbolic functions of violence and conveys its basic message about people" (Gerbner 1972, p. 45). What images of sex roles, social classes, ethnic groups, and age groups are portrayed on television? What social values are conveyed to child viewers?

A. ETHNIC GROUP IMAGES

In both children's programs and prime-time television, most ethnic minority groups in this country are virtually ignored (Barcus 1971; Mendelson & Young 1972; Ormiston & Williams 1973). Black Americans are the only group given recognition and representation. In the few appearances of members of other ethnic minorities, they are stereotyped and made ridiculous. Non-Americans are also negatively stereotyped. In children's programs, Mendelson and Young (1972) found that good characters spoke standard English while over half of the bad characters had foreign accents. In prime-time television, foreigners are more often cast as villains than are Americans (Gerbner 1972).

In response to black militancy and protest, portrayals of black Americans shifted from demeaning characterizations to roles of higher status in the late 1960s. For example, in 1968 through 1970, blacks were shown in many regular series in a variety of occupational roles that paralleled those in which whites were shown (Clark 1969; Dominick & Greenberg 1970; Roberts 1970). In effect, blacks were depicted as being just like the middle-class whites who dominate the world of television fiction. In one study of children's programs (Ormiston & Williams 1973), blacks were more often found to be secondary characters and villains than were whites. However, Mendelson and Young (1972) found that blacks on children's programs were shown with generally positive attributes. Both studies found that blacks were less often shown in any work role than were whites and they were almost never shown in managerial or leadership positions without a white coleader or companion.

B. AGE ROLES, OCCUPATIONS, AND SOCIAL CLASS

Most of the characters in prime-time television are young and middle-aged adults. Children, adolescents, and elderly people together form less than 10 % of the leading characters. There are so few elderly people on television that content analyses of their roles could not be performed (Gerbner 1972).

Just as the existence and importance of all but the young and beautiful are ignored, so are the contributions of people outside the middle class. The occupations shown are those of high status. Professional and managerial jobs are overrepresented, while occupations involving labor and service are infrequent compared with their numbers in the real world (Gerbner 1972).

C. SEX ROLES

Despite the majority of females in the population, males predominate in television programming of all kinds. The underrepresentation of women and the distortion of their roles are consistent with Gerbner's hypothesis that television characterizations serve to present symbolic messages conveying the values of the dominant culture. Females are needed for romantic or family themes, but they are not pertinent to the many other themes that appear in television fiction. The message is clear: males can engage in a wide variety of interesting and exciting activities, while females are restricted to family and romantic contexts with less variable and less important options.

In prime-time television, 70%–75% of the leading characters are male (Gerbner 1972; Tedesco 1974). The predominance of males is even more overwhelming in children's programs, particularly cartoons (Gerbner 1972; Hennessee 1971; Hoffman 1972; Streicher 1974). Sternglanz and Serbin (1973) found that about half of the 10 children's programs with the highest Nielsen ratings had too few females to analyze gender role portrayals.

The greater power, prestige, and variability of male roles are conveyed when both genders are presented. Males engage in varied and prestigious occupations while females usually have no occupation outside the home (Courtney & Whipple 1974; Tedesco 1974). When women do work, they are subservient to a man in stereotyped feminine occupations such as nursing (Cantor 1972; Hennessee 1971). Male competence and authority are also subtly conveyed in advertisements using the "voice-over" technique to describe a product off camera while other people or materials are shown visually. In samples of commercials from four stations, about 90% of the "voice-overs" were male (Courtney & Whipple 1974).

In children's programs, males are more aggressive, more constructive, and more often rewarded for whatever they do, while females are more deferent and passive, they initiate less, and they are more likely to get punished when they do (Hoffman 1972; Sternglanz & Serbin 1973).

According to Gerbner (1972), the successful use of violence is a principal symbolic means of exerting power in fiction; falling victim to violence is a demonstration of powerlessness. In his analyses (Gerbner & Gross 1973), women were less violent than men, were less successful when they were violent, and were more likely to be victims of violence. This power differential between males and females has become more sharply delineated over the last several years as the networks reduce violence slightly. The major reductions in violent actions occurred for female and minority characters, and the ratio of victimization (the margin of victims over perpetrators of violence within a given group) increased dramatically for females from 1967 to 1972. "A reduction in violent characterizations may be offset by a sharpening of the social functions of symbolic violence in demonstrating an invidious pattern of fear and power" (Gerbner & Gross 1973, p. 2).

Although youth predominates as a value for both sexes, it is more important for women than for men. In dramatic programming and commercials, the bulk of the male characters are in the age range 30–55; the largest percentage of females are in their twenties and early thirties (Aronoff 1974; Cantor 1972; Courtney & Whipple 1974). Thus, the middle-aged female is consigned to the position of low power and nonrecognition that occurs for the elderly of both sexes.

D. INFLUENCE OF TELEVISION ON SOCIAL KNOWLEDGE

To the extent that television reflects the dominant cultural values, it is difficult to determine its impact independent of the other sources to which people are exposed. Nevertheless, it appears that television portrayals influence children's attitudes, beliefs, and factual information about people. We have already noted that those who watch violent television have aggressive attitudes and believe that violent programs are realistic. Heavy viewers of television in general also have more traditional sex role stereotypes than light viewers (Beuf 1974; Frueh & McGhee, in press).

Both positive and negative stereotypes can be learned from exposure to television, films, and radio depending on the content of the programs. There is some evidence that children learn occupational information (DeFleur & DeFleur 1967; Siegel 1958), stereotypes about physical appearance (Scherer 1970), attitudes about foreigners (Himmelweit et al. 1958), and beliefs about ethnic minorities (Greenberg 1972) through television and other media. As one might expect, media influence is greatest where children have little personal contact or other sources of information about a group (DeFleur & DeFleur 1967; Greenberg 1972).

Learning and believing the images presented on television is not limited to the young and the naive. Adults who were heavy television viewers differed from light viewers in overestimating the percentage of both the white and nonwhite population employed in professional and managerial occupations and the percentage employed in law enforcement (Gross 1974).

The most notable change in television content over the last 10 years has occurred in the portrayals of black Americans. As black children are more likely than whites to believe that television portrayals are realistic and true to life (Greenberg 1972), one might expect them to be especially responsive to these altered images, but there is little information on possible improvements in self-image and self-esteem. Black children and adolescents are heavy viewers of the shows featuring blacks, and they frequently name black television characters as models (Clark 1972; Greenberg 1972). In one study, black adolescents had more positive attitudes toward a black television character who conformed to societal norms than toward a black militant (Clark 1972). It is reasonable to expect that the current portrayals of blacks in conventional, middle-class roles will lead black children to identify with such roles, but more evidence is needed.

E. SUMMARY

The social knowledge available on television represents a composite of dominant American values with little recognition of the diversity in our society. Middle-class white American male adults are portrayed as the most powerful and important members of the society. Women, foreigners, and lower-class men have a restricted set of options and little power. Most minority groups and people who are not adult, young, and beautiful are ignored almost completely. The one notable change in this picture has been an increased representation of black Americans in prestigious, relatively powerful positions.

The images and stereotypes portrayed on television appear to be important sources of children's learning, particularly about activities and groups with which they have little personal contact. A serious question must, then, be raised about the power of scriptwriters and producers who are making decisions about what values and attitudes are depicted. A related question concerns who should decide what social information is imparted through television entertainment. Should the medium reflect the world as it is, or as it might ideally be, or both? Whose ideals should be implemented? For example, Clark (1972) suggests that current portrayals of blacks may exert social control over blacks and co-opt them into white, middle-class values instead of giving true respect to their identity and value as a separate subcultural group. One solution is for television to present a wider diversity of life as it is and as it might be. Children could then be made aware of a variety of possibilities for interpersonal relations, social roles, occupational activities, and ethnic group attributes.

VIII. CONCLUDING REMARKS

The large body of literature on observational learning and television reviewed here has provided important information, but many questions remain. The focus on violent television and aggressive behavior has led to a relative neglect of prosocial television, prosocial behavior, and other kinds of social and cognitive learning from television.

The effect of violent television on behavior other than aggression is still largely unexplored. Although it appears that cooperation and other forms of positive social interaction are not reduced by violent television for young children, is this the case for older children and adolescents? Do older children who are avid fans of violent television and are frequently aggressive also have a wide repertoire of prosocial skills, or will we find a deprivation of learning? What is the relation of aggressive attitudes toward prosocial behavior? And what are the effects of violent television on such subtle but critical dimensions as the ability to tolerate frustration and irritability?

Most of the violent content studied has been derived from regular television series. Yet feature-length movies are an important part of prime-time television, and they are often quite violent. Particularly for older children and adolescents, these longer films, which allow for more development of character and plot, might have more impact than the predictable adventures of most serial characters. There is little information concerning both the content and the effect of movies on television.

The world view conveyed through the types of people, power relations, and actions that lead to success or failure may have insinuated itself into our thinking so much that it is difficult to pinpoint and study. More information is needed about the kinds of beliefs and attitudes about the real world that are cultivated by television fiction. The depiction of social and occupational roles, described in the chapter, are important to study, but other features of television presentations, such as the ways in which people show affection, express anger, resolve differences, and a host of other forms of human interactions, also need to be examined.

Exploration of the effects of prosocial television has barely begun. Most of the current programming and research is limited to preschool children; programs for older children and adolescents need to be developed and studied. Of particular importance is the question of generalization and durability of learning. Longitudinal research and follow-up studies are needed to assess the long-term effects of program content. More information is needed about the critical features of models, verbal content, and modes of presentation that enhance imitation and performance in natural settings as well as the development of training procedures that might be used by parents, teachers, clinicians, and rehabilitation workers. Finally, little is known about noncontent features of programs such as pace, photographic techniques, and methods of narration.

If the directions for new research are indicated, the directions for needed television programming are glaring. FCC Commissioner Nicholas Johnson has observed: "All television is educational television. The only question is, what is it teaching?" (Liebert et al. 1973, p. 170). There has been a reluctance on the part of the television industry and on the part of the American public to see television as an educational medium rather than a harmless form of entertainment. Once television programs are recognized as instruction, the issue of power becomes apparent. Siegel (in Liebert et al. 1973) has noted the striking contrast between the American public's preoccupation with governing the schooling of their children and their indifference to governing what children learn from commercial television. American public schools are led by elected local school boards. These mesh with county and state boards of education, whose members are public-spirited citizens, either elected or appointed by elected officials. At the federal level, we have a cabinet-level Secretary of Health, Education, and Welfare, and in his department are the

Office of Education and the National Institute of Education. Yet citizens have no voice in the governance of television. There are no elected officials, no tests of competence for writers or performers, and no potent means of influencing television instruction (Liebert et al. 1973, p. xii).

The responsibility rests heavily on researchers to inform the public that this ready form of relaxation is, in fact, a powerful teacher. The public must be alerted to the content and values being taught. They must also be informed of the great potential inherent in the medium for enhancing the quality of life for individuals and for society as a whole.

REFERENCES

Allen, M. K., & Liebert, R. M. Effects of live and symbolic deviant-modeling cues on adoption of a previously learned standard. *Journal of Personality and Social Psychology,* 1969, *11,* 253–260.

Aronoff, C. E. Sex role and aging on television. *Journal of Communication,* 1974, *24,* 124.

Bailyn, L. Mass media and children. *Psychological Monographs,* 1959, *73*(1, Whole No. 471).

Baker, R. K., & Ball, S. J. *Mass media and violence: a staff report to the National Commission on the Causes and Prevention of Violence.* Vol. *9A.* Washington, D.C.: Government Printing Office, 1969.

Ball, S., & Bogatz, G. A. *The first year of Sesame Street: an evaluation.* Princeton, N.J.: Educational Testing Service, 1970.

Ball, S., & Bogatz, G. A. Summative research of Sesame Street: implications for the study of preschool children. In A. D. Pick (Ed.), *Minnesota symposium on child psychology.* Vol. *6.* Minneapolis: University of Minnesota Press, 1972.

Ball, S., & Bogatz, G. A. *Reading with television: an evaluation of the Electric Company.* Princeton, N.J.: Educational Testing Service, 1973. 2 vols.

Bandura, A. Influence of models' reinforcement contingencies on the acquisition of imitative responses. *Journal of Personality and Social Psychology,* 1965, *1,* 589–595.

Bandura, A. *Principles of behavior modification.* New York: Holt, 1969. (a)

Bandura, A. Social-learning theory of identificatory processes. In D. A. Goslin (Ed.), *Handbook of socialization theory and research.* Chicago: Rand McNally, 1969. (b)

Bandura, A.; Grusec, J. E.; & Menlove, F. L. Some social determinants of self-monitoring reinforcement systems. *Journal of Personality and Social Psychology,* 1967, *5,* 449–455.

Bandura, A., & McDonald, F. J. Influence of social reinforcement and the behavior of models in shaping children's moral judgments. *Journal of Abnormal and Social Psychology,* 1963, *67,* 274–281.

Bandura, A., & Mischel, W. Modification of self-imposed delay of reward through exposure to live and symbolic models. *Journal of Personality and Social Psychology,* 1965, *2,* 698–705.

Bandura, A.; Ross, D.; & Ross, S. A. Imitation of film-mediated aggressive models. *Journal of Abnormal and Social Psychology,* 1963, *66,* 3–11. (a)

Bandura, A.; Ross, D.; & Ross, S. A. Vicarious reinforcement and imitative learning. *Journal of Abnormal and Social Psychology,* 1963, *67,* 601–607. (b)

Barcus, E. Saturday children's television: a report of TV programming and advertising on

Boston commercial television. ERIC Document Files No. ED 055 461. Action for Children's Television, Boston, 1971.

Bechtel, R. B.; Achelpohl, C.; & Akers, R. Correlates between observed behavior and questionnaire responses on television viewing. In E. A. Rubinstein, G. A. Comstock, & J. P. Murray (Eds.), *Television and social behavior.* Vol. *4. Television in day-to-day life: patterns of use.* Washington, D.C.: Government Printing Office, 1972.

Becker, G. Causal analysis in R-R studies: television violence and aggression. *American Psychologist,* 1972, *27,* 967–968.

Berkowitz, L. The contagion of violence: an S-R mediational analysis of some effects of observed aggression. In W. J. Arnold & M. M. Page (Eds.), *Nebraska symposium on motivation.* Vol. *18.* Lincoln: University of Nebraska Press, 1970.

Beuf, A. Doctor, lawyer, household drudge. *Journal of Communication,* 1974, *24,* 142–145.

Biblow, E. Imaginative play and the control of aggressive behavior. In J. L. Singer (Ed.), *The child's world of make-believe.* New York: Academic Press, 1973.

Bogatz, G. A., & Ball, S. *The second year of "Sesame Street": a continuing evaluation.* Princeton, N.J.: Educational Testing Service, 1971. 2 vols.

Borton, T.; Belasco, L.; & Echewa, T. Dual audio TV instruction: a mass broadcast simulation. *AV Communication Review,* 1974, *22,* 133–152.

Cantor, M. Comparison of tasks and roles of males and females in commercials aired by WRC-TV during composite week. In National Organization for Women (Eds.), *A study of the treatment of males and females in WRC-TV programming aired during a composite week.* Washington, D.C.; National Organization for Women, 1972.

CBS Broadcast Group. *A study of messages received by children who viewed an episode of* "Fat Albert and the Cosby Kids." New York: Office of Social Research, Department of Economics and Research, CBS Broadcast Group, 1974.

Chaffee, S. H. Television and adolescent aggressiveness (overview). In G. A. Comstock & E. A. Rubinstein (Eds.), *Television and social behavior.* Vol. *3. Television and adolescent aggressiveness.* Washington, D.C.: Government Printing Office, 1972.

Chaffee, S. H., & McLeod, J. M. Adolescents, parents, and television violence. Paper presented at the annual meeting of the American Psychological Association, Washington, D.C., September 1971.

Chaffee, S. H., & McLeod, J. M. Adolescent television use in the family context. In G. A. Comstock & E. A. Rubinstein (Eds.), *Television and social behavior.* Vol. *3. Television and adolescent aggressiveness.* Washington, D.C.: Government Printing Office, 1972.

Charlesworth, R., & Hartup, W. W. Positive social reinforcement in the nursery school peer group. *Child Development,* 1967, *38,* 993–1002.

Christy, P. R.; Gelfand, D. M.; & Hartmann, D. P. Effects of competition-induced frustration on two classes of modeled behavior. *Developmental Psychology,* 1971, *5,* 104–111.

Clark, C. C. Television and social controls: some observations on the portrayals of ethnic minorities. *Television Quarterly,* 1969, *8,* 18–22.

Clark, C. C. Race, identification, and television violence. In G. A. Comstock, E. A. Rubinstein, & J. P. Murray (Eds.), *Television and social behavior.* Vol. *5. Television's effects: further explorations.* Washington, D.C.: Government Printing Office, 1972.

Cline, V. B.; Croft, R. G.; & Courrier, S. Desensitization of children to television violence. *Journal of Personality and Social Psychology,* 1973, *27,* 360–365.

Coates, B., & Hartup, W. W. Age and verbalization in observational learning. *Developmental Psychology,* 1969, *1,* 556–562.

Collins, H. L. The influence of prosocial television programs emphasizing the positive value of differences on children's attitudes toward differences and children's behavior in choice situations. Unpublished doctoral dissertation, Pennsylvania State University, 1974.

Collins, W. A. Learning of media content: a developmental study. *Child Development,* 1970, *41,* 1133–1142.

Collins, W. A. Effect of temporal separation between motivation, aggression, and consequences: a developmental study. *Developmental Psychology,* 1973, *8,* 215–221

Collins, W. A.; Berndt, T. J.; & Hess, V. L. Social inferences about motives and consequences for televised aggression: a developmental study. Paper presented at the biennial meeting of the Society for Research in Child Development, Philadelphia, March 1973.

Comstock, G. A., & Rubinstein, E. A. (Eds.) *Television and social behavior.* Vol. *1. Media content and control.* Washington, D.C.: Government Printing Office, 1972. (a)

Comstock, G. A., & Rubinstein, E. A. (Eds.) *Television and social behavior.* Vol. *3. Television and adolescent aggressiveness.* Washington, D.C.: Government Printing Office, 1972. (b)

Comstock, G. A.; Rubinstein, E. A.; & Murray, J. P. (Eds.) *Television and social behavior.* Vol. *5. Television's effects: further explorations.* Washington, D.C.: Government Printing Office, 1972.

Cosgrove, M., & McIntyre, C. W. The influence of "Misterogers' Neighborhood" on nursery school children's prosocial behavior. Paper presented at the meeting of the Southeastern Regional Society for Research in Child Development, Chapel Hill, N.C., March 1974.

Courtney, A. E., & Whipple, T. W. Women in TV commercials. *Journal of Communication,* 1974, *24,* 110–118.

Cowan, P. A.; Langer, J.; Heavenrich, J.; & Nathanson, M. Social learning and Piaget's cognitive theory of moral development. *Journal of Personality and Social Psychology,* 1969, *11,* 261–274.

Davids, A. Effects of aggressive and nonaggressive male and female models on the behavior of emotionally disturbed boys. *Child Development,* 1972, *43,* 1443–1448.

Debus, R. L. Effects of brief observation of model behavior on conceptual tempo of impulsive children. *Developmental Psychology,* 1970, *2,* 22–32.

DeFleur, M. L., & DeFleur, L. B. The relative contribution of television as a learning source for children's occupational knowledge. *American Sociological Review,* 1967, *32,* 777–789.

Denney, D. R. Modeling effects upon conceptual style and cognitive tempo. *Child Development,* 1972, *43,* 105–120.

Dominick, J. R., & Greenberg, B. S. Three seasons of blacks on television. *Journal of Advertising Research,* 1970, *10,* 21–29.

Dominick, J. R., & Greenberg, B. S. Attitudes toward violence: the interaction of television exposure, family attitudes, and social class. In G. A. Comstock & E. A. Rubinstein (Eds.), *Television and social behavior.* Vol. *3. Television and adolescent aggressiveness.* Washington, D.C.: Government Printing Office, 1972.

Efron, E. A million dollar mistake. *TV Guide,* 1972, *20* (524), no. 46, pp. 8–13.

Ekman, P.; Liebert, R. M.; Friesen, W. V.; Harrison, R.; Zlatchin, C.; Malmstrom, E. J.; & Baron, R. A. Facial expressions of emotion while watching televised violence as predictors of subsequent aggression. In G. A. Comstock, E. A. Rubinstein, & J. P. Murray (Eds.), *Television and social behavior.* Vol. *5. Television's effects: further explorations.* Washington, D.C.: Government Printing Office, 1972.

Elliot, R., & Vasta, R. The modeling of sharing: effects associated with vicarious reinforcement, symbolization, age, and generalization. *Journal of Experimental Child Psychology,* 1970, *10,* 8–15.

Ellis, G. T., & Sekyra, F. The effect of aggressive cartoons on the behavior of first grade children. *Journal of Psychology,* 1972, *81,* 37–43.

Eron, L. D. Relationship of TV viewing habits and aggressive behavior in children. *Journal of Abnormal and Social Psychology,* 1963, *67,* 193–196.

Eron, L. D.; Lefkowitz, M. M.; Huesmann, L. R.; & Walder, L. O. Does television violence cause aggression? *American Psychologist,* 1972, *27,* 253–263.

Feshbach, S. Reality and fantasy in filmed violence. In J. P. Murray, E. A. Rubinstein, & G. A. Comstock (Eds.), *Television and social behavior.* Vol. *2. Television and social learning.* Washington, D.C.: Government Printing Office, 1972.

Feshbach, S. Fantasy and the regulation of aggression. Unpublished manuscript, University of California, Los Angeles, 1973.

Feshbach, S., & Singer, R. *Television and aggression.* San Francisco: Jossey-Bass, 1971.

Feshbach, S., & Singer, R. Television and aggression: a reply to Liebert, Sobol, and Davidson. In G. A. Comstock, E. A. Rubinstein, & J. P. Murray (Eds.), *Television and social behavior.* Vol. *5. Television's effects: further explorations.* Washington, D.C.: Government Printing Office, 1972.

Flavell, J. H.; Beach, D. R.; & Chinsky, J. M. Spontaneous verbal rehearsal in a memory task as a function of age. *Child Development,* 1966, *37,* 283–299.

Fletcher, A. D. Negro and white children's television program preferences. *Journal of Broadcasting,* 1969, *13,* 359–366.

Foulkes, D.; Belvedere, E.; & Brubaker, T. Televised violence and dream content. In G. A. Comstock, E. A. Rubinstein, & J. P. Murray (Eds.), *Television and social behavior.* Vol. *5. Television's effects: further explorations.* Washington, D.C.: Government Printing Office, 1972.

Friedrich, L. K., & Stein, A. H. Aggressive and prosocial television programs and the natural behavior of preschool children. *Monographs of the Society for Research in Child Development,* 1973, *38*(4, Serial No. 151).

Friedrich, L. K., & Stein, A. H. Prosocial television and young children: the effects of verbal labeling and role playing on learning and behavior. *Child Development,* 1975, *46,* 27–38.

Frueh, T., & McGhee, P. E. Sex-role development and amount of time spent watching television. *Developmental Psychology,* in press.

Gerbner, G. Violence in television drama: trends and symbolic functions. In G. A. Comstock & E. A. Rubinstein (Eds.), *Television and social behavior.* Vol. *1. Media content and control.* Washington, D.C.: Government Printing Office, 1972.

Gerbner, G., & Gross, L. P. The violence profile, V: Trends in network television drama and viewer conceptions of reality. Unpublished manuscript, University of Pennsylvania, 1973.

Goranson, R. E. Media violence and aggressive behavior: a review of experimental research. In L. Berkowitz (Ed.), *Advances in experimental social psychology.* Vol. *5.* New York: Academic Press, 1970.

Greenberg, B. S. Children's reactions to TV blacks. *Journalism Quarterly,* 1972, *50,* 5–14.

Greenberg, B. S.; Ericson, P. M.; & Vlahos, M. Children's television behaviors as perceived by mother and child. In E. A. Rubinstein, G. A. Comstock, & J. P. Murray (Eds.), *Television and social behavior.* Vol. *4. Television in day-to-day life: patterns of use.* Washington, D.C.: Government Printing Office, 1972.

Greenberg, B. S., & Gordon, T. F. Perceptions of violence in television programs: critics and the public. In G. A. Comstock & E. A. Rubinstein (Eds.), *Television and social behavior.* Vol. *1. Media content and control.* Washington, D.C.: Government Printing Office, 1972. (a)

Greenberg, B. S., & Gordon, T. F. Social class and racial differences in children's perceptions of television violence. In G. A. Comstock, E. A. Rubinstein, & J. P. Murray

(Eds.), *Television and social behavior*. Vol. 5. *Television's effects: further explorations*. Washington, D.C.: Government Printing Office, 1972. (b)

Gross, L. The real world of television. *Today's Education*, 1974, *63*, 86–92.

Grusec, J. E. Demand characteristics of the modeling experiment: altruism as a function of age and aggression. *Journal of Personality and Social Psychology*, 1972, *22*, 139–148.

Grusec, J. E. Effects of co-observer evaluations on imitation: a developmental study. *Developmental Psychology*, 1973, *8*, 141.

Hale, G. A.; Miller, L. K.; & Stevenson, H. W. Incidental learning of film content: a developmental study. *Child Development*, 1968, *39*, 69–77.

Hanratty, M. A.; Liebert, R. M.; Morris, L. W.; & Fernandez, L. E. Imitation of film-mediated aggression against live and inanimate victims. Proceedings of the 77th annual convention of the American Psychological Association, Washington, D.C., 1969.

Hanratty, M. A.; O'Neal, E.; & Sulzer, J. L. Effect of frustration upon imitation of aggression. *Journal of Personality and Social Psychology*, 1972, *21*, 30–34.

Hapkiewitz, W. G., & Roden, A. H. The effect of aggressive cartoons on children's interpersonal play. *Child Development*, 1971, *42*, 1583–1585.

Harris, M. B. Reciprocity and generosity: some determinants of sharing in children. *Child Development*, 1970, *41*, 313–328.

Harris, M. B. Models, norms, and sharing. *Psychological Reports*, 1971, *29*, 147–153.

Hartmann, D. P. Influence of symbolically modeled instrumental aggression and pain cues on aggressive behavior. *Journal of Personality and Social Psychology*, 1969, *11*, 280–288.

Hennessee, J. *Analysis of WABC-TV programming*. New York: National Organization for Women, 1971.

Hicks, D. J. Effects of co-observer's sanctions and adult presence on imitative aggression. *Child Development*, 1968, *39*, 303–309. (a)

Hicks, D. J. Short- and long-term retentions of affectively varied modeled behavior. *Psychonomic Science*, 1968, *11*, 369–370. (b)

Hicks, D. J. Girls' attitudes toward modeled behaviors and the content of imitative private play. *Child Development* 1971, *42*, 139–147.

Himmelweit, H. T.; Oppenheim, A. N.; & Vince, P. *Television and the child*. London: Oxford University Press, 1958.

Hoffman, H. Report on monitoring of children's television programming aired by WRC-TV: a comparison of male and female roles. In National Organization for Women (Eds.), *A study of the treatment of males and females in WRC-TV programming aired during a composite week*. Washington, D.C.: National Organization for Women, 1972.

Hoffman, M. L. Moral development. In P. H. Mussen (Ed.), *Carmichael's handbook of child psychology*. Vol. 2. (3d ed.) New York: Wiley, 1970.

Howitt, D. Television and aggression: a counterargument. *American Psychologist*, 1972, *27*, 969–970.

Kaplan, R. M. On television as a cause of aggression. *American Psychologist*, 1972, *27*, 968–969.

Katzman, N. I. Violence and color television: what children of different ages learn. In G. A. Comstock, E. A. Rubinstein, & J. P. Murray (Eds.), *Television and social behavior*. Vol. 5. *Television's effects: further explorations*. Washington, D.C.: Government Printing Office, 1972.

Kay, H. Weaknesses in the television-causes-aggression analysis by Eron et al. *American Psychologist*, 1972, *27*, 970–973.

Kenny, D. A. Threats to the internal validity of cross-lagged panel inference, as relation to "Television violence and child aggression: a followup study." In G. A. Comstock & E.

A. Rubinstein (Eds.), *Television and social behavior*. Vol. *3. Television and adolescent aggressiveness*. Washington, D.C.: Government Printing Office, 1972.

Klapper, J. T. The impact of viewing "aggression": studies and problems of extrapolation. In O. N. Larsen (Ed.), *Violence and the mass media*. New York: Harper & Row, 1968.

Kuhn, D. Z.; Madsen, C. H.; & Becker, W. C. Effects of exposure to an aggressive model and "frustration" on children's aggressive behavior. *Child Development*, 1967, *38*, 739–746.

Kunce, J. T., & Thelen, M. H. Modeled standards of self-reward and observer performance. *Developmental Psychology*, 1972, *7*, 153–156.

Lange, D. L.; Baker, R. K.; & Ball, S. J. *Mass media and violence: a report to the National Commission on the Causes and Prevention of Violence*. Washington, D.C.: Government Printing Office, 1969.

Larsen, O. N.; Gray, L. N.; & Fortis, J. G. Achieving goals through violence on television. In O. N. Larsen (Ed.), *Violence and the mass media*. New York: Harper & Row, 1968.

Lefkowitz, M. M.; Eron, L. D.; Walder, L. O.; & Huesmann, L. R. Television violence and child aggression: a followup study. In G. A. Comstock & E. A. Rubinstein (Eds.), *Television and social behavior*. Vol. *3. Television and adolescent aggressiveness*. Washington, D.C.: Government Printing Office, 1972.

Leifer, A. D. Children's conceptions of television. Paper presented at the biennial meeting of the Society for Research in Child Development, Philadelphia, 1973.

Leifer, A. D., & Roberts, D. F. Children's responses to television violence. In J. P. Murray, E. A. Rubinstein, & G. A. Comstock (Eds.), *Television and social behavior*. Vol. *2. Television and social learning*. Washington, D.C.: Government Printing Office, 1972.

Lesser, G. S. *Children and television: lessons from "Sesame Street."* New York: Random House, 1974.

Liebert, R. M., & Baron, R. A. Some immediate effects of televised violence on children's behavior. *Developmental Psychology*, 1972, *6*, 469–475.

Liebert, R. M., & Fernandez, L. E. Effects of vicarious consequences on imitative performance. *Child Development*, 1970, *41*, 847–852. (a)

Liebert, R. M., & Fernandez, L. E. Imitation as a function of vicarious and direct reward. *Developmental Psychology*, 1970, *2*, 230–232. (b)

Liebert, R. M.; Neale, J. M.; & Davidson, E. S. *The early window: effects of television on children and youth*. New York: Pergamon, 1973.

Liebert, R. M.; Sobol, M. P.; & Copemann, C. D. Effects of vicarious consequences and race of model upon imitative performance by black children. *Developmental Psychology*, 1972, *6*, 453–456.

Liebert, R. M.; Sobol, M. D.; & Davidson, E. S. Catharsis of aggression among institutionalized boys: fact or artifact? In G. A. Comstock, E. A. Rubinstein, & J. P. Murray (Eds.), *Television and social behavior*. Vol. *5. Television's effects: further explorations*. Washington, D.C.: Government Printing Office, 1972.

Lovaas, O. Effect of exposure to symbolic aggression on aggressive behavior. *Child Development*, 1961, *32*, 37–44.

Lovibond, S. H. The effect of media stressing crime and violence upon children's attitudes. *Social Problems*, 1967, *15*, 91–100.

Lyle, J. Television in daily life: patterns of use (overview). In E. A. Rubinstein, G. A. Comstock, & J. P. Murray (Eds.), *Television and social behavior*. Vol. *4. Television in day-to-day life: patterns of use*. Washington, D.C.: Government Printing Office, 1972.

Lyle, J., & Hoffman, H. Children's use of television and other media. In E. A. Rubinstein, G. A. Comstock, & J. P. Murray (Eds.), *Television and social behavior*. Vol. *4. Television in day-to-day life: patterns of use*. Washington, D.C.: Government Printing Office, 1972. (a)

Lyle, J., & Hoffman, H. Explorations in patterns of television viewing by preschool-age children. In E. A. Rubinstein, G. A. Comstock, & J. P. Murray (Eds.), *Television and social behavior. Vol. 4. Television in day-to-day life: patterns of use.* Washington, D.C.: Government Printing Office, 1972. (b)

Maccoby, E. E. The effects of mass media. In M. L. Hoffman & L. W. Hoffman (Eds.), *Review of child development research.* Vol. *1.* New York: Russell Sage Foundation, 1964.

Maccoby, E. E. Sex differences in intellectual functioning. In E. E. Maccoby (Ed.), *The development of sex differences.* Stanford, Calif.: Stanford University Press, 1966.

McIntyre, J. J., & Teevan, J. J. Television violence and deviant behavior. In G. A. Comstock & E. A. Rubinstein (Eds.), *Television and social behavior.* Vol. *3. Television and adolescent aggressiveness.* Washington, D.C.: Government Printing Office, 1972.

McLeod, J. M.; Atkin, C. K.; & Chaffee, S. H. Adolescents, parents, and television use: adolescent self-report measures from Maryland and Wisconsin sample. In G. A. Comstock & E. A. Rubinstein (Eds.), *Television and social behavior.* Vol. *3. Television and adolescent aggressiveness.* Washington, D.C.: Government Printing Office, 1972. (a)

McLeod, J. M.; Atkin, C. K.; & Chaffee, S. H. Adolescents, parents, and television use: self-report and other-report measures from the Wisconsin sample. In G. A. Comstock & E. A. Rubinstein (Eds.), *Television and social behavior.* Vol. *3. Television and adolescent aggressiveness.* Washington, D.C.: Government Printing Office, 1972. (b)

Mendelson, G., & Young, M. Network children's programming: a content analysis of black and minority treatment on children's television. ERIC Document Files No. ED 067 889. Action for Children's Television, Boston, 1972.

Meyer, T. P. Effects of viewing justified and unjustified real film violence on aggressive behavior. *Journal of Personality and Social Psychology,* 1972, *23,* 21–29.

Murphy, L. B. *Social behavior and child personality.* New York: Columbia University Press, 1937.

Murray, J. P. Television and violence: implications of the Surgeon General's Research Program. *American Psychologist,* 1973, *28,* 472–478.

Murray, J. P.; Comstock, G. A.; & Rubinstein, E. A. (Eds.) *Television and social behavior.* Vol. *2. Television and social learning.* Washington, D.C.: Government Printing Office, 1972.

Murray, J. P.; Nayman, O. B.; & Atkin, C. K. Television and the child: a comprehensive research bibliography. *Journal of Broadcasting,* 1971, *16,* 3–20.

Mussen, P., & Rutherford, E. Effects of aggressive cartoons on children's aggressive play. *Journal of Abnormal and Social Psychology,* 1961, *62,* 461–464.

Neale, J. M. Comment on "Television violence and child aggression: a followup study." In G. A. Comstock & E. A. Rubinstein (Eds.), *Television and social behavior.* Vol. *3. Television and adolescent aggressiveness.* Washington, D.C.: Government Printing Office, 1972.

Nelson, J. D.; Gelfand, D. M.; & Hartmann, D. P. Children's aggression following competition and exposure to an aggressive model. *Child Development,* 1969, *40,* 1085–1097.

Noble, G. Film-mediated aggressive and creative play. *British Journal of Social and Clinical Psychology,* 1970, *9,* 1–7.

O'Connor, R. C. Modification of social withdrawal through symbolic modeling. In K. D. O'Leary and S. G. O'Leary (Eds.), *Classroom management.* New York: Pergamon, 1972.

Ormiston, L. H., & Williams, S. Saturday children's programming in San Francisco, California. An analysis of the presentation of racial and cultural groups on three network affiliated San Francisco television stations. ERIC Document Files No. ED 071 440. Committee on Children's Television, San Francisco, 1973.

Osborn, D. K., & Endsley, R. C. Emotional reaction of young children to TV violence. *Child Development,* 1971, *42,* 321–331.

Parke, R. D.; Berkowitz, L.; Leyens, J. P.; West, S.; & Sebastian, R. J. Film violence and aggression: a field experimental analysis. *Journal of Social Issues,* 1974, in press.

Paulson, F. L.; McDonald, D. L.; & Whittemore, S. L. *An evaluation of "Sesame Street" programming to teach cooperation.* Monmouth, Ore.: Teaching Research, 1973.

Porro, C. R. Effects of the observation of a model's affective responses to her own transgression on resistance to temptation in children. *Dissertation Abstracts,* 1968, *28,* 3064 B.

Ridberg, E. H.; Parke, R. D.; & Hetherington, E. M. Modification of impulsive and reflective cognitive styles through observation of film-mediated models. *Developmental Psychology,* 1971, *5,* 369–377.

Roberts, C. The portrayal of blacks on network television. *Journal of Broadcasting,* 1970, *15,* 45–53.

Robinson, J. P., & Bachman, J. G. Television viewing habits and aggression. In G. A. Comstock & E. A. Rubinstein (Eds.), *Television and social behavior.* Vol. *3. Television and adolescent aggressiveness.* Washington, D.C.: Government Printing Office, 1972.

Rosekrans, M. A. Imitation in children as a function of perceived similarity to a social model and vicarious reinforcement. *Journal of Personality and Social Psychology,* 1967, *7,* 307–315.

Rosekrans, M. A., & Hartup, W. W. Imitative influences of consistent and inconsistent response consequences to a model on aggressive behavior in children. *Journal of Personality and Social Psychology,* 1967, *7,* 429–434.

Rosenhan, D., & White, G. M. Observation and rehearsal as determinants of prosocial behavior. *Journal of Personality and Social Psychology,* 1967, *5,* 424–431.

Ross, L. B. The effect of aggressive cartoons on the group play of children. Unpublished doctoral dissertation, Miami University, 1972.

Rubinstein, E. A., Comstock, G. A., & Murray, J. P. (Eds.) *Television and social behavior.* Vol. *4. Television in day-to-day life: patterns of use.* Washington, D.C.: Government Printing Office, 1972.

Savitsky, J. C.; Rogers, R. W.; Izard, C. E.; & Liebert, R. M. Role of frustration and anger in the imitation of filmed aggression against a human victim. *Psychological Reports,* 1971, *29,* 807–810.

Sawin, D. B. Aggressive behavior among children in small playgroup settings with violent television. Unpublished doctoral dissertation, University of Minnesota, 1974.

Scherer, K. R. Stereotype change following exposure to counter-stereotypical media heroes. *Journal of Broadcasting,* 1970, *15,* 91–100.

Schramm, W.; Lyle, J.; & Parker, E. B. *Television in the lives of our children.* Stanford, Calif.: Stanford University Press, 1961.

Sebastian, R. J.; Parke, R. D.; Berkowitz, L.; & West, S. Repeated and single exposure to movie violence and verbal aggression. Unpublished manuscript, University of Wisconsin, 1974.

Shirley, K. W. The prosocial effects of publicly broadcast children's television. Unpublished doctoral dissertation, University of Kansas, 1974.

Siegel, A. E. Film-mediated fantasy aggression and strength of aggressive drive. *Child Development,* 1956, *27,* 365–378.

Siegel, A. E. The influence of violence in the mass media upon children's role expectations. *Child Development,* 1958, *29,* 35–36.

Siegel, A. E., & Kohn, L. G. Permissiveness, permission, and aggression: the effect of adult presence or absence on aggression in children's play. *Child Development,* 1959, *30,* 131–141.

Singer, J. L., & Singer, D. G. Fostering imaginative play in preschool children: television and live model effects. Draft for presentation at the annual meeting of the American Psychological Association, New Orleans, August 1974.

Slaby, R. G., & Parke, R. D. Effect on resistence to deviation of observing a model's affective reaction to response consequences. *Developmental Psychology*, 1971, *5*, 40–47.

Sprigle, H. A. Who wants to live on Sesame Street? ERIC Document Files No. ED 066 221. Learning to Learn, Inc., Jacksonville, Fla., n.d.

Staub, E. The use of role playing and induction in children's learning of helping and sharing behavior. *Child Development*, 1971, *42*, 805–816.

Staub, E. Effects of persuasion and modeling on delay of gratification. *Developmental Psychology*, 1972, *6*, 166–177.

Stein, A. H., & Friedrich, L. K. Television content and young children's behavior. In J. P. Murray, E. A. Rubinstein, & G. A. Comstock (Eds.), *Television and social behavior*. Vol. 2. *Television and social learning*. Washington, D.C.: Government Printing Office, 1972.

Stein, A. H.; Friedrich, L. K.; Deutsch, F.; & Nydegger, C. The effects of aggressive and prosocial television on the social interaction of preschool children. Paper presented at the meeting of the Midwestern Psychological Association, Chicago, May 1973.

Stein, A. H.; Friedrich, L. K.; & Tahsler, S. The effects of prosocial television and environmental cues on children's task persistence and conceptual tempo. Unpublished manuscript, Pennsylvania State University, 1973.

Sternglanz, S. H., & Serbin, L. An analysis of sex roles presented on children's television programs. Paper presented at the biennial meeting of the Society for Research in Child Development, Philadelphia, 1973.

Steuer, F. B.; Applefield, J. M.; & Smith, R. Televised aggression and the interpersonal aggression of preschool children. *Journal of Experimental Child Psychology*, 1971, *11*, 442–447.

Stouwie, R. J.; Hetherington, E. M.; & Parke, R. D. Some determinants of children's self-reward behavior after exposure to discrepant reward criteria. *Developmental Psychology*, 1970, *3*, 313–319.

Streicher, H. W. The girls in the cartoons. *Journal of Communication*, 1974, *24*, 125–129.

Stumphauzer, J. S. Increased delay of gratification in young prison inmates through imitation of high-delay peer models. *Journal of Personality and Social Psychology*, 1972, *21*, 10–17.

Surgeon General's Scientific Advisory Committee on Television and Social Behavior. *Television and growing up: the impact of televised violence*. Washington, D.C.: Government Printing Office, 1972.

Surlin, S. H., & Dominick, J. R. Television's function as a "third parent" for black and white teenagers. *Journal of Broadcasting*, 1970, *15*, 55–64.

Tahsler, S. The effect of prosocial television on reflectivity-impulsivity and motor inhibition. Unpublished masters thesis, Pennsylvania State University, 1973.

Tedesco, N. S. Patterns in prime time. *Journal of Communications*, 1974, *24*, 118–124.

Thelen, M. H. The effect of subject race, model race, and vicarious praise on vicarious learning. *Child Development*, 1971, *42*, 972–977.

Thelen, M. H., & Fryrear, J. L. Effect of observer and model race on the imitation of standards of self-reward. *Developmental Psychology*, 1971, *5*, 133–135.

Thelen, M. H.; Rennie, D. L.; Fryrear, J. L.; & McGuire, D. Expectancy to performance and vicarious reward: their effects upon imitation. *Child Development*, 1972, *43*, 699–703.

Thelen, M. H., & Soltz, W. The effect of vicarious reinforcement on imitation in two social-racial groups. *Child Development*, 1969, *40*, 879–887.

Thomas, S. The role of cognitive style variables in mediating the influence of aggressive television upon elementary school children. ERIC Document Files No. ED 065 175. Unpublished doctoral dissertation, University of California, Los Angeles, 1972.

Walters, R. H., & Thomas, E. L. Enhancement of punitiveness by visual and audio-visual displays. *Canadian Journal of Psychology,* 1963, *17,* 244–255.

Walters, R. H., & Willows, D. C. Imitative behavior of disturbed and nondisturbed children following exposure to aggressive and nonaggressive models. *Child Development,* 1968, *39,* 79–89.

Ward, S. Effects of television advertising on children and adolescents. In E. A. Rubinstein, G. A. Comstock, & J. P. Murray (Eds.), *Television and social behavior. Vol. 4. Television in day-to-day life: patterns of use.* Washington, D.C.: Government Printing Office, 1972.

Wells, W. D. Television and aggression: replication of an experimental field study. Unpublished manuscript, University of Chicago Graduate School of Business, 1973.

White, G. M. Immediate and deferred effects of model observation and guided and unguided rehearsal on donating and stealing. *Journal of Personality and Social Psychology,* 1972, *21,* 139–148.

Williams, F., & Natalicio, D. S. Evaluating "Carrascolindas:" a television series for Mexican-American children. ERIC Document Files No. ED 062 367. Unpublished manuscript, University of Texas, 1972.

Williams, J. F.; Meyerson, L. J.; Eron, L. D.; & Semler, I. J. Peer-rated aggression and aggressive responses elicited in an experimental situation. *Child Development,* 1967, *38,* 181–190.

Wright, H. F. Observational child study. In P. H. Mussen (Ed.), *Handbook of research methods in child development.* New York: Wiley, 1960.

Wright, J. C. Matching communication pace with children's cognitive styles. In D. D. Hearn (Ed.), *Values, feelings, and morals, I: Research and perspectives.* Washington, D.C.: American Association of Elementary-Kindergarten-Nursery Educators, 1974.

Yando, R. M., & Kagan, J. The effect of teacher tempo on the child. *Child Development,* 1968, *39,* 27–34.

Zimmerman, B. J., & Rosenthal, T. L. Observational learning of rule-governed behavior by children. *Psychological Bulletin,* 1974, *81,* 29–42.

5 The Development of Social Cognition

CAROLYN UHLINGER SHANTZ
Wayne State University

CONTENTS

The author appreciates the helpful suggestions by Drs. John Flavell, Robert Selman, Irving Sigel, and Aletha Stein in the preparation of this review. A special acknowledgment is given to Dr. David Shantz for both his valuable criticisms of the initial draft of this chapter and his encouragement.

257

I. INTRODUCTION

A. OVERVIEW

Only a decade ago very little was known about the child's understanding of his social world (Bronfenbrenner 1963; Wallach 1963). The
scarcity of information was particularly striking in comparison with the
vast amount of information about the child's understanding of his nonsocial world. But in the last 10 years there has been a great deal of
interest and research effort devoted to the study of the development of
social cognition.

The topic of this chapter is how children conceptualize other people
and how they come to understand the thoughts, emotions, intentions,
and viewpoints of others. Research on this topic has gone under a variety
of generic labels—role taking, person perception, empathy, social cognition, and egocentrism— depending on the researcher's interest in a particular type of inference, process, and/or his theoretical orientation. For
purposes of this review, the area of social cognition refers to the child's
intuitive or logical representation of others, that is, how he characterizes
others and makes inferences about their covert, inner psychological experiences.

The study of the development of social cognition is important on two
counts. First, it provides a more complete picture of the child's cognitive
development indicating what types of concepts and processes are evident
in both the nonsocial and social domains at particular age periods. Second, the way in which children conceptualize others presumably has an
important effect on their social behavior with others. The concepts of
people held by children and adults make possible a system of sufficient
predictive utility that one can interact with others adaptively and efficiently (Kelly 1955). If one's conceptual system is not sufficiently accurate, one's interrelationships are drastically affected, as when, for example, a paranoid person construes an innocent glance to mean
malevolence, or a child views an accidental act by another to be an
aggressive provocation.

This chapter will begin with an introduction to some of the factors
involved in making social inferences and a brief summary of the primary

theories that have contributed to this area: cognitive-developmental and social psychological. The substantive research findings on the development of social cognition then will be reviewed in five content areas: children's understanding of what another person sees, feels, thinks, intends, and what the other person is like. Then two questions are posed: Are these various inferences in understanding others interrelated? How are such abilities related to other, nonsocial cognitive abilities? The next major topic concerns the relationship between social cognition and social behavior. In the final section, the major developmental changes in social understanding are reviewed and some methodological issues and implications for future research are considered.

The focus here is on the child's conception of *other* people and not the child's *self*-concept and, as such, constitutes a major limitation. There are theoretical and empirical bases for asserting that there are important relations between self- and other-concepts in both children and adults (e.g., Mead 1934; Sullivan 1953), but this literature will not be reviewed. Likewise, the child's understanding of social relations involved in religious, political, economic, and legal systems will not be covered here (see Flavell 1970). And, as the definition of social cognition implies, the review excludes the early preconceptual, unreflective social object relations of infancy.

Before proceeding to the factors in social cognition, some historical perspective is helpful to clarify the reasons for the recent interest in social cognition of children and introduce some of the issues in the area. Up to the mid-sixties, approximately, developmental psychology was particularly devoted to the study of social behavior and cognitive functioning. Social behavior was studied largely from the perspective of psychoanalytic theory or social learning theory. The latter was particularly interested in the conditions under which certain social behavior occurred and not the child's conception of other people involved in the social interaction. At the same time, cognitive development was given increasing attention as psychologists became more concerned with higher mental processes, in general, and became acquainted with Piaget's research and theory, in particular. Piaget studied primarily the child's understanding of his nonsocial, physical world, and those who replicated and extended his work largely retained this focus. However, some of Piaget's findings and theory concerning stages of cognitive development and the concepts of egocentrism (akin to Werner's "perspectivism") and decentration have been used extensively in the study of the development of social cognition. Thus, the recent work in social cognitive development has been in large measure an extension of the study of cognitive development in logical problem solving.

However, social cognition of adults, but not children, has been studied throughout this century by social psychologists. Some of the empirical work stemmed from the writings of Allport (1961), Brunswik (1947), Kelly (1955), and Mead (1934). More recently, attribution theory as developed by Heider (1958) and Kelley (1967, 1973) has contributed to this area.

Studies of adults' social understanding posed two basic questions: How accurate is the judgment about another person? and What processes are used in making social judgments? The issue of accuracy had an active research life up to the time that Cronbach (1955, 1958) and Hastorf and Bender (1952) presented methodological critiques of the area. Of several problems noted, one is particularly relevant to the findings reviewed in this chapter. Accuracy scores were shown to be a function of both the judge and person judged. Specifically, the similarity between the judge and "judgee" facilitated accurate assessments in that the judge could project his own traits, or assume similarity, and get a high accuracy score. Thus, ability was confounded with actual similarity. In addition, accuracy in judging the "generalized other" (stereotype accuracy) was quite independent of the ability to judge specific individuals (differential accuracy) (Taguiri 1969).

Although research on accuracy judgments continues, a substantial shift to studying the processes involved in adults' social judgments has occurred in recent years. This interest in processes was stimulated, in part apparently, by the work of Asch (1946), Brunswik (1947), Heider (1958), Kelly (1955), and Sarbin, Taft, and Bailey (1960). Quite recently, some social psychological theories, notably Heider's, have been used in studying children's social cognition (Baldwin et al. 1969; Sedlak & Schmidt 1973; Shaw & Sulzer 1964; Weiner & Peter 1973; Weinstein & Finley 1973). The theories that have contributed to this area of research will be described later.

B. FACTORS INVOLVED IN MAKING SOCIAL INFERENCES

In this section there will be a brief discussion of some of the factors that appear to be involved in the child's attempt to make inferences about others, regardless of the content of the inferences (i.e., thoughts, feelings, or intentions), and which presumably influence the adequacy of the child's performance.

1. The Type of Response Required

As perceivers and cognizers of the physical and social world, children and adults construct order out of the flux of stimuli, primarily by "chunking" diversity into units of similarities called concepts (Sigel 1964). Most research in social cognition is aimed at clarifying the child's concepts of people by requiring him to make a judgment about, or an assessment of, another individual. But sometimes studies require a judgment about the *relation* between two individuals or a prediction of how another person might respond to a particular situation. Specifically, the child might be asked to characterize a person with whom he has interacted in the past or has just observed, or to assess a person's current or future "internal states" (such as his intentions or feelings) and/or his future behavior. Although most studies appear to be focused on differential judgments (what a particular individual is thinking or feeling), some are assessments of stereotypic or normative inferences (what most people feel in a given situation). The processes underlying such characterizations, assessments, and predictions will be discussed later.

The bulk of research requires a verbal response from the child: he tells how he thinks another feels, what another has done or is going to do, or he writes a description of another. It is important to bear in mind at the outset that the picture of children's social cognitive development reflects both cognitive and linguistic abilities. Some research, but very little, requires nonverbal responses. For example, the child selects a facial expression to indicate what another feels in a particular situation, or selects a spatial perspective in a photograph to indicate another's viewpoint from a particular location. The child's motor and affective behavior may be used, as in some game-playing situations, to infer his representation of another individual.

2. The Information Provided about the Other

There is a great deal of diversity in the way "the other person" is presented to the child in empirical studies. The child may judge a hypothetical person, a known but absent person, or a present but unfamiliar person. Sometimes he is not given any information about the person, but rather is told about a situation from which he infers or predicts a hypothetical child's response.

The type of stimulus material varies from verbal stories about an individual or still photographs to, more recently, tape recordings or movies of people interacting. In these settings, the child is in the role of an observer of the individual(s). Other studies use an actual individual for the child to judge, often with the child in the role of a participant. For example, the child plays a game with another person and inferences are made about his ability to infer his opponent's thoughts or game strategies, or he communicates a message to another actual individual. Finally, in some studies, notably "person-perception" studies, the child has participated with another person in many situations and over time, and he is asked to characterize the absent individual.

The type and amount of information about the person given in empirical studies are often quite different from the information available in real life situations. In the latter, the person as a physical object provides a major source of "surface" cues, such as size, dress, facial expression, movement, voice quality, and verbal statements, to which the child selectively attends. Present cues may well be supplemented by information about the person from past interactions. To the extent that the child in social judgment studies is required to make inferences from impoverished cues of the person (both in type and number of cues), the generality of the responses to real life situations may well be limited.

3. The Information Provided about the Situation

The child in his everyday social life observes and interacts with people in particular situations. It is well known that the context in which an individual is observed is another major source of cues for understanding the other's current internal states and predicting how he will act. Much as the "field" affects the perception of physical objects, the situation or context affects the meaning of the person's expressions and behavior. The situation constrains the interpretation of behavior (i.e., what a person can and cannot do, does and does not do) and induces expectancies for certain behavior (Heider 1958). Indeed, quite accurate assessments of another's covert experiences and predictions of future behavior can often be made knowing only the setting the person is in without recourse to cues from the person (Barker & Wright 1955; see also Gump, chap. 2 of this volume). Children, like adults, attend to and use situational cues in their descriptions and interpretations of individual (Flapan 1968).

The amount and type of situational information presented in research studies vary greatly, from no situational information to only situational information. An example is provided by research on children's inferences about others' feelings. The child may be shown only the face of an adult in a photograph and asked to infer the emotion (Izard 1971); he may be shown a pictured situation and facial expression and told about the situation (Feshbach & Roe 1968); or he may be told about and shown a picture only of a situation (Borke 1973) from which he infers what another feels. As with "person" cues, meager situational information may substantially influence the type of response obtained.

4. The Child's Ability to Attend to Relevant Information

Given the diverse and complex stimuli provided by the person and the situation in laboratory and nonlaboratory settings, to what does the child attend in making his judgments of the other? There has been virtually no research on attentional processes in social cognition. The closest relevant information is probably the research on children's descriptions of other people. That is, of the many ways a person and his behavior can be described, how do children characterize them? Perhaps the most general finding is that young children, particularly before the age of 7 attend to highly observable, salient, surface cues of people and situations. For example, young children often use appearance and possessions of the person (Livesley & Bromley 1973): "He is tall and has two brothers and a bicycle and lives on my street." Such attention to observable qualities is consistent with Piaget's findings with regard to preschool children's attention to the surface cues of physical objects and events. For example, in making a judgment about the constancy of one of an object's attributes, such as its mass or weight, the young child uses a single, highly observable cue such as the length of the object. Likewise, the tendency to center attention on a single aspect of "external" stimuli also occurs with "internal" stimuli: the child focuses his attention on his own position, idea and feeling, to the exclusion of other possible positions, ideas, etc.

Around 7 or 8 years of age, children show a substantial change in the ways they describe people. More often the description is in terms of habits, dispositions, values, beliefs, and traits, that is, more abstract descriptions based on regularities in behavior of others across time and situations (Livesley & Bromley 1973; Peevers & Secord 1973). This change is paralleled rather well by children's apparent attentional changes in problem solving in the nonsocial domain. That is, the child is increasingly able to deploy his attention (decentration) to greater spatial and temporal "fields," a necessary condition in Piaget's view (1950) for conceptual advance in objectivity.

However, it is important to note that the differences between the younger and older children's descriptions of other people may be due to *what* cues they attend to, and/or *how* they interpret the cues attended to.

5. The Child's Processing of Relevant Information

The cognitive processes involved in interpreting cues from the person and/or situation are not yet well delineated, either for the adult or child. It appears that a variety of processes may be used, depending on the type of information available, the interpersonal task at hand, and the abilities of the judge. Allport (1961) reviewed some theories of how one knows another person. These included the imitation of the motor behavior or posture of another as a means of understanding him, the matching of another's affective state, and making inferences about another from present cues. Certainly the latter is the primary process invoked today and the most researched.

Inference may be used in its proper logical sense of syllogistic reasoning requiring concepts of compatibility and incompatibility between statements (Donaldson 1971), but more often it is used in a general way to indicate that one has "gone beyond the information given." For example, in Flavell's model (1974) of interpersonal inference, many processes are included under "inference," such as discrimination, probability judgments, and logical abilities.

Role taking is a cognitive process (or more correctly a group of processes) which has been emphasized as a major means by which one person comes to know and understand another person (Baldwin 1906; Kohlberg 1969; Mead 1934). As it is used in the field currently, role taking refers to the activity of and/or ability to take the position of another person and thereby infer his perspective. Or, more generally, role taking is "understanding the nature of the relation between the self's and other's perspectives" (Selman 1973, p. 5). As such, the term is most often opposed to Piaget's concept of egocentrism, the inability to take another's position and thus his perspective. More generally, egocentrism is the lack of differentiation between the subject and object (Elkind 1967).

Since a majority of studies reviewed in this chapter are studies of the development of role taking, some additional comments are in order. First, the term "role" is not used as most social psychologists and sociologists use it to refer to a class of shared behavorial expectations defined by a set of functions or traits, such as sex role or occupational role. While role taking may use information such as sex, age, and occupation upon which to make inferences about another's attributes, the term is used more generically to include even momentary positions or relations between two or more people. For example, at one moment a person is in the role of listener, and in the next, as speaker. Role taking occurs in both "positions" in this reciprocal relation. The speaker who wishes to communicate effectively to a listener must adapt his message to the listener's information, attitudes, vocabulary, etc. He must form his message and continually monitor the ongoing message with his listener's perspective in mind. The greater the difference in relevant information between the speaker and listener, the greater the role-taking demands. Likewise, to be a competent listener one must take the role of the speaker to determine what he means by what he says. Thus, Piaget (1926) notes, the egocentric (non-role-taking) child not only assumes he makes himself perfectly clear to his listener but also believes he understands perfectly when he is the listener. A second point can be drawn from this example: role taking is viewed as an instument or means of reaching some interpersonal goal such as informing, persuading, winning a game, or solving a social dilemma. True social interaction has been viewed as a reciprocal relation between individuals in which each person represents the goals, needs, and future actions of the other in order to act or operate in concert—to "cooperate" (Asch 1952; Piaget 1967, 1970). Third, role taking usually refers to the covert, cognitive action of assuming the perspective of another person, whereas role enactment refers to actually taking on the role attributes of another and behaving overtly as the role demands (e.g., the child playing his mother's role). Fourth, role taking is sometimes assessed by the activity or attempts to take on another's perspective rather than by the outcome of this activity, its accuracy. Finally, depending on the content of the role-taking activity, it may be referred to as affective role taking, spatial role taking, etc.

There are other processes which may be involved in understanding another person. For example, in real life situations the child makes a succession of social judgments of an individual in an ongoing sequence of behavior, often a person with whom he has interacted before. His ability and disposition to recall past behavior of the individual may influence the meaning he attributes to the individual's behavior in the current situation. Also, the child may form simple associations or find similarities between the person he is judging and other people he knows which would provide added cues for making inferences about the person. For example, the individual's age and sex may promote expectancies based on role concepts that would influence what the child attends to and infers about the other person. Research on the development of role concepts and social norms (Bigner 1973; Emmerich 1959, 1961; Emmerich, Goldman, & Shore 1971) and the stability of social-belief systems in children (Saltz & Medow 1971; Sigel, Saltz, & Roskind 1967) can only be noted here.

Finally, the possible perceptual processes and conceptual processes involved in understanding others have not been clearly differentiated; this is true, of course, in psychology in general. Social psychologists most often have used the phrase "person perception" while cognitive psychologists, not surprisingly, have preferred "social cognition." The suitability of "perception" often has been questioned because the characteristics, qualities, and covert experiences attributed to another person are not immediately given as observables. Livesley and Bromley (1973) suggest that perception has been used as a convenient term to demarcate the area from other areas within social psychology and has never had a clear descriptive or explanatory function by those using it. Be that as it may, the intuitive and logical abilities apparently used in making social judgments would seem to more closely match the usual definitions of social cognition.

C. THEORETICAL APPROACHES

1. Cognitive-Developmental Theory

Most of the research on the development of social cognition has been drawn from the theories of mental development of Piaget (1970) and Werner (1948). The assumptions of cognitive-developmental theory have been presented by Kohlberg (1969): development involves basic trans-formations of cognitive structure, defined as systems of relations, and such structuring is not the direct result of either maturation or learning. Rather it is a product of the interaction between the organism and the environment. Thus, understanding others is not merely a matter of "learning more" about people in some quantitative sense; it is organizing what one knows into systems of meaning or belief. What one learns from his experiences with others depends heavily on the structuring of those experiences by the person.

While there is no single, general theory of the development of social cognition and an attempt at such a theory is clearly beyond the scope of this chapter, there are two recent models of interpersonal inference that hold substantial promise. The most extensive model has been formulated by Selman (1973; Selman & Byrne 1974). It deals specifically with the changes in role-taking skills of the child and adolescent, conceptualized as structures or stages. The general outline of the model will be presented here with amplification in a later section. Selman suggests that prior to 6 years of age the child is egocentric in the sense that he makes no distinc-tion between his view of social situations and possible alternative views. He may know that the other *can* hold a different perspective, but he is unable to specify that perspective or merely assumes similarity between his thoughts and the other's thoughts, intentions, and the like. During middle childhood, approximately from 6 to 10 years of age, the child achieves two important representations: first he is able to infer the other's intentions, feelings, and thoughts with a good deal of accuracy. Then he becomes able to understand that he, himself, and his inner thoughts can be the object of another person's thinking. Around 10 or 11 years of age a new stage of role taking occurs in which the child under-stands that another can take one's own perspective simultaneously with one's taking of the other's perspective ("mutual role taking"). Around 12 years of age the perspective-taking ability of the adolescent extends be-yond the two-person level to that of the social system, "the generalized other." The adolescent recognizes that both he and the other know that both can remove themselves from simultaneous role taking and view its dynamics. Byrne (1973) has extended Selman's model to a new stage usually occurring after adolescence. The person is aware of the relativity of perspectives held by himself and the social group. Social "facts" are seen as being interpreted according to one's own system of analysis which, in turn, is based upon one's own culture, history, emotional state, etc.

This stage model of role taking is based largely on children's verbal responses to short stories, some involving moral dilemmas and others simple social dilemmas (e.g., should a new doctor, trying to attract patients, decorate his office lavishly or plainly?). There are other stage models of role-taking changes during early and middle childhood by DeVries (1970), Feffer (1970), and Kuhn (1972) that use different methods and which, on the whole, correspond quite well with Selman's stage descriptions. Flavell (1974) has provided a stage model describing spatial role taking from the preschool years to adolescence.

In addition to these stage constructions, Flavell (1968, 1974) has presented a general model of interpersonal inference based on an information-processing approach. It describes the sequential psychological events involved in social role taking. The four events are labeled, "existence," "need," "inference," and "application." First, the individual must be aware that he or another person might have covert, psychological events (i.e., that such events do exist). Second, the child must recognize that the present situation requires (needs) some inference about the other's psychological experience(s). Inference refers to any of the child's mental activities that result in a representation of another person's subjective experiences and activities that maintain the representation. As noted before, the term applies to simple discrimination of cues, integration of cues, probabilistic reasoning, and the like. Finally, application is defined as any subsequent behavior of the child as a consequence of his inference, such as adjusting his game strategy or accommodating his message to a particular listener about whom he has just made an inference. Flavell (1974) has used this "flow diagram" as a microgenetic description of the steps involved in a single act of role taking. It may also be viewed as a description of the sequence of an individual's development in role taking. In the latter case, Flavell has suggested a series of stages of development within the "existence" component which will be described in detail later.

2. Social Psychological Theory

There are several theories dealing with self- and other-conceptions of the adult, collectively known as attribution theory (e.g., Bem 1972; Heider 1958; Kelley 1967, 1973). The focus of attribution theory is on the inferences one makes as to why a person acts as he does, that is, causal attributions. For example, Heider proposes that the cause of an individual's action is inferred by the average adult observer as either a function of factors in the environment, or the person, or both. There are two classes of person factors, the ability attributed to the person (what he "can" do) and the intention and effort attributed to him (what he is "trying" to do). The factors are related multiplicatively: if either the ability factor or the intention and effort factors are absent, no effective action occurs. One of the few points within the theory directed at the development of various attributions concerns the individual's assignment of responsibility for an action. For example, Heider notes that Piaget's first stage of moral development indicates that children (like some adults) may blame a person for any bad consequences with which he is associated even though the consequences were unintended, whereas in the second state blame is assigned only for intended personal actions.

Kelley (1973) has elaborated the method by which the adult, the naive psychologist, makes various causal attributions. Essentially an action or effect is attributed to one of the possible causes with which it covaries. For example, an adult will attribute the cause of a particular behavior to some quality of the person if he observes the behavior in that individual in most situations and most of the time; or to situational factors, if a particular behavior covaries with a particular situation in most people most of the time. Neither Heider nor Kelley has elaborated the developmental origins of such a naive psychology, but both have noted some possible points of contact with existing developmental research.

Another area of social psychological research is generically labeled "person perception." The question addressed is how an individual describes or categorizes another person or his actions and what dispositions or traits he attributes to another. There are two primary methods used in obtaining the descriptions: providing the subject with categories, adjective checklists, rating scales, or descriptive statements which he then applies to various people; and "free-response" measures in which an individual merely describes, orally or in writing, various people.

The development of person perception has been very infrequently studied until the last decade. Both the earlier studies (Gollin 1958; Signell 1966) and some recent studies (Scarlett, Press, & Crockett 1971) were based on Werner's organismic theory. Werner (1948) holds that all development is a process of transition from global, undifferentiated states to states of greater differentiation, specification, and hierarchic integration. Likewise, a developmental shift is posited from egocentrism to perspectivism (Langer 1970; Werner 1948). The primary measures in person perception thus concerned egocentrism and the differentiation and organization of person concepts (see Rosenberg & Sedlak 1972). Some more recent developmental studies of person descriptions have not been based on any one theory (Flapan 1968; Livesley & Bromley 1973).

II. STUDIES OF THE DEVELOPMENT OF SOCIAL INFERENCE

A. WHAT IS THE OTHER SEEING?

One covert, psychological experience of another person is his visual perspective of objects in space, an experience typically not shared at the same time by another. An inference about another's perspective is the least social of all the various types of inferences to be reviewed here. It is least social in the sense that anyone and everyone at a particular location viewing a particular object or array has an identical viewpoint on it, and, indeed, a camera would capture the same viewpoint. Thus, the child is predicting the visual experience of a "generalized other" which has no variability between people. The *only* thing he has to consider about the other person is his spatial location, whereas in other types of social inference he must often take into account several aspects of the situation in order to infer the other's psychological experience, be it feelings, thoughts, or other subjective experiences.

The fact that young children have difficulty in inferring another's spatial perspective is documented by spontaneous behavior of preschoolers in natural settings and in empirical studies. For example, it is fairly common for a young child to ask an adult to identify a picture in a book but continue to orient the book to herself, apparently (though not necessarily) unaware that the adult standing opposite to her cannot see the picture. The inability to take another's viewpoint, in its literal sense, was documented in Piaget and Inhelder's classic study (1956) of spatial representation. Briefly, a landscape of three different-sized mountains was presented to children and they were asked to identify the perspective of "another" (a doll) in various locations around the landscape. Three types of responses were used: reconstruction of the scene, selection of a photograph from a set which matched the doll's location, and placement of the doll to match a particular perspective. The ability to solve this task showed a clear developmental trend, but most important, the types of errors children made were informative. The predominant error was to attribute to the doll the child's own viewpoint regardless of the doll's location, a manifestation, Piaget asserted, of a pervasive difficulty of the young child in self-other relations, namely, egocentrism. This difficulty in relational concepts has been studied in other contexts, such as the relativity of spatial concepts of "right" and "left" and words such as "brother" and "foreigner." The young child uses such words as if they represented some absolute attribute of the object rather than a relation of "being to the right of . . . " and a "brother to . . . " (Elkind 1961; Piaget 1928).

From the three-mountain task data, Piaget inferred three major stages.

The first, occurring in children 4–6 years of age, represents the familiar inability to take the doll's viewpoint and the specific error of attributing one's own viewpoint. Children in this age range seemed to have some intuitive understanding of the instructions for the task but nevertheless failed to solve it. Children younger than 4 were not usually tested since they could not understand the instructions. In fact, one of the difficulties of this assessment procedure is that a child must have some understanding that perspective varies with spatial location in order to test that very concept. That is, the child is usually given a set of pictures showing various perspectives from which he chooses one that shows another's from a given location. But the differences among the pictures are only meaningful if the child has some grasp of the concept of perspective varying with location. Thus, the task materials require an understanding of the very concept the procedures are then designed to assess. Likewise, this task may well elicit a number of "false negatives," children who fail because they have difficulty understanding the rather complex verbal instructions but who can take spatial perspectives of another.

At the onset of concrete-operational ability, typically around 6 or 7 years of age, Piaget found stage 2 performance on the standard task. There was some success in understanding that the doll saw something different than the child, but errors occurred in specifying the difference. Children tended to reverse near objects to far locations for a doll located 180° from them, for example, but failed to reverse right and left. Usually between 7 and 9 years of age children understood how viewpoints differed, with only occasional errors (stage 3). The sequence and timing of these achievements have been found in many other studies using three-object arrays (e.g., Flavell 1968; Laurendau & Pinard 1970).

Is it true, then, that children prior to 6 years of age are highly egocentric and show no appreciation of the location-perspective relation? No. That picture of development emerges when using the standard landscape task or some close variation of it. Flavell (1974) has summarized a number of studies using tasks with simplified arrays and fewer verbal skills to clarify early development in perspective taking. His analysis deals with two factors: (1) the child's identification of *what* object another sees and the more complex concept of *how* it is seen (perspective); and (2) the mode of response, that is, sensorimotor or representational. This stage analysis applies within the "existence" part of Flavell's larger model of social inference (see p. 267). Level 0 describes those objects the child expects in his environment and how they appear to him. The responses are sensorimotor-type expectancies, not representations of a visual experience of either the child or another. That is, the child behaves appropriately toward objects even though he has only a certain perspective of the object (e.g., recognition of a toy dog he is looking for even though he only sees the bottom of the paws). Operationally, a task used by Masangkay et al. (1974) with children between 2 and 5 years of age is instructive. A card with different pictures on each side is shown to the child, placed vertically, and the questions posed: "What do *you* see?" and "What do *I* see?" The level 0 child would fail the second question. However, if he were asked, "What picture is on *my* side of the card?" he might answer correctly. The child can represent objects but cannot represent another's perspective experience regarding them. It might be noted that if a child spontaneously construes "What do *I* see?" to mean "What is on my side of the card?" this could be taken as evidence of the next level of development, that is, that he understands them to be identical questions. On the other hand, if the child repeats verbatim the examiner's question to himself ("What do I see?") he may use himself as the referent to "I" and give the egocentric response, that is, he would fail to make the correct transformation of the examiner's question to "What do you (does he) see?"

Findings by Shantz and Watson (1970) illustrate the level 0 Flavell has hypothesized. Three- to 5-year-olds viewed an array in a covered box, then went to the opposite side to view the array again. They were unaware that on some trials the array rotated 180° with them. About half the children in this age range were surprised, bewildered, or amused at seeing the same perspective they had seen on the opposite side. This seemed to indicate gross expectancies in young children that objects do appear differently from different locations for the self (i.e., when the child himself moves).

Level 1 performance is based on the child's capacity for representing *what* another person sees when the child himself does not see the object, but not yet representing *how* the other person sees the object, in other words, the perspective. The child could thus correctly answer the above, "What do I see?" question. This rudimentary ability to role take, to understand what another person sees, has been found present in all 3-year-olds and about half of the 2-year-olds in a study by Masangkay et al. (1974). Using the same method, Strayer, Bigelow, and Ames (1973) found nine of 24 children between 24 and 30 months of age performed correctly on the majority of trials. This appears to be the first "laboratory" evidence of simple role taking at such a young age. Strayer et al. (1973) also found that such role-taking ability in 18–30-month-olds was related to correct use of the pronouns "I" and "you" in spontaneous communication. The notion here is that the person referred to by "I" or "you" changes with role: "I" or "me" refers to the toddler when he is speaking but to the other person when that person is speaking. However, since the role-taking task used these very pronouns the relationship between the task and spontaneous pronoun use may be spurious, indicating only that the toddler is consistently confused by the pronouns or consistently not confused by them.

At level 2, the child represents the fact that another person sees things in particular ways, that is, how things appear. The three-mountain task clearly assesses this level of role taking. The child must deal with the fact that he and the other see the same objects (three mountains) but have different visual experiences (perspectives of them). When a more simple array is used, particularly a single, meaningful object with readily nameable sides, preschool and kindergarten children have shown some ability to infer *how* the object appears from another's location (Fishbein, Lewis, & Keiffer 1972; Laubengayer 1965; Lewis & Fishbein 1969). The final spatial competency in the existence part of Flavell's inference model, level 3, is the ability to infer another's exact retinal-image percept, an ability not yet empirically tested.

In brief, the sequential achievements in visual inference appear to be the child's inferring that another sees some object the child does not see (or vice versa), an ability evident in most 3-year-olds. Next, the child is able to infer another's visual perspective for one object, typically by 5 years of age. If a group of objects is involved, as in the standard landscape task, the recognition of another's perspective is not usually attained until 7 years of age. Improvement in accuracy in specifying another's experience of interobject relations occurs gradually up to 9 years of age. However, additional task complexity elicits some continuing inaccuracies into adolescence (Flavell 1968).

Given that all findings are captives of the methods by which they are obtained, it is particularly clear in this research that the "average age of accurate spatial role taking" depends heavily on task factors and the type of response required. As already noted, the number of objects in the array (one vs. three or more) and the type of response (motor vs. representational) have significant impact on the child's response. In addition, performance on the standard landscape task has been found to be influenced by the complexity of objects in the array (Brodzinsky & Jackson 1973; Flavell 1968); the location of the other in relation to the child—180° or 90° (Piaget & Inhelder 1956; Shantz & Watson 1970); the mode of response—reconstructing, matching, or pointing (Fishbein, Lewis, & Keifer 1972; Piaget & Inhelder 1956, 1970); and even the symmetry or asymmetry of object placement in the array (Piaget & Inhelder 1970).

Findings such as these may tell more about the child's emerging spatial representation than role taking per se. That is, it may be that the content of the role-taking problem, spatial relations, has intruded as an element in the problem to such an extent that it ceases to be useful in explicating role taking as a social conceptual process. For example, of what general significance is it that the last apparent step in attaining correct perspectivism is dealing with right-left spatial relations? Or in what way does one interpret the significance for role taking that the symmetry of object relations within the array has substantial impact on performance? While these task effects might be of legitimate import to one interested in the child's emerging projective spatial representation, their social psychological significance remains obscure. Yet the consistent appearance of effects of these and other task parameters over age or in interaction with age could lead to reconceptualizing underlying processes that would have significance for the role-taking process (Wohlwill 1973). Perhaps the more immediate question is whether spatial role-taking performance, despite its dependence on various task features, relates to other types of social role taking, a question to be dealt with in a later section of this chapter.

Now that the achievements in spatial role taking have been considered, the next question concerns processes. What indications are there of the types of processes involved in solving the spatial problem? Three general approaches have been taken to clarify underlying processes: analyzing the types of errors, examining the perceptual features of the task, and examining the role of movement in space.

Analyses of the *types* of errors children make in the spatial task, as is true in other problem-solving situations, can provide information about the means by which problems are solved. For example. Coie, Costanzo, and Farnill (1973) tested children from age 5 to 11 on a three-object landscape and found that "relative success on the spatial perspective task was related to a differential disposition toward certain kinds of errors" (p. 176), both in group data and patterns of errors for individuals. Specifically, the first discrimination is the child's determining *what* objects in the array are visible from a particular location, then *how* those objects appear from a particular location, and, finally, where on the right-left dimension the objects are seen. The sequence of the first two types of errors of these children are similar to Flavell's findings of correct performance sequences with preschoolers on single objects. Some corroborative data were also found by an analysis of errors made by 3 ½–6 ½-years-olds by Shantz and Watson (1971). Egocentric errors were most frequent, as would be expected, but the next most popular error was an "impossible" perspective (i.e., the objects had been rearranged and photographed). The choice of this photograph suggested that the child understood that the doll saw something different than he and adopted a strategy of finding the "most different" photograph in the set. Much less frequently chosen in this age group were photographs with correct interobject relations that were incorrect for the location being judged. These analyses of error types suggest that there is an increasing specificity in what information the child infers. Longitudinal data are required to determine whether such a sequence applies to changes in problem solving for the individual child over time.

A second approach to clarifying processes is to examine the impact of the child's own viewpoint on his ability to correctly infer another's. In the standard procedure, for example, the child's view of the mountains is ever-present while he attempts simultaneously to imagine another's view. The perceptual features of the task may dominate the child's attempt to visualize or infer the other's viewpoint. Would a child solve the task more easily if his view were masked so as to free him of the seduction of his present view? Or might masking increase the memory load sufficiently to prevent any facilitating effect? Brodzinsky, Jackson, and Overton (1972) tested children aged 6, 8, and 10, using mask and no-mask conditions, and found that, on arrays with many objects, masking had a significant facilitative effect for the 8-year-olds only. The authors interpreted these findings as indicating that masking of the "perceptually distracting" array did not help the 6-year-olds because they lacked the underlying competency to perform the task, and the 10-year-olds had such stable competencies that masking also did not help them perform better than a no-mask condition. The middle group, the authors suggest, had emerging spatial competencies that were "activated" by the masking. A second study (Brodzinsky & Jackson 1973) using 6- and 8-year-olds replicated the findings for the 8-year-olds in the earlier study. But in the younger group, masking, instead of having no effect, produced significantly poorer performance compared with no masking. And even in the 8-year-old group masking had a significant positive effect only with objects of high internal complexity (not uniformly gray). Shantz, Asarnow, and Berkowitz (1974) found, however, that poorer performance occurred under masked conditions for both 7- and 9-year-olds in the standard landscape task using high-complexity objects. Given the differences in procedures and ages of the subjects in these studies, it is difficult to determine the reason for the discrepancy. In general, masking does not appear to have a simple, direct effect across age groups or within particular age groups. The effect seems to depend on a combination of factors: complexity of the objects, the age of the subjects, and, as will be seen later, other variables such as the movement of the child or the array. The factor of perceptual dominance in spatial problem solving appears more complex than in class-inclusion problems (Wohlwill 1968) or conservation problems (Bruner 1964).

A third approach to understanding the operations involved has been an analysis of the role of movement in space. The questions are: Does the child understand what another sees by mentally (imaginally) rotating the array to his position and "reading off" the resulting image? (strategy 1); does he mentally move himself to the other's position and "read off" the resulting image? (strategy 2); or does he systematically reverse near-far, right-left relations to infer the resulting perspective (strategy 3)? The first two strategies use visual imagery primarily, the third, logical inference.

Two studies give some indirect evidence to answer these questions, essentially by comparing difficulty levels of various "movement" conditions. Huttenlocher and Presson (1973) reported a study in which all arrays were shielded after initial viewing and children either remained stationary as in Piaget's standard task and imagined they moved to a new location or they actually moved to a new location. These conditions were combined with the presence of a fixed stick on the array or no such object. Fourth graders performed significantly better when they actually moved as compared with remaining still and presumably imagined themselves having moved, with or without a fixed stick. Egocentric errors were three times less frequent when the child moved than in the standard perspective task (shielded). The authors also found that the standard perspective task was more difficult than a "rotation" task in which the shielded landscape rotated on its own axis, but the type of movement and shielding conditions were confounded in the design.

The greater ease with which children solve the task when they move as compared with not moving was also found in a study by Shantz et al. (1974). They had six groups of 7-year-olds and six groups of 9-year-olds each solve a landscape problem under a different condition. The conditions were defined by the combination of three factors: actual movement versus imagined movement; movement of the child versus movement of the landscape; and masked versus unmasked landscape. In both age groups the best performance occurred when the child actually moved around a masked landscape or imagined the masked landscape moving; the two most difficult conditions both involved the child remaining in one place and imagining himself moving (or inferring the solution) whether the array was masked or not.

These data indicate about equal facility in solving problems involving actual movement of the landscape and imagined movement of the landscape, which suggests that the latter may be solved like the former: while the child remains stationary, he mentally rotates the landscape to his position and "reads off" the image produced (strategy 1). In these cases, the child seems to need to deal with only one relation—between himself and the array. However, in the standard task, the problem is to imagine how the landscape appears from another position—that of the "other person." Here two relations seem required—the self-array and other-array relations. The task would seem easily solved if the child would imagine himself moving to the new position and then would read off the resulting image (strategy 2). Is that what he does? Apparently not. As discussed earlier, two studies have found that with *actual* movement of the child the landscape perspective is very easily anticipated, but not in the standard task. This suggests that the child does not mentally move *himself* to the other's position. As Huttenlocher and Presson (1973) note, the symbolic movement of the self may well be very difficult for the child. Instead, the child may be mentally moving the "other" to his, the child's, position. Or, more exactly, he may take the observer-array relation and rotate that relation to his own-array relation and read off the resulting image, a complex version of strategy 1. Adults who solve the standard landscape problem report that "they rotate the entire observer-array pair until the imagined observer becomes recoupled with ego" (the subject being tested) (Huttenlocher & Presson 1973, p. 296).

The third strategy posed earlier, the systematic reversing of right-left and near-far relations for an observer opposite the child, remains a possibility. However, even among adults this "inference process" is seldom reported (Huttenlocher & Presson 1973).

These studies manipulating movement conditions represent only one means of clarifying the processes by which the child solves various landscape problems. They depend rather heavily on the assumption that tasks of equal or near-equal difficulty are solved by the same or similar processes while those of much greater difficulty are solved by different or more complex processes. Much more research is required before definitive statements can be made as to the process(es) used in spatial perspective problems.

In conclusion, the sequence of developmental achievements in visual role taking appears to be the child correctly inferring the answer to the following: "Does the other see something?" "What is it he sees?" and "How does it appear to him?" The performance of preschoolers and young school-age children, as well as the types of errors of older children, generally support Flavell's model of increasing specification of another's visual perceptions. As such, the model and data are similar to developmental findings in other areas in which children simplify both the information and the processing of information. For example, young children sometimes construe the conservation question, "Is this the same amount of water?" to be the much less complex question, "Is this the same water?" (Bruner 1964). Likewise, they often attempt to solve seriation problems involving multiple relations (such as sticks ordered from shortest to tallest) as the more simple binary category problem (grouping short sticks vs. tall sticks). But how the sequential achievements in specifying another's visual experience occur in relation to levels of cognitive functioning (sensorimotor or representational) remain to be specified. Apart from the general developmental sequence described above, there is little definitive information concerning the processes, rules, and/or strategies which make such role taking, in its various forms, possible. It should be noted, too, that inferences about another's perceptual experiences have been almost entirely concerned with visual percepts while auditory and tactual experiences have been largely unexplored (see Moore 1958).

B. WHAT IS THE OTHER FEELING?

In keeping with the focus of this chapter, the child's understanding of another's emotional experience will be reviewed with no assumption that the child himself *feels* the same emotion. This brings us immediately to the problem of the concept of empathy. It has been defined in the literature in a variety of ways (Deutsch & Madle, in press), primarily as either a cognitive response (i.e., understanding what another person is feeling), an affective response (i.e., having the same emotion as the other person), or both. The word originally meant neither: empathy was "objective motor mimicry" (Taguiri 1969).

A description of some methods might help clarify the issues surrounding the definition of empathy. In some studies, a child is presented with a brief story depicting a situation and accompanied by a picture (Borke 1971, 1973) or a series of slides (Feshbach & Roe 1968). The situations are simple ones such as attending a birthday party, losing a pet, having one's toy broken by another child, or being lost, illustrating happiness, sadness, anger, or fear. A child is asked, "How does the child in the story feel?" A correct answer has been labeled as "empathy" by Borke (1971, 1973) and as "social understanding" by Feshbach (Feshbach & Feshbach 1963; Feshbach & Roe 1968). Or the child is asked, "How do *you* feel?" the correct answer being scored as "empathy" by Feshbach. In short, empathy is, operationally, primarily a cognitive response for Borke and an affective response for Feshbach.

Two aspects of these procedures require further discussion. The notion that empathy is "feeling the same emotion as another person feels" seems to be based on the idea that the child, hearing the story and seeing a depiction of the situation, identifies with the story-child's situation, or his expressed emotion, or remembers how he felt in the same type of situation, and thereby feels the same emotion. The child is asked, "How do you feel?" and not, "How would you feel in that situation?" The researcher, in asking the first question rather than the second, is interested in what emotion the child *does* feel in response to the story-picture material and not what the child *can* feel given explicit instruction to put himself in the story-child's place. The second aspect of these procedures has to do with the stimulus materials presented to the child. In Borke's case (1971), the story-child has a blank face and the subject-child supplies a face with a particular expression (happy, sad, etc.) as his nonverbal response to the question, "How does the child in the story feel?" In Feshbach's procedures, however, the slides depict not only the situation but an expression of the "correct" emotion on the story-child's face. Thus, there are two sources of cues for the correct emotion (situational and facial) while Borke's material provides only one source of cues (situational).

There appear to be several issues embedded within the various definitions and methods used to measure empathy: whether the response is affective, cognitive, or both (Feshbach 1973); whether the child is responding to another person's situation, the other's expressive cues of an emotional state, or both; and how empathy is related to various processes. In the latter issue, for example, if empathy is defined as understanding another's feelings, is that understanding mediated by imitating another's emotional cues (affective matching), by role taking, projection, or identification? Or is empathy, defined as a shared emotional experience, mediated by understanding? Some of these questions will be dealt with in the course of reviewing the studies. Accuracy as a criterion of empathy is not an issue: all researchers score empathy only if the child is correct in matching an emotion to the situation depicted.

The developmental findings concerning empathy as "understanding how the other is feeling" will be reviewed first. Most of these data are based on Borke's Interpersonal Perception Test (1971) which consists of 23 stories, each accompanied by a picture. Only a nonverbal response, selecting a face, is required. Various studies have found that by 4 years of age children can correctly identify above a chance level those situations that typically elicit emotions of happiness, sadness, fear, and anger, although the latter two emotions tend to fluctuate in relative ease of identification (Borke 1971; Mood, Johnson, & Shantz 1974). For example, one might respond with anger or sadness at having a toy broken by another. In a cross-cultural study, Borke (1973) found that happy situations were identified with high reliability by both American and Chinese

3-year-olds, but situations involving unpleasant feelings of fear, sadness, and anger were recognized with increasing accuracy in the 4–7-year-old range. Both cultural groups at all ages had the greatest difficulty identifying angry situations. Recognition of fearful situations was found to be more advanced in Chinese middle-class than Chinese lower-class children or American children of either socioeconomic class, which Borke suggested may be due to more protectiveness by Chinese middle-class parents. A cultural difference was also found in the identification of sad situations: Chinese children between 3 and 4 were more accurate than American children.

In summary, then, simple situations which usually evoke happy responses in children are reliably identified by 4-year-olds. Between 4 and 7 years of age, there is increasing accuracy in identifying situations eliciting fear, sadness, and anger. Recognition of fearful and sad situations seems to be a function not only of age but of cultural and class membership. At the same time, some of the differences found on identification of sad situations may be due to individual differences between children in their response to frustration in a particular situation.

What is the relation between understanding how another feels and actually experiencing that same feeling? Feshbach and Roe (1968) investigated this question, using the same four emotions of anger, happiness, sadness, and fear, in children aged approximately 6–7. After each story and slide sequence depicting an emotional situation, children responded verbally in answer to, "How do *you* feel?" The situations were re-presented to half the sample of children, and they were asked, "How does this child feel?" (the story-child). They found that more children reported the depicted emotion in answering the second than the first question. The authors suggest that "empathy as a vicarious affective response may be contingent upon the comprehension of a social event, while social understanding may be independent of an affective response" (Feshbach & Roe 1968, p. 133). This hypothesis, that "cognitive empathy" is a necessary but not sufficient condition for "affective empathy," was given some support in another study using Borke's test (Mood et al. 1974). For each story, children from 3 to 5 years of age were asked both how the story-child felt and how they themselves felt. Of the total responses across emotions, 57% were correct identifications of the story-child's feelings, but only 30% of these also felt the same way as the story-child. Likewise, for the 42% of the total responses that were incorrect, only 29% felt the same way they thought (incorrectly) the story-child felt. Thus, whether a child correctly identifies how another child feels or not, there is a tendency not to feel the same way himself, as measured by this type of story test.

How should these findings be interpreted? When a child can identify how another child feels in a given situation, is that a function of role-taking skills? Probably not, or at the most, it is a very primitive form. The situations used in the Interpersonal Perception Test (Borke 1971), the Affective Situations Test (Feshbach & Roe 1968), and other methods (e.g., Deutsch, in press) are probably quite familiar to young children (i.e., having a toy snatched away, getting lost). A child may identify the correct emotion to go with a situation from his own experience or from remembering others' responses when he was an observer. Chandler and Greenspan (1972) have been critical of interpretations such as Borke's that role-taking skills are involved. Rather, they suggest, more primitive mechanisms such as projection or identification are more likely to underlie correct performance. The argument is essentially the same as that raised by Cronbach (1958) regarding interpretation of adults' accuracy judgments. When situations are familiar and/or the person judged is similar to the judger, accuracy may be the result of a simple attribution of one's own response or characteristics.

But is there evidence that similarity between the judger and judgee increases empathy in children as it does in adults? Yes, according to several studies. Boys are more empathic when judging story-boys, and girls when judging story-girls, than when making cross-sex judgments (Deutsch, in press; Feshbach & Roe 1968). And similarity of race facilitates empathy (Klein 1971). Corroborating evidence is also supplied by a study by Rothenberg (1970) in which a substantial difference was engineered between the child-subjects and those they judged: two adults in a tape-recorded dramatized vignette. For example, one vignette went, "Shall we go out to a movie tonight? . . . Oh, I forgot to tell you. I've invited some couples over for dinner tonight. . . . Oh no! I can't be ready . . . ." Thus, Rothenberg tried to maximize dissimilarity by using adults as targets and experiences the child probably had not had himself. Situational and voice cues were given for identification of four emotions, anger, happiness, anxiety, and sadness. Children aged 10 ½ were significantly more accurate in their perception of feelings and changes in feelings than 8 ½-year-olds. The fact that the 8 ½-year-olds had difficulty identifying emotions accurately, particularly when compared with the studies previously reviewed of preschoolers' accuracy in identifying the same emotions, suggests that Rothenberg's use of dissimilar targets and situations for child-judgers had a substantial impact on accuracy. Consistent but less direct evidence is provided by Flapan's findings (1968) that 6-year-olds, after viewing a film of children and adults interacting, had more difficulty spontaneously reporting or answering direct questions about the movie-adults' feelings than about the movie-children's feelings. Nine- and 12-year-olds much more often mentioned the feelings of adults and were more likely to answer questions correctly about those feelings.

Overall, these studies suggest that accurate empathy concerning simple emotions is achieved by preschool children when the situation the other person is in is familiar to the child and/or the other person is substantially similar to the child. Accurate understanding of these same emotions is not usually attained until middle or late childhood when the situations and people judged have low similarity and low familiarity to the child. Such data support the contentions of Bronfenbrenner, Harding, and Gallwey (1958), Chandler and Greenspan (1972), Flavell (1968), and Rothenberg (1970) that accuracy in judging others' emotions under conditions of high familiarity and similarity may be no more than self-descriptions.

Let us now turn to studies in which the only cue about another's emotional state is facial expression. Izard (1971) has reviewed the developmental research. Generally, preschoolers can differentiate pleasant and unpleasant emotions in photographs and can select among three photographs the one depicting a particular emotion (such as anger, joy, disgust). However, if children are required to give a specific verbal label to the expression, they are much less accurate, Izard found. The same effect was observed in children's judgments of affective situations (Feshbach & Roe 1968).

If both facial and situational cues are available, do children tend to rely more on one type of cue than another to understand another's feelings? There are few direct data. Burns and Cavey (1957) presented children aged 3–7 with a picture in which the situation was in conflict with the child's facial expression (e.g., a child smiling next to a doctor with a long needle, or frowning at a birthday party). When asked, "How does the child feel?" preschoolers' answers were more determined by the situation than the expression, but for 5–7-year-olds the expression was more often noted and the conflict recognized. As attention was not drawn equally to situational and facial cues before judgment, the relative impact of the two types of cues is not clear. Deutsch (1974a) presented short, filmed episodes in which affective expression was incongruous with the situation in some instances and congruous in others. The "situations" in this case involved such interpersonal behavior as an adult giving another adult a cup of coffee while the latter was writing. A smile by the recipient of the coffee was congruous; a frown incongruous. Preschoolers were more accurate in labeling the situation than the affect expressed, particularly in congruous episodes. Although there was greater dissimilarity of the target person to the judger than in the Burns and

Cavey study, the child's attention was not directed specifically to facial or situational cues.

These studies suggest that children's attention is more likely to be drawn spontaneously to situation cues than to facial cues and/or that verbal labels for situations are more available than verbal labels for facial cues. It seems reasonable that children would recognize the utility of situations in predicting feelings of others, particularly situations involving simple events. Taguiri (1969) has reviewed evidence that adults rely quite heavily on situations in making judgments about others and further tend to construe facial expressions to fit the situation. However, reliance on facial or situational cues might well depend upon the discriminability of the cues, the reliability of the cues as representative of certain emotions, and the particular question asked the child. For example, asking, "What were the people doing in this story?" would probably elicit situational descriptions whereas, "What were the people feeling in the story?" might elicit facial and/or situational descriptions.

The studies reviewed to this point have concerned primarily the child's ability to identify emotions usually experienced in particular situations or to identify emotions expressed facially. The child's ability to identify the *causes* of another person's feelings has been the subject of a few studies. Not surprisingly, children are much more competent at an early age in describing behavior in general (obvious emotions, actions) than inferring the reasons for the behavior (Deutsch, 1974a; Flapan 1968; Livesley & Bromley 1973; Rothenberg 1970; Whiteman 1967). Interestingly, when young children do make causal attributions they tend to use the situation to explain the feelings and thoughts of the other person. For example, Flapan (1968) found that 6-year-olds' descriptions of movie episodes did not often include causal reasoning, but when they did the situation was used as an explanation (e.g., "She felt sad because the squirrel was hurt"). There was a substantial increase in causal attributions by 9-year-olds and a greater tendency to use psychological explanations (e.g., "She felt sad because she thought her father didn't love her"). In turn, explanations of feelings and thoughts in terms of how one person in the movie perceived another occurred more regularly in 12-year-olds (e.g., "The mother changed her mind because she saw how sad her daughter felt"). Children did not abandon situational explanations but rather used psychological explanations and interpersonal perceptions as additional sources of causal attributions.

In summary, children as young as 3 years of age can recognize reliably that certain familiar situations typically elicit certain emotions such as happiness and fear. These same emotions can be reliably discriminated on the basis of facial cues only. The fact that children can match a situation to an emotion probably should not be interpreted as reflecting sophisticated causal reasoning or role taking. Such matching may be no more than an association, a co-occurrence as in children's tendency to juxtapose physical events without recognizing their causal relation (Piaget 1928), and it may represent only accurate self-description. The degree to which children attend to and use situational versus facial cues in identifying others' emotions is not clear from the data available. Accuracy seems to be partly a function of the child's familiarity with the situation the other is in and his similarity to the other person. Only in middle or late childhood can children correctly recognize emotions when judging people who are dissimilar to themselves in unfamiliar situations. During this same age period, children begin trying spontaneously to explain the reasons for others' feelings.

C. WHAT IS THE OTHER THINKING?

This section concerns the child's ability to infer what another is thinking or what another knows about a particular situation or event. Children's inferences about another's thoughts have been studied in three major research paradigms: communication behavior, game playing, and story analysis. In the first two paradigms inferences about the other (listener, opponent) are instrumental in achieving a goal (informing, winning), whereas they are not a means to an obvious goal in the third paradigm.

The communication studies investigate how the child uses the language he possesses in order to inform or persuade another. The child learns to "edit" what he wishes to express for his particular listener(s). Presumably, such editing is guided by the speaker's analysis of the knowledge and attitudes of his listener. "Taking the role" of the listener facilitates effective communication (Flavell 1968). Most research with children and adolescents on communication development has been recently reviewed by Glucksberg, Krauss, and Higgins (1975) and Looft (1972), and will not be included here.

A second paradigm is a "game" situation in which, as in the communication problems, the child is a participant. His goal of winning is helped by correctly inferring his opponent's strategies (thoughts) and, further, by recognizing that his opponent is trying to infer his thoughts. For example, DeVries (1970) had children from 3 to 7 years of age try to guess in which hand an opponent had a penny and, on some trials, to hide the penny for the opponent to guess. Five levels of role-taking skills were inferred from the hiding and guessing behavior, competitive attitude, and affective reactions during the game. The first level is characterized as the child having no awareness of individual perspective; that is, the young child may offer the penny instead of hiding it, and if he hides it he does not seem to recognize any need for deception or secrecy. At the second stage perspective differences are recognized on a *behavioral* level (probably in imitation of others). The child does not always hide the penny in the same hand. Motivational differences between opponents are not recognized yet: the child wants his opponent to find the penny just as the child wants to find it. At the third level the child may recognize such motivational differences but does not yet understand that his opponent is thinking out a guessing strategy. The child regularly alternates hands when hiding the penny, which DeVries interprets as indicating that the child is still not "thinking what the other might be thinking." At stage 4 there is irregular hiding (i.e., attempting to be unpredictable to the opponent); but, interestingly, there is not use of an irregular *guessing* pattern. Shifting from hand to hand irregularly when guessing over trials is typical of level 5. Most 6- and 7-year-olds of average intelligence and half of the bright 5-year-olds tested behaved at the stage 5 level.

Selman (1971b) also tested young children's role-taking skills, but with a different method. In a specially constructed room, the child was asked to infer what a peer could see (visual role taking) and what a peer would guess in a choice situation (inferring the other's thoughts and reasoning). The verbal responses of children 4–6-years-old were analyzed and showed four levels of rudimentary role taking. At level A the child may have a sense of the other, but does not distinguish between thoughts and perceptions of himself and the other. At level B the child clearly distinguishes himself from the other, but does not see any commonality between his thoughts and the other's. Next (level C), the child attributes his own thoughts to the other by putting himself in the other's position. Given an identity in situation with the other, he naively assumes similarity between the other's thoughts and his thoughts. At the next step, level D, performance indicates that the child is aware that the other has viewpoints based on his own reasoning, and those may or may not be similar to the child's. These levels all occur within stage 0 of Selman's larger-stage model of role taking, described in the "Introduction."

The assumption that another's thoughts are the same as one's own reaches a peak around 5 years of age, Selman found. The recognition of a difference in thoughts or strategies usually occurred around 6 years of age.

In summary, DeVries found evidence of role taking in 5-year-olds, whereas Selman found very little for that same age group. The discrepancy in abilities inferred by DeVries and Selman may be the result, in part, of different response measures. DeVries used game *behavior* and inferred the cognitive structures underlying it; that is, the child behaved *as if* he had a particular representation of the other. Selman, on the other hand, posed questions to the child and used the verbal response to infer representations. Given the limited verbal abilities of subjects this age, one might feel more confident making inferences from motor behavior than from verbalizations. But the popularity of the hiding game among children makes it possible that they imitate various hiding and guessing behavior without actually understanding the reasons for or the effects of such behavior. Thus, DeVries's method may tend to overestimate the child's competence while Selman's may tend to underestimate it. At the same time, Marvin (1974) has recently provided some interesting and relevant data on this issue. While replicating DeVries's findings on penny-hiding strategies in 4-year-olds, Marvin also found that about half the 4-year-olds made appropriate choices for a birthday gift for their mothers (when pitted against desirable toys) and had some nonegocentric concepts of social causality. The latter was tested by asking a child after his mother left the room such questions as, for example, "Can *you* [child] make mommy come back?" a typical nonegocentric response being, "No, but herself can." These abilities were absent in all 2-year-olds and most 3-year-olds, who insisted that they could make her come back. The data give more weight to the possibility that "old" preschoolers have simple role-taking skills in familiar situations.

Another game situation used with older children requires that a child predict which of two cups an opponent will choose to get some money and give a rationale for the prediction (Flavell 1968). The simplest level in predicting the other's choice is no prediction: the child is unable or unwilling to anticipate a particular choice by the opponent, or has no verbalized rationale for a predicted choice. At the second level the child attributes a motive to his opponent—financial gain. The child always predicts the other will choose the 10¢ cup rather than the 5¢ cup. He focuses only on his opponent's thoughts about the game materials. At the third level the game strategy attributed to the opponent results from the child's recognition of the monetary-gain motive plus an important additional attribution: the opponent may predict what he, the child, will do. Therefore, the child switches to the 5¢ cup. He is aware, in other words, that his own thoughts may be the object of thinking of another person ("reciprocal role taking," in Selman's terms). There is a fourth level in which the child understands that the opponent is making inferences about the child's strategy (as shown at the previous level) and, to combat it, the child will switch back to picking the 10¢ cup for the opponent's choice.

Flavell found the lowest level of performance at all age levels, including a third of the sample of 16-year-olds. It is surprising that such a high proportion of adolescents showed no ability to infer an opponent's simple thoughts. It is likely that the verbal requirements entailed in the causal attributions in this task underestimated the inference competency. The second level was typical from ages 7 to 10, approximately; the third level (entailing the recognition that one's own thoughts are an object of another's thinking) occurred most frequently for children from age 11 on. Selman (1971a) found approximately one-third of 8- and 10-year-olds used this strategy. The most complex level was seldom used at any age level tested by Flavell (1968). A structural analysis of this game strategy task is presented later.

A third approach to studying the inferences about thoughts of another uses stories in the following format: (1) the child constructs a story and then retells it from the perspective of each story-character (Feffer 1959; Feffer & Gourevitch 1960); (2) a story involving a social dilemma is presented and the child is questioned about his understanding of the dilemma from various viewpoints (e.g., Byrne 1973; Selman & Byrne 1974); and (3) a story is presented in which characters have differing types or amounts of information (Chandler & Greenspan 1972) or a variation of this method (Flavell 1968), which the child must keep differentiated.

Feffer's Role-Taking Task (1959) represents the first method. Role taking is measured essentially by the degree to which the story line remains constant but perspectives are differentiated and integrated. Feffer has suggested three levels of role taking. Children as young as 6 can "refocus" from one character to another but the story suffers: gross inconsistencies develop. Usually around 7 or 8 years of age, the child can coordinate perspectives sequentially (e.g., a father-character suggests going for a ride to which the child-character responds with excitement). About the age of 9, "simultaneous coordination" of perspectives occurs with interpersonal perceptions involved (e.g., a renter feels cheated and angry because her rent was raised while the landlady perceives her anger but feels she had no choice) (Feffer 1970; Feffer & Gourevitch 1960).

A second method presents a social conflict or dilemma. For example, a new doctor is trying to decide whether his office should be decorated luxuriously or plainly (Byrne 1973); a boy who is accustomed to calling adults by their first names is instructed not to do so with his teachers but refuses (Turiel 1966); or a girl promises her father not to climb trees but later is asked by a friend to rescue his kitten in a tree (Selman & Byrne 1974; Selman, Damon, & Gordon 1973). Social role-taking stories differ from moral role-taking stories to the extent that the former involve general social expectancies or conventions rather than moral principles.

However, the last example above where breaking a promise is at issue illustrates that social role taking and moral role taking as contents are not clearly distinguished at times. To the degree that they overlap, the result may be spuriously high correlations between social and moral role-taking performance.

Selman (1973; Selman & Byrne 1974) has presented a stage analysis of responses to social dilemmas, described in part in the "Introduction." The stages in middle childhood will be elaborated here. Stage 1 is called social-information role taking, and usually occurs between 6 and 8 years of age. The child recognizes that another may view social actions differently than he depending on the amount of information that each person has, that is, he sees others as interpreters of social situations. He also understands that he and the other can distinguish between intentional and accidental actions. At stage 2, self-reflective role taking occurs (approximately between 9 and 10 years of age) in which the child is clearly aware that he and his inner thoughts, feelings, and intentions can be the object of another's thinking. He can figuratively step outside himself and reflect on his own and the other's thinking and the other's thinking about him. Such role taking occurs only sequentially, however. At stage 3, the role taking of the child can occur simultaneously and mutually, as evidenced by children aged 10–12 in their response to social dilemmas. Additional role-taking stages in adolescence are described in the "Introduction."

Selman's model of role taking and his findings concerning the abilities of children match those of Feffer fairly well. The basic ability to understand that others may have different perspectives than oneself, Feffer's "simple refocusing" and Selman's stage 1, usually emerges around 6 years of age. The second level of sequential coordination of different perspectives (Feffer's "consistent elaboration" and Selman's stage 2) typically appears around 8 or 9 years of age. The third level in which perspectives are simultaneously and mutually assumed by each party (Feffer's "simultaneous coordination" and Selman's stage 3) is apparent in most children around 10 years of age.

A third type of story format has been constructed to determine whether a child attributes to another person information that, in fact, only the child himself has (Chandler & Greenspan 1972; Flavell 1968). For example, Flavell (1968) presented seven pictures showing a boy, walking down a street, who is suddenly threatened by a dog, climbs an apple tree for safety, and ends by sitting in the tree munching an apple. The cards showing the dog chasing the boy and his fearful expression are then deleted, leaving another possible story. The child is asked to predict what story another person, seeing only the shorter series of pictures, would tell. Poor role taking is measured by the extent to which the child's first, seven-card story intrudes on the second story. The results corroborate quite well the developmental findings obtained by other story methods.

An analysis by Flavell (1968) of the role-taking skills involved in thought inferences indicates a sequential pattern of relationships among the child's thoughts, the object of his thinking, and the other person. That is, the child's inference of others' thoughts is described in structural terms. The first level is the simple attribution to another person of a thought, feeling, or intent (e.g., "I know how you feel about that new car"). Next, the child understands that his own thoughts about something or someone can be the object of another's thinking (e.g., "I think you know what I think of it"). And the third, most complex level, is essentially the realization of the recursive nature of thinking, that the self and the other can consider another's thinking ad infinitum (e.g., "I know you must think that I can't understand your liking for soccer").

Two studies have dealt specifically with this structural model: the analysis of verbal "thinking out loud" as children plan a game strategy (Flavell 1968), reviewed earlier, and direct assessment of the understanding of recursive thinking depicted in cartoons (Miller, Kessel, & Flavell 1970). In the latter case, children described cartoons showing a person (1) thinking about two people, (2) thinking about talking between two people, (3) thinking about thinking of another person, and (4) thinking about thinking about thinking. The items were scalable with 92% of the children having a pattern of more correct responses for items lower in the scale. The first item was understood by all children from grades 1–6, but not until fourth grade was the second type correctly understood 75% of the time. Fifth and sixth graders answered the third type correctly only half the time. Two-loop recursion, the fourth type, was correctly described only a third of the time by children in the fifth and sixth grades. The authors suggest that competency in recursive thinking may be underestimated by the verbal demands of the task. Such recursive thinking ability does appear to be related to more conventional role taking tasks. Rubin (1973) found correlations around .70 between this task and two others, spatial role taking and communication role taking. Also, such ability to think about thinking seems to have formal similarity to the ability to ascend and descend class hierarchies, such as Grouping I in Piaget's model of concrete-operational thought (Miller et al. 1970). For example, in the case of one-loop recursion, "the boy is thinking that the girl is thinking of her father," the father is the object of two identical actions at the same time. And, in class hierarchies, one class is the superordinate class of two subclasses while, at the same time, it is itself a subclass of a larger superordinate class. Hence it is embedded in the hierarchy by additive operations. Such a possible relation between non-social and social logical abilities is, however, untested.

The various structural models of changing ability to infer another's thoughts warrant some comparison. Feffer's task is conceived in terms of social decentering and is analogous to spatial role taking: the object of focus, the story, must remain constant but vary in interpretation or per-spective from each character's "position" in relation to the story events. Analogously, persons around a landscape recognize the constancy of the objects and that appearances vary depending on location, each perspec-tive coordinated with one another. Flavell and Selman have models deal-ing with this "object" focus as well, but these extend to the child as participant, which allows the child to be an "object" of another's think-ing. Decentering in Selman's model extends from the child as observer and inferer about another, and as participant with another, to observer of the dyad of which he is a member and to the role of observer of the observer of the dyad. As the child becomes more cognitively mature, the model indicates, the child can increasingly "step back" from himself, his thoughts, the other person's thoughts, and the relation between himself and the other.

The developmental findings are these. By 6 years of age the child can usually infer that another may have different thoughts or knowledge than the child himself, and by middle childhood he is aware that others can think about the child's thoughts. In late middle childhood, around 10 or so, children evidence ability to infer what another is thinking while at the same time infer that the other is thinking of what the child himself is thinking. Inferential accuracy and recognition of the nature of recursive thinking continue to develop well into late adolescence. There are some discrepancies in the ages at which these various abilities have been found in different studies. For example, DeVries found the majority of 6- and 7-year-olds not only took account of the other's role but knew the other was taking account of his perspective (DeVries 1970). Such sequential role taking has been found by others to emerge in middle childhood, around 8 or 9. The discrepancy may be due to several factors, one of which is the type of response used (motor vs. verbal), as discussed before. Also, it may be that the child's inferential skills about particular types of thoughts develop at different ages, or if generalized, that the child may not recognize the utility of making such inferences in particular settings (the "need" component of Flavell's model of interpersonal inference).

The stage-model analyses of the developmental changes in inferring another's thoughts have proceeded far beyond the investigation of what processes might account for the changes. That is, there is much more information and theory on what inferences a child is able to make about another person's thoughts than how he manages to do so. The speculations of Miller et al. (1970) concerning the child's ability to conceptualize particular types of relations (e.g., nested relations and reciprocal relations) and his ability to make causal inferences (Whiteman 1967) might be fruitful sources of information about the logic involved in making such inferences.

D. WHAT IS THE OTHER INTENDING?

Considerable attention has been given in research to a particular type of thought attributed to the other: his intentions. In the flux of people's behavior toward objects and other people, adults make important inferences about the other person's goals or purposes of actions. It is the inference of what a person is *trying* to do, consciously or unconsciously. The ability to differentiate between events that are intended or not intended (accidental) and the ability to differentiate between types of intended actions, good or bad, are both clear developmental achievements.

The intentions one attributes to another serve as an important basis for praising, crediting, or blaming that person for his actions. Understanding another's intentions plays an important role in many everyday events. For example, if a child's blocks are knocked down by another child or if he is benefited in some way, the child's response to the events will be very different depending on whether he views the actions as intended or accidental (Baldwin & Baldwin 1970; Shantz & Voydanoff 1973). However, most research on intentionality has been restricted to the area of moral judgment, particularly whether one blames another for the outcome of his actions.

The major source of developmental research on intentionality is Piaget's work (1965) on moral development, and many have replicated his method in studying intentionality. Two stories are presented. In one, a child acts from bad intentions (such as malice or greed) causing a small amount of damage, while in the second story another child with good intentions (such as obedience, helpfulness, generosity) causes a large amount of damage. The general finding has been that the seriousness of the outcome is the major determiner of blame judgments up to the age of 8 or 9, whereas the intention of the actor is the basis for assigning blame in older children (Bandura & McDonald 1963; Cowan et al. 1969; Piaget 1965).

There are several problems with this method that have been noted recently (Hebble 1971; King 1971; Sedlak 1973; Turiel 1966). First, the amount of damage and the type of intention are covaried so that one cannot determine clearly the relation between these two variables for blame assignment. Second, in some stories, at least two variables are confounded: the type of intent (good or bad) and the responsibility for the outcome or consequences (accidental or intended outcome). For example, in "good-intention" stories (the child obeying, being helpful, having permissible fun), the child's actions that result in bad outcomes are always unintended (being clumsy, ignorant of some fact, negligent, etc.). In short, the outcome is accidental, unforeseen by the actor. In "bad-intention" stories, however, where the child is acting from a motive such as greed, the bad motive is paired with two different types of responsibility. In some stories, a bad outcome is directly intended by the child and foreseen by him. In other bad-intention stories, though, the outcome is as accidental as it always is in the good-intention stories. For instance, while attempting to reach a forbidden cookie, the child accidentally knocks down a cup that breaks. As Sedlak notes (1973), "The child (or adult) who is basing blame judgments on intent is sometimes required to determine whether the character intended the damage that resulted from his action, while at other times he is also required to determine whether the character was acting from a good or bad motive, independent of the happened outcome" (p. 8). That is, if the subject decides that the damage which occurred was indeed intended, then the problem is easily solved; but if he decides that the damage was not intended, he must analyze further the character's other (uncompleted) goal in the situation and then judge how acceptable that goal was. Perhaps, as Sedlak notes, the finding that a young child's moral judgments are based largely on outcome is due to the fact that the outcome is the only aspect of the story that is systematically varied.

Another problem should be noted. In some stories, the wording does not make clear whether the outcome was intended or not. For example, "First he played with the pen, and then he made a little blot on the table cloth," versus "But while he was opening the ink-bottle, he made a big blot on the table cloth" (Piaget 1965, p. 122). "Little blot" compared with "big blot" makes the amount of damage very clear, but whether the blot making was intended or accidental is difficult to determine in either story.

With these methodological problems in mind, a few studies will be reviewed first in which the responsibility for consequences (i.e., intended vs. accidental) has been clearly varied. King (1971) showed children four motion-picture sequences and determined by open-ended questions the extent to which they attributed responsibility to the actor for the consequences. The accidental versus intentional variable was paired with neutral versus negative outcomes. For example, the "accidental neutral" story showed two boys running, then one boy tripping and getting up unhurt; the "intentional negative" story showed the boys running, one pushing the other into a tree, and the pushed boy appearing hurt. There was a significant increase in judgments based on intentions from pre-school age (about 4 ½-year-olds) to kindergarten (about 5 ½-year-olds), with the younger children showing little inference about intent. Most interestingly, the presence or absence of negative consequences had *no* significant effect on correct inferences of intention for any age tested (preschool to third grade). Armsby (1971) also found that a majority of 6-year-olds used intentions as the basis for judging naughtiness of the actor. Purposeful action was compared with accidental action in each of four story-pairs, each pair having four levels of consequences (breaking one cup, 15 cups, a set of dishes, or a new television set). Three-fourths of the 6-year-olds used intentions as the basis for moral judgments rather than damage done. With more serious damage, however, judgments by 6–8-year-olds tended to rely less on intentions.

In a different content area, but using the same paired-story method, Baldwin and Baldwin (1970) found that two-thirds of a group of kinder-gartners (and virtually all of the second graders) judged a child more kind who intentionally benefited another child than one who accidently benefited another. However, Shantz and Voydanoff (1973) found that 7-year-olds did not vary their retaliatory aggression depending on wheth-er provocation in stories was purposeful or accidental, although 9- and 12-year-olds did. Having subjects merely recall the story before re-sponding resulted in greater differentiation between intentional and acci-dental provocation across all ages, but effect of recall was not significant for 7-year-olds. Thus, attentiveness and memory for purposeful or acci-dental cues in a story do not seem to account for the youngest children's failure to differentially respond; the ability to infer intentions and use that inference might be the bases, however.

In summary, the majority of studies indicated that most children by 6 years of age do distinguish between intended and accidental actions whether or not these actions have good, neutral, or negative conse-quences. However, as consequences become more extreme the distinc-tion becomes less reliable. This may be the result of the child's recogniz-ing (as do adults and the legal system) that intention is less important in assigning responsibility when outcomes are extreme. Also, it seems possi-ble that children may distinguish whether actions are accidental or in-tended prior to distinguishing between good and bad intentions. There are no longitudinal data to determine whether this is the case for individ-ual development, but cross-sectional data using group means of 5- and 7-year-olds suggest such a sequence (Irwin & Ambron 1973).

What judgments are made by children when stories are presented where all actions are purposeful and intentions and consequences are either good or bad? Costanzo et al. (1973) used such a framework for moral judgments in boys of approximately 6, 8, and 10 years of age. The consequences were good or bad, whereas in most stories in other studies the outcomes are neutral or vary in degree of badness. Also, the outcomes were social (an adult's approval or disapproval) rather than material (breaking things, hurting people, etc.). For example, in one story a boy emptied his toy box on the floor in order to arrange the toys neatly, whereas another boy did the same thing because he was cross and wanted to mess the toys up. The good and bad intentions were paired with an adult's subsequent disapproval or approval. It was found that the type of intent and type of consequences interacted. Specifically, kindergarten boys did not vary their blame judgments on good versus bad intentions when the consequences were bad (i.e., the adult's disapproval). But in positive-consequence stories (adult's approval) even the kindergartners viewed the child acting from bad intentions as naughtier than the child acting from good intentions. The type of consequences was less relevant for the older children: they based their judgments on the type of intention. It appears then that the adult's disapproval "swamped" the younger children's use of the type of intention.

In relation to the earlier summary on intended and unintended actions, it appears that children as young as 6 do distinguish between good and bad intentions when the consequences are positive but apparently do not when consequences are negative. In studies using stories that have bad versus good intent with varying degrees of damage and varying responsibility, it seems that children do consistently make blame judgments contingent on intention by 8 or 9 years of age (Breznitz & Kugelmass 1967; Hebble 1971; Johnson 1962). If situations are made more complex by varying the degree of responsibility (a planned act vs. careless act vs. an insane actor) and more extreme consequences (such as wounding or killing a person), judgments based on intentionality continue to develop in early and middle adolescence (Kugelmass & Breznitz 1968). To this point, all studies have examined conscious intentions. But it is clear that children around 8 years of age have some degree of understanding of unconscious intentions, as represented by the classic defense mechanisms of displacement, projection, denial, etc. (King 1971; Whiteman 1967). For example, children usually understand why a story-child, whose mother broke a promise to her, says nothing to the mother but spanks her doll instead.

Finally, one other variable in intentionality studies is noteworthy: the medium in which the situation is presented. All studies reported to this point have used stories (and sometimes a picture) with the exception of King's movie method (1971). Could the way in which the situations are presented have an impact on blame judgments? Chandler, Greenspan, and Barenboim (1973) address this question from their observation that research findings on intentionality based on stories did not square with young children's apparent use of intention in real life situations. They compared good versus bad intentions paired with minor or severe negative consequences. For example, one child spills a lot of paint while helping his father paint a chair, while another child spills a little paint while trying to paint the family cat. Each subject compared the two children's naughtiness in two conditions: the situations given in stories or on videotape, with the order counterbalanced. It was found that the children aged 6 ½–7 ½ based their blame judgments in the story situation largely on the severity of the consequences, whereas judgments of the videotape situation were largely based on the type of intention. The medium does seem to have an important impact on the bases children use to make blame judgments. An analysis of the amount and type of information given in movies as compared with stories would be critical to clarify the effects of the two media.

Some of the findings on moral development have been analyzed by Sedlak (1973) using Heider's theory of interpersonal behavioral judgments in adults. Her central thesis is that our understanding of moral judgments in children would be greatly enhanced by investigating the child's understanding of what a person in a given situation is able and not able to do (Heider's "can" factor), what a person is intending to do (Heider's "try" factor), and what a person in a given situation is required by standards to do (Heider's "ought" factor). Taking the one general finding that younger children tend to weight consequences more heavily than intentions in determining blame, Sedlak (1973) gives four possible interpretations. First, children may have difficulty inferring intentions of people and learn to rely on other more obvious criteria (such as damage done). Or, children may infer intent and use it as a criterion of blame as adults do but err in inferring responsibility of the person (i.e., whether the person could or could not foresee the consequences of his actions). A third possible interpretation is that children may infer intent but not differentially: they assume intention of all actors for any outcome with which they are associated ("guilt by association"). And fourth, it is possible that blame judgments are not related to responsibility inferences, that moral and causal systems develop independently for some time. There is anecdotal evidence that the inferences about "can," for example, may not be very accurate in the young child, as suggested when the child becomes enraged at the helpless parent when "Disneyworld" is preempted by a presidential address. Systematic investigation of the child's understanding of others' abilities, intentions, and environmental factors in a given situation has been rather meager (Sedlak & Schmidt 1973; Shaw & Sulzer 1964) and deserves more inquiry.

In summary, children by approximately 6 years of age appear to be able to infer whether another person's actions are intended or accidental and to use such inferences in assigning blame or credit. This tends to be the case whether the consequences of the action are good, neutral, or negative, but not when they are extremely negative. At this same age, children use information about whether intentions are good or bad if positive consequences are involved but not if consequences are negative. The latter seem to swamp inferences about and uses of intentions until middle childhood. As many published studies do not report the exact stories told to children, it is not always possible to determine whether children were required to *infer* accidental versus intended actions and/or types of intentions or whether they were given this information directly. In the latter case, the issue is their ability to use information about intentions.

E. WHAT IS THE OTHER LIKE?

This rather inelegant title subsumes the research usually called person perception, that is, how children describe other people. The data in such studies are often divided into two large categories: "overt" descriptions, including such aspects as physical appearance, possessions, and family membership, and "covert" descriptions, dealing with the other person's attitudes, abilities, and personality traits. Thus, in person-perception studies, descriptions about thoughts, feelings, and intentions are all grouped together in the covert category. So the data here cannot be discussed under different types of inferences about others. There have been several reviews of person perception in childhood and adolescence (Dubin & Dubin 1965; Livesley & Bromley 1973; Rosenberg & Sedlak 1972); therefore, only illustrative studies using free descriptions will be reviewed here.

Livesley and Bromley (1973) had 320 English boys and girls write one self-description and eight descriptions about others. As there is ample evidence of interactions between characteristics of the perceiver and the "perceived" person, children described people they knew who differed in age (adults vs. children), sex, and affective relationship (liked vs. disliked). The subjects ranged from 7-4 to 15-9, classified in eight age groups and two levels of intelligence. Each response page began with a role description, such as "a girl I know very well and like is . . .." The child selected someone to fit the specification and then wrote a description without time limits. He was instructed to describe the person carefully, to describe "what sort of person" he was, and was specifically told not to describe physical characteristics. The descriptions were analyzed for the number of statements made, the number and proportion of psychological versus nonpsychological statements, the types of statements (e.g., habits, possessions, aptitudes, social influence), and the number and proportion of traits attributed (such as being generous, honest, conceited).

Some of the major findings follow. The number and proportion of psychological descriptions increased significantly with age. Interestingly, the proportion of psychological statements increased significantly only between 7 ½ and 8 ½ years of age (from 22% to 43%). Verbal fluency is not a likely explanation since a proportional measure was used. Girls used more but not a higher proportion of psychological statements than boys. More psychological statements were made in describing males than females and in describing children than adults for all subjects. In addition, the authors noted than the "greatest increase in differentiation [number of categories] was observed between the ages of 7 and 8 years . . . and frequently the differences between the 7- and 8-year-old groups were greater than those between 8- and 15-year-olds. This is perhaps the most important finding of all; it suggests that the eighth year is a critical period in the developmental psychology of person perception" (Livesley & Bromley 1973, p. 147). There appeared to be a substantial shift in the types of categories used with increasing age. The 7-year-olds tended to focus on overt qualities such as appearance and possessions (despite the fact they were instructed not to), while children aged 8 and older used more inferential concepts, those based on regularities in behavior across time and situations (e.g., values, beliefs, dispositions). Some aspects of descriptions (number of categories, proportion of psychological statements) varied with characteristics of the person being described (e.g., adult vs. child, liked vs. disliked), or the describer (sex, intelligence), or both. Some of these findings are too complex to be reviewed here.

What *traits* do young children use in free description and how do these change over time? Livesley and Bromley (1973) found that 7-year-olds used on the average about five different traits in their descriptions of eight individuals. That number doubled over the next year. Generally, trait vocabularies grew particularly between 7 and 10 years of age. The most frequent traits were "kind" and "nice," used by half of the 320 subjects. Adjectives used by 7-year-olds tended to be vague and diffuse with a strong evaluative component (e.g., nice, good, bad, horrible) while others reflected salient value systems such as "lazy," "clever." Older children used terms that were more abstract and precise in meaning (e.g., considerate, shy, sensible) and more often referred to the perceived person's impact on other people.

Some of these same trends were found by Peevers and Secord (1973) in free-response interviews with 80 subjects from kindergarten to college age. The descriptions of liked and disliked acquaintances of the same sex as the subject were coded on four dimensions: (1) descriptiveness (from undifferentiated to dispositional); (2) personal involvement (from ego-centric to other-oriented); (3) consistency of evaluation on a good-bad dimension; and (4) depth. The latter dimension ranged from statements that were superficial and unqualified trait attributions, to a level in which the describer noted contradictory characteristics of a person or condi-tions under which particular behavior occurred, to the highest level in which an explanation for the characteristic(s) was given. The two higher levels never occurred in the descriptions given by kindergartners and third graders but did for eleventh graders and college students at low frequencies. These trends of describing what people are like and less often why they are like that (explanation) were also found by Flapan (1968) and Livesley and Bromley (1973). Peevers and Secord (1973) found that liked peers elicited other-oriented descriptions (no personal involvement) while disliked peers elicited more egocentric statements (e.g., "he hits me"), but exactly the opposite was found by Scarlett, Press, and Crockett (1971). In general, however, there is a decreasing use of egocentric and concrete descriptions with increasing age (Livesley & Bromley 1973; Peevers & Secord 1973; Scarlett et al. 1971).

As age increases, both the number of categories and the use of inferen-tial, abstract, covert categories have been found to increase in most stud-ies (Gollin 1958; Scarlett et al 1971; Supnick 1967; Yarrow & Campbell 1963), but not all (Olshan 1970; Signell 1966). Differences in methods and scaling techniques may account for some of these discrepancies.

What are some of the strengths and weaknesses of the free-description method? On the positive side, it appears to have less chance of biasing the way in which children describe people than using adjective check-lists, traits, rating scales, category statements, and the like. For example, both Livesley and Bromley (1973) and Peevers and Secord (1973) found that traits made up only about 20% of the total content of free descrip-tions. Likewise, the traits children do use often differ a good deal from those given in rating scales or checklists. If these latter techniques are used, they may well bias our understanding of children's conceptions of people by requiring attributions of adult traits. Similarly, they neglect a substantial part (80%) of children's spontaneous descriptions. On the other hand, free-description data should be interpreted as what children *do* do in describing others, and not, necessarily, what they *can* do. What they do is partly dependent upon their interpretation of the instructions "to tell what the person is like." Some investigation is needed to determine whether some of the reported differences between younger and older children's descriptions are partially due to different interpretations of instructions. For example, young children's tendency to use appearance and possessions to describe others may reflect their tendency to treat the instructions as a referential task, distinguishing an individual from other people (much as an adult would describe another by his age, residence, and occupation to identify him for a listener). In two studies some of the subjects were interviewed and "probed" about their previous descriptions. Children manifested higher levels of understanding (Flapan 1968) or more abstract attributions (Livesley & Bromley 1973) than they had revealed in spontaneous descriptions, although both studies suggest the differences were not great. Certainly, for an adult the task at hand determines largely whether he identifies another by giving a psychological profile or demographic data. The same factor could influence children's approach to description.

The studies reviewed to this point are essentially investigations of "classification schemes" children apply to people they actually know. There are a few studies (Dickman 1963; Flapan 1968) which have presented filmed social interactions among two or more people whom the children do not know to determine how children discriminate, categorize, infer, and explain the behavior observed and how they characterize the people. A study by Flapan (1968) serves as an illustration. The subjects, 6-, 9-, and 12-year-old girls, were shown one of two episodes from the movie *Our Vines Have Tender Grapes*, in which children and adults interacted around one or two major events. The children reported what happened in the viewed episode and the responses were analyzed into three categories: reporting-describing, explaining, and inferring-interpreting, with each category subdivided. The general findings were: First, with increasing age reporting of an overt action and dialogue and describing the situation gave way increasingly to attempts to explain the social interactions, which, in turn, were supplemented by inferring thoughts, feelings, and intentions of the actors (see also Rappoport & Fritzler 1969). Second, explanations changed from situational factors to psychological factors (feelings and motives) to "person-perception" explanations (the child attributed one actor's behavior to that actor's perceptions of the other actor). There was, third, a shift with age in the kinds of inferences made, in the following sequence: inferences about thoughts and intentions, inferences about feelings, then inferences about interpersonal perceptions (Flapan 1968, p. 28). Overall, the greatest changes of all kinds occurred in the age interval between 6 and 9, which is consistent with a good deal of research in both person perception and role taking. These data should be helpful in understanding related processes such as observational learning in children and the effects of television. They also complement laboratory studies about specific abilities of children, particularly role-taking skills. Certainly more study is needed of children's understanding of actual and filmed social episodes they observe and those in which they participate.

III. Social Cognition and Cognitive Abilities

A. INTERRELATIONSHIPS OF SOCIAL COGNITIVE ABILITIES

Having considered the development of various inferences about people and characterizations of them, a question arises about their relationship. For example, are more abstract person descriptions related to higher role-taking skills? There are no studies available to answer this question. It is clear that both increase with increasing age, but whether the sequential levels of role taking and sequential changes in person description are functionally related in development is not known.

The second issue concerns the generality of various types of social inference. For example, is a child who is advanced in understanding what others see also advanced in comprehending another's thoughts? Piaget suggested such generality by his very use of the construct of egocentrism. It is an inability, a lack of differentiation that is not tied to one or two manifestations but is evident in a number of "contents." Piaget studied various contents—spatial representation, moral judgment, communication skills, concepts of relational words—each with a different group of children. Because there was a substantial change in these behaviors and the changes occurred in synchrony, around 7 years of age, Piaget assumed that all of these behaviors manifested an underlying cognitive orientation—egocentrism. However, at no time was the same group of children given a variety of tasks measuring egocentrism or, conversely, role taking, to determine whether there was sufficiently high relationship among them to support the assumption of generality, that is, the convergent validity of the construct (Campbell & Fiske 1959).

Rubin (1973) studied the question of generality by testing 80 children from kindergarten to sixth grade on a battery of tests which were designed to assess the ability to take another's role. The tests were spatial role taking as measured by Flavell's method (1968), "cognitive egocentrism" measured by the degree of private speech (Kohlberg, Yaeger, & Hjortholm 1968), recursive thinking ability (Miller et al. 1970), and communicative role taking (Glucksberg & Krauss 1967). Verbal intelligence, conservation ability, and popularity were also measured. Three of the role-taking tasks—spatial, communicative, recursive thinking—were significantly intercorrelated in the .65–.73 range. With mental age or chronological age partialled out, the correlations among the three tasks remained significant, but moderate (.31–.36 range). A factor analysis revealed a principal factor accounting for 57% of the variance defined by all measures of role taking (except the private-speech measure) and conservation. The second factor represented entirely the popularity variable.

Van Lieshout, Leckie, and Smits-Van Sonsbeek (1973) examined the issue of generality with 142 3–5-year-olds. Nine tasks were used: recognition of occupational roles, recognition of role behavior of family members (Emmerich 1959), choice of a gift for another (Flavell 1968), recognition of sensory needs of another, empathy (Borke 1971), identification of another's right and left hands and feet (Elkind 1961), and three spatial perspective tasks (Flavell 1968). All tests intercorrelated significantly, except for the right/left task, and the range of correlations generally was from .20 to .48. Because of the small age range, it is unlikely that these correlations are due to age. Factor analysis revealed one major factor accounting for a third of the total variance on which all tasks loaded significantly, except for the right/left task. The authors interpreted the results as indicating that "different aspects of early childhood role-taking behavior . . . can be considered as aspects of a single construct or parallel constructs" (Van Lieshout et al. 1973, p. 14). Kingsley (1971) found significant intercorrelations among spatial, communication, and perceptual tasks for third graders but not for kindergartners.

Cowan (1967) divided children into high and low role-taking ability groups by their performance on the three-mountain task, and then assessed the degree of egocentric communication in dyads consisting of two high role takers, two low role takers, or one of each type. He found the best communication for dyads with high spatial role-taking ability and the poorest performance for dyads with low role-taking ability. However, the data were not tested for statistical significance. Other researchers using this design have not replicated Cowan's findings (Looft 1970) or have done so only partially (Ceresnie 1974). There are several other studies which have intercorrelated two or more different role-taking tasks and found no significant relationships (Finley, French, & Cowan 1973; Rothbaum 1973; Sullivan & Hunt 1967).

The studies suggest that there is, at best, only a moderate relationship among various role-taking skills. The magnitude of the correlations in the study by Van Lieshout et al. (1973), while significant, is not very high. It is not clear why some studies have found significant interrelationships and others have not, but there are several possible reasons. The magnitude of correlations among tasks is known to be influenced by the reliability of each task, the range of scores, and the difficulty level of each task. Thus, low intercorrelations might be statistical artifacts and/ or indicate that one or more of the tasks do not measure role taking, or that they do measure role taking and it is not a general ability or unitary construct. Likewise, high intercorrelations are spurious to the extent that they represent shared method variance. This might occur, for example, when all tasks require substantial verbal skills. High intercorrelations might be due more to that factor than the construct being measured. This does not seem to be the case in most studies reported here. Measures of spatial role taking, communication of messages, and recursive thinking concepts appear to be quite dissimilar in content and type of response required. Shared method variance, then, is not a likely explanation for the intercorrelations obtained. Considering the impact of various task features on some types of inference performance (e.g., spatial role taking), the intercorrelations of tasks found in some studies are unexpectedly high.

No studies have included a task of some other cognitive ability which is *theoretically unrelated* to role taking. Such an inclusion would allow a determination of whether role-taking tasks intercorrelate more highly with each other than any of them do with the theoretically independent ability (rather than comparing the intercorrelations to zero). This would afford a measure of the discriminant validity of role taking (Campbell & Fiske 1959).

In this context it is also important to note that another method of establishing the construct validity of role taking is to find a high degree of relationship with an ability predicted in Piaget's theory (1967) to be necessary (but not sufficient) for role taking to emerge—decentration. The notion is that the child's ability to deploy his attention to more than a single aspect of a situation provides the necessary elements upon which his logical abilities may (or may not) operate. However, this theoretical premise apparently has not yet been tested directly. Decentration and role taking have been used as almost synonymous concepts rather than as two processes, attentional and logical, whose relationship is to be determined. For example, a high loading of several role-taking tasks on the principal factor has been labeled a "decentration" factor but with no independent assessment of the child's ability to decenter (Rubin 1973), or decentration has been inferred from the same data as perspective taking (Feffer 1959). In neither instance has progress been made in clearly differentiating the two concepts and establishing a relation between them.

In summary, findings on the generality of role taking range from indications of no significant generality to a moderate, significant degree of generality. Depending on one's prior expectancies about the generality of cognitive abilities, the intercorrelations might be sobering or encouraging. Either reaction may be premature given the relatively small number of studies of convergent validity and the lack of studies of discriminant validity.

B. RELATION OF SOCIAL COGNITION AND OTHER COGNITIVE ABILITIES

One frequent approach to studying the relation between social cognitive and impersonal cognitive abilities is to examine the relation between intelligence, as measured by various psychometric methods and role-taking tasks. Generally, the relationship has been found to be in the low to moderate range, usually between .20 and .40 (Coie & Dorval 1973; Flavell 1968; Irwin & Ambron 1973; Rothbaum 1973; Rothenberg 1970; Rubin 1973). However, studies which have included other differential variables indicate that the IQ/role-taking correlations vary with the gender of the child (Coie & Dorval 1973; Irwin & Ambron 1973) and/or socioeconomic class (Irwin & Ambron 1973) as well as the type of intelligence test (verbal or nonverbal) (Coie & Dorval 1973; Rothenberg 1970). Likewise, the types of descriptions of people given by children vary with particular combinations of intellectual level, gender of the child, and sex of the person being described (Livesley & Bromley 1973). To date, there seem to be no data to support the view that children's social cognitive skills are "nothing more" than a reflection of their brightness as measured by conventional intelligence tests.

Even if social cognitive skills were substantially related to intelligence, the relation would not be very helpful in clarifying what processes are involved in social cognition. Most intelligence tests tap many abilities. Piaget (1970) has maintained that there is a moderate relationship between logical operation development and role-taking development since certain logical operations (e.g., reversibility) are necessary for role taking.

Some specific cognitive abilities have been studied to examine their relationship to role-taking abilities. For example, Feffer and Gourevitch (1960) gave 6–13-year-old boys Feffer's Role-Taking Task and problems of conservation and class inclusion. Significant positive correlations among measures were found when age and intelligence were controlled. Likewise, Rubin (1973) found that conservation performance correlated highly with role-taking performance, indeed as highly as the role-taking tasks intercorrelated. Swinson's data (1966) corroborate these findings. However, Hollos and Cowan (1973) reported low correlations between role taking and logical operations (class inclusion, logical multiplication, conservation tasks) in Norwegian children aged 6–9. Although social cognitive and logical abilities appear to be generally related, it is not clear, paradoxically, what particular logical abilities are involved. Some investigators cite the fact that decentration is required in tasks of conservation and class inclusion, and, using Piaget's notion that decentration is necessary for role taking, conclude that a relationship has been established between decentration and role taking. However, decentration is clearly not the only ability required to solve the part-whole problem of class inclusion or conservation. For example, in conservation solutions the child presumably not only deploys attention to several stimulus aspects but integrates the information by means of any one of several logical operations (reversibility, multiplication, or others). Which of these or other logical abilities relate to role taking is not known.

In conclusion, the studies on the generality of the child's various inferences about people differ in finding moderate generality to no generality. Role-taking skills usually relate in the low to moderate range with conventional measures of intelligence, but that relationship often varies with the sex of the child, socioeconomic status, and the type of intelligence test. The attempt to find specific, nonsocial logical skills relating to role-taking ability has not proceeded far. The most frequent relation found has been with conservation performance, but even that is not consistent. It is unlikely, on both theoretical and empirical grounds, that the role taking/conservation relationship is wholly or substantially due to decentration.

IV. SOCIAL COGNITION AND SOCIAL BEHAVIOR

A. PEER INTERACTIONS

One might well expect that there would be a good deal of information relating the child's understanding of other people to his actual social behavior, but there is not. Presumably this lack of research reflects the traditional insularity in the study of conceptual, motivational, and behavioral processes (Kagan & Kogan 1970). In fact, the relation between social cognition and interpersonal behavior may be one of the largest unexplored areas in developmental psychology today. In a recent review of research on peer interaction, Hartup (1970) observed, "There is little doubt that the changes which occur in child-child interactions during infancy and childhood are closely linked with changes in sensory-motor capacities, cognitive skills, and the development of impulse controls. . . . Role-taking would appear to be one prerequisite for the emergence of many . . . social behaviors. . . . It is inherent, for example, in cooperation and altruistic interaction" (p. 368). It would appear so, but there are few direct data to support or refute such a relation.

It has been suggested that a variety of prosocial behaviors— cooperativeness, friendliness, helping, kindness, generosity—emerge and are strengthened by the child's ability to take the role of the other (Aronfreed 1968; Kohlberg 1969; Murphy 1937; Piaget 1965). That such behaviors are influenced by situational variables (see chap. 3 in this volume) does not preclude the possibility that role-taking ability affects the ease of shaping, maintaining, and generalizing prosocial behavior. It has also been suggested that certain antisocial behavior, such as aggression against peers, may by inhibited by the aggressor taking the role of his victim (Feshbach & Feshbach 1969). Besides prosocial and antisocial behavior, only two other social variables have been studied: popularity and conformity.

The expected relation between role-taking abilities and social behavior has stemmed most directly from Piaget's theory (1965, 1967). He suggested a bidirectional causal relation: peer interaction as a necessary factor for the development of role-taking skills, and vice versa. In the first case, Piaget suggests that egocentric functioning decreases as a result of the child's confrontation with peers who differ in their wishes, perspectives, needs, and thoughts. Thus, peer interaction in general, and peer conflict in particular, is the necessary condition for role taking to emerge and stabilize. In the second case, as role-taking abilities emerge the child can engage in reciprocal social behavior, such as cooperation, discussion, and planning. To date most research has focused on establishing a relationship between certain social behaviors and role taking; only a few studies have more direct bearing on the question of causal relations.

1. Correlational Studies

In the case of prosocial behaviors, Rubin and Schneider (1973) found for 7-year-olds a significant, moderate relationship between communicative role taking and two measures of altruism, generosity and helpfulness (r's = .29 and .64, respectively, with mental age partialled out). Such a relationship does not mean, of course, that role taking is causally related to generosity and helpfulness. The fact is that helping and sharing behavior increase with age (Handlon & Gross 1959; Midlarsky & Bryan 1967), as do role-taking skills. Hartup (1970) has noted that role taking *may* cause increases in altruistic behavior, but it is also possible that increases in altruistic behavior (as a function of external rewards, perhaps) cause increases in role-taking abilities—a bidirectional view shared by Piaget. The only other prosocial behavior that has been investigated in relation to role taking is cooperative behavior, and Ceresnie (1974) found no relation between the two.

Is there any evidence of a relation between role-taking skills and antisocial behavior? Yes and no. Feshbach and Feshbach (1969) found high empathy was related to *more* aggression in 4- and 5-year-old boys, *less* aggression in 6- and 7-year-old boys, and was unrelated for girls of both age levels. Chandler (1973) found that chronically delinquent boys aged

11–13 had significant deficits in taking others' viewpoints (at a level of children half their chronological age) compared with nondelinquents at the same age. When IQ was controlled, the difference in role taking remained significant. In general, these two studies indicate an inverse relation between role-taking ability and antisocial behavior for boys older than 5.

Piaget (1926) also proposed that a child's social status or popularity is related to his ability to take another's viewpoint. Generally, the findings have indicated no relation between the two (Finley et al. 1973; Rothenberg 1970; Rubin 1973). However, Rubin (1972) found a positive relation in kindergarten and second grade, but not fourth and sixth grades. Deutsch (1974b) found that communicative role-taking ability in preschool girls was significantly related to popularity measured by the amount of positive social interaction of the child but not to popularity measured by sociometric choices. Rothenberg's findings (1970) that role taking was related not to popularity but to being described by peers as a leader, gregarious, and friendly, as well as Deutsch's data, suggest that role taking may relate to general positive interactions with others more than popularity.

Finally, conformity, indexed by responsiveness to peer influence, has been studied. Hartup (1970) suggested that the more egocentric the child, the less conforming he is, apparently because he is immune to social norms. Two studies, however, found the opposite relation in children approximately 5–8: the greater the egocentrism, the greater the conformity (Tierney & Rubin, in press; Weinheimer 1972). The reason is not at all apparent, and, in fact, the relationship may not be reliable. It is known that conformity behavior, itself, varies with the difficulty level of a task and the ambiguity of the situation. Further, conformity bears a curvilinear relationship to increasing age whereas role-taking skills tend to be more linearly related. The complexities here demand more intensive study.

2. Training Studies

Some studies have attempted to train role-taking skills to determine the effects on social behavior. Staub (1971) placed groups of kindergartners in four training conditions: role playing in helping and being helped; induction training focused on pointing out the consequences of helping; combined role play and induction training; and a control group. He found that helping a distressed girl occurred more often for girls who had only role-playing training, but for boys the combined role playing/induction training was most effective. Girls' sharing with a needy boy was not influenced by any training condition but was significantly increased for boys in the role-playing-only and induction-only groups. Generally, role playing seemed to have the most consistent effect in increasing helping (for girls) and sharing (for boys). This procedure involved both mild reinforcement for playing helpfully and the experience of reversing roles, either of which alone or together may have produced the effect on prosocial behaviors. No study has yet trained children directly and only on prosocial behavior and measured the effects on role-taking ability to test the possible causal relation in the other direction than that suggested by Staub's findings.

It is worth noting that the different effects of different training for boys and girls, as well as the complete lack of relationship between helping and sharing across conditions, may be due in part to the similarity of sex between the child and the "victim" in Staub's study (1971) (i.e., girls helping the girl and boys sharing with a needy boy). Such findings may suggest at first blush that empathy is mediating prosocial behavior since, as previously discussed, similarity of sex increases empathy. However, it is also possible that similarity of sex directly elicits prosocial behaviors without empathy being involved.

The effects of role-taking training on antisocial behavior were studied by Chandler (1973). Delinquent adolescents with demonstrated low role-taking skills were divided into three groups. The role-taking training group made up skits, took various roles, filmed the skits and viewed themselves in the films. The placebo group made animated cartoons and documentary films in which they did not act. A control group received no training. After a 10-week training program, the role-taking skills of the groups were tested, and at 18 months after training the police records of all delinquents were compared. In the first case, the trained group showed significant increases from pretesting in role-taking ability compared with changes in the other groups. The role-trained boys committed approximately half as many known delinquencies during the 18 months following training as boys in the other groups. In summary, then, this study and that by Feshbach and Feshbach (1969) suggest an inverse relation between role-taking ability and antisocial behavior for boys older than 5. And, specific role-taking training has been shown in one study to increase role-taking ability and decrease antisocial behavior. The post-training increases in role-taking skills are consistent with the notion that role taking was mediating changes in social behavior.

In this context, a few training studies have attempted to demonstrate that role-taking skills can be elicited and/or accelerated in development by appropriate training but have made no assessment of their effects on social behavior. For completeness, these studies will be briefly reviewed. Van Lieshout et al. (1973) pretested a groups of preschoolers on a variety of role-taking and empathy tests and then, during regular nursery school hours, gave training on role taking and prosocial behavior. For example, children discussed feelings of others in stories and doll play, enacted roles, and were induced and reinforced for being altruistic, comforting, and helpful to other children. With pretest role-taking ability and mental age controlled, trained children showed significantly higher role-taking abilities compared with a no-training group for the 3- and 4-year-olds, but not the 5-year-olds. Unfortunately, some aspects of training were specific to the test battery of role taking, and thus some changes may represent little more than practice effects. Beyond that, it leaves open the question of what aspect of training—role taking or prosocial behavior—produced the effects found.

Three studies have attempted to facilitate the child's ability to take the role of his listener in communications. In all cases, small groups of children communicated about designs and discussed the adequacy of the message from the listener's viewpoint. Two studies showed minimal changes in communicative role-taking ability (Fry 1966, 1969) and one found a significant increase and some generalization (Shantz & Wilson 1972). In two studies of spatial role taking the children made inferences about another's viewpoint from various locations and received feedback about the correctness of the inferences. Such a procedure resulted in positive training effects in one study (Laubengayer 1965) and no effects in the other (Douglas 1971).

Finally, the training of role taking as well as other skills in the school setting has been attempted. One example is Spivack and Shure's training (1974) of preschoolers to consider alternative ways of behaving in social problem situations, to be aware of the consequences of their behavior, and to increase their sensitivity to others' feelings, thoughts, and intentions. The authors report several studies showing improved social problem-solving ability and improved social behavior in children with such training. However, Elardo (1974), using a somewhat similar "combination" training program for 1 year with elementary school children, found no significant effects on role-taking ability or teachers' perceptions of classroom adjustment.

These training studies are essentially demonstrations of some experiences which are *sufficient* (and, in some cases, not sufficient) to elicit and accelerate the development of role-taking skills in children from preschool age to adolescence. Some training studies, in addition, have examined the effects of training on social behaviors (Chandler 1973; Spivak & Shure 1974). None of these studies indicates what experiences are *necessary* to elicit and accelerate role-taking skills or changes in social behavior. Such a question can be answered, not by training, but by "deprivation" studies (i.e., isolating what experiences when absent result in retarded role-taking ability). Because of ethical considerations, the researcher is dependent on finding naturally occurring conditions where the suspected "necessary" factors are absent.

In summary, the hypothesis of a substantial relationship between role-taking ability and social behavior has not been strongly supported to date, but neither, certainly, has it been refuted. Both correlational and training studies indicate some moderate positive relationships between role taking and prosocial behavior, such as helping and sharing, and moderate negative relationships with antisocial behavior in boys. About an equal number of training studies have produced and not produced significant gains in role-taking skills. A more coherent picture of the relation between role-taking skills and social behavior would be gained in the future by assessing a variety of social inference skills and a variety of social behaviors and examining the relationships between and within each domain.

B. FAMILY VARIABLES

Parental influences on role-taking skills have been suggested by Hoffman (1970), Kohlberg (1969), and Weinstein (1969). Hoffman found that various indices of moral development in a large number of studies are most consistently associated with predominantly "inductive" child-rearing practices, as compared with techniques using the assertion of parental power, withdrawal of love, and parental affection. Inductive practices include giving the child reasons for requiring a change in his behavior and pointing out the consequences (material and psychological) of his behavior for other people and himself. It is, in short, a more conceptually oriented than ·punishment-oriented discipline method. Piaget (1965) stressed the importance of peer rather than parental interactions in fostering role-taking skills, but he did discuss parental influences. He noted that social systems involving authority or constraint lead to a "sociocentrism closely akin to egocentrism" (Piaget 1970, p. 229), a system presumably existing in families with authoritarian child-rearing practices. Further, child-rearing practices which emphasize a system of social relations rather than a system of commands may well facilitate role taking in the child (Piaget 1965). There is some face validity to the notion that parents who verbally indicate their own and others' covert responses (feelings of sadness or pride, intentions, and thoughts) to the child's behavior might foster the child's ability to make such inferences himself and, in addition, provide a model of role taking.

Since parental induction tends to be related to moral development after the preschool years (Hoffman 1970) and moral development has been found to be highly related to role-taking skills (Byrne 1973), it might be that parental induction and role-taking abilities of the child are related. There is, however, very little direct evidence on the matter. Bearison and Cassel (1975) examined "appeal strategies" that middle-class parents use over common parent-child conflicts such as bedtime, not wanting to go to school, picking neighbors' flowers. If the parent reasons with the child, what types of reasons does he use? "Types of reasons" were conceptualized within Bernstein's sociolinguistic theory which posits that family control systems are reflected by the way parents use language. Specifically, some parents appeal to position-status factors ("all children should . . . ") and some to person factors involving the feelings, needs, intentions of particular people involved in particular situations ("the teacher will feel sad if . . . "). Bearison and Cassel found that person-oriented appeals by parents were positively related to role-taking skills in children aged 6–7. This indicates that even *within* the inductive mode parental focusing on covert events, compared with rule focusing, is associated with children's ability to take the role of the other.

Some supportive evidence is also found in a study by Dlugokinski and Firestone (1974). Third- and fifth-graders' perceived inductive discipline by their parents was associated with other-centered values and with sharing money, if the appeal to share was inductive rather than power assertive. However, Birnbaum-Steinlauf (1974) did not find any relation between 5-year-olds' role-taking abilities and their mothers' reported use of inductive discipline, nor with mothers' person-oriented appeal strategies. It may be that the children in this latter study were too young to have shown the effects of maternal inductive discipline.

Other studies have sought to clarify the relation between parental and child interactions by examining settings in which this relation differs. For example, Hollos and Cowan (1973) examined logical and role-taking skills of the children living in three different locations in rural Norway: a farm community, a village, and a town. The main difference in these environments, the authors found, was the amount of social-verbal interaction of the children with their parents and peers. On a variety of tasks, the performance of 7- and 9-year-olds revealed two primary factors: one of logical operations, showing a marked relationship to age, and a role-taking factor on which only the environmental settings had strong effects. The farm community children (low social-verbal interaction) had much lower role-taking skills than village or town children, the latter two having almost identical skills despite differences in the amount of verbal interaction between the two settings. The authors suggest that there may be a certain amount of verbal interaction that is necessary for role-taking development to proceed normally, "but beyond this threshold, the sheer amount of interaction does not affect the development of role-taking skills" (Hollos & Cowan 1973, p. 640), as Kohlberg (1969) has proposed. In relation to the discussion about training studies, the Hollos and Cowan study is the closest study to date to examine a natural "deprivation" condition in order to assess factors *necessary* for role-taking development. As in all naturally occurring conditions, however, there are a large number of correlated variables which have the potential of being the effective necessary experience, alone or in combination with that variable cited as "the major difference" between settings—the amount of verbal interaction.

Another study examined differences in social orientation of adolescents reared in two rural settings: Israeli kibbutzim and moshavim. The primary difference in these settings is the extensive peer interaction in the former and parent rearing in the latter. No significant differences were found in the adolescents' egocentrism (Long, Henderson, & Platt 1973).

Another "setting" is the family constellation which provides different role-taking opportunities depending upon the number of siblings, the age spacing between them, and their sex. Flavell (1968) speculated, for example, that a child who interacts with a sibling a few years younger may have more opportunities for role taking and role enacting, such as teaching and caring for the younger child. Rubin, Hultsch, and Peters (1971) found less role-taking ability in later-born children, but more role taking in firstborn and *only* children, the latter clearly not supportive of a direct effect of sibling position. Findings by Staub (1971) and Cicirelli (1972) provide indirect evidence that role taking may be more advanced in firstborn or older females but not firstborn or older males. Given the evidence that parents interact differently with first- and later-born children (Hilton 1967), the untangling of parental and sibling influences appears difficult at best.

To summarize, the impact of environmental factors on the development of role-taking abilities has been examined mainly in terms of the amount and/or type of verbal interactions of the child with his parents and peers. As this section amply illustrates, there have been very few studies. At best they provide a loose network of findings that have some credibility as factors facilitating role-taking development: more than a "meager" amount of verbal interaction with others, parental child-rearing techniques focused on labeling other people's covert responses to the child's behavior and a position within the family as the only or oldest child. These studies, in conjunction with several training studies cited earlier, provide data that have face validity in the sense that greater role taking seems to be fostered by the opportunity to enact various roles

(Chandler 1973; Shantz & Wilson 1972; Staub 1971) or have others' covert responses labeled by the parents (Bearison & Cassel 1975). The relationship between the child's role-taking skills and the child's "linguistic environment" needs more study, particularly as measured by the amount, the style, and the content of the verbal interactions with others.

V. Conclusions and Implications

A. THE DEVELOPMENT OF SOCIAL UNDERSTANDING

The ability to understand what another person thinks, feels, sees, and intends, and the way in which people are described are clear developmental phenomena. In general, there is a good deal more information about what a child thinks about another person than the processes by which he arrives at such conceptions. In this section, the general social cognitive achievements at various age periods will be summarized. The cited ages are only approximate guidelines to developmental timing.

The view of the preschool child as profoundly egocentric has given way to a rather different view: the preschooler has emerged as much more competent in his social understanding. He has a rudimentary understanding that others can have a different visual experience than he has, but is limited to the case where the child identifies *what* another person sees that the child himself does not see (or vice versa). That is, prior to 5 years of age he does not indicate an appreciation of perspective—*how* objects appear to another person. In addition, he demonstrates some ability to take into account certain characteristics of his listener (Shatz & Gelman 1973). In these two areas—spatial and communicative—there is evidence of a simple form of role-taking ability.

The preschooler can identify certain simple emotions that another feels from facial cues alone or from knowing only the situation the other is in if that situation is familiar to the child. He does not appear to be able to anticipate another's thoughts, as tested in simple guessing games. The way in which the preschooler characterizes people is virtually unknown. The available data (Livesley & Bromley 1973) indicate that another is usually described in terms of physical appearance, the child's interactions with the person (e.g., "he plays with me"), and with a strong evaluative orientation.

There are some important achievements in social understanding that usually appear between 5 and 7 years of age. There is a clear recognition that others can have a different spatial perspective than the child, usually limited to a simple spatial context: how one object looks from various positions. Likewise, in making inferences about others' thoughts there is an understanding that another *can* have different thoughts than the child himself. However, the child may deny he can impute any thoughts to the other or, if he attempts to do so, he is often inaccurate. Many children this age are able to discriminate accidental from intended actions of others. Further, there is some ability to distinguish good intentions from bad intentions in allocating blame if the actions are not too negative. If they are, the use of intentional information is apparently absent, and the consequences determine blame. The characterization of people in verbal descriptions indicates that the child makes little differentiation between the person and his environment: people most often are described by their appearance and possessions, and with simple evaluative traits (nice, mean, and the like).

Middle childhood is the time of some rather dramatic advances in social understanding. First, social inferences now progress to the level of the child's understanding that his own thoughts, feelings, and intentions can be the object of another's thinking. He can view simple social episodes from the position of each participant and maintain a consistency among viewpoints on the episode. When judging others' blameworthiness, he quite consistently weights the intentions more than the damage done. Increasingly accurate and reliable specification of another's spatial perspective for rather complex spatial arrays occurs. In addition, the child shows an ability to infer the feelings of others when others are in situations largely unfamiliar to him.

There is also a rather striking, parallel change in the descriptions of others from early middle childhood onward. Children describe others less in terms of their "surface" characteristics and more in terms of their covert attributes—attitudes, abilities, interests. The individual is differentiated much more in descriptions from his environment and has a unique as opposed to a stereotypic quality. In viewing filmed social episodes, the child during this age period spontaneously attends less to obvious aspects of interactions (e.g., people's movements and statements) and more to inferred inner experiences and social relations between people.

Other advances in social inference ability occur in early and middle adolescence. The perspective of the adolescent extends further to include himself, the other person, the inner experiences of each, and the relation between himself and the other as a third-party observer might understand it. In social episodes, the adolescent is much more oriented toward and accurate in making inferences about the thoughts, intentions, and feelings of each participant in the episode. Particularly, there is a spontaneous tendency to try to *explain* such thoughts and feelings, not merely to describe them. Likewise, the descriptions of others show much greater subtlety and refinement in the use of traits, the recognition of contradictory tendencies within an individual, and relating situational factors to another's behavior. The refinement, breadth, and depth of understanding others does not have, of course, an "end point."

This summary of the major, documented social cognitive competencies of children at various age periods may jar with the estimate one has from everyday interactions with them, presumably in both directions—at times an underestimation and at times an overestimation. The differences between real life social situations and laboratory situations in the amount and nature of the information, and the affective and instrumental aspects of real social situations, may well be some of the sources of such discrepancies.

B. METHODOLOGICAL AND THEORETICAL CONSIDERATIONS

There are several features of the research on social cognition that deserve analysis. First, all of the developmental changes in social inference are based on findings from cross-sectional studies. That is, the changes in social cognition are inferred from age *differences* in performance. No study has directly examined the change itself in social inference making in development using a longitudinal method. The hazards of using data from cross-sectional studies of groups of children to make statements about the individual's development have been extensively discussed (e.g., Wohlwill 1973) and demonstrated (e.g., Schaie & Labouvie-Vief 1974). Longitudinal study, even over relatively short periods, of a variety of social inferential abilities would provide needed information and a more coherent picture of developmental changes.

Although the definition of role taking appears to be generally agreed on, difficulties have arisen in determining whether certain methods are assessing role-taking skills or some related skills. This problem was encountered particularly in the research on empathy, and may well arise again as tasks in a variety of content areas are simplified for younger children in future study. The adult and child research (e.g., Bronfenbrenner et al. 1958; Cronbach 1955; Rothenberg 1970) suggests that one primary difficulty is differentiating accurate self-description from accurate role taking in judging another person. The problem seems to reside in specifying the dimensions of similarity between the child-judge and the person whom he is judging and specifying dimensions of familiarity with the other's present situation due to the child's current or previous experiences.

This is not to suggest that the child's attributions of his own thoughts and feelings are not important means of understanding others. Since as humans we are more alike than we are different, the child's assumption of similarity to others is probably often accurate. That is, egocentrism during early periods of the life span undoubtedly has an adaptive function but becomes increasingly maladaptive as the social environment demands more differentiated responses to others.

There is minimal information on the relation between social cognition and social behavior, particularly how specific social interactions influence children's social understanding and vice versa. Such research could have important implications for cognitive-developmental theory and social learning theory. For example, the specification of the social stimulus from the child's viewpoint might be useful for observational learning studies using televised aggressive episodes (e.g., Collins 1970, 1973; Collins, Berndt, & Hess 1974).

The review here has revealed some extensive work in some areas of social cognition (such as role-taking development), relatively little research in others (such as person-perception development and social causal reasoning), and no research apparently in several other areas (inferences about others' abilities and attitudes, the child's conception of how environmental contexts effect others' behavior, etc.). But, of course, the very questions posed about children's social understanding usually arise out of an implicit or explicit theoretical framework. To date, most questions come from cognitive-developmental theories of Piaget and Werner. And there appear to be some substantial parallels between nonsocial and social cognition. For example, there is the developmental trend toward conceiving of people less in terms of their surface appearance, possessions, and motor behavior and more in terms of an "underlying reality"—constructions of regularities and identities such as values, beliefs, intentions, etc.—much like (and in some synchrony with) the developmental trend toward constructing underlying stable attributes of physical objects (such as their mass and weight) despite surface variability. Or, there is the increasing spatial and temporal decentration in concepts of the physical world paralleled by the increasing "theory of social relativity" in which the child expands his social frame of reference from self, to others, to his society, to other societies now and in the past. At the same time, there is the possibility that other approaches might well enrich the very questions asked about children's social understanding. Flavell (1974) has argued that our conception of the development of many processes and concepts is partly determined by our conception of them in the mature organism, the adult (as shown in the change in linguistic theory). But the research and theories of adults' interpersonal understanding have had very little impact on developmental research. Not only would more utilization of the adult literature have the practical value of decreasing the likelihood of repeating methodological and conceptual errors in research, but the use of adult social psychological theories might make an important contribution to the process of formulating questions about interpersonal understanding of the child.

C. APPLICATIONS

Three areas of possible application of this research will be addressed. First, public education has emphasized children's understanding of their physical environment far more than their social environment, and non-social problem solving more than social problem solving. Social understanding has been allowed to develop more as a by-product of social interaction and cognitive advances. Given the implication that it has for fostering prosocial behavior and positive interpersonal attitudes, it seems particularly important that our formal education system give more direct attention in the curriculum to facilitating greater breadth and depth of social comprehension. Some studies have demonstrated the feasibility of doing so (e.g., Spivack & Shure 1973).

Second, some evidence allows speculation that parents' methods of communicating with their children in simple conflict situations have an impact on the children's ability to understand others' feelings, thoughts, and intentions. When parents focus on the contingency between children's behavior and others' covert responses and give verbal labels to those responses, children are likely to have more mature moral judgment. Some data suggest that they will have higher levels of social understanding as well. Last, social cognitive developmental findings with normal children may well be of use in clinical practice to guide social intervention (e.g., Chandler 1973; Selman 1974). Educating, child rearing, and remediating do not and cannot wait for extensive data. These applications are suggested despite obvious limitations in our understanding of the child's understanding of others.

REFERENCES

Allport, G. W. *Pattern and growth in personality.* New York: Holt, Rinehart & Winston, 1961.

Armsby, R. E. A reexamination of the development of moral judgments in children. *Child Development,* 1971, *42,* 1242–1248.

Aronfreed, J. *Conduct and conscience: the socialization of internalized control over behavior.* New York: Academic Press, 1968.

Asch, S. E. Forming impressions of personality. *Journal of Abnormal and Social Psychology,* 1946, *41,* 258–290.

Asch, S. E. *Social psychology.* New York: Prentice-Hall, 1952.

Baldwin, A. L.; Baldwin, C. P.; Hilton, I. R.; & Lambert, N. W. The measurement of social expectations and their development in children. *Monographs of the Society for Research in Child Development,* 1969, *34* (4, Serial No. 128).

Baldwin, C. P., & Baldwin, A. L. Children's judgments of kindness. *Child Development,* 1970, *41,* 29–47.

Baldwin, J. M. *Social and ethical interpretations of mental development.* New York: Macmillan, 1906.

Bandura, A., & McDonald, F. The influence of social reinforcement and the behavior of models in shaping children's moral judgments. *Journal of Abnormal and Social Psychology*, 1963, *67*, 274–281.

Barker, R. G., & Wright, H. F. *Midwest and its children*. New York: Harper & Row, 1955.

Bearison, D. J., & Cassel, T. Z. Cognitive decentration and social codes: communicative effectiveness in young children from differing family contexts. *Developmental Psychology*, 1975, *11*, 29–36.

Bem, D. J. Self-perception theory. In L. Berkowitz (Ed.), *Advances in experimental social psychology*. Vol. 6. New York: Academic Press, 1972.

Bigner, J. J. Children's discrimination of sibling role concepts. Paper presented at the meeting of the Society for Research in Child Development, Philadelphia, 1973.

Birnbaum-Steinlauf, B. Role-taking abilities of young children and maternal discipline strategies. Unpublished master's thesis, Wayne State University, 1974.

Borke, H. Interpersonal perception of young children: egocentrism or empathy? *Developmental Psychology*, 1971, *5*, 263–269.

Borke, H. The development of empathy in Chinese and American children between three and six years of age: a cross-cultural study. *Developmental Psychology*, 1973, *9*, 102–108.

Breznitz, S., & Kugelmass, S. Intentionality in moral judgment; developmental stages. *Child Development*, 1967, *38*, 469–479.

Brodzinsky, D. M., & Jackson, J. P. Effects of stimulus complexity and perceptual shielding in the development of spatial perspectives. Paper presented at the meeting of the Society for Research in Child Development, Philadelphia, 1973.

Brodzinsky, D. M.; Jackson, J. P.; & Overton, W. F. Effects of perceptual shielding in the development of spatial perspectives. *Child Development*, 1972, *43*, 1041–1046.

Bronfenbrenner, U. Developmental theory in transition. In H. W. Stevenson (Ed.), *Child psychology*. Chicago: University of Chicago Press, 1963.

Bronfenbrenner, U.; Harding, J.; & Gallwey, M. The measurement of skill in social perception. In D. C. McClelland, A. L. Baldwin, U. Bronfenbrenner, & F. L. Strodtbeck (Eds.), *Talent and society*. Princeton, N. J.: Van Nostrand, 1958.

Bruner, J. The course of cognitive growth. *American Psychologist*, 1964, *19*, 1–14.

Brunswik, E. *Systematic and representative design of psychological experiments, with results in physical and social perception*. Berkeley: University of California Press, 1947.

Burns, N., & Cavey, L. Age differences in empathic ability among children. *Canadian Journal of Psychology*, 1957, *11*, 227–230.

Byrne, D. F. The development of role-taking in adolescence. Unpublished doctoral dissertation, Harvard University, 1973.

Campbell, D. T., & Fiske, D. W. Convergent and discriminant validation by the multitrait-multimethod matrix. *Psychological Bulletin*, 1959, *56*, 81–105.

Ceresnie, S. Communication and cooperation in dyads of children of varying levels of egocentrism. Unpublished master's thesis, Wayne State University, 1974.

Chandler, M. J. Egocentrism and childhood psychopathology: the development and application of measurement techniques. Paper presented at the meeting of the Society for Research in Child Development, Minneapolis, 1971.

Chandler, M. J. Egocentrism and antisocial behavior: the assessment and training of social perspective-taking skills. *Developmental Psychology*, 1973, *9*, 326–332.

Chandler, M. J., & Greenspan, D. Ersatz egocentrism: a reply to H. Borke. *Developmental Psychology*, 1972, *7*, 104–106.

Chandler, M. J.; Greenspan, S.; & Barenboim, C. Judgments of intentionality in response to videotaped and verbally presented moral dilemmas; the medium is the message. *Child Development*, 1973, *44*, 311–320.

Cicirelli, V. G. The effect of sibling relationship on concept learning of children taught by child-teachers. *Child Development*, 1972, *43*, 282–287.

Coie, J. D.; Costanzo, P. R.; & Farnill, D. Specific transitions in the development of spatial perspective-taking ability. *Developmental Psychology*, 1973, *9*, 167–177.

Coie, J. D., & Dorval, B. Sex differences in the intellectual structure of social interaction skills. *Developmental Psychology*, 1973, *8*, 261–267.

Collins, W. A. Learning of media content: a developmental study. *Child Development*, 1970, *41*, 1133–1142.

Collins, W. A. Effects of temporal separation between motivation, aggression, and consequences: a developmental study. *Developmental Psychology*, 1973, *8*, 215–221.

Collins, W. A.; Berndt, T. J.; & Hess, V. L. Observational learning of motives and consequences for television aggression; a developmental study. *Child Development*, 1974, *45*, 799–802.

Costanzo, P. R.; Coie, J. D.; Grumet, J. F.; & Farnill, D. A reexamination of the effects of intent and consequence on children's moral judgment. *Child Development*, 1973, *44*, 154–161.

Cowan, P. A. The link between cognitive structure and social structure in two-child verbal interaction. Paper presented at the meeting of the Society for Research in Child Development, Santa Monica, Calif., 1967.

Cowan, P. A.; Langer, J.; Heavenrich, J.; & Nathanson, M. Social learning and Piaget's theory of cognitive development. *Journal of Personality and Social Psychology*, 1969, *11*, 261–274.

Cronbach, L. J. Processes affecting scores on "understanding others" and "assumed similarity." *Psychological Bulletin*, 1955, *52*, 177–193.

Cronbach, L. J. Proposals leading to analytic treatment of social perception scores. In R. Taguiri & L. Petrullo (Eds.), *Person perception and interpersonal behavior*, Stanford, Calif.: Stanford University Press, 1958.

Deutsch, F. The effects of sex of subject and story character of preschoolers' perceptions of affective responses and interpersonal behavior in story sequences: a question of similarity of person. *Developmental Psychology*, in press.

Deutsch, F. Female preschoolers' perceptions of affective responses and interpersonal behavior in videotaped episodes. *Developmental Psychology*, 1974, *10*, 733–740. (a)

Deutsch, F. Observational and sociometric measures of peer popularity and their relationship to egocentric communication in female preschoolers. *Developmental Psychology*, 1974, *10*, 745–747. (b)

Deutsch, F. & Madle, R. Empathy: historic and current conceptualizations, measurement, and a cognitive theoretical perspective. *Human Development*, in press.

DeVries, R. The development of role-taking as reflected by the behavior of bright, average, and retarded children in a social guessing game. *Child Development*, 1970, *41*, 759–770.

Dickman, H. R. The perception of behavioral units. In R. B. Barker (Ed.), *The stream of behavior*. New York: Appleton-Century-Crofts, 1963.

Dlugokinski, E. L., & Firestone, I. J. Other centeredness and susceptibility to charitable appeals: effects of perceived discipline. *Developmental Psychology*, 1974, *10*, 21–28.

Donaldson, M. Preconditions of inference. In W. J. Arnold & D. Levine (Eds.), *Nebraska symposium on motivation*. Lincoln: University of Nebraska Press, 1971.

Douglas, E. C. The effect of spatial training on spatial egocentrism. Unpublished master's thesis, University of Georgia, 1971.

Dubin, R., & Dubin, E. R. Children's social perceptions: a review of research. *Child Development*, 1965, *36*, 809–838.

Elardo, P. Project AWARE: a school program to facilitate the social development of children. Paper presented at the 4th annual H. Blumberg symposium, Chapel Hill, N. C., 1974.

Elkind, D. Children's conceptions of right and left: Piaget replication study IV. *Journal of Genetic Psychology*, 1961, *99*, 269–276.

Elkind, D. Egocentrism in adolescence. *Child Development*, 1967, *38*, 1025–1034.

Emmerich, W. Young children's discriminations of parent and child roles. *Child Development*, 1959, *30*, 403–419.

Emmerich, W. Family role concepts of children ages six to ten. *Child Development*, 1961, *32*, 609–624.

Emmerich, W.; Goldman, K. S.; & Shore, R. E. Differentiation and development of social norms. *Journal of Personality and Social Psychology*, 1971, *18*, 323–353.

Feffer, M. The cognitive implications of role-taking behavior. *Journal of Personality*, 1959, *27*, 152–168.

Feffer, M. Developmental analysis of interpersonal behavior. *Psychological Review*, 1970, *77*, 197–214.

Feffer, M., & Gourevitch, V. Cognitive aspects of role-taking in children. *Journal of Personality*, 1960, *28*, 383–396.

Feshbach, N. D. Empathy: an interpersonal process. Paper presented at the meeting of the American Psychological Association, Montreal, 1973.

Feshbach, N. D., & Feshbach, S. The relationship between empathy and aggression in two age groups. *Developmental Psychology*, 1969, *1*, 102–107.

Feshbach, N. D. & Roe, K. Empathy in six and seven year olds. *Child Development*, 1968, *39*, 133–145.

Finley, G. E.; French, D.; & Cowan, P. Egocentrism and popularity. Paper presented at the 14th Inter-American Congress of Psychology, São Paulo, 1973.

Fishbein, H. D.; Lewis, S.; & Keiffer, K. Children's understanding of spatial relations: coordination of perspectives. *Developmental Psychology*, 1972, *7*, 21–33.

Flapan, D. *Children's understanding of social interaction*, New York: Teachers College Press, 1968.

Flavell, J. H. *The development of role-taking and communication skills in children*. New York: Wiley, 1968.

Flavell, J. H. Concept development. In P. H. Mussen (Ed.), *Carmichael's manual of child psychology*. Vol. 1. New York: Wiley, 1970.

Flavell, J. H. The development of inferences about others. In T. Mischel (Ed.), *Understanding other persons*. Oxford: Blackwell, Basil, Mott, 1974.

Fry, C. L. Training children to communicate to listeners. *Child Development*, 1966, *37*, 675–685.

Fry, C. L. Training children to communicate to listeners who have varying listener requirements. *Journal of Genetic Psychology*, 1969, *114*, 153–166.

Glucksberg, S., & Krauss, R. M. What do people say after they have learned how to talk? *Merrill-Palmer Quarterly*, 1967, *13*, 309–316.

Glucksberg, S.; Krauss, R. M.; & Higgins, T. The development of communication skills in children. In F. Horowitz (Ed.), *Review of child development research*. Vol. 4. Chicago: University of Chicago Press, 1975.

Gollin, E. S. Organizational characteristics of social judgments: a developmental investigation. *Journal of Personality*, 1958, *26*, 139–154.

Handlon, B. J., & Gross, P. The development of sharing behavior. *Journal of Abnormal and Social Psychology*, 1959, *59*, 425–428.

Hartup, W. W. Peer interaction and social organization. In P. H. Mussen (Ed.), *Carmichael's manual of child psychology*. Vol. 2. New York: Wiley, 1970.

Hastorf, A. H., & Bender, I. E. A caution respecting the measurement of empathic ability. *Journal of Abnormal and Social Psychology*, 1952, *47*, 574–576.

Hebble, P. W. The development of elementary school children's judgment of intent. *Child Development*, 1971, *42*, 1203–1215.

Heider, P. *The psychology of interpersonal relations.* New York: Wiley, 1958.

Hilton, I. Differences in the behavior of mothers toward first and later-born children. *Journal of Personality and Social Behavior*, 1967, *7*, 282–290.

Hoffman, M. L. Moral development. In P. H. Mussen (Ed.), *Carmichael's manual of child psychology.* Vol. 2. New York: Wiley, 1970.

Hollos, M., & Cowan, P. A. Social isolation and cognitive development: logical operations and role-taking abilities in three Norwegian social settings. *Child Development*, 1973, *44*, 630–641.

Huttenlocher, J., & Presson, C. C. Mental rotation and the perspective problem. *Cognitive Psychology*, 1973, *4*, 277–299.

Irwin, D. M., & Ambron, S. R. Moral judgment and role-taking in children ages three to seven. Paper presented at the meeting of the Society for Research in Child Development, Philadelphia, 1973.

Izard, C. E. *The face of emotion.* New York: Appleton-Century-Crofts, 1971.

Johnson, R. C. A study of children's moral judgments. *Child Development*, 1962, *33*, 327–354.

Kagan, J., & Kogan, N. Individual variation in cognitive processes. In P. H. Mussen (Ed.), *Carmichael's manual of child psychology.* Vol. 1. New York: Wiley, 1970.

Kelley, H. H. Attribution theory in social psychology. In D. Levine (Ed.), *Nebraska symposium on motivation.* Vol. 15. Lincoln: University of Nebraska Press, 1967.

Kelley, H. H. The processes of causal attribution. *American Psychologist*, 1973, *28*, 107–128.

Kelly, G. A. *A theory of personality: the psychology of personal constructs.* New York: Norton, 1955.

King, M. The development of some intention concepts in young children. *Child Development*, 1971, *42*, 1145–1152.

Kingsley, P. Relationship between egocentrism and children's communication. Paper read at the meeting of Society for Research in Child Development, Minneapolis, 1971.

Klein, R. Some factors influencing empathy in six and seven year old children varying in ethnic background. Unpublished doctoral dissertation, University of California, Los Angeles, 1971.

Kohlberg, L. Stage and sequence: the cognitive-developmental approach to socialization. In D. A. Goslin (Ed.), *Handbook of socialization theory and research.* New York: Rand-McNally, 1969.

Kohlberg, L.; Yaeger, J.; & Hjortholm, E. Private speech: four studies and a review of theories. *Child Development*, 1968, *39*, 692–736.

Kugelmass, S., & Breznitz, S. Intentionality in Moral Judgement: adolescent development. *Child Development*, 1968, *39*, 240–256.

Kuhn, D. The development of role-taking ability. Unpublished manuscript, Columbia University, 1972.

Langer, J. Werner's comparative organismic theory. In P. H. Mussen (Ed.), *Carmichael's manual of child psychology.* Vol. 1. New York: Wiley, 1970.

Laubengayer, N. C. The effects of training on the spatial egocentrism of preschoolers. Unpublished master's thesis, University of Minnesota, 1965.

Laurendeau, M., & Pinard, A. Development of the concept of space in the child. New York: International Universities Press, 1970.

Lewis, S., & Fishbein, H. D. Space perception in children: a disconfirmation of Piaget's developmental hypothesis. Paper presented at the meeting of the Psychonomic Society, Saint Louis, 1969.

Livesley, W. J., & Bromley, D. B. *Person perception in childhood and adolescence.* London: Wiley, 1973.

Long, B. H.; Henderson, E. H.; & Platt, L. Self-other orientations of Israeli adolescents reared in kibbutzim and moshavim. *Developmental Psychology,* 1973, *8,* 300–308.

Looft, W. R. Egocentrism and its manifestations in young and old adults. Paper presented at the meeting of the Gerontological Society, Toronto, 1970.

Looft, W. R. Egocentrism and social interaction across the life span. *Psychological Bulletin,* 1972, *78,* 73–92.

Marvin, R. S. Aspects of the preschool child's changing conception of his mother. Unpublished manuscript, University of Virginia, 1974.

Masangkay, Z. S.; McCluskey, K. A.; McIntyre, C. W.; Sims-Knight, J.; Vaughn, B. E.; Flavell, J. H. The early development of inferences about the visual percepts of others. *Child Development,* 1974, *45,* 357–366.

Mead, G. *Mind, self, and society.* Chicago: University of Chicago Press, 1934.

Midlarsky, E., & Bryan, J. H. Training charity in children. *Journal of Personality and Social Psychology,* 1967, *5,* 408–415.

Miller, P. H.; Kessel, F. S.; & Flavell, J. H. Thinking about people thinking about people thinking about . . . : a study of social cognitive development. *Child Development,* 1970, *41,* 613–623.

Mood, D.; Johnson, J.; & Shantz, C. U. Affective and cognitive components of empathy in young children. Paper presented at the southeast regional meeting of the Society for Research in Child Development, Chapel Hill, N. C., 1974.

Moore, O. K. Problem solving and the perception of persons. In R. Taguiri & I. Petrullo (Eds.), *Person perception and interpersonal behavior.* Stanford, Calif.: Stanford University Press, 1958.

Murphy, L. B. *Social behavior and child personality.* New York: Columbia University Press, 1937.

Olshan, K. The multidimensional structure of person perception in children. Unpublished doctoral dissertation, Rutgers University, 1970.

Peevers, B. H., & Secord, P. F. Developmental changes in attribution of descriptive concepts to persons. *Journal of Personality and Social Psychology,* 1973, *27,* 120–128.

Piaget, J. *The Language and thought of the child.* New York: Harcourt, Brace, 1926.

Piaget, J. *Judgment and reasoning in the child.* New York: Harcourt, Brace, 1928.

Piaget, J. *The psychology of intelligence.* New York: Harcourt, Brace, 1950.

Piaget, J. *The moral judgment of the child.* (Original translation: London: Kegan Paul, 1932) New York: Free Press, 1965.

Piaget, J. *Six psychological studies.* New York: Random House, 1967.

Piaget, J. Piaget's theory. In P. H. Mussen (Ed.), *Carmichael's manual of child psychology.* Vol. *1.* New York: Wiley, 1970.

Piaget, J., & Inhelder, B. *The child's conception of space.* London: Routledge & Kegan Paul, 1956.

Piaget, J., & Inhelder, B. *Mental imagery in the child.* New York: Basic Books, 1970.

Rappoport, L., & Fritzler, D. Developmental responses to quantity changes in artificial social objects. *Child Development,* 1969, *40,* 1145–1154.

Rosenberg, S., & Sedlak, A. Structural representations of implicit personality theory. In L. Berkowitz (Ed.), *Advances in experimental social psychology.* Vol. *6.* New York: Academic Press, 1972.

Rothbaum, F. Taking the perspective of another: a study of 11 and 13 year old children. Unpublished manuscript, Yale University, 1973.

Rothenberg, B. Children's social sensitivity and the relationship to interpersonal competence, intrapersonal comfort, and intellectual level. *Developmental Psychology*, 1970, *2*, 335–350.

Rubin, K. H. Relationship between egocentric communication and popularity among peers. *Developmental Psychology*, 1972, *7*, 364.

Rubin, K. H. Egocentrism in childhood: a unitary construct? *Child Development*, 1973, *44*, 102–110.

Rubin, K. H.; Hultsch, D. F.; & Peters, D. L. Non-social speech in four-year-old children as a function of birth order and interpersonal situation. *Merrill-Palmer Quarterly*, 1971, *17*, 41–50.

Rubin, K. H., & Schneider, F. W. The relationship between moral judgment, egocentrism, and altruistic behavior. *Child Development*, 1973, *44*, 661–665.

Saltz, E., & Medow, M. L. Concept conservation in children: the dependence of belief systems on semantic representation. *Child Development*, 1971, *42*, 1533–1542.

Sarbin, T. R.; Taft, R.; & Bailey, D. E. *Clinical inference and cognitive theory.* New York: Holt, Rinehart & Winston, 1960.

Scarlett, H. H.; Press, A. N.; & Crockett, W. H. Children's descriptions of peers: a Wernerian developmental analysis. *Child Development*, 1971, *42*, 439–453.

Schaie, K. W., & Labourvie-Vief, G. Generational versus ontogenetic components of change in adult cognitive behavior: a fourteen-year cross-sequential study. *Developmental Psychology*, 1974, *10*, 305–320.

Sedlak, A. Four theoretical interpretations of the young child's objective blame judgments. Doctoral dissertation, Rutgers University, 1973.

Sedlak, A., & Schmidt, C. F. Belief systems: notes on the child's interpretation of social episodes. Computers in biomedicine. Technical Report No. 19, Rutgers University, 1973.

Selman, R. L. The relation of role-taking to the development of moral judgments in children. *Child Development*, 1971, *42*, 79–91. (a)

Selman, R. L. Taking another's perspective: role-taking development in early childhood. *Child Development*, 1971, *42*, 1721–1734. (b)

Selman, R. L. A structural analysis of the ability to take another's social perspective: stages in the development of role-taking ability. Paper presented at the meeting of the Society for Research in Child Development, Philadelphia, 1973.

Selman, R. L. Stages in role-taking and moral judgments as guides to social intervention. In T. Lickona (Ed.), *Man and morality.* New York: Holt, Rinehart & Winston, 1974.

Selman, R. L., & Byrne, D. F. A structural-developmental analysis of levels of role-taking in middle childhood. *Child Development*, 1974, *45*, 803–806.

Selman, R.; Damon, W.; & Gordon, A. The relation between levels of social role-taking and stages of justice conception in children ages four to ten. Paper presented at the meeting of the Society for Research in Child Development, Philadelphia, 1973.

Shantz, C. U.; Asarnow, J.; & Berkowitz, M. Situational and intellectual factors influencing perspective-taking performance in children. Paper read at the southeast regional meeting of the Society for Research in Child Development, Chapel Hill, N. C., 1974.

Shantz, C. U., & Watson, J. S. Assessment of spatial egocentrism through expectancy violation. *Psychonomic Science*, 1970, *18*, 93–94.

Shantz, C. U., & Watson, J. S. Spatial abilities and spatial egocentrism in the young child. *Child Development*, 1971, *42*, 171–181.

Shantz, C. U., & Wilson, K. Training communication skills in young children. *Child Development*, 1972, *43*, 118–122.

Shantz, D. W., & Voydanoff, D. A. Situational effects on retaliatory aggression at three age levels. *Child Development*, 1973, *44*, 149–153.

Shatz, M., & Gelman, R. The development of communication skills: modifications in the speech of young children as a function of listener. *Monographs of the Society for Research in Child Development*, 1973, *38* (5, Serial No. 152).

Shaw, M. E., & Sulzer, J. L. An empirical test of Heider's levels in attribution of responsibility. *Journal of Abnormal and Social Psychology*, 1964, *69*, 39–46.

Sigel, I. E. The attainment of concepts. In M. L. Hoffman & L. W. Hoffman (Eds.), *Review of child development research*. Vol. *1*. New York: Russell Sage Foundation, 1964.

Sigel, I. E.; Saltz, E.; & Roskind, W. Variables determining concept conservation in children. *Journal of Experimental Psychology*, 1967, *74*, 471–475.

Signell, K. A. Cognitive complexity in person perception and nation perception: a developmental approach. *Journal of Personality*, 1966, *34*, 517–537.

Spivack, G., & Shure, M. B. *Social adjustment of young children*. San Francisco: Jossey-Bass, 1974.

Staub, E. The use of role playing and induction in children's learning of helping and sharing behavior. *Child Development*, 1971, *42*, 805–816.

Strayer, K.; Bigelow, A.; & Ames, E. W. "I," "you," and point of view. Unpublished manuscript, Simon Fraser University, 1973.

Sullivan, E. V., & Hunt, D. E. Interpersonal and objective decentering as a function of age and social class. *Journal of Genetic Psychology*, 1967, *110*, 199–210.

Sullivan, H. S. *The interpersonal theory of psychiatry*. New York: Norton, 1953.

Supnick, E. L. Source of information as a factor affecting the impression of others. Unpublished doctoral dissertation, Clark University, 1967.

Swinson, M. E. The development of cognitive skills and role-taking. *Dissertation Abstracts*, 1966, *26*, 4082.

Taguiri, R. Person perception. In G. Lindzey & E. Aronson (Eds.), *The handbook of social psychology*, Vol. *3*, Reading, Mass.: Addison-Wesley, 1969.

Tierney, M. C., & Rubin, K. H. The relationship between egocentrism and conformity in early childhood. *Journal of Genetic Psychology*, in press.

Turiel, E. An experimental test of sequentiality of developmental changes in the child's moral judgments. *Journal of Personality and Social Psychology*, 1966, *3*, 611–618.

Van Lieshout, C. F.; Leckie, G.; & Smits–Van Sonsbeek, B. The effect of a social perspective-taking training on empathy and role-taking ability of preschool children. Paper presented at the meeting of the International Society for the Study of Behavioral Development, Ann Arbor, Mich., 1973.

Wallach, M. A. Research on children's thinking. In H. W. Stevenson (Ed.), *Child psychology*. Chicago: University of Chicago Press, 1963.

Weiner, B., & Peter, N. A cognitive developmental analysis of achievement and moral judgments. *Developmental Psychology*, 1973, *9*, 290–309.

Weinheimer, S. Egocentrism and social influence in children. *Child Development*, 1972, *43*, 567–578.

Weinstein, E. A. The development of interpersonal competence. In D. A. Goslin (Ed.), *Handbook of socialization theory and research*. New York: Rand-McNally, 1969.

Weinstein, E. L., & Finley, G. E. Egocentrism, naive psychology and the development of persuasive skills. Unpublished manuscript, University of Toronto, 1973.

Werner, H. *Comparative psychology of mental development*. New York: International Universities Press, 1948.

Whiteman, M. Children's conception of psychological causality. *Child Development*, 1967, *38*, 143–155.

Wohlwill, J. F. Responses to class-inclusion questions for verbally and pictorially presented items. *Child Development*, 1968, *39*, 449–465.

Wohlwill, J. F. *The study of behavioral development*. New York: Academic Press, 1973.

Yarrow, M. R., & Campbell, J. D. Person perception in children. *Merrill-Palmer Quarterly*, 1963, *9*, 57–72.

6 Children's Attention:
The Development of Selectivity

ANNE D. PICK, DANIEL G. FRANKEL,
AND VALERIE L. HESS
University of Minnesota

Preparation of this chapter began while the first author was a Fellow at the Center for Advanced Study in the Behavioral Sciences, Stanford, Calif., and held Special Fellowship no. 1F03HD54324 from the National Institute of Child Health and Human Development. The work was also supported by Program Project Grant no. 5P01HD05027 and Training Grant no. 5T01HD00105 from the National Institute of Child Health and Human Development to the University of Minnesota, and by Training Grant no. 5T01MH06668 from the National Institute of Mental Health to the University of Minnesota. The authors are grateful to Judith Allen, Herbert Pick, Jr., John Rieser, Philip Salapatek, and Marsha Unze for their suggestions and assistance.

I. Introduction

"Children are not inattentive when their masters say they are. They are only attending to other, perhaps more important things than these which the severely practical master is commending to their attention" (Mann 1966, p. 282). A practical adjunct to Thomas Mann's observation is the fact that asking a child to "pay attention" may even be an ambiguous request. The intent might be to direct him toward information on which he is already concentrating. Thus, a teacher of mathematics describing how to multiply numbers or a mother instructing a child how to use the kitchen stove might preface crucial points with the request to "pay attention." Though the children might already be listening and looking carefully, the purpose of the request is to ensure that they will acquire essential information. Alternatively, the same request might imply that a child should shift his concentration toward different information. When schoolchildren are listening to each other instead of to the teacher, or when the child being instructed about the stove is listening to the radio instead of to his mother, the admonition to "pay attention" is a demand for a change—probably a rapid change—in what information is heeded. Again, of course, the purpose of the request is to ensure that essential information is acquired, but in the one case the request is for continued concentration and in the other case the request is for a shift in concentration.

In fact, "attention" is a term used frequently but with a great variety of meanings. For instance, attention can be attracted or distracted, directed, captured, paid, focused, concentrated, or given. What is common to all of these uses of the term "attention" is a reference to selection. An assumption implicit in attempts to "attract attention," or to "direct attention," is that only some among all of the available objects and events in one's immediate environment will be seen, heard, thought about, and remembered. Attention implies selectivity, and to study attention is to attempt to describe how this selection occurs.

Disagreement among various descriptions of attention arises because different researchers and theorists describe different types of selective activities. Furthermore, the descriptions vary in terms of the locus of selectivity considered to be attention, whether it is selectivity of perception or of memory. All the descriptions may not turn out to be compatible; indeed, some may not even be valid. However, to avoid the ignorance of the blind men who declared the elephant to be only that which each described, we must consider the varieties of selection which have been included under the rubric of attention.

Individuals of all species are in constant interaction with their environment. In order to survive, they must exert some degree of selective control over this interaction. The degree of control varies phylogenetically, ontogenetically, between individuals, and even from one situation to another for a particular individual. For example, to avoid being inundated by an infinite amount of sensory stimulation we select only a sample of what is available to see, hear, taste, or feel. We may accomplish this selectivity by searching systematically for certain specific types of information. E. J. Gibson has described this process of "optimization of attention" (1969, p. 456) in the context of her theory of perceptual learning and development. Research on visual scanning (e.g., Salapatek & Kessen 1973; Vurpillot 1968) documents this type of selective perception. However, in many situations some information is more likely to be noticed than other information not because it is sought by the individual but because of the nature of the information itself. Sometimes, as in orientation to a sudden, loud sound, the selection may be due to simple reflexive behaviors. More often the selection reflects a complex interaction between one's present situation and past experiences. For instance, when infants attend to sights or sounds which are novel, their selection must be based on what they have seen or heard in the past. Attention based on past experience is also important in theories such as that of Zeaman and House (1963, 1974).

Even after some available information has been perceived, additional selection occurs. Not all that we notice is thought about further or remembered later. Neisser (1967) described how, through selective analysis of information, called "focal attention," only some things are thought about and remembered. Some investigators of the development of attention have cited Neisser's model as being important in interpreting their own findings about what is remembered (e.g., Hagen & Hale 1973). Also, the well-known filter models of attention, formulated by Broadbent (1958) and by Treisman (1969), are attempts to explain how some information makes its way into memory but other information does not. While these theories were not intended to account for developmental changes in attention, they too have influenced researchers interested in children's attention (e.g., Hagen & Hale 1973; Maccoby 1969).

Although there is not generally a close relation between studies of children's attention and theories of attention, a common emphasis on selectivity of functioning characterizes both theoretical and empirical efforts to understand attention. Attention will be treated in this chapter not as an independent construct, but rather as selectivity which is brought about by certain types of activity. Because such selectivity occurs in the continuous encounters of an individual in an environment, it characterizes a variety of cognitive activities—perception, memory, thought.

There are three general questions to be answered in order to arrive at some formulation about the nature of attention. The first is: What are the activities by which an individual brings about selectivity? This question focuses on how one's own behavior affects attention. A second, reciprocal question is: What type of information is acquired from the environment? This question focuses on the environmental contribution to attention. The third question is about development: How do changes in selectivity occur? We will see that there has not been uniform emphasis on these questions by investigators of children's attention. A summary of the review which follows suggests that a good deal is known about the effect of the environment on children's attention and that relatively little is known about how one's own behavior can affect attention. Also there are suggestions but little confirmation as yet about developmental trends in attention.

The plan of this chapter will be, first, to review the empirical findings about attention in infants and children and then to identify problems needing investigation in order fully to describe the development of attention in children. We separate, for review, the studies of infants' attention from those of older children because, for the most part, researchers have asked different questions about infants' attention than they have about older children's attention.

II. ATTENTION IN INFANTS

The study of infants' attention has been concerned with the question of whether infants do, in fact, attend. The research has been concentrated on the effects on attention of some specifiable types of environmental information. These types of information will be used as the basis for organizing the discussion of infants' attention.

We have suggested that one characteristic common to various descriptions of attention is selectivity. Not all selective behavior, though, is appropriately described in terms of attention. Rather, investigators have taken the view that attention reflects the infant's cognitive functioning and hence can be understood only within a psychological context of how the infant knows, understands, and perceives. However, in spite of the assumed importance of cognitive functioning for defining infants' attention, few investigators have tested specific hypotheses about the nature of attention itself. Thus, there is little clarity about where in the interaction between baby and world attention may occur. In general, investigators have asked whether, in an experimentally controlled setting, babies exhibit behaviors which seem to reflect attention. The controlled settings have often contained information presumed to be novel, discrepant, or of a certain complexity level.

A. NOVELTY

How are attention and cognition related developmentally? When and how does an infant's attention depend on what he has learned from his interaction with the world? One technique for studying the relation between attention and cognitive development has been to use novel objects or patterns. When infants attend to such things, their behavior is then considered in terms of such cognitive processes as formation of a memory model of a familiar object or pattern (Kagan 1970), or transition into a stage of more general interest in novel things (Hunt 1970).

In many studies of attention to novelty, the question has been asked whether infants of varying age demonstrate responsiveness specific to their experiences. In an early study, Fantz (1964) showed photographs and advertisements to infants between the ages of 1 and 6 months. The pictures were presented for 10 successive 1-minute periods. During each period, two pictures were shown; one was unique to that period while the other was common to all time periods. Fantz found that babies older than 2 months preferred to look at the novel picture. This result has been confirmed by other investigators, some of whom made longitudinal observations and also controlled for such variables as familiarity of bassinet (Fantz & Nevis 1967; Greenberg, Uzgiris, & Hunt 1970; Uzgiris & Hunt 1970; Weizman, Cohen, & Pratt 1971; Wetherford & Cohen 1973). Although babies younger than 2 months in Fantz's study did not prefer looking at either picture, findings from recent studies indicate that babies younger than 2 months prefer to look at the familiar item (Greenberg et al. 1970; Weizman et al. 1971; Wetherford & Cohen 1973). The developmental trend toward preference for novelty has not been equally apparent from different experimental procedures. Recently, Wetherford and Cohen (1973) found a developmental transition from preference for familiarity to preference for novelty to be more obvious when infants were studied using a cross-sectional procedure than when they were studied using a longitudinal procedure. Weizman et al. (1971) found the age of transition to a preference for novelty to be related both to sex of the infant and to the infant's familiarity with the test setting. And Fantz and Nevis (1967) observed the transition from preference for familiarity to preference for novelty to be more abrupt when familiarization occurred in a short time than when it occurred over a longer period of time.

The developmental trend toward a preference for novelty has been interpreted as reflecting a significant maturation of central nervous system structures at about 2 months of age (e.g., Kagan 1970). This interpretation was supported by findings of Fagan, Fantz, and Miranda (1971), who compared preferences of premature babies with those of full-term babies and found that both groups preferred novelty at 50 weeks conceptual age. The maturation presumably permits the infant to form an enduring internal image of what she has seen and/or heard. Clearly, if an infant cannot remember what she has just seen and/or heard, she will probably not respond to something familiar as something known; all things will be novel.

There are some findings which cast doubt on neurological maturation as an explanation for memory capacity which is present at 2 months. There is evidence, from studies of habituation, of memory in newborns. Habituation occurs when infants attend less—often by looking less—to something that has become familiar to them. Friedman (1972) observed newborn babies habituating to checkerboard patterns; some of the babies also increased their fixation time for a novel stimulus. McGurk (1970) observed infants as young as 6 weeks habituating to objects in one orientation and then renewing their responsiveness to the objects placed in another orientation. Finally, Horowitz (1974) and her colleagues conducted a series of studies in which they observed that infants as young as 7 weeks—or even, in one study, 5 weeks—showed a response decrement indicative of habituation. In many other studies habituation has not been demonstrated in infants younger than 2 months, and Horowitz and her colleagues suggested that this may be due to procedural difficulties. They therefore developed a methodology for studying habituation in very young infants which minimizes arbitrary conditions and maximizes sensitivity to individual differences among infants.

Even though attention to novelty depends on cognitive functions like memory, it is surprising that the objects and patterns used in these studies have rarely been designed with a view to the infant's cognitive abilities. For example, among the items used have been "a red plastic bulb with a stem topped with a clown's face" (McCall & Kagan 1970, p. 92), "a . . . lime green barbell" (Wetherford & Cohen 1973, p. 418), and "three match boxes covered with colorful wrapping paper and attached at equal intervals to the edge of the base by three-inch strings" (Uzgiris & Hunt 1970, p. 111). More appropriate items might be simple geometric figures that can be scanned adequately by young infants (Salapatek 1969) or displays which provide information that is important for survival or that represent information available normally to the infant. With different items, a preference for novelty may be demonstrated more easily even for infants younger than 2 months of age. More careful and representative selection of stimulus items may well change the generalizations we make about infant attention.

In sum, it is apparent that infants older than 2 months attend to visual novelty. While this behavior may reflect neurological maturation, it also seems as though procedural artifacts may mask more fragile but essentially similar behaviors in younger infants. The question of whether infants younger than 2 months are responsive to novelty may have more to do with the specific items they are shown than with their ability to remember and hence to attend.

B. DISCREPANCY

Does infants' attention to novelty depend on the *degree* to which the new information deviates from the familiar? This question has been asked by a number of investigators in the form of the hypothesis that "stimuli moderately discrepant from the schema elicit longer orientations than do either minimally discrepant (that is, familiar) events or novel events that bear no relation to the schema" (Kagan 1970, p. 828). Thus, the hypothesis predicts a curvilinear, "inverted-U" relation between attention and discrepancy of a stimulus item from an internal representation (the schema). The internal representation allows the infant to recognize things seen previously. The hypothesis has also been understood to imply that infants' cognitive development proceeds by comprehension of moderately new information (Kagan 1970). The effect of degree of novelty or discrepancy on infants' attention has often been assessed using preference measures (McCall 1973; McCall et al. 1973). Though preferences imply attention, they do not, by themselves, necessarily provide accurate information about how things are represented internally, or about how representations are acquired.

It is, in fact, very difficult to assess adequately the discrepancy hypothesis. An absence of the predicted relation between attention and discrepancy does not necessarily prove that the hypothesis is incorrect. The stimuli may simply be inappropriate. Since discrepancy is defined by reference to what the individual infant knows or prefers, selection of appropriate stimulus items requires (*a*) a prior assessment of what the infant has observed and thus may have represented and remembered, and (*b*) the establishment of a scale by which to describe degree of discrepancy. These requirements have not generally been met. Investigators instead have expected that infants would internalize a picture-like trace of an object or pattern as that item is known by the experimenter; then, it has been expected that the infants would respond as predicted to items discrepant in degrees determined by adults (McCall et al. 1973; McCall & Kagan 1967a). The fact that babies don't always behave in this way does not mean that the hypothesis is incorrect.

There is one further difficulty in assessing the discrepancy hypothesis. Thomas (1971) pointed out that the hypothesis assumes that a single dimension describes the ordering of the stimulus items and the basis for responding. But attention to discrepancy might be determined by variation in several dimensions; the hypothesis could be true even while the relation between attention and discrepancy could not be described by one dimension.

Some investigators have observed a curvilinear relation between infants' attention and degree of discrepancy. McCall and Kagan (1967a) habituated 3-month-old infants to a standard item, a mobile, which was a linear array of three-dimensional X's, Y's, and blocks against a black-rimmed white background. The infants viewed the mobile at home for approximately 30 days. Then, at about 4 months of age, the infants were shown three new mobiles which were previously judged by a group of adults to vary in amount of discrepancy from the standard. There was no relation between the visual measures of attention and degree of discrepancy. However, for the female infants, but not for the males, magnitude of heart rate deceleration (another measure of attention) was related as predicted to discrepancy. The absence of a general, straightforward relation between infants' attention and discrepancy characterizes many similar studies (Hopkins et al. 1971; McCall & Melson 1969; Super et al. 1972). It is difficult to derive general support for the discrepancy hypothesis from findings which are specific to one sex or one measure.

Some investigators have sought to explain the specificity of results by demonstrating a general relation between presumed completeness of habituation and attention to discrepancy (McCall 1971, 1973; McCall et al. 1973; McCall & Kagan 1970; McCall & Melson 1970b). McCall & Kagan (1970) for example, classified 4-month-old infants as slow-habituators, rapid-habituators, and short-lookers (those whose visual fixations were too short to provide habituation data), and they found that the short-lookers and the rapid-habituators attend more to greater discrepancy. McCall et al. (1973) then suggested that an incomplete internal representation or memory of the standard stimulus item, a consequence of insufficient habituation, might be responsible when the predicted relation between attention and discrepancy is not observed. Twelve-week-old and 18-week-old infants were again classified as rapid- and slow-habituators after they met a criterion of habituation. Attention was related curvilinearly to degree of discrepancy for the rapid-habituators but not for the slow-habituators. Thus, even though all the infants presumably formed an adequate memory of the standard stimulus (i.e., met a criterion of habituation), the curvilinear relation still did not describe the behavior of all the infants. General support for the discrepancy hypothesis thus continues to be lacking.

Infants' attention to discrepancy has also been studied with auditory patterns. Melson and McCall (1970) familiarized 5-month-old girls to an eight-note sequence of tones. Then two discrepant patterns were presented, each of which was a reordered sequence of the same tones. The infants who habituated rapidly also responded differentially, in terms of heart rate deceleration, to the two new sequences.

Horowitz (1972) habituated 6-month-old boys to a two-tone sequence which was then presented in one of four modified forms. These forms were constructed to permit the experimenter to determine, and not merely to assume, what the babies had learned during the habituation period. The results suggested that there were differences among the infants in what was learned and remembered. Some infants remembered the first note, some remembered the second, and some remembered the fact that two notes had been heard. Horowitz suggested that " . . . an infant's internal model of the standard stimulus may not be the same as the experimenter-defined standard from which the degree of discrepancy accorded to a test stimulus is usually assessed. In fact, in light of the present findings I remain perplexed over the degree of approximation achieved by experimenter-defined descrepancy levels in ordering data from some previous investigations. . . . It may well be that some infants are capable of responding to particular stimuli in a manner approximating that of the 'naive' experimenter" (p. 51).

In summary, infants attend to some forms of discrepancy; the behavior is more obvious, the older the infant. The relation between infants' attention and discrepancy remains unspecified; as yet it is neither general nor robust. A major difficulty in describing the relation is the need to assess what an individual baby remembers and knows.

C. PATTERNS

So far in this review we have considered evidence that as infants become familiar with their world, they attend more systematically to it. Studies of novelty and discrepancy seem to confirm hypotheses that changes in attention may reflect developing intellectual processes. But what parts of objects or patterns can infants attend to so that they can begin to know their world and recognize what they already have learned? Are infants, even at birth, capable of organizing what they are seeing and/or hearing in order to explore their environment systematically rather than randomly? Do infants attend to well-defined aspects of their environment? These questions have provided a focus for many investigations of infants' attention. The review of this research will be divided into sections on geometric patterns, ecologically relevant patterns, and auditory patterns.

1. Geometric Patterns

Do infants attend to pattern? Very young infants, even newborns, not only can attend to contoured pattern (e.g., Fantz 1963), but also can discriminate pattern movement and seem to prefer to watch patterns that move. Haith (1966) reported that newborns showed greater suppression of nonnutritive sucking (another measure of attention) when a light appeared to move than when it appeared to remain stationary. Ames and Silfen (1965) reported that infants as young as 11 weeks preferred to view a moving rather than a stationary checkerboard pattern. Attention to movement has been confirmed for 2 to 6-month-olds (Cohen 1969) and for 6-, 9-, 13-, and 18-month-olds (Lewis, Goldberg, & Campbell 1969). In spite of the evidence that infants are so greatly interested in pattern movement, in most studies stationary patterns have been used.

What aspects of stationary patterns do infants attend to? Recently, several investigators have tried to explain why infants at approximately 2 months of age begin to prefer a bull's-eye pattern over a striped pattern (e.g., Fantz & Nevis 1967). Bond (1972b) designed patterns that would allow comparisons of the independent and interactive effects on attention of curvature and concentricity. She measured the visual fixations of 3 to 4.5-month-old infants, and she concluded that the preference for the bull's-eye occurred because the infants attended to curvature. Ruff and Birch (1974) compared the effects of three variables on infants' attention to the bull's-eye: curvature, concentricity, and number of line orientations within the stimulus. They tested 3-month-old infants with 10 patterns representing combinations of values of the three variables. In contrast to Bond, Ruff and Birch concluded that (a) all of the variables were interesting to 3-month-old infants, and (b) the preference for the bull's-eye occurred because the infants attended to all three variables. Finally, Maidel and Karmel (1973) tried to assess the effects on attention to the bull's-eye of overall and central contour density. They failed even to find a developmental trend toward preference for the bull's-eye when they compared preferences of 5 to 6-week-old infants with those of 8 to 10-week-old infants. Differences in contour density of patterns did affect the infants' attention, and Maisel and Karmel suggested that the bull's-eye preference might depend in part on contour density.

Evidence about other aspects of patterns which may elicit attention has been provided by Spears (1964), who found that the ordering of 4-month-olds' preferences for colored geometric forms was better described by shape than by color. Cohen, Gelber, & Lazar (1971) showed that infants can attend to form and to color. After habituation, 4-month-old boys attended to patterns that differed from a standard pattern either in form or in color, and they attended most to patterns in which both components had been changed. Similar findings have been reported for 3-month-old infants (Saayman, Ames, & Moffett 1964).

Complexity is an aspect of patterns thought to be important for infant attention. Unfortunately, complexity is an unwieldy construct, and its operational definitions have been varied. Some definitions have referred to physical indices like number of light-dark transitions (Hershenson 1964) or amount of black-white contour per unit area (Greenberg & O'Donnell 1972). Other definitions have referred to ratings by adults (Zelazo & Komer 1971) or to ratings by the experimenters themselves (Kagan & Lewis 1965). Because of the variety of definitions, Hutt (1970) advises about the concept of complexity: "Acknowledging that it is a useful short-hand term but no more, we may have to suspend, at least temporarily, the use of the term and discipline ourselves instead to specify *which* dimension of the independent variable is being manipulated and *how*" (p. 138).

Often, complexity has been defined as the number of squares in a black-and-white checkerboard pattern. In an early study, patterns with 2 × 2, 8 × 8, and 24 × 24 checks were shown to babies from 3 weeks of age (Brennan, Ames, & Moore 1966). The 3-week-old babies preferred the least complex pattern; the 8-week-old babies preferred the intermediate stimulus; and the 14-week-old babies preferred the most complex stimulus. In a replication of that study using a longitudinal procedure, babies did not show consistent individual developmental trends toward attention to increasing complexity (Horowitz 1969). But subsequent observations of individuals as well as of groups (e.g., Greenberg 1971; Greenberg & O'Donnell 1972) do support the earlier interpretation of a developmental trend toward preference for greater complexity.

Complexity has also been studied using patterns which are random shapes varying in the number of independent turns or angles. Hershenson, Munsinger, and Kessen (1965) showed newborn infants shapes with 5, 10, or 20 turns. Fixation time was a curvilinear function of complexity;

the infants preferred the middle-value pattern. Munsinger and Weir (1967) used more stimulus patterns in testing infants between 9 and 41 months of age and found preference to be linearly related to complexity for all the age levels tested. McCall and Kagan (1967b), on the other hand, did not observe any relation between their measures of visual attention and number of turns when they studied 4-month-old infants. Again, there is a disappointing lack of generality to the findings.

Attempts have been made to unify the various interpretations of complexity proposed by investigators of infants' attention. Karmel (1969a, 1969b) suggested that contour is the important stimulus characteristic. In two studies he demonstrated that infants' visual fixations were influenced not by complexity—the random or redundant arrangement of a stimulus pattern—but by the amount of contour within the stimulus pattern (Karmel 1969a, 1969b). Karmel suggested that there is a curvilinear relation, an inverted-U function, between attention and the square root of total contour, and he showed that findings from previous studies (Brennan et al. 1966; Greenberg & O'Donnell 1972; Hershenson 1964) conform to this inverted-U function (Karmel 1969b, 1974). Since the peaks of the curve shift with increasing age to higher values of contour, there is also evidence of a developmental progression toward preference for greater complexity. (Recently, Karmel [1974] has suggested that attention does not depend only on the total amount of contour shown to the infant. Instead, attention is related to contour density, the size of the stimulus pattern, the distance between the infant and the pattern, and the retinal angle subtended by the contours of the pattern.) The importance of contour for assessing the effects of complexity has also been verified with 4-month-olds (McCall & Kagan 1967b) and with 5-month-old girls (McCall & Melson 1970a).

Karmel (1969a, 1969b) suggested that the basis for the curvilinear relation of attention to contour might be an optimal level of stimulation for cells responsive to contour. He pursued this suggestion by measuring visually evoked potentials elicited by brief presentations of checkerboard patterns. He found that one component of the potential, amplitude of the P_2 peak, was related curvilinearly to density of the square root of stimulus contour (Karmel, Hoffman, & Fegy 1974). Furthermore, the peak of the curve shifted toward greater contour density as the age of infants increased. The shift in curve peaks represents a striking correspondence between neurological and psychological functioning, although, of course, the meaning of the correspondence remains to be identified.

There are findings not congruent with Karmel's hypothesis. McCall (1971) noted, for example, that Fantz (1965) found infants' fixation times to vary with different arrangements of squares even when contour and area remained constant. Moffett (1969), too, found infants' viewing time to vary for patterns with different arrangements of lines. And Spears (1964) was unable to use contour to order a series of stimuli in accord with demonstrated preferences. In short, it may well be that several dimensions besides contour are subsumed under the construct complexity. Jones-Molfese (1972) noted that even the feasibility of ordering preferences according to one dimension does not preclude the possibility that " . . . a linear combination of different physical attributes of the patterns" (p. 1295) may also account for such ordering.

In summary, even at an early age, infants attend to patterns, colors, and shapes—both stationary and moving—in their environment. As they grow older, they show increased interest in patterns that are increasingly complex. The specific stimulus dimensions which are the source of this interest include contour and perhaps other characteristics as well.

If a baby attends visually to some pattern in its environment, it must look at that pattern. Thus, another way to study what the infant attends to in its environment is to observe how it looks at its world, how it explores and searches visually. In empirical studies of visual scanning the infants' patterns of eye movements are photographed while they are looking at stimuli like solid black triangles or black-white outline circles. The techniques are highly sophisticated, involving infrared corneal photography (Haith 1969; Salapatek & Kessen 1966). Typical measures have included dispersion of gaze, location of gaze, and pattern of ocular orientation.

In an early study, Salapatek and Kessen (1966) showed infants less than 8 days of age an equilateral triangle in a central area of their visual field. The infants not only reduced their overall scanning in the presence of the stimulus, but they also restricted their scanning to part of the triangle, mostly to its vertex. Selection of vertices was not quite so obvious in the results of a subsequent study in which circular as well as triangular stimuli were used (Salapatek 1968). Newborns in that study tended again to view only part of the figure, but the parts selected were central portions and contour as well as angles. The infants' horizontal scanning also decreased differently for different-sized figures. Selective fixation of parts of the stimulus was again in evidence in a study (Salapatek & Kessen 1973) in which newborns were given a rather long exposure to a plane triangle placed in several orientations. While all of the infants concentrated at least sometimes on a single feature, some of them also looked at several features, thus demonstrating early individual differences in scanning behavior.

How do scanning patterns change with age? Salapatek (1969) studied the scanning behavior of infants between approximately 1 and 2.5 months of age. Older infants (8 to 10 weeks), though generally regarding the contour, tended to look more often than did younger infants (4 to 6 weeks) at the central portion of geometric outline shapes. In addition, the older babies scanned a greater amount of the contour than did the younger babies. In a second study, outline geometric shapes were either embedded within or placed next to each other. The older infants tended more often than did the young infants to view the embedded, internal figures. Developmentally, infants seem to acquire increased flexibility in scanning which enables them to select more and different features of their environment.

2. Ecologically Relevant Patterns

Many investigators have stressed the need for careful control of stimulus patterns in studying infants' attention; fewer have been concerned with the relevance of the pattern for the infants who view or hear it. There have been some attempts to model a meaningful three-dimensional world and to observe whether infants discriminate variables that specify important information like the approach of an object or the sudden drop-off of terrestrial support. Campos, Langer, and Krowitz (1970) investigated infants' attention to loss of visual support by placing babies 1.5 to 3.5 months of age on both sides of a visual cliff (a glass-topped table with two textured surfaces at different distances underneath [Walk & Gibson 1961]). They found that the infants' orienting behavior (heart rate deceleration) and looking time were greater when they were on the deep side than when they were on the shallow side. Subsequently, Schwartz, Campos, and Baisel (1973) found that the heart rate of babies 5 months of age decelerated when they were on the deep side, while the heart rates of babies 9 months of age accelerated when they were on that same side. It was suggested that the older infants were no longer attending to the deep side but rather were reacting with fear.

Ball and Tronick (1971) studied infants' attention to impending collision by showing a symmetrically expanding shadow to infants between 2 and 11 weeks of age. They reported defensive behaviors like a pulling back of the head for babies across the age range. This response has also been reported for newborns who observed the approach of real objects (Bower, Broughton, & Moore 1970). The newborns' response to an optical expansion pattern, though, was less intense than their response to the real objects. Hruska and Yonas (1971) presented an optical expansion pattern to infants 2 to 4, 5 to 7, and 8 to 10 months of age and recorded the babies' heart rate patterns. The heart rate of infants younger than 7 months typically decelerated while that of infants older than 8 months typically accelerated. These results—together with those of Schwartz et al. (1973)—suggest the interesting hypothesis that attention precedes fear developmentally. When babies younger than a half year or so are placed in a visibly dangerous situation, they react by attending; when older babies are placed in the same situation, they react with fear. In order to know that something in the environment is threatening, an infant must attend to those parts of the environment that indicate danger. At least in some cases, learning how to attend may be a prerequisite for learning to be afraid. These studies certainly do seem to suggest that future research on the development of fear may benefit from defining what in the environment lets an infant know that danger is near and/or imminent.

3. Auditory Patterns

What kinds of auditory patterns can infants attend to? Most information about attention to auditory patterns is found in results of studies in which auditory patterns have been used to study habituation (e.g., Eisenberg, Coursin, & Rupp 1966), heart rate change (e.g., Porges, Arnold, & Forbes 1973), and arousal state (e.g., Ashton 1971). For example, Kearsley (1973) assessed cardiac deceleration of newborn infants to pure tones and to white noise. Frequency, intensity, and length of rise time of the tones were varied systematically. Kearsley found that the infants attended not to the components of the tones but rather to the total stimulus event; combinations of the three factors—frequency, intensity, and rise time—elicited the greatest deceleration. Moffitt (1973), on the other hand, assessed infants' habituation and did find evidence that babies 20 to 24 weeks of age do attend to intensity.

At present, the information about infants' attention to auditory patterns is too meager and the methodological problems too far from solution to allow general suggestions about developmental trends (Kessen, Haith, & Salapatek 1970). Much of the information is based on habituation research, and the focus of most of that research has been on methodological issues (Jeffrey & Cohen 1971). Methodological studies can suggest limitations on interpretations, but they do not necessarily sample a sufficient range of stimuli for assessing attention capabilities. (See Graham and Jackson [1970] for discussion of habituation studies that record changes of heart rate.)

Attention to one important type of auditory pattern—speech—has received much notice in recent years. The study of this problem has been greatly influenced by findings from the Haskins Laboratories, where impressive spectographic techniques have been developed for analyzing and synthesizing speech sounds (Liberman et al. 1967). The spectographic techniques have provided evidence that (a) perception of at least some phonemes (stop consonants) may not be based on discrimination of an easily defined invariant acoustic pattern, and (*b*) adult perception of these phonemes may be categorical: even though the acoustic patterns of a specific phoneme may vary, the sounds cannot be discriminated much better than they can be categorized. An important question to ask about infants, then, is whether they discriminate phonemes categorically. Typically, habituation procedures have been used to study this question (Eimas et al. 1971; Moffitt 1971; Morse 1972; Trehub & Rabinovitch 1972). Eimas et al. (1971) found some of the most compelling evidence for a linguistic discrimination. They presented synthetic /b/ and /p/ sounds to 1- and 4-month-old infants. The acoustic difference for sounds which were the same phoneme was as great as the acoustic difference for sounds which were different phonemes. But after habituation, infants attended only when they heard a sound from a new phoneme category, and they did not attend to sounds equally different from the habituation sound but from the same phoneme category. Similar findings have been obtained by Trehub and Rabinovitch (1972), although they did not provide a control of sounds from the same category as that of the habituation sound.

The acoustic property that distinguishes phonemes which differ only in place of articulation—/b/ versus /g/, for example—also seems to be perceived categorically by adults, and again there is evidence that 20 to 40-week-old infants (Moffitt 1971) and 40 to 54-day-old infants (Morse 1972) can discriminate such phonemes. Thus, it appears that infants can attend to linguistically important properties of acoustic stimuli. These studies of infant speech perception suggest that classes of language sounds may well conform to biological constraints and that the young infant may therefore be equipped at birth to begin to isolate sounds into those categories which will be meaningful for learning a language. A biological endowment may provide the infant with unique tools for perceiving speech sounds as a special type of acoustic stimulation. The findings indicate that the young infant may be able to learn properties of its native language long before it can be differentially reinforced for having produced recognizable utterances in that language.

Recently Horowitz (1974) and her colleagues have developed an intermodal method for studying infants' attention to auditory stimuli; they observe infants' looking at visible stimuli which are presented simultaneously with auditory stimuli. Horowitz has argued persuasively that such intermodal functioning reflects important aspects of an infant's natural learning environment. For instance, Horowitz and her colleagues found that babies of approximately 8 weeks of age can attend to some aspect or aspects of voices in order to discriminate between a mother's and a stranger's voice and that infants 8 to 9 weeks old can attend to properties that correspond to changes in voice tone quality. The intermodal method, because of its ecological validity, may provide an important new tool for evaluating what an infant can listen and attend to.

D. PROCEDURES FOR STUDYING INFANT ATTENTION

In most studies of infants, behaviors demonstrating either preference or habituation have been used as indices of attention. The preference procedure has become popular primarily due to the work of Berlyne (1958) and of Fantz (e.g., Cohen 1973; Fantz 1958). A basic reason for using preferences as indices of attention is the assumption that if there is a preference for one of two items, the two have been compared and one has been selected.

There are three difficulties in interpreting infants' preferences for one of two objects or patterns. One is that the absence of a preference does not necessarily correspond with an inability to detect a difference (e.g., Gibson & Olum 1969). McGurk (1970) provided an example of this difficulty when he compared infants' preferences for novelty with their sensitivity to novelty. The infants, from 6 to 26 weeks of age, showed no preference for either of two orientations of a plaster face model or of a funnel-like object. The same infants, however, responded to the objects in a novel orientation after tiring of viewing them in the original orientation. Clearly, they could detect the difference in orientation in spite of showing no preference for one or the other orientation.

A second difficulty of interpretation occurs when infants do seem to demonstrate a preference because they respond differently to two items. A difference in response to the two items need not reflect a preference for one of them. For instance, such a difference could occur if the baby were "captured" or drawn to the one item while it responded to the other item as part of the background or context (Hershenson, Kessen, & Munsinger 1967). To circumvent this difficulty, Hershenson et al. (1967) suggested a set of criteria which would allow response differences to be interpreted as preferences. For instance, they suggested that if the response differences for at least three items allow those items to be described as an ordered set, then the environmental basis for the response differences can be defined by the ways in which the items vary.

A third difficulty of interpreting preferences is to specify the psychological basis for the preference. Karmel (1969a) proposed that infants' preferences for items with varying amounts of contour might reflect optimal amounts of stimulation for neuronal spiking activity. More recently, Bond (1972b) has speculated that the preference for bull's-eye patterns shown by infants of approximately 2 months of age might be a consequence of neurological maturation. (See also Ruff and Birch [1974], who also suggest neurological hypotheses for the bull's-eye effect.) While such hypotheses may be correct in identifying neurological prerequisites for preferences, as yet we cannot characterize adequately the relation between neurological and psychological functioning unless we assume the relation is one of simple correspondence.

Habituation has been the other favored procedure for studying infants' attention. Habituation, it will be recalled, refers to a response decrement that occurs as a result of repeated or prolonged exposure to a stimulus. The popularity of this procedure may be due to the assumption that habituation is mediated by cortical processes and that therefore one can make inferences about perceptual and cognitive functioning and development. (For an excellent review of habituation research with human infants, see Jeffrey and Cohen [1971]). Habituation has been demonstrated most often with two types of stimulus items: (*a*) items chosen by the experimenter (e.g., Super et al. 1972) and (*b*) items preferred by the infant subjects (e.g., Saayman et al. 1964).

Use of the habituation procedure is complicated by the necessity for certain controls. Before habituation can be assumed to account for a response decrement, it must be possible to reject explanations based on habituation-like behavior, for example, sensory fatigue. In an excellent theoretical discussion of habituation and dishabituation, Thompson and Spencer (1966) suggested nine criteria for judging whether it is appropriate to interpret a response decrement as habituation. When Jeffrey and Cohen (1971) reviewed the literature on infants' habituation, they noted that few of these criteria had been met by the procedures of any single study. They suggested, though, that most of the criteria are met if one evaluates many studies together. They also argued that habituation is demonstrated adequately simply by a renewed response to a novel or slightly discrepant stimulus item. They wrote: "Whether this effect should be called dishabituation is not nearly as critical as is the fact that experimental situations with proper controls can provide a solid basis for inferences about perceptual and cognitive development . . ." (p. 70). Proper control procedures usually include either showing that the novel or discrepant item does not ordinarily elicit greater responsivity than does the habituated item (e.g., Wetherford & Cohen 1973) or counterbalancing the two items (McCall et al. 1973).

It is sometimes difficult to interpret the meaning of habituation, since it is not easy to specify to what the infant has become habituated. For instance, it cannot be assumed that the infant forms a memory trace of the entire stimulus item as it is known to the experimenter. In fact, there is some evidence that infants may become habituated only to a part of the item (Caron, Caron, & Caldwell 1971; Collard & Rydberg 1972). D.

J. Miller (1972), for example, first assessed infants' initial fixation on three components of a standard figure which was then used for familiarization (e.g., the dots, cross, and circular outline of a complex geometric figure). She then showed the standard figure and the components again and compared the durations of the infants' pre- and postfamiliarization fixations. She found that the infants' viewing times decreased for the component most preferred initially (i.e., looked at longest), did not change for the component second most preferred, and increased slightly for the component least preferred. Also, fixations of the standard figure increased in duration toward the end of the habituation trials and into the testing trials. Miller suggested that these findings might reflect increased attention to components less salient than those that earlier had become familiar. Clearly, it would have been wrong to assume that a response decrement reflected habituation to the entire figure.

Many behaviors and activities have been used to assess infants' attention with the habituation procedure. They include amount of limb movement (Collins, Kessen, & Haith 1972), magnitude of heart rate change (McCall & Kagan 1970), frequency of smiling (Zelazo & Komer 1971), latency of turning toward a stimulus figure or object (Cohen 1972), total looking time (Fagan 1970), and mean fixation time (Greenberg 1971). We know little about which of these measures are comparable or complementary and which are not; however, theoretical constructs can provide a context for examining the relations among measures—as is evident in the work of Cohen (1972, 1973). He suggested that latency of head turning and duration of visual fixation may not provide equivalent reflections of global attention, and so he distinguished between orienting—indexed by head turning—and information gathering—indexed by fixation. An alternative strategy for assessing relations among measures is to compute intercorrelations among the measures (e.g., Wilson & Lewis 1971). These statistical relations are useful because they can suggest hypotheses about meaningful behavioral relations.

In summary, procedures for inducing preferences or habituation are most frequently used to study infants' attention. In using both procedures it is assumed that attentional behaviors reflect the infant's cognitive functioning and not merely his ability to discriminate or detect differences. However, it is often difficult to justify this assumption. Furthermore, even demonstrating a cognitive contribution to the behavior still does not always specify what precisely has been attended to.

E. SUMMARY

In a well-known statement, William James suggested that the infant's world is a confusion of sensory intrusions. One would likely not expect,

on the basis of such a characterization, that an infant could systematically organize his or her world by attending to specific aspects of the environment. But from recent evidence it does seem clear that infants respond selectively to objects and events around them and that they
thereby do actively influence what constitutes their effective environment. Indeed, even the newborn infant can be surprisingly selective (e.g.,
Friedman 1972; Salapatek 1969).

When Elizabeth Bond (1972a) reviewed the literature on young infants' perception of form, she concluded that the form perception of the
infant, which depends on selective responding to the environment, may
be quite similar to the perception of the adult. The evidence that is as yet
available would appear to support a parallel conclusion for attention.
Certainly, such a conclusion cannot be rejected. But how then does the
selectivity of attention change developmentally? As infants get older,
they not only select or detect new or different things, but they do so
more efficiently. Earliest forms of selectivity may be primarily determined by neural functions while later forms may be increasingly influenced by experience. Neither of these developments, however, requires
an assumption of change in attention—selectivity is common to the behavior of infants of all ages. If older infants can attend to greater degrees
of novelty, discrepancy, and complexity, their ability to attend may well
be due to changes in their ability to remember and understand.

In general, infant attention has been conceptualized and studied only
indirectly. There has been emphasis on the effects of situational manipulation on behaviors that presumably reflect attention. In order to investigate directly and to understand attention and its development, it may be
necessary to develop comprehensive theories that more adequately accommodate the cognitive and perceptual context of the selective behavior. Theories can help determine which behaviors should be observed
and how these behaviors should be compared as expressions of attention.

III. ATTENTION IN YOUNG CHILDREN

With rare exceptions (e.g., Watson & Danielson 1969) attention in
children between 18 months and 3 years has not been studied. This
chronological discontinuity underlies the distinction made in this chapter
between research on infants' and on young children's attention. A review
of research on young children's attention does not lend itself to the same
organization pattern as that on infants' attention. One reason for this is,
of course, that more research techniques are available for use with children than with infants. Further, we shall find that research with children
beyond infancy has not been so focused on selective responsiveness to
specific environmental information. Instead, investigators use the term

attention to refer to various selective aspects of memory, perception, learning, and motivation. Our review of research on attention in young children will therefore be organized in terms of the cognitive requirements for the children who have been the subjects of that research. In this way, we hope to be able to identify some of the aspects of cognitive functioning in which the selectivity we are calling attention to occurs.

A. ATTENTION IN MEMORY

Attention occurs in many phases of perceptual and cognitive functioning. Some information about objects and events is seen and heard, and other information is not. Further, some information which has been noticed is remembered and some is forgotten. This selectivity in memory has been studied extensively by investigators of children's attention. A typical procedure is to present, for a short time, items to be viewed (or heard) and remembered. The conditions of presentation vary in ways which affect the ease or adequacy of remembering, and attention is inferred from discrepancies between what has been presented and what is remembered. Relations between the presentation conditions and what is remembered provide knowledge about conditions which facilitate or hamper attention. Such conditions then can be used to help children remember important information.

1. Recalling

When related items are presented together, as a unit, children's recall is facilitated, presumably because they can notice and remember the relevant category or class as well as the separate items. Kobasigawa and Orr (1973) asked kindergartners to recall drawings of various animals, vegetables, furniture, and vehicles. When the members of a category were presented together, more drawings were recalled than when the drawings were not presented in a systematic arrangement. Simple labeling of the category did not provide additional facilitation for children from kindergarten to fifth grade (Kobasigawa & Middleton 1972). However, recall is aided by instructing children to think about ways in which a collection of items "goes together" or is related (Rosner 1971) and, for children as young as 3 years, recall is aided by physically moving items into a systematic arrangement (Lampel 1973).

Categories also facilitate recall for children as young as preschool age when the items are words or objects instead of pictures (Denney & Ziobrowski 1972; Scribner & Cole 1972; Steinmetz & Battig 1969). The form of an item does affect the ease with which it can be recalled. Cole, Frankel, and Sharp (1971) showed children items as pictures, as objects, or as words and found better recall for the objects and pictures than for the words. The modality of presentation also may affect recall. Murray and Roberts (1968) found that children's recall for digits was facilitated when they listened to rather than looked at the numbers.

Generally, chronological age and measured recall are positively related and conditions which facilitate recall are effective over a fairly wide age range. Some conditions, however, may not have similar effects for children of different ages. In one study nursery school children, first graders, and fifth graders were shown a collection of pictures with instructions either to look at the pictures or to study the pictures in order to remember them (Appel et al. 1972). The older children recalled more items under the second instructions than under the first, whereas the younger children recalled approximately the same number of items under either set of instructions. In another study, kindergartners did recall more items when instructed to prepare for recall than when not so instructed (Wright 1973). If there are developmental changes in the ways in which children seek and remember information about their environment, then we should expect to find that some conditions affect attention differently for children of different ages. We should also find that, in settings such as classrooms, conditions which affect recall in children of one age may be ineffective for children of another age.

2. Recognizing Identity

Children's skill in recognizing things seen or heard before is also used as an index of attention. Sheer accuracy of recognition varies greatly for different types of material. For instance, it is easier for children to recognize realistic pictures that they have seen previously than to recognize abstract pictures (Nelson 1971). Preschoolers shown a series of pictures and asked to say about each one whether they had seen it before were nearly 100% accurate and were even accurate as long as 1 month later (Brown & Scott 1971). On the other hand, second graders were only 60% accurate and fourth graders 86% accurate in a similar task in which the items were not pictures but words read by the experimenter (Poteat & Kasschau 1969). In general, it is easier for children to recognize items which they have seen than to recognize the same items if they have been heard (Entwisle & Huggins 1973; Kirsner 1972). Young children also recognize objects they have seen better than objects they have felt (Goodnow 1971a), but children as young as preschool age recognize objects seen and felt better than objects which are only seen (Wolff 1972). Weiner and Goodnow (1970) suggested that handling or feeling an object in addition to looking at it directs visual attention and that some three-dimensional objects tend to attract notice more than do comparable two-dimensional objects.

If children name items when they are presented, the items subsequently are recognized more easily than if they are not named. Ward and Legant (1971) found that naming facilitates preschoolers' recognition of pictures and also of color patches. In fact, naming facilitates preschoolers' recognition of color samples even after a delay of days between presentation and recognition (Kimball & Dale 1972). Also, instructions to visualize or to imagine items facilitate their recognition by children at least from nursery school age (Millar 1972) through fourth grade (London & Robinson 1968; Robinson & London 1971). Instructions to imagine things may actually be functionally equivalent to instructions to name them. Both may lead children to visualize and to verbalize, which together may enhance items for later remembering. When we show children things which we want them to recognize later, we may help them by asking that they say the names of the items and also visualize them.

The length of time available to see items also affects how well they can be recognized. Young children require a longer time than do adults to recognize a given number of items (Haith, Morrison, & Sheingold 1970; Haith, Morrison, Sheingold, & Mindes 1970). Sheingold (1973) suggested that the locus of this difference is not in initially acquiring information about what items are present, but in maintaining that information in order to report it. If the time interval between seeing the items and recognizing them is sufficiently short, young children's recognition is as accurate as adults! In other words, this difference in attention between children and adults occurs in memory and not in perception. Thus, when children do have to recognize items over a long interval, it is all the more important that we provide them with whatever memory aids we can.

3. Recognizing Sequence

In many studies of attention children are asked to remember not the identity of items previously seen but the order in which the items occurred. A typical procedure is to lay out a series of picture cards, one at a time, in front of the child. Then the cards are covered and the child is shown a picture which is identical with one in the array, and he is asked where, in the array, that picture is to be found. One factor consistently found to affect children's performance in this task is the order of presentation. Children about 7 years of age and older remember items early or late in the series better than items which are in the middle of the series (Donaldson & Strang 1969). Younger, preschool-age children, however, only have better memory for items late in the series (Atkinson, Hansen, & Bernbach 1964). These age differences in the "recency" effect as well as in the "primacy" effect (advantage for items presented early in the series) are modifiable by a number of other factors, for example, the number of items in the array (Bush & Cohen 1970; Siegel & Allik 1973), the rate of presentation of the items, and the form in which they are presented—as spoken words or visible pictures (Siegel & Allik 1973). Presenting items in groups rather than evenly spaced temporally and spatially also helps children older than preschool age remember location (Harris & Burke 1972; McCarver 1972).

We have noted above that naming helps children recall the identity of items they have seen. Such naming also helps children remember the locations of items (Bush & Cohen 1970; Conrad 1972), but the effect is most pronounced for recent items and naming may even hinder remembering items shown early in a series (Hagen & Kingsley 1968; McCarver & Ellis 1972). This difference in the effects of naming depending on what children are trying to remember suggests that a device intended to help children remember certain information is most useful when it is related obviously to the memory task, that is, when the device directs the child to select the intended information. A name refers to an item's identity and not necessarily to its location or position. And saying its name seems, indeed, to help children remember its identity, but saying its name does not necessarily help them remember its location. Saying its position or location should help in that task. Recalling or rehearsing the sequence of all items as each new item is presented does assist preschool children to remember the early items (Bernbach 1967; Kingsley & Hagen 1969), especially if the experimenter ensures that the children recite the order correctly (Hagen, Hargrave, & Ross 1973). Thus, if we want children to remember a series of items in which the sequence is important, we should ask them to recite the order in which the items occur and not just their names.

One other factor which affects how well children can remember sequences of items has been ignored until recently. That factor is the features of the items themselves, that is, their form, color, etc. Odom and Corbin (1973) have found that the ease with which children can remember a sequence of items depends on the salience of particular features which must be remembered.

4. Remembering Relevant and Incidental Information

Much of what children remember is material which neither they nor an experimenter specifically intended to be remembered. Hence, it is important to identify conditions in which children remember information without specific instructions or direction to do so. The most systematic investigation of attention to incidental information is that of Hagen and Hale (1973). They have used tasks like those just considered, tasks in which children are asked to learn the position of pictures presented serially, in an array. However, after the children's memory of the relevant information—that is, location of the pictures—has been assessed, measures are obtained of other, incidental information which the children might have acquired about the pictures while learning their location. Relations between children's memory for the two types of information reflect attention to relevant and to irrelevant, or incidental, aspects of the task.

In an early study in this investigation (Maccoby & Hagen 1965), children from first through seventh grades were shown a series of pictures on backgrounds of different colors. The children were asked to learn the location in the series of each background color. After their memory for that information had been assessed, they were then asked to identify the pictures which went with each background color. Performance on the central task improved with age; the older children remembered much more about the locations of the background colors than did the younger children. Memory for the incidental information, however, did not change with age, except to decline between fifth and seventh grades. Similar results were obtained in a subsequent study in which the materials were cards depicting pairs of objects, an animal and a household object, and in which the task was to learn the sequence of the animals, while the incidental information was the household object paired with each animal (Hagen 1967). Again, older children remembered more of the relevant information than did younger children, but the children's memory of the incidental information was not related to their age. Such findings have been interpreted as reflecting a developmental change toward increasingly precise attention. Older children are better able than younger children to remember only the information which they have been directed to learn.

Children's attention in these tasks is affected by some specific characteristics of the materials used. A preliminary procedure of Maccoby and Hagen's study was to ask children to learn the sequence of the pictures and then to assess their memory of the background colors as the incidental information. That procedure was halted because the children remembered little or nothing of the background colors (Maccoby & Hagen 1965, p. 283), perhaps because the background colors simply were not salient features of the pictures. When salience has been assessed directly, it is found that children remember incidental information that is highly salient much better than information that is not (Odom 1972). The particular features which are most salient are not necessarily the same for children of different ages (Odom 1972, p. 288), and so developmental changes in the extent to which children remember relevant and incidental information reflect, in part, changes in the relative salience of different features (Hale & Morgan 1973).

Naming each item as it is presented decreases memory of the inciden-

tal unnamed item (Wheeler & Dusek 1973). Another important characteristic is the location of the picture on a card. When the materials are
pairs of pictured objects (e.g., a household object and an animal), sepa-
rating the pictures on the card impairs children's memory for the incidental picture; however, consistent or inconsistent placement of the two
pictures on the card does not affect memory of the incidental picture
(Druker & Hagen 1969). It may even be that without any spatial separation between the picture designated as relevant and the one designated
irrelevant, age trends in memory for the two types of material may be
similar. Hale and Piper (1973) found that when children 8 and 12 years
of age were asked to learn the location of colored shapes when shape was
designated as relevant, the children's memory for the incidental colors
increased with age instead of being unrelated to age. However, when the
shapes were shown on colored backgrounds, or beside color patches, the
usual age trends were observed. The older children remembered more of
the relevant information than the younger children did, but there was
relatively little change with age in memory of the incidental material.

These effects of the spatial relations between relevant and irrelevant
items on what children remember about the items may reflect differences
in how the children implicitly interpret the task. When the items are
separated and the relevant item specified, children remember just what
they have been directed to remember—the location of the relevant items.
However, when the items are not separated, they may not even function
as two items for the child. When the child is asked to learn the order of
shapes which are different colors, there is no reason to ignore the colors,
and they might well aid in remembering the sequence of the shapes.
Garner (1970) has noted that just because an experimenter can describe
two (or more) features of items or objects, it does not follow that a
subject will treat those features separately. Spatial relations may be important in determining whether different features are perceived and remembered separately or together, as a unit.

Despite the numerous studies of children's memory for relevant and
incidental information, the findings are limited in generality. The reason
is that in all the studies described so far, the relevent information was the
sequence of items in a two-dimensional array. Before we can make general statements about how children select relevant from irrelevant information to remember, we need to know whether sequences sufficiently
represent the types of information usually designated as relevant for
young children. In the few additional studies in which something besides
a sequence was designated relevant, the materials still have been two-
dimensional, and so we know little about how children remember relevant information about three-dimensional objects (Deichmann, Speltz, &
Kausler 1971; Siegel & Corsini 1969; Siegel & Stevenson 1966).

In summary, children become better able, with development, to remember information which they have been instructed to learn. Whether they also remember incidental and irrelevant information about things depends on a number of factors: what the irrelevant information is and whether it is salient, whether the irrelevant information is separated in space from what is relevant, and also whether what is relevant has been named. In general, factors which enhance the relevant material help children to remember it exclusively.

5. Imagery

The effect of imagery on retention has been of interest partly because it has been suggested that very young children may not be able to use imagery to help themselves remember things (Rohwer 1970). However, Reese (1972) found that when pairs of pictures were drawn so as to depict a relation between them, nursery school children's learning was facilitated. The presumption is that the children imagined the objects in their relation in order to remember them. Merely describing the relation does not have the same effect as when the relation is actually depicted (Jones 1973), although specific instructions to imagine relations among items does help children remember them (Clarkson et al. 1973; Danner & Taylor 1973; Yuille & Catchpole 1973). A device which is especially effective is for the experimenter or the child actually to manipulate the objects so that they interact in relation to each other (Wolff & Levin 1972; Wolff, Levin, & Longobardi 1972). Perhaps any technique which encourages the child to notice the relation between items will enable him to use that relation, via imagery, to remember the items.

6. Observational Learning

Much behavior as well as information that a child learns is not explicitly taught to him. Rather, he learns by observing, remembering, and imitating other people's behavior. This often repeated fact has become something of a cliché. Yet until recently the mechanisms of such learning had not been investigated thoroughly (Kuhn 1973).

In studies of observational learning (e.g., Bandura, Ross, & Ross 1963), the child's memory of what he has seen another person—a model—do is assessed, and what he remembers is assumed to reflect what he has attended. Often the child is not instructed to attend to any particular feature of the model. The procedure for studying observational learning therefore is similar to that for studying children's memory for incidental information as compared to information which they have been instructed to learn (see above). In fact imitating another person and identifying with a model have been viewed as instances of acquiring incidental information (Bandura & Huston 1961). Sometimes (e.g., Coates & Hartup

1969) the child's attention is directed to the model's behavior by asking him to describe the behavior just after it occurs. This procedure is similar to instructing the child to name items to be recalled (see above, Recognizing Identity), and the effects are similar as well: nursery-school-age children who describe the behavior of a model remember it better than do children who do not describe it.

Investigators of observational learning usually consider attention to be perceptual selectivity, although they assess attention in terms of what is remembered. Bandura (1969), for example, cites attention along with retention, motor reproduction, and motivation as the four processes which account for observational learning. According to Bandura and Jeffrey (1973), attention and retention are the processes which control learning, while motor reproduction and motivation affect performance. Bandura describes the role of attention by noting that "simply exposing persons to distinctive sequences of modelled stimuli does not in itself guarantee that they will attend closely to the cues, that they will necessarily select . . . the most relevant events, or will even perceive accurately the cues to which their attention has been directed" (Bandura 1969, p. 136).

Liebert and Fernandez (1970a, 1970b) have suggested that directly rewarding and punishing the observer affect what he imitates, but that vicarious consequences to the model affect the observer's attention and therefore what he learns. They showed 6- and 7-year-old children a model whose behavior in a specific task was either rewarded, punished, or had no consequences. Then the children performed the same task. Children who themselves were rewarded directly performed the task more like the model than did other children, regardless of whether they had seen the model rewarded or punished. But children who had seen the model punished or rewarded remembered more about the model's behavior than did children who had not observed any consequences to the model. The vicarious reward directed the children to notice the model's behavior, and they remembered more. Similarity of the observer and the model is another factor which affects children's attention to a model. Rosekrans (1967) showed boys, 11 to 14 years of age, a film of a boy described either as similar or dissimilar to themselves. The boys both imitated more and remembered more when the model was described as similar than when he was described as dissimilar.

In two early studies, Maccoby sought to describe the relation among similarity, attention, and observational learning (Maccoby & Wilson 1957; Maccoby, Wilson, & Burton 1958). In the first study seventh graders were found to identify with and to recall more behaviors of models of the same sex than of models of the opposite sex. In the second study, young adults were found to look more at models in a film who were the same sex than at models of the opposite sex. Unfortunately the adults' memory of what they had seen was not assessed; likewise, the children's eye movements, in the first study, were not recorded, so the relation among similarity, attention, and learning still has to be inferred. In a subsequent study of the development of observational learning, children from 4, 7, and 10 years did not understand better the behaviors of models of the same sex than of those of the opposite sex (Leifer et al. 1971), so gender may be a more important determinant of similarity for older than for younger children.

The role of attention in observational learning has rarely been examined directly. Friedrich and Stein (1973) investigated the effects on preschoolers of watching prosocial and aggressive television shows, and they asked whether measures of attention are correlated with measures of observational learning. Attention to the television show was assessed by a time sampling procedure on a binary basis (attending or not attending) according to three criteria: orientation of head and eyes to the television screen, no speaking, and no gross arm or leg movements. Interobserver agreement was very high, but there was no apparent relation between attention and observational learning, possibly, the authors noted, because they assessed only where the children were looking and not whether they were listening to the show. Distractability, they thought, might be a useful index of attention.

Yussen (1974) did use distraction to assess directly the effect of attention on observational learning. Preschoolers and second graders watched a model making choices among sets of items. Each time the model made his choice, a slide of a mountain landscape scene was shown in another part of the room. Some children were told to remember what the model did while others were told simply to watch him. Frequency and duration of orienting toward the model were recorded as measures of attention, and the children's recall of the model's behavior was also assessed. Looking at the model and recall were positively related; children who were instructed to remember recalled more of the model's choices and attended more frequently to the model than did children not so instructed. The instructions to remember presumably directed the children to attend to the relevant aspects of the model's behavior.

7. Summary

Children remember more relevant information, including social information, as they get older. There are some specific techniques which can be used to help children remember. For instance, carefully instructing children about what is relevant, naming or having the children name what is relevant, or having them form images of what is relevant all serve as aids to memory. Also, aspects of the to-be-remembered objects or events themselves are important: whether what is to be remembered is salient, the physical arrangement of the material, and the order in which it is presented. Some of these techniques and factors function not only to increase children's memory of relevant material but also to degrade their memory of irrelevant or incidental material.

All of the findings presented so far have been considered as evidence about attention in memory primarily because selectivity in memory is what was assessed. However, it would not be reasonable to conclude that the locus of the selectivity demonstrated in these studies is exclusively in memory. When what is measured is what is remembered about things seen or heard, then we know that some things have been attended and some have not; we know that selectivity has occurred. What we cannot know is whether the locus of that attention is in memory, in perception, or, as is likely, in both.

Next, we will consider evidence about children's attention from tasks different from those described until now. Specifically, in the tasks next discussed the measure of attention is not what children remember about what they have seen or heard, but rather what features of material they notice and *use* to perform a task. Hence, these studies provide evidence about attention in perception. As will be seen, however, the tasks of these studies too require selectivity in many phases of cognitive functioning, and it is only the procedure for assessing attention which leads to their being classified as they are—as perceptual attention.

B. ATTENTION IN PERCEPTION

Objects in the real world usually differ in many features or attributes. Depending on the occasion, different features may be important for children to notice in order to classify objects or solve problems. On his first encounter with a chessboard and chess pieces, a child may only notice the color of each piece. Later, if he learns to play chess, he will, of course, have to attend to many other attributes of the chessmen. A goal of much of the research on children's learning is to discover to what characteristics of things children do attend. Often in this research, two-dimensional rather than three-dimensional objects are used, but the purpose is still to identify factors which affect children's choices about functional features.

1. Matching

A fundamental judgment children can make about objects is whether they are similar or different. What features do children use in order to make such decisions? Are there preferences for using certain features, and do preferences change with age? Early and often-cited findings were that when children judge the visual similarity of items varying in color and shape, young children tend to use color as a basis for the judgment but children after preschool or kindergarten age tend to use shape rather than color (Brian & Goodenough 1929; Suchman & Trabasso 1966). Preferences can influence not only which features are compared but also how quickly they can be compared (Odom & Guzman 1972). The features which children use frequently as a basis for judged similarity are also judged quickly. Conversely, features infrequently used are judged slowly—as though such features take a long time to find or to notice. Some factors which may facilitate children's use of certain features for matching are handling objects (Goodnow 1969), labeling (Katz, Albert, & Atkins 1971), and talking about or sorting objects (Butters 1969; West & Abravanel 1972).

The generality of young children's preferences depends on a number of factors: the specific colors available in the case of color preferences (Brown & Campione 1971) and whether the items are solidly colored or just colored in outline (Corah 1966b); the particular collection of features available (Corah & Gross 1967; McGurk 1972) and prior experience with the available features (Corah 1966a; Medin 1973). Preferences are generally stable (Silleroy & Johnson 1973)—as long as 6 months for first graders (Offenbach, Baecher, & White 1972)—and they are relatively resistant to moderate changes in discriminability of the available features (Gliner et al. 1969; Smiley 1972a, 1972b).

What affects the accuracy with which children use particular features for classifying or matching things? Brightness and saturation affect the accuracy with which 3-year-olds can match colors (Heider 1971). Nursery school children can match three-dimensional objects more accurately than two-dimensional items (Kraynak & Raskin 1971), possibly because there are more features available in the former. Familiarity with features also may affect the accuracy of young children's matching (Frith 1971).

Sometimes developmental changes in accuracy of matching depend simply on whether the children know the "rules of the game." A striking example is provided in a study by Goodnow (1971b). She used a task which requires children to listen to a series of taps of a pencil and to identify a comparable pattern from among series of dots on paper. Age changes in accuracy in this task have been attributed to the development of spatial integration (e.g., Birch & Belmont 1965). Goodnow tested children from kindergarten through second grade and showed that the inaccuracy of the younger children has to do with whether they know that temporal intervals between sounds can be represented by spatial intervals between dots on a paper. Knowledge of the rule enables attention to be directed to the appropriate information. An implication of such findings is that when children are asked to make careful comparisons among pictures or objects—as they often are in school tasks—special care must be taken to ensure that they understand exactly what details they are supposed to be judging.

There are developmental changes in how children search for features on which to base judgments of similarity or difference (Braine 1965). For instance, older children (and adults) tend visually to scan a geometric form from the top down, whereas younger children begin at a "focal" feature and scan down. There are also age differences in accuracy of matching depending on where the relevant feature is located on the form.

Besides facilitating attention to an object's features, handling or tracing also facilitates accurate visual matching in children as young as nursery school age, and the effect of handling is greater than the effect of a study period of simply looking at the items to be matched (Henning & Kornreich 1971; Jones 1972). Perhaps tracing an object or handling it while simultaneously looking at it helps accentuate its characteristics—especially if one is skilled at tracing and does not have to concentrate solely on the motor activity itself (Williams 1969).

When matching objects by hand is compared directly with matching objects by vision, visual matching almost always is more accurate than manual matching, and children improve in accuracy of visual matching earlier than they do in manual matching (Cronin 1973; Gliner et al. 1969; Jackson 1973; Millar 1971; Pick, Pick, & Klein 1967), especially when the matching requires successive comparisons (Rose, Blank, & Bridger 1972). Thus, exercises such as tracing letters whose purpose is to acquaint children with the details of a contour should be done while the shape is in full view.

Differences in how search is usually carried out by hand and by eye have been suggested as one basis for observed differences in accuracy of performing tasks by hand and by eye (Goodnow 1971c). Other accounts have relied on deficits of one sort or another—either in integration of information from different modalities (Birch & Belmont 1965) or in remembering information acquired by hand (Rose et al. 1972). Goodnow's suggestion is that modality effects are a function of how information is acquired via the eye and the hand, and specifically, whether the exploration results in acquiring the relevant or critical information for the task. Several investigators have observed children's manual search patterns and have found developmental changes in patterns of exploring or scanning with the hands (Cirillo, Wapner, & Rand 1967). For instance, young children tend not to explore more than one feature of a geometric form unless specifically told to do so, whereas older children seem more likely to explore more than one feature regardless of their instructions (Ginsburg 1967).

The wider-ranging exploration of the older children seems to contradict the generalization proposed from the studies of attention in memory (see above) that older children select more precisely than do younger children. However, we can suggest that children's patterns of exploration become increasingly specific to the current task; in some cases this requires precision and in other cases it does not. This suggestion is supported by the findings of Lehman (1972), who tested children from kindergarten through sixth grade on matching tasks with objects varying in shape and in texture and found the older children much better than the younger children at directing their search efficiently and appropriately. For instance, when the children were told what the relevant feature was, their search, which was manual, was mostly directed to that feature—more so for the older children than for the kindergartners. When the children were not told what feature was relevant and when the two features were redundant so that only one needed to be explored in order to make a correct judgment, older children searched for only one feature early in the task whereas younger children began to search in this way only later in the task. Also, preferences, which were assessed before the task began, affected the younger children's search patterns. The search patterns of these children were much more focused when their preferred feature was relevant than when it was irrelevant. The older children, however, could focus and direct their search regardless of their preferences for the features.

These findings suggest that children become better able to explore flexibly; there is increasing ability with age to search, at least manually, in a way which is specific and appropriate to the task. For instance, in matching tasks, it is useful to explore broadly in order to find the most relevant features. Other factors besides patterns of exploration affect children's accuracy in using features to match objects—their preferences, their knowledge of the task, and the nature of the objects themselves. Young children may have difficulty noticing the relevant details of objects. Arranging the items with this in mind may help them.

2. Discovering Relevant Features

When children first learn to read or write letters, they often confuse letters like *d* and *b* or *m* and *w*. In these cases it appears the children have not yet learned to focus on the critical aspects of the letters so as to be able to distinguish between them. Often children have to figure out or discover for themselves what information is relevant for performing a task or solving a problem. In a common laboratory version of such a task, children are shown two or three items and told that one is "correct" and that they must figure out for themselves which is the correct one. How do children learn to attend to the relevant features in such a task? The experimental settings which have been used to study this question vary in the extent to which it is obvious what features might be the relevant ones. A task with a wide range of features which might be relevant is a version of the party game "20 questions." Mosher and Hornsby (1966) showed children from 6 to 11 years a collection of items and asked the children to figure out which item the tester was thinking of. The children could ask only questions which could be answered by "yes" or "no," and the questions they asked reflected the features they were attending to. The types of questions asked by children of different ages varied. Younger children asked questions about each item separately, whereas older children asked "constraint-seeking" questions, indicating they were attending to features of the collection of items. If the collection is systematically rather than randomly arranged, and also if the children are trained—either by practice in asking strategic questions or by discussing the items with the experimenter—more constraint-seeking questions are asked (Denney, Denney, & Ziobrowski 1973; Van Horn & Bartz 1968) even by nursery school children (Nelson & Earl 1973).

Discrimination learning—In many situations the potential number of relevant features available to the child is limited. For example, when a child is taught to obey traffic signals when crossing a street, the color of the light is what he must attend to and the number of features is limited. A laboratory task in which the number of potentially relevant features is limited is one in which children are shown only two or three things and asked to choose one. Usually, the children are told only whether they are right or wrong after each choice, and the experimenter is interested .n how many times the items must be presented before the children can consistently choose the correct item. Several factors, all of which make the correct item stand out in relation to the incorrect item, facilitate consistent choice of the correct item by young children (Rieber 1966). For example, if a special feature such as a mark identifies the correct item, or if children name the correct item, they quickly learn to choose that item. However, if that same special feature identifies the incorrect item instead or if children name the incorrect item, they are slow to learn what is correct (Carmean 1969; Sainsbury 1971). Three-dimensional items—especially if they can be handled—are easier for children to learn than two-dimensional items (Etaugh & Van Sickle 1971; Falk 1968), and pictures are learned more quickly than words (Rowe 1972). Finally, irrelevant features are less distracting if they do not vary across items than if they do vary (Brown, Scott, & Urban 1972). In general, devices which emphasize the crucial features seem to help children in these tasks.

Sorting by categories— sometimes, instead of discovering a single correct item, children are asked to sort a collection of items into two (or more) groups. Usually, the potentially relevant features for such sorting are obvious—to experimenters at least—and they are trying to find out what conditions help children discover and use particular features as a basis for such sorting. The ability to classify items into categories has been deemed an important step toward cognitive maturity, since it indicates the child's ability to formulate and use concepts (Inhelder & Piaget 1964). When 4- and 5-year-old children simply are told what to look at, their performance is facilitated (Schell 1971); however, children can often sort things without being able to explain the basis for the sorting. The effect of the instruction is to direct them more quickly to attend to the feature that is relevant.

It is easier for children to learn to sort pictures into categories if the pictures are left in view after they have been sorted. Leaving them in view also makes it easier for children to learn to sort them into new categories (Kendler & Ward 1971). Such a procedure increases the likelihood that children will notice what the relevant features are. Training nursery school children in simple sorting tasks, that is, tasks in which only one obvious feature is relevant, helps them be able to use more than one relevant feature for sorting—a task which would otherwise be too difficult for them (Clarke & Cooper 1966).

When words rather than pictures are sorted, some features are easier for nursery school and kindergarten children to attend to and use than others. For example, if the items of one group share a conceptual relation, that is, if the conceptual relation is the relevant feature of the words, the members of that group are easier to identify than if a rhyming relation is relevant (Hall 1971). Likewise, when the items are sounds rather than words, some features—for example, frequency—are easier for children to attend to and use than are others—for example, intensity (Pishkin & Rosenbluh 1966).

Do preferences predict what features young children will use spontaneously in a sorting task? Not in a straightforward way (Olmsted & Sigel 1970); however, when the experimenter tells the child what feature to use, the child's preference may affect the ease with which he can comply. Odom and Mumbauer (1971) found that first graders, most of whom preferred form rather than color, made more errors when instructed to sort using color than did older children. Such age differences did not occur when the children used form. When children are given training designed to enhance the relevant feature, they quickly overcome any bias of preference for an irrelevant feature (Rollins & Castle 1973; Silleroy & Johnson 1973). In tasks in which children must use more than one feature for sorting, preference for one of the relevant features does not facilitate learning (Overton & Jordon 1971), but careful instructions about the rules of the game do (Jacobs & Vandeventer 1971).

Discrimination shift learning.—For these tasks, pairs of items are constructed from combinations of two types of features, for example, color (red, blue) and shape (triangle, circle). Each time one pair—red triangle and blue circle—is presented to the child, he is supposed to choose one. Similarly, when the other pair—blue triangle and red circle—is presented, he chooses the one he thinks is correct. The experimenter can designate, for a given child, whether color or shape is relevant for defining the correct items. The child has to learn to choose the correct item of each pair, and he can do this consistently by discovering and using the relevant feature—much as he would in a sorting task. (These tasks involve a second phase, called shift learning, in which the basis for choice may be changed, but that phase is not relevant here.) A child's preference affects the ease with which he learns this task; he is aided if his preferred feature is relevent (Seitz & Weir 1971; Smiley 1972a, 1972b; Trabasso, Stave, & Eichberg 1969). However, the effect of preference may be minimal, since in one study of 6-year-old children, preference was related to speed of learning only when the preference was assessed prior to the learning task (Tighe et al. 1970). In other words, the preference test itself, with its requirement for matching items, may bias children to search for a particular feature. Such an effect may account for why a small amount of training designed to enhance particular relevant features will overcome a child's bias or preference for attending to some other feature.

Conditional sorting.—Even young children often have to make sophisticated judgments about what information is important and should be attended to. Interesting instances of such judgments occur when children decide that behaviors allowed in one setting (e.g., with babysitters or indulgent grandparents) are not acceptable in another (e.g., with parents). Researchers have tried to construct experimental analogs of such situations with sorting tasks in which children have to use more than one feature in a constrained or conditional way. Such a problem might be defined: when feature *A* is present, feature *B* is relevant; when feature *A* is not present, feature *C* is relevant. Such problems, not surprisingly, are more difficult for children of kindergarten and first-grade age than for older children (Walk & Saltz 1965). However, there are a number of aids which help young children solve them: pointing to the features present in each item (Johnson, Warner, & Lee 1970), presenting items together which follow the same rule (Willoughby 1973), watching a model solve the problem (Zimmerman & Bell 1972), and talking about the features which happen to be relevant (Scholnick 1971). However, some kinds of talking or discussion do not help young children with these problems. For instance, describing how someone else sorts the items does not help children learn the solution (Zimmerman & Bell 1972), nor does simply noting the location of features (Scholnick 1971). The successful aids probably are those which direct the child to attend to the relevant features. A technique like noting where features are located is not useful because it is not the location of features which has to be attended to and used in order to solve the problem.

Oddity learning.—Oddity learning is usually not thought of as a sorting task. However, in solving an oddity problem, children must discover relevant features and use them in much the same way as in other sorting tasks. In an oddity problem, the child is asked to identify the different or odd member of a collection, the one that "just doesn't belong," in the words of the "Sesame Street" jingle. Sometimes all the items but one are physically identical, and sometimes all but one are members of the same category. Such problems generally are easy to solve, even for nursery school children (Gaines 1970; Scott 1970). Distraction, in the form of a mirror near a child's head, has been found to hamper oddity learning in kindergarten-age children but to facilitate such learning in children a couple of years older (Turnure 1970). The effect, though, is specific to the type of distraction; when phonograph records were played instead, oddity learning was hampered for both older and younger children. Sometimes the feature used by the child to identify the odd item is not the feature intended by the experimenter (Aiken & Williams 1973), as, for example, when an experimenter wants children to use features defining a category and the children use features like shape or color or size to identify the odd item.

Instructions.—Even the specific word used in instructing young children can affect what features they attend to. Fein (1972) taught kindergartners and third graders to choose consistently the larger of two items varying in size. Then she showed the children two new items, both larger than the original pair but also differing in size, and asked the children to choose one of the new pair. She asked some children to choose the "correct" one of the new pair; others she asked to choose the "same" one of the new pair; still others she asked to choose the "middle-sized" one. She wanted to know whether the children would choose according to the size relation they had learned—that is, whether they would choose the larger number of the new pair—or whether they would choose the one which was actually closer in size to the one they had learned was correct. The children's choices turned out to depend on the specific words used to instruct them about the new pair. Kindergartners told to choose the "correct" or the "same" item tended to choose the larger member of the new pair. The older children chose the larger member of the new pair primarily if they were told to choose the "correct" one. Each of these words presumably directed the children to attend to and use one rather than another feature, and the effects differed for the younger and older children. Similar effects of specific words were found for preschool children who were asked to learn to associate labels with sticks varying in length (Salzinger, Salzinger, & Patenaude 1970). Half the children learned to associate the numbers 1, 2, 3, and 4 with sticks of four different lengths; the other children learned to associate four color names to the same four sticks. Subsequent tests demonstrated that children who had learned color names had attended to the absolute sizes of the sticks, and children who had learned numbers had attended to the relative sizes of the sticks. When adults talk to children with the aim of explaining something, it is important not only that the words used be understood by the children, but also that the words direct the children's attention as intended.

3. Search Strategies

The general questions asked so far are: what factors influence the child's selection of information from the environment, and do these factors affect attention differently depending on the age of the child? We can also ask how the child goes about selecting such information. Do his strategies change with the task? Do young children search differently, that is, in different patterns or with different strategies, than do older children? Findings from studies relevant to these questions will be considered next. The procedures used vary greatly in spite of the fact that the number of such studies is far fewer than studies addressing the first set of questions. However, a common aspect of the procedure of studies of search strategies is that the child performing the task *knows* what he is looking or listening for. This is in contrast to most of the tasks discussed in the last few sections in which the child has to find out what the relevant information is. Whereas instructions, practice, salience, and other factors we have discussed in preceding sections are important influences on what children of all ages attend to, studies of search strategies have revealed important developmental differences in children's attention.

Age differences in accurately detecting the mere presence of something such as a letter have been attributed to differences in the sheer speed with which information can be processed by children of different ages (Liss & Haith 1970; L. Miller 1971, 1972). In addition to speed and accuracy, are there developmental differences in strategies of search? The answer to that question depends on the particular information being sought. For example, Miller (1973) asked children from first through sixth grades and adults to search through an array of letters briefly presented, looking for a particular letter, and to report the location of that letter. The younger children were much more accurate in reporting targets in some locations than in others, whereas the older children showed no such effects. In this case, the younger children may have been searching less systematically and efficiently than the older children in the limited amount of time available. However, in other studies, in which children had to search for a particular letter instead of the location of letters, there were no developmental differences in search strategies (Gibson et al. 1972; Gibson & Yonas 1966).

Developmental changes in strategies of attention have been observed when children have been asked not to search through a list but, rather to compare two things (Vurpillot 1968). Pick, Christy, and Frankel (1972) asked second and sixth graders to compare either the shapes or the colors of colored wooden animal shapes. In one task, the children were told which features to compare just prior to viewing the pair. In a second task, the children viewed the pair for a limited time and then were told which feature to compare. The older children were faster than the younger children in both tasks, but the effect of age on comparison speed was greater for the first task than for the second task. The older children were better able than the younger children to take advantage of knowing what to look for in that task.

In a subsequent study (Pick & Frankel 1973), potentially distracting features were added to the pairs midway in both tasks. The distraction did not affect children's comparisons in the task in which they knew what to look for. However, in the second task, the distracting features affected the children's comparison speed, and the effects were different for the two age groups. Specifically, the effects were temporary for the older children and more general for the younger children. The distracting features seemed to affect the efficiency of the younger children's strategies of search. In a third study (Pick & Frankel 1974), second and sixth graders compared a variety of features of pairs of objects, and it was observed that the older children were more able to adjust their strategies so as to search for different features on each trial than were the younger children. These findings provide evidence of a developmental trend toward matching search strategies precisely to the requirements of a task.

Selective listening, listening for one message rather than another, has also been studied in children and may be another task in which developmental changes in strategies of attention can be observed. Maccoby (1967) and Maccoby and Konrad (1966, 1967) asked children of different ages to repeat one of two messages which they heard simultaneously. In general, accuracy increases with age, and children of a wide age range are more accurate when they are told before hearing the messages which one to repeat than when they are told after they have heard the messages. For this auditory attention task, unlike the visual task, knowing beforehand what is relevant is equally helpful for younger and older children. That is also true for factors such as familiarity and structuredness of the message. Distraction, though, does affect auditory attention differently for children of different ages. Competing voices, for example, disrupt concentration on the relevant message more for younger than for older children (Doyle 1973).

4. Summary

Children attend most easily to relevant features when they are accentuated, for example, when they are preferred or pointed to or discussed. Accentuating what is irrelevant often makes it more difficult for children to attend to and use what is relevant. Children often must search for relevant information, and there is evidence of a developmental trend toward improved efficiency of such activity. In some cases this may actually mean that the older child engages in more search activity than the younger child, while in other situations the older child is better able to ignore, or disregard, irrelevant information. Through the use of either strategy, attention to important information is facilitated.

C. MOTIVATION AND REINFORCEMENT OF ATTENTION

Some theorists (Kahneman 1972) have been particularly interested in demonstrating relations between physiological arousal and attention. Smock and Rubin (1964) tested a hypothesis of Easterbrook (1959): that small increases in arousal, indicated by physiological measures such as GSR or heart rate, lead to increased attention to relevant features and decreased attention to irrelevant features. Smock and Rubin asked children 9 to 12 years old to indicate the position of a pattern after they had seen it very briefly. The patterns varied in complexity, and arousal was manipulated by instructions. Some children, in an incentive condition, were told that they could win prizes by playing well; others were told simply how to play the game. The hypothesis was supported, since the children were more accurate in the incentive condition than in the other condition.

Canon (1967) also studied the relation between children's motivation and attention. However, Broadbent (1958) rather than Easterbrook provided the theoretical basis in this case. Broadbent suggests that motivation influences attention by affecting the probability that certain features will be selected. Canon hypothesized that social isolation should increase children's attention to social information even at the expense of accuracy in some socially irrelevant task. Two groups of children were asked to perform a memory task after one group had experienced 20 minutes of isolation from other children (and adults). Both groups of children had to do the memory task while listening either to a tape recording of a woman telling a story (social distraction) or to a tape recording of mechanical sounds, for example, bell, siren, typewriter (nonsocial distraction). The nonisolated children performed equally well with both types of distraction, while the isolated children performed better with the nonsocial than with the social distraction, presumably because these children were listening to the story. The isolated children were, of course, deprived of many things besides people, and the decrement in their performance with social distraction may have occurred because the story was interesting and not specifically because it was social.

Yet another theoretical position, Zeaman and House's (1963) model of discrimination learning, has provided different bases for a study of the relation of motivation and attention (Witryol, Lowden, & Fagan 1967). Briefly, it is suggested that prior reinforcement history affects the probability of attending to the features of a discrimination learning task. To explore that suggestion, children first learned to choose items consistently on the basis either of their form or of their color. Their choice of one feature was rewarded with a high-incentive reinforcer. When presented later with other items, the children learned to choose correctly more rapidly if the relevant feature had been previously associated with a high-incentive reward.

Is it necessary to introduce a motivational concept to mediate observed effects of children's attention on their behavior? Attention, in the studies of motivational effects reviewed so far, is a differential response presumed to be based on differences in motivation. The difficulty in operationally and conceptually describing separate effects of motivation and attention is seen in a study by Witte and Grossman (1971). They posed a question frequently asked: do rewards and punishments have different effects on children's learning? Several investigators (Ahammer & Goulet 1969; Ratliff 1972; Schroth 1970) have found that punishment, either alone or in combination with reward, usually results in better performance than does reward alone. To account for this effect, Penney (1967) has suggested that reward distracts attention from relevant features of the task and so retards learning. On the other hand, Stevenson, Weir, and Zigler (1959) believe that punishment increases attention to relevant features of the task, and so facilitates learning. And Brackbill and O'Hara (1958) put forth the view that punishment improves performance by increasing motivation.

Witte and Grossman (1971) hoped to find a basis for choosing between motivational and attentional accounts of the effects of punishment. They tried to measure attention and motivation directly in a discrimination task in which punishment, reward, or reward and punishment were used to reinforce children's choices. Kindergarten children learned to select with their hands, and without looking, one of two differently shaped blocks. The child reached through a curtain and felt the blocks, which rested on platforms of a scale. He indicated his choice by pushing down on one block. Reward was a token, and punishment was a loud noise. The force of his push was the measure of motivation, and the amount of exploration of the blocks was the measure of attention. As predicted, the children's performance was affected by the type of reinforcement; reward retarded learning in comparison to conditions including punishment. Attention was related to reinforcement; the children explored the forms more when punishment was used than when reward alone was used. Motivation, as reflected in strength of pushing, was unrelated to performance and to reinforcement. Thus, the results were interpreted as evidence that attention and not motivation is the basis for the effects of punishment on learning.

One might question whether push force is adequate as a measure of motivation. Nonetheless, it may be unnecessary to invoke motivational drive states to account for reinforcement effects if reinforcement is considered from a different point of view. Some discussions of reinforcement (Kohlberg 1969; Stevenson 1972) stress its information value. Thus reinforcement is informative about what features are relevant for correct performance of a task—as the experimenter has defined correct performance. Reinforcement can affect discovery of relevant features. What, then, are the conditions of reinforcement which facilitate discovery of those features? Spence and Segner (1967) tested children from first through fourth grades in a discrimination learning task in which the children were told the information value of each reinforced choice. Thus a child in a reward-only condition was told that his correct answers would be rewarded while incorrect answers would have no consequences. The authors hypothesized that usually under conditions of reward alone children do not realize that their nonrewarded responses are incorrect. Both verbal (e.g., "no" and "yes") and nonverbal (buzzer and candy) reinforcers were used, and the conditions of learning included reward only, punishment only, and both reward and punishment. Children whose reinforcement was verbal performed equally well in all conditions, indicating the importance of having children understand the meaning of the reinforcement consequences of their behavior. However, children whose reinforcement was nonverbal did not perform as well when their choices were rewarded only as they did when punishment was used—in spite of the fact that they understood the reinforcement contingencies.

These results led Spence and Segner to posit that material reinforcers like candy, when used alone as rewards, distract the child from attending to other aspects of the task. Spence and Segner rejected an explanation based on motivation—that there is greater motivation to avoid punishment than to get a reward—because the children who received candy only did not perform as well as did the children who received verbal reward only. If motivation were responsible for the effect of the candy, then it would have to be asserted that elementary school children are less motivated to get candy than to receive verbal reinforcement, an assertion unlikely to be believed by any parent of an elementary school child! The distracting effect of material rewards was further demonstrated (Spence 1970) using a verbal discrimination task with elementary-school-age children of varying socioeconomic classes. Selection and use of appropriate reinforcers for children should be guided by consideration of information value rather than only incentive value. High-incentive material reinforcers like candy may actually have a detrimental effect on children's behavior.

Further information about the function of reinforcement is provided by McCullers and Martin (1971). They suggested that reinforcers with low incentive value only provide information, whereas reinforcers with high value provide both information and motivation. They tested fourth graders in a discrimination task in which the reinforcers had either high or low value, based on rankings of the items previously provided by the children themselves. Some children in each group were given information about reinforcement contingencies while the rest of the children were not. One group of children received only verbal feedback. No learning occurred when the low-value item was used as reward and without information about the reinforcement contingencies, since such reinforcers neither directed attention nor provided information. Learning occurred in all the other conditions; the best performance occurred with positive verbal reinforcement when the child understood the meaning of the reinforcing events. The information provided by reinforcement, then, rather than its incentive value, seems to determine how it directs attention.

The effects of reinforcement in the form of approval or disapproval has also been examined by Allen, Spear, and Lucke (1971), Spear (1970), and Spear and Spear (1972). In one study first, second, fifth, and sixth graders learned a two-choice discrimination task with either praise, silence, or criticism from an adult as reinforcement. All children were informed about the correctness of their choice on each presentation by a red light above the correct item. In general, with criticism as reinforcement, the children took most time to make each choice, but they also learned in the fewest number of presentations. Younger children learned slowly with silence as reinforcement, while older children learned fastest with silence. The authors suggest that silence is confusing for young children, who need evaluative comments to direct their attention to the task. Older children, on the other hand, evaluate their own performance, and so the information provided by the light about correctness of their choice is sufficient to direct their attention to the task. For these children adult comments divert or distract attention.

If reinforcement affects learning because it directs attention to some features of the task, then a delay period between response and reinforcement might be predicted to reduce the effectiveness of reinforcement. Such findings have been reported (Stevenson 1972, pp. 171–174), and then the question is asked: How does delaying reinforcement affect attention? The answer seems to be simply that the information value of reinforcement is reduced when it is delayed. For instance, when children are instructed to attend to the important aspects of a task during the delay, the effects of the delay are reduced or eliminated (Fagan & Witryol 1966; Wright & Smothergill 1967). Goldstein and Siegel (1972) found children's learning to be facilitated when the items of a discrimination problem were made available during a delay before reinforcement, and they argued that the effect is not due to additional implicit responses being made during the delay. This contention is supported by Berch (1970), who recorded eye movements during the delay but found no relation between rate of learning and orienting responses. Rather, the effect seems to occur simply because the items are available to be noticed.

Witte and Johnson (1973) found that when punishment, as reinforcement, was delayed, children's learning was impaired, whereas, as noted above, immediate punishment facilitates learning. They hypothesized that the impairment of learning after delayed punishment reflected either motivation or attention, so they measured how much the children looked at items and how strongly they pressed a lever to indicate their choice. Strength of lever pressing was not related to the other findings, and these investigators too concluded that the effect of delay was not on motivation.

In summary, reinforcement of children's choices in discrimination tasks affects their learning most directly by providing information. Reinforcement directs their attention to certain aspects and features of the task. This interpretation of reinforcement effects does not stress the motivational or incentive value of the reinforcing events. Rather, reinforcement affects the probability that the child will notice the important features of the task. A final set of findings illustrates this effect of reinforcement on attention. Barnhart (1968) investigated the effects on children's learning of adults as agents of reinforcement. He suggested that when an adult reinforces a child, the effect is not on the child's motivation; rather, the adult then can give the child information about how to behave. Second-grade children learned to choose one of two items consistently when either an adult or a light identified the correct choice. Candy as a reward reinforced correct choices. On a second similar task, either the source of information (social or nonsocial) remained the same as in the first task or it was reversed. The children learned the first task faster when the source of information was nonsocial than when it was social. However, they learned the second task faster if the source of information was the same as in the first task than if it changed. The author concluded that young children can be trained to attend to a variety of sources of information, both social and nonsocial. Reinforcement tells the child what information is important to acquire.

If reinforcement is informative, then how or even whether the child interprets this information is crucial in determining reinforcement effects. Practitioners of reinforcement could do well to keep the cognitive maturity of the child in mind when choosing and applying reinforcements. The developmental changes in cognition documented by theorists like Piaget or Gibson suggest that the ability of children to make such interpretations changes with age. Yet none of the research concerned with reinforcement has been conducted from a developmental perspective, perhaps because it is based on a psychological tradition stressing general laws of behavior assumed to operate not only across ages but across species. The one study discussed which does consider developmental changes, that of Spear and Spear (1972), indicates that such investigations would be worthwhile. The effectiveness of any reinforcement will be determined by how well it assists children in noticing and using the important features of the situation.

IV. CONCLUSIONS

Attention has not been a neglected topic either in theoretical or in empirical inquiries about infants' and children's behavior. It is operationalized differently by different experimenters and conceptualized differently in various theories. However, fundamental to any investigation of attention is the idea of selectivity in some aspect of cognitive functioning—selective perception, selective memory, even selective thought. We have not considered selective thought here, but only because the experimental evidence is not at hand. Surely, however, even quite young children can attend to their thoughts, and possibly also to the process of thinking (Miller, Kessel, & Flavell 1970). What we have discussed here is the available information about selectivity in infants' and children's perception and memory. We have defined attention in this way in order to bring together findings relevant to a number of different formulations about infants' and children's attention.

We know that as early as the first few weeks of life the infant can show some degree of selectivity in his interaction with his environment. As yet some very serious practical and conceptual limitations prevent us from understanding the full extent and meaning of this selectivity. Nonetheless, that there is such demonstrable selectivity is in itself significant, indicating that the child is always an active seeker after information.

Fewer practical problems restrict us in investigating attention in older children. We have some indication of the selective process in children's cognitive functioning. Studies in which aspects of the environment are manipulated to make them more likely to be perceived or remembered contribute to our understanding of how experiences with one's immediate environment can influence attention. There is empirical support for a number of suggestions based on common sense. For instance, factors like familiarity of materials, method of presentation, and use of instructions can facilitate or hamper selectivity of perception and memory.

We also find that there are important changes with age in the ways children regulate and direct their own attention. One developmental trend is toward greater efficiency in strategies of search and exploration. Looking specifically at relations between perception and memory may help us discover how patterns of search become integrated.

Other specific recommendations for new inquiry include more concern with the representativeness and appropriateness—in short, the ecological validity—of settings in which we study children's attention. For instance, we know a great deal about children's attention to two-dimensional materials, materials which may be compared to some school-related situations, and about children's attention in rather artificial laboratory settings. We know less about children's attention to three-dimensional objects and in more realistic home or school situations. As we overcome these research limitations, we shall be able to help children acquire and use more efficient and appropriate strategies of attention.

REFERENCES

Ahammer, J., & Goulet, L. Intrapair conceptual similarity and verbal reinforcement combinations as determinants of discrimination learning and retention in children. *Child Development*, 1969, *40*, 859–868.

Aiken, L. S., & Williams, T. M. A developmental study of schematic concept formation. *Developmental Psychology*, 1973, *8*, 162–167.

Allen, S,; Spear, P.; & Lucke, J. Effects of social reinforcement on learning and retention in children. *Developmental Psychology*, 1971, *5*, 73–80.

Ames, E. W., & Silfen, C. K. Methodological issues in the study of age differences in infants' attention to stimuli varying in movement and complexity. Paper presented at the meeting of the Society for Research in Child Development, Minneapolis, 1965.

Appel, L. F.; Cooper, R. G.; McCarrell, N.; Sims-Knight, J.; Yussen, S. R.; & Flavell, J. H. The development of the distinction between perceiving and memorizing. *Child Development*, 1972, *43*, 1365–1381.

Ashton, R. State and the auditory reactivity of the human neonate. *Journal of Experimental Child Psychology*, 1971, *12*, 339–346.

Atkinson, R. C.; Hansen, D. N.; & Bernbach, H. A. Short-term memory with young children. *Psychonomic Science*, 1964, *1*, 255–256.

Ball, W., & Tronick, E. Infant responses to impending collision: optical and real. *Science*, 1971, *171*, 818.

Bandura, A. *Principles of behavior modification*. New York: Holt, 1969.

Bandura, A., & Huston, A. Identification as a process of incidental learning. *Journal of Abnormal and Social Psychology*, 1961, *63*, 311–318.

Bandura, A., & Jeffrey, R. Role of symbolic coding and rehearsal processes in observational learning. *Journal of Personality and Social Psychology*, 1973, *26*, 122–130.

Bandura, A.; Ross, D.; & Ross, S. Imitation of film-mediated aggressive models. *Journal of Abnormal and Social Psychology*, 1963, *66*, 3–11.

Barnhart, J. Acquisition of cue properties by social and nonsocial events. *Child Development*, 1968, *39*, 1237–1245.

Berch, D. Visual orientation in children's discrimination learning under constant, variable, and covariable delay of reinforcement. *Journal of Experimental Child Psychology*, 1970, *9*, 374–387.

Berlyne, D. E. The influence of the albedo and complexity of stimuli on visual fixation in the human infant. *British Journal of Psychology*, 1958, *49*, 315–319.

Bernbach, H. A. The effect of labels on short-term memory for colors with nursery school children. *Psychonomic Science*, 1967, *7*, 149–150.

Birch, H. C., & Belmont, L. Auditory-visual integration, intelligence, and reading ability in school children. *Perceptual and Motor Skills*, 1965, *20*, 295–305.

Bond, E. Perception of form by the human infant. *Psychological Bulletin*, 1972, *77*, 225–245. (a)

Bond, E. Selective attention in the human infant: the bull's-eye effect. Unpublished doctoral dissertation, George Washington University, 1972. (b)

Bower, T. G. R.; Broughton, J. M.; & Moore, M. K. Infant responses to approaching objects: an indicator of response to distal variables. *Perception and Psychophysics*, 1970, *9*, 193–196.

Brackbill, Y., & O'Hara, J. Relative effectiveness of reward and punishment for discrimination learning in children. *Journal of Comparative and Physiological Psychology*, 1958, *51*, 747–751.

Braine, L. G. Age changes in the mode of perceiving geometric forms. *Psychonomic Science*, 1965, *2*, 155–156.

Brennan, W.; Ames, E. W.; & Moore, P. W. Age differences in infants' attention to patterns of different complexities. *Science*, 1966, *151*, 354–356.

Brian, C. R., & Goodenough, F. L. The relative potency of color and form perception at various ages. *Journal of Experimental Psychology*, 1929, *12*, 197–213.

Broadbent, D. E. *Perception and communication*. London: Pergamon, 1958.

Brown, A. L., & Campione, J. C. Color dominance in preschool children as a function of specific cue preferences. *Child Development*, 1971, *42*, 1495–1500.

Brown, A. L.; Scott, K. G.; & Urbano, R. C. Psychophysically scaled cue differences, learning rate, and attentional strategies in a tactile discrimination task. *Journal of Experimental Child Psychology*, 1972, *13*, 283–302.

Brown, A. L., & Scott, J. S. Recognition memory for pictures in preschool children. *Journal of Experimental Child Psychology*, 1971, *11*, 401–412.

Bush, E. S., & Cohen, L. B. The effects of relevant and irrelevant labels on short-term memory in nursery school children. *Psychonomic Science*, 1970, *18*, 228–229.

Butters, N. Changes in equivalence judgments following verbal, perceptual, or functional practice conditions. *Child Development*, 1969, *40*, 1179–1192.

Campos, J. J.; Langer, A.; & Krowitz, A. Cardiac responses on the visual cliff in prelocomotor human infants. *Science*, 1970, *170*, 196–197.

Canon, L. K. Motivational state, stimulus selection and distractability. *Child Development*, 1967, *38*, 589–596.

Carmean, S. L. Effects of pattern of auxiliary activity on discrimination learning of children. *Child Development*, 1969, *40*, 927–934.

Caron, R. F.; Caron, A. J.; & Caldwell, R. C. Satiation of visual reinforcement in young infants. *Developmental Psychology*, 1971, *5*, 279–289.

Cirillo, L.; Wapner, S.; & Rand, G. Differentiation of haptic exploration in two age groups. *Psychonomic Science*, 1967, *9*, 467–468.

Clarke, A. M., & Cooper, G. M. Transfer in category learning of young children: its relation to task complexity and overlearning. *British Journal of Psychology*, 1966, *57*, 361–373.

Clarkson, T. A.; Haggith, P. A.; Tierney, M. C.; & Kobasigawa, A. Relative effectiveness of imagery instructions and pictorial interactions on children's paired-associate learning. *Child Development*, 1973, *44*, 179–181.

Coates, B., & Hartup, W. Age and verbalization in observational learning. *Developmental Psychology*, 1969, *1*, 556–562.

Cohen, L. B. Observing responses, visual preferences and habituation to visual stimuli in infants. *Journal of Experimental Child Psychology*, 1969, *7*, 419–433.

Cohen, L. B. Attention-getting and attention-holding processes of infant visual preferences. *Child Development*, 1972, *43*, 869–879.

Cohen, L. B. A two process model of infant visual attention. *Merrill-Palmer Quarterly*, 1973, *19*, 157–180.

Cohen, L. B.; Gelber, E. R.; & Lazar, M. A. Infant habituation and generalization to differing degrees of stimulus novelty. *Journal of Experimental Child Psychology*, 1971, *11*, 379–389.

Cole, M.; Frankel, F.; & Sharp, D. Development of free recall learning in children. *Developmental Psychology*, 1971, *4*, 109–123.

Collard, R. R., & Rydberg, J. E. Generalization of habituation to properties of objects in human infants. *Proceedings of the Annual Convention of the American Psychological Association*, 1972, *7*, 81–82.

Collins, D.; Kessen, W.; & Haith, M. Note on an attempt to replicate a relation between stimulus unpredictability and infant attention. *Journal of Experimental Child Psychology*, 1972, *13*, 1–9.

Conrad, R. The developmental role of vocalizing in short-term memory. *Journal of Verbal Learning and Verbal Behavior*, 1972, *11*, 521–533.

Corah, N. L. The effect of instruction and performance set on color-form perception in young children. *Journal of Genetic Psychology*, 1966, *108*, 351–356. (a)

Corah, N. L. The influence of some stimulus characteristics on color and form perception in nursery-school children. *Child Development*, 1966, *37*, 205–212. (b)

Corah, N. L., & Gross, J. B. Hue, brightness, and saturation variables in color-form matching. *Child Development*, 1967, *38*, 137–142.

Cronin, V. Cross-modal and intramodal visual and tactual matching in young children. *Developmental Psychology*, 1973, *8*, 336–340.

Danner, F. W., & Taylor, A. M. Integrated pictures and relational imagery training in children's learning. *Journal of Experimental Child Psychology*, 1973, *16*, 47–54.

Deichmann, J. W.; Speltz, M. B.; & Kausler, D. H. Developmental trends in the intentional and incidental learning components of a verbal discrimination task. *Journal of Experimental Child Psychology*, 1971, *11*, 21–34.

Denney, D. R.; Denney, N. W.; & Ziobrowski, M. J. Alterations in the information-processing strategies of young children following observation of adult models. *Developmental Psychology*, 1973, *8*, 202–208.

Denney, N. W., & Ziobrowski, M. Developmental changes in clustering criteria. *Journal of Experimental Child Psychology*, 1972, *13*, 275–282.

Donaldson, M, & Strang, H. Primacy effect in short-term memory in young children. *Psychonomic Science*, 1969, *16*, 59–60.

Doyle, A. B. Listening to distraction: a developmental study of selective attention. *Journal of Experimental Child Psychology*, 1973, *15*, 100–115.

Druker, J. F., & Hagen, J. W. Developmental trends in the processing of task-relevant and task-irrelevant information. *Child Development*, 1969, *40*, 371–382.

Easterbrook, J. A. The effect of emotion on cue utilization and the organization of behavior. *Psychological Review*, 1959, *66*, 183–201.

Eimas, P. D.; Siqueland, E. R.; Jusczyk, P.; & Vigorito, J. Speech perception in infants. *Science*, 1971, *171*, 303–306.

Eisenberg, R. B.; Coursin, D. B.; & Rupp, N. R. Habituation to an acoustic pattern as an index of differences among human neonates. *Journal of Auditory Research*, 1966, *6*, 239–248.

Entwisle, D. R., & Huggins, W. H. Iconic memory in children. *Child Development*, 1973, *44*, 392–394.

Etaugh, C. F., & Van Sickle, D. Discrimination of stereometric objects and photographs of objects by children. *Child Development*, 1971, *42*, 1580–1582.

Fagan, J. F. Memory in the infant. *Journal of Experimental Child Psychology*, 1970, *9*, 217–226.

Fagan, J. F.; Fantz, R. L.; & Miranda, S. B. Infants' attention to novel stimuli as a function of postnatal and conceptual age. Paper presented at the meeting of the Society for Research in Child Development, Minneapolis, 1971.

Fagan, J., & Witryol, S. Effects of instructional set and delay of reward on children's learning in a simultaneous discrimination task. *Child Development*, 1966, *37*, 433–438.

Falk, C. T. Object and pattern discrimination learning by young children as a function of availability of cues. *Child Development*, 1968, *39*, 923–931.

Fantz, R. L. Pattern vision in young infants. *Psychological Record*, 1958, *8*, 43–47.

Fantz, R. L. Pattern vision in newborn infants. *Science*, 1963, *140*, 296–297.

Fantz, R. L. Visual experience in infants: decreased attention to familiar patterns relative to novel ones. *Science*, 1964, *146*, 668–670.

Fantz, R. L. Visual perception from birth as shown by pattern selectivity. *Annals of the New York Academy of Science*, 1965, *118*, 793–814.

Fantz, R. L., & Nevis, S. The predictive values of changes in visual preference in early infancy. In J. Hellmuth (Ed.), *Exceptional infant*. Vol. *1. The normal infant*. Seattle: Special Child Publications, 1967.

Fein, G. The effect of within-pair variation and instructions on the transposition behavior of kindergarten and third grade children. *Journal of Experimental Child Psychology*, 1972, *14*, 379–397.

Friedman, S. Habituation and recovery of visual response in the alert human newborn. *Journal of Experimental Child Psychology*, 1972, *13*, 339–349.

Friedrich, L., & Stein, A. Aggressive and prosocial TV programs and the natural behavior of preschool children. *Monographs of the Society for Research in Child Development*, 1973, *38* (4, Serial No. 151).

Frith, U. Why do children reverse letters? *British Journal of Psychology*, 1971, *62*, 459–568.

Gaines, R. Children's selective attention to stimuli: stage or set? *Child Development*, 1970, *41*, 979–992.

Garner, W. R. The stimulus in information processing. *American Psychologist*, 1970, *25*, 350–358.

Gibson, E. J. *Principles of perceptual learning and development*. New York: Appleton-Century-Crofts, 1969.

Gibson, E. J., & Olum, V. Experimental methods of studying perception in children. In P. H. Mussen (Ed.), *Handbook of research in child development*. New York: Wiley, 1960.

Gibson, E. J.; Tenney, Y. J.; Barron, R. W.; & Zaslow, M. The effect of orthographic structure on letter search. *Perception and Psychophysics*, 1972, *11*, 183–186.

Gibson, E. J., & Yonas, A. A developmental study of the effects of visual and auditory interference on a visual scanning task. *Psychonomic Science*, 1966, *5*, 163–164.

Ginsburg, H. P. Attention to information as a function of age and specificity of problem. *Journal of Child Psychology and Psychiatry*, 1967, *8*, 41–50.

Gliner, C. R.; Pick, A. D.; Pick, H. L.; & Hales, J. J. A developmental investigation of visual and haptic preferences for shape and texture. *Monographs of the Society for Research in Child Development*, 1969, *34* (6, Serial No. 130).

Goldstein, S. B., & Siegel, A. W. Facilitation of discrimination learning with delayed reinforcement. *Child Development*, 1972, *43*, 1004–1011.

Goodnow, J. J. Effects of active handling, illustrated by uses for objects. *Child Development*, 1969, *40*, 201–212.

Goodnow, J. J. Eye and hand: differential memory and its effect on matching. *Neuropsychologia*, 1971, *9*, 89–95. (a)

Goodnow, J. J. Matching auditory and visual series: modality problem or translation problem? *Child Development*, 1971, *42*, 1187–1201. (b)

Goodnow, J. J. The role of modalities in perceptual and cognitive development. In J. P. Hill (Ed.), *Minnesota symposium on child psychology*. Vol. *5*. Minneapolis: University of Minnesota Press, 1971. (c)

Graham, F. K., & Jackson, J. C. Arousal systems and infant heart rate responses. In H. W. Reese & L. P. Lipsitt (Eds.), *Advances in child development and behavior*. Vol. *5*. New York: Academic Press, 1970.

Greenberg, D. J. Accelerating visual complexity levels in the human infant. *Child Development*, 1971, *42*, 905–918.

Greenberg, D. J., & O'Donnell, W. J. Infancy and the optimal stage of stimulation. *Child Development*, 1972, *43*, 639–645.

Greenberg, D. J.; Uzgiris, I. D.; & Hunt, J. McV. Attentional preference and experience, III: Visual familiarity and looking time. *Journal of Genetic Psychology*, 1970, *117*, 123–135.

Hagen, J. W. The effect of distraction on selective attention. *Child Development*, 1967, *38*, 685–694.

Hagen, J. W., & Hale, G. A. The development of attention in children. In A. D. Pick (Ed.), *Minnesota symposium on child psychology*. Vol. 7. Minneapolis: University of Minnesota Press, 1973.

Hagen, J. W.; Hargrave, S.; & Ross, W. Prompting and rehearsal in short-term memory. *Child Development*, 1973, *44*, 201–204.

Hagen, J. W., & Kingsley, P. R. Labeling effects in short-term memory. *Child Development*, 1968, *39*, 113–122.

Haith, M. The response of the human newborn to visual movement. *Journal of Experimental Child Psychology*, 1966, *3*, 235–243.

Haith, M. Infrared television recording and measurement of ocular behavior in the human infant. *American Psychologist*, 1969, *24*, 279–283.

Haith, M. M.; Morrison, F. J.; & Sheingold, K. Tachistoscopic recognition of geometric forms by children and adults. *Psychonomic Science*, 1970, *19*, 345–347.

Haith, M. M.; Morrison, F. J.; Sheingold, K.; & Mindes, P. Short-term memory for visual information in children and adults. *Journal of Experimental Child Psychology*, 1970, *9*, 454–469.

Hale, G. A., & Morgan, J. S. Developmental trends in children's component selection. *Journal of Experimental Child Psychology*, 1973, *15*, 302–314.

Hale, G. A., & Piper, R. A. Developmental trends in children's incidental learning: some critical stimulus differences. *Developmental Psychology*, 1973, *8*, 327–335.

Hall, J. W. Young children's memory encoding reflected in verbal discrimination learning and recognition memory performance. *Psychonomic Science*, 1971, *25*, 91–93.

Harris, G. J., & Burke, D. The effects of grouping on short-term serial recall of digits by children; developmental trends. *Child Development*, 1972, *43*, 710–716.

Heider, E. R. "Focal" color areas and the development of color names. *Developmental Psychology*, 1971, *4*, 447–455.

Henning, J. S., & Kornreich, L. B. A developmental study of the effects of pretraining on a perceptual recognition task. *Child Development*, 1971, *42*, 2117–2119.

Hershenson, M. Visual discrimination in the human newborn. *Journal of Comparative and Physiological Psychology*, 1964, *58*, 270–276.

Hershenson, M.; Kessen, W.; & Munsinger, H. Pattern perception in the human newborn: a close look at some positive and negative results. In W. Wathen-Dunn (Ed.), *Models for the perception of speech and visual form*. Cambridge, Mass.: M.I.T. Press, 1967.

Hershenson, M.; Munsinger, H.; & Kessen, W. Preference for shapes of intermediate variability in the newborn human. *Science*, 1965, *147*, 630–631.

Hopkins, J. R.; Zelazo, P.; Kagan, J.; Lyons, K.; & Minton, C. The discrepancy hypothesis. Paper presented at the meeting of the Society for Research in Child Development, Minneapolis, April 1971.

Horowitz, A. Habituation and memory: infant cardiac responses to familiar and discrepant auditory stimuli. *Child Development*, 1972, *43*, 43–53.

Horowitz, F. D. Learning and individual differences. In L. P. Lipsitt & H. W. Reese (Eds.), *Advances in child development and behavior*. Vol. 4. New York: Academic Press, 1969.

Horowitz, F. D. (Ed.) Visual attention, auditory stimulation, and language discrimination in young infants. *Monographs of the Society for Research in Child Development*, 1974, *39* (5 and 6, Serial No. 158).

Hruska, K., & Yonas, A. Developmental changes in cardiac responses to the optical stimulus of impending collision. Paper presented at the meeting of the Society for Psycho-physiological Research, Saint Louis, 1971.

Hunt, J. McV. Attentional preference and experience, I: Introduction. *Journal of Genetic Psychology*, 1970, *117*, 99–117.

Hutt, C. Specific and diversive exploration. In H. W. Reese & L. P. Lipsitt (Eds.), *Advances in child development and behavior.* Vol. 5. New York: Academic Press, 1970.

Inhelder, B., & Piaget, J. *The early growth of logic in the child.* New York: Harper & Row, 1964.

Jackson, J. P. Development of visual and tactual processing of sequentially presented shapes. *Developmental Psychology*, 1973, *8*, 46–50.

Jacobs, P. I., & Vandeventer, M. The learning and transfer of double-classification skills by first graders. *Child Development*, 1971, *42*, 149–159.

Jeffrey, W. E., & Cohen, L. B. Habituation in the human infant. In H. W. Reese (Ed.), *Advances in child development and behavior.* Vol. 6. New York: Academic Press, 1971.

Johnson, P. J.; Warner, M. S.; & Lee, D. R. Effects of enforced attention and stimulus phasing upon rule learning in children. *Journal of Experimental Child Psychology*, 1970, *9*, 388–399.

Jones, B. Facilitation of visual perception through voluntary movement in elementary school children. *Journal of Experimental Child Psychology*, 1972, *14*, 408–415.

Jones, H. R. The use of visual and verbal memory processes by three-year-old children. *Journal of Experimental Child Psychology*, 1973, *15*, 340–351.

Jones-Molfese, V. Individual differences in neonatal preferences for planometric and stereometric visual patterns. *Child Development*, 1972, *43*, 1289–1296.

Kagan, J. Attention and psychological change in the young child. *Science*, 1970, *170*, 826–832.

Kagan, J., & Lewis, M. Studies of attention in the human infant. *Merrill-Palmer Quarterly*, 1965, *11*, 95–127.

Kahneman, D. *Attention and effort.* New York: Appleton-Century-Crofts, 1972.

Karmel, B. Z. Complexity, amounts of contour, and visually dependent behavior in hooded rats, domestic chicks, and human infants. *Journal of Comparative and Physiological Psychology*, 1969, *69*, 649–657. (a)

Karmel, B. Z. The effect of age, complexity, and amount of contour on pattern preferences in human infants. *Journal of Experimental Child Psychology* 1969, *7*, 339–354. (b)

Karmel, B. Z. Contour effects and pattern preferences in infants: a reply to Greenberg and O'Donnell (1972). *Child Development*, 1974, *45*, 196–199.

Karmel, B. Z.; Hoffmann, R. F.; & Fegy, M. J. Processing of contour information by human infants evidenced by pattern-dependent evoked potentials. *Child Development*, 1974, *45*, 39–48.

Katz, P. A.; Albert, J.; & Atkins, M. Mediation and perceptual transfer in children. *Developmental Psychology*, 1971, *4*, 268–276.

Kearsley, R. B. The newborn's response to auditory stimulation: a demonstration of orienting and defensive behavior. *Child Development*, 1973, *44*, 582–590.

Kendler, H. H., & Ward, J. W. Single versus cumulative presentation of stimuli to kindergartners in reversal shift behavior. *Developmental Psychology*, 1971, *5*, 420–426.

Kessen, W.; Haith, M. M.; & Salapatek, P. H. Human infancy: a bibliography and guide. In P. H. Mussen (Ed.), *Carmichael's manual of child psychology.* New York: Wiley, 1970.

Kimball, M. M., & Dale, P. S. The relationship between color naming and color recognition abilities of preschoolers. *Child Development*, 1972, *43*, 972–980.

Kinglsey, P. R., & Hagen, J. W. Induced versus spontaneous rehearsal in short-term memory in nursery school children. *Developmental Psychology*, 1969, *1*, 40–46.

Kirsner, K. Developmental changes in short-term recognition memory. *British Journal of Psychology*, 1972, *63*, 109–117.

Kobasigawa, A., & Middleton, D. E. Free recall of categorized items by children at three grade levels. *Child Development*, 1972, *43*, 1067–1072.

Kobasigawa, A., & Orr, R. R. Free recall and retrieval speed of categorized items by kindergarten children. *Journal of Experimental Child Psychology*, 1973, *15*, 187–192.

Kohlberg, L. Stage and sequence: the cognitive developmental approach to socialization. In D. Goshin (Ed.), *Handbook of socialization theory and research*. Chicago: Rand-Mc-Nally, 1969.

Kraynak, A. R., & Raskin, L. M. The influence of age and stimulus dimensionality on form perception by preschool children. *Developmental Psychology*, 1971, *4*, 389–393.

Kuhn, D. Imitation theory and research from a cognitive perspective. *Human Development*, 1973, *16*, 157–180.

Lampel, A. K. The child's memory for actional, locational, and serial scenes. *Journal of Experimental Child Psychology*, 1973, *15*, 266–277.

Lehman, E. B. Selective strategies in children's attention to task-relevant information. *Child Development*, 1972, *43*, 197–209.

Leifer, A. D.; Collins, W. A.; Gross, B.; Taylor, P.; Andrews, L.; & Blackmer, E. Developmental aspects of variables relevant to observational learning. *Child Development*, 1971, *42*, 1509–1516.

Lewis, M.; Goldberg, S.; & Campbell, H. A developmental study of information processing within the first three years of life: response decrement to a redundant signal. *Monographs of the Society for Research in Child Development*, 1969, *34* (9, Serial No. 133).

Liberman, A. M.; Cooper, F. S.; Shankweiler, D. P.; & Studdert-Kennedy, M. Perception of the speech code. *Psychological Review*, 1967, *74*, 431–461.

Liebert, R., & Fernandez, L. Effects of vicarious consequences on imitative performance. *Child Development*, 1970, *41*, 847–852. (a)

Liebert, R., & Fernandez, L. Imitation as a function of vicarious and direct reward. *Developmental Psychology*, 1970, *2*, 230–232. (b)

Liss, P. H., & Haith, M. M. The speed of visual processing in children and adults: effects of backward and forward masking. *Perception and Psychophysics*, 1970, *8*, 396–398.

London, P., & Robinson, J. P. Imagination in learning and retention. *Child Development*, 1968, *39*, 803–816.

McCall, R. B. Attention in the infant: avenue to the study of cognitive development. In D. N. Walcher & D. L. Peters (Eds.), *Early Childhood, the development of self-regulatory mechanisms*. New York: Academic Press, 1971.

McCall, R. B. Encoding and retrieval of perceptual memories after long-term familiarization and the infant's reaponse to discrepancy. *Developmental Psychology*, 1973, *9*, 310–318.

McCall, R. B.; Hogarty, P. S.; Hamilton, J. S.; & Vincent, J. H. Habituation rate and the infant's response to visual descrepancies. *Child Development*, 1973, *44*, 280–287.

McCall, R. B., & Kagan, J. Attention in the infant: effects of complexity, contour, perimeter, and familiarity. *Child Development*, 1967, *38*, 939–952. (a)

McCall, R. B., & Kagan, J. Stimulus-schema discrepancy and attention in the infant. *Journal of Experimental Child Psychology*, 1967, *5*, 381–390. (b)

McCall, R. B., & Kagan, J. Individual differences in the infant's distribution of attention to stimulus discrepancy. *Developmental Psychology*, 1970, *2*, 90–98.

McCall, R. B., & Melson, W. H. Attention in infants as a function of magnitude of discrepancy and habituation rate. *Psychonomic Science*, 1969, *17*, 317–319.

McCall, R. B., & Melson, W. H. Amount of short-term familiarization and the response to auditory discrepancies. *Child Development*, 1970, *41*, 861–869. (a)

McCall, R. B., & Melson, W. H. Complexity, contour, and area as determinants of attention in infants. *Developmental Psychology*, 1970, *3*, 343–349. (b)

McCarver, R. B. A developmental study of the effect of organizational cues on short-term memory. *Child Development*, 1972, *43*, 1317–1325.

McCarver, R. B., & Ellis, N. R. Effect of overt verbal labeling on short-term memory in culturally deprived and nondeprived children. *Developmental Psychology*, 1972, *6*, 38–41.

Maccoby, E. E. Selective auditory attention in children. In L. Lipsitt & C. Spiker (Eds.), *Advances in child development and behavior*. Vol. *3*. New York: Academic Press, 1967.

Maccoby, E. E. The development of stimulus selection. In J. P. Hill (Ed.), *Minnesota symposium on child psychology*. Vol. *3*. Minneapolis: University of Minnesota Press, 1969.

Maccoby, E. E., & Hagen, J. W. Effects of distraction upon central versus incidental recall: developmental trends. *Journal of Experimental Child Psychology*, 1965, *2*, 280–289.

Maccoby, E. E., & Konrad, K. W. Age trends in selective listening. *Journal of Experimental Child Psychology*, 1966, *3*, 113–122.

Maccoby, E. E., & Konrad, K. W. Effect of preparatory set on selective listening: developmental trends. *Monographs of the Society for Research in Child Development*, 1967, *32* (4, Serial No. 112).

Maccoby, E. E., & Wilson, W. Identification and observational learning from films. *Journal of Abnormal and Social Psychology*, 1957, *55*, 76–87.

Maccoby, E. E.; Wilson, W.; & Burton, R. Differential movie-viewing behavior of male and female viewers. *Journal of Personality*, 1958, *26*, 259–267.

McCullers, J. C., & Martin, J. A. G. A reexamination of the role of incentive in children's discrimination learning. *Child Development*, 1971, *42*, 827–838.

McGurk, J. The role of object orientation in infant perception. *Journal of Experimental Child Psychology*, 1970, *9*, 363–373.

McGurk, J. The salience of orientation in young children's perception of form. *Child Development*, 1972, *43*, 1047–1052.

Maisel, E. B., & Karmel, B. Z. Failure to replicate the bull's-eye preference effect in infants. Paper presented at the meeting of the Society for Research in Child Development, Philadelphia, 1973.

Mann, T. *Joseph and his brothers*. (Trans. H. T. Lowe-Porter) New York: Knopf, 1966.

Medin, D. L. Measuring and training dimensional preferences. *Child Development*, 1973, *44*, 359–362.

Melson, W., & McCall, R. B. Attentional responses of five-month girls to discrepant auditory stimuli. *Child Development*, 1970, *41*, 1159–1171.

Millar, S. Visual and haptic cue utilization by preschool children: the recognition of visual and haptic stimuli presented separately and together. *Journal of Experimental Child Psychology*, 1971, *12*, 88–94.

Millar, S. Effects of instructions to visualize stimuli during delay on visual recognition by preschool children. *Child Development*, 1972, *43*, 1073–1075.

Miller, D. J. Visual habituation in the human infant. *Child Development*, 1972, *43*, 481–493.

Miller, L. K. Developmental differences in the field of view during tachistoscopic presentation. *Child Development*, 1971, *42*, 1543–1551.

Miller, L. K. Visual masking and developmental differences in information processing. *Child Development*, 1972, *43*, 704–709.

Miller, L. K. Developmental differences in the field of view during covert and overt search. *Child Development*, 1973, *44*, 247–252.

Miller, P. H.; Kessel, F. S.; & Flavell, J. H. Thinking about people thinking about people thinking about . . . : a study of social cognitive development. *Child Development*, 1970, *41*, 613–623.

Moffett, A. Stimulus complexity as a determinant of visual attention in infants. *Journal of Experimental Child Psychology*, 1969, *8*, 173–179.

Moffitt, A. R. Consonant cue perception by twenty- to twenty-four-week-old infants. *Child Development*, 1971, *42*, 717–731.

Moffitt, A. R. Intensity discrimination and cardiac reaction in young infants. *Developmental Psychology*, 1973, *8*, 357–359.

Morse, P. A. The discrimination of speech and nonspeech stimuli in early infancy. *Journal of Experimental Child Psychology*, 1972, *14*, 477–492.

Mosher, F. A., & Hornsby, J. R. On asking questions. In J. Bruner, R. Olver, & P. Greenfield (Eds.), *Studies in cognitive growth*. New York: Wiley, 1966.

Munsinger, H., & Weir, M. W. Infants' and young children's preference for complexity. *Journal of Experimental Child Psychology*, 1967, *5*, 69–73.

Murray, D. J., & Roberts, B. Visual and auditory presentation, presentation rate, and short-term memory in children. *British Journal of Psychology*, 1968, *59*, 119–125.

Neisser, U. *Cognitive psychology*. New York: Appleton-Century-Crofts, 1967.

Nelson, K. E. Memory development in children: evidence from nonverbal tasks. *Psychonomic Science*, 1971, *25*, 346–348.

Nelson, K. E., & Earl, N. Information search by preschool children: induced use of categories and category hierarchies. *Child Development*, 1973, *44*, 682–685.

Odom, R. D. Effects of perceptual salience on the recall of relevant and incidental dimensional values: a developmental study. *Journal of Experimental Psychology*, 1972, *92*, 285–291.

Odom, R. D. & Corbin, E. W. Perceptual salience and children's multidimensional problem solving. *Child Development*, 1973, *44*, 425–432.

Odom, R. & Guzman, R. D. Development of hierarchies of dimensional salience. *Developmental Psychology*, 1972, *6*, 271–287.

Odom, R. D., & Mumbauer, C. C. Dimensional salience and identification of the relevant dimension in problem solving: a developmental study. *Developmental Psychology*, 1971, *4*, 135–140.

Offenbach, S. I.; Baecher, R.; & White, M. Stability of first-grade children's dimensional preferences. *Child Development*, 1972, *43*, 689–692.

Olmsted, P. P., & Sigel, I. E. The generality of color-form preference as a function of materials and task requirements among lower-class Negro children. *Child Development*, 1970, *41*, 1025–1032.

Overton, W. F., & Jordan, R. Stimulus preference and multiplicative classification in children. *Developmental Psychology*, 1971, *5*, 505–510.

Penney, R. Effect of reward and punishment on children's orientation and discrimination learning. *Journal of Experimental Psychology*, 1967, *75*, 140–142.

Pick, A. D.; Christy, M. D.; & Frankel, G. W. A developmental study of visual selective attention. *Journal of Experimental Child Psychology*, 1972, *14*, 165–175.

Pick, A. D., & Frankel, G. W. A study of strategies of visual attention in children. *Developmental Psychology*, 1973, *9*, 348–357.

Pick, A. D., & Frankel, G. W. A developmental study of strategies of visual selectivity. *Child Development*, 1974, *45*, 1162–1165.

Pick, H. L., Pick, A. D., & Klein, R. E. Perceptual integration in children. In L. P. Lipsitt & C. C. Spiker (Eds.), *Advances in child development and behavior*. Vol. *3*. New York: Academic Press, 1967.

Pishkin, V., & Rosenbluh, E. S. Concept identification of auditory dimensions as a function of age and sex. *Psychonomic Science*, 1966, *4*, 165–166.

Porges, S. W.; Arnold, W. R.; & Forbes, E. J. Heart rate variability: an index of attentional responsivity in human newborns. *Developmental Psychology*, 1973, *8*, 85–92.

Poteat, B. W. S., & Kasschau, R. A. Generalization in short-term recognition of auditory verbal stimuli. *Psychonomic Science*, 1969, *17*, 358–359.

Ratliff, R. G. Two-choice discrimination learning in children as a function of punishment modality and reinforcement combination. *Journal of Experimental Child Psychology*, 1972, *14*, 365–371.

Reese, H. W. Imagery and multiple-list paired-associate learning in young children. *Journal of Experimental Child Psychology*, 1972, *13*, 310–323.

Rieber, M. Role of stimulus comparison in children's discrimination learning. *Journal of Experimental Psychology*, 1966, *72*, 263–270.

Robinson, J. P., & London, P. Labeling and imaging as aids to memory. *Child Development*, 1971, *42*, 641–644.

Rohwer, W. D., Jr. Images and pictures in children's learning: research results and instructional implications. In H. W. Reese (Chm.), Imagery in children's learning: a symposium. *Psychological Bulletin*, 1970, *73*, 393–403.

Rollins, H., & Castle, K. Dimensional preference, pretraining, and attention in children's concept identification. *Child Development*, 1973, *44*, 363–366.

Rose, S. A.; Blank, M. S.; & Bridger, W. H. Intermodal and intramodal retention of visual and tactual information in young children. *Developmental Psychology*, 1972, *6*, 482–486.

Rosekrans, M. Imitation in children as a function of perceived similarity to a social model and vicarious reinforcement. *Journal of Personality and Social Psychology*, 1967, *7*, 307–315.

Rosner, S. The effects of rehearsal and chunking instructions on children's multitrial free recall. *Journal of Experimental Child Psychology*, 1971, *11*, 93–105.

Rowe, E. J. Discrimination learning of pictures and words: a replication of picture superiority. *Journal of Experimental Child Psychology*, 1972, *14*, 323–328.

Ruff, H., & Birch, H. B. Infant visual fixation: the effect of concentricity, curvilinearity, and number of directions. *Journal of Experimental Child Psychology*, 1974, *17*, 460–473.

Saayman, G.; Ames, E. W.; & Moffett, A. R. Response to novelty as an indicator of visual discrimination in the human infant. *Journal of Experimental Child Psychology*, 1964, *1*, 189–198.

Sainsbury, R. The "feature positive effect" and simultaneous discrimination learning. *Journal of Experimental Child Psychology*, 1971, *11*, 347–356.

Salapatek, P. Visual scanning of geometric figures by the human newborn. *Journal of Comparative and Physiological Psychology*, 1968, *66*, 247–258.

Salapatek, P. The visual investigation of geometric pattern by the one and two month old infant. Paper presented as part of the symposium on pattern perception at the meeting of the American Association for the Advancement of Science, Boston, December 1969.

Salapatek, P., & Kessen, W. Visual scanning of triangles by the human newborn. *Journal of Experimental Child Psychology*, 1966, *3*, 155–157.

Salapatek, P., & Kessen, W. Prolonged investigation of a plane geometric triangle by the human newborn. *Journal of Experimental Child Psychology*, 1973, *15*, 22–29.

Salzinger, S.; Salzinger, K.; & Patenaude, J. Effect of verbal response class on shift in the preschool child's judgment of length in response to an anchor stimulus. *Developmental Psychology*, 1970, *2*, 49–57.

Schell, D. J. Conceptual behavior in young children: learning to shift dimensional attention. *Journal of Experimental Child Psychology*, 1971, *12*, 72–87.

Scholnick, E. K. Use of labels and cues in children's concept identification. *Child Devel-*

opment, 1971, *42*, 1849–1858.

Schroth, M. Effect of informative feedback on problem solving. *Child Development*, 1970, *41*, 831–837.

Schwartz, A. N.; Campos, J. J.; & Baisel, E. J., Jr. The visual cliff: cardiac and behavioral responses on the deep and shallow sides at five and nine months of age. *Journal of Experimental Child Psychology*, 1973, *15*, 86–99.

Scott, M. W. Transfer in nursery school children between two relational tasks. *Developmental Psychology*, 1970, *3*, 145.

Scribner, S., & Cole, M. Effects of constrained recall training on children's performance in a verbal memory task. *Child Development*, 1972, *43*, 845–857.

Seitz, V., & Weir, M. W. Strength of dimensional preferences as a predictor of nursery-school children's performance on a concept-shift task. *Journal of Experimental Child Psychology*, 1971, *12*, 370–386.

Sheingold, K. Developmental differences in intake and storage of visual information. *Journal of Experimental Child Psychology*, 1973, *16*, 1–11.

Siegel, A. W., & Allik, J. P. A developmental study of visual and auditory short-term memory. *Journal of Verbal Learning and Verbal Behavior*, 1973, *12*, 409–418.

Siegel, A. W., & Corsini, D. A. Attentional differences in children's incidental learning. *Journal of Educational Psychology*, 1969, *60*, 65–70.

Siegel, A. W., & Stevenson, H. W. Incidental learning: a developmental study. *Child Development*, 1966, *37*, 811–818.

Silleroy, R. S., & Johnson, P. J. The effects of perceptual pretraining on concept identification and preference. *Journal of Experimental Child Psychology*, 1973, *15*, 462–472.

Smiley, S. S. Instability of dimensional preference following changes in relative cue similarity. *Journal of Experimental Child Psychology*, 1972, *13*, 394–403, (a)

Smiley, S. S. Optional shift behavior as a function of dimensional preference and relative cue similarity. *Journal of Experimental Child Psychology*, 1972, *14*, 313–322. (b)

Smock, C., & Rubin, B. Utilization of visual information in children as a function of incentive motivation. *Child Development*, 1964, *35*, 109–117.

Spear, P. S. Motivational effects of praise and criticism on children's learning. *Developmental Psychology*, 1970, *3*, 124–132.

Spear, P. S., & Spear, S. A. Social reinforcement, discrimination learning, and retention in children. *Developmental Psychology*, 1972, *7*, 220.

Spears, W. C. Assessment of visual preference and discrimination in the four-month-old infant. *Journal of Comparative and Physiological Psychology*, 1964, *57*, 381–386.

Spence, J. T. The distracting effects of material reinforcers in the discrimination learning of lower- and middle-class children. *Child Development*, 1970, *41*, 103–112.

Spence, J. T., & Segner, L. Verbal versus nonverbal reinforcement combinations in the discrimination learning of middle- and lower-class children. *Child Development*, 1967, *38*, 29–38.

Steinmetz, J. I., & Battig, W. F. Clustering and priority of free recall of newly learned items in children. *Developmental Psychology*, 1969, *1*, 503–507.

Stevenson, H. W. *Children's learning.* New York: Appleton-Century-Crofts, 1972.

Stevenson, J.; Weir, M.; & Zigler, F. Discrimination learning in children as a function of motive-incentive condition. *Psychological Reports*, 1959, *5*, 95–98.

Suchman, R. G., & Trabasso, T. Color and form preference in young children. *Journal of Experimental Child Psychology*, 1966, *3*, 177–187.

Super, C. M.; Kagan, J.; Morrison, F. J.; Haith, M. M.; & Weiffenbach, J. Discrepancy and attention in the five-month infant. *Genetic Psychology Monographs*, 1972, *85*, 305–331.

Thomas, H. Discrepancy hypotheses: methodological and theoretical considerations. *Psychological Review*, 1971, *78*(3), 249–259.

Thompson, R. F., & Spencer, W. A. Habituation: a model phenomenon for the study of neuronal substrates of behavior. *Psychological Review*, 1966, *73*, 16–43.

Tighe, L. S.; Tighe, T. J.; Waterhouse, M. D.; & Vasta, R. Dimensional preference and discrimination shift learning in children. *Child Development*, 1970, *41*, 737–746.

Trabasso, T.; Stave, M.; & Eichberg, R. Attribute preference and discrimination shifts in young children. *Journal of Experimental Child Psychology*, 1969, *8*, 195–209.

Trehub, S. E., & Rabinovitch, M. S. Auditory-linguistic sensitivity in early infancy. *Developmental Psychology*, 1972, *6*, 74–77.

Treisman, A. M. Strategies and models of selective attention. *Psychological Review*, 1969, *76*, 282–299.

Turnure, J. E. Children's reactions to distractors in a learning situation. *Developmental Psychology*, 1970, *2*, 115–122.

Uzgiris, I. C., & Hunt, J. McV. Attentional preference and experience, II: An exploratory longitudinal study of the effect of visual familiarity and responsiveness. *Journal of Genetic Psychology*, 1970, *117*, 109–121.

Van Horn, K. R., & Bartz, W. H. Information seeking strategies in cognitive development. *Psychonomic Science*, 1968, *11*, 341–342.

Vurpillot, E. The development of scanning strategies and their relation to visual differentiation. *Journal of Experimental Child Psychology*, 1968, *6*, 632–650.

Walk, R. D., & Gibson, E. J. A comparative and analytical study of visual depth perception. *Psychological Monographs*, 1961, *75*, No. 15.

Walk, R. D., & Saltz, E. J. Discrimination learning with varying numbers of positive and negative stimuli by children of different ages. *Psychonomic Science*, 1965, *2*, 95–96.

Ward, W. C., & Legant, P. Naming and memory in nursery school children in the absence of rehearsal. *Developmental Psychology*, 1971, *5*, 174–175.

Watson, J. S., & Danielson, G. An Attempt to shape bidimensional attention in 24-month-old infants. *Journal of Experimental Child Psychology*, 1969, *7*, 467–478.

Weiner, B., & Goodnow, J. J. Motor activity: effects on memory. *Developmental Psychology*, 1970, *2*, 448.

Weizman, F.; Cohen, L. B.; & Pratt, R. J. Novelty, familiarity and the development of infant attention. *Developmental Psychology*, 1971, *4*, 149–154.

West, H., & Abravanel, E. Evidence for class-concept mediation of perceptual sets in preschool children. *Child Development*, 1972, *43*, 1242–1248.

Wetherford, M. J., & Cohen, L. B. Developmental changes in infant visual preferences for novelty and familiarity. *Child Development*, 1973, *44*, 416–424.

Wheeler, R. J., & Dusek, J. B. The effects of attentional and cognitive factors on children's incidental learning. *Child Development*, 1973, *44*, 253–258.

Williams, J. P. Training kindergarten children to discriminate letter-like forms. *American Educational Research Journal*, 1969, *6*, 510–514.

Willoughby, R. H. Age and training effects in children's conditional matching to sample. *Child Development*, 1973, *44*, 143–148.

Wilson, C. D., & Lewis, M. A developmental study of attention: a multivariate approach. Paper presented at the meeting of the Eastern Psychological Association, New York, 1971.

Witryol, S.; Lowden, L.; & Fagan, J. Incentive effects upon attention in children's discrimination learning. *Journal of Experimental Child Psychology*, 1967, *5*, 94–108.

Witte, K., & Grossman, E. The effects of reward and punishment upon children's affection, motivation, and discrimination learning. *Child Development*, 1971, *42*, 537–542.

Witte, K., & Johnson, R. Children's discrimination learning as related to delayed punishment. *Bulletin of the Psychonomic Society*, 1973, *2*(3), 146–148.

Wolff, R. The role of stimulus-correlated activity in children's recognition of nonsense forms. *Journal of Experimental Child Psychology*, 1972, *14*, 427–441.

Wolff, P., & Levin, J. R. The role of overt activity in children's imagery production. *Child Development*, 1972, *43*, 537–547.

Wolff, P., Levin, J. R.; & Longobardi, E. T. Motoric mediation in children's paired-associate learning: effects of visual and tactual contact. *Journal of Experimental Child Psychology*, 1972, *14*, 176–183.

Wright, J., & Smothergill, D. Observing behavior and children's discrimination learning under delayed reinforcement. *Journal of Experimental Child Psychology*, 1967, *5*, 430–440.

Wright, J. M., von. Relation between verbal recall and visual recognition of the same stimuli in young children. *Journal of Experimental Child Psychology*, 1973, *15*, 481–487.

Yuille, J. C., & Catchpole, M. J. Associative learning and imagery training in children. *Journal of Experimental Child Psychology*, 1973, *16*, 403–412.

Yussen, S. Determinants of visual attention and recall in observational learning by preschoolers and second graders. *Developmental Psychology*, 1974, *10*, 93–100.

Zeaman, D., & House, B. J. The role of attention in retardate discrimination learning. In N. R. Ellis (Ed.), *Handbook of mental deficiency*. New York: McGraw-Hill, 1963.

Zeaman, D., & House, B. J. Interpretations of developmental trends in discriminative transfer effects. In A. D. Pick (Ed.), *Minnesota symposium on child psychology*. Vol. 8. Minneapolis: University of Minnesota Press, 1974.

Zelazo, P. R., & Komer, M. J. Infant smiling to nonsocial stimuli and the recognition hypothesis. *Child Development*, 1971, *42*, 1327–1339.

Zimmerman, B. J., & Bell, J. A. Observer verbalization and abstraction in vicarious rule learning, generalization, and retention. *Developmental Psychology*, 1972, *7*, 227–231.

7 Problems and Prospects in the Study of Learning Disabilities

JOSEPH TORGESEN
University of Michigan

385

I. INTRODUCTION

Over the last 15 years, there has been a phenomenal growth of interest in children of normal intelligence who do not learn normally in the classroom. Expansion of concern for these children is reflected not only in vastly increased research efforts but also in the creation of new institutions and educational practices. A large and growing parent-professional group called the Association for Children with Learning Disabilities has been established to help publicize the problems and create help for children who fit this category. The area of learning disabilities is currently recognized as a specialty area within the field of education. At present, both research and educational efforts on behalf of these children are being supported by an increasing amount of federal and state legislation.

Perhaps the most significant accomplishment of the past 15 years lies in the increased awareness of parents, educators, and other child professionals that school learning can be limited by certain special disabilities even though the child may be of normal or above-normal general intelligence. In other words, failure to learn academically does not necessarily imply the kind of general impairment in intellectual capacity which can seriously limit life opportunities. Beyond the recognition that special disabilities exist, however, very little is actually known about the kinds of problems which prevent children from learning effectively. Remedial procedures have been developed, but their current inadequacy reflects the lack of knowledge in the field.

This chapter is not intended to be an exhaustive review of research progress in the study of learning-disabled children. Rather, it is aimed at examining some of the factors which have limited our progress in understanding and helping children with learning problems. Specific consideration is given to research on one particular kind of learning failure, the inability to learn to read. This research is examined selectively with a view to understanding what generalizations are possible, what criticisms are necessary, and what guidelines for future research seem advisable.

II. Basic Conceptual Issues

In order to place the research reviewed here in the proper context, it is necessary to consider several general issues that have continually presented difficulties in studies of learning disability. The problems of defining the subject of study, establishing proper goals for research, and understanding the concept of ability deficit are important in any consideration of current knowledge about disordered learning. Much of the present confusion in the field is due to a lack of clarity centered in these issues, and any research program directed toward adding useful knowledge about learning disabilities must deal with them.

A. THE PROBLEM OF DEFINITION

Perhaps the most important problem in the field of learning disabilities is that of definition. Those who originally coined the term "learning disabilities" understood that it was not to represent a diagnostic category but was merely to serve the purpose of loosely organizing a disparate group of problems under one heading (Kirk 1963). It was also offered to parents as a more positive label for children who had previously been called "minimally brain damaged," "perceptually handicapped," or "encephalopathic." However, what started out as a general term has evolved into a new category of pathology. This development is unfortunate because a term as loosely defined as "learning disabilities" has little use in diagnosis or research.

One widely accepted definition of learning disabilities includes within the same general category disorders of "listening, thinking, talking, reading, writing, spelling, or arithmetic" (McCarthy & McCarthy 1969). On the surface at least, such disorders would include a range of childhood pathology from schizophrenia, to aphasia, to specific problems in perception! While broad definitions allowing large numbers of children to be placed within a specific category are undoubtedly effective in generating supportive legislation and educational programs, they are also destructive of efforts to build adequate theory or conduct integrated programs of research. In fact, attempts to develop coherent and unified explanations for such a diversified range of phenomena have contributed to both the superficial theoretical developments and disorganized empiricism which are so characteristic of the field today.

In addition to the large range of individual differences inadequately accounted for by the use of a general term such as "learning disability," one must also contend with the broad variety of situations in which a failure to learn may occur. In the strictest sense, there really is no such thing as a study of "learning disabilities" because of the necessity for specifying certain aspects of learning failure in the selection of subjects. Children are selected for study because of a discrepancy between reading achievement and intelligence, because they perform poorly on various indices of language development, or because their teachers identify them as ineffective in the classroom—not because they have "learning disabilities."

By far the most widely used criterion for selecting subjects in studies of disordered learning is a failure to learn to read. However, it should be clearly recognized that learning to read very likely requires unique combinations of skills and is not representative of all learning tasks. Several lines of evidence support such a conclusion. Roberts (1968–1969), for example, has reviewed work indicating that the abilities required in a given learning situation depend on both the content of the material to be learned and the way it is presented. Even different stages of accomplishment on the same task may require different abilities. Other work on the interrelationships among different kinds of learning in children (Friedrick et al. 1971) also indicates that any attempt to identify relationships between human ability patterns and learning performance "must acknowledge the specificity of functions involved in performance on different kinds of learning tasks" (p. 172). It therefore seems to be appropriate to describe those who read poorly as demonstrating failure on a specific task rather than as having a general "learning disability." Sound investigation of the psychological processes involved in reading failure will very likely demonstrate their involvement in other kinds of learning problems, but this has yet to be established. At present, it seems best to study the skills relevant to learning specific tasks without attempting to unify them under the learning-disability rubric.

In selecting topics for review in this chapter, it was decided to concentrate on research which used reading achievement as the major index of learning ability. Since this classification includes at least 70% –80% of the recent work in the area, restricting the range of studies to those investigating failure in learning to read should increase the coherence of the review without unduly restricting its scope.

Considering only one form of learning failure, however, does not solve all of the problems of definition. The reading-disabled population is itself a heterogeneous one, being composed of children with many different kinds of problems. In addition, reading is a very complex task made up of separate components that require a variety of skills in their performance (MacGinitie 1969). Children may be classified as poor readers because they have difficulty on any one of several different kinds of activities required for good reading. Methods of dealing with some of these definitional issues will be considered in a later discussion of research methodology. For the present, the definition offered by Eisenberg (1966) is taken to characterize generally the research population considered here. He states that "specific reading disability may be defined as the failure to learn to read with normal proficiency despite conventional instruction, a culturally adequate home, proper motivation, intact senses, normal intelligence, and freedom from gross neurological defect" (p. 360). For the purpose of this review, then, a "learning disability" is specifically the failure to learn to read.

B. GOALS OF RESEARCH

Research on learning disabilities in general, and reading disability in particular, has been directed toward accomplishment in three major areas. Investigators have sought to obtain (1) knowledge necessary to attribute failure to certain causes, (2) data useful for prediction of learning failure, and (3) information relevant to the remediation of learning problems.

It is important to understand how the choice of certain goals and research procedures limits the usefulness of the data obtained. For example, the vast literature which has attempted to implicate one or another form of brain dysfunction in the etiology of disordered learning has not yet provided practical information that is relevant to educational or remedial procedures (Bateman 1964). Even if definite relationships are established between some specific form of brain damage and reading failure, the remedial specialist still must plan an educational program on the basis of current behavioral observations. Present etiological formulations are probably more relevant to prevention than to remediation of learning problems.

The other two goals of research are closely related to one another. In fact, the less complicated of these goals, prediction, will probably be accomplished most effectively when knowledge relevant to the remediation of learning difficulties is more clearly established. The development of predictive indices emerges as a separate goal because of the lack of knowledge concerning psychological process variables important to learning in the classroom. Prediction does not necessarily require theoretical understanding of the processes involved in learning failure, but may occur if measures are found that have substantial empirical relationships with later school achievement or failure (Campbell 1960). In point of fact, most of the work on learning disabilities which is directed toward developing information useful for remediation is actually more suited to the development of predictive indices. Research on the psychological correlates of learning disability has uncovered a broad variety of deficits in children who have school learning problems, but has failed to provide a clear interpretation of these differences in terms of relevant psychological processes.

Over 30 years ago, one of the pioneers in the study of learning disabilities, Heinz Werner (1937), pointed out the utility of describing abilities in terms of processes rather than test scores. The distinction between test scores and psychological processes is the distinction between *what* an individual does and *how* he does it. A description of processes involves the specification of a sequence of events or behaviors that are involved in the accomplishment of a given task. Psychometric studies do not establish a description of behavior in process terms because they do not typically allow examination of the various steps involved in performance. Glanzer (1967) has discussed the reasons why knowledge of simple performance differences does not contribute to effective remedial procedures:

A set of measurements shows that one individual is worse than another on some measure. In some cases these measurements might help predict performance on a criterion task. The measurements could therefore be used for purposes of selection. They do not, however, give a basis for doing anything about the performance. They do not tell how the subject should be trained to improve his performance. They do not tell how the situation should be changed to make the criterion performance easier. Since they do not give a basis for doing anything about the performance, they do not give a basis for understanding or analysis of the performance. [P. 198]

If, however, research on the performance problems of learning-disabled children were able to establish knowledge about basic process deficits, such information would be useful for both prediction and remediation. Consider, for example, the relationship among attention, memory, and perceptual skills on many tasks. If a child is distractible, or unable to focus attention on the important features of a stimulus array, estimates of his "perceptual skills" will be lowered. Or, if one were interested in memory ability and used perceptually complex stimuli to assess it, performance might be affected by the child's perceptual skills. The investigation of psychological processes requires the careful and systematic manipulation of task characteristics so that the potential influence of different skills areas on the final performance is varied. In this way, an understanding of which components of the total process are most important in causing failure is established. Such information is crucial to the development of more effective remedial procedures. Knowledge of basic process deficits would be useful for prediction, particularly if the developmental course of these deficits were clearly understood.

C. THE CONCEPT OF ABILITY DEFICIT

A point of confusion in most attempts to study populations identified by their failure to perform to a "normal" standard is the distinction between *ability* and *performance* deficits. This distinction is particularly important in the study of learning or reading disability because research in this area has tended to invoke the concept of ability quite uncritically in explaining performance differences on specific tasks. Since "ability" is essentially an inferential construct which is never measured directly, one must be concerned about issues of construct validity if one is to use it correctly and without danger of serious error (Cronbach & Meehl 1955). As discussed in greater detail later, writers on learning disabilities have paid little attention to validating the constructs of "ability" which they use so ubiquitously.

1. Source of Ability Deficits

Those who investigate performance deficits generally acknowledge that they can be caused by a lack of ability related to the task or failure to apply efficiently those abilities or capacities which are present. There are two general ways in which basic ability deficits may occur. Maher (1963), who identifies ability deficits with the concept of structure, states that "structural differences between organisms may arise either through the effect of the environment operating on existing structure, or because of predetermined structural characteristics the nature of which are subsumed under the study of genetics" (p. 226).

A number of theorists (Bender 1958; Critchley 1970) have suggested that reading disability may be related to subtle organizational and integrative disturbances at a neurological level. These disturbances are thought to be caused by abnormal central nervous system development which is transmitted genetically. Evidence from modern behavioral genetics suggests that a broad variety of individual differences in cognitive ability may be derived from differences in genetic structure (Hirsh 1963).

The interaction of the organism with its environment can affect abilities at either the physical or psychological level. Physical damage to the brain as the result of injury or a disease process has been implicated repeatedly as one cause of reading failure (Clements 1966). There is also an accumulation of evidence to suggest that proper development of brain structure and functioning may be adversely affected by inadequate diet during the period from conception through the early years of childhood (Birch & Gussow 1970; Scrimshaw & Gordon 1968).

At the psychological level, Hunt (1961) has discussed ways in which deficient early learning and experience can limit intellectual growth. In his view, early experience leads to the establishment of certain central processes which are necessary for intellectual performance. Deficiencies in these processes can affect learning ability on a broad variety of tasks. Other theorists (Gagne 1968) have suggested that ability deficits may also be related to improper development of specific subskills or subprocesses necessary for more complex learning. Learning experiences are cumulative, so rules and principles learned at one stage are essential to learning at another.

Within the learning disability tradition, such people as Kephart (1960) are identified with efforts to conceptualize ability deficits in terms of relationships between simple and complex learning. Zamm (1973) has recently made an attempt to relate reading difficulties to a lack of early experience which emphasizes integrative skills.

2. Other Factors Which Influence Performance

In addition to the organism's abilities or capabilities, factors which influence the application or use of skills also have important effects on performance. In this latter category, the variable which has been studied most extensively is motivation. The effects of motivation on performance are very complex. A variety of factors ranging from the age and social class of the child to the sex of the one offering the reward can alter the effects which motivational variables have on children's learning performance. Many performance differences between subjects of differing social class or age which are initially interpreted as differences on some basic ability dimension often disappear when reinforcement conditions are altered to increase the motivation of the group which learned less effectively (Stevenson 1973). Different kinds of behavioral sets can also influence performance within specific task settings. A slight change in training procedures, task organization, or characteristics of the examiner may significantly influence achievement so that performance levels within specific task settings may not accurately reflect capacity (Bortner & Birch 1970).

Anxiety in the testing situation also can influence level of performance. When measured by certain paper-and-pencil tests, anxiety has been shown to relate to both reading achievement and performance on experimental tasks (Feldhusen & Klausmeier 1962; Stevenson & Odom 1965). In these studies it is assumed that the main basis for the performance differences demonstrated is not a basic difference in capacity between anxious and nonanxious subjects. The differences are usually attributed to the distracting (Wine 1971) or constricting (Easterbrook 1959) effects of anxiety that interfere with the utilization of skills relevant to the task.

3. Consequences for Research on Learning Disabilities

It is clear that reading achievement, as well as performance on tasks used to study psychological variables related to reading failure, may be influenced by individual differences in several different areas. Effective remedial treatment will ultimately depend on an understanding of the separate contributions of each of these variables to reading failure. For example, if reading failure for a given individual is mainly the result of anxiety which distracts him from the task at hand, it may be most effective to deal with the anxiety rather than focusing on the failure through intensification of instruction. If one's failure to read is related to disorganization in brain processes not subject to treatment, it may be hopeless to expect and train for reading achievement beyond a certain minimal level. On the other hand, if a failure in reading is due to the poor learning of certain basic skills, remediation may represent a fairly straightforward problem of training in the deficient skills.

It should be recognized that the separate kinds of influences on performance under discussion here do not operate in isolation. Long-standing emotional and motivational problems will certainly affect the attainment and consolidation of simple skills necessary for reading. Reading failure will likewise affect the emotional and aspirational level of most children. Brain damage probably distorts learning at many levels (Deutsch & Schumer 1967), and a failure to experience certain kinds of early learning opportunities is thought by some (Hebb 1949) to lead to a physiological condition involving permanent incapacity for learning.

Consideration of these kinds of developmental interactions points out a bewildering array of possible influences which may contribute to reading failure. At present, it seems most useful to make a clear distinction between emotional-motivational factors and "ability" factors without attempting to isolate specific causes for ability deficits. Without a clear description of the psychological processes associated with reading failure, questions about the etiology of ability deficits are premature. Only as a number of clearly described psychological differences between good and poor readers are identified can real progress be made in understanding the antecedent conditions responsible for each. What are now thought of as more or less unitary processes may actually be complexly composed of a variety of subprocesses which are each affected in different ways by psychological and developmental factors.

III. REVIEW OF RECENT RESEARCH

The studies reviewed in this section were selected because of certain similarities in their approach to the problem of disordered learning. Most of the research has been conducted since 1960, and its central focus has been to identify the psychological characteristics associated with a failure to learn to read. Explicitly excluded from this review are studies which have investigated various kinds of brain dysfunction (Clements 1966), emotional and personality disorders (Newman, Dember, & Krug 1973; Pearson 1952), and genetic-constitutional factors (Critchley 1970) as possible causes of learning problems. Although this research contains many potentially valuable insights about "learning-disabled" children, limitations of space do not allow its inclusion in this review. The work considered here is of a decidedly atheoretical, task-oriented nature and is not explicitly concerned with the investigation of etiological factors. The studies are organized according to the psychological functions or sensory modalities with which they are concerned. Specific limitations are discussed as they apply to each area of research, with more general conceptual and methodological criticisms offered after all areas have been reviewed.

A. VISUAL-PERCEPTUAL AND PERCEPTUAL-MOTOR FUNCTIONING

The study of perceptual functioning has long been an important area of research in investigations of reading and learning disabilities. In fact, of all the cognitive deficits associated with slow learning in children of normal intelligence, perceptual problems have been studied most extensively (Hallahan & Cruickshank 1973). Within the general area of perception, the study of visual and visual-motor performance has received the greatest emphasis. Although work on the perceptual problems of disabled readers has provided a theoretical and empirical base for many different approaches to the remediation of learning problems, it has recently been the subject of criticism on several counts (Cohen 1969, 1970; Mann 1970).

One of the most important problems in this area is understanding what is meant by the term "perception." The problem of defining perception is not unique to the field of learning disabilities, but failure to appreciate the complexity of the term has created many problems in the interpretation of research in the area. A failure to distinguish clearly between visual-perceptual and visual-motor functioning is one recurring point of confusion in studies of reading disability (Zach & Kaufman 1972).

1. Perceptual-Motor Functioning

One measure which is assumed to assess perceptual-motor development is the Bender Motor Gestalt Test (Bender 1938). The relationship between this test, which requires the subject to copy a series of designs, and reading achievement has been investigated quite extensively. In general, children with reading problems have been found to perform poorly on the Bender when compared to children who read normally (DeHirsh, Jansky, & Langford 1966; Keogh & Smith 1967; Koppitz 1963; Lachman 1960; Owen et al. 1971). However, the consistent association of poor Bender performance and low achievement in reading does not necessarily mean that poor readers have "special" disabilities in perceptual-motor coordination.

For example, the studies by Keogh and Smith (1967) and Koppitz (1963) contained no controls for differences in general intelligence between good and poor readers. The Bender scoring system used in both of these studies generates scores which relate significantly to measures of intelligence. Since reading level is also related to intelligence (Leton 1962), it is possible that the relationship between Bender performance and reading achievement is the result of differences in general intellectual level between good and poor readers. Controls for intelligence are essential in any effort to isolate the unique disabilities associated with failure to learn to read.

Interpretation of the relationship between Bender scores and reading skill is also made difficult by lack of knowledge about the skills which are actually measured by the Bender test. In their study of 304 elementary and high school students, Owen et al. (1971) found that poor readers, although they did poorly on the Bender, were just as accurate as normal children in recognizing their errors. It was concluded that the poor readers experienced problems in the integration of temporal sequences and organization of responses rather than in visual perception per se. With kindergarten children as subjects, DeHirsh et al. (1966) concluded that the predictive validity of Bender performance related not to the specific skills it measured but "to the extent which it measured integrative ability" (p. 38).

Because of its relationship to reading achievement, the Bender gestalt test appears to be useful in predicting certain aspects of school achievement. It is not clear, however, exactly which aspects of cognition measured by this test are important for learning in school. Thus poor performance on the Bender test may be indicative of deficiencies in cognition which are more general than simple perceptual-motor coordination.

2. Visual-Perceptual Skills

The relationship between visual perception and learning ability has also been studied with measures containing no motor component. In a well-controlled study using retarded and normal readers of similar general intelligence, Lyle and Gogen (1968) investigated the recognition of visual forms. Letters, lines in various orientations, and word forms were presented to children in the second and third grades. The children were required to pick the form they had seen from an array of forms which were presented at various intervals following the initial stimulus. The poor readers did less well on all the tasks and recall intervals. The difficulty faced by retarded readers was attributed to their inability to decode the stimuli rapidly enough for storage and recognition.

Two studies using one of Gibson's (1969) perceptual learning tasks illustrate a common difficulty in comparing results from one study of learning-disabled children with another. Whipple and Kodman (1969) used fourth- and fifth-grade retarded readers and normal control subjects and found that the disabled readers were inferior on the perceptual learning task. Walters and Doan (1962), on the other hand, used seventh and eighth graders with the same task and found no difference between good and poor readers. The populations in these two studies differed not only in age but on other very important selection criteria. Whereas Whipple and Kodman used retarded readers of normal IQ who were 8–24 months retarded on the Wide Range Achievement Test, Walters and Doan used an IQ test and *one* subtest (comprehension) of another reading test to classify their subjects as advanced, average, and poor readers. Such differences in selection criteria make it extremely difficult to assess the reasons for conflicting results.

The hypothesis that a child's inclination to use visual rather than tactile imagery can influence his skill in reading was the basis for a study reported by Erickson (1969). Seventh-grade subjects were tested on their ability to form a correct visual image of a figure after being exposed to successive partial views of it. The failure of retarded readers on this task was attributed to their lack of "visual attitude." Unfortunately, Erickson presents no real evidence that the task used in this study is actually a valid measure of the construct he uses to explain his results.

Using a reversal of the normal procedure for selecting subjects, Alexander and Money (1965) studied reading achievement in children with known perceptual deficiencies. The subjects were girls with Turner's syndrome, a cytogenetic defect resulting in a form of "space-form blindness." These girls, who all showed defects in space-form perception and directional orientation, were essentially normal in reading skills. The authors concluded that if perceptual disabilities are involved in reading retardation, "they must be specifically related to the language function and its symbolic written representation rather than to general cognitional function" (p. 984). Results like these suggest that the relationship between reading achievement and perceptual functioning is the result of deficits in a specific subset of perceptual skills.

3. Conclusions

The relationship between perceptual functioning and reading ability is undoubtedly a complex one. There is evidence, however, that retarded readers do less well on "perceptual" tasks than do those who have attained normal reading skills. Although the empirical relationship between performance on these tasks and reading achievement may make them useful in predicting which children will have problems in reading, they do not provide much direction in the development of remedial techniques. For example, Skubic and Anderson (1970) concluded that the tests of perceptual-motor skills most strongly related to reading were those which depended highly on general integrative capacity and ability to understand the purposes of the task and engage in purposeful action. Other authors (Blank 1968; Bridger 1970) have shown that the actual cognitive deficits assessed by "perceptual" tasks are open to serious question. Thus it is unclear from these studies what a deficit on any given task actually means in terms of the specific abilities or behavior which need additional training in order to improve reading ability.

B. MEMORY FUNCTIONS

Most modern conceptions of memory functions include a distinction between long-term and short-term memory. Both have obvious importance for learning. Most of the work on memory functions in reading-disabled children has been concerned with their short-term memory abilities. An early review of psychological characteristics related to reading disability (Johnson 1957) emphasized that there was clear evidence for a relationship between a "short memory span" and reading retardation. Memory span has usually been measured by requiring the subject to recall lists of digits, letters, or other stimuli which are presented for short periods of time either visually or aurally.

Several recent studies have confirmed and extended the general finding that reading-disabled children do poorly on memory tasks when
compared to normal readers. Katz and Deutsch (1967) used a sample of
lower-class black children and found that poor readers performed poorly
on both visual and auditory memory span tasks. When memory skills
within the two modalities of presentation (visual or auditory) were compared, inconsistent results were obtained. The relative superiority of visual or auditory memory seemed to depend on the specific stimuli used.
Both good and poor readers remembered auditory materials better when
the stimuli were digits. However, when memory for words was tested
with the words being represented visually in picture form, the children
remembered the visual stimuli better.

One major problem with this study is that its results may not be applicable beyond the specific sample studied. Though it is certainly important to understand the psychological deficits associated with poor reading in all cultural and economic groups, there may be little comparability
of process deficits between groups (Senf & Feshbach 1970).

Two other studies (Kluever 1971; Senf & Freundl 1972) have shown
that poor readers, in comparison to control subjects, do progressively
worse on memory tasks as the material to be remembered becomes more
difficult. Kluever compared the performance of good and poor readers
on 16 different "memory" tests. Normal readers were generally superior
to retarded readers in memory performance and became progressively
better than poor readers as the material became more meaningful and
complex. The relative abilities of 9-year-old reading-disabled and normal
children to remember visually and aurally presented lists of digits were
studied by Senf and Freundl. Poor readers made more total errors on all
lists and did disproportionately worse as the length of lists was increased.
A careful analysis of error patterns also indicated that the reading-disabled children performed more erratically than the control subjects.
These results suggest that processes other than simple memory deficits
may contribute to the lower performance of poor readers on this kind of
task.

Although only a small sample of the available studies has been reviewed here, their results were consistent with the general finding that
reading-disabled children do poorly on short-term memory tasks when
compared to normal readers. Once again, however, the meaning of these
results is less than clear. In Kluever's (1971) study, for example, it was
emphasized that poor readers were particularly deficient on tasks involving complex and linguistically meaningful material. An analysis of the
functional requirements of these tasks suggests that they involve many
cognitive operations in addition to memory skills. The more complex

material may not have been discriminated or recognized as easily by the poor readers, so the tasks may be something other than simple tests of memory.

Recent work on the development of memory in children (Flavell 1970) has emphasized that performance on memory tasks is related significantly to more general cognitive abilities and motivational variables. Specifically, the ability and disposition to apply certain strategies like active rehearsal and "chunking" are seen as crucial to success on many kinds of short-term memory tasks. It is impossible to interpret differences on many memory span tasks because the poor performance may result from any one or a combination of deficits in memory subprocesses. Acquisition strategies, retention rate, and accuracy of retrieval are several of the separate functions involved in performance on memory tasks. Interpretation of memory deficits is also complicated by the particular susceptibility of performance on memory tasks to influence by factors like anxiety level, curiosity, and attention (Belmont & Butterfield 1969).

C. VERBAL ABILITIES

1. Verbal-Performance Discrepancies

A common finding in studies of reading-disabled children is that they show lower verbal than performance scores on intelligence tests which measure both kinds of skills (Heinicke 1972). In an early study using a clinical population, Rabinovitch et al. (1954) compared subjects diagnosed as "primary" reading retardates with children identified as being low in reading achievement because of emotional disturbance. These authors found that their "primary" group had an average verbal score 22.1 points below performance, while the discrepancy, in the same direction, for the other group was 8.8.

Many studies that have attempted to discover stable subtest patterns for retarded readers on tests of intelligence like the WISC have supported the idea that reading disability is associated with a verbal-performance discrepancy. A review of 20 studies of the intelligence test performance of retarded readers (Huelsman 1970) showed that about 60% of disabled readers have higher performance than verbal scores. The actual discrepancies between scores, however, were typically not as large as those reported by Rabinovitch (Rabinovitch et al. 1954) for his "primary" group.

In his own study of the problem, Huelsman found that 61% of his group of retarded readers had higher performance than verbal scores, while only 38% of normal readers had verbal-performance discrepancies in the same direction. In the same study, 20% of reading-disabled fourth graders had performance scores at least 15 points higher than their verbal scores.

These studies, although they provide important insight into general relationships between verbal skill and reading achievement, are only a small beginning. The verbal and performance measures are far too gross to lead to any clear conceptualizations of the way a child's disabilities interact with the process of learning to read. There is a crucial need to focus on more precisely defined linguistic skills in order to understand how they facilitate or impede learning and problem solving.

2. Specific Verbal Skills

A study of specific verbal labeling skills in retarded readers was reported by Blank, Weider, and Bridger (1968). They used 6-year-olds at the end of first grade, and contrasted the ability of good and poor readers to remember and match temporally presented patterns of flashing lights. It was reasoned that temporal patterns cannot be retained through the use of visual imagery, so the child is forced to use verbal symbols to help him remember the patterns. The results clearly showed that the poor readers were less effective than the good readers in remembering temporal patterns, while they had no particular difficulties with other patterns which were presented spatially. The authors concluded that the disabled readers were deficient in the use of symbolic mediation, which would affect their performance on a wide variety of learning tasks.

Four separate studies (Bartel, Grill, & Bartel 1973; Denner 1970; Guthrie 1973; Vogel 1974) have reported inconsistent results concerning the syntactic skills of poor readers. The ability to use syntax involves an awareness of the rules which govern the placement of words in sentences. In each of the studies cited here, "syntactic ability" was measured in a different manner. Two of the studies reported that poor readers were deficient in syntactic skills, while results from the other two indicated that they were not. Although the methodological differences in these studies are probably sufficient to account for the disparate results, it is interesting to note that the two studies which examined the pattern of errors made by good and poor readers were the ones which found no differences between them. In one of these latter reports, the reading-disabled children made more errors, but their percentage of syntactic errors was no higher than that of the normal children. On the other hand, the studies which found differences between the two reading groups used the total score on several different kinds of tests to assess syntactic skills. This pattern of results raises the possibility that poor readers may be deficient in various kinds of language performance but may be similar to normal readers in their basic language competencies.

A major step in the assessment of more specific verbal processes has been taken by Kirk and his colleagues in the development of the Illinois Test of Psycholinguistic Abilities (Kirk & Kirk 1971). This test is composed of 12 subtests which purportedly measure different aspects of verbal functioning. One fairly consistent finding emerging from research with the ITPA is the relationship between scores on subtests at the "automatic" level of functioning and reading achievement. The "automatic" and "representational" levels of the ITPA supposedly correspond to two general organizational levels of linguistic functioning. The "representational" level involves responses which are mediated by various intervening processes and which involve the construction of meaning. In contrast, the "automatic" level refers to responses which are more a product of integrated habit chains and less involved with higher-level cognitive processes.

Particular difficulties on tests at the automatic level were reported by Kass (1966) for retarded readers in the second, third, and fourth grades. Golden and Steiner (1969) also reported difficulties for second- and third-grade poor readers on subtests measuring sound blending, auditory sequential memory, and auditory closure, which are all at the automatic level of processing. Finally, Kirk and Kirk (1971) report a study by Macione (1969) in which poor readers were lower than normal readers on four subtests, all at the automatic level.

These results are interesting when viewed in the context of recent work on the role of automaticity in reading improvement (LaBerge & Samuels 1973). LaBerge and Samuels state that "it is this capability of automatic processing which we consider critical for successful operation of multi-component complex skills like reading" (p. 3). Fries (1962) has also referred to an early stage in reading in which "the responses to the visual patterns become habits so automatic that the graphic shapes themselves sink below the threshold of attention" (p. 132). In addition, difficulties in the establishment of fully automatized responses have been noted in "perceptually handicapped" children (Frostig 1972). Although it remains to be shown that these investigators are all expressing the same idea by the word "automatic," there is a common emphasis on the formation of integrated habit chains which occur rapidly and without investment of higher-level cognitive resources. In any event, this example illustrates the possible utility of more precisely described problem areas in the functioning of reading-disabled children.

D. INTERMODAL INTEGRATION AND EQUIVALENCE

1. Early Studies

One aspect of psychological functioning receiving increasing attention in the study of reading disabilities is the ability to integrate, associate, or establish equivalence between stimuli from different sensory modalities. Birch and Belmont (1964, 1965) were the first investigators to look at individual differences in the ability to integrate information from different sensory modalities. Because a whole series of studies by Birch and others has used more or less the same basic task, it will be described in some detail. The subject is first presented with an auditory sequence of taps which occur in various patterns. After each pattern is presented aurally, the subject is required to identify a series of dots which represent the same pattern visually. As Birch and Belmont have used it, the test is not strictly an intermodal task, as the subject is able to see the experimenter's pencil as it taps out the pattern.

In one of their first studies with the task, Birch and Belmont (1964) used 200 Scottish schoolchildren, aged 9 ½–10 ½, and found that scores on the audiovisual task were significantly related to reading achievement. In another study (Birch & Belmont 1965), the subjects were 220 elementary school children between the ages of 5 and 12. Except for the youngest and oldest children, audiovisual performance was significantly related to IQ. For this sample, audiovisual performance was most closely related to reading in the younger children. In neither of these studies did the authors employ statistics to assess the strength of the audiovisual task relationship to reading with the relationship between IQ and reading partialed out. Using better controls for IQ, Beery (1967) also found a significant relationship between reading level and ability to match auditory and visual patterns. Tasks using either an auditory or a visual standard discriminated between retarded and normal readers.

Because of conceptual ambiguities in the audiovisual task used by Birch, several other investigators (Rudnick, Sterritt, & Flax 1967; Sterritt & Rudnick 1966) used variants of it in studies of reading disability in third- and fourth-grade children. These subjects were given a pure auditory-visual task with the sound source hidden from the subject, a visual-visual pattern matching task, and the standard pencil tapping test. With fourth graders, multiple regression techniques showed the audiovisual task to be the only one that accounted for a significant portion of the reading score variance beyond that accounted for by mental age. When the same tasks were given to third graders, however, the auditory-visual and visual-visual tasks both related significantly to reading with IQ partialed out. The pencil tapping test did not predict significantly beyond intelligence level. The authors belive that these results show audiovisual integration to be more important in reading as the child becomes older, with visual perceptual processes coming to assume a less important role.

2. Alternate Interpretations

Blank and Bridger (1966, 1967) have challenged the idea that the results outlined above indicate retarded readers have a difficulty in intermodal integration at the perceptual level. They investigated the hypothesis that performance on the intermodal task varies with facility in using verbal labels as mediators of the transfer between temporal (auditory) and spatial (visual) tasks. A study with 9-year-old children demonstrated that retarded readers did less well in converting temporal to spatial patterns within the same sensory modality than a group of IQ-matched normal readers (Blank & Bridger 1966). There were no differences in the simple ability to perceive visually presented patterns of dots. However, the retarded readers were less able to report accurately the exact sequence and patterning of a series of flashing lights. Both normal and poor readers attempted to apply some sort of verbal labels to the sequences, but the poor readers did it less accurately.

In another set of studies (Blank et al. 1968) involving 6-year-olds at the end of first grade, essentially the same results were obtained. No differences emerged between retarded readers and normal children on- tasks that required the matching of spatial patterns, but when the sequences to be matched were temporal, the retarded readers did less well. Blank and Bridger interpret their findings as indicating that the difficulty experienced by the retarded readers on the intermodal matching task is due to complex conceptual inadequacies rather than differences in perceptual integration. It is the normal readers' ability to code abstract characteristics of the stimuli verbally that enables them to succeed at the task.

3. Theoretical Issues

The two series of studies just outlined raise important theoretical questions about the concept of intermodal integration in the study of reading disability. Is it a phenomenon dependent for its development on the growth of complex neurological connections and subject to disturbance at a neurological level? Or does it depend on the abstraction and utilization of essentially amodal, relational information by complex cognitive processes? There are theorists on both sides of the issue. Gibson (1969) has developed the hypothesis, consistent with her general theory of perceptual learning, that intermodal transfer is made possible by the abstraction from stimuli of distinctive features which are essentially amodal. These distinctive features do not depend on the particular mode of input for their meaning, and the information they contain is relational. On the other hand, Birch and Lefford (1963) have developed some ideas placing the ability to integrate stimuli from the various modalities within an evolutionary-genetic framework which suggests specific neurological development. It is likely that both neurological development and certain cognitive processes involved in abstraction and symbolization mediate the integration and association of material from different senses. It is not clear from the previously discussed research, however, which of these factors, or others that might be relevant, is most crucial to performance on the specific tasks which have been used to assess integrative ability.

4. Other Studies of Integrative Ability

In a complex and carefully designed series of experiments, Senf and his associates (Senf 1969; Senf & Feshbach 1970) have investigated further the relationship between reading achievement and the ability to integrate visual and auditory stimuli. Because this work helps further illustrate the complexities of interpretation in studies which investigate psychological deficits, it is considered here in some detail. Senf (1969) selected his population carefully. The experimental group was a clinical sample of 48 boys between 8 and 15 years of age who were functioning at least 1½ years below grade level in language or reading skills. The sample was screened for normal intelligence, adequate perceptual functioning, and lack of severe emotional problems. There was a control group matched on age and IQ. These subjects were given the Bisensory Memory Task under a variety of experimental conditions. On this task, three pairs of visually and aurally presented digits are given at either ½- or 2-second intervals. Each pair consists of one auditory and one visual stimulus presented simultaneously. The subjects are required to recall the stimuli either by modality of presentation or in pairs.

The most basic finding from three separate studies in the original monograph (Senf 1969) was that reading-disabled children were less able to recall the stimuli in pairs than were the normal control subjects. In a condition which involved a pretest induction to see the stimuli in audio-visual pairs, the normal children showed a developmental increase in the number of correctly recalled stimulus pairs, while children with learning disorders showed no such increase. Except for the youngest children, there were no consistent differences in the children's ability to recall the stimuli by modality.

The major interpretation which Senf (1969) makes of his data involves a possibly greater independence of memory traces in learning-disabled children for inputs from different sensory modalities. It is essentially an explanation which centers around deficits in the ability to integrate stimuli from different senses. Senf acknowledges that other explanations for these data are possible. The learning-disabled children may have been more anxious in the situation and thus less inclined to attempt the more difficult pair order of recall. Neufeldt (1966) has shown that retardates are less flexible in adopting new strategies to categorize material for recall on a dichotic listening task. It is possible, because of their similar history of failure, that reading-disabled children, like the retardates, may be less flexible in adopting new strategies for performance on the Bisensory Memory Task.

The difficulty in paired recall may also have resulted from an inability to control the focus of attention. The most powerful organizing feature of the stimuli was the modality in which they were presented—in 74% of all responses during a free-recall condition, the subjects organized their answers by sensory modality rather than recalling the stimuli in audiovisual pairs. In other words, when left to themselves, the subjects tended to recall the auditory stimuli in one group and the visual stimuli in another rather than recalling audiovisual pairs together. Thus the difficulty experienced by the learning-disabled children may have been in breaking up the dominant perceptual organization of the task.

Because the paired-recall deficit on the Bisensory Memory Task involves visual and auditory materials, it is easy to interpret a deficit in pairing skills as an inability to integrate stimuli from different sensory modalities. However, the poor performance of the reading-disabled subjects on this task might just as well be due to a basic lack of ability or inclination to pair *any* kind of simultaneously presented material. The research of Blank and Bridger (1966) indicates that some difficulties on intersensory integration tasks may be due to general cognitive difficulties in handling temporal sequences. Thus the poor performance of retarded readers may also be the result of general difficulties in ordering and sequencing complex stimuli.

Two more recent studies (Vande Voort & Senf 1973; Vande Voort, Senf, & Benton 1972) indicate that the problems experienced by poor readers are not unique to intermodal matching tasks, but also occur on a variety of tasks which require subjects to match stimuli within the same sensory modality. Deficits in decoding skills, short-term memory, and attention are all offered as explanations for the kinds of performance problems shown by retarded readers. The authors correctly point out that studies of integrative ability have not isolated the specific skills which underlie the failure of disabled readers to perform adequately on intermodal matching or memory tasks.

In research on normal psychological processes, this kind of extended discussion of questions about interpretation might be regarded as premature or superfluous. Difficulties take care of themselves as research on particular questions accumulates. However, in a field like learning-disability research, where findings may be translated into training programs which acquire a weight and inertia of their own (Bardon 1971), the tentative nature of most research conclusions must be clearly recognized.

E. LEARNING ABILITY

One aspect of the reading-disabled child's functioning which has received inadequate attention is his learning ability. If one defines learning as a relatively permanent change in behavior resulting from experience or practice, studies of learning ability may be differentiated from those in which already existing patterns of behavior are investigated. Reading-disabled children are identified by their failure on a very complex task which is performed in a relatively uncontrolled environment. Since there is good evidence that many simple learning tasks relate significantly to learning in school (Stevenson et al. 1968), the use of laboratory tasks in well-controlled situations may be one important way to gain better understanding of the specific variables which affect learning in reading-disabled children. The use of different tasks may also provide clues in identifying particular kinds of learning ability which are deficient in retarded readers.

1. Paired-Associate Learning

The paired-associate task has probably been used most often to study the learning performance of retarded readers. Otto (1961) investigated the abilities of good, average, and poor readers of normal intelligence in learning associations between geometric forms and nonsense syllables. Subjects were children in the second, fourth, and sixth grades, and confirmation of correct responses was given in three different ways. The three conditions involved presentation of the form "name" (*a*) aurally, (*b*) aurally and visually, and (*c*) aurally, visually, and kinesthetically. The poor readers took longer to learn the paired-associate list in every condition, with the differences being greater at the younger ages. There were, however, no differences between the three groups of readers when they were subsequently required to relearn the list. Once the list was learned, it was retained equally well by good and poor readers.

The relative efficiency of visual and aural learning in children with reading problems was investigated in research by Budoff and Quinlan (1964) and Estes and Huizinga (1974). Estes and Huizinga did not use a control group of normal readers, but they did specify the characteristics of their research population very carefully. The subjects, who varied from 8 to 12½ years old, were divided into groups and required to learn paired-associate lists which involved either simple words presented aurally or a picture and a word presented visually. For these subjects, learning occurred more rapidly in the visual mode.

In contrast to these results, Budoff and Quinlan (1964) found that second-grade good and poor readers both learned better when paired-associate lists of simple words were presented aurally. However, the visually presented list in this study was slightly different from that used by Estes and Huizinga (1974). Whereas these latter investigators required their subjects to learn associations between pictures and simple words, the visually presented paired-associate lists used by Budoff and Quinlan were made up of simple words only. The differences in relative efficiency between visual and aural learning found in these two studies are very likely the result of specific differences in the stimulus materials used. Studies with normal children also show that findings of greater efficiency in aural than visual learning or vice versa depend on whether the visual stimuli are words or pictures (Hill & Hecker 1966; Shapiro 1966).

2. Other Kinds of Learning Tasks

In addition to the ability to learn paired associates, other kinds of learning studied in retarded readers include discrimination, serial, and symbolic learning. Whipple and Kodman (1969) assessed the relative abilities of good and poor readers to learn discriminations under two different conditions. They employed a two-choice discrimination task, with the stimuli to be discriminated presented either simultaneously or in sequence. Reading-disabled children learned more slowly in both cases and were more significantly influenced by the complexity of the task than were normal readers.

The serial learning abilities of good and poor readers were studied by Katz and Deutsch (1964). Lower-class black children in the first, third, and fifth grades were asked to learn eight-item lists of visually presented pictures, aurally presented words, or combinations of pictures and words. Although the different reading groups did equally well on the visual materials, the poor readers, especially in the first grade, learned the aurally presented list more slowly. Katz and Deutsch interpreted their results to mean that deficient auditory learning processes were an important cause of reading failure. As mentioned earlier, however, the unique characteristics of the sample in this investigation make it difficult to generalize these results to other groups of poor readers.

The major conclusion from two separate studies using a symbolic learning task was that additional incentives or tangible rewards may be particularly helpful in increasing learning performance in reading-disabled children (Walters & Doan 1962; Walters & Kosowski 1963). In both of these studies, retarded and normal readers were divided into two groups. One group of children received rewards for correct choices, while the other did not. The retarded readers in both conditions learned the correct responses more slowly than the normal readers. However, the performance of retarded readers was more sensitive to the presence of tangible rewards. Their scores improved more when rewards were given, and this effect was more pronounced as task difficulty was increased. These results suggest that changes in the reward structure of the classroom may be an important source of help to some reading-disabled children.

3. Qualitative versus Quantitative Differences

The preceding discussion has emphasized that reading-disabled children learn less rapidly than normal children on a variety of experimental tasks. Do these children simply learn more slowly, or do they learn differently than normal readers? In an attempt to answer this question, Camp (1973) studied the learning performance of severely retarded readers who were between the ages of 8 and 18. The children were started at different levels within a highly structured reading program designed to teach single words and paragraph reading. They were tutored from one to five times weekly and given token rewards for correct responses. The children moved through a series of lessons as they learned the new words in each lesson to the required level of accuracy. Response records were kept for each child, and acquisition curves were prepared which plotted cumulative errors in the vocabulary and paragraph-reading parts of each lesson against the total number of lessons completed. The major result, which is apparent from figure 1, is that the learning curves of all the children had very similar shapes.

A heterogeneous collection of retarded readers had been expected to produce learning curves with different shapes. The differently shaped curves would have reflected the aberrant learning processes of children who failed in reading for different reasons. The similarly shaped curves, which differed only in the rates of learning they represented, led Camp to conclude that there were no important differences in the learning processes of the children in her group.

The major problem in Camp's (1973) research, which is also found in other work on the learning performance of reading-disabled children, is that the measures used are far too gross to be sensitive to individual differences in learning processes. The curves she obtained represent cumulative performance in learning a wide variety of words and different word classes. However, there might be children with particular difficulties in learning abstract words, or others who have idiosyncratic deficiencies in learning words with certain beginning or ending letters or letter combinations. These qualitative differences in performance would be obscured by the inclusion of all types of stimuli within one category. A helpful addition to this study would have been an examination to see if any of the children had particular difficulties with certain kinds of words.

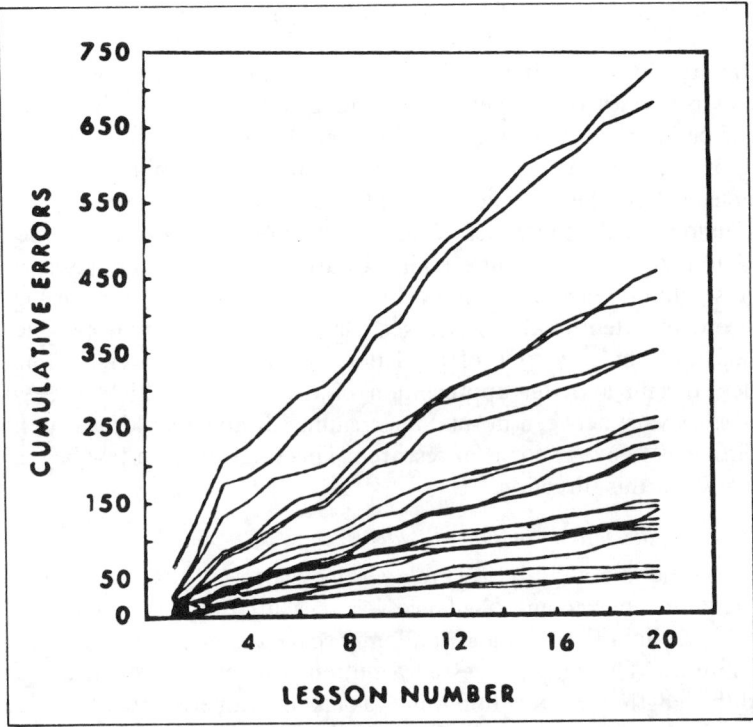

FIGURE 1.—Cumulative Error curves for children receiving lessons 1–20 (Camp 1973, p. 68).

General models for the kind of analysis of learning performance which is required in studies of reading-disabled children are provided in the work of McGuire (1961) and Zeaman and House (1963). McGuire's model of paired-associate learning, for example, indicates that failure to learn may be related to either attentional or associative problems. This kind of analysis is important because development of effective remedial approaches depends on specific knowledge of the psychological processes and task variables which contribute to performance differences, rather than the simple demonstration that such differences exist.

F. ATTENTION

Children who fail to learn normally in the classroom are often described as having problems in attention. In fact, one of the earliest constellations of traits associated with learning problems, the "Strauss syndrome" (Strauss & Lehtinen 1947), identified inattention as a central difficulty of the learning-disabled child. Although research on the attentional processes of "hyperactive" and generally defined learning-disabled children has expanded rapidly, there has been much less investigation of attention in the newer research on reading disability. Attentional problems have been typically employed as post hoc explanations of anomalous results in studies of other psychological functions. While it is undoubtedly true that one's ability to attend to a task and its requirements will influence performance in many different situations, using the concept of attentional deficit as a "last resort" explanation which is called upon only in time of need does not increase understanding. In order to gain a better appreciation of the ways in which attentional processes vary between normal and reading-disabled children, attention itself needs to be the focus of research. There have been a few beginning attempts in this direction.

1. Attentional Deficits in Poor Readers

Noland and Schuldt (1971) related one aspect of attention, vigilance, to reading achievement. Vigilance was measured by a simple apparatus in which a light flashed on at randomly spaced intervals over a period of 30 minutes. The subject pressed a button whenever the light came on, and the length of his reaction time was taken as an estimate of his degree of vigilance. The reading-disabled children detected significantly fewer of the light stimuli than the control group, and Noland concluded that they were deficient in the ability to sustain attention to a task.

As part of their large-scale investigation of the psychological correlates of reading disability in lower-class black children, Katz and Deutsch (1967) used two tasks which were supposed to measure different aspects of attention. Results from one task, the Bi-modal Reaction Time test, were interpreted to mean that poor readers had a special difficulty in shifting attention between auditory and visual modalities. While all subjects had longer response times to stimuli which were preceded by stimuli in a different modality, the retarded readers had particular difficulties in this condition. There were also suggestions from this study that retarded readers might be uneven in their vigilance to auditory and visual materials.

In another study, attention was measured by direct observation of sixth-grade children in their classroom (Lahaderne 1968). A checklist was used to record attentive behaviors of the students in four different classrooms over a period of several months. The children were also given questionnaires to assess their attitudes toward school. There was no relation between attention paid in class and attitudes about school. However, with level of intelligence controlled, attention was significantly related to reading achievement. The fact that other forms of achievement were less strongly related to attention suggests that the ability or inclination to pay attention plays a particularly important role in learning a complex skill like reading.

Three short studies illustrate other ways in which the relationship between reading skill and attention has been studied. Attwell, Orpet, and Meyers (1967) used a nine-point scale in rating various behaviors of kindergarten children as they took a battery of tests. The measure of attention they used related significantly ($r = .43$) to reading comprehension scores of the same children in the fifth grade. Santostefano, Rutledge, and Randall (1965) reported some evidence that good readers are not as affected by distracting stimuli as poor readers. Finally, Maccoby (1967), as an addition to her general study of the development of selective listening abilities in children, tested good and poor readers on one of her complex listening tasks. She found no differences in selective listening ability between the two groups and suggested that measures which assess willingness to sustain attention for longer periods of time may show a relationship to reading achievement.

2. Conclusions

Even though the number of studies is small, it seems appropriate to conclude that children with reading problems may be differentiated from normal control children by tasks or indices designed to measure attention. However, there remain many open questions about the attentional deficits of retarded readers. Are children who fail to learn to read inattentive in all situations or only in some? Is their inattention the result of active or passive processes? What kinds of stimuli are particularly distracting to them? A study by Bryan (1974) showed that children in a learning-disabled class were inattentive in some situations and not in others, while Lasky and Tobin (1973) found that children with "suspected" disabilities were particularly distracted by linguistic stimuli in the environment. Although these studies did not use subjects who were defined formally as reading disabled, they suggest that the structure of attentional deficits in children with learning problems is complex. As researchers become better acquainted with the theoretical and empirical complexities involved in the construct of attention, one hopes that a more satisfying picture of attentional deficits and their consequences may be constructed.

IV. Implications for Research and Practice

This review has emphasized that recent research on the psychological functioning of reading-disabled children leaves us with many unanswered questions. We have much yet to learn about the specific kinds of processes which prevent children from learning normally. The task of making effective applications of research to practice is just beginning. On the other hand, the research of the past 15 years has made some very substantial contributions to the field of learning disabilities, and these contributions must be assimilated if further progress is to be made.

As in other areas of psychology, research and theory about learning disorders must respond to evidence that the variables leading to disability in learning are very complex. Terms like "verbal ability" or "perceptual functioning" are no longer useful in research and practice. These general terms must be broken down into more specific kinds of processes whose direct relationship to specified learning tasks may be studied and conceptualized more clearly. Instead of talking about the relation between perception and reading ability, for example, we need to identify the particular subsets of perceptual skills which are important to the reading process at different stages of learning.

Knowledge gained from past research can be used to ask more sophisticated questions about the variables that influence learning in disabled children. For example, hypotheses about the relative efficiency of aural or visual learning can be considered in light of what is known about the influence of certain content and procedural variables in the learning task. Those who work with learning-disabled children need to be made aware of the dangers in specifying the superiority of one kind of learning environment without understanding also the narrow range of conditions in which it may be superior.

Perhaps the strongest conclusion from the preceding review is that the reading-disabled population of children may be differentiated from those who learn normally on a broad variety of performance measures. Most studies also find a fairly large overlap between good and poor readers on the performance measures used. Both of these conditions point to the heterogeneity of the population under study.

Research methods for dealing with the problem of excessive heterogeneity in the reading-disabled population will be discussed later. For the practitioner, heterogeneity in research populations has prevented the discovery of knowledge which has direct treatment implications. In other words, past research does not provide sufficient knowledge to allow reliable classification of reading-disabled children into different treatment groups. The present situation requires that each child with learning problems be treated individually and not be placed prematurely into any ill-defined and poorly understood treatment categories. It is also clear that large investments of money and energy in the development of remedial programs which emphasize only one aspect of learning failure are inappropriate. If a school district or remedial clinic operates on the assumption that the problems of all reading-disabled children are similar, the chances that it will fail to meet the needs of a large majority of its clientele are very high.

The last 15 years of research on learning disabilities have also shown that many attempts to train "abilities" as a means to general improvement on tasks like reading may have been premature. Efforts to train certain perceptual or perceptual-motor abilities as a means to reading improvement may be taken as a case in point. These programs have assumed not only that the perceptual deficits were real and correctly identified, but also that ability training is more beneficial to reading than reading practice itself (Mann & Phillips 1967). The work reviewed in this chapter does not increase one's faith in our present skill in identifying "ability" deficits, and work on the efficacy of ability training is inconclusive at best (Hallahan & Cruickshank 1973). Even where reading improvement as the result of perceptual training is noted, it is not clear whether better perception leads to better reading, or whether improvement in other skills like attention and memory is involved (Chall 1970).

Our present knowledge of the psychological functions of learning-disabled children does not allow the translation of evidence for specific performance deficits into ability training programs at more than a very superficial level. Those who establish training programs for reading-disabled children that concentrate on one particular pattern of deficits should recognize the tentative nature of present research conclusions. All such programs need to be subject to very careful evaluative research. Others who have recognized the problems involved in using current techniques to construct training programs for particular abilities include Christopelos (1969), Dykstra (1967), Mann (1971), and Silberberg and Silberberg (1969).

The current status of knowledge does not provide a firm basis for the development of programs to intervene directly at the level of deficient processes or ability. It is nevertheless true that the research has shown the problems of learning-disabled children to be very real. There is a group of children who have special problems which prevent them from learning normally in the classroom. How may they be helped most effectively in the light of present knowledge?

Frostig (1972) has given one answer which seems responsive to the current level of knowledge about learning-disabled children. She states: "Although perceptual training may often need to be the focus of a development or remedial program, it cannot be divorced from training in language, sensory-motor functioning, higher thought processes, affective and social behavior, and integrative abilities. In addition it must be kept in mind that . . . training in memory and attention are of great importance, and that any technique which helps the child to direct his attention more appropriately is valuable" (p. 7). The program of instruction which she presents may employ perceptual materials as a content medium, but it also involves simple and explicit instruction in the kinds of general language and problem-solving skills that are necessary for school achievement.

The advantage of using normal curriculum in training academic skills has also been pointed out by Mann (1970). Programs which develop special tasks to train deficient abilities may actually be teaching skills irrelevant to reading. A more effective approach, in the light of present knowledge, would require instruction and practice in regular academic skills which is structured to compensate for or help strengthen suspected areas of deficit. Such an approach seems realistic at present because it does not depend too heavily on unproven assumptions about the importance of specific abilities for performance in school or the effectiveness of current diagnostic techniques in identifying which children are deficient in those abilities.

A major theoretical justification for research on the psychological functions of learning-disabled children involves the assumption that specific and identifiable disabilities are responsible for their failure to learn normally in the classroom. Associated with this assumption is the idea that instruction or training programs which are responsive to intraindividual differences in cognitive functioning will increase learning efficiency. Neither of these assumptions is supported unequivocally by the current state of knowledge in the study and remediation of learning disabilities. The value of a general theoretical orientation, however, cannot always be ascertained by examining a particular technology which is thought to be derived from it (Bortner 1971). It is possible that current problems of application in the field of learning disorders derive not from inadequate general theory but from inadequate technology. Since research can contribute to both theory and technology, it is important to consider ways in which the quality of research can be improved. We turn now to an examination of general research issues in the study of reading disabilities.

V. GENERAL RESEARCH ISSUES

In the research investigating psychological correlates of reading failure, it is possible to find specific weaknesses in almost any study one cares to examine closely. These weaknesses exist because certain practicalities involved in experimentation often require compromises which trade strength in one area for weakness in another. If the problems in studies of disordered learning were the result of carefully considered compromise, there would be less reason for concern about research progress than is presently manifest. The difficulties in much of the work which has just been reviewed, however, are the result of *general* conceptual and methodological problems which, because they are widespread have a significant limiting effect on research achievements. This section focuses on problems in three major areas: the methods by which subjects are selected and described, issues in the design and execution of experiments, and sources for new hypotheses in the study of reading failure.

A. SUBJECT SELECTION AND DESCRIPTION

One of the most serious problems in research on learning disabilities in children lies in the confusion and lack of consistency involved in the selection of subjects. The lack of clearly described procedures, along with a failure to consider the special effects which any given procedure may have on research outcome, makes it nearly impossible to integrate findings from different studies. There are at least four critical dimensions to the subject-selection problem.

1. Measurement of Reading Failure

The most basic consideration in the selection of subjects is the measurement of reading failure itself. How is reading disability operationally defined? The conceptual definition of reading disability usually describes it as a failure to learn to read despite normal intelligence and adequate instruction. Studies of reading failure have operationalized this definition by assuming adequate instruction and comparing intelligence and reading level. If the child's intelligence is in the normal range and he does not read close to grade level, he is said to have a reading disability. In addition to level of intelligence, most researchers also attempt to control for physical attributes (vision and hearing) and emotional factors which also may affect reading level. Problems in defining reading disability operationally result from difficulties in deciding on the level of deficit which can be called a disability, and from variation in the measures used to assess reading level.

Subjects are often selected for studies of learning disorders in reading because their reading grade level is behind their actual grade level by a specified number of years. Many investigators have used a discrepancy of 2 years to define the reading-disabled population, while others have used different figures depending on the age of the child. Another method often used to identify poor readers involves the use of deviation scores. A measure of reading achievement is given to a group of children, and those who score a certain number of standard deviations below the mean are arbitrarily designated as reading disabled. Both of these methods have specific consequences for the kinds of populations which are used in individual studies.

The use of a fixed grade-level discrepancy to define reading disability at different ages results in a progressively larger proportion of children in each succeeding grade level who are identified as failures. Data reported by Gates and MacGinitie (1965) indicate that, for a national sample of children, a 2-year discrepancy is found in 2% of third graders and 30% of ninth graders! Ullman (1969) suggests that even if a grade-levels-behind formula is adjusted for different age levels, the percentage of children identified at each grade level as reading disabled still fluctuates significantly. Thus there is danger that, at different age levels, the groups of children who are identified as having reading problems may be different from one another in many important respects.

The use of deviation scores to identify poor readers overcomes some of the problems which accompany the grade-level-discrepancy criterion, but it also creates others. Although the same proportion of problem readers will be identified at each age, the use of relative standards of achievement can lead to differences between studies in the actual level of achievement that is associated with reading failure. In a good school district and among children of upper socioeconomic status, the lowest 20% of readers may actually be reading at grade level. In conditions at the opposite extreme and at the same actual grade level, however, the same deviation score may indicate children who cannot read at all. This would result, of course, in very different behaviors being included under the same label, which might lead to different conclusions about the nature of reading disability in each case.

It is not possible at present to decide with certainty which of these methods, or others that might be discussed, is the best one to use in selecting research populations. However, it is important that researchers become acquainted with the consequences involved in choosing to select subjects by any given criteria. This kind of knowledge not only will be helpful in defining the limits of research but also should help investigators make clearer comparisons between studies.

Another area of concern in operationalizing the definition of reading disability involves differences in measures of reading skill. A study of retarded readers' ability to form concepts (Braun 1963) can be used to illustrate one of the main problems in this area. The subjects were divided into reading groups according to their performance on the comprehension section of the Gates Reading Survey. Performance on this test certainly involves more than simple reading skill, for the subject must be able to formulate and use the ideas present in the material to answer questions. Although it is reasonable to define useful reading skill in terms of the ability to comprehend written material, other research using a simple word-recognition or oral reading task to measure reading may have found a different relationship between "reading skill" and the ability to form concepts. A study by Barrett (1965), for example, found that certain measures of visual discrimination predicted reading ability less well when it was measured by paragraph reading than when word recognition skills were used as the criterion of reading achievement.

The range of indices used to assess reading skill is large. It varies from word recognition tasks to comprehensive tests which include measures of ability to identify the mood of a paragraph or story. Although there is some relation between these various measures of reading skill, it is not perfect and is often quite low. It is very difficult to interpret studies investigating similar problems but using different indices of reading ability because the different tests, measuring somewhat different skills, very likely identify different populations as reading disabled.

The specific problems involved in operationalizing reading disability by the use of different tests may be viewed more generally as an expression of a failure to conceptualize and classify *different* kinds of reading failure. If reading disability is recognized as a general term, and subclassifications are made on the basis of the kinds of errors in reading the child makes, then, instead of creating confusion, different kinds of tests may actually bring order to the study of reading failure. That is, tests of different reading skills may be the means by which discrete disability classes are distinguished. The establishment of such disability classes, if it were done within the context of a general theoretical orientation, would allow systematic study of more specific relationships between types of reading failure and various psychological processes. In addition, such a classification scheme would contribute significantly to the comparability of studies and, as a result, to orderly research progress.

2. Controls for General Intelligence

Since reading ability bears a strong positive relationship to IQ (Leton 1962), the isolation of a specific disability in reading, as distinguished from general intellectual impairment leading to poor reading, implies that level of intelligence must be controlled. However, this statement should be qualified. Rabinovitch (1959), for example, suggests that reading problems are related to a disorder of symbolic function, which implies some verbal disability. To control for intelligence with a purely verbal test would eliminate much of the variance in verbal skills which he sees as an underlying cause of reading failure. Also, if older subjects are used, their reading failure will certainly have depressed their general knowledge and ability to deal with the kinds of items on verbal intelligence tests. Control with a verbal measure would therefore eliminate the most severe cases from one's population, even though they might perform normally on measures of nonverbal skills. Investigators who ascribe a large role to verbal processes in reading failure often use the performance scale of a test like the Wechsler Intelligence Scale for Children (WISC) to identify poor readers with otherwise normal intellectual ability.

There is one major problem with this approach to controlling level of general intelligence. A failure to control verbal intelligence in studies of reading disability would seem to make inevitable the discovery of process deficits related to verbal skills. The possibility of obtaining a distorted view of the importance of verbal processes in reading problems is therefore present. On the other hand, if verbal IQ were used as the control instead of performance, subjects might be selected whose reading retardation was related to various kinds of perceptual-performance deficits.

Kinsbourne and Warrington (1963), in fact, have identified one group of reading-disabled individuals with normal verbal and low performance scores, and another group with normal performance and low verbal achievement. The difficulties of the former group were related to various perceptual problems, while those of the latter were demonstrated on various verbal learning tasks. There is no immediately apparent solution to this dilemma. It will most probably be resolved as one or another of these methods of control proves most fruitful in studying the major proportion of reading failures.

The problems in deciding whether to use the performance or verbal scales of the WISC to control for IQ is a specific instance of the more general problem related to the quality of intelligence measures used as controls. Studies that use a measure as good as the WISC are actually in the minority. Many studies use measures like the Porteous Maze Test or the Peabody Picture Vocabulary Test that measure a very narrowly defined range of intellectual functioning and abilities. It is possible that many studies of reading failure which use these kinds of measures to control for intelligence find performance deficits in poor readers that are supposedly unrelated to IQ simply because the range of behavior controlled by the measures is so narrow. Although the deficits may be real, they should not be given special status as specific disabilities simply because they are not related to some unreliable or narrowly defined intelligence measure. It is clear that the kind of measure one uses to control for general intelligence will have an important effect on the types of process deficits one identifies as belonging uniquely to disabled readers. This is another way of saying that the concept of "specific reading disability" is largely a psychometric creation.

The concept of specific disability arises because general intelligence, as measured by IQ tests, does not adequately assess potential for all kinds of learning or performance. Stevenson et al. (1968) have shown that measures of general intelligence, although they are related to performance on a broad variety of learning tasks, do not predict performance on each of them with equal effectiveness. If, as in much of the research on learning disabilities, the concept of general intelligence is reified so that it becomes an "entity" within the individual, awareness of the discrete abilities sampled by different tests is submerged and confusion results. Any ability which is not measured by a particular test is given status as a "special" disability.

Current approaches to the control of general intelligence in studies of reading disability are limited by our imperfect understanding of the range of cognitive processes contributing to intelligent behavior. We do not have a clear picture of the mental abilities involved in performance on the various kinds of intelligence measures. Ideally, the skills which are controlled in research on reading problems should be specified without reference to an "entity" like general intelligence, the meaning of which is imperfectly understood. Realistically, however, this kind of approach is very difficult at present. Perhaps the best one can do, given the current state of knowledge, is to be aware of the general issues involved in selecting a particular test to control for "general intelligence." More specific discussion of ways in which the concept of intelligence can lead to confusion in thinking about achievement differences can be found in Liverant (1960), Thorndike (1963), and Tuddenham (1963).

3. Clinical versus Nonclinical Populations

A third issue regarding the selection of subjects for research on reading disability is whether the disability should be investigated in clinical or "normal" populations. A clinical population is one in which the subjects have been referred for special treatment or remediation because of subnormal or abnormal performance. Research using children in this kind of population usually involves a comparison of their performance with that of "normal" children on some specified set of tasks. Another approach entails the selection of children from a defined group of classrooms or schools. These children are tested for reading ability, and, with some effort to exclude children of subnormal intelligence, those who do well in reading are compared against those who do poorly. There are fairly clear advantages and disadvantages for each method.

Children in a clinical sample, because they have been identified as a special population, may be influenced in their performance by the labels which are attached to them (Clausen 1967). This difficulty is not entirely alleviated by the classroom selection method because those who are identified as poor readers have probably also had a variety of stigmatizing experiences, although the effect may not be as severe as for a clinical sample. With clinical samples, it is very difficult to control background factors like classroom atmosphere or teaching style which may have effects on reading progress. The use of all the children in a classroom or school makes it easier to control these factors.

In order for research results to be generalized to populations larger than the specific sample from which they are obtained, subjects in the sample must not be systematically different from the general population. Because studies using nonclinical samples may easily select subjects randomly, it is fairly easy for them to meet the formal requirements for generalization of results. On the other hand, the kinds of difficulties present in a given clinical sample are often related to the program emphasis of the center to which they are referred and biases in the referring source (Goldfarb 1970). However, as long as these sources of bias are recognized, the uniqueness of any given sample may actually have positive effects for research in reading disability.

An important problem in research on learning disabilities is the heterogeneity of most subject populations. The study of psychological variables related to reading skills in a large, randomly selected population of children may provide some hints about general kinds of problems which are most often associated with reading failure. Because of the heterogeneity of the sample, however, it is much more difficult to investigate the specific relationships of any given variable or psychological process to reading failure. Thus one might select a clinical sample *because* the subjects in it had been previously identified as having similar kinds of problems. This would facilitate the further study of specific process differences both between reading-disabled and normal children and between different kinds of reading-disabled subjects. However, one would have to be very careful about generalizations made to larger populations.

One further argument that is often used to favor clinical samples recommends the study of severe instances of a problem in order to gain an understanding of processes which may not be shown as clearly in less severe cases. It is probably true that severe cases of reading disability are more likely to be found in clinical samples than in those where the subjects are selected by tests from a larger population functioning within normal limits. However, there is certainly no guarantee that the specific kinds of disability leading to severe reading retardation will be at all similar to those which produce lesser degrees of failure. Thus, it would be incorrect to assume that study of severe cases of reading disability will lead to information which may be generalized to less retarded populations.

4. Age Differences

Another important variable in subject selection is age. Studies using subjects at one age may identify deficits associated with reading disability which are different from those found at other ages. A few developmental studies have shown that poor reading achievement tends to be related to different skills at different ages (Reed 1968; Sabatino & Hayden 1970). After reviewing a broad spectrum of research on reading retardation, Benton (1962) concluded that perceptual difficulties may be related to transient reading difficulty at younger ages, while older disabled readers have more complex conceptual and verbal difficulties. A variety of authors (Beery 1967; Katz & Deutsch 1967; Rudnick et al. 1967) have produced evidence which is taken to indicate that auditory and visual-auditory integration processes become particularly important for reading achievement sometime in the middle elementary school years, while strictly visual processes decline in importance. Thus, although any conclusions about underlying process deficits must remain tenuous, there is evidence that the tasks which differentiate between normal and retarded readers are different at different ages.

How are age differences in the variables associated with reading failure to be interpreted? One alternative is suggested by Blank and Bridger (1966). They favor a developmental interpretation of reading disability and point to the fact that almost all tasks that differentiate good and poor readers are sensitive to developmental level. Thus poor readers simply develop more slowly in a variety of areas than do normal readers. They can be identified at a given age by their failure on any task "which requires sustained concentration, but which has not reached its asymptote in development" (p. 846). The same children will fail on different tasks at different ages, rather than different children failing at various stages of reading because of specific and discrete disabilities.

On the other hand, it is possible that specific kinds of disability interact with stage of reading so that a child can learn one set of reading skills easily and yet have difficulty on other reading tasks that require abilities in which he is weak. For example, some poor readers may reach a normal asymptote on certain kinds of tasks related to beginning reading, yet never achieve normal levels in complex skills required for advanced reading. Other children might be identified as poor beginning readers because of deficits in visual skills which are only gradually overcome. These same children could progress rapidly at later stages of reading so that they would no longer be classified as reading disabled.

A clearer understanding of age-related changes in the factors associated with reading problems can best be attained through the use of developmental paradigms in reading-disability research. Studies of the developmental course of disabilities can help us understand which deficits are most basic and which ones are related to one another in the development of the child (Senf & Feshbach 1970).

Both longitudinal studies, which chart the development of a single sample of children through time, and cross-sectional designs, which compare the performance of different age groups at one point in time, would contribute significantly to a more comprehensive understanding of deficiencies associated with reading failure. One clear advantage of longitudinal studies would be their ability to investigate whether there are different children in the retarded reading groups at different ages. If there are, then reading disability at any given age would appear to be a function of a variety of specific disabilities which are unrelated to one another in development. If the same children are identified as reading failures at different ages, and these children seem to have different deficits at different ages, then their difficulties may be traced to some basic developmental abnormality which affects performance on a variety of tasks at different ages (Blank & Bridger 1966).

B. PROBLEMS OF EXPERIMENTAL DESIGN AND INTERPRETATION

In addition to very complex problems in the selection and description of subjects, researchers in the field of learning disabilities also face challenges in the area of experimental design and interpretation. The review of research in this chapter leads one to be wary of simple correlational approaches to the study of psychological factors involved in reading disability. Studies that simply compare the performance of good and poor readers on certain tasks have demonstrated that reading disability is associated with a broad range of performance deficits. However, the interpretation of these performance deficiencies is sufficiently unclear that their meaning for remedial procedures is difficult to ascertain.

1. Psychological Processes

In the earlier discussion of research goals, it was suggested that knowledge of the psychological processes involved in deficient performance can lead directly to correct remedial procedures. By studying dynamic processes rather than the static products of psychometric tests, investigators achieve better insight about how to affect performance. The fact that a child fails a test tells nothing about why he failed it or how to improve his performance. On the other hand, if differences in performance are observed as the result of experimental manipulations, the experimenter has provided a demonstration both "of what to do and how to do it" (Thorndike 1963, p. 21).

The paradigm seen to be most useful in studying the process deficits of poor readers is one in which the effects on performance of certain variables are observed. Psychological processes are best studied as changes in performance resulting from manipulation of independent variables. The emphasis in studies of psychological processes, then, is not on the association between reading disability and performance deficits per se, but rather on the ways in which reading-disabled subjects respond to variables which affect the behavior or psychological functioning of normal children.

2. Construct Validity

Researchers in the field of learning disabilities have suggested many different concepts to account for the performance deficits of children who learn slowly. A variety of specific "perceptual" problems, difficulties in "integrative" ability, and deficiencies in "memory" processes have all been identified as traits of poor readers. When given the status of traits, these constructs are assumed to represent sufficient and accurate descriptions of underlying disabilities which prevent reading-disabled children from learning normally in a variety of situations. However, when test scores or performance is interpreted as a measure of hypothetical attributes of the individual, issues of construct validity are involved (Campbell 1960).

As difficult as they are to develop, well-formulated constructs are essential to the creation of useful knowledge about the problems of disabled readers. The crucial link between data from the laboratory or experiment and its useful application in the field must be clearly described and well-understood constructs. "Constructs, because they may be imbedded in theory and have application to broader areas of psychological functioning, are necessary if one is to develop a clear view of expected behavior under a broad variety of circumstances" (Cronbach & Meehl 1955, p. 290). In other words, constructs are the medium by which researchers communicate their message to teachers and clinicians.

Unfortunately, most learning-disability researchers have relied on their own subjective analysis of what a given test measures in developing their concepts of disability. Many have committed the "stimulus error," which involves the mistake of identifying test responses and the processes they supposedly measure with the names of the tests which elicit and measure them. For example, the Bender Motor Gestalt Test (Bender 1938) is commonly assumed to measure "perceptual-motor coordination." It is a paper-and-pencil test. Fleishman (1967), who has studied eye-hand coordination in normal subjects, suggests that one's ability on this dimension depends strongly on how it is measured. An apparatus test provides a different measure than does a paper-and-pencil test. How much of the Bender's relationship to school achievement depends on the method of measurement, and how much on the specific perceptual motor abilities it supposedly measures?

Stevenson, Friedrichs, and Simpson (1970) have pointed out that "the discussion of children's learning is dependent upon an understanding of the processes underlying performance on a task, rather than upon an analysis of the structure of the task" (p. 636). Too often in the study of learning problems, poor performance on a measure of "perception" or "short-term memory" is taken to mean that a child needs training in perceptual development or memory skills before he can function on tasks requiring higher-level processes. Such training is often based on oversimplified ideas of what the tests in question really measure and disregards many other factors which might determine performance on any given test. Although there are no shortcuts to the clarification of relationships between experimental measures and the concepts they are supposed to represent, effort in this direction is vital to more productive research on the problems of children who cannot read.

There are many ways to approach the issue of construct validity. Mann and Phillips (1967) suggest that the validity of the psychometric instruments used to identify disabilities needs to be formally evaluated. Another approach, which avoids the arduous task of validating large numbers of recently developed tests, involves the use of well-established experimental paradigms in reading-disability research. Just as the meaning of test scores is made clearer by formal validation procedures, so is the theoretical base for interpreting performance within experimental paradigms made stronger by their repeated use. For example, the use of procedures which have been employed repeatedly to study normal development would certainly enable more meaningful interpretations of results than if a new test or experimental procedure were developed to study the same phenomena.

A third way to approach the issue of construct validity is through the use of multiple operationalism. This is a simple concept, involving the main stipulation that one should attempt to show the independence of one's measurements from a specific method of measurement or set of materials. Practically all studies of learning disability have employed a single measure of the construct under study. However, when only one operation is used to define a construct, it is difficult to determine whether individual differences measured by the operation are due to "real" trait differences, or whether they are the result of specific responses to a certain kind of task. Campbell and Fiske (1959) have discussed the necessity of defining one's concepts in more than one way in order to insure that psychological processes are defined by something more than a specific measurement method.

The best effects of a multiple-operational approach are not achieved by many different researchers studying similar problems in slightly different ways, for too many variables are left uncontrolled. The greatest fruits of this approach will come as more studies are designed which use multiple measures in systematic ways on carefully selected and controlled populations.

3. Need for Systematic Research Programs

In addition to the considerations outlined above, deficiencies in the constructs employed by learning-disability researchers are also related to a lack of systematic research programs in the field. Once an experimental effect has been demonstrated, it is almost always necessary to conduct further investigations in order to identify which aspects of the experimental treatment are most essential to the effect. This is the normal course of science (Campbell & Stanley 1963).

Unfortunately, research in the field of learning disabilities has not typically followed the orderly "course of science" but has consisted of isolated experiments which receive no follow-up to clarify and refine explanatory hypotheses. Since the number of rival hypotheses by which results can be explained is not reduced systematically through subsequent research, interpretations of the differences between good and poor readers remain vague and tenuous.

Within the field of learning disabilities, the research of Senf and his associates (Senf 1969; Senf & Feshbach 1970; Senf & Freundl 1971) provides a good example of the kind of research program recommended here. Senf was able to eliminate several different explanations for his results on the role of attention and memory processes in reading failure by systematically varying experimental conditions. Such research is difficult because it requires careful analysis of a variety of explanatory hypotheses as well as a substantial investment of time and resources. It is, however, one very important means by which research can begin to establish more clearly confirmed constructs in theories of reading disability.

4. Heterogeneity of Research Populations

The most pressing problem for research on learning and reading disabilities is that of sample definition. Intimately connected to the way in which past research has typically defined its sample population is the problem of heterogeneity. Because the variety of problems experienced by children assigned the "reading-disabled" label is so great, research has been able to find very few correlates of membership in this class which can be used to understand deviant processes and establish remedial procedures. The findings of many studies are weakened by the fact that the disabled sample is heterogeneous with regard to the dependent variable under study, so that only low-order relationships are established.

In their treatment of general issues in the classification of deviant populations, Zigler and Phillips (1961) point out that complaints about the heterogeneity of sample populations are really pleas for the establishment of new classificatory principles. If the established way of classifying subjects in studies of reading disability has not led to the discovery of useful class correlates, then perhaps it is time to develop new classification schema.

There are two general problems involved in the use of the term "reading disabled" to describe research populations. It is, first of all, an unreliable way to classify subjects. The definition of reading disability has changed over time, it varies from area to area within the United States and throughout the world, and it lacks clear and explicit class principles. This unreliability of classification makes it difficult to compare results from one study to another. Differences in results can always be ascribed to differences in the populations under study.

The second difficulty involved in defining research populations simply as reading disabled is related to the basic rationale by which classification is justified. People or things are usually classified in the hope of attaining certain goals. An appropriate goal in the classification of children with reading problems is to identify groups who have similar process deficiencies and to whom certain remedial procedures may commonly be applied. The problem at present is that "reading disability," the predictor class used in most recent research, is at a more general conceptual level than the variables it is supposed to predict (Senf 1974). There is little hope of finding remedial procedures or process deficits applicable to all poor readers simply because the range of individual variation within the class is too great.

What is needed, then, are ways to classify children with learning problems so that the classes formed are more homogeneous with regard to the variables one desires to predict. Classification principles must be made not only more specific but also more explicit so that children may be reliably assigned to various classes. Senf (1974) has reported beginning attempts in the formation of a classification scheme useful for research in the general area of learning disabilities. In this work, the use of both theory and statistical procedures is involved in order to generate classes whose validity may be assessed by further empirical research.

Related to the general procedure of identifying subgroups within a given sample is the practice of analyzing data for individuals rather than groups. This represents another approach to the problem of heterogeneity. Although such an approach presents unique methodological problems (Jensen 1967), they are not insurmountable. In certain cases, analyzing the performance of individuals rather than pooling it for group analysis has led to important new insights about individual differences in performance (Trabasso & Bower 1968; Zeiler 1967).

In studies of learning disability, the data are typically reported as average differences between normal and disabled groups. If the substance of these differences is being contributed by only a few individuals in the population, or if the averaged performance figures are typical of only a minority of subjects, then the possibility of misinterpretation is strong. For example, Huelsman (1970) analyzed the WISC subtest patterns of a large number of fourth-grade good and poor readers. As a group, poor readers had low scores on the information, arithmetic, and coding subtests. However, examination of individual protocols showed that *none* of the poor readers had significantly low scores in all three areas. Only about 6% had low scores in two areas, and 64% were not significantly deficient in any of the areas. These results not only underline the heterogeneity of the reading-disabled group, but they also show that averaged performance figures may not be accurate when used to describe the abilities of individual children. As a means to clearer assessment of individual differences among learning-disabled children, careful examination of individual response styles may be helpful.

5. Establishing Proper Controls

A basic problem in all types of experimentation is that of control. In reading-disability research, as in all work which attempts to understand the psychological differences involved in deviant functioning, two types of control are important. It is first important to have the control of "normal" functioning. One may demonstrate that certain variables have specified effects on the task performance of reading-disabled children, but unless the effects can be contrasted with those occurring in a normal group of subjects, there is no evidence that they have any particular association to reading failure. In other words, to have a sound base for attributing poor reading to a particular mode of psychological functioning, one must demonstrate that that mode is not characteristic of those who read well.

Most recent studies of reading disability have employed control groups in the sense that they have contrasted the performance of good and poor readers on a given test. However, many of these studies are subject to multiple interpretations because they fail to equate the comparison groups on important individual difference variables other than those under direct investigation. This is the second type of control, and its objective is to reduce the number of plausible rival hypotheses in explaining the data.

An important factor which often affects the study of deviant groups is the tendency of investigators to see these groups only in terms of their main deviant characteristic. In the study of mental retardation, for example, mentally retarded subjects are often seen only in terms of their lower intellectual level, and other social and personality factors are not given proper attention. Many performance differences between mentally retarded and normal subjects which were previously thought to be the result of dissimilar cognitive processes, may be explained equally well in terms of personality and motivational differences between the groups (Zigler 1967, 1969). Many of the differences between good and poor readers which have been demonstrated in various task settings may also prove to be the result of emotional-motivational factors that are secondary to the reading disability.

Recent work on the effects of anxiety level will be taken as a case in point. Both Feldhusen and Klausmeier (1962) and Hill and Sarason (1966) have demonstrated that, with level of intelligence controlled, measured anxiety is inversely related to reading ability by the fifth and sixth years of school. In the Hill and Sarason study, children who went from high to low anxiety between first and fifth grade achieved a mean difference of 18.7 months in reading level over those who went from low to high anxiety in the same period. It is not important to the present discussion whether anxiety was a response to reading failure or vice versa. What is important is the empirical finding that poor readers were more anxious on the measures used.

Using very similar measures of anxiety, Stevenson and Odom (1965) found that anxious subjects did more poorly on several different kinds of experimental learning tasks, and Sieber, Kameya, and Paulson (1970) found that anxiety was related negatively to performance on a short-term memory task. These findings point to the twin conclusions that (*a*) samples of reading-disabled children may be more anxious than normal control subjects, and (*b*) many performance deficits may be more closely associated with level of anxiety than they are with the cognitive disabilities supposedly underlying reading failure.

Research on the role of anxiety in learning also indicates that high anxiety may be more strongly related to deficiencies on verbal than on other kinds of tasks, and it may affect the performance of boys more than girls. These findings are interesting in view of the facts that verbal deficiencies are commonly found in learning-disabled children and that more boys than girls are referred with these problems.

There are many other noncognitive variables which may covary with reading disability and affect performance on experimental tasks. It is crucial that more attention be paid to these kinds of variables in controlling differences between normal and reading-disabled groups. In addition to providing more easily interpreted results, such an approach might provide important information about subtle interactions between cognitive and emotional factors in reading failure.

C. SOURCES OF RESEARCH HYPOTHESES

In selecting a specific problem or approach to the study of reading disability, one may gather ideas from a wide range of ongoing research.

1. Research on Process in Normal Reading

One area that seems immediately important as a source of ideas about psychological processes which may be implicated in reading failure is the study of reading itself.

LaBerge and Samuels (1973), for example, have presented a complex model of the reading process which describes the role of several important variables. Recent studies of attentional processes (Egeth & Bevan 1973; Moray 1970) have shown that the human organism has a limited capacity to process different kinds of information at the same time. It is also true, however, that stimuli which are overlearned or have special significance to the observer may be processed without attention being focused on them. Recognizing that reading is a complex process requiring the simultaneous utilization of many different kinds of information, LaBerge and Samuels have attempted to specify the way in which automatic functioning reduces the load on attention so that efficient reading results. Many different psychological variables are important in this system, but the most basic one is the ability to acquire automatic responses to stimuli at several different levels. There are individual differences in this ability which may interact with other factors involved in learning to read.

One positive feature of LaBerge and Samuels's work is their attempt to develop measures of the psychological processes they describe. If their model is a good description of variables important to the development of normal reading skills, then the measures which they use to define their variables have obvious utility for the study of process deficits in reading-disabled children. Furthermore, if process deficits are specified within a clearly defined model of the development of reading skill, the model can also provide a rich source of ideas for remedial procedures. The recent work of Gibson and her associates (Gibson 1965, 1973) further underlines the fact that research on reading in normal children can make valuable contributions to both methodology and theory in the study of reading disabilities.

2. Clinical Studies

Reading failure has been a clinical problem for many years, and large numbers of children with reading problems have been tested and ob-

served by clinical psychologists and psychiatrists. While it is often difficult to interpret the significance of clinical observations because of the
uncontrolled conditions under which they are usually made, clinical material can serve as a rich source of ideas for those attempting to make
more systematic and controlled observations. Because they start with the
child himself, clinical observations may point to problems of central
importance which are missed by more rigid research approaches that
operate within a specific theoretical or methodological bias.

One interpretation of reading failure which has been receiving increased emphasis is that generated by the clinical work of such investigators as Critchley (1970) and Rabinovitch (1968). These workers have
identified a certain pattern of deficits which they believe to be centrally
important in reading failure. Critchley states that "within the heterogeneous community of poor readers there exists a syndrome comprising a
specific difficulty in learning the conventional meaning of verbal symbols, and also in correlating sound with symbol in appropriate fashion"
(p. 24).

Rabinovitch and Ingram (1962) describe the "process" deficits associated with the syndrome in this way: "Analysis of the child's reading
performance indicates difficulties in both visual and auditory areas, and
directionality also tends to be impaired. Visual recognition and discrimination on a perceptual level are intact, but letter forms and combinations
cannot be translated into meaningful concepts. In a similar way in the
auditory sphere, differences in vowel sounds are appreciated when presented orally, but the sounds cannot be translated into their letter symbols. . . . The difficulty then, is in symbolization in both visual and
auditory fields" (p. 435). Rabinovitch (1968) suggests that the problems
of reading-disabled children are related to general language and conceptual disabilities which affect performance in areas other than reading.
They have difficulty in translating orientational and perceptual concepts
into symbols, their syntax is often poor, and their visual and auditory
memory processes are impaired.

These descriptions of the cognitive deficits involved in reading disability have weight and significance because they are the product of close
observation of many cases extending over a long period. However, a
major problem with these approaches, from the present point of view, is
that they define the disability most clearly in terms of the reading task
itself. Deficits in areas like visual memory are inferred from failure on
parts of the reading task which are assumed to require certain abilities.
Difficulties in the use of single tasks to identify specific ability deficits
have already been discussed. When an extremely complex task such as
reading is used to identify ability deficits, difficulties of interpretation
are greatly compounded by the very complexity of the task.

In addition, clinical descriptions of ability deficits associated with reading failure are formulated in terms that are too general. Boder (1968), for example, discusses "phonetic ability" as though it were a primary and unitary cognitive dimension. One result of most recent research on cognitive functioning is that variables like visual and auditory memory, or the ability to use verbal symbols, cannot be described as unitary functions. There are a variety of subprocesses which are important to performance in each area.

Critchley (1968) has pointed out the critical need to define more clearly the parameters associated with the kind of reading failure described in his work. One need particularly acute at present involves the development of studies directed toward specification of the various psychological processes that may underlie the more globally described clinical deficits.

3. Research on Normal Development

One way to avoid misleading conclusions about which psychological processes or functions are implicated when a child fails a task is to understand which psychological mechanisms are important to normal functioning on the task. Learning-disability research has paid insufficient attention to recent advances in the study of cognition and learning in children. In the face of this research, many of the concepts and procedures used to study learning disorders appear to be simply out of date. Research on disordered learning has followed too closely the thinking within its own tradition and thus has failed to utilize effectively the burgeoning research in the study of normal development.

Although much of developmental research has the same atheoretical, task-oriented flavor that has already been described in this review, there are segments of it which have some theoretical sophistication and allow the kind of systematic, variable-oriented study which was discussed earlier. The use of research paradigms that have theoretical descriptions or models of performance associated with them would certainly help foster more systematic study and might also make the knowledge contributed by learning-disability research more cumulative.

Research on normal psychological functioning can also help those studying learning disorders appreciate more fully the complexity of the psychological functions they are investigating. It is clear from research on attention, for example, that failure on one kind of task supposedly measuring attentional processes does not mean the child has a general attentional deficit. Moray (1970) has identified seven different names for attention and indicates that tasks measuring several of them have very low relationships to one another. Research on perceptual development points to a much more complicated relationship between tactual and visual perception than is currently espoused by many learning-disability theorists (Pick, Pick, & Klein 1967). In addition, Gibson's (1969) theory of perceptual learning indicates that a broad variety of cognitive processes are involved in perceptual functioning.

Finally, recent research in child development has enriched our understanding of the interrelatedness of various cognitive processes at many different levels. Much of the newer work has come to view the functioning of specific processes as embedded in and influenced by general cognitive development. Norman's (1969) view that no psychological process can be studied in isolation is supported by the work of Flavell (1970) and others (Belmont & Butterfield 1969; Hagen 1971) on the development of memory. These authors have come to view memory functioning as something like "applied cognition" (Flavell 1971). The use of certain strategies and other active problem-solving techniques is seen as crucial to performance on many kinds of memory tasks. In view of this work, low performance on a given task must be viewed in the broader context of a child's ability to adapt his total resources to the requirements of the task rather than as indicating a deficit in some specific psychological process.

VI. Concluding Remarks

This review has raised and explored a number of the most important issues involved in studying children with reading disabilities. In viewing the research, it is important to maintain a skeptical attitude without being unduly pessimistic. Certainly the research has serious problems in design and execution, but it also has led to the accumulation of knowledge that can lead to better work in the future.

A critical examination of past efforts to study the problem of disordered learning is necessary in order to understand the limitations of present knowledge. A certain humility in those who work with learning-disabled children is required in order that the potential for positive achievement in the future is not destroyed by current failures to meet unrealistic expectations. At the same time that it makes us aware of current limitations, a skeptical look at previous research provides a way to break with tradition in order that these limitations may be overcome. This chapter has considered a number of the many possible research emphases that may bring more order and coherence to the study of learning failure in children.

A general theme emerging from the discussion of many separate issues emphasizes the advantages which accrue from an awareness of the range of choices available in the solution of any particular problem. Any given choice has certain consequences for experimental results, and the range of alternatives and their sequelae needs to be better understood. Although specific answers to the various methodological questions raised in this review are not often available, an awareness of alternatives is important so that the selection of a given method is a matter of conscious choice rather than unreasoned necessity.

The discussion of new research approaches has been both incomplete and idealistic. The problems are in fact much more complex than I have presented them as being. The politics of research and the emphasis on originality in experimental design and problem conception dictate that no consensus will likely be reached on very many of the issues which I have discussed.

The relationship between research and application is also complicated by many factors not fully appreciated in this discussion. Implicit in this presentation has been the assumption that the identification of specific deficits in the learning and cognitive processes of reading-disabled children would lead fairly simply to remedial procedures that might apply to individual children. Such an assumption not only is contrary to the actual events of the past but also fails to take account of the complexity of individual functioning. Even if specific process deficits are identified, the expression of the deficit and its effect on reading achievement will certainly vary with the matrix of personal traits within which it is embedded.

The greatest usefulness of research may not be in the construction of specific remedial techniques, but in the contribution which it makes to the cataloging and proper description of the variety of human abilities. Once clinicians and educators are aware of the relevant dimensions along which children's abilities may vary, they can begin to construct programs that make allowances for the unique problems of each child with learning difficulties. If good research is successful in demonstrating the vital necessity for considering different learning styles and unique ability patterns in the educational process, then its contributions to children with learning disability will have been significant.

REFERENCES

Alexander, D., & Money, J. Reading ability, object constancy, and Turner's syndrome. *Perceptual and Motor Skills,* 1965, *20,* 981–984.

Attwell, A.; Orpet, R. E.; & Meyers, E. C. Kindergarten behavior ratings as predictors of academic achievement. *Journal of School Psychology,* 1967, *6,* 43–46.

Bardon, J. I. The babe and the bathwater: the case for discrimination between use and abuse. *Journal of Special Education,* 1971, *5,* 31–34.

Barrett, T. C. Visual discrimination tasks as predictors of first grade reading achievement. *Reading Teacher*, 1965, *18*, 276–282.

Bartel, N. R.; Grill, J. J.; & Bartel, H. W. The syntactic-paradigmatic shift in learning disabled and normal children. *Journal of Learning Disabilities*, 1973, *6*, 518–523.

Bateman, B. Learning disabilities—yesterday, today, and tomorrow. *Journal of Exceptional Children*, 1964, *31*, 167–177.

Beery, J. W. Matching of auditory and visual stimuli by average and retarded readers. *Child Development*, 1967, *38*, 827–833.

Belmont, J. W., & Butterfield, E. C. The relations of short term memory to development and IQ. In L. P. Lipsitt & N. Reese (Eds.), *Advances in child development and behavior.* Vol. *4.* New York: Academic Press, 1969.

Bender, L. A visual motor gestalt test and its clinical use. *American Orthopsychiatric Association Research Monograph*, 1938, No. 3.

Bender, L. Problems in conceptualization and communication in children with developmental alexia. In P. M. Hoch & J. Zubin (Eds.), *Psychopathology of communication.* New York: Grune & Stratton, 1958.

Benton, A. L. Dyslexia in relation to form perception and directional sense. In J. Money (Ed.), *Reading disability: progress and research needs in dyslexia.* Baltimore: Johns Hopkins University Press, 1962.

Birch, H. G., & Belmont, L. Auditory-visual integration in normal and retarded readers. *American Journal of Orthopsychiatry*, 1964, *34*, 852–861.

Birch, H. G., & Belmont, L. Auditory-visual integration, intelligence and reading ability in school children. *Perceptual and Motor Skills*, 1965, *20*, 295–305.

Birch, H. G., & Gussow, J. D. *Disadvantaged children: health, nutrition, and school failure.* New York: Harcourt, Brace & World, 1970.

Birch, H. G., & Lefford, A. Intersensory development in children. *Monographs of the Society for Research in Child Development*, 1963, *28* (5, Serial No. 89).

Blank, M. Cognitive processes in auditory discrimination in normals and retarded readers. *Child Development*, 1968, *39*, 1091–1101.

Blank, M., & Bridger, W. H. Deficiencies in verbal labeling in retarded readers. *American Journal of Orthopsychiatry*, 1966, *36*, 840–847.

Blank, M., & Bridger, W. H. Perceptual abilities and conceptual deficiencies in retarded readers. In J. Zubin (Ed.), *Psychopathology of intelligence.* New York: Grune & Stratton, 1967.

Blank, M.; Weider, S.; & Bridger, W. H. Verbal deficiencies in abstract thinking in early reading retardation. *American Journal of Orthopsychiatry*, 1968, *38*, 823–834.

Boder, E. Developmental dyslexia: a diagnostic screening procedure based on three characteristic patterns of reading and spelling. In M. P. Douglas (Ed.), *Claremont reading conference: thirty-second yearbook.* Claremont, Calif.: Claremont University Center, 1968.

Bortner, M. Phrenology, localization, and learning disabilities. *Journal of Special Education,* 1971, *5*, 23–29.

Bortner, M., & Birch, H. G. Cognitive capacity and cognitive competence. *American Journal of Mental Deficiency,* 1970, *74*, 735–744.

Braun, J. S. Relation between concept formation ability and reading achievement at three developmental levels. *Child Development*, 1963, *34*, 675–682.

Bridger, W. H. Cognitive factors in perceptual dysfunction. *Research Publication of the Association of Nervous and Mental Disease*, 1970, *48*, 266–271.

Bryan, T. S. An observational analysis of classroom behaviors of children with learning disabilities. *Journal of Learning Disabilities*, 1974, *7*, 35–43.

Budoff, M., & Quinlan, D. Reading progress as related to efficiency of visual and aural learning in the primary grades. *Journal of Educational Psychology,* 1964, *55,* 247–252.

Camp, B. W. Learning rate and retention in retarded readers. *Journal of Learning Disabilities,* 1973, *6,* 65–71.

Campbell, D. T. Recommendations for APA test standards regarding construct, trait, or discriminant validity. *American Psychologist,* 1960, *15,* 546–553.

Campbell, D. T., & Fiske, D. W. Convergent and discriminant validation by the multitrait-multimethod matrix. *Psychological Bulletin,* 1959, *56,* 81–105.

Campbell, D. T., & Stanley, J. C. *Experimental and quasi-experimental designs for research.* Chicago: Rand-McNally, 1963.

Chall, J. S. Learning and learning to read: current issues and trends. In F. A. Young & D. B. Lindsley (Eds.), *Early experience and visual information processing in perceptual and reading disorders.* Washington, D.C.: National Academy of Sciences, 1970.

Christopelos, F. Programming for children with learning disabilities. *Journal of Learning Disabilities,* 1969, *2,* 45–48.

Clausen, J. A. Mental deficiency: development of a concept. *American Journal of Mental Deficiency,* 1967, *71,* 27–45.

Clements, S. D. Minimal brain dysfunction in children. NINDB Monograph No. 3, Department of Health, Education, and Welfare, 1966.

Cohen, S. A. Studies in visual perception and reading in disadvantaged children. *Journal of Learning Disabilities,* 1969, *2,* 498–503.

Cohen, S. A. Cause versus treatment in reading achievement. *Journal of Learning Disabilities,* 1970, *3,* 163–166.

Critchley, M. Topics worthy of research. In A. H. Keeney & V. T. Keeney (Eds.), *Dyslexia: diagnosis and treatment of reading disorders.* Saint Louis: Mosby, 1968.

Critchley, M. *The dyslexic child.* Springfield, Ill.: Thomas, 1970.

Cronbach, L. J., & Meehl, P. E. Construct validity in psychological tests. *Psychological Bulletin,* 1955, *52,* 281–301.

DeHirsch, K.; Jansky, J.; & Langford, W. S. *Predicting reading failure.* New York: Harper & Row, 1966.

Denner, B. Representational and syntactic competence of problem readers. *Child Development,* 1970, *41,* 881–887.

Deutsch, C. P., & Schumer, F. Brain-damaged children: a modality oriented exploration of performance. Final report to the Vocational Rehabilitation Administration, Department of Health, Education, and Welfare, 1967.

Dykstra, R. The use of reading readiness tests for prediction and diagnosis: a critique. In T. C. Barrett (Ed.), *The evaluation of children's reading achievement.* Newark, Del.: International Reading Association, 1967.

Easterbrook, J. A. The effect of emotion on cue utilization and the organization of behavior. *Psychological Review,* 1959, *66,* 183–201.

Egeth, H., & Bevan, W. Attention. In B. B. Wolman (Ed.), *Handbook of general psychology,* New York: Prentice-Hall, 1973.

Eisenberg, L. Reading retardation: psychiatric and sociological aspects. *Pediatrics,* 1966, *37,* 352–365.

Erickson, R. C. Visual-haptic aptitude: effect on student achievement in reading. *Journal of Learning Disabilities,* 1969, *2,* 256–260.

Estes, R. E., & Huizinga, R. J. A comparison of visual and auditory presentations of a paired-associate learning task with learning disabled children. *Journal of Learning Disabilities,* 1974, *7,* 44–51.

Feldhusen, J. R., & Klausmeier, H. J. Anxiety, intelligence, and achievement in children of low, average, and high intelligence. *Child Development,* 1962, *33,* 403–409.

Flavell, J. H. Developmental studies of mediated memory. In H. W. Reese & L. P. Lipsitt (Eds.), *Advances in child development and behavior.* Vol. *5.* New York: Academic Press, 1970.

Flavell, J. H. What is memory development the development of? *Human Development,* 1971, *14,* 272–278.

Fleishman, E. A. Individual differences and motor learning. In R. M. Gagne (Ed.), *Learning and individual differences.* Columbus, Ohio: Merrill, 1967.

Friedrich, A. G.; Hertz, T. W.; Moynahan, E. P.; Simpson, W. E.; Arnold, M. R.; Christy, M. P.; Cooper, C. R.; & Stevenson, H. W. Interrelations among learning and performance tasks at the preschool level. *Developmental Psychology,* 1971, *4,* 164–172.

Fries, C. C. *Linguistics and reading.* New York: Holt, Rinehart & Winston, 1962.

Frostig, M. Visual perception, integrative functions, and academic learning. *Journal of Learning Disabilities,* 1972, *5,* 5–15.

Gagne, R. M. Contributions of learning to human development. *Psychological Review,* 1968, *75,* 177–191.

Gates, A. I., & MacGinitie, W. H. Gates-MacGinitie Reading Tests (Teacher's Manual, Levels A, B, C, & D). New York: Teachers College Press, 1965.

Gibson, E. J. Learning to read. *Science,* 1965, *148,* 1066–1072.

Gibson, E. J. *Principles of perceptual learning and development.* New York: Appleton-Century-Crofts, 1969.

Gibson, E. J. Trends in perceptual development: implications for the reading process. Paper presented at the Minnesota Symposium in Child Development, Minneapolis, October 1973.

Glanzer, M. Individual performance, R-R theory, and perception. In R. M. Gagne (Ed.), *Learning and individual differences.* Columbus, Ohio: Merrill, 1967.

Golden, N. E., & Steiner, S. R. Auditory and visual functions in good and poor readers. *Journal of Learning Disabilities,* 1969, *2,* 476–481.

Goldfarb, W. Childhood psychoses. In P. H. Mussen (Ed.), *Carmichael's manual of child psychology,* Vol. 2. New York: Wiley, 1970.

Guthrie, J. T. Reading comprehension and syntactic responses in good and poor readers. *Journal of Educational Psychology,* 1973, *65,* 294–299.

Hagen, J. W. Some thoughts on how children learn to remember. *Human Development,* 1971, *14,* 262–271.

Hallahan, D. P., & Cruickshank, W. M. *Psycho-educational foundations of learning disabilities.* Englewood Cliffs, N.J.: Prentice-Hall, 1973.

Hebb, D. O. *The organization of behavior.* New York: Wiley, 1949.

Heinicke, C. M. Learning disturbance in childhood. In B. J. Wolman (Ed.), *Manual of child psychopathology,* New York: McGraw-Hill, 1972.

Hill, S. D., & Hecker, E. E. Auditory and visual learning of a paired-associate task by second grade children. *Perceptual and Motor Skills,* 1966, *23,* 814.

Hill, K. T., & Sarason, S. B. The relation of test anxiety and defensiveness to test and school performance over the elementary school years: a further longitudinal study. *Monographs of the Society for Research in Child Development,* 1966, *31* (2, Serial No. 104).

Hirsh, J. Behavior genetics and individuality understood. *Science,* 1963, *142,* 1436–1442.

Huelsman, C. B. The WISC subtest syndrome for disabled readers. *Perceptual and Motor Skills,* 1970, *30,* 535–550.

Hunt, J. M. *Intelligence and experience.* New York: Ronald, 1961.

Jensen, A. R. Varieties of individual differences in learning. In R. M. Gagne (Ed.), *Learning and individual differences.* Columbus, Ohio: Merrill, 1967.

Johnson, M. S. Factors related to reading disability. *Journal of Experimental Education,* 1957, *26,* 1–26.

Kass, C. E. Psycholinguistic disabilities of children with reading problems. *Exceptional Children,* 1966, *32,* 533–539.

Katz, P. A., & Deutsch, M. Modality learning and reading achievement. *Perceptual and Motor Skills,* 1964, *19,* 627–633.

Katz, P. A., & Deutsch, M. Auditory and visual functioning and reading achievement. In M. Deutsch (Ed.), *The disadvantaged child.* New York: Basic, 1967.

Keogh, B. K., & Smith, C. E. Visuo-motor ability for school prediction: a seven-year study. *Perceptual and Motor Skills,* 1967, *25,* 101–110.

Kephart, N. C. *The slow learner in the classroom.* Columbus, Ohio: Merrill, 1960.

Kinsbourne, M., & Warrington, E. K. Developmental factors in reading and writing backwardness. *British Journal of Psychology,* 1963, *54,* 145–156.

Kirk, S. A. Behavioral diagnosis and remediation of learning disabilities. Paper presented at the 1st annual meeting of the Conference on Exploration into the Problems of the Perceptually Handicapped Child, Chicago, 1963.

Kirk, S. A., & Kirk, W. D. *Psycholinguistic learning disabilities.* Urbana: University of Illinois Press, 1971.

Kluever, R. Mental abilities and disorders of learning. In H. R. Myklebust (Ed.), *Progress in learning disabilities.* Vol. 2. New York: Grune & Stratton, 1971.

Koppitz, E. M. *The Bender Gestalt test for young children.* New York: Grune & Stratton, 1963.

LaBerge, D., & Samuels, S. J. Toward a theory of automatic information processing in reading. Technical Report No. 3, Minnesota Reading Research Project, University of Minnesota, 1973.

Lachman, F. M. Perceptual-motor development in children regarded in reading ability. *Journal of Consulting Psychology,* 1960, *24,* 427–431.

Lahaderne, H. M. Attitudinal and intellectual correlates of attention: a study of four sixth grade classrooms. *Journal of Educational Psychology,* 1968, *59,* 320–324.

Lasky, E. Z., & Tobin, H. Linguistic and non-linguistic competing message effects. *Journal of Learning Disabilities,* 1973, *6,* 243–250.

Leton, D. A. Visual-motor capacities and ocular efficiency in reading. *Perceptual and Motor Skills,* 1962, *15,* 407–432.

Liverant, S. Intelligence: a concept in need of re-examination. *Journal of Consulting Psychology,* 1960, *24,* 101–110.

Lyle, J. G., & Gogen, J. Visual recognition, developmental lag, and strephosymbolia in reading retardation. *Journal of Abnormal Psychology,* 1968, *73,* 25–29.

McCarthy, J. J., & McCarthy, J. F. *Learning disabilities.* Boston: Allyn & Bacon, 1969.

Maccoby, E. Selective attention in children. In L. P. Lipsitt and C. C. Spiker (Eds.), *Advances in child development and behavior.* Vol. 3. New York: Academic Press, 1967.

MacGinitie, W. H. Evaluating readiness for learning to read: a critical review and evaluation of research. *Reading Research Quarterly,* 1969, *4,* 396–410.

McGuire, W. J. A multiprocess model for paired-associate learning. *Journal of Experimental Psychology,* 1961, *62,* 335–347.

Macione, J. R. Psychological correlates of reading disability as defined by the Illinois Test of Psycholinguistic Abilities. Unpublished doctoral dissertation, University of South Dakota, 1969.

Maher, B. A. Intelligence and brain damage. In N. R. Ellis (Ed.), *Handbook of mental deficiency.* New York: McGraw-Hill, 1963.

Mann, L. Perceptual training: misdirections and redirections. *American Journal of Orthop-*

sychiatry, 1970, *40,* 30–38.

Mann, L. Psychometric phrenology and the new faculty psychology: the case against ability assessment and training. *Journal of Special Education,* 1971, *5,* 3–14.

Mann, L., & Phillips, W. A. Fractional practices in special education: a critique. *Exceptional Children,* 1967, *33,* 311–317.

Moray, N. *Attention: selective processes in vision and hearing.* New York: Academic Press, 1970.

Neufeldt, A. H. Short-term memory in the mentally retarded: an application of the dichotic listening technique. *Psychological Monographs,* 1966, *80* (12, Whole No. 620).

Newman, C. J.; Dember, C. F.; & Krug, O. "He can but he won't": a psycho-dynamic study of so-called "gifted underachievers." *Psychoanalytic Study of the Child,* 1973, *28,* 83–129.

Noland, E. C., & Schuldt, W. J. Sustained attention and reading retardation. *Journal of Experimental Education,* 1971, *40,* 73–76.

Norman, D. A. *Memory and attention.* New York: Wiley, 1969.

Otto, W. The acquisition and retention of paired-associates by good, average, and poor readers. *Journal of Educational Psychology,* 1961, *52,* 241–248.

Owen, F. W.; Adams, P. A.; Forrest, T.; Stolz, L. M.; & Fisher, S. Learning Learning disorders in children: sibling studies. *Monographs of the Society for Research in Child Development,* 1971, *36* (4, Serial No. 144).

Pearson, G. H. J. A survey of learning difficulties in children. *Psychoanalytic Study of the Child,* 1952, *7,* 322–386.

Pick, H. L.; Pick, A. D.; & Klein, R. E. Perceptual integration in children. In L. P. Lipsitt & C. C. Spiker, (Eds.), *Advances in child development and behavior.* New York: Academic Press, 1967.

Rabinovitch, R. D. Reading and learning disabilities. In S. Arieti (Ed.), *American handbook of psychiatry.* Vol. *1.* New York: Basic, 1959.

Rabinovitch, R. D. Reading problems in children: definitions and classifications. In A. H. Keeney & V. T. Keeney (Eds.), *Dyslexia: diagnosis and treatment of reading disorders.* Saint Louis: Mosby, 1968.

Rabinovitch, R. D.; Daw, A. L.; DeJong, R. N.; Ingram, W.; & Withey, L. A research approach to reading retardation. *Research Publications of the Association of Nervous and Mental Disease,* 1954, *34,* 363–396.

Rabinovitch, R. D., & Ingram, W. Neuropsychiatric considerations in reading retardation. *Reading Teacher,* 1962, *5,* 433–439.

Reed, J. C. The ability deficits of good and poor readers. *Journal of Learning Disabilities,* 1968, *1,* 44–49.

Roberts, D. M. Abilities and learning: a brief review and discussion of empirical studies. *Journal of School Psychology,* 1968–1969, *7,* 12–21.

Rudnick, M.; Sterritt, G. M.; & Flax, M. Auditory and visual rhythm perception and reading ability. *Child Development,* 1967, 581–587.

Sabatino, D. A., & Hayden, D. L. Variation in information processing behaviors. *Journal of Learning Disabilities,* 1970, 4, 404–412.

Santostefano, S.; Rutledge, L.; & Randall, P. Cognitive styles and reading disability. *Psychology in the Schools,* 1965, *2,* 57–62.

Scrimshaw, M. S., & Gordon, J. E. (Eds.), *Malnutrition, learning, and behavior.* Cambridge, Mass.: M.I.T. Press, 1968.

Senf, G. M. Development of immediate memory for bisensory stimuli in normal children and children with learning disorders. *Developmental Psychology Monographs,* 1969, *1* (6, Pt. 2).

Senf, G. M. Issues surrounding classification in learning disabilities. Paper presented at annual national convention, Association for Children with Learning Disabilities, Houston, Texas, March 1974.

Senf, G. M., & Feshbach, S. Development of bisensory memory in culturally deprived dyslexic and normal readers. *Journal of Educational Psychology,* 1970, *61,* 461–470.

Senf, G. M., & Freundl, P. C. Memory and attention factors in specific learning disabilities. *Journal of Learning Disabilities,* 1971, *4,* 94–106.

Senf, G. M., & Freundl, P. C. Sequential auditory and visual memory in learning disabled children. Paper presented at the meeting of the American Psychological Association, Honolulu, 1972.

Shapiro, S. S. Aural paired-associates learning in grade-school children. *Child Development,* 1966, *37,* 417–424.

Sieber, J. E.; Kameya, L. I.; & Paulson, F. L. Effect on memory support on the problem-solving ability of test anxious children. *Journal of Educational Psychology,* 1970, *61,* 159–168.

Silberberg, N. E., & Silberberg, M. C. Myths in remedial education. *Journal of Learning Disabilities,* 1969, *2,* 209–217.

Skubic, V., & Anderson, M. The interrelationship of perceptual-motor achievement, academic achievement, and intelligence of fourth grade children. *Journal of Learning Disabilities,* 1970, *3,* 413–420.

Sterritt, G. M., & Rudnick, M. Auditory and visual rhythm perception in relation to reading ability in fourth grade boys. *Perceptual and Motor Skills,* 1966, *22,* 859–864.

Stevenson, H. W. *Children's learning.* New York: Appleton-Century-Crofts, 1973.

Stevenson, H. W.; Friedrichs, A. C.; & Simpson, W. E. Interrelations and correlates over time in children's learning. *Child Development,* 1970, *41,* 625–637.

Stevenson, H. W.; Hale, G. A.; Klein, R. E.; & Miller, L. K. Interrelations and correlates in children's learning and problem solving. *Monographs of the Society for Research in Child Development,* 1968, *33* (7, Serial No. 123).

Stevenson, H. W., & Odom, R. D. The relationship of anxiety to children's performance on learning and problem solving tasks. *Child Development,* 1965, *36,* 1003–1012.

Strauss, A. A., & Lehtinen, L. *Psychopathology and education of the brain-injured child.* New York: Grune & Stratton, 1947.

Thorndike, R. L. *The concepts of over and under achievement.* New York: Teachers College Press, 1963.

Trabasso, T., & Bower, G. H. *Attention in learning: theory and research.* New York: Wiley, 1968.

Tuddenham, R. D. The nature and measurement of intelligence. In L. Postman (Ed.), *Psychology in the making.* New York: Knopf, 1963.

Ullman, C. A. Prevalence of reading disability as a function of the measure used. *Journal of Learning Disabilities,* 1969, *2,* 556–558.

Vande Voort, L., & Senf, G. M. Audio visual integration in retarded readers. *Journal of Learning Disabilities,* 1973, *6,* 49–58.

Vande Voort, L.; Senf, G. M.; & Benton, A. L. Development of audiovisual integration in normal and retarded readers. *Child Development,* 1972, *4,* 1260–1272.

Vogel, S. A. Syntactic abilities in normal and dyslexic children. *Journal of Learning Disabilities,* 1974, *7,* 47–53.

Walters, R. H., & Doan, H. Perceptual and cognitive functioning of retarded readers. *Journal of Consulting Psychology,* 1962, *26,* 355–361.

Walters, R. H., & Kosowski, I. Symbolic learning and reading retardation. *Journal of Consulting Psychology,* 1963, *27,* 75–82.

Werner, H. Process and achievement—a basic problem of education and developmental psychology. *Harvard Educational Review,* 1937, *7,* 353–368.

Whipple, C. I., & Kodman, F. A study of discrimination and perceptual learning with retarded readers. *Journal of Educational Psychology,* 1969, *60,* 1–5.

Wine, J. Test anxiety and direction of attention. *Psychological Bulletin,* 1971, *76,* 92–104.

Zach, L., & Kaufman, J. How adequate is the concept of perceptual deficit for education? *Journal of Learning Disabilities,* 1972, *5,* 36–41.

Zamm, M. Reading disabilities: a theory of cognitive integration. *Journal of Learning Disabilities,* 1973, *6,* 41–47.

Zeaman, D., & House, B. J. The role of attention in retardate discrimination learning. In N. R. Ellis (Ed.), *Handbook of mental deficiency.* New York: McGraw-Hill, 1963.

Zeiler, M. D. Stimulus definition and choice. In L. P. Lipsitt and C. C. Spiker (Eds.), *Advances in child development and behavior.* Vol. *3.* New York: Academic Press, 1967.

Zigler, E. Familial mental retardation: a continuing dilemma. *Science,* 1967, *155,* 292–298.

Zigler, E. Developmental vs. difference theories of mental retardation and the problem of motivation. *American Journal of Mental Deficiency,* 1969, *73,* 536–546.

Zigler, E., & Phillips, L. Psychiatric diagnosis: a critique. *Journal of Abnormal and Social Psychology,* 1961, *63,* 607–617.

8 The Development of Deaf Children

KATHRYN P. MEADOW

University of California, San Francisco

CONTENTS

The author wishes to acknowledge the assistance of Iris Daigre and Anthony Bass in the preparation of this chapter. The suggestions of John W. Hagen, E. Mavis Hetherington, Lloyd Meadow, and Hilde S. Schlesinger have been extremely helpful in successive revisions of the manuscript. Support from Maternal and Child Health (grant no. MC-R-060160-04-0) and the Office of Education, Bureau for the Education of the Handicapped (grant no. OEG-0-74-1141) made much of this work possible. Material in the chapter will be revised and incorporated into a book titled *Deafness and Child Development*, to be published by the University of California Press.

441

I. Introduction

Deaf children have much to teach the student of human development. Whether the focal interest is medicine, physiology, audiology, genetics, linguistics, psychology, anthropology, or sociology, new perspectives on behavioral puzzles can be gained from a knowledge of the global consequences of auditory loss. Likewise, the developmental approach to the study of behavior provides a needed perspective to practitioners working in the field of deafness. Historically, professionals trained to work with deaf children know little about deaf adults, and vice versa. Understanding of developmental aspects throughout the life cycle could do much to reduce the conflict that currently surrounds the formulation of educational policy.

The consequences of early childhood deafness are so far-reaching and varied that some rudimentary knowledge of the linguistic, cognitive, social, and psychological aspects of development are necessary if understanding of any one specialized area is to be possible. In addition to providing an overview of key research results, this chapter will provide basic information to allow the nonspecialist to evaluate published research more intelligently. Demographic and medical variables contribute special dimensions and requirements to problems of research methodology. Sample selection and description have critical importance for the understanding of results. The politics of the medical and educational treatment of the deaf child create a pervasive influence on the climate in which research of deaf children is conducted and reported. For more than 200 years practitioners in the field of deafness have engaged in a bitter controversy about the relative benefits and disadvantages attending the use of oral and manual communication with deaf children. These discussions have proceeded on the basis of very limited research evidence. The polemic attached to the conflict and the impassioned commitment with which participants pursue their points of view make scientific objectivity both difficult and suspect.

Another factor influencing the paucity of developmental research with deaf children is the relatively low incidence of profound auditory loss. Total population estimates vary from 200,000 to 2 million persons in the United States with some hearing impairment (Frisina 1959). Differences in estimates are related to definitions. The larger figures include hard-of-hearing persons and those deafened in adulthood. In 1969 the incidence of profound childhood deafness was estimated to be about 60 per 100,000 population (Rainer, Altshuler, & Kallmann 1969). Data from the National Census of the Deaf Population conducted in 1971 was reported with prevalence rates as follows: prelingual deafness (onset prior to age three) 100 per 100,000 population; prevocational deafness (onset prior to age nineteen) 203 per 100,000 population (Schein & Delk, 1974). There were 46,000 deaf children enrolled in 674 special schools and classes in 1971 (Craig 1972). This is an increase from 10,000 in 1900 (Schein & Bushnaq 1962) and is less than 0.1% of all schoolchildren. The theoretical importance of this group is greater than its numbers would indicate.

Even though the size of the deaf population is very small, it consists of numerous subgroups. One of the difficulties in conducting research into any aspect of the development of the deaf child is the necessity to consider a large number of variables in the selection of research subjects and/or in the treatment of data. The combination of the small number of available subjects and the greater need for selectivity means that behavioral scientists must often compromise if they are to carry out research at all. One reason for the many areas of contradictory results from various studies is that researchers include different kinds of subgroups in their studies. The experimental group is labeled "deaf" when in actuality there may be as many differences *within* the deaf group as between the deaf and the hearing control children. The sophisticated consumer of research on deaf children must be aware of the important differentiating variables if he is to have a basis for evaluating research findings.

II. BACKGROUND VARIABLES

A. DEGREE AND NATURE OF HEARING LOSS

Auditory loss is measured in decibels, or units of sound. An individual's responses to sound, introduced to him at varying cycles per second and at increasing levels of intensity, give a picture of his hearing threshold, called an audiogram. The conventional summary of this audiogram is the average hearing threshold in the frequencies where most speech sounds are produced (500, 1,000, and 2,000 cycles per second). An individual whose average hearing threshold in the speech range is 80 decibels would be considered profoundly deaf and will probably hear only loud sounds. A person with a hearing loss of from 60 to 80 decibels is labeled severely deaf or even hard-of-hearing. He may identify some sounds and may distinguish vowels, but he is unable to perceive consonants (Silverman 1966). Recently, more attention has been given to the hearing threshold outside the speech range, at both higher and lower frequences. Children who have some intact high-frequency hearing often given the impression of normal peripheral hearing (Fry 1966; Hirsh 1966; Ross & Matkin 1967). Additional residual hearing at low frequencies (125 or 250 cycles) can also provide additional auditory clues for the deaf child even though these frequencies are outside the speech range. In general, if children are defined as "deaf" in a research sample, they should have an average hearing loss in the speech range of at least 80 decibels. Additional information should be given about the nature of the audiometric configuration wherever possible.

B. TRAINING AND USE OF RESIDUAL HEARING

It is rare that deafness is total. While there are few if any deaf children whose hearing level cannot be improved with proper amplification, it is still impossible to restore normal hearing by means of electronic aids. The gain from a hearing aid is usually about 30 decibels, although in some cases it may be as much as 60. The researcher should provide information on the hearing loss of his study population both with and without hearing aids. Ability to make use of residual hearing is determined by a complex interplay of hearing-loss pattern, proper fit and prescription of hearing aids, as well as educational, psychological, and social factors. Hearing aids and batteries must be checked and maintained if they are to continue to provide maximum benefit. Two different studies of the functioning of hearing aids worn by large groups of deaf children showed that more than half were not in working order (Porter 1973; Zink 1972). Some deaf children and adults refuse to wear a hearing aid (Schein 1968). Early auditory training can help in the utilization of residual hearing, but delays in diagnosis and prescription frequently occur (Elliott & Armbruster 1967; Fellendorf & Harrow 1970; Jackson & Fisch 1958). The importance of utilization of existing hearing and the presence of early training are becoming especially important as control variables with the development of new techniques for early screening and identification (Downs & Sterritt 1967; Glorig 1971; Goldstein &

Tait 1971) and new developments in hearing aids (Erber 1971; Ling 1971; Stein 1973).

C. AGE AT ONSET OF DEAFNESS

Age at onset of deafness is a critical research variable, since the later the onset the more likely it is that the child had acquired language before he lost his hearing. The 1920 census definition included as deaf all persons who lost their hearing before the age of 8 (U.S. Census 1928, 1931). With earlier identification and remedial procedures, the critical definition has become "prelingual deafness." The cutoff is often defined as 2 years of age. However, there is increasing speculation that receptive language heard in the early months of an infant's life was a positive influence on his future language development and his utilization of residual hearing (Fry 1966; Lenneberg 1967).

Of the 34,000 deaf students surveyed in 1971 for whom information on age at onset was available, 79% were reported to have been deaf at the time of birth. An additional 11% were deaf by the time they were 1 year of age. Only 7% were reported as becoming deaf after the age of 2. However, for the 24,000 children for whom the age at diagnosis was reported, 34% were older than 2 years when their deafness was confirmed (Office of Demographic Studies 1973).

D. ETIOLOGY OF DEAFNESS

Etiology of deafness is important to the behavioral scientist for a number of reasons. Some conditions that cause deafness are relatively unlikely to do additional damage to the human organism. Others, such as maternal rubella, may create wide-ranging physical and intellectual handicaps. Parents react differently to their deaf child in ways that may be related to the reasons for his deafness. Parents who are knowledgeable about the probable cause of a handicap seem to be more capable of coping with the guilt, shame, and sorrow that accompany the diagnosis than parents who are not knowledgeable (Davis 1961, 1963; Meadow 1968b). However, in one-third to one-half the cases of deafness, there is no known cause (Barton, Court, & Walker 1962; Hicks 1970; Rainer et al. 1969; Schein 1968; Vernon 1968). For reasons that are not entirely clear, children whose deafness is of unknown origin are more likely to be identified as exhibiting problem behavior at school (Schlesinger & Meadow 1972).

There are more than 60 types of hereditary hearing loss (Konigsmark 1972), all of which have more than one major gene involved (Fraser 1964; Kloepfer, Laguaite, & McLaurin 1970; Sank 1969). Eight to 10%

of all deaf children have a deaf mother and/or deaf father (Office of Demographic Studies 1973; Rainer et al. 1969). Although some forms of hereditary deafness have associated anomalies (Fraser 1964), it is a fairly safe assumption that when there is presumptive evidence of hereditary deafness there is less chance of additional damage to the central nervous system than is related to other etiologies of deafness.

Other kinds of damage often occur in children whose deafness results from complications resulting from Rh incompatability. About 70% of the Rh deaf children surveyed in one study were multiply handicapped, over half of these with cerebral palsy (Vernon 1967c). Perinatal anoxia and traumatic instrumentation are also associated with multiple handicaps (Schlesinger 1971). Prematurity is sometimes listed as the cause of deafness, usually because the premature infant also suffered anoxia. Almost one-fifth of Vernon's (1967b) large sample of deaf children were born prematurely.

Deafness resulting from maternal rubella can be particularly complicated. Before the epidemic of 1963–1965, an estimated 10% of childhood deafness was caused by rubella (Vernon 1967a). A later study found 40% of one population to be rubella-deaf (Hicks 1970). Several studies have confirmed that there is a characteristic flat or basin-shaped audiological pattern in rubella-deaf children (Anderson, Barr, & Wedenberg 1970; Fitzgerald, Sitton, & McConnell 1970; Jackson & Fisch 1958; Vernon 1967a). In this type of loss, where more residual hearing remains in the high sound frequencies, the child gets more benefit from amplification than he does when his hearing loss follows a different pattern. Some observers believe that the rubella-deaf child is more likely to experience pain from the amplification of sound. However, this was not true of children studied by Hicks (1970) or by the Vanderbilt group (Fitzgerald et al. 1970). Rubella-deaf children are believed to be more hyperactive and atypical in a number of ways. Again, these anomalies have not been found in several research populations (Bindon 1957; Hicks 1970). Levine (1951) and Vernon (1967a), on the other hand, report that there were more signs of brain damage among their rubella children. Chess, Korn, and Fernandez (1971) assert that the assumption of an organically-determined hyperkinetic syndrome has been challenged and that the behaviors displayed by children with cerebral dysfunction are now thought to be extremely varied.

Deafness occurring after birth due to inflammatory disease or its aftermath has shown the most drastic decrease of all causative factors. Many of the viral diseases previously implicated have been eliminated by vaccines or their consequences lessened through antibiotics (Schlesinger 1971). One study showed that the proportion of children adventitiously deafened had decreased from 50% to 30% from 1929 to 1959 (Kent 1962).

Etiology of deafness is important in research related to the cognitive development of deaf children since four of the five known leading causes of deafness (prematurity, meningitis, maternal rubella, and Rh incompatability) are also major etiological factors in brain damage (Vernon 1968). The presence of multiple handicaps can affect all areas of development for the deaf child. The effect may be both direct, in terms of functional difficulties, and indirect, in terms of family, community, and societal reactions.

E. EDUCATIONAL SETTING

The two major educational settings in which deaf children are placed are state residential schools and day classes located in regular public schools for hearing children. Smaller numbers are found in private residential or day schools and in public day schools attended only by deaf children. Both the reasons for and the developmental consequences of the various educational settings make research specification (and sometimes sample separation) important. Most obvious is the far-reaching effect of living at home within the family versus living in a dormitory separated from the family unit. A second important difference is the minority status of deaf students in a day class compared with an entire school milieu composed of other deaf pupils.

There are also traditional differences between public day and residential schools in the relative usage and acceptance of oral and manual communication. The state residential schools have long been a focal point of the deaf subculture (Meadow 1972). Almost all deaf parents with deaf children prefer to send their children to the residential schools. Some teachers and counselors in the residential schools are deaf, whereas it is rare to find deaf teachers in day schools. Most residential schools accept the use of sign language in the classroom, at least in the upper grades. This practice means that children who are least able to learn through oral methods of speech and lipreading, because of more profound hearing loss or additional mental, physical, or emotional handicaps, may be sent to the residential schools. Thus it is not surprising that a number of studies have concluded that deaf day students perform at a higher level academically than comparison groups of residential students (Barker 1953; Pintner & Reamer 1920; Quigley & Frisina 1961; Upshall 1929).

Meadow compared the academic achievement scores and social/psychological adjustment ratings of pupils in residential schools and day classes (Schlesinger & Meadow 1972). The residential school group was divided according to parents' hearing status. Comparisons where differences were statistically significant favored the residential students with deaf parents on the following dimensions: self-image, maturity, independence, sociability, popularity with peers and adults, adjustment to deafness, written language ability, communicative confidence, use of intellectual potential. Comparisons favored the day school students, all of whom had hearing parents, on the dimensions of appropriate sex-role behavior and speech. On almost all of the comparisons the residential students with hearing parents scored, or were rated, lowest of the three groups. These findings suggest that there is an important interaction effect between school and family variables and that perhaps the issue of residential versus day schooling cannot be evaluated meaningfully when only one factor is considered.

F. FAMILY CLIMATE

Both structural and affective variations of families with deaf children serve to differentiate subgroups in important ways. The hearing status of the deaf child's parents can summarize a large number of family differences. Deaf parents are less likely to define the diagnosis of deafness in their child as a tragic crisis (Meadow 1967). Hearing parents, however, like the parents of children with other kinds of handicaps, often express feelings of incompetence, self-doubt, and sorrow (Cummings, Bayley, & Rie 1966; Meadow 1968b; Mindel & Vernon 1971; Zuk 1962). In some cases the integration of the family is threatened, and the balance of previous relationships is destroyed (Farber 1960; Jordan 1962).

Deaf parents usually communicate with their deaf children by means of sign language as a matter of course, while hearing parents with very few exceptions use only oral means of communication (Collins 1969; Meadow 1967; Rainer et al. 1969; Stuckless & Birch 1966). Deaf children with hearing parents are more apt to receive early amplification, auditory training, and preschool education (Meadow 1967). Because of their social, educational, and linguistic deprivation, deaf parents are likely to have fewer social and economic resources compared with the hearing parents of deaf children. Perhaps for the same reason it has been suggested that deaf children of deaf parents are more likely to come from "problem families" (Brill 1960). Depending on the kind of research undertaken, the hearing status of deaf children's parents might influence the kinds of predictions that were made about their development.

Deaf children with hearing parents are much more numerous, comprising about 90% of the total number of deaf children. Within this larger group, too, there are variables that separate families into important subgroups. It would seem likely that various racial and ethnic groups might view a child's handicap generally, and a communication handicap specifically, in differing ways. Parents from middle and upper social strata are likely to have expectations for verbal and academic achievements that are difficult or impossible for deaf children to meet. Thus, the interaction of various family characteristics with the characteristics described in previous pages can combine to create additional categories of subgroups.

G. SUMMARY

1. The incidence of profound childhood deafness is relatively low. Approximately 46,000 deaf children are enrolled in special schools and classes in the United States, representing less than one-tenth of 1% of the total number of schoolchildren. In designing and evaluating developmental research with deaf children, it is important to consider the relevance of various subgroups to the possible range of findings.

2. Most important to consider is the degree of the child's hearing loss. A child whose hearing loss averages 80 decibels in the speech range is considered to be profoundly deaf. One with a hearing loss of from 60 to less than 80 decibels is considered to be severely deaf or hard-of-hearing. However, additional residual hearing at lower or higher frequencies may provide auditory clues leading to better functioning.

3. Proper amplification may increase the hearing threshold from 30 to 60 decibels. Early auditory training may increase the child's ability to utilize residual hearing. Information on both aided and unaided hearing loss should be included in the description of any research population.

4. Age at onset of deafness is a crucial variable in the selection of research subjects. Children who are deaf at birth and those who are deafened after the acquisition of language form two distinctly different subgroups.

5. Etiology of deafness is important in terms of implications for additional physical and mental handicaps and in terms of parental attitudes regarding the child's handicap. Where the cause of deafness is unknown, parental anxieties are accelerated.

6. The deaf child's placement in a residential or a day school setting may be related to his degree of hearing loss and his school performance. It affects his interaction with his family, with deaf and hearing peers, and with deaf adults. Also associated with the educational setting is the relative use and acceptance of oral and manual communication, with most day schools utilizing oral-only instruction.

7. The hearing status of the deaf child's parents influences their acceptance of his deafness and their use of oral and manual communication with him. Racial, ethnic, linguistic, and socioeconomic factors also create important subgroups within the total population of deaf children.

It would be difficult if not impossible to consider every important variable when formulating a research design and planning the selection of deaf children as research subjects. However, both the researcher and the consumer need to be aware of the intricate interplay of all these factors in order to recognize those that are critical for any particular investigation.

III. Language Development in Deaf Children

It cannot be emphasized too strongly that the basic deprivation of profound congenital deafness is the deprivation of language and not the deprivation of sound. To those who are unfamiliar with deafness and its consequences, this statement may not have full and immediate impact. It reflects the deaf child's inability to communicate in a fully meaningful way about his needs, his thoughts, his feelings, his experiences. It also means that the significant others in his environment cannot communicate their thoughts, demands, questions, reasons. Often the uninitiated social scientist or lay person believes that the worst consequence of deafness is some degree of unintelligible speech, or a need to resort to written notes in order to clarify some difficult point. We take for granted the fact that a 4-year-old hearing member of any culture has a complete working grasp and knowledge of his native language—a knowledge that he has absorbed, processed, and assimilated without formal didactic tutoring. For most deaf children, a limited grasp of oral communication is acquired at the cost of hour upon hour of intensive tutoring, investment of time, and recurring frustration. Methods of teaching language to deaf children have been the subject of bitter controversy for a period of 200 years or more (Bender 1960; Levine 1969a; Schlesinger 1969). The conflict in this area is an important part of the social and cultural context of the deaf child's development because it influences all the developmental issues related to deafness. The observation that the limits of one's language coincide with the limits of one's world has special meaning for language-deprived children and their parents.

There are several previously published reviews of language development in deaf children (Bonvillian, Charrow, & Nelson 1973; Cooper & Rosenstein 1966; Rosenstein 1961). Each of these can be useful for readers who wish to pursue the subject further. Here, research on language development and deafness is presented under four major headings: "First Language Acquisition," "Acquisition of a 'Second Language,'" "Written Language Used by Deaf Children," and "Evaluation of the Linguistic Milieus of Deaf Children."

A. FIRST LANGUAGE ACQUISITION

In considering the acquisition of language by deaf children, it is helpful to differentiate among three groups of children: (1) those whose deaf parents use the American Sign Language (Ameslan) as their preferred means of everyday communication, at least within the home, and whose socialization therefore takes place through manual communication; (2) those whose (hearing or deaf) parents use a simultaneous combination of signed and spoken English when they communicate with their deaf child; (3) those whose (hearing) parents use spoken English as their only means of communication with their deaf child and who hope and expect that the child's eventual sole communicative mode is oral English.

1. Linguistic Input: American Sign Language

To be considered in this section are those few studies of language acquisition in deaf children whose linguistic socialization takes place through parental use of American Sign Language, or Ameslan. Ameslan is used by approximately three-quarters of deaf American adults (Rainer et al. 1969). It is a language comprised of combinations of symbolic gestures deriving meaning from the shape of the hand, the location of the hand in relation to the body of the signer, and the movement of the hand or hands. Many of the individual signs symbolize concepts rather than individual words. The derivation of some of the signs was iconic; that is, they were apparently based on natural pantomime gestures. Ameslan has long been a stigmatized language. Many have insisted that it was not a language at all. Linguists have only recently begun to study Ameslan seriously and have found that it does have all the characteristics of language, although there are some differences deriving from the crossing of modalities (Bellugi & Klima 1972, 1975; McCall 1965; Stokoe 1960; Stokoe, Casterline, & Croneberg 1965). Parents who make use of Ameslan, as "native signers," are with rare exception deaf themselves. This does not mean, however, that *all* deaf parents use Ameslan to communicate with their deaf children. Some deaf parents themselves use only or mostly spoken English as their primary mode of communication. Other deaf parents may use Ameslan with each other but use only spoken English with their deaf child (Stuckless & Birch 1966). A special characteristic of Ameslan as a "native" or "first" language is that the deaf parents of deaf children have in most cases acquired *their* Ameslan from other deaf children in a residential school after the usual and perhaps optimum age of language acquisition. Their own experiences with early language, and with early family interaction, may have been sparse and even painful. Their ideas about parent-child interaction and linguistic socialization may be quite different from those of the hearing parents whose children were the subjects of previous linguistic studies. It is only recently that the language acquisition of young deaf children has received any systematic attention and analysis. There are only three studies available of features of Ameslan acquisition. These were reported by Bellugi (1972), by Hoffmeister and Moores (1973), and by Schlesinger

(Schlesinger & Meadow 1972). Schlesinger followed two children of deaf parents. Ann was observed periodically from 8 months to 22 months of age (Schlesinger & Meadow 1972, pp. 54–68). Karen was observed from age 2-10 to age 3-6 (Schlesinger & Meadow 1972, pp. 70–74). Ann's mother was also the child of deaf parents. She used English syntax in her written English and alternated between English and Ameslan syntax in her signed/spoken communications. Ann's father was more likely than her mother to utilize Ameslan syntax in all his communication.

At the age of 10 months, Ann made some first approximation of recognizable signs; at 12 months she signed "pretty" and "wrong"; at 14 months she added "cat" and "sleep" to her vocabulary and combined "bye sleep." When Ann was 17 months old, nine two-sign combinations were recorded. At age 19 months, she had a vocabulary of 117 signs and five manual letters of the alphabet. At age 19 ½ months, her recorded vocabulary was 142 signs and 14 manual alphabet letters. Thus, Ann had more than 100 signs at the age when Lenneberg (1967) estimates that a normal hearing child will have acquired no more than 50 spoken words.

Numerous examples are cited in which Ann used one-word utterances in holophrastic ways just as hearing children use spoken words initially. For example, at age 15 months, she used the sign for smell to mean "I want to go to the bathroom"; "I am soiled, please change"; and "I want the pretty smelling flower." Schlesinger observed a number of immature variations in Ann's early signs comparable with the baby talk found in the early language of hearing children. The nonstandard variations might be in hand configuration, in placement, or in movement. Thus, context plus the remaining standard features were important in deciphering the meaning of the signed utterance.

Schlesinger emphasizes that style and feeling of the linguistic input have equal importance with the content. The enjoyment apparent in the language interaction in which Ann and her mother participated were a striking contrast with that observed for many deaf children and their mothers. She suggests that understanding of early meaning, combined with an enjoyment of mother-child communicative events, may represent a necessary feature of normal language development. This theme is elaborated in a later paper on the language development of deaf children (Schlesinger 1972).

The language of the second child in the Schlesinger study, Karen, was analyzed from a body of 200 combinations of two or more signs collected over a period of 8 months. The primary focus of this analysis was a comparison with previously published accounts of children's open and pivot word combinations. Pivot words had been defined as a small group of words used frequently by the young child presumably either first *or* last in two-word combinations. The pivot word would be combined with an unlimited number of open words. Pivot words are more like adult function words (e.g., prepositions), while open words are more like adult content words (e.g., nouns and verbs). Schlesinger's data supported those of several other investigators who were beginning to question the strict definition of the pivot in child language. Karen's pivot signs were found to occur alone as well as in combination with other open signs and in combination with other pivots. Likewise, pivot signs were found sometimes first and sometimes last in two-sign combinations (Schlesinger & Meadow 1972).

Bellugi (1967) was among the first to study the process of child language acquisition among hearing children. More recently she has looked at the (sign) language acquisition of deaf children. A report based on these studies suggests that deaf children learning sign language are systematic, regular, and productive in their language just as were the hearing children studied earlier (Bellugi & Klima 1972). One child, Pola, provided their initial data on sign language acquisition. Her sign vocabulary apparently covered the full range of concepts expressed by hearing children of a comparable age. Like hearing children, Pola appeared to overgeneralize linguistic rules initially, applying them too broadly at first, but later learning appropriate restrictions on the general linguistic rules. Before she was 3 years old, Pola used spontaneously the signs for name, stay, tomorrow, will, where, who, what, how, dead, know, understand, none, nothing, don't know, and letters of the manual alphabet. Her early sign combinations expressed the full range of semantic relations found in the expressions of hearing children. The increase in the length of her signed expression matched the increase seen in hearing children. Bellugi and Klima conclude (1972) that in spite of the difference in modality the milestones of language development may be the same in the deaf as in the hearing child.

Hoffmeister and Moores (1973) studied the initial language interaction of Alice and her deaf mother at 1-month intervals from the time she was 25 months old until she was 28 months of age. Eight 30-minute videotapes were transcribed and analyzed for the development of the use of the "pointing action" by Alice. The authors concluded that the pointing action was a separate linguistic unit, glossed as "that" or "this." As such it was used in a way very similar to the use of demonstrative pronouns by normal hearing children, but with more apparent precision of meaning. Although normal hearing children use pointing as a gesture, with Alice variations in pointing indicated differential meanings. From their observations of Alice, Hoffmeister and Moores conclude that specific reference, through the pointing action referring to "this" or "that," is an initial stage of sign language acquisition.

The differences between Alice's pointing "sign" and the pointing "gesture" used by hearing children would seem to be difficult to decipher. However, Bellugi and Klima (1975) are working on this very problem with adult signers. That is, they are attempting to develop criteria for differentiating between pantomime and sign. They have observed that certain elements must remain recognizable and constant if a gesture is to be considered to be a specific sign. While Hoffmeister and Moores seem to be observing the same phenomenon in Alice's "this" and "that," the exact differences are nebulous and difficult to pinpoint.

2. Linguistic Input: Bimodal English

A few children who are deaf receive a simultaneous combination of signed plus spoken English as their earliest parental language input. They are the children whose (usually hearing) parents have elected to learn manual communication in some modified version of American Sign Language. Until the very recent past, the use of sign language in any form was seen as an admission of failure on the part of the deaf child, his parents, and his teachers. Since manual communication was believed to interfere with the acquisition of speech and lipreading skills, parents feared to use either nonsystematic gestures or systematic signs. In recent years, the phrase "total communication" has come to be utilized to refer to a communicative mode that combines speech, lipreading, amplification, and the simultaneous use of one of several manual sign systems. Schlesinger (1974) has suggested the term "bimodalism" as a substitute. The manual sign systems are derived from the basic signs of American Sign Language. The variations in the different systems are for the purpose of providing a means for signing a direct and precise gloss of spoken English rather than utilizing the different syntax of American Sign Language. The initial efforts in this direction began in 1962 with the work of Anthony (1966). Bornstein (1973) summarizes four major and competing sign systems currently being developed by groups in different parts of the United States: Signing Exact English, Seeing Essential English, Linguistics of Visual English, and Signed English (Gustason, Pfetzing, & Zawolkow 1972; Kannapell, Hamilton, & Bornstein 1969; O'Rourke 1970). The four systems differ in several ways, but primarily in the extent to which they incorporate traditional signs and in the method for forming the auxiliary verbs, pronouns, articles, and so forth that are not used in American Sign Language. The Rochester Method is another variant of the total communication idea. It utilizes a combination of speech and simultaneous finger spelling (Scouten 1967).

Schlesinger followed the language development of two children, Ruth and Marie, whose hearing parents were utilizing signed and spoken English as well as hearing aids and speech training. Ruth was observed and videotaped from the age of 2-8 to 3-5. Her deafness had been diagnosed at the age of 9 months, and her parents began to learn and to use total communication when she was 15 months old. At 3 years of age, Ruth's vocabulary included a total of 348 words; at 3-4 she had a vocabulary of 604 words, including one or more in each form class. On the basis of three tests of grammatical complexity administered when Ruth was 3, Schlesinger concluded that Ruth was following the same order of grammatical emergence in signed and spoken language that hearing children have previously demonstrated (Schlesinger & Meadow 1972).

Marie was adopted by a hearing family at the age of 6 ½ months and diagnosed as a deaf child before the age of 12 months. Her parents began to use manual communication with her when she was 3-1; she was followed by Schlesinger from the age of 3-4 to 5-3 (Schlesinger & Meadow 1972, pp. 82–86). Data on Marie's language showed that she was incorporating English syntax, using appropriately such characteristics as plurals and tense that are not part of Ameslan (e.g., "popped" and "broken" at 3-4; glasses, teachers, potatoes, shared, stabbed, working at age 3-5 ½). Marie's mother played many finger-spelling anagram games with her. At the age of 4-5 Marie demonstrated that she was able to transfer her finger-spelling games to reading material. Marie also gave evidence of the acquisition of negation in the same sequence as has been observed in hearing children in the past. Her lipreading score at age 3-10 ½ was well above the average score for a 5-year-old.

Analysis of early linguistic samples from these children demonstrated the similarities in their acquisit on of bimodal language and the acquisition of spoken English by hearing children. Schlesinger's report of data collected somewhat later in the acquisition process illustrates a fascinating difference between these bimodal deaf children and previously observed hearing children. The difference is related to the perceptual salience of various morphemes in visual and auditory modalities. Hearing children typically acquire the "ing" ending for the present progressive before they learn to use the accompanying auxiliary verb (e.g., "girl running" is used for a period before "girl is running"). Apparently hearing children using oral or spoken language pay more attention to the endings of words. This principle did not apply as forcefully for some of the bimodal youngsters studied and may be related to the perceptual salience of various morphemes in the visual or the auditory mode. The perceptual salience appears to be directly related to the amount of residual hearing and to the precision and frequency with which the child's parents use the morphemic modulations in sign language. Thus the child with the most useable residual hearing acquired the "ing" ending very much as hearing children do, although the auxiliary verb appeared more quickly in the deaf child. Another child subject who is *profoundly* deaf acquired the "ing" and the auxiliary simultaneously. The third youngster, also profoundly deaf but whose linguistic input was less precise for the morphemic modulations, persisted in the use of the auxiliary alone with no trace of the "ing" form for a long period of time. Schlesinger relates these data to Brown's (1973) idea that the relatively late acquisition of the possessive form in hearing children may result from the indistinct and frequently slurred nature of the spoken form.

3. Linguistic Input: Oral English Only

By far the largest number of deaf children (practically all those with hearing parents, or approximately 90% of the total number) have had their initial exposure to language through oral or spoken English. Most parents and educators are committed to the "oral-only" approach to language acquisition for deaf children. There are several methods used. One, called acoupedics, places exclusive reliance on training the deaf child to use his residual hearing. This is also called the unisensory approach because all visual cues, including lipreading, are avoided. Mothers are counseled that they must not accept the idea that their children cannot hear because this implies resignation and will lead eventually to reliance on gestures. Proponents indicate that the program is designed for children who have an average aided hearing loss of less than 60 decibels (Pollock 1964). The Verbotonal approach, developed by Guberina in Yugoslavia, also emphasizes the use of residual hearing (Craig, Craig, & DiJohnson 1972).

Most educators, however, include lipreading within their definition of oral-only approaches to language acquisition. There is a strong commitment to the belief in an exclusively oral environment, which means the conscious elimination of any meaningful gestures from the child's linguistic input during the critical period of language development (DiCarlo 1964). For example, the deaf child would not be allowed to *wave* goodbye because the wave is a meaningful gesture (John Tracy Clinic 1954). The reasoning behind the oral-only approach is that the deaf child who is permitted to use an easier gesture communication system will not work to acquire the harder oral skills of lipreading and speech. Despite the firm convictions attached to what Furth (1966b) has called the myth of least effort, it is only recently that any attempts have been made to test the theory empirically. (These attempts are described in section D below).

Most of the many studies of various aspects of the language development and deficiencies of deaf children have as their subjects children whose early linguistic input was largely unintelligible and therefore meaningless. Much of what is written about language development of the young deaf child is based on nonsystematic observational anecdotal material. There is, it would seem, unanimous consensus that the young deaf child exposed to the difficult spoken English environment is extremely impoverished. DiCarlo comments (1964) that a 5-year-old deaf child probably has fewer than 25 words in his vocabulary unless he has had intensive language instruction. Hodgson (1953) believes that only the unusual 4- or 5-year-old deaf child knows as many as 200 words, whereas the hearing child can be expected to know about 2,000 words at that age. The normal hearing child has been estimated to produce and respond to three words at age 1, 272 words at age 2, 896 words at age 3, and 1,540 words at age 4 (Vetter 1970).

Schlesinger and Meadow (1972) collected language data for 40 deaf and 20 hearing preschoolers. They found that 75% of the deaf children had a language age of 28 months or less when their mean age was 44 months. All of the hearing children scored at the expected age level.

The usual booming buzzing confusion of language is greatly increased for the deaf child. For the orally trained deaf child, reinforcement is not selective. Because his verbalizations are usually grossly distorted and often misunderstood, he often receives inappropriate and contradictory reactions from others. These inconsistent responses to his speech often produce bewilderment and may actually inhibit his future efforts to produce spoken language. He finds it more difficult to generalize, he fails to develop linguistic discrimination, he lacks both primary and secondary reinforcement for his language. It is not surprising that his vocabulary and his language are grossly retarded (DiCarlo 1964). The painfully laborious nature of language acquisition in these circumstances may help to explain not only the impoverished nature of the deaf child's language, but also the absence of any systematic studies of deaf children whose input is spoken English. Furthermore, it has been suggested that discouraging the deaf child's attempts to communicate through the use of natural gestures may well dampen his curiosity about the world around him, thus impeding his capacity for formal cognitive development (Chess et al. 1971).

McNeill (1965) has speculated about the possible effect of the difficulty and delay experienced by deaf children in language acquisition. He suggests that the capacity to acquire language may be transitory, peaking between the ages of 2 and 4, and declining after that. McNeill also points to the greater difficulty experienced in the acquisition of a second language after puberty. These points lead him to observe that early language acquisition for the deaf child is especially crucial.

The production of speech cannot be separated from the reception of speech. Too often, in discussions of deaf children, this is forgotten. There are three aspects to speech development: the learning of motor skills, the mastery of cues for recognition, and the building of linguistic knowledge that is basic to both production and reception (Fry 1966). Available studies of the development of speech and speechreading (or lipreading) skills in deaf children have been conducted, with few exceptions, with oral-only children as subjects. These studies often equate speech development with language development.

Apparently the initial vocalizations of deaf infants have the same tonal quality as those of hearing infants. The one published study touching on early vocalization included only one deaf infant, however (Lenneberg, Rebelsky, & Nichols 1965). The researchers analyzed tape recordings of babies in deaf and in hearing homes. They concluded that crying and cooing depend upon maturational readiness rather than on environmental stimulation. Anecdotal accounts indicate that while deaf babies cry and coo normally at birth, the cooing gradually lessens and is no longer heard after the age of about 6 months. Of seven children whose speech development was followed beginning when they were between the ages of 11 and 32 months, none was judged to have normal vocal quality at the beginning of their training (Lach et al. 1970). After 12 months of training, five of the seven were judged to have normal voices. However, none of the children had produced more than 10 words during the year of training.

The interdependence of all linguistic skills is illustrated when studies of the speechreading skills of deaf children are evaluated. Speechreading has been found to correlate with both written language and with reading ability, although these correlations have not been entirely consistent from one study to another. O'Neill and Davidson (1956) found no relationship to reading but Craig (1964), Myklebust (1960), and Neyhus (1969) report significant positive correlations. Speechreading has received a great deal of attention from researchers attempting to unravel the mystery of the relative abilities of deaf persons to utilize this method. Of the many factors investigated, amount of residual hearing is the only one which continues to bear an unequivocal positive relationship to the ability to read lips (Donnelly 1969; Farwell 1975). It may well be that the contradictory nature of the results of investigations of other areas may be due to inconsistencies in the selection of research subjects in terms of some of the subtleties of the audiological variables.

Variability of reported correlations between IQ test scores and speechreading ability is great. Most researchers have reported low positive but nonsignificant correlations (Butt & Chreist 1968; Lewis 1972; O'Neill & Davidson 1956; Reid 1947; Simmons 1959). Others have considered the influence of visual synthesis, visual closure, visual memory, concept formation, and rhythm. Most studies report positive correlations between speechreading and chronological age. The fact that the correlations are generally low indicates, however, that speechreading is not a naturally developing compensatory phenomenon. The effects of training on speechreading ability are also unclear. However, training does not appear to have long-term positive effects on speechreading proficiency (Black, O'Reilly, & Peck 1963; Craig 1964; Heider & Heider 1940).

B. ACQUISITION OF A "SECOND LANGUAGE"

Because of the atypical way in which most deaf children acquire (or fail to acquire) a first language, the question of what constitutes a second language for them is somewhat murky. Despite the fact that most deaf children receive no signed linguistic input from their parents, most of them know at least some formal or recognizable signs by the time they are 11 years old. Apparently these formal signs are learned from signing peers, usually the deaf children of deaf parents. Whether these signs are a first or a second language is a moot point. In some cases the formal signs used within a specific group of deaf children appear to have evolved from natural gestures that are group-specific. The one study of this kind of language was conducted in a very interesting way by Tervoort (1961). He studied 24 American and 24 Dutch-speaking children, residential school students ages 7–12 years. Dyads of age-mates were filmed during 10-minute conversational units. These children, apparently, did not have access to a formal sign language system; that is, their language input from adult models was through oral or spoken language, but their peer group communication was by means of gestures.

Tervoort observed that a natural gesture, which he calls a motivated sign, is a concrete imitation of some object within the visual field. It is based on true imitation and associative recognition on the part of both children. At this stage, the gesture is strictly situation-bound. However, this motivated sign may and often does develop into a formal sign. In order to qualify as a formal sign, it must be dissociated from the object that was the immediate stimulus for the motivated sign. Some signs formalize slowly because their imitative character stays so evident. Others are only natural to those to whom the motivation is known. Frequently gestures that seem natural actually are formal in use. Formality (freedom of motivation by the object) is a prerequisite of any language symbol and is a prerequisite for multidimensional use—that is, with abstract, metaphoric, ironic, or idiomatic meaning.

Tervoort's study is extremely interesting because it shows the ways in which deaf children had developed or were developing their own formal-

ized signs. Apparently, the development was slower than it is when a
formal language symbol is transmitted directly. Thus, Tervoort's subjects
had signs that were dissociated from the stimulus object in meaning.
They were not yet at the stage of formality that requires or that allows
for more subtle uses of language for metaphor or humor. We do know
from Bellugi and Klima's work (Bellugi 1972; Bellugi & Klima 1972,
1975) that American Sign Language allows for the use of metaphor,
humor, irony, and abstraction in "rich profusion."

Charrow and Fletcher (1974) studied the acquisition of English as a
second language by deaf children. They selected 13 deaf students of deaf
parents in a residential school and matched them for IQ and hearing loss
with 13 deaf students of hearing parents. Mean age was 17-9, with the
"hearing-parent" group more than 12 months older, on the average, than
the "deaf parent" group. The Test of English as a Foreign Language
(TOEFL) was administered to all the students. Significant differences
favoring the students with deaf parents were computed on three of the
four subtests and for the total scores. Their assumption that the subjects
with deaf parents were learning a second language (English) at school
seems warranted since all of them had learned Ameslan earlier at home.
It becomes difficult to evaluate the meaning of the results from this point
of view, however, because we have no way of knowing from their data
the extent to which the school English constituted a first or a second
language for the subjects with hearing parents.

C. WRITTEN LANGUAGE USED BY DEAF CHILDREN

The nature of the language (usually written) of the deaf child has been
the subject of several studies. These often take the form of analyzing the
type and number of errors made by deaf children in their written language productions. Since these are reported in terms of statistics, some
samples of the kind of language that may be expected may help the
reader realize some of the difficulties inherent in conducting research
with deaf children. The examples given below (Fusfeld 1958) were taken
from papers written by deaf high school students applying for admission
to Gallaudet College in Washington, D.C., one of the few college programs for the deaf in the world:

I began to love it as to be my favorite sport now.
She told him that there was a fitted place to put.
To his disappointed, his wife disgusted of what he made.
Many things find in Arkansas.
She is good at sewing than she is at cooking.
The doctor believes that a sickness woman would live within three or
    four weeks.

The backfield players must follow the play what the captain say.
This room was small and many furniture lay crowdly.
I was happy to kiss my parents because they letted my playing football.

The kinds of language errors illustrated above pervade the compositions of deaf children. Pintner and Paterson (1916) made one of the earliest studies of the practical consequences of linguistic deprivation among the deaf. They utilized a test, the Easy-Directions Test, consisting of 20 simple printed directions such as: "Cross out the *g* in tiger." "What comes next after *D* in the alphabet?" "Draw a line around the three dots: ... ..." The investigators submit that these directions demand very little actual knowledge but rather test the ability to comprehend simple language. Form A of the test was administered to 366 deaf pupils and 308 hearing pupils; form B was administered to 289 deaf pupils and 313 hearing pupils. Students ranged in age from 9 to 20. From the age of 9 on the hearing children achieved perfect scores with almost no exceptions. However, the average deaf child never reached that point. At the age of 9 the median score for deaf children was 1 correct. This performance increased slowly to a median score of 7 for the 20-year-olds. Thus, the deaf child barely reaches the median of the 8-year-old hearing child and never approximates the score of the 9-year-old.

The written language of deaf and hearing children was analyzed by Heider and Heider (1940) through 1,118 compositions based on a short motion picture. They summarized their conclusions as follows:

1. The sentences of the deaf are shorter than those of the hearing.
2. The deaf use more simple sentences.
3. No significant differences were found in the total length of compositions.
4. In general the compositions of the deaf resemble those of less mature hearing children.
5. If different forms of subordination in sentence structure are analyzed as to difficulty, it is found that the more difficult forms are used less by the deaf than by the hearing.

The whole picture indicates a simpler style, involving relatively rigid, unrelated language units that follow each other with little overlapping of structure or meaning. The Heiders' research subjects were students at the Clarke School for the Deaf in Massachusetts—a highly selective private institution so the performance level of these students was no doubt considerably above that of the majority of deaf children who attend public schools.

Myklebust (1960) reported a complex analysis of stories written in response to the Picture Story Language Test. He administered this instrument to 200 deaf children (divided between residential and day school students) and to 200 hearing children, matched for IQ score and age. He selected 40 children, 20 of each sex at ages 7, 9, 11, 13, and 15. Every word in each of the 400 stories was counted and classified according to parts of speech. The deaf children were found to use a higher proportion of nouns at all age levels. The naming level type of written language persisted, and, if noun usage is taken as the criterion, the language of the deaf was substantially more concrete than that used by the hearing. Verbs were the second most commonly used, articles third, and pronouns fourth for both groups. However, the deaf children almost never used pronouns until after age 9, whereas the hearing children used an extensive list of adjectives by the age of 7. Prepositions were not used with equal frequency by the deaf children until age 15. The deaf group used virtually no adverbs, while hearing children began using them at age 9.

The cloze procedure has been used to evaluate the linguistic ability and style of deaf children. This procedure was devised originally to measure readability of textbooks. The investigator deletes (for example) every fifth word in a passage and asks his subjects to fill in the missing words. Moores (1970a) selected a group of deaf students, mean age 16-10 and a mean reading achievement score of 4.8. He then recruited a group of hearing fourth and fifth graders (mean age 9-10) with a mean reading achievement score of 4.8 (grade level). Three passages of 250 words each, selected from fourth-, sixth-, and eighth-grade texts with every fifth word deleted, were presented to the two groups of students with instructions to fill in the missing words. The deaf students' scores for verbatim reproduction at the respective grade levels were 41%, 16%, and 15%. Hearing students scored 52%, 30%, and 19% ($p < .001$). When the same data were analyzed for form class reproduction rather than verbatim accuracy, the hearing students' scores were significantly higher than the deaf students' for the fourth- and sixth-grade texts. Differences for the eighth-grade text passage were not significant. Moores concluded that even when the deaf students' language was grammatically correct it was stereotyped and redundant, and that the students exhibited restricted repetitive modes of expression as well as limited vocabulary. He believes that the language ability of deaf students differs from that of the hearing both quantitatively and qualitatively. Not only does their language develop at a slower rate, but deaf children also develop patterns and constructions which produce utterances not normally found in hearing children.

Cohen (1967) also utilized the cloze technique to analyze language ability of deaf and hearing children. Her subjects were matched for reading ability. They were instructed to paraphrase a written passage, then to restore deleted words to the original passage, to a paraphrase written by a deaf child, and to a paraphrase written by a hearing child. Hearing subjects found deaf stories significantly less predictable than the original stories or those written by hearing subjects. Deaf subjects found different types of material equally predictable. It was hypothesized that differences between deaf and hearing performances were due to the fact that the hearing were better users of English than the deaf and therefore showed greater differentiation between good and poor language samples.

Odom and Blanton (1967) presented phrasally defined language segments to groups of deaf and hearing fifth and twelfth graders. Some received eight verb phrases, some received eight noun phrases, some received the same words in scrambled (nonsense) order. Hearing subjects recalled the verb phrases better than nonphrasal segments containing the same words, as was expected from previous experiments. Deaf students showed no differential performance. The investigators make the tentative suggestion that they do not have the same mechanism or processes operating with regard to English structure as do hearing subjects.

Boothroyd (1971) conducted an exploratory investigation of eight young deaf children (students in Lower School Program at the Clarke School for the Deaf). On the basis of their recall of meaningful and nonsense forms, he concluded that if one takes a child's apparent performance at face value one is likely to overestimate his true language capacity and to expect a much higher level of functioning than that of which he is capable. He observed that the children were working in their classrooms with complex syntactical forms, whereas their spontaneous language would lead one to believe that their internal language model was still fairly rudimentary.

It seems possible, from most of the studies cited above, that the traditional formats for evaluating the language of hearing children yield results that provide a picture of language levels inflated beyond reality. Perhaps the spontaneous language examples quoted at the beginning of this section reflect the true impoverishment of the expressive language of deaf children. When they are given a task where the linguistic structure is already provided, as in the cloze procedure, they need not rely on their own grasp of syntactical principles.

D. EVALUATION OF THE LINGUISTIC MILIEUS OF DEAF CHILDREN

The data describing the language acquisition and linguistic achievements of deaf children leave no doubt that most profoundly deaf children do not have a command of language that enables them to function on a high level. There are few studies that serve to evaluate the various methods and philosophies about language acquisition for deaf children, even though this would seem to be one of the most critical research areas in terms of implications for training and education.

There are three studies that have been designed to evaluate (among other variables) the language of deaf children exposed to differing linguistic input in their school settings. Two of these were conducted by Quigley (1968); the other is underway presently and is being conducted by Moores, McIntyre, & Weiss (1972). In one of Quigley's studies, he was able to incorporate the random assignment of children to the experimental classroom where the Rochester Method (simultaneous use of speech and finger spelling) was used. Comparison subjects were exposed to the Oral Method (speech only). Test instruments were administered to the 32 participating students at the end of each of 5 years. Results were somewhat variable from one year to another, and differences were often directional rather than statistically significant. Nevertheless the children exposed to finger spelling showed better speechreading ability, scored higher on reading tests, and achieved higher scores on three of the five measures of written language ability. Quigley's second evaluation study included more than 200 subjects from six residential schools. Experimental schools used speech plus finger spelling; comparison schools used speech plus manual signs. In this case, the children exposed to finger spelling achieved a generally higher language level than did those whose teachers used the combined method.

Moores et al. (1972) have reported the results of the first 2 years of an evaluation study of preschool children in seven different programs utilizing oral-only methods, finger spelling plus speech, or total communication. To date they have found that children in three of the seven programs are performing relatively well in all areas of linguistic competence. The three programs have five elements in common: all have a heavy cognitive or academic orientation, all use some form of manual as well as oral communication in the classroom, classroom activities tend to be structured and organized, auditory training activities are included in on-going classroom events, and parents view the program as a combination of oral and manual and are comfortable with the communicative mode used by the school.

The fear that development of signed language will discourage the development of oral language has been a major specter in the field of deaf education. The few studies that exist do not support this view, however. Montgomery (1966) reported positive significant correlations between the manual communication rating and the Donaldson Lipreading Test results for 59 Scottish students he tested. A number of studies comparing the language proficiency of the deaf children of deaf parents with that of the deaf children of hearing parents have shown that the deaf children of deaf parents have significantly better scores on reading and written language, with no statistical differences on tests of speech and lipreading skill (Meadow 1968a; Quigley & Frisina 1961; Stuckless & Birch 1966; Vernon & Koh 1970). Of course, there are factors in addition to the early communicative mode operating in the deaf and hearing families, so that it is impossible to assume that early manual communication is the only factor influencing the higher language achievements of the children with deaf parents.

The final study considered provides evidence related to the educational issues under consideration. It is a report of the language development of two deaf children exposed to both oral and manual communication during the critical early years of language acquisition. If the two systems of communication are competitive rather than mutually supportive, or if "speech fails to develop in children exposed to signs," these children could be expected to reflect this.

Schlesinger made counts of the expressive language modes for two deaf children of hearing parents whose language was studied intensively (see table 1).

TABLE 1

Use of Speech and Sign Language by
Two Deaf Children (%)

Subject and Age	Speech Only	Signs Only	Both
Ruth:			
2–11	10	22	68
3–1	24	19	57
3–3	29	4	66
Marie:			
3–4	12	79	9
3–10	4	81	14
4–8	18	58	24

At successive ages, Ruth's use of speech alone increased while her use of signs alone decreased. Her combined use of signs and speech remained approximately the same. Marie, on the other hand, increased her relative usage of speech both alone and together with signs, while her use of signs alone decreased significantly (Schlesinger & Meadow 1972, p. 86). In comparing the two children, the differences in the relative usage of varying communicative modes is striking. Ruth consistently used a smaller proportion of signs only and a larger proportion of speech and signs together, compared with Marie. There are a number of possible explanations for the discrepancies. First, Ruth consistently had amplification more appropriate for her hearing loss than did Marie, and her parents were more consistent in maintaining her hearing aids in working order.

Second, Ruth's parents were more committed than Marie's to the idea that the combination of speech and signs was the optimum communicative input. The differing viewpoints of the parents may well have been perceived by Ruth and Marie and influenced their linguistic modes. Third, Ruth's mother used a combination of speech and signs consistently with her while Marie's mother slipped into the use of signs alone more often. These factors, and perhaps others too, helped to form the linguistic milieus of the two children. Emotional and attitudinal influences on the communicative modes and styles of deaf children have special importance that is frequently ignored in discussions of communicative outcomes.

E. SUMMARY

1. The basic deprivation of deafness is the difficulty it produces for the process of normal language acquisition. This includes the basic inner language abilities as well as the more superficial oral language skills of speech and speechreading.

2. Language acquisition was reviewed for three categories of deaf children whose linguistic milieus and parental inputs differed. The first group includes deaf children of deaf parents who use the American Sign Language, or Ameslan, only in the home. The few existing studies illustrate some of the variations that occur when linguistic socialization takes place in a visual rather than an auditory mode, relying on some features of visual salience. Initial holophrastic usage, progress in combining two or more signs, usage of pivot and open signs, and overgeneralization of first-learned language rules were all similar to observations reported for hearing children.

3. Deaf children of deaf or hearing parents who use some simultaneous combination of signed and spoken English develop bimodal expressive language. Vocabulary growth, grammatical complexity, and syntactical structure all progress in the same way as in hearing children.

4. Deaf children whose parents use oral English only have not received systematic study in terms of the process of their language acquisition. Studies of the language proficiency of these children at various ages make it clear that acquisition is painfully slow. Linguistic retardation continues through adolescence and remains a factor among most deaf adults.

5. Analyses of the written language of deaf children have shown that the vocabulary is limited and sentence structure is simpler and more rigid than for hearing children of the same ages.

6. Analyses of studies that can be utilized for either direct or inferential evidence about the efficacy of various methods of linguistic socializa-

tion for deaf children show no reason to support continuing dedication to an oral-only approach. Children exposed to early manual or simultaneous manual-oral input appear to develop more adequate inner language with no reduction in their abilities to use speech and speech reading for communication than do children not so exposed.

IV. COGNITIVE DEVELOPMENT IN DEAF CHILDREN

The cognitive development of the deaf child has been a provocative and challenging area for study. The relationship between language and thought, problems related to the attainment of concepts, perceptual-motor processes, attributes of memory functioning, performance on tests of intelligence, and academic achievement have been considered through studies of deaf children. Rosenstein (1961) provided a good review and commentary on earlier studies of perception, cognition, and language development in deaf children. He concluded then that there was no clear picture of the performance level of deaf children in the perceptual or cognitive domain. This continues to be true more than a decade later, even though much important research has been published during this time. Confusion of terms, reliance on research populations with characteristics that can well confound results, difficulties in designing testing procedures that do not confuse linguistic and cognitive variables—all add to the research problems. However, the natural experiment of deafness offers a unique opportunity to examine learning theories. Conversely, the theories raise questions about the inadequate mastery of verbal/spoken language by prelingually deaf children (Vernon & Rothstein 1968).

A. SPECIAL PROBLEMS OF RESEARCH METHODOLOGY

Some of the problems attendant upon research with deaf children have special importance when cognitive development is under study. The difficulties of finding homogeneous subgroups are many and varied. So, too, are problems of gathering background data that will enable the researcher to control statistically for important intervening variables. For example, it is apparent that we can expect a higher incidence of motor disturbances among deaf children because of the increased possibility of central nervous system damage, related to the original condition causing deafness. If the researcher interested in cognitive development decides to rely on nonverbal tasks in order to reduce confounding from low linguistic achievement, these often require gross or fine motor coordination that may also be impaired. It is important, especially when questions related to memory and retention are being investigated, to sort out difficulties of test administration and language availability and modality from problems of information processing. Earlier studies particularly, but some contemporary ones as well, fail to acknowledge that sign language is available to many deaf children as a possible means of communication in a testing situation. For the most part there has been little appreciation and less research investigation of the necessity for a different interpretation of responses to signed and spoken or written stimuli.

The general question of the degree to which deaf children constitute a group without language is an extremely complex one for studies of the cognitive domain. Earlier, it was assumed that sign language as used by the deaf community did not constitute a true language, and perhaps not even a complex symbolic system. As discussed in the previous section, this view is no longer tenable in view of current research. The degree to which deaf schoolchildren have achieved receptive and expressive proficiency in sign language varies tremendously in relation to their age, their school setting, and the hearing status of their parents. Some measure of sign language achievement needs to be available in evaluating the cognitive performance of deaf subjects. The degree to which deaf children acquire spoken language is also variable. Blank (1965) has pointed out, in a discussion of some of these research issues, that deaf children are exposed to intensive oral language training, beginning as early as age 2 or 3. Some respond well and learn a good deal of language. (These children are more likely to be found in private schools or in public day schools rather than residential school programs.)

Problems of finding or developing materials that will allow for the assessment of cognitive or intellectual development without the confounding factor of language sometimes appear insurmountable. Even if tasks are constructed that seem relatively independent of linguistic ability, the problem of administration remains. If the examiner must communicate instructions that are even slightly complicated it is difficult to be certain that apparent understanding is real. Many deaf children have learned that they are rewarded in many ways for "agreeing" with adults. The set for compliance that is often found can be a dangerous trap for a researcher.

The difficulties inherent in communicating complex tasks to deaf children have led, perhaps inevitably, to the design of tasks that seem too simplistic for the measurement of complex concepts, particularly when research with deaf children is designed to investigate issues of the relationship between language and thought. Sigel (1964) has raised the question of the level of difficulty of tasks in Piagetian research with hearing children. He suggests that comprehension of a principle should be tested by the introduction of a series of tasks, graded in level of difficulty, in order to gain an understanding of individual differences among children.

This problem is perhaps even more important when deaf children are research subjects.

The research on cognitive development in deaf children will be considered under five different headings: intelligence as measured on IQ tests; attainment of concepts; academic achievement; perceptual and motor functioning; and studies of sensory compensation (the substitution of one sensory mode for another) in information processing.

B: INTELLIGENCE AS MEASURED BY IQ TESTS

The traditional way of assessing level of cognitive development is by evaluation of performance on standardized tests purporting to reflect intellectual ability. An early review of studies done with deaf schoolchildren between 1900 and 1930 concluded that these children were retarded 3–4 years in comparison with hearing children and that they usually scored in the low 90s when tested with performance IQ scales (Pintner, Eisenson, & Stanton 1941). Vernon (1969b) reviewed a large number of studies and concluded that deaf and hard-of-hearing children have essentially the same distribution of intelligence as the general population, even though the mean score for deaf children may be slightly below that for hearing children.

There is an extensive body of literature available on the special characteristics of particular tests and the problems of the administration of these tests to deaf children (Hiskey 1956; Levine 1960, 1969b; Mira 1962; Myklebust 1960). Some of those tests used frequently include the Leiter International Performance Scale, the Ontario School Ability Examination, and the Nebraska Test of Learning Aptitude (also referred to as the Hiskey-Nebraska). One study (Mira 1962) indicated that the Hiskey-Nebraska yielded consistently inflated scores compared with the Leiter. It is apparent from several of these studies that the scores of young deaf children are highly unreliable.

The most widely used IQ test for deaf children is the Performance Scale of the Wechsler Intelligence Scale for Children (WISC). This is considered to yield fairly valid IQ scores for deaf children aged 9–16. Because of the difficulties of administering verbal tests, the Verbal Scale is usually omitted from the battery, and an IQ score is calculated on the basis of the Performance Scale alone, often administered through pantomimed instructions. The wide use of this scale, both for assessing the intelligence of deaf children, and for equating research samples, gives special importance to a study reported by Graham and Shapiro (1953). These researchers decided to evaluate the effect of pantomimed (nonverbal) instructions on children's scores on the WISC Performance Scale. They selected three groups of 20 children each, aged 6–12 years. One group had a marked hearing loss (60 decibels or greater); the other two groups included only children with normal hearing. The deaf children and one group of hearing children received pantomimed instructions. The other group of hearing children received standard (i.e., verbal) instructions. The three groups were matched on several demographic characteristics and equated for intelligence as measured by the Goodenough Draw-a-Man test.

The hearing children who received standard instructions performed at a significantly higher level on the overall performance scale and on three of the subtests: picture arrangement, coding, and mazes. The scores of the hearing children who received pantomimed instructions were significantly higher than the scores of the deaf children for picture arrangement, coding, and mazes, but the deaf group scored higher on object assembly. The authors point out that the hearing children receiving pantomimed instructions may have been at a special disadvantage because they were not able to utilize their usual communicative mode. Apparently it did not occur to them to consider if this might also be true for the deaf children, some of whom might have been accustomed to utilizing sign language. The major point of the study, however, is that there appears to be a disadvantage to children receiving pantomimed instructions, even on a test that is supposedly nonverbal.

In summary, it can be said that deaf children usually score within the normal range on intelligence tests, although mean scores are somewhat lower than those of hearing children. This is true provided that the tests administered are nonverbal ones that do not require a high level of language either for administration or for response. Given the fact that many deaf children can be expected to have additional difficulties interfering with intellectual development and the problems inherent in test administration, this conclusion is surprising. The apparently normal intellectual capacity of most deaf children is not reflected in their academic achievement, however, as will be seen in the following section.

C. ACADEMIC ACHIEVEMENT

Two recent large-scale testing efforts have been conducted to evaluate the academic achievement levels of deaf students. The first was undertaken in 1959 (Wrightstone, Aronow, & Moskowitz 1963), the second in 1971 (Office of Demographic Studies 1972, 1973). The 1959 survey was designed to develop reading norms for deaf pupils. The Metropolitan Achievement Test, Elementary Level, Form B, was administered to 5,307 deaf students in 73 special schools for the deaf (or schools with special classes for the deaf) in the United States and Canada. Students were between the ages of 10.5 and 16.5 years at the time of test; 52% were boys, 48% were girls. Mean hearing loss was 84 decibels. Furth analyzed these data (1966a), selecting grade level 4.9 as a minimal functional reflection of literacy. "On the basis of this, looking at the results of a comprehensive survey of reading ability of deaf children, one per cent of 654 deaf children age 10 ½ to 11 ½ scored at grade 4.9 or better . . . seven per cent of those 13 ½ to 14 ½ scored 4.9 or better; twelve per cent of those 15 ½ to 16 ½ scored 4.9 or better" (Furth 1966a, p. 461).

The most recent nationwide achievement-testing effort was conducted by the Office of Demographic Studies of Gallaudet College in 1969 and 1971. Stanford Achievement Tests were administered to 19,000 students in 288 programs for hearing-impaired children. Analysis of about 17,000 scores indicated that these children showed better achievement in reading than in other academic areas during the first 3 years of schooling. Beyond grade 3, achievement in spelling and in arithmetic was better than achievement in reading. The age of the children tested was about 12.5 years, which means their median grade level might be placed at 6.5. However, the average achievement level on arithmetic-computation subtests was grade 4.1; average achievement level on the paragraph-meaning subtest was grade 3.0. Highest scores on these two subtests, achieved by the 19-year-olds in both cases, were 4.4 and 6.7, respectively. These findings illustrate the exceedingly slow increment of achievement between ages 12 and 19 years. Also, it is evident that in the decade between these two major surveys of educational achievement among deaf children there was no apparent improvement in their overall attainment of the functionally useful ability to read.

Smaller studies of special populations of deaf children add dimensions to understanding educational achievement. Fiedler (1969) studied students at the Clarke School in Massachusetts. This population can be expected to be among the highest achieving, since it is from a private school where admission and retention of students can be more selective than in public school programs.

Although only 20 students were involved, the longitudinal nature of the study conducted over a 10-year period, the careful individual testing, and the prestige of the school in educational circles make this an important study. The subjects were the 20 children entering the three youngest classes at the school in 1951. Their ages ranged from 4-5 to 5-7 at that time. When these students were tested 10 years later, three of the girls (27%) and six of the boys (67%) were found to be retarded educationally by 5 years or more (p. 149). Only three of the 20 students "were not retarded academically" (p. 13). "In addition to the three extremely poor learners, three girls and three boys, 16 years old, were educationally retarded from 5 to 5 ½ years on achievement tests, as compared with the mean retardation of four years for the entire group. Thus, they were functioning at the fifth to sixth grade level according to median test scores, but at only the fourth grade level on subtests of paragraph and word meaning" (p. 65). The students' scores on the WISC performance scales ranged from 90 to 142 (p. 170).

A number of studies comparing the deaf children of deaf parents with those of hearing parents included comparisons of academic achievement. These studies are important as a group as well as individually, since the direction of the findings favors the deaf children of deaf parents in each instance. In each of these studies attempts were made to control for intelligence as measured by IQ tests. Mean IQ scores were above average in all cases. Differences in scores for the two groups of students were statistically significant in each of the studies.

In a study of graduates from the California School for the Deaf, Riverside, from 1956 to 1971 it was concluded that mean grade-level scores were 7.0 for students with hearing parents, compared with scores of 8.4 for students of deaf parents (Balow & Brill 1972). Two studies used matched pairs of students. In one (Stuckless & Birch 1966), differences in Metropolitan Achievement Test reading scores were computed, and students with deaf parents were found to score higher than students with hearing parents. The other (Meadow 1968a) reported that the mean differences between the two groups on the Stanford Achievement Test were 2.1 years for reading, 1.3 years for arithmetic scores, and 1.3 years for overall grade-level scores. Differences favored students with deaf parents in each case. A third study (Vernon & Koh 1970) also used a matched-pair design, but included the children with hearing parents only when there was presumptive evidence of hereditary deafness. This criterion effectively controlled for the possibility of differences due to the etiological basis of deafness.

Significant differences favoring the deaf children with deaf parents were found on the following subtests of the Stanford Achievement Test: paragraph meaning, word meaning, reading average, and general average. The consistent results of these several studies, all showing significant differences in the academic achievement of deaf students with deaf parents and those with hearing parents, illustrate the importance of family milieu and communication patterns in the overall functioning of deaf children.

D. ATTAINMENT OF CONCEPTS

In the two previous sections material has been reviewed that shows first, the apparently normal intellectual potential of deaf children and second, the acutely subnormal school achievement of deaf children.

Here, material is presented that may provide some explanatory link between these two discrepant areas by examining the *process* by which deaf children attain concepts that enable them to engage in logical thought.

Much of the recent research on cognitive development in children has been based on the work of Jean Piaget. Hans Furth has utilized a Piagetian approach in his extensive research on the cognitive development of deaf children. Furth's reviews (1964, 1971) and his classic book, *Thinking without Language* (1966b), are important references. His basic conclusion is summarized in the title of his book: logical, intelligent thinking does not need the support of a linguistic symbol system; intelligence is not dependent on language, but language is dependent on the structure of intelligence (p. 228).

Furth and others have investigated a large number of concepts necessary to logical thinking in their attempts to understand how and when these operations, or thought processes, develop. Some of the operations identified and investigated are outlined briefly below.

The *concept of classification* summarizes the process that results in the logical combination of items that are similar or the same in homogeneous groups. For example, a child might be given a group of six objects that differ in shape and color, or in size and texture, and asked to "put together the things that go together." If he can consistently group the objects that are the same color, or the same shape, or the same shape *and* color, he is beginning to attain the concept of classification. The *concept of seriation* refers to the ability to combine items in logical order on the basis of differences between them. For example, the child might be presented with a number of forms that are shaped identically but are of varying sizes. If the child can consistently order the forms serially in ascending or descending order, he is discovering the concept of seriation. The *concept of conservation* refers to the idea that the weight, or volume, or quantity of a given amount of liquid or mass does not change as long as nothing is either added to or subtracted from the substance. For example, a child might be shown a tall narrow glass filled with water. While he watches, the experimenter pours the water into a short wide glass. If the child consistently asserts that the quantity of water has remained the same, he has fulfilled one of the requirements for mastery of the concept of conservation.

An overview of studies comparing the performance of deaf children with that of hearing children on tasks reflecting concept attainment indicates that deaf children perform as well as hearing children during the earlier ages and stages of cognitive development. In Piaget's framework, children progress from the preoperational stage, in which they are unable consistently to utilize concepts to draw logical conclusions, to the stage of concrete operations, in which they are able to engage in logical thought about nonsymbolic materials. Finally, at the most advanced stage of formal operations they are able to utilize abstract, symbolic logic for the solution of problems. For example, Templin (1950) found that the scores of the deaf and the hearing children whom she studied did not differ significantly for any of her subtests related to classification. However, the scores of the hearing children on the subtests related to analogy were significantly higher than the scores of the deaf children. Templin suggests that analogies are less likely to be discerned concretely in daily life and that this fact may explain the differences in the scores for the deaf and the hearing children. Other studies showing equivalence of deaf and hearing children include Rosenstein's (1960). He compared 60 deaf children with 60 hearing children aged 8–12 on nonverbal tasks requiring classification abilities and found no differences between the two groups. Essentially the same results were reported by Kates, Yudin, and Tiffany (1962), who investigated concept attainment in deaf and hearing adolescents.

In one of Furth's first published studies (1961a), the classification behavior of 180 deaf and 180 hearing subjects aged 7–12 was examined. The children were presented with three kinds of classification tasks: one required them to classify objects that were the same, another required the classification of objects with others that were similar, the third required grouping together objects that had opposite characteristics. The deaf children and the hearing children performed equally well on the first two kinds of tasks, reflecting the ability to manipulate the concepts of sameness and similarity. However, while 96% of the hearing children were able to complete successfully the task reflecting mastery of the concept "opposite," only 78% of the deaf children were able to do so. Furth suggests that the hearing subjects did not "truly" understand the concept of opposition any more completely than did the deaf subjects, but that their mastery of language enabled them to give the impression that they did. This explanation would seem to be weak, particularly when the whole thrust of Furth's investigation (and the eventual conclusion that he drew) was that language in and of itself had little influence on the development of logical thought.

An alternative explanation is suggested from the framework of Blank's (1974) paper on the cognitive functions of language in the preschool years. She found that the tasks with which deaf children had the greatest difficulty were those where the instructions could not be communicated by means of gestures. In her experiments, Blank found ways of training the deaf children to grasp what they were to do. However, she reports that it took only a few seconds to communicate the information to the hearing children whereas 5 minutes were required to train the deaf children in the correct procedures. Thus, one of the functions of language is seen to be the communication of requests that have no visible referent. Another is the reverse ability of the experimenter to comprehend what his deaf subjects are communicating. Unless both of these language functions can be performed, the experimenter is unable to say if the deaf child has grasped the concept or not.

Additional evidence supporting the notion of the equivalence of deaf and hearing children during the earlier stages of cognitive development, with a widening gap at later ages, is derived from another of Furth's studies (1963). Deaf and hearing college students were tested in this study, in which tasks were administered requiring the mastery of the more difficult concept of transfer (i.e., the subject is required to transfer his knowledge gained from one situation and utilize it by extrapolation in a different situation). The deaf students participating in the experiment did not perform as well as the hearing students on the tasks requiring transfer. Furth suggests that the absence of verbal or language ability in the deaf subjects is not related *directly* to mastery of the concept but rather that deficient language produced an inability to utilize prior set or knowledge. However, the implication remains that if linguistic abilities of the two groups were equivalent their cognitive attainment might be equivalent as well.

Both Best (1970) and Silverman (1967) report results that suggest that greater grasp of language allows for a higher standard of performance on cognitive tasks on the part of deaf children. Silverman matched deaf and hearing children on the basis of reading-achievement scores and found that this procedure eliminated differences in their abilities to engage in more complex abstract reasoning. Best compared the performance of three groups of deaf children with varying exposure to signed and spoken language with the performance of hearing children on a variety of classification tasks. Generally speaking, performance correlated with exposure to language. The hearing children performed most effectively. Those deaf children with most exposure to both oral and manual language performed better than did the other deaf children. Of additional interest is Best's finding that all groups were found to progress through the same stages of cognitive development and to use the same strategies for problem solving. However, the progress of the hearing children appeared to be more rapid than did that of the deaf children. Also, correct verbal reasoning usually accompanied correct performance on the tasks, although there was no evidence that this relationship was a causal one.

The concept of conservation is generally seen as more difficult than some others and one that is mastered later. Three studies of conservation in deaf children are now considered (Furth 1966b; Oleron & Herren 1961; Templin 1967). All found deaf children to be retarded in mastery of the concept compared with hearing children, although their results differed in some important respects. Oleron and Herren studied the conservation of weight and volume and found deaf subjects to be retarded by approximately 6 years in comparison with the hearing controls. Furth studied the conservation of weight in deaf children with a mean age of 8-5. He found that the performance of the deaf children was similar to that of hearing first graders with a mean age of 6-10—less than 2 years retarded. Templin reported differing findings at a first and a second administration of tasks measuring the conservation of weight in deaf and hearing subjects. At the initial testing the 12- and 14-year-old subjects were retarded by about 2 years compared with hearing subjects. The 11-year-old deaf subjects were retarded by 5 years compared with the hearing controls. The second administration of the materials revealed about a 6-year retardation for the 14-year-old deaf subjects.

The suggested explanation for the differences between Templin's results and those of Furth and Oleron and Herren points again to the importance of the administration of any procedures to deaf children. She observes that kinesthetic cues were built into the administrative procedures designed by Furth but were not included in the other studies. There is a possibility that by requiring the subjects to actually handle the clay Furth emphasized the kinesthetic rather than the cognitive aspect of the conservation of weight task.

The way in which *experience* may serve as an intervening variable, helping to determine the relationship of language and cognitive development, provides another important issue. In Best's study (1970), described above, the degree of language exposure of the deaf subjects was varied through selection of children with differing experiences both at school and within the family. Templin (1950) utilized a similar, although less complex, design by choosing two groups of deaf children and two groups of hearing children. In both cases one group attended day schools, the other group attended residential schools. Templin was interested in testing the hypothesis that environmental restrictions on experience would be related to restrictions on the ability to perform abstract reasoning. Environmental restrictions were seen either as internally imposed (i.e., the limitation of deafness) or as externally imposed (i.e., the limitation of a residential institution). Several tests of abstract reasoning were administered to pairs of residential and day students matched for age, grade placement, IQ score, and sex. The mean hearing loss for the deaf residential students was greater than that for the deaf day students. When this factor was controlled, scores of the two deaf groups did not differ significantly. Thus, it seems that the apparent relationship between attendance at a residential school and poor reasoning ability is spurious. The important explanatory variable is, rather, the extent of the hearing loss. The ability to reason declines as the extent of the hearing loss increases.

Scores of the deaf and the hearing children did not differ significantly for any of the subtests related to classification. However, the scores of the hearing children on the subtests related to analogy were significantly higher than the scores of the deaf children. Templin suggests that analogies are less likely to be experienced in daily life and that this may explain the differences found in the scores for the deaf and the hearing children. So she is suggesting, as did Furth in the study cited above, that *experience* is the intervening variable between language and cognition. There are at least two difficulties in this explanation. First, it appeared that the reason for Templin's inclusion of the two residential school groups as part of her research design was to evaluate the effect of experience on the ability to reason. That is, children in a residential institution might be expected to have a more narrow range of experience than children living at home and attending a day school. Second, if language deprivation leads to experiential deprivation that in turn leads to deficient or retarded cognitive development, we would not be convinced that language had no influence on thought. Rather, we would have evidence of the indirect *manner* in which language influences thinking.

In spite of the many studies that have been completed that investigate the attainment of concepts by deaf children, it is obvious that there are still many unanswered questions and unresolved problems.

E. MEMORY STUDIES

Memory has been used as indication of cognitive ability, and a number of studies have been reported with deaf children. Again, many of these results seem contradictory. Goetzinger and Huber (1964) found that their hearing subjects performed better than the deaf on delayed recall but not on immediate recall. Doehring and Rosenstein (1960) found no differences among deaf and hearing children in ability to recognize and reproduce letters, trigrams, and four-letter words that were exposed briefly. Furth (1961b) found no differences between deaf and hearing children in visual memory at ages 7–10 years but found marked differences favoring 11- and 12-year-old hearing children.

A number of studies have been reported that give some indications about the conditions under which deaf children are deficient or equivalent compared with hearing peers. Blair (1957) matched groups of deaf and hearing children for IQ, age, and sex, and then administered several visual memory tests to the 53 pairs of children. The deaf children performed significantly better than the hearing children on the Knox Cube Test and on the Memory-for-Designs Test. The hearing children had consistently higher scores on all four of the memory-span tests. Blair suggests that the memory-span tasks require greater mental abstraction and conceptualization and that these areas are more difficult for deaf children. However, Olsson and Furth (Furth 1966b) also compared deaf and hearing adolescents and adults on memory-span tasks. They found that the deaf subjects differed minimally from the hearing when the task involved memory for forms, whereas their performance was at a significantly lower level when the task involved digits. This relatively better ability to retain forms leads to a consideration of a study by Odom, Blanton, and McIntyre (1970), who found that deaf children were more likely to remember words for which there were sign language equivalents than they were to remember words for which there were no sign language equivalents. Words in the two groups were equated for length and for frequency as judged by the Thorndike-Lorge list. These several studies indicate that there are a number of factors that must be considered in evaluating memory in deaf and hearing children. Available symbol systems, divergent motor, kinesthetic, visual, and auditory cues in the stimulus materials, differing levels of experience related to language exposure, all must be considered.

Another illustration of these factors is apparent in a study by Blanton, Nunnally, and Odom (1967). They found that deaf subjects were more likely than hearing subjects to remember graphemically related words— that is, words that were related in terms of their visual appearance. Hearing subjects were more likely than deaf subjects to remember the words that were related by sound. Similarly, a study on retention of words judged to be easy or difficult to pronounce (Blanton & Nunnally 1967) showed that hearing children were significantly better able than deaf children to retain the difficult words. This finding illustrates again the fact that material related to the experiences of deaf children is retained better than material that is divorced from their experiences.

The question of whether cues presented simultaneously in different modalities have a distracting or a facilitating influence on retention and recall is an important one. Bruininks and Clark (1970) experimented with groups (12 each) of disadvantaged retarded, disadvantaged normal, and advantaged normal first graders (none with hearing impairments). Pictures were used as stimuli in the presentation of lists of noun pairs to control for differences in reading ability. Performance of all groups under visual and combined auditory-visual conditions was significantly higher ($p < .01$) than that attained under the auditory condition alone.

Previous research reviewed by these authors indicated that most studies have shown that a visual presentation is superior to an auditory presentation of verbal materials when nonmeaningful materials are employed. In a study of 29 deaf children (Ross et al. 1972) better lipreading scores (using the Word Intelligibility by Picture Identification Test) were achieved when combined visual-auditory modalities were utilized than when either modality alone was used in test administration. Twenty of the children obtained higher combined modality scores than they did for either the visual or the auditory modality alone. Moores (1970b) comments that the question of interference versus efficacy of bimodal presentations for deaf children has not been studied enough to draw definitive conclusions. He believes that severity of the hearing loss may be one important variable.

Another possible clue to an explanation of differential responses to bimodal presentations by deaf children is provided by Conrad's research results (1970, 1971). In his first studies, Conrad analyzed the errors in immediate written recall of letters by deaf boys when these were read silently and when they were recited aloud. He concluded that one group relied primarily on articulatory coding while another group relied on visual coding. In an extension of this research, Conrad (1971) found that the subjects who were classified as relying on articulatory coding scored higher in a test of reading comprehension when they read the test material aloud. Those who were classified as relying on a visual code scored higher when they read silently. Conrad does not speculate about the basis for the difference in coding modalities, but his findings relating learning or performance to the "fit" of presentation of materials and ability to learn from them suggest that the same kind of presentation may not be efficient for all deaf children. Some may benefit more from one mode, some from another.

F. PERCEPTUAL AND MOTOR FUNCTIONING

Studies of the perceptual and motor functioning of deaf children have been designed to investigate the bases for their differential cognitive development, to learn about the cognitive results of sensory deprivation, and to investigate human capacity for modal compensation or the substitution of one sensory modality for another.

Several investigators have used the Bender Gestalt Test with deaf children. Gilbert and Levee (1967) found that deaf children produced more errors than did hearing children of similar age and intelligence. They interpret this finding to suggest a higher incidence of brain damage in the deaf children. However, the results of Keogh, Vernon, and Smith (1970) indicate that the Bender Gestalt Test may have limited accuracy for the individual determination of brain damage in deaf children. Disturbances in motor functioning of deaf children have been reported as measured by a Balance Board (Pintner et al. 1941), and by the Heath Railwalking Test for evaluation of locomotor coordination (Myklebust, Neyhus, & Mulholland 1962). Another study (Boyd 1967) found significant differences favoring hearing children over deaf children on the Oseretsky Scale for evaluation of equilibrium, coordination, and speed. A larger proportion of the deaf children than the hearing children in this study were also found to be left-handed.

Questions about the possibly competing or facilitating effects of presentation of material to deaf children in a variety of modes have been largely neglected by researchers. This is unfortunate, because research based on perceptual-motor evidence might help to solve some of the educational controversies around cross-modal teaching techniques. There is one report (MacDougall & Rabinovitch 1971b) of an experiment conducted to determine the role of auditory and kinesthetic cues produced by overt verbalizations in a learning situation. The group of hearing children and one of the two groups of deaf children used speech to learn lists of pictures, words, and nonsense syllables. The second deaf group used signing and finger spelling as the verbalization method. Verbalization in neither the auditory nor the kinesthetic modality resulted in an improvement in the performance of any of the three groups.

A different approach to this question is represented in two animal studies (MacDougall & Rabinovitch 1971a, 1972). These experiments were suggested by a study of blinded animals that reopened the "sensory-compensation hypothesis" when it was found that the weight and biochemical activity of nonvisual areas of the cortex of blinded or visually deprived animals was greater than that found in sighted control animals (Rosenzweig 1966). The effect was particularly pronounced when animals were raised in an enriched environment. MacDougall and Rabinovitch studied *behavioral* (rather than tissue) differences in rats deafened by ototoxic drugs, congenitally deaf mice, and normally hearing littermates. No differences were found in simple or in complex learning in either normal or "enriched" environments. "These results suggest that early auditory deprivation does not lead to the development of increased visual perceptual ability. This may mean that the anatomical and physiological changes found (in the cited study) are not manifested at the behavioral level, or, different effects may be produced when the deprivation is in the auditory rather than the visual modality" (MacDougall & Rabinovitch 1971a).

The second study reported by these researchers dealt with the effect of early auditory deprivation on the exploratory behavior of mice. At 2 months of age the deaf and hearing mice, raised in an enriched environment, showed no differences in their patterns of exploratory behavior. However, when tested at maturity, they showed different patterns. These findings suggest to the investigators that the deaf mice learned to use their intact senses in a unique way to obtain information and stimulation from the environment (MacDougall & Rabinovitch 1972).

Findings reported by Sterritt, Camp, and Lipman (1966), comparing the auditory and the visual information processing of nine deaf and nine hearing children, would argue against the thesis that children with a hearing loss compensate by achieving superior visual skills. The deaf children were inferior in their discrimination of visual temporal patterns compared with the hearing subjects.

Most of the research evaluating sensory compensation has concentrated on auditory versus visual stimuli. A few studies have evaluated possible tactile compensation; none has evaluated the possibility of haptic compensation. This approach might be a meaningful effort since it has been pointed out (Schlesinger & Meadow 1972) that cortical areas controlling vocal and hand movements are adjacent in the brain. It has been reported (Rosenstein 1957) that blind children, as a group, performed better in the tactile perception of rhythmic patterns than did deaf, normal, and aphasic groups. Also, blind and normal children improved on successive trials whereas the deaf and aphasic children did not. In a study of the transfer of a concept from visual to tactile modalities, however, deaf children were found to be more proficient at utilizing tactual cues than were the hearing children with whom they were compared (Blank & Bridger 1966). On the other hand, Schiff and Dytell (1971) reported that deaf and hearing subjects performed similarly on a battery of tactual perception tests. The researchers concluded from this that acoustical storage of information does not necessarily have to precede cross-modal identification. This appears to be still another area where additional research would be useful to the understanding of the cognitive development of deaf children.

G. SUMMARY

1. Studies of the cognitive development of deaf children are particularly liable to pitfalls of research methodology. Special attention must be given to the possibility of central nervous system impairments in groups of deaf children, with related built-in deficits in perceptual-motor abilities. Baseline data on language ability, either spoken or signed, should be accumulated for deaf subjects to allow for analysis and interpretation of test-performance results. Both signed and spoken language levels of prospective subjects are important in reaching decisions about design

and administration of test instruments. Inattention to these methodological details undoubtedly contributes to the picture of conflicting results and consequent differences in assessment of the manner and level of cognitive development in deaf children.

2. Deaf children usually score within the normal range on intelligence tests, although mean scores are somewhat lower than those of hearing children. This finding, however, is true only when tests are administered with nonverbal instructions and do not depend on spoken responses.

3. The general level of academic achievement in deaf children is much below that which could be expected from performance on tests of cognitive development. Reading achievement especially is below par. The most recent nationwide assessment of academic achievement showed that the highest average achievement by any age group on paragraph meaning was at grade level 4.4. The highest average achievement by any age group on arithmetic computation was at grade level 6.7. Deaf children of deaf parents consistently perform at a higher level of tests of academic achievement than do the deaf children of hearing parents.

4. Considerable evidence indicates that deaf children learn concepts in the same sequence and in the same manner as do hearing children. However, the ages at which these processes occur are later than with normally hearing children. The influence of innate intellectual ability on the attainment of concepts is an open question, particularly since it is confounded by the possibility of secondary effects of auditory and experiential deprivation in depression of ability to perform on tests of intelligence.

5. Deaf children appear to have particular difficulty in attainment of the concept of opposition but show relatively little retardation in the attainment of the concepts of sameness and symmetry. Tasks related to classification skills are easier for deaf children to perform than tasks related to analogy. Superordinate reasoning, allowing individuals to combine a number of concepts parsimoniously for the solution of problems, appears to be more difficult for deaf children. The question of the relationship between language and thought has been explored through interpretation of comparative performance of deaf and hearing children on conceptual tasks. Some argue that the relatively high performance of deaf children demonstrates that thought develops independently of language. Others counter that this is shown to be true only when specific and relatively limited definitions of both thought and language are utilized.

6. Comparisons of deaf children with hearing peers on memory tasks show conflicting results, often seemingly related to the type of test mate-

rial utilized. For example, deaf children are more likely to retain words that have a sign equivalent, and they are more likely to remember geometric forms than digits than are hearing children. The patterns of their word associations are similar to those of hearing children of a younger age.

7.   Deaf children are more likely than hearing children to have problems with equilibrium and balance, stemming from the same etiological basis as their hearing handicap. Disturbances in laterality are also more likely among deaf than among hearing children.

8.   There have been a few efforts made to evaluate the comparative efficacy of auditory, visual, and bimodal cues on the comprehension of deaf children. Results are contradictory, but the direction of the effect seems related to the degree of hearing loss. Ability to attend to one or another presentation mode may be related to inherent or learned "set" that differs idiosyncratically from one individual to another.

9.   The hypothesis that deprivation in one sensory modality leads to compensation in functioning in another modality has been investigated in some animal studies. Although blind animals appeared to compensate in nonvisual areas of the brain, the same did not hold true for deaf animals. Even though the deaf animals did not seem to be more sensitive in other perceptual areas, they did use their intact senses in unique ways to obtain information and stimulation from the environment.

V. Social and Psychological Development in Deaf Children

The difficulties that deaf children experience in the spheres of linguistic and cognitive development are reflected in the areas of their social and psychological development as well. In this section the topics of social development, self concept, personality development, and emotional and behavioral disorders are reviewed.

A. SOCIAL DEVELOPMENT

1. Social Maturity

The concept of social maturity is difficult to define and to study. It is concerned with the definitions we have of behavior that is appropriate for particular ages and stages of development. However, when a child is handicapped it is quite likely that "significant others" in his environment scale down their expectations for his social achievements. One way of viewing social development in younger children is to evaluate their ability to care for their own needs as they move toward greater independence and self-reliance. The Vineland Social Maturity Scale was designed to measure increasing ability in the areas of self-help, self-direction, locomotion, occupation, communication, and social relations (Doll 1965).

Several early studies of deaf children used this scale. Avery (1948), Burchard and Myklebust (1942), Myklebust (1960), and Streng and Kirk (1938) all found that deaf children received lower scores on this scale than did hearing children of comparable ages. Many of the studies reported before 1950 utilized large numbers of children with varying degrees of hearing impairment included in the same groups. Changing pictures of etiology, early educational treatment, and audiological advances make these earlier studies less meaningful in terms of reflecting the kinds of behavioral responses that could be expected from deaf children today. However, the basic theoretical issues remain much the same. Many of these early studies are reviewed by DiCarlo and Dolphin (1952).

Schlesinger and Meadow (1971) utilized the Vineland Scale in a study of 40 deaf preschoolers. They found a strong positive relationship between the Vineland score and an Index of Communicative Competence. (This index included the Mecham Language Development Scale score; teachers' ratings for expressive and receptive communication, speech, and lipreading; and two communication ratings devised from videotaped mother-child interaction.) Sixty-five percent of the children who scored below the median on the Vineland also scored below the median for communicative competence, while 75% scoring above the Vineland median also scored above the median for communication.

Myklebust (1960) reports a study using the Vineland Scale with results that are similar to those of Burchard and Myklebust (1942). He surveyed 150 deaf children in a public residential school (aged 10–21 years). The mean social quotient (norm = 100) was 85.8. On the basis of these data, plus additional data collected independently from preschool deaf children, Myklebust concluded that the gap between the social maturity of deaf and hearing children widens with increasing age. The social quotient for the preschool group and for the other age groups up to 15 years was slightly above 90. For the age groups from 15 to 21 years there was a gradual decline in social quotient: at 15 it was 82.2, at 17 it was 80.4, and at 19 it was 76.2. Myklebust's conclusion should be regarded with caution because of the special nature of his population. All the older children in his sample were students in residential schools. Furthermore, those who were older than 18 may well have been a special group, remaining in school precisely because they were less mature than their peers who had graduated.

Barker and his colleagues (1953) have hypothesized that the social immaturity seemingly characterizing deaf children (and adults) may result from the high proportion who attend residential schools, where the development of independence and responsibility may be stifled.

Meadow's studies of different subgroups of deaf children allow some inferences about the various factors that play into the low level of social maturity that has been found across so many studies of deaf children. On the basis of teachers' ratings of 54 matched pairs of deaf children in a residential school, she (Meadow 1968a) reported that deaf children of deaf parents were rated significantly higher than the deaf children of hearing parents on the dimensions "maturity," "independence," and "ability to take responsibility." In a later extension of this research, Schlesinger and Meadow (1972) found that deaf students living at home and attending day schools or classes received ratings intermediate to those of the two residential school groups. That is, the deaf children of deaf parents in the residential settings were rated highest, the deaf children of hearing parents in nonresidential school settings received intermediate ratings, and deaf children of hearing parents in residential settings were rated significantly below the two other groups.

It is suggested by these findings that parents' attitudes and child-rearing practices may contribute most to the slow development of social maturity in their deaf children but that residential living, with the absence of family contact and the close supervision leading to few opportunities for independence, adds an additional causative factor. It must be noted, however, that a true test of the effect of the residential setting would have required the inclusion of a fourth group of children in Meadow's design: deaf children of deaf parents attending a *day school.* This group did not exist, simply because the overwhelming majority of deaf parents send their deaf children to residential schools. (About 1% of all deaf children of those in day schools contacted by Meadow had deaf parents.)

There are a number of studies that give some insight into the dynamics of the protectiveness families have for their deaf children that very likely contributes to their retarded social development.

Chess et al. (1971) collected material on levels of self-help functioning from mothers of 243 rubella children. Although 30% of these children had no hearing loss, and some had no other identifiable handicap, their data are important for our purposes because it appears that the parents' *definition* of the child's fragility may be a major critical variable regardless of the actual level of the child's physical abilities. The most striking thing about their data is the discrepancy between what the children were actually capable of doing and the self-help tasks that they performed on a regular basis. Half the children for whom information was obtained were able to do at least 80% of the activities necessary for dressing themselves. However, fewer than half of the children actually performed 25% of these activities.

These findings are elaborated by a consideration of Gordon's (1959) attempt to relate maternal attitudes toward independence to deaf children's social maturity. He studied 19 mothers and their deaf children (2 ½–6 years old). He used the discrepancy between scores on the Merrill-Palmer (a performance IQ test) and the Vineland Social Maturity Scale as the measure for maturity level, and McClelland's Thematic Apperception Test plus Winterbottom's independence training attitude questionnaire to reflect maternal attitudes. Gordon concluded that the more important influences on the handicapped child are not the maternal attitudes regarding handicap but rather those toward children in general. Specifically, it is reported that (1) attitudes favoring early independence in normal children were found in the mothers of deaf children who showed relatively large Merrill-Palmer/Vineland discrepancies; (2) independence training attitudes toward deaf children and discrepancies between attitudes toward deaf and normal children were not associated with the child's maturity level; (3) mothers with low need achievement tended to be moderate in their independence training attitudes toward normal children, while high need achievement mothers tended toward the extreme positions of favoring very early or very late independence; (4) high need achievement mothers favored significantly later independence in deaf children than did low need achievement mothers. It is also suggested that the mother who encourages early independence in her hearing child is free to devote more interest to the handicapped child. Gordon's results stimulate a more general question about the roots of achievement motivation in mothers for their children. Possibly it is those mothers whose children are not progressing at an optimum developmental rate who begin to concentrate on encouraging the child in areas where he has difficulty. Parents of deaf children are sometimes made more anxious by teachers who try to encourage them to work harder for the child's achievement.

Meadow (1967) interviewed deaf parents and hearing parents about various practices that might reflect the encouragement of independence in deaf children. Almost half of the deaf parents stated that a deaf child should be allowed to play independently in the immediate neighborhood before the age of 5, while only 15% of the hearing parents responded in this way. The hearing parents were more reluctant to grant "neighborhood independence" to *both* deaf and hearing children than were deaf parents. Meadow suggests that the hearing parent, in his eagerness to "treat the deaf and hearing child alike" may achieve this goal by scaling down expectations for the hearing child rather than by giving the deaf child the same degree of independence.

Stinson (1974) studied the attitudes of a group of 31 mothers of hearing-impaired boys compared with 33 mothers of boys with normal hearing. It is suggested by his findings that mothers of the hearing subjects tended to react to the pressures, burdens, and restrictions of child rearing by increasing their demands on their children, while mothers of the hearing-impaired subjects responded by relaxing demands. He also studied maternal and child behavior in task situations designed to reflect (1) verbal and (2) nonverbal achievement orientation and motivation. While intense demands for the acquisition of nonverbal skills were optimal for acquisition of the achievement motive for the hearing subjects, moderate demands for the attainment of verbal skills worked more effectively with the hearing-impaired subjects. Too early or too late expectations for language appeared to limit acquisition of the achievement motive in the hearing-impaired subjects. Instituting demands of appropriate intensity may be difficult, especially when the mother must use different standards in judging her child's progress than if the child had normal hearing.

There is a good deal of pressure on the parents of deaf children to provide the children with early training and education. One study found that 80% of the deaf sample had received some form of early preschool education (Meadow 1967). Traditionally, the deaf child's problem has been viewed in an educational context. His mother is trained by educators to be his teacher. Added to the strain of communicative frustration is the strain of extended demands on the mother's time and attention. Three studies of early mother–deaf child interaction illustrate the outcome of this thrust. Schlesinger and Meadow (1972) found the mothers of preschool deaf children to be significantly less permissive, more intrusive, more didactic, less creative, less flexible, and as showing less approval of their children in comparison with ratings of a group of mothers interacting with their hearing children. No significant differences were observed between the two groups of mothers in terms of their enjoyment of the child, their effectiveness in achieving his cooperation, and the degree to which they appeared to be relaxed and comfortable in the study situation.

Some of the ways in which child-rearing practices differ in families with young deaf children are illustrated in Schlesinger and Meadow's (1972) interviews with parents of preschool deaf children. Parents of deaf children reported the deaf child's need (or their own felt need) for more constant supervision in order to protect him from accidents. These parents reported a narrower range of disciplinary techniques, a heavier reliance on spanking for discipline, and more areas of expressed frustration around child rearing generally. A constant concern of the parents of deaf children was whether they were expecting too much or too little from the deaf child and whether they were being overprotective or underprotective.

When the behavior of the deaf and the hearing children was com-

pared, the deaf children were rated as appearing significantly less buoy-
ant or happy, showing less enjoyment of the interaction with their mothers, less compliant, exhibiting less pride in mastery, and less creative or
imaginative. No significant differences were found for apparent comfort
in the situation, frequency of body movement, independence, attentiveness, or curiosity. When the deaf children were divided into two groups
according to their scores on an Index of Communicative Competence it
was found that the deaf children with better communicative skills were
rated very close to the hearing children with respect to buoyancy and
enjoyment of the interaction. They were differentiated from the less
competent deaf children on degree of compliance, pride in mastery, and
creativity as well.

Collins (1969) classified 40% of the behavior of the mothers of deaf
children as "directing." Goss (1970) found mothers of deaf children to
give directions significantly more often than the control mothers of hearing children. Schlesinger and Meadow conclude that mothers of deaf
children are significantly more intrusive than mothers of hearing children. Bell (1964) reviewed five studies of families containing children
with various kinds of handicaps. In each of the five studies, mothers
scored higher for intrusiveness as measured by the Parental Attitude
Research Inventory, a questionnaire used extensively in previous research (Schaefer & Bell 1958). Bell suggested that an intrusive attitude
may be induced in a mother as an effect of a limitation in coping ability
in her child. The reciprocal nature of mother-child interaction is clarified
and its importance magnified when the deaf child and his mother are the
focus. The mother's dilemma in finding the balance between withholding
appropriate opportunities for developing independence in the deaf child
and in exposing him unnecessarily to the dangers imposed by his handicap is one that has major implications for socialization and child development theory. The role of the father in families with deaf children has
been studied very little. There is some evidence that fathers may interact
less frequently with their handicapped children than mothers (Jordan
1962). Fathers of deaf children seem to experience more difficulty in
learning sign language (or are less able to spend the time to develop
expertise). The meaning of a physical handicap differs among both
mothers and fathers, depending on the sex of the child (Schlesinger &
Meadow 1972).

2. Social Interaction

Social development and language acquisition are intertwined. It is to
be expected that deaf children whose language development is retarded
will have fewer opportunities for social interaction, both within the family and outside it. The feelings of others about aborted attempts at com-

munication are negative and lead to frustration, creating a spiral leading to more and more isolation from the fabric of social interaction.

Parents interviewed by Schlesinger and Meadow (1972) reported some sense of frustration about their inability to communicate with their children. Most stated that it was the child's inability to understand them rather than their own inability to understand the child that was felt to be most frustrating. Of the 16 mothers studied by Collins (1969), 13 reported that they could communicate with their preschool deaf child only about things or events that were present in time and/or space. Only one mother said that her child communicated about absent things or events; the others indicated that immediacy was a prerequisite for the child's inability to communicate.

Research conducted by Heider and Heider (1941) at the Clarke School illustrates some of the specific ways in which imperfect language interferes with social interaction. They observed 53 pairs of deaf preschool children during periods of unrestricted play and compared these observations with those of 22 pairs of hearing children. Additional data were collected on film. A striking feature of these observations was the difference in the ability of the two groups of children to utilize references to future time in organizing and coordinating their ongoing interaction. They felt that the ability of the hearing children to refer to future activities or expectations of future events played a major role in their definition of the present. The global, nonspecific, amorphous character of the interaction between the pairs of deaf children was also striking compared with that of the hearing children. The deaf children were able to announce only in a very general way the meaning and intent of their ongoing activity.

This limitation to present actions creates the possibility for much anxiety in deaf children. If their parents are unable to communicate to them the probable course of future events, and to reassure them about the outcome of current disturbing happenings, the possibilities for growth of distrust are numerous. Expectations will often be shaken and events assume more hostile meaning. The Heiders point out from their observational data that deaf children are handicapped in dealing with the qualities of objects or situations beyond what is immediately perceived. In the face of communicative deficits, it is difficult to know whether this handicap is apparent or real. It is certainly apparent, as evidenced by Schlesinger and Meadow's data showing that 95% of deaf children and their parents limited communication to topics with a visual reference. In comparison, the hearing children made at least a passing comment referring to a nonvisible object, and 15% had a prolonged conversation about something outside the visual range (Schlesinger 1972).

The handicap of the inability to refer to linguistically complex meanings may also handicap the development of imaginary play requiring fantasy and role taking. Heider and Heider remark that in their subjects imaginary play was restricted in terms of the possible level of action, because elaborate pantomime was needed to communicate a role where a single word would serve this purpose for a hearing child. Possibility, which is used by the hearing child to indicate what he is able to do, can be implied by the deaf child, although in a far less specific way, by a kind of general bragging with reference to himself. Evaluating statements are limited: degrees of specificity are difficult to express, as are personal and impersonal expressions of approval. Another block to the development of positive patterns of social interaction is the fact that references to internal events are difficult: specific references to thinking, knowing, guessing, and to perceptual processes like watching, looking, or wanting. These references or ideas can only be expressed in very general ways by the deaf child.

In a later study, Heider (1948) compared the personal relationships of 66 pairs of hearing and 48 pairs of deaf children. Their interaction was studied after each pair was offered a game which only one child could use at a time. It was found that the interaction of the hearing pairs was more highly organized and showed greater continuity of structure. The ways in which language was used to enable one child to gain control of the situation without arousing either aggression or withdrawal on the part of the other gave fresh appreciation of its function in social relationships. At the same time these data brought into sharp focus the question of the effect of the more diffused, less structured, less sharply oriented social relations of the younger deaf child on the development of his personality.

Moores et al. (1972) made observations of the communication patterns among preschool deaf children in connection with their evaluation research. These children (average age about 5 years) depended primarily on gestures when communicating with each other, unless they were in preschool programs utilizing standardized sign language.

Van Lieshout (1973) conducted systematic observational research in a study of peer interaction comparing 34 prelingually profoundly deaf children and 34 hearing children (mean ages were 60 months and 61 months, respectively). Observations of social interactions in small groups were conducted under a time-sample scheme on two different occasions 6 months apart. Teacher ratings were also collected. The hearing children were rated as more sociable than the deaf children, and they had more social interactions than the deaf children, especially in the categories of verbal interaction and mutual attention. However, the deaf children exhibited more social interactions of an expressive kind: that is, more physical contact, approval, and negative interactions. During both periods of measurement, deaf children spent more time in noninteraction than did the hearing children. The deaf children had more physical contact than the hearing children at both periods of measurement. These differences in the interaction experienced by deaf and hearing children as they related to peers is undoubtedly one of the factors that contributes to findings of the self-image or the self-concept of the deaf child.

B. SELF-CONCEPT

Social development and self-concept go hand in hand. As a child begins to be an object to himself, as he sees himself reflected in the appraisals of others, he begins to understand both their behavior and his own. The importance of the development of self-boundaries, of distinguishing oneself as having an identity separate from that of others, is a basic psychoanalytic concept. The concept of identity is of great significance for behavioral scientists. Positive self-image is generally agreed to be essential to mental health. In spite of general agreement among behavioral scientists about the importance of the self-concept, there is no consensus about how to define, study, or measure it. When the subjects of interest are deaf children, problems of research methodology are magnified. Problems of definition and interpretation emerge with special clarity as well. Several investigators have compared the self-concept or self-image of deaf children with that of hearing children.

Brunschwig (1936) used a sentence-completion test to gather data on the self-image of deaf and hearing children; Craig (1965) utilized drawings to elicit sociometric choice data from which she extrapolated summaries of self evaluations; Gillies (1968) collected drawings of the child and of another person and interpreted them for self-image. All three of these researchers concluded that deaf children rated themselves significantly more positively than did the hearing children with whom they were compared.

Because of the language difficulties encountered in administering written sentence completion tests to profoundly deaf children, we must question the data collected by Brunschwig. If her subjects were indeed able to provide adequate sentences, it is likely that they were postlingually deaf and/or hard-of-hearing rather than deaf. The early date of the research makes this a good possibility, for reasons discussed previously. In a study completed more recently (Titus 1965), it was concluded that the sentence completion technique was unsuitable for eliciting self-image data from a group of profoundly deaf students in a residential school. This reviewer has attempted the same technique in pretest efforts to develop a self-image test with equally negative results.

Craig's population of 48 subjects consisted of three groups: a deaf group from a residential school, a deaf group attending a day school, and a hearing group attending regular public school. The children (9 ½–12 years old) were asked to decide which members of their class would choose them to sit near them or go to the beach and which of their classmates they would choose. Scores were derived for accuracy of self-perception, direction of errors of self-perception, and self-acceptance and sociability. The deaf children, both in day and in residential schools, were significantly less accurate in their self-perceptions than were the hearing children. The deaf children in the residential school rated themselves significantly more positively than did the children in the two other groups.

Meadow's research on self-image (Meadow 1969; Schlesinger & Meadow 1972), provides an interpretation for the studies of Brunschwig, Craig, and Gillies, primarily because her research design permitted analysis in terms of various subgroups of deaf children. A disadvantage is that no comparable data were collected from hearing children. Meadow (1969) originally studied 58 pairs of deaf children attending a residential school. Pairs were matched for age, sex, hearing loss, and IQ score. One member of each pair had deaf parents, the other member had hearing parents. After experimentation with a number of different testing techniques, a graphic cartoon-like test was developed using written adjectives plus illustrations of the manual signs for descriptive adjectives. For older children the test was administered in small groups. For younger children testing was individual. In all cases a combination of signs and speech was used. The deaf children with deaf parents (all of whom utilized manual communication with the children from an early age) had significantly higher, more positive scores than did the deaf children of hearing parents.

Later this study was expanded to include a group of 56 deaf students attending day schools (Schlesinger & Meadow 1972). All of these children had hearing parents. Too few students with deaf parents were available to include the logical fourth group in the research design. The average self-image test scores for the day pupils were almost identical with those of the residential school pupils with hearing parents—significantly less positive than the scores of the residential pupils with deaf parents. None of the hearing parents had used manual communication in any form when their children were young. Only a few hearing parents of the teenage children either used or approved the use of sign language.

The differences in apparent level of self-image between the deaf children with deaf and hearing parents can be interpreted in a variety of ways. The identity match in terms of handicap, providing the deaf child with a positive role model, is one possible contributing factor. The availability of sign language as a communicative mode is a second explanatory factor. The symbolic value and role-modeling function of sign language is yet a third possible factor.

In his interpretation of Brunschwig's findings of the apparent self-judgments of superiority on the part of deaf children, Barker (1953) suggests that if these responses do indeed reflect real feelings of well-being, they may result from the fact that children in schools for the deaf are praised frequently for relatively minor accomplishments. He notes, too, that the full force of cultural restraints and coercions associated with physical handicap is not felt until adulthood.

Craig's subjects were no older than 12 years of age. It may be that this "full force of cultural restraints" had not yet been brought to play with them, thus accounting for the high level of self-image of the deaf children compared with the hearing children in her study. Another factor of possible importance, not checked by Meadow, may be related to the frequent transfer of deaf children from day schools to residential schools at or about the age of 13. If a number of her subjects had indeed transferred from a day school setting, where they had been a distinct minority among a large population of hearing peers, to a residential school setting where they could identify with all their classmates and with some of their teachers on the dimension of deafness, their self-image might well shoot upward, thus accounting for the sharp discrepancy between the older and the younger students of hearing parents in the residential school. On the other hand, those deaf students who remain in day schools during the critical transitional adolescent years may feel their minority status even more sharply with a resultant decline in self-image which is reflected in the lower scores of the older day students.

Other variables investigated by Meadow in relation to the self-image scores included family climate, school achievement scores, and communication scores. Positive relationships were reported between each of these three variables and self-image. In addition, it was found that those deaf parents who were particularly active in the deaf community had children with significantly more positive self-images, as measured by Meadow's test. That is, if the deaf parents belonged to deaf social clubs, had many deaf friends, belonged to organizations such as the National Association of the Deaf, and subscribed to publications such as the *Deaf American,* their deaf children's self-conceptions were more likely to be positive. Thus there may either be a directly positive effect on the children of the parents' interaction with other deaf persons, or the deaf parents who felt more positive about their own identity were more likely to form these associations and also to communicate positive feelings regarding themselves to their children. Still a third possibility is that the support of the community was a positive influence independent of the family (Meadow 1967).

C. PERSONALITY STUDIES

Research on personality characteristics of deaf children has most often been conducted through the use of personality inventories. One of the major reasons for using these instruments is they seem simpler to administer than some other kinds of test instruments. However, the simplicity of the inventories is more apparent than real. Another type of instrument is the rating scale, completed by teachers or others in direct contact with the deaf child. These, too, have limitations for personality assessment. Early studies of personality development using inventories and rating scales showed, with few exceptions, that deaf children were rated, or that they displayed, more adjustment problems than did hearing children. Instruments used included, for example, the Bernreuter Personality Inventory (Pintner 1933, Welles 1932) and the Haggerty-Olson-Wickman Behavior Rating Scale (Burchard & Myklebust 1942; Getz 1953; Springer 1938).

Levine (1956) used a projective technique (Rorschach Test) for an in-depth study of personality characteristics of 31 girls aged 15–18. The subjects were all students at the Lexington School for the Deaf in New York City, had a hearing loss greater than 70 decibels in the better ear, and had hearing parents. All were rated as "normal deaf students" by three different teachers. That is, they were without any severe behavioral problems and were not considered to be unusual. Levine found few indications of anxiety, depression, or inner tension in the records of the adolescent girls tested. The incidence of egocentric and immature responses was very high. The most outstanding points were the singular absence or sparseness of signs of emotional disturbance and the adequate range of scoring factors in the responses.

Levine concluded that there was evidence of an impoverished capacity for inner creation, a meagerness of inner life, and an absence of the inner controls that should develop from it. Many records were characterized by indications of conscious control and respect for reality. Also typical were responses indicative of impulsiveness, easy irritability, egocentricity, and suggestibility. Levine's findings have been supported in a variety of ways in projective tests administered to other groups of deaf children by several investigators. For example, Hess (1960) describes his 28 deaf subjects, between 8 and 10 years of age, as being more rigid in new situations and less aware of the individuality of others. They were seen as more impulsive, having superficial interpersonal contacts, and as more egocentric, compared with 48 "well adjusted" and 49 "maladjusted" hearing children.

The Make A Picture Story test (Schneidman 1952) used in the previous study was also used by Bindon (1957) and by Neyhus (1964), with results that support those of Levine and Hess in a number of respects. Bindon administered the Make A Picture Story test to groups of rubella-deaf, non-rubella-deaf, and normal-hearing 15-year-olds. She found no differences between the rubella and non-rubella groups. However, when she compared the records of the rubella-deaf with those of the normal-hearing, the responses of the deaf children were rated inferior in terms of maturity of the responses. They were the responses typical of much younger children. Neyhus (1964) analyzed the Make A Picture Story test responses of 80 deaf adults aged 18–65 (average, 37). He concluded that the personality pattern that emerged was one reflecting restriction in breadth of experience, rigidity and confusion in thought processes, and an inability to integrate experiences in meaningful ways. He also found evidence of difficulties in forming interpersonal relationships and feelings of social isolation. However, Neyhus, like the other authors who have studied personality in deaf persons, concluded that there was little or no evidence of overt mental illness.

D. EMOTIONAL AND BEHAVIORAL DISORDERS

Our major source of information about the prevalence of extreme behavioral disorders in a deaf population is the work of Rainer, Altshuler, Kallmann, and their colleagues at the New York Psychiatric Institute (1966, 1969, 1971). These investigators concluded that the incidence of schizophrenia was not appreciably different in the deaf and in the hearing populations of New York State. However, they reported that the prevalence of "problems of living" appeared to be considerably higher in the deaf population. These problems appeared as higher arrest rates, marital/sexual and vocational difficulties, and difficulties related to low educational attainment. The basis for the New York material on mental disorders was records of 230 psychotic individuals, comprising the entire deaf population of New York State mental hospitals in 1958. The 120 schizophrenic cases constituted 52% of all deaf patients, a close approximation to the 57% of nondeaf patients with the same diagnosis (Altshuler & Rainer 1969).

Altshuler and Rainer noted the relative absence of severe endogenous depression among their deaf patients. Vernon (1969c) reports a different experience with patients seen at a Chicago clinic, where about 6% of the patient population had a primary diagnosis of depression, and depressive affect was seen as a component in many other cases. The Chicago group felt that the high prevalence of denial (often related specifically to the nature of their handicap) was often a mask or defense against depression among deaf patients. Vernon believes that depression is not insignificant in the deaf population, particularly among those deaf persons whose abilities and educational attainments lead them to feel frustrated by the realistic absence of opportunity for achievement.

While Altshuler and Rainer (1969) noted the relative absence of paranoid symptoms in their deaf-patient population, it may be that the popular belief that deaf persons are more likely to exhibit paranoid behavior is based on an accurate perception of deafened and hard-of-hearing persons. Indeed, Vernon concludes that "paranoid behavior or suspiciousness is probably somewhat more common among the deaf mentally ill than corresponding hearing populations. This seems especially true of the hard of hearing and the adventitiously deafened" (1969c, p. 27).

The New York group also had extensive experience in out-patient treatment of deaf adolescents and adults (Rainer & Altshuler 1966, 1971). Their descriptions of typical clusters of symptoms found in their deaf patients include many of the same personality characteristics found in populations of nondisturbed children and adults cited in the preceding section. They noted a general lack of understanding and empathy for others, egocentricity, coercive demands to have their own wishes gratified, and a lack of awareness of the effect of their behavior on other people. There were many instances of impulsive acting-out kinds of behavior, with few instances of self-imposed restraint. The kinds of problems observed in adolescent students referred for treatment in a residential school for the deaf were characterized as "primary behavior disorders of childhood" and "adjustment reactions of adolescence." The boys aged 13–16 years seemed exceedingly preoccupied with violence and fears. Girls seemed somewhat more mature than the boys. Both boys and girls displayed wide lack of knowledge about sexual functioning and about relationships with the opposite sex.

Like the New York group, the California group, at the Langley Porter Neuropsychiatric Institute, found difficulties in fitting deaf patients into the standard psychiatric diagnostic nomenclature. The experience of the clinicians in the San Francisco Bay Area (reported in Schlesinger & Meadow 1972, pp. 163–195) paralleled in many respects the earlier reports from New York. Illustrative data from case materials are presented, as they are in reports by Basilier (1964), and Williams (1970).

Schlesinger and Meadow (1972) also collected data on the prevalence of behavioral disorders at one residential school for the deaf. This study was done by means of a questionnaire distributed to teachers and counselors who were asked to identify children in their care whom they considered to be severely emotionally disturbed. Definitions and descriptions were offered that matched those used in a similar survey of all schoolchildren in Los Angeles County. School personnel were also asked to identify those students with more moderate behavioral problems. About 12% of the 516 students in the school were identified as severely disturbed; an additional 20% were seen as having problems of a lesser degree. These figures were five times and 2½ times, respectively, as high as the figures gathered for all (hearing) students in Los Angeles County.

E. SUMMARY

1. Many independent studies, done over a period of 40 years, have found deaf children to be less *socially mature* than hearing children. Deaf children of deaf parents have been found to be relatively more mature than the deaf children of hearing parents with whom they were compared. Residential school life appears to be related to social immaturity as well. A number of findings indicate that parents of handicapped children generally, and deaf children specifically, are reluctant to grant them the freedom and independence that would encourage independence and consequent maturity. These attitudes are often coupled with strong pressures for achievement in areas of speech training that are particularly difficult for the deaf child. The didactic and intrusive nature of mothers' interactions with their deaf children may be induced by the realistic assessment of reduced coping ability in the child. These interaction patterns may then lead to exacerbated dependence and even more retarded social maturity in the deaf child.

2. Delayed language acquisition experienced by most deaf children leads to more limited opportunities for *social interaction* and to frustration for them and their parents. An inability to communicate future plans limits the child, his parents, and his peers in structuring social life. They are handicapped in dealing with the qualities of objects and with abstract relationships. Imaginary play is limited, the expression of necessity and possibility is difficult, as is reference to internal events. All these linguistic features contribute to the reduced social interaction of deaf children.

3. Studies of the self-concept or self-image of deaf children, compared with hearing peers, indicate that their ideas about themselves are perhaps inaccurate—that is, that they have inflated ideas about their capabilities and the opinions held about them by others. Self-image studies of subgroups of deaf children have shown that the deaf children of deaf parents feel more positively about themselves than the deaf children of hearing parents with whom they were compared. Deaf children with hearing parents who attend residential schools have less positive self-

concepts than their peers who attend day schools. This suggests that the opportunity for interaction with other deaf children in a protective setting, and the opportunity to use adult deaf teachers and dormitory counselors as models, may be important to the development of positive feelings about themselves.

4. Personality inventories have consistently shown that deaf children have more adjustment problems than hearing children. When deaf children without overt or serious problems have been studied, they have been found to exhibit characteristics of rigidity, egocentricity, absence of creativity, absence of inner controls, impulsiveness, suggestibility, and lack of empathy.

5. Studies of the characteristics of overtly disturbed deaf individuals have shown exaggerated instances of the "problems of living" created by the kinds of personality characteristics described in the paragraph above. However, it is most interesting that the incidence of severe emotional/behavioral disorders is no higher in the deaf population than in the hearing population when measured by incidence of hospitalized patients and by known cases of schizophrenia. The incidence of problem behavior in a school for the deaf, however, has been found to be much higher than is to be expected. It would appear that paranoid symptoms are more often found among persons who are hard-of-hearing and adventitiously deafened. There are conflicting reports about the incidence of paranoid and depressive symptoms among groups of deaf mental patients.

VI. CONCLUSION

Profound congenital deafness creates a global handicap affecting the total development of a child. Consideration of the deficits and the consequences for the deaf child and for his family can lead the developmental scientist to a heightened appreciation of the influence of communicative deprivation. It is perhaps impossible and certainly misleading to separate the linguistic, the cognitive, the social, and the psychological aspects of the deaf-child's development. In a general sense, this is true for any child. However, an inadequate understanding of the blanketing effect of the auditory handicap can lead not only to less able research but also to major errors of design, analysis, and interpretation.

The linguistic deprivation encountered by most deaf children remains with them throughout their lives, if proficiency in standard written or spoken forms of English are the criteria for judgment. The influence of this deficit on the ability to participate in everyday family and educational activities is far-reaching and frustrating for both the child and his family. Intellectual activities are usually conducted through and evaluated in terms of the standard language of the majority hearing culture. As would be expected, most deaf children and deaf adults do not perform at a level that enables them to achieve satisfactorily in a competitive society.

Socialization and social development take place primarily through verbal communication. Rules of behavior, and the reasons for the rules, are transmitted verbally. Children who do not understand what is expected of them, and why, are at a major disadvantage. It is not surprising that they are found to have more than their share of psychological problems. The surprising thing is that the human organism can adapt as well as most deaf children do.

The general statements about the linguistic, cognitive, social, and psychological deprivation of deaf children assume early impoverishment of communication between the child and significant others in his environment. Some evidence has been cited to indicate that this early deprivation is neither as complete nor as devastating for deaf children who are exposed to auxiliary, visual modes of communication in the early years as compared with those who are not so exposed. Little experimental evidence is available, primarily because of the ongoing and bitter battles among educators about the consequences of nonoral communication. In the very recent past, however, this climate has been changing, and there should be additional opportunities for controlled scientific research. Thus, not only do deaf children have much to teach students of human development, behavioral scientists have unusual opportunities to contribute to the optimum development of these children in the future.

REFERENCES

Altshuler, K. Z., & Rainer, J. D. Distribution and diagnosis of patients in New York State mental hospitals. In J. D. Rainer, K. Z. Altshuler, & F. J. Kallmann (Eds.), *Family and mental health problems in a deaf population* (2d ed.) Springfield, Ill.: Thomas, 1969.

Anderson, H.; Barr, B.; & Wedenberg, E. Genetic disposition—a prerequisite for maternal rubella deafness. *Archives of Otolaryngology,* 1970, *91,* 141–147.

Anthony, D. A. Signing essential English. Unpublished master's thesis, Eastern Michigan University, 1966.

Avery, C. The social competence of pre-school acoustically handicapped children. *Journal of Exceptional Children,* 1948, *15,* 71–73.

Balow, I. H., & Brill, R. G. An evaluation study of reading and academic achievement levels of sixteen graduating classes of the California School for the Deaf, Riverside. Mimeographed report, Contract No. 4566, State of California, Department of Education, 1972.

Barker, R. G., with Wright, B. A.; Meyerson, L.; & Gonick, M. R. *Adjustment to physical handicap and illness: a survey of the social psychology of physique and disability.* (Bulletin 55, rev.) New York: Social Science Research Council, 1953.

Barton, M. E.; Court, S. D.; & Walker, W. Causes of severe deafness in school children in Northumberland and Durham. *British Medical Journal,* 1962, *1,* 351–355.

Basilier, T. Surdophrenia; the psychic consequences of congenital or early acquired deafness: some theoretical and clinical considerations. *Acta Psychiatrica Scandinavica,* 1964, *40* (Supplementum 180), 362–372.

Bell, R. Q. The effect on the family of a limitation in coping ability in the child: a research approach and a finding. *Merrill-Palmer Quarterly,* 1964, *10,* 129–142.

Bellugi, U. The acquisition of negation. Unpublished doctoral dissertation, Harvard University, 1967.

Bellugi, U. Studies in sign language. In T. J. O'Rourke (Ed.), *Psycholinguistics and total communication: the state of the art.* Washington, D.C.: American Annals of the Deaf, 1972.

Bellugi, U., & Klima, E. S. The roots of language in the sign talk of the deaf. *Psychology Today,* 1972, *6,* 661–64, 76.

Bellugi, U., & Klima, E. S. *Aspects of sign language and its structure.* Cambridge, Mass.: M.I.T. Press, 1975.

Bender, R. E. *The conquest of deafness.* Cleveland: Press of Western Reserve University, 1960.

Best, B. Development of classification skills in deaf children with and without early manual communication. Unpublished doctoral dissertation, University of California, Berkeley, 1970.

Bindon, D. M. Personality characteristics of rubella deaf children: implications for teaching of the deaf in general. *American Annals of the Deaf,* 1957, *102,* 264–270.

Black, J. W.; O'Reilly, P. P.; & Peck, L. Self administered training in lipreading. *Journal of Speech and Hearing Disorders,* 1963, *28,* 183–186.

Blair, F. X. A study of the visual memory of deaf and hearing children. *American Annals of the Deaf,* 1957, *102,* 254–263.

Blank, M. Use of the deaf in language studies: a reply to Furth. *Psychological Bulletin,* 1965, *63,* 442–444.

Blank, M. Cognitive functions of language in the preschool years. *Developmental Psychology,* 1974, *10,* 229–245.

Blank, M., & Bridger, W. H. Conceptual cross-modal transfer in deaf and hearing children. *Child Development,* 1966, *37,* 29–38.

Blanton, R. L., & Nunnally, J. C. Retention of trigrams by deaf and hearing subjects as a function of pronunciability. *Journal of Verbal Learning and Verbal Behavior,* 1967, *6,* 428–431.

Blanton, R. L.; Nunnally, J. C.; & Odom, P. B. Graphemic, phonetic, and associative factors in the verbal behavior of deaf and hearing subjects. *Journal of Speech and Hearing Research,* 1967, *10,* 225–231.

Bonvillian, J. D.; Charrow, V. R.; & Nelson, K. E. Psycholinguistic and educational implications of deafness. *Human Development,* 1973, *16,* 321–345.

Boothroyd, A. Some aspects of language function in a group of lower school children. Sensory Aids Research Project Report No. 6, C. V. Hudgins Diagnostic and Research Center, Clarke School for the Deaf, Northampton, Mass., 1971.

Bornstein, H. A description of some current sign systems designed to represent English. *American Annals of the Deaf,* 1973, *118,* 454–463.

Boyd, J. Comparison of motor behavior in deaf and hearing boys. *American Annals of the Deaf,* 1967, *112,* 598–605.

Brill, R. G. A study in adjustment of three groups of deaf children. *Exceptional Children,* 1960, *26,* 464–466.

Brown, R. *A first language, the early stages.* Cambridge, Mass.: Harvard University Press, 1973.

Bruininks, R. H., & Clark, C. Auditory and visual learning in first-grade educable mentally retarded and normal children. Research Report No. 13, Research, Development and Demonstration Center in Education of Handicapped Children, University of Minnesota, November 1970.

Brunschwig, L. *A study of some personality aspects of deaf children.* (Contributions to education, No. 687) New York: Teachers College Press, Columbia University, 1936.

Burchard, E. M. L., & Myklebust, H. R. A comparison of congenital and adventitious deafness with respect to its effect on intelligence, personality, and social maturity. *American Annals of the Deaf,* 1942, *87,* 140–154, 241–251, 342–360.

Butt, D., & Chreist, F. M. A speechreading test for young children. *Volta Review,* 1968, *70,* 225–235.

Charrow, V. R., & Fletcher, J. D. English as the second language of deaf children. *Developmental Psychology,* 1974, *10,* 463–470.

Chess, S.; Korn, S. J.; & Fernandez, P. B. *Psychiatric disorders of children with congenital rubella.* New York: Brunner/Mazel, 1971.

Cohen, S. R. Predictability of deaf and hearing story paraphrases. *Journal of Verbal Learning and Verbal Behavior,* 1967, *6,* 916–921.

Collins, J. L. Communication between deaf children of pre-school age and their mothers. Unpublished doctoral dissertation, University of Pittsburgh, 1969.

Conrad, R. Short-term memory processes in the deaf. *British Journal of Psychology,* 1970, *61,* 179–195.

Conrad, R. The effect of vocalizing on comprehension in the profoundly deaf. *British Journal of Psychology,* 1971, *62,* 147–150.

Cooper, R. L., & Rosenstein, J. Language acquisition of deaf children. *Volta Review,* 1966, *68,* 58–67.

Craig, H. B. A sociometric investigation of the self-concept of the deaf child. *American Annals of the Deaf,* 1965, *110,* 456–478.

Craig, W. N. Effects of pre-school training on the development of reading and lipreading skills of deaf children. *American Annals of the Deaf,* 1964, *109,* 280–296.

Craig, W. N. (Ed.) Directory of programs and services. *American Annals of the Deaf,* 1972, *117,* 41–356.

Craig, W. N.; Craig, H. B.; & DiJohnson, A. Pre-school verbotonal instruction for deaf children. *Volta Review,* 1972, *74,* 236–246.

Cummings, S. T.; Bayley, H. C.; & Rie, H. E. Effects of the child's deficiency on the mother: a study of mothers of mentally retarded, chronically ill and neurotic children. *American Journal of Orthopsychiatry,* 1966, *35,* 595–608.

Davis, F. Deviance disavowal: the management of strained interaction by the visibly handicapped. *Social Problems,* 1961, *9,* 120–132.

Davis, F. *Passage through crisis: polio victims and their families.* Indianapolis: Bobbs-Merrill, 1963.

DiCarlo, L. M. *The deaf.* Englewood Cliffs, N.J.: Prentice-Hall, 1964.

DiCarlo, L. M., & Dolphin, J. Social adjustment and personality development of deaf children: a review of literature. *Exceptional Children,* 1952, *18,* 111–118.

Doehring, D. G., & Rosenstein, J. Visual word recognition by deaf and hearing children. *Journal of Speech and Hearing Research,* 1960, *3,* 320–326.

Doll, E. A. *Vineland Social Maturity Scale: condensed manual of directions.* Circle Pines, Minn.: American Guidance Service, 1965.

Donnelly, K. An investigation into the determinants of lipreading of deaf adults. *International Audiology,* 1969, *8,* 501–508.

Downs, M. P., & Sterritt, G. M. A guide to newborn and infant hearing screening programs. *Archives of Otolaryngology,* 1967, *85,* 15–22.

Elliott, L. L., & Armbruster, V. B. Some possible effects of the delay of early treatment of deafness. *Journal of Speech and Hearing Research,* 1967, *10,* 209–224.

Erber, N. P. Evaluation of special hearing aids for deaf children. *Journal of Speech and Hearing Disorders,* 1971, *36,* 527–537.

Farber, B. Family organization and crisis: maintenance of integration in families with a severely mentally retarded child. *Monographs of the Society for Research in Child Development,* 1960, *25* (1, Serial No. 75).

Farwell, R. M. Speechreading, a review of the research. *American Annals of the Deaf.* 1975 (in press).

Fellendorf, G., & Harrow, I. Parent counseling, 1961–1968. *Volta Review,* 1970, *72,* 51–57.

Fiedler, M. F. Developmental studies of deaf children. *ASHA Monographs Number 13.* Vol. 5. Washington, D.C.: American Speech and Hearing Association, 1969.

Fitzgerald, M. D.; Sitton, A. B.; & McConnell, F. Audiometric, development, and learning characteristics of a group of rubella deaf children. *Journal of Speech and Hearing Disorders,* 1970, *35,* 218–228.

Fraser, G. R. Profound childhood deafness. *Journal of Medical Genetics,* 1964, *1,* 118–151.

Frisina, D. R. Statistical information concerning the deaf and the hard of hearing in the United States. *American Annals of the Deaf,* 1959, *104,* 265–270.

Fry, D. B. The development of the phonological system in the normal and the deaf child. In F. Smith & G. A. Miller (Eds.), *The genesis of language: a psycholinguistic approach.* Cambridge, Mass.: M.I.T. Press, 1966.

Furth, H. G. Influence of language on the development of concept formation in deaf children. *Journal of Abnormal and Social Psychology,* 1961, *63,* 386–389. (a)

Furth, H. G. Visual paired-associates task with deaf and hearing children. *Journal of Speech and Hearing Research,* 1961, *4,* 172–177. (b)

Furth, H. G. Classification transfer with disjunctive concepts as a function of verbal training and set. *Journal of Psychology,* 1963, *55,* 477–485.

Furth, H. G. Research with the deaf: implications for language and cognition. *Psychological Bulletin,* 1964, *62,* 145–164. (Reprinted with an addendum in S. P. Quigley [Ed.], *Language acquisition.* Washington, D.C.: A. G. Bell Association for the Deaf, 1966.)

Furth, H. G. A comparison of reading test norms of deaf and hearing children. *American Annals of the Deaf,* 1966, *111,* 461–462. (a)

Furth, H. G. *Thinking without language: psychological implications of deafness.* New York: Free Press, 1966. (b)

Furth, H. G. Linguistic deficiency and thinking: research with deaf subjects, 1964–1969. *Psychological Bulletin,* 1971, *76,* 58–72.

Fusfeld, I. S. How the deaf communicate—written language. *American Annals of the Deaf,* 1958, *103,* 255–263.

Getz, S. *Environment and the deaf child.* Springfield, Ill.: Thomas, 1953.

Gilbert, J., & Levee, R. F. Performances of deaf and normally-hearing children on the Bender Gestalt and the Archimedes Spiral Tests. *Perceptual and Motor Skills,* 1967, *24,* 1059–1066.

Gillies, J. Variations in drawings of "a person" and "myself" by hearing-impaired and normal children. *British Journal of Educational Psychology,* 1968, *38,* 86–88.

Glorig, A. Routine neonate hearing screening: summary and evaluation. *Hearing and Speech News,* 1971, *39,* 4–7.

Goetzinger, C. P., & Huber, T. C. A study of immediate and delayed visual retention with deaf and hearing adolescents. *American Annals of the Deaf,* 1964, *109,* 297–305.

Goldstein, R., & Tait, C. Critique of neonatal hearing evaluation. *Journal of Speech and Hearing Disorders,* 1971, *36,* 3–18.

Gordon, J. E. Relationship among mother's achievement, independence training attitudes, and handicapped child's performance. *Journal of Consulting Psychology,* 1959, *23,* 207–213.

Goss, R. N. Language used by mothers of deaf children and mothers of hearing children. *American Annals of the Deaf,* 1970, *115,* 93–96.

Graham, E. E., & Shapiro, E. Use of the performance scale of the W.I.S.C. with the deaf child. *Journal of Consulting Psychology,* 1953, *17,* 396–398.

Gustason, G.; Pfetzing, D.; & Zawolkow, E. *Signing exact English.* Rossmoor, Calif.: Modern Signs Press, 1972.

Heider, F., & Heider, G. M. Studies in the psychology of the deaf, No. 1 Psychological Division, Clarke School for the Deaf. *Psychological Monographs,* 1940, *52,* No. 232.

Heider, F., & Heider, G. M. Studies in psychology of the deaf. *Psychological Monographs,* 1941, *53,* No. 242.

Heider, G. M. Adjustment problems of the deaf child. *Nervous Child,* 1948, *7,* 38–44.

Hess, W. Personality adjustment in deaf children. Unpublished doctoral dissertation, University of Rochester, 1960.

Hicks, D. E. Comparison profiles of rubella and non-rubella deaf children. *American Annals of the Deaf,* 1970, *115,* 86–92.

Hirsh, I. J. Teaching the deaf child to speak. In F. Smith & G. A. Miller (Eds.), *The genesis of language.* Cambridge, Mass.: M.I.T. Press, 1966.

Hiskey, M. C. A study of the intelligence of deaf and hearing children. *American Annals of the Deaf,* 1956, *101,* 329–339.

Hodgson, K. W. *The deaf and their problems: a study in special education.* London: Watts, 1953.

Hoffmeister, R. J., & Moores, D. F. The acquisition of specific reference in the linguistic system of a deaf child of deaf parents. Research Report No. 53, Research, Development and Demonstration Center in Education of Handicapped Children, University of Minnesota, August 1973.

Jackson, A. D. M., & Fisch, J. Deafness following maternal rubella: results of a prospective investigation. *Lancet,* 1958, *2,* 1241–1244.

John Tracy Clinic. Correspondence course for parents of little deaf children. Mimeographed. Los Angeles: John Tracy Clinic, 1954.

Jordan, T. E. Research on the handicapped child and the family. *Merrill-Palmer Quarterly,* 1962, *8,* 243–260.

Kannapell, B. M.; Hamilton, L. B.; & Bornstein, H. *Signs for instructional purposes.* Washington, D.C.: Gallaudet College Press, 1969.

Kates, S. L.; Yudin, L.; & Tiffany, R. K. Concept attainment by deaf and hearing adolescents. *Journal of Educational Psychology,* 1962, *53,* 119–126.

Kent, M. S. Differential educational needs in the habilitation and rehabilitation of the deaf. *American Annals of the Deaf,* 1962, *107,* 523–529.

Keogh, B. K.; Vernon, M.; & Smith, C. E. Deafness and visuo-motor function. *Journal of Special Education,* 1970, *4,* 41–47.

Kloepfer, H. W.; Laguaite, J.; & McLaurin, J. W. Genetic aspects of congenital hearing loss. *American Annals of the Deaf,* 1970, *115,* 17–22.

Konigsmark, B. W. Genetic hearing loss with no associated abnormalities: a review. *Journal of Speech and Hearing Disorders,* 1972, 37, 89–99.

Lach, R.; Ling, D.; Ling, A. H.; & Ship, N. Early speech development in deaf infants. *American Annals of the Deaf,* 1970, *115,* 522–526.

Lenneberg, E. H. *Biological foundations of language.* New York: Wiley, 1967.

Lenneberg, E. H.; Rebelsky, F. G.; & Nichols, I. A. The vocalizations of infants born to deaf and to hearing parents. *Human Development,* 1965, *8,* 23–37.

Levine, E. S. Psychoeducational study of children born deaf following maternal rubella in pregnancy. *American Journal of Diseases of Children,* 1951, *81,* 627–635.

Levine, E. S. *Youth in a soundless world: a search for personality.* New York: New York University Press, 1956.

Levine, E. S. *The psychology of deafness: techniques of appraisal for rehabilitation.* New York: Columbia University Press, 1960.

Levine, E. S. Historical review of special education and mental health services. In J. D. Rainer, K. Z. Altshuler, & F. J. Kallmann (Eds.), *Family and mental health problems in a deaf population* (2d ed.) Springfield, Ill.: Thomas, 1969. (a)

Levine, E. S. Psychological testing: development and practice. In J. D. Rainer, K. Z. Altshuler, & F. J. Kallmann (Eds.), *Family and mental health problems in a deaf population* (2d ed.) Springfield, Ill.: Thomas, 1969. (b)

Lewis, D. N. Lipreading skills of hearing impaired children in regular schools. *Volta Review,* 1972, *74,* 303–311.

Ling, D. Conventional hearing aids: an overview. *Volta Review,* 1971, *73,* 343–352, 375–383.

McCall, E. A generative grammar of signs. Unpublished master's thesis, University of Iowa, 1965.

MacDougall, J. C., & Rabinovitch, M. S. Early auditory deprivation and sensory compensation. *Developmental Psychology,* 1971, *5,* 368. (a)

MacDougall, J. C., & Rabinovitch, M. S. Imagery and learning in deaf and hearing children. *Psychonomic Science,* 1971, *22,* 347–349. (b)

MacDougall, J. C., & Rabinovitch, M. S. Early auditory deprivation and exploratory activity. *Developmental Psychology,* 1972, *7,* 17–20.

McNeill, D. The capacity for language acquisition. In Vocational Rehabilitation Administration, Research on behavioral aspects of deafness, Proceedings of a National Research Conference on behavioral aspects of deafness, New Orleans, May 1965.

Meadow, K. P. The effect of early manual communication and family climate on the deaf child's development. Unpublished doctoral dissertation, University of California, Berkeley, 1967.

Meadow, K. P. Early manual communication in relation to the deaf child's intellectual, social, and communicative functioning. *American Annals of the Deaf,* 1968, *113,* 29–41. (a)

Meadow, K. P. Parental responses to the medical ambiguities of deafness. *Journal of Health and Social Behavior,* 1968, *9,* 299–309. (b)

Meadow, K. P. Self-image, family climate, and deafness. *Social Forces,* 1969, *47,* 428–438.

Meadow, K. P. Sociolinguistics, sign language and the deaf sub-culture. In T. J. O'Rourke (Ed.), *Psycholinguistics and total communication: the state of the art.* Washington, D.C.: American Annals of the Deaf, 1972.

Mindel, E. D., & Vernon, M. *They grow in silence—the deaf child and his family.* Silver Spring, Md.: National Association of the Deaf, 1971.

Mira, M. P. The use of the Arthur Adaptation of the Leiter International Performance Scale and Nebraska Test of Learning Aptitude with pre-school deaf children. *American Annals of the Deaf,* 1962, *107,* 224–228.

Montgomery, G. W. G. The relationship of oral skills to manual communication in profoundly deaf students. *American Annals of the Deaf,* 1966, *111,* 557–565.

Moores, D. F. An investigation of the psycholinguistic functioning of deaf adolescents. *Exceptional Children,* 1970, *36,* 645–654. (a)

Moores, D. F. Oral vs. manual. . ."old prejudices die hard, but die they must." *American Annals of the Deaf,* 1970, *115,* 667–669. (b)

Moores, D. F.; McIntyre, C. K.; & Weiss, K. L. Evaluation of programs for hearing impaired children: report of 1971–72. Research Report No. 39, Research, Development and Demonstration Center in Education of Handicapped Children, University of Minnesota, September 1972.

Myklebust, H. R. *The psychology of deafness, sensory deprivation, learning and adjustment.* New York: Grune & Stratton, 1960.

Myklebust, H. R.; Neyhus, A; & Mulholland, A. M. Guidance and counseling for the deaf. *American Annals of the Deaf,* 1962, *107,* 370–415.

Neyhus, A. The social and emotional adjustment of deaf adults. *Volta Review,* 1964, *66,* 319–325.

Neyhus, A. *Speechreading failure in deaf children.* Washington, D.C.: Office of Education, Department of Health, Education, and Welfare, 1969.

Odom, P. B., & Blanton, R. L. Phrase-learning in deaf and hearing subjects. *Journal of Speech and Hearing Research,* 1967, *10,* 600–605.

Odom, P. B.; Blanton, R. L.; & McIntyre, C. K. Coding medium and word recall by deaf and hearing subjects. *Journal of Speech and Hearing Research,* 1970, *13,* 54–58.

Office of Demographic Studies. Academic achievement test results of a national testing program for hearing impaired students: United States, 1971. Data from the annual survey of hearing impaired children and youth. Series D, No. 9. Washington, D.C.: Gallaudet College, 1972.

Office of Demographic Studies. Further studies in achievement testing, hearing impaired students: United States, Spring 1971. Data from the annual survey of hearing impaired children and youth. Series D, No. 13. Washington, D.C.: Gallaudet College, 1973.

Oleron, P., & Herren, H. L'acquisition des conservations et langage: étude comparative sur des enfants sourds et entendants. *Enfance,* 1961, *14,* 203–219.

O'Neill, J. J., & Davidson, J. L. Relationship between lipreading and five psychological factors. *Journal of Speech and Hearing Disorders,* 1956, *21,* 478–481.

O'Rourke, T. J. *A basic course in manual communication.* Silver Spring, Md.: National Association of the Deaf, 1970.

Pintner, R. Emotional stability of the hard of hearing. *Journal of Genetic Psychology,* 1933, *43,* 293–311.

Pintner, R.; Eisenson, J.; & Stanton, M. *The psychology of the physically handicapped.* New York: Crofts, 1941.

Pintner, R., & Paterson, D. G. The ability of deaf and hearing children to follow printed directions. *Pediatric Seminary,* 1916, *23,* 477–497.

Pintner, R., & Reamer, J. F. A mental and educational survey of schools for the deaf. *American Annals of the Deaf,* 1920, *65,* 451.

Pollack, D. Acoupedies: a unisensory approach to auditory training. *Volta Review,* 1964, *66,* 400–409.

Porter, T. A. Hearing aids in a residential school. *American Annals of the Deaf,* 1973, *118,* 31–33.

Quigley, S. P. *The influence of fingerspelling on the development of language, communication, and educational achievement in deaf children.* Urbana/Champaign: University of Illinois, Institute for Research on Exceptional Children, 1968.

Quigley, S. P., & Frisina, D. R. Institutionalization and psychoeducational development of deaf children. *Council for Exceptional Children Research Monographs,* 1961(3, Series A).

Rainer, J. D., & Altshuler, K. Z. *Comprehensive mental health services for the deaf.* New York: New York State Psychiatric Institute, Columbia University, 1966.

Rainer, J. D., & Altshuler, K. Z. *Expanded mental health care for the deaf: rehabilitation and prevention.* Washington, D.C.: Government Printing Office, 1971.

Rainer, J. D.; Altshuler, K. Z.; & Kallmann, F. J. (Eds.) *Family and mental health problems in a deaf population* (2d ed.) Springfield, Ill.: Thomas, 1969.

Reid, G. W. A preliminary investigation of the testing of lipreading achievement. *Journal of Speech and Hearing Disorders,* 1947, *12,* 77–82.

Rosenstein, J. Tactile perception of rhythmic patterns by normal, blind, deaf and aphasic children. *American Annals of the Deaf,* 1957, *102,* 399–403.

Rosenstein, J. Cognitive abilities of deaf children. *Journal of Speech and Hearing Research,* 1960, *3,* 108–119.

Rosenstein, J. Perception, cognition, and language in deaf children. *Exceptional Children,* 1961, *27,* 276–284.

Rosenzweig, M. R. Environmental complexity, cerebral change, and behavior. *American Psychologist,* 1966, *21,* 321–332.

Ross, M.; Kessler, M. E.; Phillips, M. E.; & Lerman, J. W. Visual, auditory, and combined mode presentations of the WIPI Test to hearing impaired children. *Volta Review,* 1972, *74,* 90–96.

Ross, M., & Matkin, N. D. The rising audiometric configuration. *Journal of Speech and Hearing Disorders,* 1967, *32,* 377–382.

Sank, D. Genetic aspects of early total deafness. In J. D. Rainer, K. Z. Altshuler, & F. J. Kallmann (Eds.), *Family and mental health problems in a deaf population* (2d ed.) Springfield, Ill.: Thomas, 1969.

Schaefer, E. S., & Bell, R. Q. Development of a parental attitude research instrument. *Child Development,* 1958, *29,* 339–361.

Schein, J. D. *The deaf community: studies in the social psychology of deafness.* Washington, D.C.: Gallaudet College Press, 1968.

Schein, J. D., & Bushnaq, S. Higher education for the deaf in the United States, a retrospective investigation. *American Annals of the Deaf,* 1962, *107,* 416–420.

Schein, J. D., & Delk, M. T., Jr. *The deaf population of the United States.* Silver Springs, Md.: National Association of the Deaf, 1974.

Schiff, W., & Dytell, R. S. Tactile identification of letters: a comparison of deaf and hearing children's performances. *Journal of Experimental Child Psychology,* 1971, *11,* 150–164.

Schlesinger, H. S. Beyond the range of sound. *California Medicine,* 1969, *110,* 213–217.

Schlesinger, H. S. Prevention, diagnosis, and habilitation of deafness: a critical look. In D. Hicks (Ed.), *Medical aspects of deafness.* Proceedings, National Forum IV, Council of Organizations Serving the Deaf, Atlantic City, 1971.

Schlesinger, H. S. Meaning and enjoyment: language acquisition of deaf children. In T. J. O'Rourke (Ed.), *Psycholinguistics and total communication: the state of the art.* Washington, D.C.: American Annals of the Deaf, 1972.

Schlesinger, H. S. The acquisition of sign language. Unpublished manuscript, Department of Psychiatry, University of California, San Francisco, 1974.

Schlesinger, H. S., & Meadow, K. P. Deafness and mental health: a developmental approach. Multilithed. San Francisco: Langley Porter Neuropsychiatric Institute, 1971.

Schlesinger, H. S., & Meadow, K. P. *Sound and sign: childhood deafness and mental health.* Berkeley: University of California Press, 1972.

Schneidman, E. S. *Manual for the Make A Picture Story method.* New York: Society for Projective Techniques and Rorschach Institute, 1952.

Scouten, E. L. The Rochester method, an oral multisensory approach for instructing prelingual deaf children. *American Annals of the Deaf,* 1967, *112,* 50–55.

Sigel, I. E. The attainment of concepts. In M. L. Hoffman & L. W. Hoffman (Eds.), *Review of child development research.* Vol. 1. New York: Russell Sage Foundation, 1964.

Silverman, R. T. Categorization behavior and achievement in deaf and hearing children. *Exceptional Children,* 1967, *34,* 241–250.

Silverman, S. R. Rehabilitation for irreversible deafness. *Journal of the American Medical Association,* 1966, *196,* 843–846.

Simmons, A. A. Factors related to lipreading. *Journal of Speech and Hearing Research,* 1959, *2,* 340–352.

Springer, N. N. A comparative study of behavior traits of deaf and hearing children of New York City. *American Annals of the Deaf,* 1938, *83,* 255–273.

Stein, L. A cure for deafness: reality or myth. *American Annals of the Deaf,* 1973, *118,* 670–671.

Sterritt, G. M.; Camp, B. W.; & Lipman, B. S. Effects of early auditory deprivation upon auditory and visual information processing. *Perceptual and Motor Skills,* 1966, *23,* 123–130.

Stinson, M. S. Maternal reinforcement and help and the achievement motive in hearing and hearing impaired children. *Developmental Psychology,* 1974, *10,* 348–353.

Stokoe, W. C., Jr. *Sign language structure: an outline of the visual communication systems of the American deaf.* (Studies in linguistics, occasional papers, 8) Buffalo, N.Y.: Department of Anthropology and Linguistics, University of Buffalo. 1960.

Stokoe, W. C., Jr.; Casterline, D. C.; & Croneberg, C. G. *A dictionary of American Sign Language on linguistic principles.* Washington, D.C.: Gallaudet College Press, 1965.

Streng, A., & Kirk, S. A. The social competence of deaf and hard of hearing children in a public day school. *American Annals of the Deaf,* 1938, *83,* 244–254.

Stuckless, E. R., & Birch, J. W. The influence of early manual communication on the linguistic development of deaf children. *American Annals of the Deaf,* 1966, *111,* 452–460, 499–504.

Templin, M. *The development of reasoning in children with normal and defective hearing.* Minneapolis: University of Minnesota Press, 1950.

Templin, M. Methodological variations in language research with deaf subjects. *Proceedings of International Conference on Oral Education of the Deaf.* Vol. 2. Washington, D.C.: Alexander Graham Bell Association, 1967.

Tervoort, B. T. Esoteric symbolism in the communication behavior of young deaf children. *American Annals of the Deaf,* 1961, *106,* 436–480.

Titus, E. S. The self-concept and adjustment of deaf teenagers. Unpublished doctoral dissertation, University of Missouri, 1965.

U.S. Census. *The deaf-mute population of the United States, 1920.* Washington, D.C.: Government Printing Office, 1928.

U.S. Census. *The blind and deaf-mutes in the United States, 1930.* Washington, D.C.: Government Printing Office, 1931.

Upshall, C. C. *Day schools vs. institutions for the deaf.* Teachers College, Columbia University contributions to education, No. 389. New York: Bureau of Publications, Teachers College, Columbia University, 1929.

Van Lieshout, C. F. M. The assessment of stability and change in peer interaction of normal hearing and deaf pre-school children. Paper presented at the 1973 biennial meeting of the International Society for the Study of Behavioral Development, Ann Arbor, Mich., August 21–25, 1973.

Vernon, M. Characteristics associated with post-rubella children: psychological, educational, and physical. *Volta Review,* 1967, *69,* 176–185. (a)

Vernon, M. Prematurity and deafness: the magnitude and nature of the problem among deaf children. *Exceptional Children,* 1967, *34,* 289–298. (b)

Vernon, M. Rh factor and deafness: the problem, its psychological, physical, and educational manifestations. *Exceptional Children,* 1967, *34,* 5–12. (c)

Vernon, M. Current etiological factors in deafness. *American Annals of the Deaf,* 1968, *113,* 1–12.

Vernon, M. *Multiply handicapped deaf children: medical, educational, and psychological considerations.* (CEC Research Monograph) Washington, D.C.: Council for Exceptional Children, 1969. (a)

Vernon, M. Sociological and psychological factors associated with hearing loss. *Journal of Speech and Hearing Research,* 1969, *12,* 541–563. (b)

Vernon, M. The final report. In R. R. Grinker, Sr. (Ed.), *Psychiatric diagnosis, therapy and research on the psychotic deaf.* Chicago: Institute for Psychosomatic and Psychiatric Research and Training, Michael Reese Hospital, 1969. (c)

Vernon, M., & Koh, S. D. Early manual communication and deaf children's achievement. *American Annals of the Deaf,* 1970, *115,* 527–536.

Vernon, M., & Rothstein, D. A. Prelingual deafness, an experiment of nature. *Archives of Genetic Psychiatry,* 1968, *19,* 361–369.

Vetter, H. J. *Language behavior and psychopathology.* Chicago: Rand-McNally, 1970.

Welles, H. H. Measurement of certain aspects of personality among hard of hearing adults. *Teachers College Contributions to Education,* 1932, No. 545.

Williams, K. E. Some psychiatric observations in a group of maladjusted deaf children. *Journal of Child Psychology and Psychiatry,* 1970, *11,* 1–18.

Wrightstone, J. W.; Aronow, M. S.; & Moskowitz, S. Developing reading test norms for deaf children. *American Annals of the Deaf,* 1963, *108,* 311–316.

Zink, G. D. Hearing aids children wear: a longitudinal study of performance. *Volta Review,* 1972, *74,* 41–51.

Zuk, G. H. The cultural dilemma and spiritual crisis of the family with a handicapped child. *Exceptional Children,* 1962, *28,* 405–408.

9 Child Abuse:
An Interdisciplinary Analysis

ROSS D. PARKE
AND CANDACE WHITMER COLLMER
Fels Research Institute

CONTENTS

The chapter was prepared with the support of National Science Foundation grant SOC72-05220 A03 to Ross D. Parke. Thanks to a number of individuals for critical comments and suggestions on earlier drafts of this chapter, including Frank Falkner, E. Mavis Hetherington, Robert D. Kavanaugh, C. Henry Kempe, Gerald R. Patterson, John B. Reid, Douglas B. Sawin, Suzanne K. Steinmetz, and Murray A. Straus. A special note of appreciation to the members of the 1974 Summer Seminar on Child Abuse at the Institute of Child Development, University of Minnesota, who contributed significantly to the clarification of the conceptual foundations of this chapter. The group included Susan Adelson, Pauline Banford, Wyndol Furman, Royal G. Grueneich, Michael C. Lougee, Janice R. Mokros, and Brian E. Vaughn. Finally, thanks to Frances Hall and Cathy Prinslow for their able assistance in preparation of the manuscript.

I. Introduction

Few problems in recent times have aroused the concern of American society to the extent of child abuse. It is a shocking fact that many thousands of children are beaten, sexually molested, and neglected annually in the United States. The purpose of this paper is to provide a review and analysis of the problem of physical abuse of children. Attention will be paid to an evaluation of alternative theoretical models that have been proposed to account for child abuse. Finally, treatment programs aimed at reducing the incidence of abuse will be examined. "Child abuse," as a term, can cover many different forms of maltreatment of children. This review is restricted to the use of excessive physical force by parents usually in the home environment. The use of extreme forms of physical discipline by school teachers and other school authorities is outside the scope of this review. Similarly, sexual abuse of children by adults will not be considered in this chapter.

II. Toward a Definition of Child Abuse

A variety of definitions of child abuse have been offered and none is free of ambiguities. There are parallels between attempts at defining child abuse and defining other types of social behavior such as aggression. There are two principal approaches to the definition of physical abuse. First, abuse can be defined in terms of outcomes, which serves to focus attention on the injuries. From this perspective, abuse would be defined as "behavior that results in injury of another individual." The advantage of this type of definition is that certain objectively quantifiable levels of injury could be established as standards for invoking the label of child abuse and inferences about the injuring agent's intent or motives would be minimized. Buss (1961) has advocated this approach in defining aggressive behavior. However, there are serious limitations to this type of definition. In this case, children receiving accidental injuries would be grouped with those who were victims of intentionally inflicted injuries. Consider the following example: parent A in a moment of anger pushes child A against a table corner injuring his head, while parent B in the course of a friendly game pushes child B who falls and injures his head. Both children are injured, and by an objective definition both parents would be described as abusive. But it is obvious that we need a definition that excludes accidental occurrences.

The second approach to definition of physical abuse recognizes the need to include the concept of intentionality. Kempe and Helfer (1972) give recognition to the concept of intentionality in their definition of abuse: ". . . any child who received nonaccidental physical injury (or injuries) as a result of acts (or omissions) on the part of his parents or guardians" (p. 1). While this does eliminate accidental occurrences of injury, many would object to this definition because of the difficulties encountered by the use of the concept of intentionality. The introduction of intent into the definition raises a serious problem, since intent is not part of the observable behavior but can most often be inferred from antecendent conditions and context. This type of definition involves more than an observable act or sequence of behavior which can be reliably measured, since the observer must also make judgments or inferences concerning the actor's intention. Neither laymen nor professionals are very accurate in judging another person's intentions, and thus problems of the reliability and validity of judgments of intent often arise.

A third approach to defining child abuse recognizes that physical abuse is not a set of behaviors but, rather, a culturally determined label which is applied to behavior and injury patterns as an outcome of a social judgment on the part of the observer (Walters & Parke 1964). Intention is merely one criterion that we typically employ in deciding whether an interpersonal exchange between an adult caretaker and a child is abusive. In making this judgment, an observer takes into account a variety of factors, including the antecendents of the response, the form and intensity of the response, the extent of the injury, and the role and status of the agent and victim of the behavior. In short, an injury will be labeled abuse in one situation or in one child or in one social class, and the same injury may not be judged abuse in another situation, child, or social class. For example, is an injury incurred by a child from a poor family more likely to be labeled abuse than a similar injury incurred by a child from a middle-class family? Even an objective definition of child abuse in terms of injuries must include standards concerning the severity of outcome which, in turn, are culturally defined. From this viewpoint, the definition of child abuse will vary with social class and the cultural background of the defining individual. Child abuse is a community-defined phenomenon, which must be viewed in the context of community norms and standards governing the appropriate conduct of adults in their interactions with their own and others' children. To date, insufficient attention has been paid to the development of an empirically derived set of standards based on community consensus concerning the rights of children and parents. An adequate definition of child abuse must give explicit recognition to the community-defined bases of the phenomenon.

To illustrate the confusion that may arise if a definition deviates from commonly accepted community standards of appropriate parental behavior, consider the definition offered by Gil in "Violence against Children": "Physical abuse of children is the intentional, nonaccidental use of force, on the part of a parent or other caretaker interacting with a child in his care aimed at hurting, injuring or destroying that child" (Gil 1970, p. 6). There are serious conceptual problems with Gil's definition, which flow in part from a failure to distinguish between actual community attitudes toward the use of physical punishment as a technique of discipline and one's own ideological views concerning the acceptability of these disciplinary techniques. Included in this definition are "all uses of physical force aimed at hurting, injuring or destroying a child irrespective of the degree of seriousness of the act and/or the outcome" (Gil 1970, p. 6). However, is it useful to include all parents who use physical force in the form of physical punishment in a definition of abuse? It is not merely from the viewpoint of community standards that this approach can be questioned. Consider the following estimates: Stark and McEvoy (1970) report that 93% of parents surveyed use physical punishment although some use it only rarely and only on young children. In contrast, Gil estimates that approximately 2.3%–3.7% of the population are subject to abuse. Therefore, it is questionable whether a definition which includes over 90% of the population is sufficiently discriminating to be useful.

A final problem of definition flows from the assumption that physical abuse is a single phenomenon; in fact, as we will note in the later sections, there are many types of physical abuse—whether defined in terms of the situations that elicit abuse, or in terms of the parents who abuse, or in terms of the types of injuries and victims.

For purposes of this review a modification of the Kempe-Helfer definition of child abuse will be employed: any child who receives nonaccidental physical injury (or injuries) as a result of acts (or omissions) on the part of his parents or guardians that violate the community standards concerning the treatment of children.

III. SCOPE OF THE PROBLEM

A. RATE OF INCIDENCE

At present the exact scope of child abuse is unknown. However, there are a number of statistics that help define the magnitude of the problem. There are two principal sources of data: hospital and community agency reports and a recent national survey (Gil 1970). Kempe (1971) estimated that there were as many as six incidents of physical abuse per 1,000 births in the United States. And, more recently, Kempe (1973) estimates that approximately 60,000 children were seriously abused during 1972. Fontana (1973) suggests that the annual rate is 1.5 million cases of child abuse. However, to illustrate the seriousness of the reporting problem— since the inception of a central registry in New York in 1966, the local rate of abused children has increased 549%. Similarly, in 1968, there were 11,000 cases of child abuse filed in all state registries, but by 1972 the number doubled. Whether this increase in reported cases of child abuse reflects a real increase in the problem is questionable. Apparent increases in child abuse rates may, in part, be due to shifts in public and professional awareness and knowledge of child abuse in conjunction with more stringent reporting laws and better legal protection for persons who report cases of abuse.

In light of the potential error in utilizing agency estimates, other techniques for estimating the incidence of child abuse have been employed. Another approach to the incidence problem comes from Gil (1970), who conducted a national survey to determine public awareness of child abuse. Gil assumed that members of the community know of cases of child abuse, even though these cases are never reported to professional authorities or at least never appear in the incidence statistics. In conjunction with the National Opinion Research Center, Gil surveyed a sample of 1,520 people which represented the total noninstitutionalized population of the United States over 21 years old or under 21 and married. They were asked "whether they personally knew families involved in incidents of child abuse resulting in physical injury during the prior 12 months." Forty-five individuals or 3% of the sample of 1,520 people reported such knowledge of 48 different incidents. Extrapolating from this outcome to the total U. S. population of 110 million and allowing for a margin of error, Gil estimated that there were between 2.53 and 4.07 million adults throughout the United States who personally knew families involved in incidents of child abuse during the preceding year. These figures, as Gil notes, must be interpreted cautiously, since there may be some overlap in the cases of abuse known to different respondents. More recently, Light (1973) has offered a more conservative estimate of physical abuse by applying a series of corrective assumptions to Gil's original data. By assuming that each respondent in the survey knew more than one family and were differentially acquainted with other families, and by further adjustment for the average number of abused children per family (1.6), Light estimates that there are approximately 500,000 abused children in the United States. In any case, the numbers of abused children are sufficiently large to justify a major effort to determine the causes of this phenomenon. These figures should not imply that child abuse is a peculiarly American phenomenon. Other English-speaking countries, such as Canada (Harrison 1968; Van Stolk 1972), Australia (Committee Report 1967), and Great Britain (Skinner & Castle 1969), report incidents of child abuse. In Britain, estimates are that, of 500,000 infants born, 3,000 will be seriously injured or deprived. Similarly, non-English-speaking countries, such as Germany, report similar problems (Torgerson 1973, cited by Bellak & Antell 1974).

B. SOURCES OF UNRELIABILITY IN ABUSE ESTIMATES

Most approximations of the incidence of child abuse in the United States probably underestimate the actual rate of occurrence. What are the reasons for the vast discrepancy between actual reported figures of child abuse and the frequencies reported by Gil's interviewees concerning their knowledge of abuse cases? There are a number of possible reasons. First, parents may simply not take the child or infant for medical attention. Second, parents who are repeated abusers may shift hospitals and/or physicians in order to reduce the likelihood that their child's repeated injuries will form the basis for classification as abuse, but instead be seen as accidents. Third, the types of injuries that are inflicted may sometimes not easily be detected. Fourth, the physician may fail to report the case to a central registry and so no record is available. (Becker [1973; cited by Light 1973] noted that of 3,000 reported cases of child abuse collected from New York City's Central Registry only eight were reported by physicians). Fifth, definitions of abuse vary across geographic areas and across public health personnel, and the reported instances of abuse vary from state to state. Another reason may stem from recognition of our potential for abuse, which is confirmed by the results of Gil's survey (1970). Fifty-eight percent of Gil's sample assumed that "almost anybody could at some time injure a child in his care," while over 22% thought that they "could at some time injure a child." Even more striking is the finding that nearly 16% of the interviewed admitted coming very close to injuring a child in their care. This recognition of our vulnerability may lead to a "tacit agreement among us not to meddle in each other's private matters" (Zalba 1971, p. 61). In addition, as Zalba notes, there is a prevailing strong conception of children as property, and some reluctance to intervene may flow from this view of parental rights in the treatment of children.

In light of the fact that large numbers of abused children go undetected, suggestions to improve our identification of abused children have been offered. Kempe (1973) has suggested that the United States develop a system of national health visitors, similar to the visitor system in operation in Aberdeen, Scotland.

We suggest that a health visitor call at intervals during the first months of life upon each young family and that she become, as it were, the guardian who would see to it that each infant is receiving his basic health rights. . . . It is my view that the concept of the utilization of health visitors would be widely accepted in this country. Health visitors need not have nursing training, and intelligent, successful mothers and fathers could be readily prepared for this task at little cost. . . . In those areas where it is not practical to have health visitors health stations could be established in neighborhood fire houses. [Kempe; cited by Light 1973, p. 568]

While this may, in fact, be an economically feasible means of improving our detection rates, there are some serious problems with large-scale screening programs that may outweigh the benefits. Light (1973), in a thoughtful discussion of this issue, raises three general potential difficulties that merit consideration. Evaluation of the massive screening must be viewed in the context of the incidence of abuse. If a very high proportion of children were abused, then the expense, inconvenience, and even minimal harm incurred in the detection process could be easily justified. However, abuse, fortunately, has a low base rate and, therefore, the costs to the large majority of nonabused children must be weighed against the cost of the nondetection of a small number of abused children. Light illustrates this problem by a consideration of the implications of using X-ray techniques as standard diagnostic procedures to detect abuse. "If one child in a hundred is really abused, then even if this case were detected via x-ray, 99 would be needlessly exposed to x-ray diagnosis. . . . It is not clear that the benefit of detecting the one case outweighs the cost of cumulative exposure of the other ninety-nine children" (Light 1973, p. 568).

Second, the relative incidence of abuse in contrast to the incidence of other health problems must be considered. Is the cost of abuse detection in the best overall interests of children? There may be other problems that are more serious, such as nutrition. On the other hand, there is no reason to restrict a large-scale screening examination to the detection of only one type of problem.

The final problem is the most serious one, namely, the error rate in detection. Two types are possible: false negatives, whereby the test fails to detect an abused child, and false positives, whereby the test suggests that a child is abused when this is not the case. Light (1973) empirically demonstrated the fact that with a low base rate event, such as child abuse, even small margins of error will result in high levels of false positives. Even in a situation where an abused child is detected 90% of the time and nonabuse is correctly detected 95% of the time, 85% of the parents who are accused of abuse would be falsely accused. This possibility of false detection does not necessarily, of course, undermine the usefulness of a national health examiniation for detection of abuse. However, diagnostic personnel require excellent training in order to minimize detection error. Light recommends an alternative approach that will reduce some of the detection error—a multiple-stage checking procedure. "At the first stage, where large numbers of children are examined, the primary focus should be on avoiding false negatives, missing real cases of abuse. But, subsequent stages should steadily work towards winnowing out questionable cases, leaving the focus at the final stage on avoiding false positives, and the resulting false accusation of parents" (Light 1973, p. 571). A final consideration, of course, is the type of intervention that would follow from the detection. If the intervention involved advice and aid in child care, and increasing the family's awareness of community resources and services, without any direct accusation, the false detection would not be so serious. More intrusive intervention, however, raises serious questions concerning the privacy rights of parents.

IV. Approaches to Understanding Child Abuse

There have been three approaches to understanding child abuse. The first and most predominant model derives from psychiatric analyses of the abusing parent. The distinctive feature of this approach is the focus on the parent as the principal cause of the abuse; it is assumed that the abusive parents have a set of personality characteristics that distinguish them from other parents. In addition, there is the implicit assumption that abusive parents are abnormal or "sick" and therefore require extensive psychiatric treatment in order to overcome their "illness." A second model of child abuse is sociological. In this case the causal focus shifts from the parent to the social environment. Abuse is assumed to be a result of the stress and frustration encountered by parents in their daily attempts to cope with their social environment. From this viewpoint, alleviation of the stress encountered, particularly by lower-class parents, is the main recommendation for the reduction of abuse. A third approach is a social-situational model of child abuse. This shares with the sociological model the common assumption that child abuse can be best understood by an examination of external environmental events that impinge on families. The level of analysis is, however, different. This approach assumes that a detailed exploration of the patterns of interaction between family members will be useful. In this model, the child as an active participant and elicitor of abuse is given full recognition. Specification of the events that elicit and maintain the use of physically punitive tactics in interpersonal control in the family context and the isolation of the specific circumstances under which abusive incidents occur are the aims of this type of analysis. In the following sections, the main supporting data for each of these three approaches will be discussed as well as the unique treatment implications of each model.

A. PSYCHIATRIC MODEL OF CHILD ABUSE

There are a variety of approaches subsumed under the psychiatric model. First, abusive parents may be classified into traditional psychiatric diagnostic categories such as schizophrenia or manic-depressive psychosis. In this case, the abusive behavior is viewed as a manifestation of a broader underlying psychosis. Although some psychotic individuals are responsible for child abuse, estimates indicate that less than 10% of the child-abusive adults can be classified as mentally ill (Kempe 1973). In fact, as Spinetta and Rigler (1972) note:

There has been an evolution in thinking regarding the presence of a frank psychosis in the abusing parent. Woolley and Evans (1955) and Miller (1959) posited a high incidence of neurotic or psychotic behavior as a strong etiological factor in child abuse. Cochrane (1965), Greengard (1964), Platou, Lennox and Beasley (1964) and Simpson (1967, 1968) concurred. Adelson (1961) and Kaufman (1962) considered only the most violent and abusive parents as having schizophrenic personalities. Kempe et al. (1962), allowing that direct murder of children betrayed a frank psychosis on the part of the parent, found that most of the abusing parents, though lacking in impulse control, were not severely psychotic. By the end of the decade, the literature seemed to support the view that only a few of the abusing parents showed severe psychotic tendencies (Fleming, 1967; Laupus, 1966; Steele & Pollock, 1968; Wasserman, 1967). [Spinetta & Rigler 1972, p. 299]

And the trend has continued. Blumberg (1974) recently noted that viewing the abusive parent as psychotic was a misconception of a psychiatric analysis of child abusing. "Psychosis is very rarely a factor in child abuse. The number of children harmed or killed by schizophrenic parents is only a very small fraction of the total" (Blumberg 1974, p. 22).

1. Personality Characteristics of Abusive Parents

Although psychiatric classification of abusive parents is on the wane, attempting to discover distinctive personality characteristics is still a fashionable strategy. Typically, this involves the listing of personality traits that characterize abusive parents derived either from clinical interviews and diagnosis or from a set of standardized test instruments.

The most systematic and well-controlled study of personality attributes of child-abusing mothers has been reported by Melnick and Hurley (1969). Using largely lower-class black mothers, they compared groups of 10 abusive and 10 control mothers, matched for age, social class, and education, on 18 personality variables. The tests used in the study were the California Test of Personality (CTP), the Family Concept Inventory (FCI), the Manifest Rejection Scale (index of general harshness of parental disciplinary policies), and 12 TAT cards. The abusing mothers revealed lower self-esteem (CTP), less family satisfaction (FCI), a higher pathogenic index (TAT), less need to give nurturance (TAT), higher frustration of need dependence (TAT), and a less openly rejectant stance toward children.

Even this well-controlled study has the serious limitation of being based on a small and highly select sample (lower-class black mothers), and the generalizability of these findings is questionable. Whether similar traits are applicable to fathers, middle-class parents, or other ethnic groups is unknown. Moreover, the lack of differences was also striking: the two groups of mothers did not differ on 12 of the 18 personality dimensions.

Various other investigators have offered their own descriptions of abusing parents ranging from rigid and domineering (Johnson & Morse 1968), to impulsive, immature, self-centered, and hypersensitive (Kempe et al. 1962). However, there has been little success in constructing a consistent set of personality traits. After an extensive analysis of the literature on personality characteristics, Spinetta and Rigler (1972) concluded that "a review of opinions on parental personality and motivational variables leads to a conglomerate picture. While the authors generally agree that there is a defect in the abusing parent's personality that allows aggressive impulses to be expressed too freely (Kempe et al. 1962; Steele & Pollock 1968; Wasserman 1967), disagreement comes in describing the source of the aggressive impulses" (Spinetta & Rigler 1972, p. 299). In another recent review, Gelles (1973) found that, of 19 traits noted by various investigators, there was agreement by two or more authors on only four traits, with the remaining 15 characteristics being unique to one particular author.

Although specific traits may be difficult to isolate, other investigators have attempted to discover clusters of traits that might characterize the abusive parent more adequately then the single-trait approach (Delsordo 1963; Merrill 1962; Zalba 1967). At present, there has been no attempt to empirically validate or cross-validate these typologies and so their usefulness in detecting high-risk parents *or* in economically representing and organizing findings from other investigations of personality traits remains to be determined.

A variety of other problems limit the usefulness of currently available studies of personality characteristics. With a few exceptions (e.g., Melnick & Hurley 1969), there are no comparison groups of nonabusers that are drawn either from other types of clinical populations or from nonclinical normal populations. Consequently, it is impossible to assess whether these personality traits are unique to child-abusing adults. Even psychiatric advocates such as Steele and Pollock comment, "Such adjectives are essentially appropriate when applied to those who abuse children, yet these qualities are so prevalent among people in general that they add little specific understanding" (Steele & Pollock 1968, p. 109). Second, the samples of abusive individuals employed in developing the lists of traits may be unique. "Most of the data are gathered from cases that medical or psychiatric practitioners have at hand. Thus, the sample cannot be considered truly representative of child abusers since many or most are not seen in clinics" (Gelles 1973, p. 614). These criticisms do not imply that more carefully conducted studies may not reveal specific and unique personality traits that can be useful in the screening and detection of potential child-abusing adults. However, in light of the accumulating evidence of the limited relationship between personality traits and actual behavior (Mischel 1968, 1973), this does not appear to be a very fruitful approach.

One final comment: the only general conclusion that Spinetta and Rigler (1972) were able to draw was that "a general defect in character—from whatever source—is present in the abusing parent allowing aggressive impulses to be expressed too freely" (1972, pp. 300–301). This kind of tautological explanation is, unfortunately, too often characteristic of a personality approach. Since nearly all research on child abuse is ex post facto, one wonders about the usefulness of re-describing the abusive parent as being low in aggression control. That descriptive characterization should be the starting point in attempting to understand the behavior and is not, in any sense, an explanation. Re-labeling is not a substitute for adequate explanation.

2. Child-rearing Histories of Abusing Parents

Although there is only limited agreement on the particular personality characteristics of abusive parents, there is more consensus on the distinctive child-rearing attitudes of abusing parents. It has been reported by a wide range of investigators that abusing parents were very frequently abused and neglected as children (Curtis 1963; Kempe et al. 1962; Steele & Pollack 1968; cf. Spinetta & Rigler 1972 for an extensive summary of this literature). Moreover, as children they may have experienced more than just exposure to physically abusive patterns. Perhaps more important as a factor in the occurrence of their own abusive behavior later was their childhood deprivation of basic mothering. Steele and Pollock (1968), in their classic psychiatric examination of abusive parents, view "the lack of mothering," defined as "a lack of the deep sense of being cared for and cared about from the beginning of one's life," as "a most basic factor in the genesis of parental abuse" (p. 112). Not only have abusive parents learned patterns of aggressive behavior as children, but also they have experienced a "pattern of demand, criticism, and disregard designed to suit the mother and leave the [child] out" (p. 112). It is assumed that this pattern of demanding, aggressive behavior experienced in childhood leads to abusive parental behavior in adulthood. A number of other studies generally confirm the intergenerational consistency of abuse; it is clear that the parent's own child-rearing history is an important determinant of abuse. In a later section, the manner in which rearing with physically punitive tactics contributes to parental abusive behavior will be discussed in more detail.

3. Summary

In this section, the psychiatric approach to child abuse was outlined. This approach emphasizes the parent as the principal cause of abuse and assumes that there are personality characteristics that distinguish abusive parents. Implicit in this approach is the assumption that abusive parents are abnormal or ill. The failure to identify distinctive personality factors casts some doubt on the utility of the psychiatric approach. Finally, the child-rearing histories of abusive parents revealed a consistent picture of aggressive, physically punitive childhood experiences.

B. SOCIOLOGICAL MODEL OF CHILD ABUSE

From a sociological perspective, the focus is not on individual differences as in the psychiatric model but on the social values and social organization of the culture, the community, and the family as contributors to child abuse. It is assumed that an examination of the social-cultural context in which abuse occurs offers a useful perspective for understanding child abuse.

First, it is assumed that child abuse can be understood by an examination of "the society's basic social philosophy and value premises" (Gil 1974, p. 12) and more specifically by an examination of the prevailing cultural attitudes toward violence and the use of physical force as a form of control in interpersonal interactions. Second, it is assumed that position of the family in the social-economic hierarchy is an important key to understanding child abuse. Underlying the assumption is a cumulative stress model, which suggests that the degree of stress and frustration encountered by individuals in different positions in the social structure is a determinant of abuse. Finally, it is assumed that the structure and organization of the family and the family relationship to sources of community support are relevant determinants of child abuse. In this section, a critical examination of each of these three facets of the sociological model are presented.

1. The Cultural Attitude to Violence as a Contributor to Child Abuse

It has been proposed that the level of child abuse in American society is, in part, due to our cultural sanctioning of physical force for resolving interpersonal conflict (Gil 1970). To assess the accuracy of this proposal, first, let us examine the level of violence in American society (Palmer 1972; Pinkney 1972). Comparisons of our rate of violent murder with other countries is instructive. In the United States there were nearly 20,000 murders known to the police in 1972 or a rate of 8.9 per 100,000 inhabitants (Kelley 1973), whereas the rate is only one-tenth as high in England (Geis & Monahan 1975). Similarly, the assault-and-battery rate for Canada in 1968 was 28.6 per 100,000, while the U. S. rate was 141 per 100,000 (Steinmetz 1974a). Similarly, cross-cultural comparisons of the level of television violence indicate that the United States is, again, higher than other countries such as Sweden, Israel, or Britain. (Liebert, Neale, & Davidson 1973). In a careful analysis of the content of TV programs over a 5-year period, Gerbner (1972) found that over 75% of the programs contained violence. Elsewhere in this volume, Stein and Freidrich summarize the effects of this type of exposure: both behavior and attitudes are shaped by this type of TV programming. In fact, there is a consistently presented moral lesson that children and adults are repeatedly exposed to, namely, that violence is an appropriate means for resolving conflict. Moreover, there are other forms of institutionalized violence that are commonly executed by corporate and government officials (such as failures to enforce pollution standards and permitting dangerous drugs to be profitably marketed) (see Geis & Monahan 1975 for a fuller discussion of these subtler forms of violence).

There is other evidence that suggests that the levels of violence in a

society are reflected in the levels of violence in the family. More generally, the conflict resolution strategies that are predominant at a societal
level appear to be mirrored in family interaction patterns. First, let us
examine the cross-cultural data. Bellak and Antell (1974), in a comparison of German, Italian, and Danish cities, found that the higher suicide
and homicide rates corresponded to an equally higher level of both parental and child aggression. Similarly, Steinmetz (1974a) in a U. S.-Cana-
da comparison found lower levels of intrafamilial aggression in Canada,
where the levels of criminal aggressive activity are also lower.

Closer examination of familial violence reveals striking degrees of interrelationship among marital conflict tactics, disciplinary techniques,
and the methods employed by children in settling sibling conflicts. Steinmetz (1974b) found that families who use verbal and physically aggressive tactics for resolution of husband-wife disputes tend to use similar
types of techniques in disciplining their children; the children, in turn,
tend to duplicate these tactics in their sib/sib relationships.

In light of these replicated patterns of violence across societal, media,
and familial levels, it is not surprising that physical punishment is a
widely used disciplinary and child-rearing technique in American society. Stark and McEvoy (1970) report that 93% of all parents use physical
punishment, although some use it only rarely and only on young children. In fact, one investigation (Korsch et al. 1965) revealed that in their
sample of 100 Los Angeles mothers one-quarter of the mothers were
spanking their infants in the first 6 months of life and nearly half were
spanking their infants by the end of the first year. However, other studies
(Steinmetz 1974c; Straus 1971) report that physical punishment is not
restricted to young children. For example, Straus found that 52.3% of the
subjects in his adolescent sample had experienced actual or threatened
physical punishment during their last year of high school. Further, professional groups, as well as parents, advocate the use of physical punishment. Viano (1974) found that two-thirds of the educators, police, and
clergy questioned condoned physical discipline in the form of hand-
administered spanking, while over 10% of the police and clergy condoned spanking children for disciplinary purposes with belts, straps, and
brushes! Finally, recent studies indicate that physical punishment as a
disciplinary technique is used at all social class levels (Erlanger 1974),
which is, of course, contrary to earlier reports of social class differences
in punitiveness (Bronfenbrenner 1958). In general, these social class differences in punitiveness have been overstated.

Is the widespread use of physical punishment as a child-rearing technique in American society a factor in the level of child abuse? Gil argues
the case as follows: "A key element to understanding child abuse of

children in the United States seems to be that the context of child rearing does not exclude the use of physical force toward children by parents and others responsible for their socialization. Rather, American culture encourages in subtle and at times not so subtle ways the use of 'a certain measure' of physical force in rearing children" (Gil 1970, p. 134).

Some support for this viewpoint comes from studies of other cultures where there is no sanctioning of physical punishment as a child-rearing tactic. Recent visitors to China (Sidel 1972; Stevenson 1974) report only rare use of physical punishment, little aggression among children, and no incidents of child abuse. More direct evidence comes from comparisons of the child-rearing tactics used by Taiwan parents in controlling their 4–5-year-old children with disciplinary practices of white American parents (Niem & Collard 1971). The Chinese parents reported using any form of physical punishment less than half as often as American parents and spankings were only one-quarter as frequent among the Chinese families. Alternatively, the Chinese families used love-oriented discipline twice as often as American parents. While a number of factors may account for these findings, temperament differences indicating the greater soothability and less emotional lability among Chinese newborns may, in fact, make these children less troublesome (Freedman & Freedman 1969). Goode (1971) has noted a similar situation in Japan, where physical punishment is not a common disciplinary tactic and child abuse is infrequent. Similarly, parents in a number of other cultures where there are few reports of child abuse such as the Arapesh (Mead 1935) and the Tahitians (Levy 1969) raise their children without physical punishment.

In summary, these cross-cultural examples suggest that variations in the cultural level of violence are reflected in family violence and particularly in the prevalence of physical punishment as a child-rearing technique. Whether these variations in disciplinary practices are, in fact, responsible for different levels of child abuse is left unanswered. However, the ways in which physical punitiveness *can* lead to child abuse will be examined in more detail in a later section—the social-situational analysis of child abuse.

Next we shift from a cultural level of analysis to an examination of the relationship between the individual's position in the social hierarchy and child abuse.

2. Social Stress, Social Class, and Child Abuse

One of the assumptions underlying the sociological model of child abuse is that stress and frustration elicit abusive behavior; second, it is assumed that the degrees of stress are related to the social status of the individual, with lower socioeconomic groups experiencing greater amounts of environmental stress. To test these assumptions, it is necessary to examine the relationship between social class and child abuse. First, child abuse is not restricted to a single socioeconomic class in particular; it is not merely a lower-class phenomenon. It is one of the myths of a middle-class social science that intrafamily violence is concentrated in the lower socioeconomic groups (Steinmetz & Strauss 1974). A number of investigators have reported cases of child abuse in both middle- and upper-class families (Allen, Ten Bensel, & Raile 1968; Boardman 1962; Bryant et al. 1963; de Francis 1963; Gillespie 1965; Helfer & Kempe 1968, 1974; Helfer & Pollock 1968; Laury 1970; Nurse 1964; Steele & Pollock 1968; Ten Bensel & Raile 1963; Young 1964).

However, the results of the recent Gil survey (1970) have given renewed impetus to a class-linked view of child abuse. Since this study has been very influential, it is important to examine this investigation critically. In 1967 and 1968, Gil executed a nationwide survey of child abusers in order to provide a comprehensive demographic sketch of child-abusing adults and their victims. To increase the accuracy of his survey, standardized reporting forms were developed for use by central registries of child abuse in each state. Approximately 6,000 cases were studied in 1967 and a new and slightly larger sample was examined in 1968. Gil analyzed detailed socioeconomic data using a subsample of 1,380 abusive parents; the results suggested quite clearly that child abuse is more likely among lower-class parents: over 48% of the abusers had an annual income of under $5,000, while the percentage of all U. S. families at this income level is only 25.3. In addition, Gil reported that the abusive adults tend to be poorly educated: for mothers, less than 1% were college graduates, 4.4% had some college, and 17% were high school graduates. The majority had not completed high school (41%), and 24% had less than 9 years of schooling. A similar picture is present for fathers, with 32% not completing high school and another 24% having had less than 9 years of formal education. In light of the careful, comprehensive nature of the Gil survey, should we conclude that child abuse is more prevalent at lower socioeconomic levels? It is probably premature to draw this conclusion, since there are many reasons which make it difficult to secure reliable estimates of the incidence of child abuse across social classes. First, middle-class families are less likely to use the services of public agencies, clinics, and hospitals in the event of abuse; rather, they are able to afford the services of a private physician, who, in turn, may fail to report the incident in order to protect the family's privacy. Consideration of the Gil survey in view of this possibility casts some doubt on the extent to which all social class groups are represented in the survey results. The official sources reporting the incidents were principally hospitals (49%), police (23%), and public social agencies (8%). Private physicians and private social agencies reported only 2.9% of the cases. The importance of these figures stems from the fact that these private sources are more likely to be utilized by middle- and upper-class abusing adults. In short, lower-class abusers may be overrepresented in the Gil data. There are other reasons that preclude any strong conclusions about social class and child abuse. The living conditions (i.e., single-family dwellings) of middle-class parents may decrease the likelihood of detection by neighbors and others in the community. Third, community agencies may be less likely to intervene in middle- and upper-class homes (Solomon 1973). Fourth, some writers (Elmer 1967; Paulson & Blake 1969; Young 1964) note that higher socioeconomic class parents may be more deceptive and suspicious and make greater effort to conceal their abusive behavior.

Another set of data which casts doubt on a class-linked model of abuse comes from Gil's (1970) national survey of opinion and attitudes toward abuse. Gil inquired how his respondents thought they would react upon learning of an incident of abuse in their neighborhood. Only 7% would not involve themselves, and there were few social class differences. There is no evidence to support the view that lower-class adults are indifferent to the occurrence of abuse or are more likely to condone abuse than adults from higher social classes. At present, no clear-cut conclusions concerning the incidence of abuse across social class can be drawn. However, it is clear that some abuse does occur at all social class levels.

The particular source of stress that may elicit abuse, on the other hand, may be class-related. To date most of the literature has focused on those sources of stress that are more likely to affect lower-class families, such as unemployment, poor housing, and limited income. While we will examine these factors as possible contributors of abuse, it should be noted that the general stress model of abuse is not limited to the lower social class; middle-class families may encounter a variety of stresses which, in turn, may contribute to abuse. Job-elicited tension, marital disputes, and disobedient children are not limited to a single class; and more attention could profitably be paid to these sources of stress that are common to families at all social class levels.

3. Housing and Living Conditions

Is there a relationship between the type of housing and the type of parental disciplinary tactics generally and child abuse specifically? Unfortunately, systematic evidence of the impact of different physical aspects of the environment on the choices of socializing tactics of adults is nearly totally absent. Although earlier studies of crowding in animals (Calhoun 1962) found clear relationships between crowding and aggression, caution must be exercised in generalizing these findings to humans (Lawrence 1974). Some recent studies (Loo 1972) report no increase in interpersonal aggression among children of nursery school age as the amount of physical play space decreases. On the other hand, recent studies with adults suggest that reducing physical space may, in fact, influence propensities to aggression, particularly in males (Freedman 1973).

More relevant to the housing-discipline relationship is a study by Roy (1950) who found a direct relationship between the permissiveness of child-rearing attitudes as a function of the number of rooms in the house: fathers were more likely to endorse the use of power-assertive disciplinary tactics as household space decreased. However, the effect held only for fathers: mothers' attitudes did not vary with the availability of space. Whether parents and other socializing agents actually employ different types of disciplinary techniques as a function of house size is still to be determined. Other data (Newson & Newson 1968) derived from a study of English mothers found that punishment of lower-class children was significantly more frequent in unimproved and more densely populated housing. Frequency of interaction between parent and child may be higher in congested living quarters, thereby increasing the probability of conflict. Mitchell (1971), in a well-controlled study of high-density housing in Hong Kong, found that there is more hostility among families who live on upper floors of high-rise apartment buildings than those who reside on lower floors. The assumption is that lower-floor dwellers can more easily escape their living conditions by their easier access to outside areas. Living conditions may contribute to abuse in a variety of ways other than through modifying child-training practices. (See the chapter on ecology and development by Paul Gump in this volume for other relationships between housing and parental and child behavior.)

Parent interaction with neighbors may be affected by architectural and other housing variables (Festinger, Schachter & Back 1950; Mitchell 1971). Mitchell found that high-density housing discourages interaction and friendship practices among neighbors and friends; the higher the density, the less likely a family is to interact—even after family income is controlled. Social isolation—a factor that has been implicated in abuse (Young 1964)—may, in part, be determined by housing conditions.

There is little evidence that directly links housing and abuse; however, as we will note below, housing conditions may interact with other factors such as unemployment to jointly determine child abuse. But, first, unemployment as a contributor to abuse will be discussed.

4. Unemployment

A number of investigators have reported that unemployment may contribute to child abuse. Gil (1970) reported that only 52.5% of the fathers
in his sample were employed throughout the year preceding the abuse
incident. Twenty-seven percent of the fathers were unemployed part of
the time, while 5.3% were unemployed for the whole year. In the case of
working mothers, only 30.1% were consistently employed. Perhaps most
important is the fact that nearly 12% of the fathers were actually unemployed at the time of the abuse incident, which, as Gil points out, is three
times as high as the national unemployment rate. These unemployment
figures were even higher for nonwhite fathers. Galdston (1965) and
Young (1964) report similar findings in support of the unemployment–
child abuse relationship.

Nor is it limited to child abuse; rather, unemployment appears to be
related to other forms of intrafamily violence as well. Steinmetz and
Straus (1974) note that there was a sharp rise in wife beating in England
during a 6-month period when unemployment rapidly increased. More
generally, this suggests that it is not just unemployment per se, but unexpected and sudden unemployment that would be most likely to elicit
violent behavior. Support for this proposition derives from recent applications of expectancy theory to analyses of violence among the poor
(Baron 1970; Berkowitz 1972; Gurin & Gurin 1970). There are a number
of reasons for these relationships. First, a father who is unemployed is
available in the home a larger portion of time, thereby increasing the
probability of conflict arising either between husband and wife or father
and children. Second, if available, the father may assume a greater role
as disciplinarian than before. Third, some theorists (O'Brien 1971) have
interpreted the unemployment–child abuse relationship in terms of status loss for the father. Viewing status as deriving from occupational
achievement, failure to maintain job status may lead to attempts to assert
greater authority in the family as a way of re-establishing his status and
self-esteem. "Violent behavior was found to be most common in families
where the husband was not achieving well in the work earner role and
where the husband demonstrated certain status characteristics lower
than those of his wife. This was viewed as a special form of status inconsistency. . . . Violent behavior represented the use of coercive, physical
force by the husband in an effort to re-affirm his superior ascribed sex-
role status vis-à-vis the other family members" (O'Brien 1971, p. 698).
Fourth, unemployment may be associated with other frustrating circumstances such as lack of monetary resources. Steinmetz and Straus (1974)
argue that unemployment may not directly affect the female, since her

status is less likely to be job-defined; however, the reduced resources associated with unemployment that make her role as homemaker more difficult to fulfill adequately may be a source of dissatisfaction.

These relationships between intrafamily aggression and unemployment are consistent with other findings concerning job satisfaction. Gil (1974) has argued that the serious work alienation experienced by large segments of the working force may be a contributor to child abuse and other forms of familial violence. Some indirect evidence in support of Gil's position derives from McKinley's (1964) finding that the lower the job satisfaction, the higher the percentage of fathers who employed harsh punishment with their children—a relationship that held across social class levels. In summary, both unemployment and general job dissatisfaction are significant factors in child abuse.

In the next section, the relationships between the structure and organization of the family and child abuse will be examined.

5. *Family Size and Ordinal Position*

Another factor that is related to child abuse is family size. This would be expected on the assumption that an above-average number of children would be stressful for a caretaker. A number of investigators have found this relationship.

Gil (1970) has found that the proportion of families with three or more children is higher among families of child abuse than among the total U.S. population. In fact, the proportion of families with four or more children was nearly twice as high for his sample as for all families in the U.S. population. He also found that the proportion of larger families among nonwhite families in his sample was significantly higher than among white families.

Young (1964), in a rather broad-based sample of 180 families of abuse and neglect, found that only 20% of these had fewer than three children, and 37% had between six and 12 children. Johnson and Morse (1968), in their study of 101 children in Denver, found that two-thirds of the families had three or fewer children; 33% had four or more children; 2% had eight or more. Although these figures are certainly less extreme than Young's, they still indicate larger families among abusive families than families in the United States as a whole. Elmer (1967), looking at 20 abusive families, four nonabusive families, and seven unclassified (possible abuse?) families, found that the abusive families had a greater average number of children than the other groups and than the general population.

Light (1973) has offered the most extensive analysis of this problem in

TABLE 1

FAMILY SIZE AND BIRTH ORDER IN THREE COUNTRIES

U.S.A.

Number of Children	Abusing Families; Percentage in Gil Survey	U.S. Census Family Size Distribution Families /ith Children under 18
1................	18.0	31.8
2................	22.3	29.7
3............⸳...	20.2	18.9
4 or more........	39.5	19.6
	100.0	100.0

New Zealand

Number of Children	Abusing Families; Percentage in DSW Survey	New Zealand Family Size Distribution Families with Children under 18
1................	13.5	33.2
2................	19.2	30.8
3................	20.8	21.9
4 or more........	46.5	14.1
	100.0	100.0

England

Number of Children	Abusing Families; Percentage in NSPCC Survey	England Family Size Distribution Families with Children under 18
1................	23.1	34.4
2................	44.8	33.2
3................	19.2	20.5
4 or more........	12.9	11.9
	100.0	100.0

SOURCE.—Richard Light, "Abuse and Neglected Children in America: A Study of Alternative Policies," *Harvard Educational Review* 43 (November 1973): 574. Copyright © 1973 by President and Fellows of Harvard College.

a comparison of the family size of child abusers in three countries: United States, New Zealand, and England. As table 1 illustrates, in all three countries approximately one-third of families who have children under 18 years of age have only a single child. However, the percentage of one child abusing families is much lower: 18% in the United States, 13.5% in New Zealand, and 23% in England. On the other end of the scale, 39.5% of U.S. abusing families have four or more children, which is twice as high (19.6%) as the national average for all U.S. families. Similarly, in New Zealand, 46.5% of the abusing families have a large family of four or more children in contrast to a national average in New Zealand of 14.1%.

In summary, family size appears to be a contributor to child abuse; alternatively, it is possible that parents who are unable to judge adequately the number of children they can properly care for may, in addition, be potentially abusive as well.

While a number of different investigators have noted that the child's ordinal position in the family hierarchy may play a role in abuse, few clear-cut conclusions are possible (Brett 1967; Cameron, Johnson, & Camps 1966; Tuteur & Glotzer 1966). Part of the difficulty in evaluating the conflicting evidence is the failure of the majority of studies to control for family size, a clear correlate of abuse.

6. Family-Community Relationships: Social Isolation as a Factor in Child Abuse

To the extent that abuse is the outcome of a mounting set of stresses, the availability of structural arrangements that can provide support in times of stress and/or some periodic alleviation of or sharing of responsibility for children may be an important determinant. In modern society, there has been a general trend in family structure from the extended family to a self-contained, nuclear family living arrangement. In addition there have been trends toward greater mobility, social isolation, and anonymity. Whether abusive parents are products of these general trends is unclear; however, there are considerable data which suggest that abusive parents are socially isolated with few personal or community-based relationships. Young (1964) found that 95% of her severe-abuse families and 83% of her moderate-abuse families had "no continuing relationships with others outside the family." Friendships that did develop usually ended after a few weeks or months in a violent quarrel and ensuing bitterness. Moreover, 85% of her abusive families showed no membership or participation in an organized group. Merrill (1962), too, found that 50% of his abusive families had no formal group association, and 28% had only one group association, which was most frequently the church. Elmer (1967) found a difference between abusive and nonabusive mothers on her anomie scale—a scale that measured distrust of society, retreat from society, and resulting isolation. In support of the self-imposed isolation view, Lenoski (1974), in a large and careful study, found that 89% of abusive parents who had telephones had unlisted numbers; in contrast, only 12% of the nonabusive parents had unlisted telephone numbers. In addition, this investigator found that 81% of his abuse families preferred to resolve crises alone in contrast to 43% of the nonabuse parents. However, other evidence suggests that this isolation may not be completely voluntary. Merrill (1962) reported that abuse families are not fully accepted by their communities: 36% were accepted only moderately well and 47% only minimally, while Schloesser (1964) found that a number of her families were actually rebuffed by the community.

Several other investigators have found a high mobility among these families (Gil 1970; Schloesser 1964), with the result being the same—few nearby relatives or other roots in the community. The special point of mobility is the consequent disappearance of the extended family, a social group that in the past provided a built-in protection in the immediate environment. The contemporary nuclear family is often adrift from its original community, and the loss of the extended family probably plays a role in psychosocial isolation. Elmer (1967) has also mentioned the extended family, more common among Negro mothers than white, as a possible reason why the birth of a premature child seems less stressful to Negro than white mothers. However, it is more than merely the presence of relatives. The type of contact between white and black mothers and their relatives also differs: instrumental support in the form of babysitting and housecleaning was more characteristic among black than white mothers (Giovannoni & Billingsley 1970). Finally, it should be noted that the extended family is just one more contextual support missing from abusive parents' lives. As Bakan (1971) points out: "Although certain natural forces may be conducive to making parents care for their children, nonetheless there must be adequate contextual supports for the parents in this enterprise. In the relative absence of social support, one may expect that contrary impulses arise, even if they are not always acted out" (1971, pp. 89–90).

Abusive parents not only isolate themselves from the community, but abusive parents, according to Young (1964) are more likely than neglectful parents to prevent the child from developing relationships or friendships with other individuals outside the home and immediate family. The kind of community isolation that characterized the parents' own social behavior is apparently imposed on their children as well. Second, abusive families consistently denied normally accepted activities to children; the parents refused to allow children to participate in the usual recreational and educational opportunities, such as organized sports, parties, and informal neigborhood activities. The development of ordinary childhood friendships with peers is impossible under these circumstances. The family pattern of isolation has both immediate and long-range implications. To the extent that a cumulative stress model of abuse is appropriate, whereby a parent may become increasingly upset by a continuing number of minor misbehaviors, any set of factors that maintain the child in the immediate presence of the parent is likely to increase the possibility of abuse. Since childhood friendships often provide the basis for future adult friendships, the fact that the child is prevented from developing a network of friends merely increases the family isolation. Since social skills, including empathetic capacities, are learned through interactions with peers, the child's social development may be curtailed (Hartup 1970). Observations of the peer interactions of young abused children (under 4 years of age) in a nursery school setting confirms this expectation (Galdston 1971). There is little social interaction among the children, except unpredictable aggression among the boys. Galdston describes the abused children as "listless, apathetic, and uninterested in other children, toys or adults" (1971, p. 339).

Finally, preventing the child from forming friends makes it more likely that the child will continue a similar pattern of isolation as an adult. In summary, social isolation of both parent and child is characteristic of abusive families; again, the direction of causality is not clear. Possibly, abusive parents isolate themselves to avoid detection; on the other hand, abusive parents may lack the social skills that are necessary to form and maintain friendships and community ties. There is a third alternative, namely, that others may avoid abusive and potentially abusive parents because acquaintances may disapprove of the way in which these parents treat their children.

7. Toward Multiple-Cause Prediction of Abuse

In prior sections, the sociological variables that may contribute to abuse have been considered separately. However, it is unlikely that any single factor, *alone*, will be successful in accounting for abuse. Two recent investigators have moved to multiple-factor models of abuse.

First, Light (1973) has reported a statistically sophisticated re-analysis of Gil's original findings, using a multidimensional contingency table analysis which permits a preliminary isolation of two-variable relationships that discriminate abusing from nonabusing families. Light's analysis is a significant advance, since it introduces appropriate comparisons with nonabusing families. Much of the descriptive material in the child abuse literature is difficult to evaluate because such comparison rates in the nonabusing population are absent. A number of preliminary, but suggestive, findings emerged from the Light re-analysis. First, the unem-

ployment status of the father was a discriminating variable but interacted with housing variables: "Abusing families where the father is unemployed are much more likely to live in an apartment than in a house
relative to comparable non-abusing families where the father is unemployed. . . . Second, abusing families with an unemployed father/or a
less educated father are much less likely to 'share their quarters' with
other persons or families" (Light 1973, p. 587). Abusing families where
the father is unemployed tend to have more children. Similarly, abusing
families with less educated mothers or fathers tend to have more children. Finally, among abusing families, the father's unemployment status
is related to the type of target; if the father is unemployed, abuse is more
likely to be directed against a very young child. If the father is employed,
abuse is more likely to be directed against an older child. Father's employment is the variable that shows up most often in the Light re-analysis and is consistent with a sociological emphasis on family stress due to
unemployment.

Another multifactor approach to child abuse has recently been reported by Garbarino (1975). One of the problems that plague research on
child abuse is the inconsistency in reporting across counties, cities, and
states. In 1964, New York State established a reporting law which requires reporting of incidents or suspected incidents of child abuse to
county social service agencies; in turn, county rates of abuse are collected in a Central Registry Office. Garbarino, as a test of a sociological
view of child abuse, examined variations in rates of child abuse as a
function of a number of socioeconomic and demographic variables
across 58 counties in New York State. U.S. Census data were used to
characterize the socioeconomic status of the counties in the sample in
order to evaluate the contribution of (1) family mobility or transcience,
(2) general economic development, (3) educational level, (4) rural-urban
differences, and (5) the socioeconomic situation of mothers in the county. In addition, the rates of child abuse in each county were available.

This data base permitted a test of the hypothesis that the socioeconomic support system for the family in each county is directly associated
with the rate of child abuse/maltreatment for that county: where support
systems are better, where the family has more human resources, the rate
of child abuse/maltreatment will be lower, and vice versa (Garbarino
1975, p. 9). First, use of a standard correlational approach, in which the
separate contribution of each economic factor to child abuse was considered, yielded only a few significant relationships. The percentage of
women with children under 18 in the labor force was positively related to
abuse($r = .42$), while the median income of families headed by a female

and the median income of all families were both negatively related to child abuse ($r = -.40$ and $-.27$, respectively). However, by the use of a multiple-regression approach, which controls for the intercorrelation among the socioeconomic and demographic indices, Garbarino was able to account for an impressive portion of the variance in child abuse across counties. Table 2 presents the results of this analysis, which suggests that five indices accounted for 36% of the total variance. This study provides impressive support for a sociological social stress analysis of child abuse; again, however, it should be noted that the child abuse incidence data were derived from public agency sources which overrepresent lower socioeconomic classes. Nevertheless, this study does suggest that environmental stress induced by variations in the availibility of socioeconomic resources—even within lower-class groups—is related to child abuse.

TABLE 2

Multiple Regression of Correlates of Child Abuse (Rate per 10,000 Population)

(1) Percentage of women in the labor force who have children under 18 years of age...	$r = .42$
(1) + (2) Median income of households headed by females............	$r = .47$
(1) + (2) + (3) Percentage of 3–4-year-olds enrolled in schools.........	$r = .55$
(1) + (2) + (3) + (4) Percentage of 18–19-year-olds enrolled in schools	$r = .58$
(1) + (2) + (3) + (4) + (5) Percentage who are high school graduates..	$r = .60$

Source:—Garbarino 1975.

While neither of these studies can be viewed as definitive without replication, the multiplicative model of abuse underlying these investigations should be adopted in future studies. While single variables may be easier for conceptual and empirical analysis, only by moving beyond single-variable approaches will significant progress be made in understanding child abuse—a clearly multidetermined phenomenon.

8. Summary

In this section the sociological approach to child abuse which emphasizes the social-cultural context of abuse was presented. The prevailing condoning attitude toward violence in the American culture is assumed to be a determinant of abuse. Of particular importance for an understanding of child abuse is the widespread acceptance of physical punishment as a child-rearing technique. While abuse rates do vary across cultures, it is difficult to accurately assess the extent of abuse across social classes within our own culture. A variety of stress factors, such as unemployment and poor housing, were found to correlate with abuse rates. More attention should be paid to the types of stress in middle-class families that may elicit child abuse. The relationships between structure and organization of the family and child abuse were examined. Both family size and the child's ordinal position may be related to child abuse. While abuse rates are lower in small families, the current data on ordinal position of the child permit no firm conclusion. The isolation from the rest of the community is another characteristic of abusive families. Finally, it was argued that multiple-factor models of abuse are necessary, and some illustrative data in support of this approach were offered.

C. SOCIAL-SITUATIONAL MODEL OF CHILD ABUSE

Social-situational factors may contribute in a variety of ways to child abuse. First, the social situation in which the child is reared may determine the extent to which he himself is abusive as an adult. Second, the type of interaction patterns between child and adult or husband and wife may yield clues concerning the conditions under which potentially abusive patterns develop and the specific stimuli which serve to trigger or elicit abusive behavior. Third, a social-situational analysis may yield clues concerning the factors which may maintain abusive patterns. Let us examine each of these facets of a social-situational analysis.

1. The Eliciting and Accelerating Phases of Abuse

The effects of punitive child rearing.—A number of studies have documented the observation that abusive parents were themselves abused as children. This is a special manifestation of a more general relationship which suggests that the use of physical punishment by parents is associated with high aggression outside the home as children and as adults (Erlanger 1974). Probably these patterns are learned through imitation, and there is now a large body of research documenting the effects of exposure to aggressive models on the subsequent aggressive behavior of observers (see Stein & Freidrich, this volume). Translated into the disciplinary context, Bandura (1967) expressed this relationship as follows: "When a parent punishes his child physically for having aggressed toward peers, for example, the intended outcome of this training is that the child should refrain from hitting others. The child, however, is also learning from parental demonstration how to aggress physically. And the imitative learning may provide the direction for the child's behavior when he is similarly frustrated in subsequent social interactions" (1967, p. 43).

Similarly, adult physically punitive disciplinary patterns are probably shaped by early exposure to these patterns in childhood. Consistent exposure to these patterns may serve to sanction these types of behavior so that the adults view physical discipline as normative behavior for child rearing. Second, inhibitions against the use of physical force generally are lessened as a result of the legitimacy of physical punishment in child rearing.

This early establishment of physically punitive tactics as legitimate techniques for the solution of conflict may, in part, aid in understanding the relationship between physical punishment and child abuse. To the extent that physical punishment is used as a control tactic, this general class of physically violent responses, such as hitting, will be well rehearsed and high in the repertoire of available responses. A number of studies (e.g., Davitz 1952) have shown that, under conditions of stress and frustration, predominant responses are likely to be emitted; in short, the typical use of physically punitive responses in disciplinary contexts makes it more likely that these same types of responses will be employed in anger-eliciting situations. This assumes, of course, that some abuse occurs under circumstances where adults may react impulsively and involuntarily and cause injury that was not fully anticipated. Just as in murder, abuse is not necessarily rational and deliberate. As Berkowitz recently argued: "Most homocides are 'spontaneous acts of passion' arising from fights over trivial issues. Relatively few are the product of thought-out determination to kill (Mulvihill and Tumin, 1969; Wolfgang, 1968). These violent outbursts are often too impulsive, too quick and involuntary to be greatly affected by the aggressor's belief as to what will be the outcome of their behavior, beyond the simple idea they will hurt their victim. . . . In their rage they strike out without much thought" (1974, p. 165). At least some child abuse may begin in a similar, nondeliberate fashion, and it is assumed that the ready availability of aggressive responses used in a disciplinary context makes abuse more likely.

There are other reasons for the physical punishment–child abuse relationship. There is an interesting discrepancy between attitude and usage in the realm of physical punishment. Many who use physically punitive tactics tend to disapprove of these techniques. In contrast, in the past, there was less discrepancy between attitudes and usage. As a result of this cultural shift in attitude, the manner in which physical punishment is employed makes the contemporary use of this type of discipline potentially more dangerous than in the past. When punishment was viewed as an appropriate and justifiable tactic, it was used in a more measured and deliberate fashion. As a disciplinary technique, punishment was delivered not necessarily in anger but under controlled circumstances in which both victim and punishing agent were aware of the reason for the action and the limits of the dosage. Not only was punishment likely to be more effective in achieving control, due to the clear understanding concerning the relationship between the disapproved act and the punishment, but under these controlled circumstances of delivery, escalation—as might occur under conditions of anger—would be less likely to occur. Physical punishment in contemporary child rearing, especially in middle-class homes, is more typically an impulsive, angry reaction than a deliberate, disciplinary action. This discrepancy in terms of norms and actual usage may be creating the potential for abuse.

Inconsistent use of discipline.—Another reason for the possible link between physical punishment and child abuse is the inconsistent fashion in which physical punishment is employed by abusive parents. A pattern of inconsistent discipline is typical of abusing parents. Young (1964) reported that virtually all of the abusing families were inconsistent in disciplining their children (100% of the severe-abuse and 91% of the moderate-abuse families). Similarly, 88% of the severe-abuse and 81% of the moderate-abuse families showed "no consistent expectations" for their children; in less than one-quarter of the abusive families were the children given any defined responsibilities. These findings indicate a total absence of guidelines or consistent discipline in the abusive families. Discipline is consistent instruction and must conform with some established rules or standards; these standards must have continuity. In contrast, parental punishment of children in the abused families was divorced from the specific behavior of the children; it became, in effect, punishment for its own sake. "The severity and brutality of parental abuse and its lack of corrective purpose distinguish it clearly from the customary concept of punishment of children" (Young 1964, p. 181). Moreover, the reasons which these parents gave for their behavior were typically inappropriate and illogical, nor did they recognize any discrepancy between the intensity of the punishment and the minor seriousness of the child's misbehavior.

An examination of the marital roles of the parents reveals further inconsistency. Young found that "parents have defined responsibilities" in only 33% of the severe-abuse and 21% of the moderate-abuse families. Each of the following categories held true for about 60% of the severe group: "one parent imposes controls," "one parent plans use of money," "one parent makes all or most decisions," However, in 88% of the families "neither parent takes responsibility for decisions," which indicates a marked separation of authority and responsibility in the abuse families; the parent making the decisions shifts the responsibility for them; the result is poor child control and a low level of predictability for the child. Neither parent nor child can depend on any consistent interaction pattern.

Elmer (1967) reported similar findings in her comparison of abusive and nonabusive families. In terms of household organization, the abusive mothers were low in comparison to the nonabusive mothers. In terms of discipline, she found that the nonabusive families tended to use a few types of discipline consistently; in contrast, the abusive families used a broad range of tactics in an inconsistent manner.

What are the effects of inconsistent discipline? Data from field studies of delinquency have yielded a few clues concerning the consequences of inconsistency of discipline. Glueck and Glueck (1950) found that parents of delinquent boys were more "erratic" in their disciplinary practices than were parents of nondelinquent boys. Similarly, the McCords (e.g., McCord, McCord, & Howard 1961) have found that erratic disciplinary procedures were correlated with high degrees of criminality. Inconsistent patterns involving a combination of love, laxity, and punitiveness, or a mixture of punitiveness and laxity alone, were particularly likely to be found in the background of their delinquent sample.

Laboratory studies of the effects of inconsistent punishment on children's aggression have indicated that intermittent punishment administered by a single agent is a less effective technique than consistent punishment for controlling aggressive behavior (Parke & Deur 1972). Nor is it simply intraagent inconsistency that produces poor control; as Stouwie (1972) has demonstrated, inconsistency between two socializing agents also leads to ineffective control of children's behavior.

Other investigations indicate that inconsistent discipline has long-term implications for the control of child behavior. Parents and other socializing agents often use consistent punishment after inconsistent punishment has failed to change the child's behavior. To investigate the effectiveness of consistent punishment after the child has been treated in an inconsistent fashion was the aim of another study by Deur and Parke (1970). Specifically, these investigators found that children who are inconsistently disciplined by occasionally being rewarded and at other times punished for aggressive behavior persisted in their aggressive behavior for a longer period—under conditions of either extinction or consistent punishment—than boys who had not previously experienced the inconsistent treatment. The implication is clear: the socializing agent using inconsistent punishment builds up resistance to future attempts to either extinguish deviant behavior or suppress it by consistently administered punishment.

The acceleration of low-intensity punishment to high-intensity levels.— There is another outcome of the inconsistent use of punishment that may aid in understanding the punishment-abuse relationship, namely, the acceleration of low-intensity punitive responses into more intense and therefore potentially abusive responses. This acceleration process is, in fact, one of the central problems that must be faced by a social-situational analysis. In other words, how are high-intensity responses shaped up so that they are available for elicitation under stressful conditions? The erratic use of punishment and the resulting weak control of behavior may be one factor in accounting for acceleration. As the child's behavior persists in the face of inconsistent handling, the parents, in order to control the child's behavior, may accelerate the intensity of their punitive tactics. Since other research (Parke 1969) indicates that high-intensity punishment is more effective than low-intensity punishment, the socializing agent may, in fact, be reinforced for their use of high-intensity tactics. However, if the punishment is erratic, only momentary control will be achieved and the parent may, in turn, resort to a more intense punishment on some future occasion. It is quite possible that abusive levels of punishment could develop out of this type of parent-child interaction in a disciplinary context.

Patterson has conceptualized a related type of interaction pattern in which there is acceleration of aversive stimuli exchanged by participants as the coercion process (Patterson & Cobb 1971, 1973; Patterson & Reid 1970). According to this view, when one person presents an aversive stimulus, the second person is likely to respond with an aversive stimulus if the initial aversive stimulus appears alterable. The aversive interchange continues and escalates in intensity until one person withdraws his aversive stimulus; at this point, the other person would withdraw his aversive stimulus. The coercion paradigm provides a fruitful framework for elucidating the contribution of the child's behavior to the development of parental abuse patterns. The coercion paradigm describes how the intensity of parental disciplinary responses could be escalated in response to aversive stimuli presented by the child until physical abuse results. Studies (Patterson & Cobb 1971) in the home context illustrate this process. In detailed observations of the interaction patterns among family members, they found that aversive stimuli such as commands or teasing accelerated the probablity that the target child would hit; similarly, hitting increased hitting in the victim. In a related study (Patterson & Cobb 1973), they isolated the clusters of stimuli that elicited either social aggression (physically aggressive behavior or teasing) or hostility (negativism, disapproval, humiliation, whining). A specific example will illustrate the nature of this stimulus control. The baseline probability of hit was .003, but if a younger sister teased the target child, the probability increased to .067. In turn, if the subject hit the sister and she returned the hit, the probability of another hit was .44. These examples illustrate the manner in which the intensity of responses can be accelerated in dyadic interaction contexts.

Although Patterson's work has implicated peers and siblings as shapers of aggression, these high-intensity aggressive responses on the part of children may, in turn, elicit high-intensity disciplinary tactics from parents in order to suppress these behaviors. It is hypothesized that the success that a parent may have in inhibiting highly disruptive behaviors through the use of high-intensity tactics serves to maintain these tactics. Patterson and Cobb spell out the possible implications of their model for abuse as follows:

In the case of mothers, it is hypothesized that there are many grown women with no past history of Hitting, who are shaped by interactions with infants and children to initiate physical assaults. Presumably the shaping process is analogous to that provided by children, for children. The mother learns that Hits terminate aversive child behavior. She may then be trained to display behavior of increasingly high amplitude as a function of contingencies supplied by children. We also suspect that many of the child homicides reported are in fact the outcome of such training programs. A young woman, unskilled in mothering, is trained by her own children to carry out assaults that result in bodily injury to her trainers. [Patterson & Cobb 1971, p. 124]

In fact, Reid (1974, personal communication) has indicated that approximately one-quarter of the parents of the aggressive boys in these studies would be classified as abusive. In a later section, ways of modifying parent and child behaviors that are maintained by this coercion process will be examined.

An illustration of the combined operation of both coercion and inconsistent discipline in the development of tantrum behavior in an 8-year-old child is provided by Bernal et al. (1968). They noted that the child is able to force maternal compliance by verbal and physical threats; in turn, the mother's acquiescence in the face of the threats increased the probability of further threatening and tantrum behavior. Control attempts typically took the form of an occasional severe spanking, but these spankings were inconsistently delivered and provided little unambiguous information concerning the nature of inappropriate behavior. In addition, threats to punish were seldom accompanied by follow-up punishment. As noted above, inconsistent punishment is ineffective in controlling behavior. This erratic use of punishment and the exercises in hollow threatening combined with submission in the face of high-magnitude noncompliant tactics served to accelerate the child's behavior; in turn, to control these behaviors, the parent may accelerate the punitive tactics in attempting to inhibit the behavior. In combination, the concepts of inconsistent discipline and coercion suggest a reasonable framework within which the acceleration of parental punishment to abusive levels can be understood.

Generalization.—Why is the child often a victim of intrafamily violence? While abuse may be directly triggered by children's behavior, abuse, on other occasions, may be the outcome of husband-wife violence. Particularly in cases where there are strong norms limiting this type of conflict, the child may become a victim. Alternatively, aggression may be directed toward the child when extreme dominant-submissive patterns between the parents prevent a passive parent from directly expressing aggression toward the spouse. In fact, Terr (1970) has reported exaggerated dominant-submissive patterns in abusive families. Fenigstein and Buss (1974) recently provided evidence in support of the concept of selective aggression against a weak victim. Adults were angered and then given the opportunity to deliver a mildly noxious stimulus to a confederate who was associated with the insulting experimenter or aggress in a more intense manner against a nonassociated individual. The angered subjects preferred the target that allowed the display of the most intense aggression rather than the victim most similar to the original anger inducer. A similar process may operate in family contexts.

2. Maintaining Conditions for Abuse

Another question that requires attention are the conditions that maintain repeated abuse. There are many reasons for the finding that patterns of abuse are maintained. One aspect of this maintenance issue is post-abuse justification. In light of apparent harm, adults may engage in a series of tactics designed to minimize, justify, or shift responsibility for the abuse. An understanding of these processes may also aid in understanding the low reporting rate among abusing parents.

Justification of abuse.—A common tactic is justification of abuse in terms of higher principles. The abuse is viewed as part of necessary and morally justified discipline, the intent of the discipline being to establish appropriate social and moral conduct (Steele & Pollock 1968). In such cases, cooperation with authorities is often low; authorities are viewed as interfering with parental rights to choose their own methods of discipline and child care. In such cases, guilt and remorse which, in turn, may serve to inhibit later abusive attacks (Berkowitz 1962) are lacking, which, in turn, will increase the probability of future abuse.

Minimization of abuse.—Another factor which may maintain abuse is the minimization of the incident and the selective forgetting of the consequences (Bandura 1973). Individuals often execute acts of harmful abuse under conditions of anger in spite of the fact that these acts are inconsistent with their expressed values. Brock and Buss (1964) have shown that individuals who display aggressive acts of which they disapprove tend to selectively recall information concerning the potential benefits of such behavior while being less able to remember the harmful effects.

Shifting of responsibility.—There are other factors as well. The parent may blame the child for his behavior: "the child drove me to it," By shifting responsibility to the victim, there is a decreased likelihood of the abusive parent modifying his behavior. This shifting of responsibility may take other forms, such as displacing responsibility to another family member such as a spouse *or*, alternatively, not sharing responsibility with a spouse. Characteristic of severely abusive families is an unwillingness to take responsibility for decisions (Young 1964, p. 168).

Partner reactions to abuse.—Another factor that contributes to the maintenance of abuse is the reaction of a partner or spouse. Peer reaction can both maintain and inhibit aggressive behavior. In a situation in which adults were required to deliver increasingly harmful aggressive responses to a victim, the presence of two supportive peers increased the level of aggressiveness that the subject was willing to display. Alternatively, the presence of partners who refuse to escalate their level of aggressiveness served to lower the subject's aggressive behavior (Milgram 1974). In the abuse context, the reactions of a spouse or coobserver can clearly modify the extent of abuse and the probability of repeated occurrence. While abuse may, in part, be more likely in single-parent homes due to the lack of a partner who can intervene and prevent serious acceleration of punishment to damaging levels, no simple prediction is possible without exploration of the attitudes of the partner. However, it may be that abuse is often maintained due not to explicit approval by the partner but simply by the partner's indifference or nonreaction. Nonreaction in situations involving serious harm may, in fact, function as positive reinforcement or approval (Bandura 1965).

Derogation of victim.—Derogation of the victim is another device used to justify family violence. By attributing a sufficient number of negative characteristics to the victim, any dissonance associated with the abuse can be reduced. Young (1964) has reported that over 90% of the severely abusive families engaged in verbally abusive language such as name calling, insulting, and mockery. For example, "parents stated bluntly that they hated the children . . . others remarked they had never liked them. A parent referred frequently to his son as 'crazy,' 'the idiot' or a child was repeatedly told he was 'dumb.' In other cases a parent emphasized how physically ugly a child was or called him 'the criminal' " (Young

1964, p. 159). These reactions characterized 85% of the severe-abuse families, 55% of the moderately abusive families, and only 40% and 22% of the severe- and moderate-neglect families. It is easy to attack a victim whom you have despised and labeled in ways that make him undesirable.

There is another aspect that merits consideration. Not only do physically abusive parents derogate the child victim, but there is a high degree of verbal abuse and criticism. The high rate of verbal aggression may not only serve to justify physical violence but, in fact, may stimulate the parents to engage in physical violence. A number of experimental studies (Loew 1967; Parke, Ewall, & Slaby 1972) have demonstrated that speaking aggressively may stimulate and make more likely subsequent physically aggressive actions as well. Straus (1974) has recently found that there is a close positive relationship between verbal and physical violence in husband-wife conflicts.

Pain feedback.—Another factor that may play an important role in regulating the degree of abusive behavior is the pain feedback from the victim. Pain cues may function either to maintain an ongoing aggressive sequence or inhibit the attacker's aggression. In well-socialized adults, pain feedback from the victim will decrease the intensity of an aggressive attack (Baron 1971; Buss 1966). In fact, aggression is even more readily inhibited if the attacker is directly exposed to the visual and auditory signs of suffering. Although knowledge that a prior action caused another person to suffer can inhibit (Buss 1966), the pain cues that the victim displays during an aggressive encounter can also function to reduce the intensity of the attack (Baron 1971). Moreover, the inhibitory impact of pain feedback is most marked when the aggressor can directly witness the visual and auditory pain cues of the victim (Milgram 1974). In an abusive exchange between parent and child where the parent is directly exposed to the suffering of the child, why does the pain feedback not function as an inhibitor? There are a number of possible reasons. First, Feshbach and Feshbach (1969) have demonstrated that the inhibitory effect of pain feedback may be dependent on the development of empathy; research on abusive parents (Spinetta & Rigler 1972) suggests that abusive parents are relatively low in empathy and, therefore, may be unresponsive to the signs of suffering in their victims. In part, it may be due to the failure of the abusive parent to react with inhibition to low-intensity signs of suffering that permits the escalation of punitiveness to abusive extremes. In nonabusive parents, early and subtler signs of pain function to regulate and prevent extremely harmful forms of aggression from occurring. There is evidence which indicates that highly aggressive individuals, particularly if angered, may accelerate the intensity of their attacks in response to the sight of pain on the part of the victim. Hartmann (1969) exposed juvenile delinquent males to a film which graphically displayed the suffering of a victim of an aggressive attack. In contrast to those exposed to a film emphasizing the instrumental features of an aggressive encounter, the boys who watched the pain-cues film more vigorously attacked an opponent when they were angered. The delinquents with the longest records of prior offenses were most strongly affected by the pain cues. It appears that individuals who have well-established aggressive patterns of behavior may be particularly likely to react to a victim's suffering with strong attacks.

Summary.—In this section the social-situational model of child abuse was outlined. This approach stresses the ways in which abusive patterns may develop from the use of physically punitive discipline. It was demonstrated that the abusing parents' own history of physically punitive rearing predisposes them to employ similar tactics in controlling their own children. A variety of factors, including parental inconsistency in the execution of discipline, were examined to explain the possible manner in which low-intensity punitive responses are accelerated into more intense abusive behaviors. On occasion, the child may be the victim of the generalization of husband-wife violence. Next, a series of processes which account for the maintainance of child abuse were examined. Post-abuse justification in terms of higher principles, minimization of the harm, derogation of the victim, and shifting of responsibility were noted as tehniques that may account for the maintainance of abusive patterns. The role that the partner may play in the maintainance process was also discussed.

D. THE CHILD'S ROLE IN ABUSE

A serious shortcoming in both the psychiatric and sociological models is their failure to give adequate recognition to the interactive nature of child abuse. It is insufficient to view abuse from a unidirectional viewpoint, whereby the main cause is located in either the parent or in external social circumstances. One important feature of the social-situational approach is the recognition that both partners, the child victim as well as the parent, need to be considered if child abuse is to be fully understood. In particular, the role that the child himself may play in eliciting abuse needs to be more closely examined. With few exceptions (Milowe & Lowrie 1964; Sameroff & Chandler 1975), this issue has received little attention in the past. A number of clinical investigators have pointed to the *selectivity* of abuse; not all children are abused, but usually only a single child within a family is selected for the abusive treatment.

The child may contribute to his own abuse in a variety of ways. First, there may be some genetically determined physical and behavioral characteristics of the child that may make it more likely that he will be abused. Second, the child may develop behaviors through interaction with parents and peers that make him a likely target for abuse. Alternatively, as a result of physical abuse, the child may develop behavior patterns which, in turn, elicit more abuse from his caretakers or possibly from other caretakers, who themselves may not have originally maltreated the child. Abuse, in other words, may shape up behavior patterns which increase the likelihood of further abuse. As Bakan (1971) notes, "the well taken care of child attracts positive responses. The child who is abused and neglected becomes ugly in appearance and behavior and invites further abuse and neglect" (p. 109). Of particular importance are the altered behavior patterns that may invite further abuse. While there are reports of the same child being abused in different foster homes (McKay, cited by Milowe & Lourie 1964), even professional personnel, such as nurses, find abused children difficult to manage and care for. A statement by Bain (cited by Bakan 1971) illustrates the reaction of nurses in one hospital setting: "We began discovering that the child in the bed farthest from the nurse's station was sometimes a child that fitted into this syndrome. . . . Somehow these children establish the same relationship to the nurses (as to their parents). When you walk through the ward you can judge by the number of toys on beds; these children have less toys. You can count the pictures in their rooms. Somehow the response they're getting from the nurse is less warm" (p. 110). It is clear that the child can contribute to his own abuse. Now let us examine the ways in which this may occur in more detail.

1. The Infant as a Target of Abuse

The birth of the newborn infant is often a stressful event which can affect the relationships among family members. There are many tasks that must be mastered, including not only routine caretaking but modifying schedules and activities to accomodate another individual. As Bakan (1971) notes: "the coming of the child tends to disturb the total equilibrium of the life of the parents, including the possibility of the child's creating disturbances in the sexual sphere, the social sphere, the occupational sphere and the total income of the parent. . . . Children constitute a burden calling for sacrifices on the part of the adult" (Bakan 1971, p. 90). Ryder (1973), in a unique longitudinal assessment of the impact that a new infant has on family relationships, confirmed this conclusion. Women who had a child, compared with those who did not, were less satisfied with their marriage and specifically reported that their husbands were not paying sufficient attention to them. The problem of adjusting to a newborn infant is exaggerated under a number of circumstances which may make abusive reactions more likely. For example, these dissatisfactions are probably exaggerated in the case of a child who is the product of an unwanted pregnancy—"a pregnancy which began before marriage, too soon after marriage, or at some time felt to be extremely inconvenient" (Kempe et al. 1962) and a number of studies (Birrell & Birrell 1968; Nurse 1964) have documented this conclusion. Moreover, as noted earlier, the arrival of another child in an already large family may strain the resources of the family so greatly that the new infant is abused.

Bell's (1968) distinction between parental upper- and lower-limit-control behaviors may be useful for understanding how the infant's behavior may contribute to his abuse. Upper-limit-control behavior of the parent includes those responses which regulate and reduce behavior of the child which exceeds parental expectations and standards of intensity, frequency, and competence for the child's age. Conversely, lower-limit-control behavior is that which stimulates child behavior which is below parental standards. Bell predicts, for example, that the parent will exhibit upper-limit-control behavior in response to excessive and sustained crying by an infant or to impulsive and hyperactive behavior by a child, whereas lethargic and apathetic behavior should elicit lower-limit-control behavior. Viewed from this vantage point, successful socialization involves the maintenance of the child's behavior within the upper and lower boundaries acceptable to the parent.

Many characteristics of the child could affect the frequency and threshold of parental upper- and lower-limit-control behavior and thus influence the probability of the occurrence of the coercive process (Patterson & Cobb 1973) that we described earlier. For example, infants who exhibit excessive and sustained crying may present particularly frequent and strong aversive stimuli to the mother and thus elicit upper control behavior.

There are individual differences in irritability and soothability which may be congenitally based (Freedman & Freedman 1969; Wolff 1969); moreover, there are wide individual differences in the ways in which distress can be successfully inhibited (Birns, Blank , & Bridger 1966). Typically, crying decreases over the first year of life (Bell & Ainsworth 1972; Parmalee 1972), and successful control of infant crying is a prerequisite for successful maintenance of the parent-infant dyad. However, failure to inhibit crying effectively can lead to a breakdown in the parent-child relationship. Robson and Moss (1970) noted decreases in mother-infant attachment after the first month as a result of sustained irritability (crying, fussing). Similarly, Bell and Ainsworth (1972) reported relationships between failure to control infant crying effectively and maternal withdrawal in the latter part of the first year. The breakdown of the affectional relationship may be the first step toward a potentially abusive outcome. To the extent that a mother withdraws and interacts less with her infant, the less likely that she will be able to notice and respond to low-intensity precursors of crying. Responding to the early cues may avert the high-intensity aspects of the sequence, such as agitated crying (Bell 1974), which, in turn, is probably more difficult to inhibit than the lower levels of distress. Unfortunately, the full-blown crying may be reinforced by maternal attention involved in attempting to inhibit it (Etzel & Gewirtz 1967). The result is a situation wherein the infant is shaped up to use high-intensity cues to elicit a maternal response; the parent, in turn, may also resort to high-intensity behaviors to control this aversive behavior. Initially, the maternal behavior may produce little harm and be of low intensity; however, as the infant sustains the crying, the mother may escalate her responses. This escalation may continue until eventually the mother uses high-intensity and harmful tactics in a desperate attempt to terminate her infant's crying.

Another important factor is the clearness or readability of the cues which an infant provides his mother. If an infant presents weak or unclear signals about the internal or external stimuli controlling his behavior (Korner 1974), his mother may have difficulty in determining how to terminate his aversive stimuli effectively, and thus the probability of the coercive process occurring may be increased. With respect to parents, a mother who is unskilled at detecting an infant's signals may have great difficulty in soothing her infant. Similarly, a mother who lacks a wide, flexible range of effective caretaking and disciplinary techniques is likely to have increased chances of becoming involved in the coercion process, simply because she possesses few effective means of terminating her infant or child's undesirable behavior. Alernatively, "Too often mothers cannot or will not respond to their infants' cues, either for reasons of their own psychology and needs or because of convictions they hold as to what contributes 'good childcare.' Such factors within the mother can seriously impede the beginning mother-child interaction and result in a mismatch of the pair" (Korner 1974, p. 117). Still another attribute of the mother which may affect her upper-limit-control behavior is her expectations of the child. The mother who sets excessively high standards for her child or who tolerates only very low-intensity aversive stimuli may be more likely to escalate her behavior to abusive levels when the child presents her with aversive stimuli.

Another way in which mismatching can occur is in terms of the mother and infant preferred modes of interaction. Some babies resist such forms of physical contact as being embraced, hugged, and held tight

(Schaffer & Emerson 1964). This apparently genetically based interaction style may cause serious disruptions for certain types of mothers who prefer cuddly infants. Possible mismatches between parental styles may conceivably be an early precursor of poor attachment formation and possible later abuse. As Steele and Pollock (1968) note in their discussion of abusive parents: "Some parents are disappointed when they have a placid child instead of a hoped-for more reactive, responsive baby. Other parents are equally distressed by having an active, somewhat aggressive baby who makes up his own mind about things when they had hoped for a very placid compliant infant" (1968, p. 129).

Current research aimed at isolating the ways in which parent-infant dyads adapt (Osofsky & Danzger 1974; Parke & O'Leary 1975) should prove fruitful in the early identification of potential breakdowns in the parent-infant dyad.

However, lower limit control behaviors, which may occur in response to a lethargic and unresponsive infant, or in an infant who fails to meet parental expectations of normal development, may also contribute to the development of abusive patterns. For example, Robson & Moss (1970) found that an infant who was late in exhibiting smiling and eye-to-eye contact elicited violent reactions in the mother and was later found to have suffered relatively serious brain damage (cited by Bell 1974). In addition, abuse is more likely in the case of the passive or lethargic infant or one who is developmentally retarded in their expression of new behaviors, because these characteristics may interfere with the development of a positive parent-child relationship. To the extent that an affectional tie between a caretaker and infant may function as a deterrent to the expression of abusive behaviors the infant who exhibits lower-limit behaviors may be a more likely candidate for abuse. The low birth weight infant that we will discuss in the next section is an example of this type of infant.

2. The Low Birth Weight Infant: A Special Target for Abuse?

An infant who is particuarly likely to be abused is the low birth weight infant. Low birth weight, of course can take a variety of forms: (*a*) infants born at term to mothers of small stature, (*b*) infants born at or near term but markedly underweight as a result of intrauterine malnutrition, or (*c*) infants born after a relatively short gestation period. A baby of low birth weight born to a small mother may be a result of genetic factors and have low morbidity rates (Douglas, cited by Caputo & Mandell 1970). As Caputo and Mandell note, however, it is important to consider birth weight in conjunction with other variables such as gestational age. An infant whose birth weight is well below the mean for his gestational age (small-for-dates babies) is presumed to show retarded fetal growth and demonstrate prenatal and postnatal characteristics different from those of low birth weight infants of low gestational age. Unfortunately, too little attention has been paid to distinctions among low birth weight infants in terms of their potential for abuse.

The most convincing evidence of the association between low birth weight and child abuse comes from a study by Klein and Stern (1971). Using hospital records between 1960 and 1969, these investigators retrieved all charts containing diagnoses of "battered child syndrome," which was defined as "frank unexplained skeletal trauma or severe bruising or both, or such neglect as to lead to severe medical illness or immediate threat to life" (1971, p. 15). Of the 51 cases retrieved, 39 cases, or 76%, had been full-term infants and 12, or 23.5%, had been low birth weight infants (less than 2,500 grams). This proportion of low birth weight infants is significantly higher than the normal rate for low birth weight of 7%–8%. However, since mothers of low socioeconomic status are more likely to have children of low birth weight, Klein and Stern reexamined the birth weight–abuse relationship while controlling for the rate of low birth weight infants among lower-class mothers. Even employing a revised rate of 10% as the incidence of low birth weight for low socioeconomic mothers, the abuse incidence of 23.5% was still significantly higher than the expected percentage.

Other investigators have reported similar relationships. Simons et al. (1966) found that 20% of the abused babies in their New York sample for whom birth records were available were under 5 ½ pounds at birth—a percentage which is approximately twice that of the city as a whole. Similarly, Fontàna (1968) reported that over 50% of the 25 maltreated children in his sample were of low birth weight, while Elmer and Gregg (1967) found 30% of their sample were under 2,400 grams at birth.

Some reasons for the low birth weight–child abuse relationship.—There are many factors that may account for the greater susceptibility of the low birth infant to abuse. Two sets of issues will be discussed: (1) the characteristics of the low birth weight infants that may make the caretaking task more difficult and (2) the structural arrangements surrounding the birth of a low birth weight infant, particularly parent-infant separation.

Characteristics of low birth weight infants.—The survival rate of the low birth weight infant has increased greatly in recent years due to advances in medical care and technology (Caputo & Mandell 1970; Klaus & Fanaroff 1973). While these advances are laudable, many of these "new" survivors often have serious medical difficulties as well as a higher rate of short-term and long-term developmental problems than normal infants. In a comprehensive review of the consequences of low birth weight, Caputo and Mandell (1970) point out a number of outcomes that may make the low birth weight infant more susceptible to parental abuse. It should be noted that some of the outcomes may alter the parent-child relationship in the early postpartum months, while others may not affect the parent-child dyad until the child is beyond infancy. Of course, the disturbances in parent-child interaction may, in fact, be important contributors to disturbances in later years. First, we will examine some of the short-term effects of low birth weight.

There are clear cultural norms concerning appropriate size, weight, and appearance for newborn infants; the parents' responsiveness is, in part, determined by the extent to which the infant's physical characteristics conform to parental expectations. In fact, there are certain characteristics of the normal human infant's face, such as the concavity of the face and the height of the eyes, which are responded to discriminatively and positively by adults (Brooks & Hochberg 1960). The low birth weight premature infant violates many parental expectations; it is not merely a matter of timing, but possibly it is the smallness and underdeveloped appearance of the premature infant which contributes to his eventual abuse as a result of parental failure to develop strong attachment to this "unattractive" infant.

Low birth weight infants place greater demands on their parents than normal infants. For example, feeding disturbances are more common among low birth weight infants. Due to their low weight, these infants must be fed more often, and especially in the case of very low birth weight infants, special feeding techniques may be necessary (Klaus & Fanaroff 1973). In addition, premature infants may cry more and be more irritable (Elmer 1967). In part, these difficulties may stem from the fact that medical problems are often associated with prematurity and low birth weight. For example, Klein and Stern (1971) reported that nine of their 12 low birth weight infants had major neonatal problems (e.g., exchange transfusion, pneumonia, birth asphyxia). In contrast, only 15 out of the 39 normal birth weight infants had medical or developmental complications. In turn, these infants may make more demands on their parents and caretaking may be a more difficult task.

In addition, low birth weight infants may continue to disappoint their parents, since their developmental progress in motor, social, and cognitive spheres is often retarded during at least the first 2 years (Wright 1971). These infants may develop more slowly in terms of social behavior as indexed by the Vineland Social Maturity Scale (Moore 1966); others report that prematures make fewer vocalizations prior to 8 months of age (Lezine 1958). Due to the slower development of social responsiveness, the infant may elicit less positive attention from his caretakers and be viewed as less interesting. On the motor and cognitive side, premature infants tend to walk later and use sentences later than controls (Rabinowitz, Bibace, & Caplan 1961). Nor are the problems restricted to infancy. Caputo and Mandell (1970) have noted a variety of post infancy problems including hyperactivity and childhood accidents. Finally, language development, reading, arithmetic, and spelling are often poorer among low birth weight infants. Although research is badly needed to specify the exact characteristics of the low birth weight infant that elicit parental abuse, it is clear that the burden, stress, and disappointment associated with the birth and care of a low birth weight infant could increase the probability of abuse. The low birth weight–abuse relationship is even more plausible in light of the extremely high and unrealistic expectations that many abusive parents have for their children's developmental progress (Steele & Pollock 1968); the discrepancy between parental expectations and child behavior is particularly marked in the case of the low birth weight infant.

Early maternal-infant separation.—There is another factor that merits consideration in untangling the low birth weight–abuse relationship, namely, the prolonged separation between mother and premature infant in the early postpartum period. It is assumed that the early postpartum period is important for the development of parent-infant attachment. Second, it is assumed that according to the extent to which there is parent-infant attachment, the likelihood of abusive behavior being directed toward the infant would be reduced. Finally, it is assumed that a caretaker who has the opportunity to form an attachment with his infant will be more sensitive to the infant's needs and signals and, therefore, more likely to effectively control potentially abuse-eliciting behaviors, such as irritability and crying.

The recent human research is based on earlier studies with animals (Collias 1956; Hersher, Moore, & Richmond 1958) which demonstrated that mothers may reject their young if they were separated from their newborn infants immediately after birth. These human studies of the effect of separation of mother and infant in the early postpartum period indicate that the type and amount of social interaction between mothers and their newborns during the immediate postpartum period have significant effects on the mother's subsequent attitudes and behavior toward her infant.

Evidence for the influence of mothers' early contact with their premature infants and their later caretaking skills is reported by Leifer, Leiderman, and Barnett (1970). Mothers who were given an opportunity to care for their premature infants in the intensive-care nursery were found to be significantly more skillful in a subsequent feeding session observed during the fifth visit to the discharge nursery than were the mothers who had not been permitted interaction with infants during the infant's earlier stay in the intensive-care nursery. Other research (Seashore et al. 1973) indicates that early separation results in lowered self-confidence among primiparous mothers in their performance of instrumental tasks (diapering, feeding, bathing) as well as social tasks (calming baby, recognizing infant's needs, showing affection).

Opportunities for early contact affect maternal attachment behavior as well as maternal attitudes. Mothers who were permitted physical contact with their premature infants beginning in the first days of life were found to spend significantly more time engaged in cuddling and *en face* behaviors during feeding just preceding discharge than mothers who first handled their babies after 20 days of age (Kennell, Gordon, & Klaus 1970). Other studies indicate that early contact mothers engage in more holding and ventral contact at 1-week discharge and more ventral contact at 1-month postdischarge (Leifer et al. 1970; Leifer et al. 1972). Separation mothers often held their infants at some distance from them, while the early contact mothers more often held their infants cradled close to their body or on their chest or shoulder. Further, the contact mothers exhibited a pattern of looking at the infant, talking to the infant, and refraining from looking and talking to others more often than the separated mothers. Supplementary data reported for these contact and separated mothers indicate that early separation may be associated with a greater incidence of relinquishing custody of infants, greater incidence of divorce, and unsuccessful attempts at breast feeding. For instance, two of the mothers in the separated premature group relinquished custody of their infants after discharge from the hospital. Furthermore, six cases of divorce occurred in the sample with five of them being in the separated group and the other one in the contact group. This last finding suggests a striking correlation between giving birth to a premature infant and family stress, although the causal patterns have not yet been identified.

Finally, Fanaroff, Kennell, and Klaus (1972) have shown that maternal visiting for low birth weight infants is predictive of later maternal treatment of their infants. Among the mothers with a low visiting record, there was higher incidence of battered and failure-to-thrive infants than among the mothers who visited their low birth weight infants during the hospitalization period.

Although the effect of postpartum separation of mother and low birth weight infant has been emphasized in this section, it should be noted that separation may occur more frequently with different types of delivery, such as Caesarean sections. Possibly the early mother-infant separation that may accompany this type of delivery is, in part, responsible for Lenoski's (1974) recent finding that 30% of the abused children in his sample, in contrast to 3.2% of the nonabused children, were delivered by Caesarean section.

Overall, the findings reviewed above provide strong evidence to support the contention that the amount of early maternal involvement with infants has a significant influence on mothers' attitudes about their parenting role, their skill in caring for their infants, and patterns of social interactions with infants. In turn, these factors may, in part, account for the greater tendency of premature infants to become the victims of abuse. Perhaps, as Parke and O'Leary (1975) note, father-infant attachment would be enhanced as well with greater opportunities for paternal visiting during the early postpartum period. Similarly, if the father has the opportunity to learn and practice his caretaking skills during this period, he may be more likely to share with his wife in the caretaking of his infant. This may serve to relieve the mother of some of this responsibility and reduce the probability of tension-elicited abuse.

3. The Older Child's Role in Abuse

It is not just the infant that contributes to his own abuse; the child may elicit abuse from his caretakers at a variety of points throughout his development. In our earlier discussion, the child's role in escalating discipline was noted. In this section, some further examples of the role played by the child in his own abuse will be presented. As in infancy, the older child's appearance, general tempo, or style as well as his specific behavioral reactions are important factors.

Just as appearance of the infant may be an important determinant of the degree of attachment, and thereby may indirectly affect the probability of parental abuse of children, physical attractiveness can modify the disciplinary tactics that adults employ with older children. A recent study by Dion (1974) illustrates this relationship. Female adults viewed a videotape of an interaction between another adult and an ostensibly attractive or unattractive 8-year-old child. When given the opportunity to penalize the child for incorrect responses on a picture-matching task, the adults penalized the unattractive boy more than the attractive boy. The degree of punitiveness, then, may in part be determined by the physical attractiveness of the vicitm and, by implication, may affect the child's potential for abuse.

It is not merely physical attractiveness that determines disciplinary choices, but certain behavior patterns may be influential as well. Activity level is one pattern recently examined by Stevens-Long (1973) and is of particular interest because of the relationships between prematurity and later activity level patterns, and prematurity and abuse. Parents responded to videotapes of sequences depicting either an overactive, underactive, or an average-active child. The adults were required to select an appropriate disciplinary tactic (ranging from reward and affection to corporal punishment) when the child misbehaved at a number of points during the videotape sequence. More severe discipline was selected for the overactive child than for the underactive and average-active child. In summary, highly active children may elicit more extreme forms of discipline from their caretakers.

Another manner in which the child may contribute to the selection of severe disciplinary tactics is, of course, by his own reactions to being disciplined. In a recent examination of this issue, Parke, Sawin, and Kreling (1974) asked adults to monitor a child in a nearby room via a closed circuit videotape arrangement. The adults were to discipline the child whenever the child misbehaved; the reaction of the child to the adult discipline was systematically varied in one of the following ways: (1) the child ignores the adult, (2) the child makes reparation, (3) the child pleads with the adult, or (4) the child behaves in a defiant manner. When the child misbehaved on a future occasion, the adult disciplinary choice was affected by the child's prior reaction to being disciplined. The children who had reacted with defiance received the harshest discipline while those who had made a reparative response received less severe discipline. The implication of the study is clear: children's reactions in a disciplinary context can clearly modify adult behavior and may serve to maintain and/or increase adult punitiveness.

These brief examples demonstrate a clear relationship between child characteristics and behavior and adult punitiveness. In future research, closer attention needs to be paid to the role that the child may play in eliciting abusive reactions from his caretakers.

4. Summary

The child may contribute to his own abuse in a variety of ways. There may be some genetically determined physical and behavioral characteristics of the child that may predispose the child to abuse. Alternatively, the child may develop behaviors through interaction with parents and peers that make him a likely target for abuse. The infant as a target of abuse was discussed; abuse was viewed as an outcome of the demands that infants place on caretakers. Special attention was given to the low birth weight infant, who is particularly likely to be abused. Some of the characteristics of the low birth weight infant, including appearance and slow maturation, were viewed as contributing factors. In addition, mother-infant separation in the early postpartum period which may interfere with the development of mother-infant attachment was viewed as a further factor accounting for the abuse of the low birth weight infant. Finally, it was argued that the older child's appearance, temperament, and behavioral reactions to discipline may contribute to the development of parental abusive patterns.

V. Control of Abuse

Control of child abuse can be viewed in short- and long-term perspectives. Short-term control involves some type of crisis intervention, which may prevent an imminent case of abuse from occurring. Telephone hot lines, crisis nurseries, and day-care drop-off centers are examples of short-term control. Similarly, temporary removal of the abused child from the home may be viewed as another form of short-term control.

However, in light of the large number of abused children reported annually, removal and placement cannot be viewed as an economically feasible solution to the abuse problem. Long-term control has the more ambitious aim of restructuring the social interaction patterns of the family members that may be the cause of abuse or the modification of either the child's or the parent's attitudes, values, personality, and/or behavior which are viewed as causing the abuse. The particular form that long-term intervention and control assume will vary with the idiosyncratic theoretical views of the intervention agent. Next we will examine the implications of each of the three main approaches—psychiatric, sociological, and social-situational—for the control of abuse. Not all of these possible control methods have been employed; however, it seems useful to explore fully the range of techniques that could prove useful in the planning of control programs. Finally, the existing programs will be reviewed, and some evaluation of their effectiveness will be offered.

A. PSYCHIATRIC APPROACH

To the extent that the psychiatric model of abuse focuses primarily on the character and personality deficiencies of the parents, the main aim of psychiatric treatment is the modification of parental personality. Psychiatric intervention can assume a variety of forms ranging from individual psychotherapy to various types of group therapy, usually under the direction of a psychiatric or psychological professional. The recommended form of therapeutic intervention varies widely across professionals. Choices among therapies are probably as much a function of the prior theoretical orientation of the therapist as a function of an examination of the dynamics of the child abuse. Estimates concerning the success of various forms of psychotherapy vary widely. Green (1973) estimates that, with proper combined therapeutic modalities and under optimum conditions, about 80% of abusing parents can be rehabilitated. However, as Blumberg (1974) has commented: "The truth must be faced realistically that about 20 to 50 percent of all cases, depending on time, place and facilities, are untreatable" (p. 27).

Perhaps the most thoroughly instituted and evaluated program of psychiatric intervention is the Steele-Pollock program in Denver, Colorado. In their words:

Our method of study was clinical, patterned basically after the usual methods of psychiatric diagnosis and therapeutic interviews with an attempt to reach as deeply as possible into the patient's personality. In addition to the directly psychiatric procedure, great use was made of interviews and home visits by our social worker, whereby information could be obtained about general modes of living and of actual day-by-day interactions between parents and between parents and child. Contacts were made not only with the attacking parent but also with the spouse. This was often inevitable, as it was not always possible at first to know who had attacked the child. Later such contacts were maintained or instituted because the uncovering of problems in the marriage made it obvious that treatment of both parents was highly desirable. Interviews, usually rather informal, were held whenever possible with attacker's parents and other relatives, and occasionally we had the chance to see an abusing mother with her own mother in a joint interview and to observe their interaction. From such sources we obtained information which corroborated, corrected, or elaborated with memories which the attacker had of his own childhood and upbringing. A battery of psychological tests was done on most of our attacking parents and in some instances, on the non-attacking spouse as well. [Steele & Pollock 1968, p. 105]

The duration of contact varied, with most parents being seen over a period of months and several for as long as 3–5 years. Some patients were hospitalized in the early stages of therapy, while other patients were seen on a regular basis of 1–3 times per week. One important feature was the continued availability of the therapist by telephone. These investigators reported that three-quarters of their 60 patients showed significant "improvement" which was defined as:

. . . when dangerously severe physical attack of the infant was eliminated and milder physical attack in the form of disciplinary punishment was either eliminated or reduced to a non-injurious minimum. Of equal significance was a reduction in demand upon and criticism of children accompanied by increased recognition of a child as an individual with age-appropriate needs and behavior. Further signs of improvement in the parents were increased abilities to relate to a wider social milieu for pleasureable satisfaction and source of help in time of need rather than looking to their children for such responses. We did not always try nor did we always succeed in making any change in all of the psychological conflicts and character problems of our patients. [Steele & Pollock 1968, p. 145]

Although the Denver program has successfully suppressed abusive behavior, the durability of the treatment effects has not been established. However, Pollock and Steele (1972) suggest that "the parents are not automatically protected from future trouble" (p. 21) as a result of therapeutic intervention and recommend that the parents be able to reinstitute contact in case of future crises.

Although the program developed from a traditional psychiatric model, the type of therapy is multifaceted and nonorthodox in many respects. In spite of the emphasis on modification of patient personality, considerable stress is placed on reprogramming the "basic pattern of child rearing." The use of home observations which permitted an assessment of the parent-child interaction patterns may have increased the success of these efforts to modify child rearing. In short, this was not an intervention program whose sole emphasis was on the modification of parental personality through the development of a positive patient-client relationship.

In evaluating the effectiveness of any intervention effort, the cost in parent and change-agent time and money needs to be carefully considered. Second, the practical utility of intervention programs must be evaluated in terms of the feasibility of wide-scale application to groups at both local and state or even national levels. Regardless of the eventual judgment concerning the effectiveness of individual psychotherapy as a treatment for child-abusing parents, there are serious practical limitations to this approach. The amount of therapist time, client time, and monetary outlay places severe limitations on the type of individuals for whom this technique can be used. Generally, this type of intervention will be restricted to the treatment of middle- and upper-class clients; in light of the apparent disproportionate number of lower-class abusers, the method must be viewed as one of limited wide-scale utility. In terms of state or national intervention, both cost and therapist availability make this approach unlikely.

B. SOCIOLOGICAL APPROACH

There are many implications for control that are derived from a sociological perspective. The most articulate spokesman for wide-ranging changes in societal values and the social structure is Gil (1970, 1974), who recently stated that "primary prevention of child abuse, on all levels, would require fundamental changes in social philosophy and value premises in societal institutions and in human relations" (Gil 1974, pp. 22–23). It would also require a reconceptualization of childhood, of children's rights, and of child rearing. It would necessitate rejecting the use of force as a means for achieving societal ends, especially in dealing with children. It would require the elimination of poverty and of alienating conditions of production, major sources of stress and frustration which tend to trigger abusive acts toward children in adult-child interaction. And, finally, it would necessitate the elimination of psychological illness.

Specifically, Gil has offered a number of general suggestions that are aimed to

unconditional elimination of poverty by assuring to all members of society, without discrimination, equal opportunity to the enjoyment of life through:
(*a*) adequate income derived from employment whenever feasible, or assured by means of a system of nonstigmatizing guaranteed-income maintenance based on legal entitlement rather than on charity and bureaucratic discretion;
(*b*) comprehensive health care and social services;
(*c*) decent and adequate housing and neighborhoods, free from the stigmatizing milieu and conditions of many existing public-housing programs;
(*d*) comprehensive education fitting inherent capacities and assuring the realization of each person's potential;
(*e*) cultural and recreational facilities. [Gil 1970, p. 145]

While few would argue with Gil's recommendations that the elimination of poverty should be a national priority, the extent to which this level of solution will aid in the reduction of child abuse is unknown. First, this general set of recommendations is based on the assumption that child abuse is a poverty-related phenomenon; earlier, we raised serious questions concerning whether this is, in fact, the case. To the extent that child abuse is a class-free phenomenon, this general solution deals only with a portion of the problem. Abuse still occurs in families where poverty is not a problem and source of stress. Even if Gil's analysis and recommendations are correct, they would require extensive supplementation to aid in the control of non-poverty-based abuse. Second, even if there is a link between poverty and abuse, can we necessarily assume that the reduction of poverty will result in abuse reduction? For example, possibly there are third-order factors which are related to both abuse and poverty which are, in fact, responsible for the apparent correlation. Third, Gil seems to be following a repeated tendency to blame any problem that poverty-level individuals may have on the low level of income; this is a solution that is recommended for nearly all of the problems of the poor. It is questionable whether these general solutions or panaceas are any longer adequate. Fourth, the solution is highly impractical; there can be general commitment to the elimination of poverty, but alternative solutions that are more practical to implement and more *specifically* related to the question of abuse per se would seem to be required.

Gil (1970) has made a series of more specific proposals that are more directly related to the analysis of child abuse. First, comprehensive family planning programs and legal medical abortions are recommended. Both of these suggestions flow from prior research which suggests that child abuse is more frequent in large families and in the case of unwanted children. Second, Gil recommends family-life education and counseling programs for both teenagers and adults that are aimed at providing realistic information concerning the tasks and demands of marriage and child rearing. This would serve to avoid the unrealistic expectations for children that characterize many abusive parents (cf. Steele & Pollock 1968). Another suggestion offered by Gil has been incorporated into many of the current child abuse control programs, namely, support services for mothers, which serve to relieve the stress of child care. The assumption underlying this suggestion is that "no mother should be expected to care for her children around the clock 365 days a year" (Gil 1970, p. 147). Specifically, Gil recommends:

A range of high quality, neighborhood-based social, child-welfare, and child-protective services geared to the reduction of environmental and internal stresses on family life, and especially on mothers who carry major responsibility for the child-rearing function. Such stresses are known to precipitate incidents of physical abuse of children, and any measure that would reduce these stresses would also indirectly reduce the incidence of child abuse. Family counseling, homemaker and housekeeping services, mother's helpers and baby-sitting services, family and group day-care facilities for preschool and school-age children are all examples of such services. [1970, p. 147]

These suggestions are well grounded in the prior sociological analysis and would appear to offer considerable promise for the control of child abuse. Programs, such as nursery schools and day-care centers, may serve not only to relieve parents of their child care responsibilities, but to provide an opportunity for the child to learn new patterns of social interaction as a result of exposure to peers as well as a new set of adults. To the extent that the abusive behavior in some cases may be due to the child's behavior, opportunities for modifying child behavior patterns in these nonhome contexts may, in turn, alter the parent-child interaction patterns in the home situation. Specific techniques for the modification of child behavior will be discussed in the next section, which concerns the implications of the social situational approach for the control of abuse.

C. SOCIAL-SITUATIONAL APPROACH

There are certain distinctive features of a social-situational approach to the control of child abuse. First, it assumes that the cause of abuse is not in the individual, but in the social situation which, in turn, may be maintaining certain patterns of behavior. In contrast to a psychiatric approach which stresses modification of the verbal output of the "patient" in a nonhome setting, this approach focuses on the modification of *observable behavior* in the home context. Therefore, the locus of change is the setting in which the abuse occurs; the content of the treatment is the actual observed behavior of the parent. Third, the assumption is that there is usually a high degree of interdependence between the abusing parent and the victim and, therefore, both parent and child must be treated; although for some phases of treatment the child and parent may be worked with separately, it is assumed that any separate changes in one partner will alter the behavior of the other partner in the dyad.

1. Techniques for the Modification of Child Behavior

As noted earlier in this chapter, children themselves sometimes may elicit abusive behavior from their caretakers by persisting in noxious and deviant behavior; it is in the service of attempting to control this undesirable behavior that abuse may occur. Therefore, an examination of effective tehniques for controlling children's behavior which avoid the use of punitive tactics that may tend to escalate to abusive levels is worthwhile.

First, a brief comment about punishment. Punishment can be an effective technique for controlling children's behavior, if it is carefully administered (Parke 1970). However, the effectiveness of punishment is dependent on a variety of parameters such as the timing, intensity, consistency of the punishing event, as well as the nature of the relationship between the punishing agent and the recipient of punishment (Parke 1972). While it would be possible to teach parents more effective ways of using punishment as a control tactic, physical punishment has a series of undesirable side effects which severely curtail its value as a technique of parental control (Parke 1972). As noted above, the punished child may model the behavior of the punitive parent and display increased aggression. A variety of studies (Ulrich 1966) have demonstrated that the pain associated with the administration of physical punishment may itself lead to an increase in aggression. Another undesirable consequence of punishment is the effect on the agent-child relationship. As a result of punishment, the child may be motivated to avoid the punishing parent. Consequently, the socialization agent may no longer be able to direct or influence the child's behavior. In a recent experimental study, Redd, Morris, and Martin (1975) demonstrated that children preferred work and play with adults who had previously treated them in a positive or neutral fashion and avoided a previously punishing adult. The implication is clear: punishment may be an effective modification technique, but the use of punishment by adults may lead the child to avoid that socializing agent and therefore undermine the adult's effectiveness as a future influence on the child's behavior.

Conditions such as crowded living arrangements often prevent the child from physically escaping the presence of the agent. Continued use of punishment in an inescapable context, however, may lead to passivity and withdrawal (Seligman, Maier, & Solomon 1969) or adaptation to the punishing stimuli themselves. In any case, whether escape is possible or not, the quality of the agent-child relationship may deteriorate if punishment is used with high frequency; punishment administered by such an agent will, therefore, be less effective in inhibiting the child.

The undesirable effects of physical punishment mentioned here probably occur mainly in situations where the disciplinary agents are indiscriminately punitive. In child-rearing contexts where the agent rewards and encourages a large proportion of the child's behavior, even though selectively and occasionally punishing certain kinds of behavior, these side effects are less likely to be found (Walters & Parke 1967).

There are many alternative techniques that can be employed to successfully control children's behavior that avoid the negative consequences of physical punishment. Extinction (Williams 1959), reinforcement of incompatible responses (Brown & Elliot 1965), time-out (Hawkins et al. 1966), and verbal reasoning (Parke 1970, 1974) are effective techniques for improving parental control of children's behavior. Extinction involves the nonreinforcement of the undesirable response; in the study by Williams (1959), the crying behavior of an infant was diminished by systematically ignoring this behavior. The effectiveness of reinforcement of incompatible responses is illustrated in a study by Brown and Elliot (1965). Adults were instructed to ignore aggressive responses while rewarding cooperative behavior. Through these procedures, the amount of aggressive behavior was reduced. Another technique is "time-out," which involves the removal of the child from the situation for a brief time period. A number of investigators have demonstrated the usefulness of this control tactic for modification of deviant child behaviors in home situations. Hawkins et al (1966) trained mothers to use these procedures to control aggressive behavior. Risley and Baer (1973) discuss a variety of these behavior-modification techniques in detail. Finally, Parke (1974) has demonstrated that children's deviant behavior can be effectively inhibited by the provision of verbal rationales.

These techniques may be utilized by an outside therapist or change agent who can modify the child's behavior with the aim of reducing the deviant behavior that may be eliciting the punitive and possibly abusive behavior. However, it is assumed that abusive behavior of parents will be more adequately modified through a program of parental retraining. In the next section, techniques for modifying parental control tactics will be examined.

2. Techniques for the Modification of Parental Disciplinary Behavior

Programs for parental retraining have a two-level focus. First, the parents themselves who are using physically punitive tactics need to be provided with a new repertoire of training tactics that will be effective in child control and, therefore, be adopted by them to replace their punitive behavior. Second, through the use of these techniques, the child behaviors which may be eliciting highly punitive parental reactions will be altered. As noted above, social learning principles of operant conditioning have been utilized in the development of extremely effective techniques for modification of children's behavior, and, more recently, these same principles, in conjunction with modeling techniques (Bandura 1969), have been employed in developing strategies for the effective retraining of parents to employ nonpunitive control tactics.

To illustrate this approach to the modification of parent and child behaviors, we will examine a comprehensive program for the retraining of parents of aggressive children developed by Patterson (1974). This program is of particular relevance to child abuse since one-fourth of the parents in the program would be classified as abusive. This treatment program is based on social learning principles, particularly operant conditioning concepts, in which the relationships between parental reactions and deviant behavior are the focus. It is assumed that much deviant behavior is maintained by parental and peer reactions; therefore, by making the parents aware of these relationships and by giving them the opportunity to learn and rehearse alternative techniques for dealing with their children, the deviant behavior can be brought under better control. A number of steps are involved. First, the parents are required to study a programmed text on social learning–based child-management techniques. The book emphasizes that child behavior can be controlled and in nontechnical language explains social learning principles such as reinforcement, shaping, generalization, coercion, extinction, and punishment. The parents must complete the book before proceeding with the treatment. In the next phase of the program, the parents are taught to carefully define, track, and record a series of targeted deviant and/or prosocial child behaviors. This involves defining in a precise fashion the exact behavior, to note the elicitors and consequences that accompany a response, and, finally, to record the occurrences. During this phase they are monitored frequently by telephone.

The third stage involves a parent training group, where modeling and role-playing procedures are used to illustrate appropriate techniques. There are two aims in this phase: (1) to teach the parents to reinforce and encourage prosocial appropriate behaviors and (2) to reduce the rate of occurrence of deviant behaviors. To accomplish the first aim, the parents are taught to recognize and reinforce in a consistent way instances of acceptable behavior. The complementary set of procedures involves the use of time-out for deviant behavior. Time-out is a procedure whereby a child is removed for a specified period from the reinforcing environment and placed in isolation. Usually a bathroom is used for this purpose. This is an effective technique for reducing deviant behavior in children; moreover the parent, who may use more severe punitive techniques, is provided with alternative and effective procedures for child control. In group-training situations which consist of 3–4 sets of parents, these behavior management skills are directly modeled, and the novice parents engage in supervised role playing of these same skills. Usually 8–12 weekly sessions are sufficient. Where necessary, training sessions are conducted in the home with the experimenters modeling the appropriate parenting skills. A final aspect of the program consists of learning to construct contracts which specified contingencies for a list of problem behaviors occurring at home and/or at school. In addition, Patterson combines these procedures with a set of classroom interventions.

To assess the effectiveness of the program, detailed observations by trained observers of the interaction patterns between the parents and the deviant child are made in the home situation. A careful assessment of 27 families indicated that there was a significant decrease in deviant behavior from the baseline across the treatment phase. Follow-up assessments revealed that there was an increase in noxious behavior for half of the families during the month following the cessation of treatment; however, by providing families with a "booster shot" of approximately 2 hours of extra treatment, the deviant behavior was reduced. Most important, the results suggest that the effects induced by the training were relatively stable over 1 year. Finally, in contrast to long-term psychiatric therapy, this type of intervention program was relatively economical: the cost in terms of therapist contact time was 31.4 hours for the family training intervention.

The success of this program is impressive and clearly documents the feasibility of retraining parents to use nonpunitive modification tactics for effective child control. Part of the reason for the long-term stability of the changes is that, as the child's behavior improves, the relationship between parent and child may improve and the negative attitude to the child may diminish. The child may become a more attractive and valued family member and, as such, a less likely target for abuse.

These effects have been partially replicated by Johnson et al. (1974). Based on the fact that some of these families were abusive, there is an indication that these procedures are applicable to the modification of abusive parental behaviors. Recently, a child abuse intervention program in Los Angeles (Savino & Sanders 1973) adopted a social learning approach in retraining parents and is utilizing the Patterson and Guillon text, *Living with Children* (1968). Whether exposure to social learning principles through the text alone, without the extensive modeling and role-playing components that are part of the full-scale Patterson program, will be effective remains unknown without careful follow-up documentation of the success rate of this program.

The Patterson program should serve as a model for future intervention attempts in terms of the careful assessment, programmatic intervention, and detailed documentation of outcomes. The Patterson work illustrates that it is possible to introduce adequate assessment and evaluation procedures as part of an intervention program in this area.

3. Techniques for Anger Control

Another approach recognizes the fact that not all parental abusive behavior is, in fact, due to annoying and disruptive behavior of a child; many other sources of frustration may be present in the environment, and an examination of techniques for lessening anger in the face of potentially anger-eliciting stimuli is useful. What techniques are useful for anger control?

A number of techniques have been suggested including (*a*) reinforcement of nonangry responses, (*b*) role playing and modeling of nonangry reactions, and (*c*) desensitization in the presence of the anger-evoking stimuli.

An early study by Davitz (1952) illustrates the role of reinforcement in the anger-reduction process. In this experiment, children were reinforced for either nonangry cooperative responses or angry aggressive reactions; when they were subsequently frustrated by an adult, the children who had previously been reinforced for their nonangry cooperative behavior reacted with little anger and aggression relative to the other children who were encouraged for their angry responses. Clearly, reactions to frustration can be modified by reinforcement of alternative, nonangry responses. Using a related approach, Mahoney (1971) directly rewarded hyperaggressive boys for remaining calm and noncombative in the face of peer harassment. The magnitude of the rewards varied in relation to the length of time that the victim was able to maintain his composure and equanimity.

Just as parental behaviors can be reprogrammed successfully through the use of modeling and role-playing techniques, anger reactions in the face of frustrating and other anger-eliciting cues can often be modified by the use of these same techniques. The assumption underlying this approach is that new, alternative nonangry modes of reacting in anger-eliciting situations can be learned successfully by exposure to models who demonstrate these new reactions. Second, it is assumed that the observer needs practice and rehearsal of these new behaviors, and if these new behaviors are rewarded, the reactions become a habitual part of the response repertoire. As Bandura (1973) has noted: "Given adequate demonstration, guided practice and success experiences, this method is almost certain to produce favorable results" (p. 253).

Gittelman (1965) has successfully employed these techniques in modifying the aggressive-angry reactions of children. After constructing a hierarchy of annoying situations, the children then enacted these situations and rehearsed nonviolent tactics for handling them. This type of anger-control tactic will probably be most effective when combined with an extensive modeling component which involves exposure to a wide range of models who demonstrate nonaggressive and nonangry solutions to conflictful and frustrating problems. Chittenden (1942) also has demonstrated the usefulness of modeling and rehearsal in modifying aggressive behavior in children. More recently, modeling and behavioral rehearsal techniques have been applied to the modification of anger in adults. Rimm et al. (1974) successfully treated males who had a history of expressing anger in an anti-social manner. These investigators employed group assertive training, which involves the modeling and rehearsal of appropriate nonaggressive solutions to a potentially anger-eliciting problem.

Another technique for anger control is desensitization by which the anger-evoking stimuli lose some of their anger-eliciting potency. Herrell (1971) successfully employed this technique in a chronically assaultive adult. By providing relaxation instructions while the person imagined the anger-eliciting scenes, the anger reactions were reduced.

The comparative effectiveness of these different approaches for anger control merits investigation in future research. Similarly, the effectiveness of these techniques in modifying the angry reactions of abusive adults needs to be examined.

4. Techniques for Increasing Social Contacts

One of the characteristics of abusive adults is their isolation from other members of the community. In a series of recent studies, modeling techniques have been successfully employed in the modification of social isolation behavior. There are two assumptions underlying this research: (1) the social isolate may be fearful of other individuals and/or (2) the isolate may lack the necessary social skills to successfully initiate and maintain social contacts. These techniques have been successfully applied to both children and adults. O'Conner (1969) exposed children who displayed extreme social withdrawal, characterized by isolation from both adults and other children, to a film of a child interacting with other individuals. The film model gradually increased the degree of social interaction as the film progressed. In contrast to a control film of nonsocial behavior, the children exposed to the experimental film increased their degree of subsequent social participation. With adults, McFall and Twentyman (1972) have employed a combination of modeling and behavioral rehearsal to overcome shyness and increase social assertiveness in young men. Rimm and Masters (1974) have presented a comprehensive review of the application of modeling techniques to the modification of social deficits. These techniques could be extremely useful for modifying the social isolation that often characterizes abusive adults. By teaching them new social skills, they will be better able to form friendships and seek social support in crisis situations.

5. Increasing the Awareness of Harmful Effects

Another tactic that is probably most effectively employed in conjunction with modeling and behavioral rehearsal techniques involves increasing the awareness of the harmful effects of abusive behavior. Some abusive parents tend to minimize the harm that they have caused. As a first step in sensitizing them to the impact of their behavior, vivid videotape and film displays of both abused and battered children as well as depictions of different adults abusing their children could be shown. These films would have to be accompanied by commentary which highlights the unjustifiability of this behavior and which underlines the negative, harmful outcomes for the children. Note that two components are involved here: first, an increased sensitivity to the harmful effects of excessive physical treatment and, second, the explicit labeling of the observed outcome as "bad" and unjustified. This latter labeling may serve to un-

TABLE 3

CURRENT INTERVENTION PROGRAMS

Name of Program Location and Date Begun	Individual Psychotherapy with a Psychiatrist, Psychologist, or Social Worker	Individual Lay Therapy or Parent Aide	Group Therapy or Parent Groups	Child-Care Instruction	Day-Care Crisis Nursery	Medical Care	24-Hour Hotline	Research Prof. Training Public Education
Kentucky Welfare Dept. Protective Services, Louisville, 1958	Casework with social worker		Parent group led by social worker mtgs. twice/month	Child care taught in parent mtgs.				
University of Colorado Med. Ctr., Child Abuse Study, Denver, 1962	With psychiatrist 1–3 times/week + social worker						Staff accessible 24 hours	Research prof. training public education
Massachusetts Dept. of Pub. Welfare Div. of Child Guardianship, Boston, 1967	Casework with social worker				1971-est. day-care program			
Parents' Center Project, Boston, 1968	Home visits by social worker on request		Group therapy led by social worker once/week		Day-care program	For children 6 mos.–3 yrs.		Research prof. training

	Individual	Group	Child care	Telephone	Other
Mothers Anonymous (Parents Anonymous), Redondo Beach, Calif., 1970..........	Individual relationship with another member possible	Group meetings led by member once/week		Self-referral hotline + members call each other	
C.A.L.M. (Child Abuse Listening Mediation), Santa Barbara, Calif., 1970..................	Volunteer lay therapists			2 nonprof. directors take calls	Community Education
UCLA, Neuropsychiatric Inst., Child Abuse Project, Los Angeles, 1971..................		Groups led by "surrogate parents" once/week	Child care in in group mtgs. lessons at home on request		Research
P.S.S. (Parental Stress Service), Berkeley, 1972	Volunteer lay therapists		Volunteers will baby-sit	Volunteers take calls	

TABLE 3 (*Continued*)

Name of Program Location and Date Begun	Individual Psychotherapy with a Psychiatrist, Psychologist, or Social Worker	Individual Lay Therapy or Parent Aide	Group Therapy or Parent Groups	Child-Care Instruction	Day-Care Crisis Nursery	Medical Care	24-Hour Hotline	Research Prof. Training Public Education
Children's Trauma Ctr., Oakland, Calif., 1972..	Available		Group, family, marital counsel			Special trauma clinic & follow up	Staff accessible 24 hrs.	Prof. train. community education
Child Protection Team Univ. of Colorado Med. Ctr., Denver, 1972		Lay therapists make 1–2 visits/week	"Families anonymous," semi-self-help group	Homemaker & visiting nurse available	Crisis nursery		Prof. take calls	Research prediction prof. train. public education
S.C.A.N. (Suspected Child Abuse & Neglect), Little Rock, Ark., 1972	Intensive supportive therapy	Lay therapists			Day-care & crisis nursery			
Child Abuse Project, Maricopa County Hospital, Phoenix, 1973	Some individual counseling	Lay therapists	Group therapy led by volunteer		Crisis nursery	Medical care if parents accept soc. serv.	Volunteers take calls	Public education

C.A.P.E. (Child Abuse Prevention Effort), Philadelphia, 1973......		Anonymous parent groups led by professional once/week	Professional volunteers take calls	Research public educ.
S.P.S. (Spotlight on Parental Stress), Oakland, Calif., 1973..	Volunteer lay therapists		Crisis phone	
Family Focus, Birmingham, Ala., 1973	Family aids	Through nursery schools	Listening service supervised by prof.	Speaker on money management
CALL (Child Abuse Listening Service), Santa Monica, Calif., 1974.........	Makes referrals to parent group or Child Trauma Prevention Program at UCLA		Listening service	

dermine some parental attempts to justify their behavior in light of higher-order disciplinary principles.

In part, both the specific teaching of new control tactics and the modification of attitudes involve the induction of new norms and standards that were not learned during their own socialization.

6. Summary

In this section the implications of each of the three main approaches—psychiatric, sociological, and social-situational—for the control of abuse were presented. Under the psychiatric model, individual and group therapy has been utilized to modify the behavior of abusive parents. From a sociological perspective, on the other hand, a variety of recommendations aimed at the alleviation of stress induced by poverty conditions were discussed. Support services for mothers, such as day-care centers and homemaker programs, would seem to offer particular promise. Next, the implications of the social-situational model for the control of abuse were examined. Techniques for nonpunitive management of children's behavior were discussed as well as ways of training parents to utilize these alternative tactics. Approaches for increasing anger control in abusive adults were examined, as well as techniques for the modification of the pattern of social isolation that characterizes many abusive families.

D. CURRENT INTERVENTION PROGRAMS

In this section, we will outline a variety of current innovative programs and services which have been developed to attempt to control child abuse. These are supplements to a wide network of state and local welfare and social work agencies and child protection services which have traditionally handled abuse and neglect problems; these traditional approaches are reviewed elsewhere (Davoren 1974; Glazier 1971; Kempe & Helfer 1972). There are a number of different types of intervention programs that merit distinction: (1) parent groups which provide group discussion and support for child-abusing parents, (2) home support personnel who provide assistance in the home environment, (3) crisis services such as hotlines, (4) drop-off nurseries and day-care centers, (5) child-care instruction, and (6) public education. Typically, intervention programs have one or more of these different approaches represented as the outline of current programs in table 3 indicates.

1. Parent's Groups

Parent groups provide child abusers with the opportunity to meet others with similar problems and feelings to discuss personal experiences relating to themselves, their children, and their marriage. Meetings are usually held weekly for 2 hours, and may be with or without a professional leader. Group members report that they profit from the helpfulness of knowing that other people have problems and feelings similar to their own (McFerran 1958). Another positive aspect of parent groups is the opportunity for meaningful social experience for otherwise isolated people (Feinstein, Paul, & Esmiol 1964). No systematic assessment of the effectiveness of this approach is available.

Parents Anonymous is a self-help group which maintains independence from professional help. An attempt is made in the meetings to help one another by presenting positive behavioral alternatives to problem situations such as child abuse. Group cohesiveness is fostered by members using each other for support and guidance, helping each other without judgment, moralization, or stigma (Parents Anonymous 1972). Group members share phone numbers and are encouraged to contact each other any time for relief of stress or to report positive experiences. Kempe and Helfer (1972) have offered a series of suggestions for strengthening these self-help group programs, including: (1) the development of group intervention skills for the session leaders; (2) affiliation with a hospital or community-based child abuse consultation team as a backup resource for special cases; (3) assistance in providing child-rearing education for members; (4) a follow-through program for drop-outs; and (5) a program to aid parents in improving their relationships with their children.

Parent group programs with professional leadership may use the model of surrogate parent leaders. A child abuse program at UCLA uses two surrogate parent co-therapists, a male clinical psychologist and a female psychiatric nurse (Paulson & Chalef 1973; Saving & Sanders 1973). The surrogate parent model is seen as useful for work with abusing parents since it facilitates identification and modeling of parent surrogate roles.

2. Home Support Programs

Parent Aides, one of the most innovative recent intervention programs, was developed by Kempe and Helfer (1972) as an off-shoot of the highly successful "foster grandparent program" sponsored by OEO in the 1960s. This parent aide program is a lay therapist intervention effort whose participants function as family friends for abusing parents. In contrast to the typical social worker load of 15–30 cases, an aid is assigned to only one or two families. Their main function is to provide advice and support for the family over an extended period of 8–12 months on a regular basis, usually in the parents' home. The aide is always available by phone 24 hours a day, 7 days a week, and the parent is encouraged to make use of the aide, especially during a crisis. Attempts are made to match aides and families by race, education, and social and economic class on the assumption that this similarity would facilitate family acceptance of the aide's intervention. The focus of the aide's work is the parents and their problem; the child is viewed as secondary. In the Kempe-Helfer program the parent aides receive support and advice through bi-weekly group therapy sessions as well as ongoing supervision by a social worker.

How successful has the program been? Unfortunately, no statistical data are available to date, but "clinical results have been outstandingly good at a fraction of the cost of employing psychiatrists and social workers as therapists" (Kempe & Helfer 1972, p. 44).

The homemaker service can serve the function of relieving the mother and/or sharing with the mother the responsibility of managing the children and the household duties. A number of agencies have employed these homemakers, but, again, data concerning their effectiveness are lacking.

3. Hotline Services

Using the successful model of emergency telephone lines for suicide cases as a guide, hotlines for potential child abusers have expanded rapidly in the last few years. The public is made aware of these 24-hour emergency hotlines for potential or actual child abusers through a variety of media including radio, TV, billboards, and newspapers. A newspaper ad sponsored by the CALM program states: "Is your child abused, neglected? Let us share your problems. Keep CALM in mind, call . . . for help" (Pike 1973). The aim of the hotlines is generally twofold. First, through the availability of support in a crisis situation, the hotline service aims to prevent abuse before it occurs. Second, it serves as a referral agency for either potential or actual abusing parents and attempts to encourage parental involvement in some type of more long-range program such as a parent group or counseling service. The types of personnel staffing the hotlines as well as the types of referral vary widely across the country. Some programs use trained volunteers for hotlines while others use only professionals for hotline work and volunteers as lay therapists.

4. Crisis Nurseries and Drop-off Centers

Crisis nurseries provide the parent in a crisis situation with 24-hour emergency short-term care for infants. Crisis nurseries originated because of the frequent observation that a major contributing factor to child abuse is the escalation of the parents' stress when faced with the task of caring for their children with no relief from those responsibilities. The Denver program's crisis nursery includes admission of the mother and infant "rooming in" fashion, so that the mother can be helped to develop parenting skills (Kempe & Helfer 1972; National Center for the Prevention and Treatment of Child Abuse and Neglect 1973). Another closely related service is the drop-off day-care center, which permits an older child to be left under professional supervision at times when the parent is under stress.

5. Child-Care Instruction

Since many abusive parents have been found to share common misunderstandings about child rearing (Spinetta & Rigler 1972), instruction in child rearing and normal child development are included in several programs. In some programs child care is taught in parent group meetings while in other programs it is taught individually in the home. Emphasis is on the practical aspects of child care such as toilet training and discipline. The UCLA child abuse program offers home instruction in behavior modification, teaching the parents the principles of reinforcement. A closely related project in Seattle (Slaby 1974), stressing similar principles of behavior management through the use of positive reinforcement, provides parent training through supervised practice of child-management techniques in a clinic setting. Early results indicate that this program is a promising approach; in fact, Slaby (1974, personal communication) reports that the program has been effective even when other group intervention efforts, such as "Parents Anonymous" have failed to modify parental behavior.

6. Public Education

Another service of child abuse programs is public education, which is aimed at increasing public awareness and knowledge concerning the scope and nature of child abuse. In addition to lectures, pamphlets, and films on child abuse, some programs provide information on the problems of normal parenting. For example, CALM offers a film-discussion program to adolescents in high school, which aims to expose future parents to some of the realities and responsibilities of parenthood. In view of the fact that most adolescents have a vague and unrealistic conception of the parental role, this type of public education is extremely valuable.

7. The Effectiveness of Current Intervention Programs

Although there have been many claims on behalf of these various intervention efforts, there has been insufficient systematic evaluation of the effectiveness of these different programs. Two strategies are necessary. First, the current programs need to introduce an evaluation component as part of their ongoing intervention effort. Second, a specific series of field-experimental intervention programs need to be established.

These programs should include a systematic introduction of various types of intervention strategies both singly and in combination. Evaluation would be an integral part of this effort whereby abuse rates would be assessed at time points before, during, and after treatment to document the impact of the program. Then we would know not only which aspects of current programs are critical, but also the optimal combination of services that are most effective. Evaluation should not be restricted only to the treatment sample and the formal control groups, but should include assessments of other groups of parents in the community to determine the secondary effects of introducing abuse-control programs into a community on such issues as knowledge of abuse, attitudes toward abuse, readiness to report abusing adults, and, of course, rates of actual child abuse.

One approach to program assessment would involve the use of comparable counties as units for introducing different types of programs. With careful baseline assessments and follow-up evaluation, the relative effectiveness of various approaches could be determined. It is to be hoped that these evaluations would permit some conclusions concerning the relative effectiveness not only of various newly instituted child abuse programs but also provide some evaluation of their success in comparison to more traditional social service work approaches to this problem.

In future research, a clear distinction needs to be made between the functions and possibly the clientele served by different types of programs or program components. Short-term crisis intervention procedures such as hotlines and drop-off child-care centers need to be distinguished from long-term programs which aim to effect substantial changes in child-rearing practices. Both are probably necessary, but little is known about the relative impact of these different levels of intervention, nor is there information concerning the types of individuals which are best served by these different approaches. The general question concerning the criteria for matching intervention programs for different types of abusers needs serious attention.

Another issue concerns the type of parents who are consumers of these new innovative programs. Are they the same types of adults that would usually be seen by Social Welfare Services or are they a new breed of adults who otherwise would remain undetected since they are middle class and, therefore, unlikely to use community welfare agencies. For example, CALM has reported a self-referral rate of 61% in 1973—a figure which is significantly higher than the self-referral rate in most city and state welfare agencies. In short, it is not clear whether the rate of detection of abusers has shifted to include new individuals or whether the same types of clientele are merely using different sources of assistance. With increasingly sophisticated reporting centers, some evaluation of the secular shifts in the type of clientele that are being serviced by different types of programs may be possible.

While these increases in self-referral are encouraging, they raise a serious issue concerning the role of client-motivation variables in these programs. If the majority of parents who participate in child abuse programs are self-selected volunteers, they may have already made a commitment to alter their abusive behavior prior to the onset of the program. Although they may not change without assistance from the intervention program, they are probably more willing to comply with the demands of the program that are critical for behavior alteration than unmotivated parents. A number of therapists have noted the importance of client motivation in determining the success of an intervention program. For example, Moorehead (1970), in describing the key element of successful treatment of parents in a London child abuse program, stated that, once the parents can ask for and receive help, the vicious circle which leads to a battered child may be broken. Galdston (1971), reporting the outcome of the Parent's Center Project's recruitment of families, mentions that of the 42 families referred to the project, 19 withdrew before or after the intake interview. He readily acknowledges the motivation factor of the 23 families who remained in the program stating, "thus our parents appear to be the most motivated" of the initial group (p. 342). The critical issue is this: if current programs are successful, to what extent is their success due to the overrepresentation of motivated parents? While these new programs may prove to be valuable for abuse control, the effectiveness of these efforts may not be generalizable to unmotivated parents.

It is clear that careful, systematic evaluation of both programs and their clientele is urgently required to determine whether these programs are, in fact, fulfilling their goals of successful modification of abusive parental behavior.

8. Prediction of Abuse

One other recent innovation in the area of child abuse concerns prediction. There have been two recent attempts at a priori prediction of child abuse. Kempe (1973) reported an ongoing project in Aberdeen, Scotland, of postpartum prediction of child abuse. Data are collected by health visitors who systematically visit every home in the city to assist mothers in caring for their new infants. To identify potentially abusive mothers, the nurses ask a short set of questions concerning the maternal attitudes and feeding of their 8-week-old infant. The following are examples of the types of questions:

1. Does your baby cry excessively and does it make you feel like crying?
2. Do you dislike having somebody watch you feed the baby or take care of this baby?
3. Does your older child know when you're upset and does she take care of you at this time?

They then study every child in the city that has an accident or fails to thrive. Kempe writes, "I can tell you now that people who are going to have children who have accidents, inflicted or otherwise, answer these questions very differently from matched controls who enter the study because they had a child born the same day who had not had an accident." And once you identify a family that is at risk, you can successfully intervene (Kempe 1973). Unfortunately, systematic statistical reports of the results of this study are not yet available.

Another prediction attempt is being executed by the Denver Child Protection Team to establish criteria for identifying and helping mothers who appear to be at risk and unable to make positive healthy attachments to their children. Screening of pregnant women begins in the Ob-Gyn Clinic. Women who have unreasonable levels of expectation toward newborns and who seem to have problems with basic "mother-crafting" are observed during labor, delivery, and in the postpartum period. If it is felt that the mother is "high risk," she is randomly placed in one of two groups: an intervene group or a nonintervene group. The hospital contacts are documented and success of intervention is measured by the mother's ability to utilize intensive follow-up care (National Center for the Prevention and Treatment of Child Abuse and Neglect 1973).

Again, no data are available on the predictive success of this program; however, in light of our earlier discussions concerning the early mother-infant interaction context as a setting in which abusive patterns may develop, this approach appears to be well founded and promising. These prediction studies are among the most important recent innovations in the area of child abuse. If they are successful in identifying potential abusive caretakers, education programs for parents can begin immediately after birth and, hopefully, short-circuit the development of patterns of interaction which may lead to later abuse. Moreover, it is probably easier to prevent the development of these patterns of interaction than to modify them after they have been well established.

It is likely that there will be a considerable risk of overprediction in studies of abuse prediction. The problem of prediction in the area of child abuse has a conceptual and statistical parallel in another area that shares the common characteristics of being (*a*) low in frequency among the population and (*b*) multiply determined. Perhaps the best parallel to use to illustrate the problems of prediction comes from the closely related issue of the prediction of adult interpersonal violence. These studies addressed the question of whether it is possible to predict recidivism among parolees with a history of interpersonal violent offenses. In one attempt to predict violence, Kosol, Boucher, and Garofalo (1972) used a wide range of clinical and psychological measures as well as a "meticulous reconstruction of the family history elicited from multiple sources—the patient himself, his family, friends, neighbors, teachers, and employers and court, correctional and mental hospital records" (p. 383), and the percentage of false prediction was high. Only one-third of those predicted actually committed an act of violence, while 65% did not. As Monahan (1973) concluded after a careful review of the violence prediction studies: "Of those predicted to be dangerous, between 65% and 99% are false positives . . . violence is vastly overpredicted whether simple behavioral indicators are used or sophisticated multivariate analyses are employed and whether psychological tests are administered or thorough psychiatric examinations are performed. . . . The fact that even in these groups, with higher base rates for violence than the general population, violence cannot be validly predicted bodes very poorly for predicting violence among those who have not committed a criminal act" (1973, p. 8). Since these studies were aimed at detection of repeaters, it is assumed that the current attempts at the prediction of potentially abusive, but currently nonabusive, parents may be even more difficult. In light of the probable high rate of overprediction, an intervention program would have to be sufficiently broadly based so that all participants would benefit from the program—regardless of whether or not they would have actually abused their children at some later date. The types of education programs for child care and child rearing aimed at high-risk adolescent mothers would probably be suitable. The recent "infant stimulation" program initiated by Badger, Elass, and Sutherland (1974) at the Cincinnati General Hospital is prototypic of this approach; young teenage mothers are recruited during their hospital stay to attend weekly group discussion classes which are aimed at teaching mothers how to interact with and stimulate their infants. This type of program serves to provide important information about normal infant development which serves to correct unrealistic expectations and, second, through direct instruction, role playing, and modeling, the mothers learn to be effective caretakers.

9. Summary

A series of innovative intervention programs which are currently operating were examined. These include lay group therapy programs, homemaker services, emergency hotlines, crisis nurseries, as well as child-rearing and public education programs. Although these approaches are promising, no formal assessments concerning the effectiveness of these programs are available. Finally, some of the recent prediction attempts were described and the difficulties associated with successful prediction were discussed.

VI. EPILOGUE

It is clear that much has been learned since Kempe's classic paper in 1962 brought the problem of child abuse to national attention. A number of issues are still to be addressed if significant progress is to be made in future research in this area. The most pressing need at present is for greater concern for rigorous evaluation and assessment of all facets of the child abuse problem.

First, the interaction patterns among family members in abusive families need to be carefully observed and compared with nonabusive families to determine whether distinctive patterns can be isolated. These assessments should include husband-wife, sib-sib, as well as parent-child interaction patterns. Similar types of observational investigations need to be executed in nonhome settings to determine whether children in abusive families show different patterns in their interactions with peers and other adults. These observational studies should by supplemented by other assessment techniques, such as structured family intervention, to permit a closer examination of the decision-making strategies and problem-solving strategies of abusive and nonabusive families. Of particular urgency is the extensive investigation of middle-class as well as lower-class families. Whether the conditions that give rise to abuse are similar or different across social classes is a problem that merits much closer examination.

While new innovative programs spring up across the country in reaction to the increased awareness of the problem of child abuse, too little attention is paid to a careful evaluation of the short- and long-term impact of these programs. Recent methodological advances in evaluation research (Campbell 1969) permit meaningful, but unobtrusive, assessment of the impact of action-oriented intervention programs. To supplement already established efforts, carefully designed field intervention experiments are badly needed in which comparable areas of the country receive different types of programs. By comparing the rates of child abuse in the different areas, we will be able more adequately to determine the effectiveness of various types of intervention efforts. Without this type of systematic experimental intervention, little solid information will be available on which to make policy decisions for the establishment of statewide and countrywide programs of abuse control. In addition, considerable work is required to evaluate the effectiveness of a variety of group and individual intervention strategies, such as programs for modification of parental disciplinary tactics and for improving anger control of abusive parents.

The same criteria that are applied to the descriptive studies and the intervention programs hold for the prediction studies. While these appear promising, careful evaluation of the predictive accuracy is necessary if these procedures are to be refined and improved.

The best interests of children will be served only to the extent that the problem of child abuse is viewed, not just as a human tragedy, but also as a problem that is amenable to careful and rigorous research and analysis. Only through better understanding of the problem will we be better able to protect our children.

REFERENCES

Adelson, L. Slaughter of the innocents. *New England Journal of Medicine*, 1961, *264*, 1345–1349.

Allen, H. D.; Ten Bensel, R. W.; & Raile, R. B. The battered child syndrome. *Minnesota Medicine*, 1968, *51*, 1793–1799.

Badger, E.; Elsass, S.; & Sutherland, J. M. Mother training as a means of accelerating childhood development in a high risk population. Unpublished manuscript, University of Cincinnati, 1974.

Bakan, D. *Slaughter of the innocents.* San Francisco: Jossey-Bass, 1971.

Bandura, A. Influence of model's reinforcement contingencies on the acquisition of imitative responses. *Journal of Personality and Social Psychology*, 1965, *1*, 589–595.

Bandura, A. The role of modeling processes in personality development. In W. W. Hartup & L. Smothergill (Eds.), *The young child: reviews of research.* Washington, D. C.: National Association for the Education of Young Children, 1967.

Bandura, A. *Principles of behavior modification.* New York: Holt, Rinehart & Winston, 1969.

Bandura, A. *Aggression: a social learning analysis.* New York: Prentice-Hall, 1973.

Baron, R. A. Magnitude of victim's pain cues and level of prior anger arousal as determinants of adult aggressive behavior. *Journal of Personality and Social Psychology*, 1971, *17*, 236–243.

Baron, R. M. The SRS model as a predictor of Negro responsiveness to reinforcement. *Journal of Social Issues*, 1970, *26*, 61–82.

Becker, T. T. Presentation to the American Medical Association, New York City, June 25, 1973.

Bell, R. Q. A reinterpretation of the direction of effects in studies of socialization. *Psychological Review*, 1968, *75*, 81–95.

Bell, R. Q. Contributions of human infants to caregiving and social interaction. In M. Lewis & L. A. Rosenblum (Eds.), *The effect of the infant on its caregiver.* New York: Wiley, 1974.

Bell, S. M., & Ainsworth, M. D. Infant crying and maternal responsiveness. *Child Development*, 1972, *43*, 1171–1190.

Bellak, L., & Antell, M. An intercultural study of aggressive behavior on children's playgrounds. *American Journal of Orthopsychiatry*, 1974, *44*, 503–511.

Berkowitz, L. *Aggression: a social psychological analysis*. New York: McGraw-Hill, 1962.

Berkowitz, L. Frustrations, comparisons, and other sources of emotional arousal as contributors to social unrest. *Journal of Social Issues*, 1972, *28*, 77–91.

Berkowitz, L. Some determinants of impulsive aggression: role of mediated associations with reinforcements for aggression. *Psychological Review*, 1974, *81*, 165–176.

Bernal, M. E.; Duryee, J. S.; Pruett, H. L.; & Burns, B. J. Behavior modification and the brat syndrome. *Journal of Consulting and Clinical Psychology*, 1968, *32*, 447–455.

Birns, B.; Blank, M.; & Bridger, W. H. The effectiveness of various soothing techniques on human neonates. *Psychomatic Medicine*, 1966, *28*, 316–322.

Birrell, R. G., & Birrell, J. H. W. The maltreatment syndrome in children: a hospital survey. *Medical Journal of Australia*, 1968, *2*, 1023–1029.

Blumberg, M. L. Psychopathology of the abusing parent. *American Journal of Psychotherapy*, 1974, *28*, 21–29.

Boardman, H. E. A project to rescue children from inflicted injuries. *Social Work*, 1962, *7*, 43–51.

Brett, D. I. *The battered and abused child syndrome*. Berkeley: University of California Press, 1967.

Brock, R. C., & Buss, A. H. Effects of justification for aggression and communication with the victim on postaggression dissonance. *Journal of Abnormal and Social Psychology*, 1964, *68*, 403–412.

Bronfenbrenner, U. Socialization and social class through time and space. In E. E. Baccoby, T. M. Newcomb, & E. L. Hartley (Eds.), *Readings in social psychology*. New York: Holt, 1958.

Brooks, V., & Hochberg, J. A psychophysical study of "cuteness." *Perceptual and Motor Skills*, 1960, *11*, 205.

Brown, P., & Elliott, R. The control of aggression in a nursery school class. *Journal of Experimental Child Psychology*, 1965, *2*, 103–107.

Bryant, H. D.; Billingsley, A.; Kerry, G. A.: Leefman, W. V.; Merrill, E. J.; Senecal, G. R.; & Walsh, B. G. Physical abuse of children—an agency study. *Child Welfare*, 1963, *42*, 125–130.

Buss, A. H. *The psychology of aggression*. New York: Wiley, 1961.

Buss, A. H. The effect of harm on subsequent aggression. *Journal of Experimental Research in Personality*, 1966, *1*, 249–255.

Calhoun, J. B. Population density and social pathology. *Scientific American*, 1962, *206*, 139–150.

Cameron, J. M.; Johnson, H. R. M.; & Camps, F. E. The battered child syndrome. *Medicine, Science and the Law*, 1966, *6*, 2–21.

Campbell, D. T. Reforms as experiments. *American Psychologist*, 1969, *24*, 409–429.

Caputo, D. V., & Mandell, W. Consequences of low birth weight. *Developmental Psychology*, 1970, *3*, 363–383.

Chittenden, G. E. An experimental study in measuring and modifying assertive behavior in young children. *Monographs of the Society for Research in Child Development*, 1942, *7*, (1, Serial No. 31).

Cochrane, W. A. The battered child syndrome. *Canadian Journal of Public Health*, 1965, *56*, 193–196.

Collias, N. E. The analysis of socialization in sheep and goats. *Ecology*, 1965, *37*, 228–239.

Committee of Investigation into Allegations of Neglect and Maltreatment of Young Children. Report to the Honorable the Chief Secretary and the Honorable the Minister of Health. Melbourne: Chelsea House, December 1967.

Curtis, G. Violence breeds violence. *American Journal of Psychiatry*, 1963, *120*, 386–387.

Davitz, J. R. The effects of previous training on postfrustration behavior. *Journal of Abnormal and Social Psychology*, 1952, *47*, 309–315.

Davoren, E. The role of the social worker. In R. E. Helfer & C. H. Kempe (Eds.), *The battered child* (2d ed.) Chicago: University of Chicago Press, 1974.

de Francis, V. Parents who abuse. *PTA Magazine*, November 1963.

Delsordo, J. D. Protective casework for abused children. *Children*, November–December, 213–218.

Deur, J. L., & Parke, R. D. The effects of inconsistent punishment on aggression in children. *Developmental Psychology*, 1970, *2*, 403–411.

Dion, K. K. Children's physical attractiveness and sex as determinants of adult punitiveness. *Developmental Psychology*, 1974, *10*, 772–778.

Douglas, J. W. B. Mental ability and school achievement of premature children at eight years of age. *British Medical Journal*, 1956, *1*, 1210–1214.

Elmer, E. *Children in jeopardy: a study of abused minors and their families.* Pittsburgh: University of Pittsburgh Press, 1967.

Elmer, E., & Gregg, G. S. Developmental characteristics of abused children. *Pediatrics*, 1967, *40*, 596–602.

Erlanger, H. S. Social class differences in parents' use of physical punishment. In S. K. Steinmetz & M. A. Straus (Eds.), *Violence in the family.* New York: Dodd, Mead, 1974.

Etzel, B. C., & Gewirtz, J. L. Experimental modification of caretaker-maintained high rate operant crying in a six and a twenty week old infant: extinction of crying with reinforcement of eye contact and smiling. *Journal of Experimental Child Psychology*, 1967, *5*, 303–317.

Fanaroff, A. A.; Kennell, J. H.; & Klaus, M. H. Follow-up of low birth weight infants—the predictive value of maternal visiting patterns. *Pediatrics*, 1972, *49*, 287–290.

Feinstein, H. M.; Paul, N.; & Esmiol, P. Group therapy for mothers with infanticidal impulses. *American Journal of Psychiatry*, 1964, *120*, 882–886.

Fenigstein, A., & Buss, A. H. Association and affect as determinants of displaced aggression. *Journal of Research in Personality*, 1974, *7*, 306–313.

Feshbach, N., & Feshbacn, S. The relationship between empathy and aggression in two age groups. *Developmental Psychology*, 1969, *1*, 102–107.

Festinger, L.; Schachter, S.; & Back, K. Social pressures in informal groups: a study of human factors in housing. New York: Harper, 1950.

Fleming, G. M. Cruelty to children. *British Medical Journal*, 1967, *2*, 421–422.

Fontana, V. J. Further reflections on maltreatment of children. *Pediatrics*, 1973, *51*, 780–782.

Freedman, D. A., & Freedman, N. Behavioral differences between Chinese-American and European-American newborns. *Nature*, 1969, *224*, 1227.

Freedman, J. L. The effects of population density on humans. In J. T. Fawcett (Ed.), *Psychological perspectives on population.* New York: Basic, 1973.

Galdston, R. Observations on children who have been physically abused and their parents. *American Journal of Psychiatry*, 1965, *122*, 440–443.

Galdston, R. Violence begins at home: the parent's center project for the study and prevention of child abuse. *American Academy of Child Psychiatry*, 1971, *10*, 336–350.

Garbarino, J. Some ecological correlates of child abuse: the impact of socioeconomic stress on mothers. *Child Development*, 1975, in press.

Geis, G., & Monahan, J. The social ecology of violence. In T. Lickona (Ed.), *Man and morality*. New York: Holt, Rinehart & Winston, 1975, in press.

Gelles, R. J. Child abuse as psychopathology: a sociological critique and reformulation. *American Journal of Orthopsychiatry*, 1973, *43*, 611–621.

Gerbner, G. The violence profile: some indicators of the trends in and the symbolic structure of network television drama, 1967–1970. Unpublished manuscript, Annenberg School of Communications, University of Pennsylvania, 1972.

Gil, D. G. *Violence against children: physical child abuse in the United States*. Cambridge, Mass.: Harvard University Press, 1970.

Gil, D. G. A holistic perspective on child abuse and its prevention. Paper presented at a conference on child abuse and neglect at the National Institute of Child Health and Human Development, Washington, D.C., June 1974.

Gillespie, R. W. The battered child syndrome: thermal and caustic manifestations. *Journal of Trauma*, 1965, *5*, 523–524.

Giovannoni, J. M., & Billingsley, A. Child neglect among the poor: a study of parental adequacy in families of three ethnic groups. *Child Welfare*, 1970, *49*, 196–204.

Gittelman, M. Behavior rehearsal as a technique in child treatment. *Journal of Child Psychology and Psychiatry*, 1965, *6*, 251–255.

Glazier, A. E. (Ed.), *Child abuse: a community challenge*. East Aurora, N. Y.: Henry Stewart, 1971.

Glueck, S., & Glueck, E. *Unraveling juvenile delinquency*. Cambridge, Mass.: Harvard University Press, 1950.

Goode, W. J. Force and violence in the family. *Journal of Marriage and the Family*, 1971, *33*, 624–636.

Green, A. A. Psychiatric study and treatment of abusing parents. Paper presented at the 122d annual convention of the American Medical Association, June 1973.

Greengard, J. The battered child syndrome. *American Journal of Nursing*, 1964, *64*, 98–100.

Gurin, G., & Gurin, P. Expectancy theory in the study of poverty. *Journal of Social Issues*, 1970, *26*, 83–104.

Harrison, P. *Never enough—75 years with the Children's Aid Society of Ottawa*. Ottawa: Children's Aid Society, 1968.

Hartmann, D. P. Influence of symbolically modeled instrumental aggression and pain cues on aggressive behavior. *Journal of Personality and Social Psychology*, 1969, *11*, 280–288.

Hartup, W. W. Peer interaction and social organization. In P. H. Mussen (Ed.), *Carmichael's manual of child psychology*. Vol. 2. New York: Wiley, 1970.

Hawkins, R. P.; Peterson, R. F.; Schweid, E.; & Bijou, S. W. Behavior therapy in the home: amelioration of problem parent-child relations with the parent in a therapeutic role. *Journal of Experimental Child Psychology*, 1966, *4*, 99–107.

Helfer, R. E., & Kempe, C. H. (Eds.). *The battered child*. Chicago: University of Chicago Press, 1968.

Helfer, R. E., & Kempe, C. H. (Eds.). *The battered child*. (2d ed.) Chicago: University of Chicago Press, 1974.

Helfer, R. E., & Pollock, C. B. The battered child syndrome. *Advances in Pediatrics*, 1968, *15*, 9–27.

Herrell, J. M. Use of systematic desensitization to eliminate inappropriate anger. *Proceedings of the 79th annual convention of the American Psychological Association*. Washington, D. C.: American Psychological Association, 1971.

Hersher, L.; Moore, A. U.; & Richmond, J. B. Effect of postpartum separation of mother and kid on maternal care in the domestic goat. *Science*, 1958, *128*, 1342–1343.

Johnson, B., & Morse, H. A. Injured children and their parents. *Children*, 1968, *15*, 147–152.

Johnson, S. M.; Wahl, G.; Martin, S.; & Johanssen, S. How deviant is the normal child: a behavioral analysis of the preschool child and his family. In R. D. Rubin, J. P. Brady, & J. D. Henderson, *Advances in Behavior Therapy*. Vol. *4*. New York: Academic Press, 1974.

Kaufman, I. Discussion of physical abuse of children. Presented at national conference on social welfare sponsored by Children's Division, American Humane Association, New York, June 1, 1962.

Kelley, C. *Crime in the United States—1972*. Washington, D. C.: Government Printing Office, 1973.

Kempe, C. H. Pediatric implications of the battered baby syndrome. *Archives of Disease in Childhood*, 1971, *46*, 28–37.

Kempe, C. H. A practical approach to the protection of the abused child and rehabilitation of the abusing parent. *Pediatrics*, 1973, *51* (Pt. 3), 804–812.

Kempe, C. H., & Helfer, R. E. *Helping the battered child and his family*. Lippincott, 1972.

Kempe, C. H.; Silverman, F. N.; Steele, B. B.; Droegemueller, W.; & Silver, H. K. The battered-child syndrome. *Journal of the American Medical Association*, 1962, *181*, 17–24.

Kennell, J. H.; Gordon, D.; & Klaus, N. H. The effect of early mother-infant separation on later maternal performance. *Pediatric Research*, 1970. (Abstract 150)

Klaus, M. H., & Fanaroff, A. A. *Care of the high-risk neonate*. Philadelphia: Saunders, 1973.

Klein, M., & Stern, L. Low birth weight and the battered child syndrome. *American Journal of Diseases of Childhood*, 1971, *122*, 15–18.

Korner, A. F. The effect of the infant's state, level of arousal and ontogenetic stage on the caregiver. In M. Lewis and L. A. Rosenblum (Eds.), *The effect of the infant on its caregiver*. New York: Wiley, 1974.

Korsch, B.; Christian, J.; Gozzi, E.; & Carlson, P. Infant care and punishment: a pilot study. *American Journal of Public Health*, 1965, *55*, 1880–1888.

Kosol, H.; Boucher, R.; & Garofolo, R. The diagnosis and treatment of dangerousness. *Crime and Delinquency*, 1972, *18*, 371–393.

Laupus, W. E. Child abuse and the physician. *Virginia Medical Monthly*, 1966, *93*(1), 1–2.

Laury, G. V. The battered child syndrome: parental motivation, clinical aspects. *Bulletin of New York Academy of Medicine*, 1970, *46*, 676–685.

Lawrence, J. E. S. Science and sentiment: overview of research on crowding and human behavior. *Psychological Bulletin*, 1974, *81*, 712–720.

Leifer, A. D., Leiderman, P. H., & Barnett, C. R. Mother-infant separation: affects on later maternal behavior. Unpublished manuscript, Stanford University, 1970.

Leifer, A. D.; Leiderman, P. H.; Barnett, C. R.; & Williams, J. A. Effects of mother-infant separation on maternal attachment behavior. *Child Development*, 1972, *43*, 1203–1218.

Lenoski, E. F. Translating injury data into preventive and health care services—physical child abuse. Unpublished manuscript, University of South California School of Medicine, Los Angeles, 1974.

Levy, R. I. On getting angry in the Society Islands. In W. Caudill & T. Y. Lin (Eds.), *Mental health research in Asia and the Pacific*. Honolulu: East-West Center Press, 1969.

Lezine, I. The psychomotor development of young prematures. *Etudes Neo-Natales*, 1958, *7*, 1–50.

Liebert, R. M.; Neale, J. M.; & Davidson, E. S. *The early window: effects of television on child and youth*. New York: Pergamon, 1973.

Light, R. Abuse and neglected children in America: a study of alternative policies. *Harvard Educational Review*, 1973, *43*, 556–598.

Loew, C. A. Acquisition of a hostile attitude and its relationship to aggressive behavior. *Journal of Personality and Social Psychology*, 1967, *5*, 335–341.

Loo, C. M. The effects of spatial density on the social behavior of children. *Journal of Applied Social Psychology*, 1972, *2*, 372–381.

McCord, W.; McCord, J.; & Howard, A. Familial correlates of aggression in nondelinquent male children. *Journal of Abnormal and Social Psychology*, 1961, *62*, 79–93.

McFall, R. M., & Twentyman, C. T. Four experiments on the relative contribution of rehearsal, modeling, and coaching to assertion training. *Journal of Abnormal Psychology*, 1972, *61*, 199–218.

McFerran, J. Parents' groups in protective services. *Children*, 1958, *5*, 223–228.

McKinley, D. G. *Social class and family life.* New York: Free Press, 1964.

Mahoney, M. J. A residential program in behavior modification. Paper presented at the fifth annual meeting of the Association for the Advancement of Behavior Therapy, Washington, D. C., September 1971.

Mead, M. *Sex and temperament in three savage tribes.* New York: Morrow, 1935.

Melnick, B., & Hurley, J. Distinctive personality attributes of child-abusing mothers. *Journal of Consulting and Clinical Psychology*, 1969, *33*, 746–749.

Merril, E. J. *Protecting the battered child.* Denver: Children's Division, American Humane Association, 1962.

Milgram, S. *Obedience to authority.* New York: Harper & Row, 1974.

Miller, D. S. Fractures among children. *Minnesota Medicine*, 1959, *42*, 1209–1213.

Milow, I., & Lourie, R. The child's role in the battered child syndrome. *Society for Pediatric Research*, 1964, *65*, 1079–1081.

Mischel, W. *Personality and assessment.* New York: Wiley, 1968.

Mischel, W. Toward a cognitive social learning reconceptualization of personality. *Psychological Review*, 1973, *80*, 252–283.

Mitchell, R. E. Some social implications of high density housing. *American Sociological Review*, 1971, *36*, 18–29.

Monahan, J. The prediction and prevention of violence. Proceedings of the Pacific Northwest Conference on Violence and Criminal Justice. Issaquah, Wash, 1973.

Moore, J. L., Jr., Reporting of child abuse. *Journal of the Medical Association of Georgia*, 1966, *55*, 328–329.

Moorehead, C. Seven-man team helps parents of battered babies. *Times Educational Supplement*, 1970, *12*, 2897.

Mulvihill, D. J., & Tumin, M. M. Crimes of violence. *Staff report to the National Commission on the Causes and Prevention of Violence.* Washington, D.C.: Government Printing Office, 1969.

National Center for the Prevention and Treatment of Child Abuse and Neglect. *National Child Protection Newsletter*, 1973, *1*, 1–3.

Newson, J., & Newson, E. Four years old in an urban community Chicago: Aldine, 1968.

Niem, T. C., & Collard, R. Parental discipline of aggressive behaviors in four year old Chinese and American children. Paper presented at the annual meeting of the American Psychological Association, Washington, D.C., 1971.

Nurse, S. M. Familial patterns of parents who abuse their children. *Smith College Studies in Social Work*, 1964, *35*, 11–25.

O'Brien, T. E. Violence in divorce-prone families. *Journal of Marriage and the Family*, 1971, *33*, 292–298.

O'Conner, R. D. Modification of social withdrawal through symbolic modeling. *Journal of Applied Behavior Analysis*, 1969, *2*, 15–22.

Osofsky, J. D., & Danzger, B. Relationships between neonatal characteristics and mother-infant interaction. *Developmental Psychology*, 1974, *10*, 124–130.

Palmer, S. *The violent society*. New Haven, Conn.: College and University Press, 1972.

Parents Anonymous, Inc. Procedures and concepts manual. Redondo Beach, Calif.: National Parent Chapter, 1972.

Parke, R. D. Effectiveness of punishment as an interaction of intensity, timing, agent nurturance, and cognitive structuring. *Child Development*, 1969, *40*, 213–235.

Parke, R. D. The role of punishment in the socialization process. In R. A. Hoppe, G. A. Milton, & E. C. Simmel (Eds.), *Early experiences and the processes of socialization*. New York: Academic Press, 1970.

Parke, R. D. Some effects of punishment on children's behavior. In W. W. Hartup (Ed.), *The young child*. Vol. 2. Washington, D.C.: National Association for the Education of Young Children, 1972.

Parke, R. D. Rules, roles and resistance to deviation in children: explorations in punishment, discipline and self control. In A. Pick (Ed.), *Minnesota symposia on child psychology*. Vol. *8*. Minneapolis: University of Minnesota Press, 1974.

Parke, R. D., & Deur, J. L. Schedule of punishment and inhibition of aggression in children. *Developmental Psychology*, 1972, *7*, 266–269.

Parke, R. D., Ewall, W., & Slaby, R. G. Hostile and helpful verbalizations as regulators of nonverbal aggression. *Journal of Personality and Social Psychology*, 1972, *23*, 243–248.

Parke, R. D., & O'Leary, S. Family interaction in the newborn period: some findings, some observations, and some unresolved issues. In K. Riegel & J. Meacham (Eds.), *The developing individual in a changing world*. Vol. 2. *Social and environmental issues*. The Hague: Mouton, 1975.

Parke, R. D., Sawin, D. B., & Kreling, B. The effect of child feedback on adult disciplinary choices. Unpublished manuscript, Fels Research Institute, 1974.

Parmalee, A. H., Jr. Development of states in infants. In C. Clemente, D. Purpurpa, & F. Mayer (Eds.), *Maturation of brain mechanisms related to sleep behavior*. New York: Academic Press, 1972.

Patterson, G. R. Interventions for boys with conduct problems: multiple settings, treatments and criteria. *Journal of Consulting and Clinical Psychology*, 1974, *42*, 471–481.

Patterson, G. R., & Cobb, J. A. A dyadic analysis of "aggressive" behavior. In J. P. Hill (Ed.), *Minnesota symposia on child psychology*. Vol. 5. Minneapolis: University of Minnesota Press, 1971.

Patterson, G. R., & Cobb, J. A. Stimulus control for classes of noxious behavior. In J. S. Knutson (Ed.), *The control of aggression: implications from basic research*. Chicago: Aldine, 1973.

Patterson, G. R., & Gullion, M. E. *Living with children*. Champaign, Ill.: Research Press, 1968.

Patterson, G. R., & Reid, J. B. Reciprocity and coercion: two facets of social systems. In C. Newunger & J. Michael (Eds.), *Behavior modification in clinical psychology*. New York: Appleton-Century-Crofts, 1970.

Paulson, M., & Blake, P. The physically abused child: a focus on prevention. *Child Welfare*, 1969, *48*, 86–95.

Paulson, M. J., & Chaleff, A. Parent surrogate roles: a dynamic concept in understanding and treating abusive parents. *Journal of Clinical Child Psychology*, 1973, *2*, 38–40.

Pike, E. L. C.A.L.M.: A timely experiment in the prevention of child abuse. *Journal Clinical Child Psychology*, 1973, *2*, 43–45.

Pinkney, A. *The American way of violence*. New York: Random House, 1972.

Platou, R. V.; Lennox, R.; & Beasley, J. D. Battering. *Bulletin of the Tulane Me Faculty*, 1964, *23*, 157–165.

Pollock, D., & Steele, B. A therapeutic approach to the parents. In C. H. Kempe & R. E. Helfer (Eds.), *Helping the battered child and his family*. Philadelphia: Lippincott, 1972.

Rabinowitz, M. S.; Bibace, R.; & Caplan, H. Sequela of prematurity: psychological test findings. *Canadian Medical Association Journal*, 1961, *84*, 822–824.

Redd, W. H.; Morris, E. K.; & Martin, J. A. Effects of positive and negative adult-child interactions on children's preferences. *Journal of Experimental Child Psychology*, 1975, *19*, 153–164.

Rimm, D. C.; Hill, G. A.; Brown, N. N.; & Stuart, J. E. Group assertiveness training in treatment of inappropriate anger expression. *Psychological Reports*, 1974, *34*, 791–798.

Rimm, D. C., & Masters, J. C. *Behavior therapy: techniques and empirical findings*. New York: Academic Press, 1974.

Risley, T. R., & Baer, D. M. Operant behavior modification: the deliberate development of behavior. In B. M. Caldwell & H. N. Riciutti (Eds.), *Review of child development research*. Vol. *3*. Chicago: University of Chicago Press, 1973.

Robson, K. S., & Moss, H. A. Patterns and determinants of maternal attachment. *Journal of Pediatrics*, 1970, *77*, 976–985.

Roy, K. Parent's attitudes toward their children. *Journal of Home Economics*, 1950, *42*, 652–653.

Ryder, R. G. Longitudinal data relating marriage satisfaction and having a child. *Journal of Marriage and the Family*, 1973, *35*, 604–606.

Sameroff, A. J., & Chandler, M. J. Perinatal risk and the continuum of caretaking casualty. In F. D. Horowitz, E. M. Hetherington, S. Scarr-Salapatek, & G. Siegel (Eds.), *Review of child development research*. Vol. *4*. Chicago: University of Chicago Press, 1975.

Savino, A. B., & Sanders, R. W. Working with abusive parents: group therapy and home visits. *American Journal of Nursing*, 1973, *73*, 482–484.

Schaffer, H. R., & Emerson, P. E. Patterns of response to physical contact in early human development. *Journal of Child Psychology and Psychiatry*, 1964, *5*, 1–13.

Schloesser, P. The abused child. *Bulletin of Menninger Clinic*, 1964, *28*, 260.

Seashore, M. J.; Leifer, A. D.; Barnett, C. R.; & Leiderman, P. H. The effects of denial of early mother-infant interaction on maternal self-confidence. *Journal of Personality and Social Psychology*, 1973, *26*, 369–378.

Seligman, M. E. P.; Maier, S. F.; & Solomon, R. L. Unpredictable and uncontrollable aversive events. In F. R. Brush (Ed.), *Aversive conditioning and learning*. New York: Academic Press, 1969.

Sidel, R. *Women and child care in China*. New York: Hill & Wang, 1972.

Simons, B.; Downs, E. F.; Hurster, M. M.; & Archer, M. Child abuse: epidemiological study of medically reported cases. *New York State Journal of Medicine*, 1966, *66*.

Simpson, K. The battered baby problem. *Royal Society of Health Journal*, 1967, *87*, 168–170.

Simpson, K. The battered baby problem. *South African Medical Journal*, 1968, *42*, 661–665.

Skinner, A. E., & Castle, R L. *Seventy-eight battered children: a retrospective study*. London: National Society for the Prevention of Cruelty to Children, 1969.

Slaby, D. Program description and progress report. Children's Day School and Parent Training Programs, Department of Behavioral Sciences, Children's Orthopedic Hospital, Seattle, June 1974.

Solomon, T. History and demography of child abuse. *Pediatrics*, 1973, *51*(Pt. 2).

Spinetta, J. J., & Rigler, D. The child-abusing parent: a psychological review. *Psychological Bulletin*, 1972, *77*, 296–304.

Stark, R., & McEvoy, J. Middle class violence. *Psychology Today*, 1970, *4*, 52–65.

Steele, B. F., & Pollock, D. A psychiatric study of parents who abuse infants and small

children. In R. E. Helfer & C. H. Kempe (Eds.), *The battered child*. Chicago: University of Chicago Press, 1968.

Steinmetz, S. K. Intra-familial patterns of conflict resolution: United States and Canadian comparisons. Paper presented at the annual meeting of the Society for the Study of Social Problems, Montreal, 1974. (a)

Steinmetz, S. K. Normal families and family violence: the training ground for abuse. Paper presented at Research NIH conference on child abuse and neglect, Bethesda, Md., June 1974. (b)

Steinmetz, S. K. Occupational environment in relation to physical punishment and dogmatism. In S. K. Steinmetz & M. A. Straus (Eds.), *Violence in the family*. New York: Dodd, Mead, 1974. (c).

Steinmetz, S. K., & Straus, M. A. (Eds.) *Violence in the family*. New York: Dodd, Mead, 1974.

Stevens-Long, J. The effect of behavioral context on some aspects of adults disciplinary practice and affect. *Child Development*, 1973, *44*, 476–484.

Stevenson, H. W. *Society for Research in Child Development Newsletter*, Fall 1974.

Stouwie, R. J. An experimental study of adult dominance and warmth, conflicting verbal instructions, and children's moral behavior. *Child Development*, 1972, *43*, 959–972.

Straus, M. A. Some social antecedents of physical punishment: a linkage theory interpretation. *Journal of Marriage and the Family*, 1971, *33*, 658–663.

Straus, M. A. Leveling, civility, and violence in the family. *Journal of Marriage and the Family*, 1974, *36*, 13–19.

Ten Bensel, R. W., & Raile, R. B. The battered child syndrome. *Minnesota Medicine*, 1963, *46*, 977–982.

Terr, L. C. A family study of child abuse. *American Journal of Psychiatry*, 1970, *127*, 665–671.

Tuteur, W., & Glotzer, J. Further observations on murdering mothers. *Journal of Forensic Sciences*, 1966, *2*, 373–383.

Ulrich, R. E. Pain as a cause of aggression. *American Zoologist*, 1966, *6*, 643–662.

Van Stolk, M. The battered child in Canada. Toronto: The Canadian Publishers, 1972.

Viano, E. C. Attitudes towards child abuse among American professionals. Paper presented at the biennial meeting of the International Society for Research on Aggression, Toronto, 1974.

Walters, R. H., & Parke, R. D. Social motivation, dependency and susceptibility to social influence. In L. Berkowitz (Ed.), *Advances in experimental social psychology*. New York: Academic Press, 1964.

Walters, R. H., & Parke, R. D. The influence of punishment and related disciplinary techniques on the social behavior of children: theory and empirical findings. In B. A. Maher (Ed.), *Progress in experimental personality research*, Vol. *4*. New York: Academic Press, 1967.

Wasserman, S. The abused parent of the abused child. *Children*, 1967, *14*, 175–179.

Williams, C. D. The elimination of tantrum behavior by extinction procedures. *Journal of Abnormal and Social Psychology*, 1959, *59*, 269.

Wolff, P. H. The natural history of crying and other vocalizations in early infancy. In B. M. Foss (Ed.), *Determinants of infant behavior*. Vol. *4*. New York: Wiley, 1969.

Wolfgang, M. Crime: homicide. In D. L. Sells (Ed.), *International encyclopedia of the social sciences*. Vol. *3*. New York: Macmillan, 1968.

Woolley, P. V., & Evans, W. A., Jr. Significance of skeletal lesions in infants resembling those of traumatic origin. *Journal of the American Medical Association*, 1955, *158*, 539–543.

Wright, L. The theoretical and research base for a program of early stimulation, care and training of premature infants. In J. Hellmuth (Ed.), *Exceptional infant: Studies in abnormalities*. New York: Brunner/Mazel, 1971.

Young, L. *Wednesday's children: a study of child neglect and abuse*. New York: McGraw-Hill, 1964.

Zalba, S. R. The abused child. *Social work: a typology for classification and treatment*, 1967, 70–79.

Zalba, S. R. Battered children. *Transaction*, 1971, *8*, 58–61.

Author Index

591

Subject Index